NBC Handbook of Pronunciation

NBC
Handbook of

PRONUNCIATION

FOURTH EDITION

Revised and updated by
Eugene Ehrlich and Raymond Hand, Jr.

Introduction by Edwin Newman

1817

H A R P E R & R O W , P U B L I S H E R S , New York
Cambridge, Philadelphia, San Francisco, London
Mexico City, São Paulo, Singapore, Sydney

NBC HANDBOOK OF PRONUNCIATION *(Fourth Edition)*. Introduction copyright © 1984 by Harper & Row, Publishers, Inc. Copyright © 1984 by Harper & Row, Publishers, Inc. All rights reserved. Printed in the United States of America. No part of this book may be used or reproduced in any manner whatsoever without written permission except in the case of brief quotations embodied in critical articles and reviews. For information address Harper & Row, Publishers, Inc., 10 East 53rd Street, New York, N.Y. 10022. Published simultaneously in Canada by Fitzhenry & Whiteside Limited, Toronto.

Designer: C. Linda Dingler

Library of Congress Cataloging in Publication Data

Bender, James F. (James Frederick), 1905–
  NBC handbook of pronunciation.

  1. English language—Pronunciation—Handbooks,
manuals, etc. 2. Television broadcasting—Handbooks,
manuals, etc. 3. Americanisms—Handbooks, manuals, etc.
I. Ehrlich, Eugene H. II. Hand, Raymond. III. National
Broadcasting Company, inc. IV. Title. V. Title: N.B.C.
handbook of pronunciation.
PE1137.B573 1984   421'.52'0202   84-47592
ISBN 0-06-181142-4

---

84 85 86 87 88 10 9 8 7 6 5 4 3 2 1

Contents

Preface to the Fourth Edition

More than forty years have passed since initial publication of the *NBC Handbook of Pronunciation,* compiled originally by James F. Bender, who also prepared the second edition. Thomas Lee Crowell, Jr., prepared the third edition, which appeared after his untimely death more than twenty years ago.

All through these many years, the *NBC Handbook* has served as the standard reference work on pronunciation in General American speech. In preparing this new edition, the editors have striven to maintain the quality of the earlier editions and, in the tradition of the editors who preceded them, have once again expanded the scope of the volume. As a result, the total number of entries now exceeds 21,000 commonly used words and proper names as well as perennially difficult names from history and the arts.

One significant departure from the third edition is the modified pronunciation scheme employed. Because modern readers may lack thorough understanding of the International Phonetic Alphabet, the fourth edition offers a readily understandable respelling system to indicate pronunciation. In addition, the fourth edition supplies indications of secondary stresses as well as primary stresses within words. Needless to say, many proper names included in past editions are no longer in current use, so they have been removed to make room for names of greater value for today's speakers. Finally, pronunciations preferred in the past but no longer commonly heard have been replaced.

Despite the many changes made in the work of the previous editors, the *NBC Handbook* still adheres to the fundamental principle that guided the earlier efforts: to record "the pronunciations used by educated persons in the greater part of the United States, rather than to insist upon arbitrary standards of pronunciation unrelated to those commonly heard." True to this principle, the editors of the Fourth Edition supply American pronunciations of foreign names that have gained widespread use in our country. Where foreign names have not yet been Americanized, the pronunciations that are given approximate the pronunciations heard in the countries in which the names originate. Again in adherence to the practices of the earlier editors, the present editors supply a single pronunciation for each entry rather than a bewildering variety of acceptable pronunciations. This reflects the belief held by all the editors of the *NBC Handbook* that those who consult the book want assistance in pronunciation rather than justification for a particular pronunciation.

The editors wish to acknowledge the help of four United Nations interpreters in pronouncing certain proper names: Hossam Fakhr, Mikhail Farafonov, Judit Foldenyi, and Jacqueline Mitchell. For assistance in pronouncing African proper names, we acknowledge the assistance of the following consular officials: Janvière Baziyaka, Vlok Delport, Pholile Legwaila, Sam Nutakor, Mintsa Zue Ondo, Sulaiman Masamba Sisé, and Richard Waiguchu. We especially wish to thank Hayden Carruth for his assistance in making possible the computerization of this book.

Eugene Ehrlich
Raymond Hand, Jr.

September 1984
Pleasantville, New York

Introduction

This book might have been called *Pronunciation Can Be Fun*.
That sort of title has often been used, of course. Almost every-
thing but auto-da-fé has been described as fun for the sake of
a book title. The fact is, nonetheless, that pronouncing words
correctly can be fun. There is nothing snobbish or elitist about
it, any more than there is in doing anything else correctly.
Perhaps another word also applies. There is satisfaction to be
had from correct pronunciation, particularly when one comes
upon an unfamiliar word or name, sets out on uncharted seas,
and makes it! It's an exhilarating feeling.

As a broadcaster for three and a half decades, I may have a
special view of this. An obligation does rest on people in my
position to speak correctly, not only in matters of grammar and
usage, but in pronunciation, as well. So it is that NBC has a
pronunciation handbook, honored in the breach rather than in
the observance though it may sometimes be.

Not that I mean to suggest that my own record in such matters is spotless. It took a letter from an annoyed listener to turn
me from saying AN tī to the preferred AN tee. Another listener
objected to my saying depot with a short *e*. That, he wrote, was
a pronunciation often used by Americans who had spent time
in Europe. In the United States, he wrote, we say DEE poh.

I remember, too, doing the evening news one night and for
some reason saying LEE mə (as in Lima, Peru, where at that
time I had never been) rather than LĪ mə (as in Lima, Ohio,

where I had also never been) when indeed it was Lima, Ohio, that was, thanks to a devastating storm, in the news.

Mentioning anti, depot, and Lima does not mean that my on-the-air transgressions were limited to these. Another I remember was not on the air and probably could not have been: the place involved, a town in Scotland named Kirkcudbright, is not in the news very often. One day, in the NBC London office, an employee showed it to me on a map as the place where she had been born.

"Ah, Kirkcudbright," said I, taking the name at face value.

From the hoots of laughter that followed eventually emerged kər KOO bree.

It was a lesson of sorts, like learning that Natchitoches, Louisiana, is pronounced, roughly, NAK ə TOSH; that Biloxi, Mississippi, is bə LUK see; that Schaghticoke, New York, which the alert may find eighteen miles north of Albany, is SKAT ə KOHK; that Houston Street in New York City might elude, or annoy, a Texan as HOW stən Street; and that it is not uncommon for people born in that Wisconsin city to make it, roughly, MWAW kee.

There is, of course, no harm in asking how something is pronounced, or in looking it up. That is why books of this kind exist. That is why *this* book, which is as authoritative as we could make it, exists. It is intended to be useful not only to people who make their living as I do. It is for anybody who speaks in public, habitually, occasionally, or once in a great while. We want it to help the person, for example, who finds that he or she must deliver a book review to a local literary club, or the mother or father with something to say at the PTA meeting. In fact, it is for anyone who engages in conversation, or even in interior monologues. There is no reason to be wrong just because you're talking to yourself.

This handbook is not highbrow, but it is designed to promote correctness. Does correctness matter in this day and age? As much as ever, it seems to me, for correctness does more than add precision, which is desirable in itself; it helps us to understand and get along with one another. Much in our time is not easy to comprehend in the best of circumstances; mispronunciation only makes things harder. Besides, where is the sense of accomplishment in saying, "dimunition" when the word is "diminution"? Or in writing "diffuse" when "defuse" is required? Correct pronunciation would rule that out. When a leading American newspaper tried to show that Congressional salaries were too low, it said that some members of the House and Senate lived in "gentile poverty," which is very different from what was intended, "genteel poverty." Knowing the pronunciation of "gentile" would have ruled that mistake out. Nor is an expatriate a former patriot. Again, correct pronunciation would have precluded that error. When mistakes are *not* made, I am not, as a television correspondent put it, "jubulant." Correct pronunciation would have spared us that.

But, someone may say, dictionaries also provide pronunciations. Why not use them? Indeed they do provide pronunciations. This book, however, uses a simpler guide to pronunciation than dictionaries do. Moreover, it specializes in pronunciation and focuses on words frequently mispronounced. A major part of the list of words pronounced—greatly expanded since the last edition—is the names and places that are in the news and likely to stay there, names and places that pop up on the air, in your newspaper, in conversation. These pronunciations are for anybody who thinks that being correct about these things is worthwhile.

This is the first new edition of the *NBC Handbook of Pronunciation* since 1964. That is much too long an interval. The earlier editions came out much more rapidly: between 1945 and 1964, there were three of them. Since 1964—though we are not quite in another world—a great deal has happened. With its influence on the language, its spawning of new words, the computer very nearly alone makes an updated edition necessary.

Moreover, twenty years, in educational terms, is—from the beginning of primary school through graduation from college—more than a generation. As for names in the news, some of them come and go quickly—who now remembers Joaquin Balaguer, Antonin Novotny, Phoumi Nosavan, Duncan Sandys, Anthony Celebrezze?—while others show remarkable durability. Andrei Gromyko has been prominent, even unavoidable, since 1943; Habib Bourguiba became newsworthy (from our point of view) in 1954; Joseph Mobutu, now Mobutu Sese Seko, in 1960; Sophia

Loren, in the early 1950s. But twenty years is a long time in news. The cast of characters has substantially changed. The *Handbook* should change as well.

Mistakes in pronunciation stay in the mind of a broadcaster. Clearly, they do not equally oppress people in other lines of work, nor should they. Yet, even for those others, or most of them, mispronunciation is unfortunate. For one thing, it embarrasses people who hear it and wonder whether to offer a correction. For another, it is hardly a recommendation, since it suggests not knowledge but rather its absence. I heard a well-known broadcaster (not on NBC) speak of Michelangelo's *Pietà* which he pronounced PEE ah TAH when, of course, Pieta (pronounced PEE ay TAH) is correct. Not the end of the world, granted. Still, how revealing it was, what evidence, in a single word, of pretended knowledge—and of pretension.

Failure to pronounce something correctly must, it seems to me, impair the confidence of others in the mispronouncer. At any rate, it does for those who know that there was a mispronunciation. It always shakes me when I hear someone who has to deal with nuclear energy, still more with nuclear weapons, say "nucular." This mistake has been with us since August 1945, when the nuclear age may be said to have begun (and, unfortunately, the nucular age, as well).

Nuclear/nucular is a special case. The word, correctly pronounced, somehow is too much for a fair part of the population, and education and experience seem to have nothing to do with it. President Eisenhower, for one, could not get it right. Neither could President Carter (though he, a former officer aboard nuclear-powered submarines, made it NOO kee ər). As this introduction was being written, Walter Mondale was busily engaged in his campaign for the 1984 Democratic presidential nomination and saying "nucular," which makes one wonder how other and lesser members of the Carter administration found it tactful to pronounce the word during Cabinet meetings. In any case, thirty-four years should be enough to establish that nuclear has only one *u*, and that an *e* has willfully worked its way into it.

In March 1983, Secretary of State George Shultz, testifying before a Congressional committee, referred to the Caribbean island of Grenada as grə NAH də. Others in high positions, including one of the stars of the "intelligence community" and many broadcasters, were still making that mistake even after Grenada was invaded months later. It was not reassuring.

In the same way, if a television anchorman (not on NBC) puts the accent on the wrong syllable when naming an Italian politician who has been on the scene for at least thirty years, one suspects that his knowledge of world affairs is thin, and his interest even more so. This is also the case when a grandly titled "diplomatic correspondent" (let's forget about the network affiliation at this point) goes wrong on the name of a Swedish prime minister who has been prominent for fifteen years. If another news anchor takes the accepted English pronunciation of the Italian city Padua, a pronunciation associated with *The Taming of the Shrew* and *Kiss Me, Kate,* and tries to make it sound Italian when the Italian (Padova) is spelled and pronounced differently, one can only be sad over the lack of knowledge and curiosity thus displayed.

I admit that if an anchorman turns assembly into a four-syllable word—ə SEM bə lee—I do not conclude that he is ignorant of what the United Nations General Assembly is and what it does. Nevertheless, it is unpleasant to listen to him, and there ought to be some pleasure in listening to the language being spoken.

Am I arguing, then, that broadcasters ought to be careful about pronunciation so that they can fool the public? In a way, yes. Broadcasters do it in their own interest. But a broadcaster also has an obligation. He—or she—is a teacher of sorts. The obligation of newspeople is not only to give the news accurately; it is also to say it correctly. Others are listening, so we presume. They should not be misled.

Should you be ashamed of yourself if you mispronounce something? Sometimes it can be so disconcerting that you can't help being ashamed. But we are not suggesting sackcloth and ashes, or seclusion. We do recommend making fewer mistakes. This handbook can help. The rules are not ironclad. No punishment, condign (in which the last syllable, taking paradigm as a paradigm, comes out dine rather than din) or otherwise, will be visited upon those who err or otherwise do not conform. My late colleague, Frank McGee, on coming to the word "sit," made it what sounded to me more like "set." No doubt this was Frank's Oklahoma upbringing asserting itself. I said "sit," but hearing "set" never bothered me, and I suppose this must have been true in reverse with Frank. For my part, it was pleasant to hear the *i* turned into an *e*. It was a reminder of how large and varied a country this is, and how important, and often attractive, its regional differences are.

It is not the purpose of a pronunciation guidebook to blot out such differences. One's instinctive reaction on hearing the Cairo in Illinois pronounced KAIR oh is that it is ridiculous; likewise when Bogota, transported from Colombia to New Jersey, is stressed on the second syllable rather than the third. But that feeling wears off. Differences of that kind make life more interesting. Nor could they be blotted out, even if we foolishly wanted to do that. It is also true, of course, that these differences should not be artificially induced. They ought to be natural, not affected. A handbook gives the correct pronunciation, or to put it more exactly, the preferred pronunciation. But no handbook will make New Yorkers say New Orleans the way the locals do, and vice versa. One hears a good deal about the homogenization of America, but southern speech remains (in its numerous variations) southern, and New England speech New England, and so on. The pronunciation scheme employed in the text of the *NBC Handbook* takes regional distinctions into account, as you will see when you begin to use the book. The flavor given the vowel sounds in English varies from region to region, and the pronunciation scheme recognizes this inalienable right.

Not long ago, the telephone rang in my hotel room in Dallas. It was the limousine service entrusted by my hosts with the task of getting me to the airport next morning. The name of the company was Regal but the notable Texas accent at the other end of the line made it RAY gal, and it took me some time to catch on. Still, it was delightful, because the Raygal was authentic.

It is not easy to know why some departures from the norm, or the preferred, are more readily tolerated than others. Euphony may have something to do with it. "Raygal" for Regal I found charming. On the other hand, I went through half my life saying AHR inj (which I now consider not delightful) when I referred to a well-known citrus fruit. It wasn't until a Californian took pity on me (it was in Greece, as it happened, where we were working for the Marshall Plan) or perhaps couldn't stand it any longer, that I learned that the fruit was an OR inj. After all, I didn't say "ahr" for "or," did I? This incident had a side benefit: I stopped saying Flahrida.

Nor is it easy to know why some departures from the preferred are thought to drum up business. Apparently it grows out of the belief that a colloquial, down-to-earth pronunciation will endear the product or service advertised to the masses. This accounts for the popularity of "gonna" in television commercials, as in "You're gonna like us," which was used by an airline, and "Bet you're gonna want one," which was used by an automobile manufacturer. Honesty compels me to add that NBC, pronunciation handbook or no pronunciation handbook, used "You're gonna like it a lot" as an advertising slogan in 1975. It was NBC's program schedule that people were gonna like a lot.

A variation on this is the dropped g at the end of *ing* words, so that an airline proclaims that it is "doin' what we do best," the makers of a mint to freshen the breath turn nothing into nothin', and a shampoo, so its creators believe, will capture a larger share of the market if it is recommended for bouncin' and behavin' hair, bouncing and behaving evidently being thought to suggest a stuffy attitude.

It seems to me that if "gonna" is thought to lead people to throw themselves frenziedly onto the product advertised, then "omina" cannot be far behind. "Omina" is a pronunciation, heard most often in New York, of "I'm going to," or as some might put it, "I'm gonna." You will hear people say, "Omina catch the next train," or "Omina have dinner out tonight." This is not the same usage as "Omina hurry" (I'm in a hurry), and it is certainly not the same pronunciation as the "Ah" that some Southerners find in "I."

Foreign names pose a particular problem, which is the reason why names of persons and places are given so much attention in this book. I remember—another mistake comes back to me now—that as the newscaster on the "Today" show in 1961 I stumbled so often over the name of the president of the Philippines that I began to regret not having contributed to his opponent's campaign fund. And there was Nikita Khrushchev, now long gone and largely forgotten, who used to give news broadcasters a particularly difficult time. How far should we have gone in trying to approximate the Russian pronunciation, especially the opening Khr, which sounded something like a clearing of the throat? For that matter, will we ever know if Krushchev's successor pronounced his name Brezhnev or Brezhnyev? And was the last letter pronounced *v, ff,* or something in between?

One answer, not entirely satisfactory but still an answer, is that tradition also has a place in these affairs, tradition and usage. Consider the Fontainebleau Hotel in Miami Beach. The former Paris correspondent for NBC News arrives determined to give it the full treatment, French all the way, and not to yield to the benighted who say Fountainblue. But no taxi drivers use the French pronunciation. Why should they? None of their customers do. Nobody at the hotel calls it anything but Fountainblue. Neither do the correspondent's colleagues. "If they want to call it Fountainblue," he snarls, "why don't they spell it that way?" Eventually he subsides. Fontainebleau seems affected. Fountainblue it is.

In other words, some things are simply because they are, not necessarily because they should be. This book is, therefore, a guide not only to what is preferred; it is a guide also to what is feasible, what is done. Perfect consistency does not exist in these matters. Least of all does it exist in a tongue that draws on as many sources as English does, and has so great a variety of speakers.

What we are saying, valued reader, is that if you follow the guidelines laid down in this book, you will be all right; you'll get along; you won't make a fool of yourself. You may even sound comfortably, but not oppressively, learned.

Now a few words of explanation. There are approximately 21,000 words in this book. How were they chosen? They were chosen according to standards established in earlier editions of this book, which means that they are:

1. Words, especially proper names, most frequently used by broadcasters.
2. Common words often mispronounced.
3. Words from history and the arts that have proved to be difficult to pronounce over the years.

Some of these words have more than one acceptable pronunciation. In each case, we have chosen only one, not to be pedantic but for the sake of simplicity. As for the method of indicating what the pronunciation should be, simplicity, in the sense of ease of understanding, is again what we have tried for. Earlier editions of the *NBC Handbook of Pronunciation* contained two ways of noting pronunciation, the International Phonetic Alphabet and respelling. The IPA is clearer and more universally understood than the diacritical markings used to indicate pronunciation in dictionaries, but it was, nonetheless, largely ignored by those who used the *Handbook*. It was the respelling on which readers leaned.

For that reason, we are using only the respelling method in this edition. Doing so saves time, saves space, and rules out confusion. Broadly speaking, the pronunciation we recommend is that of General American Speech, that which is acceptable to, and used by, the great mass of competent Americans who use the language well—you, we trust, among them.

EDWIN NEWMAN
January 1984

Guide to Pronunciation

With few exceptions, the *NBC Handbook of Pronunciation* employs letters of the English alphabet to make the sounds required to pronounce the entries in the word list. The exceptions are the schwa (ə) and the barred *i*.

The schwa, which is used in the International Phonetic Alphabet, indicates the indistinct vowel sound in the first syllable of *ago* and in the second syllables of *taken, stencil, salmon,* and *circus*.

The barred *i* is used to indicate the vowel sound in such words as *die, high, my, quite,* the *y* in *analyze,* the *i* in *terrorize,* and other words containing the long i sound.

Stressed syllables are printed in capital letters. Boldfaced capital letters indicate a primary stress. Thus, *venture* is pronounced **VEN** chər. Smaller boldfaced capital letters indicate a secondary stress. Thus, *Pennsylvania* is pronounced **PEN** səl **VAY** nyə, and *aviary* is pronounced **AY** vee **ER** ee.

Pronunciations of foreign words and names given in the *NBC Handbook* are only approximations. It is difficult to represent all the sounds found in Russian, French, Spanish, and other languages whose words and names are in frequent use in the United States. In addition, most Americans who have not studied foreign languages find it almost impossible to make some of the sounds essential in pronouncing words and names from those languages. The Russian *r* and German *ch* are but two of many examples. In this handbook, therefore, no attempt is made to reproduce such sounds faithfully. Instead, the pronunciations given are those of educated American speakers with no special competence in foreign languages.

There is a single exception. A great number of French words that have made their way into the American vocabulary require a pronunciation of *n* that is quite unlike our own, and the special *n* sound is called to the reader's attention in pronunciations where it occurs. If readers of the *NBC Handbook* are unfamiliar with this sound, they are best advised to consult someone who speaks French. Through repeated demonstrations plus trial, error, and correction, this difficult sound can be mastered. The presence of a French final *n,* as it is called here, indicates that the vowel sound before the *n* is made with the nasal passages open, as in the French words *garçon* and *vin,* rather than with the nasal passages closed, as in the English words *fan* and *tone.*

A final note on foreign pronunciations: in certain Oriental languages no syllable is stressed more than any other. For this reason the reader will often encounter polysyllabic Oriental words and names pronounced without stress of any syllable. In pronunciations of other Oriental terms, stresses are shown. This is because the latter group comprises words and names that have been spoken by Americans for so long that stresses are normally used by most educated persons. Thus, *Tokyo* is pronounced **TOH** kee **OH**, while *Nakasone* is nah kah soh ne.

Abbreviations Used in This Book

a	adjective
adv	adverb
fem	feminine
masc	masculine
n	noun
pl	plural
sing	singular
US	United States
USSR	Union of Soviet Socialist Republics

Pronunciation Key

ə *as in* ago, taken, stencil, salmon, circus
a *as in* apt, sap
ah *as in* calm, father
ahr *as in* ark, dark, harm
air *as in* care, pair
aw *as in* all, saw
ay *as in* ail, say, tame
b *as in* bob, box, nab
ch *as in* chest, church, preach
d *as in* dud, dug, sad
e *as in* bet, egg
ee *as in* easy, me
eer *as in* beer, ear, tier
f *as in* far, fluff, thief
g *as in* gave, grog, hag
h *as in* half, he
i *as in* is, quick
ī *as in* my, tie
j *as in* jump, judge, magic
k *as in* cuff, kluck
l *as in* left, lull
m *as in* come, merry, mom
n *as in* now, nun, span
French final n *as in* garçon, vin
ng *as in* hang, sing, singer
o *as in* hot, on, sock

oh *as in* clone, coat, oat
oi *as in* boy, toil
oo *as in* soon, too
oor *as in* cure, poor, tour
or *as in* for, tore, warn
ow *as in* cow, ouch
p *as in* put, pop, wrap
r *as in* hear, rap, rare
s *as in* sap, spice, twice
sh *as in* hush, sheep, shush
t *as in* pat, tip, toot
th *as in* bath, fourth, thin
th *as in* bathe, father, this
u *as in* supper, up
ur *as in* first, her, spur
uu *as in* book, foot, full
v *as in* live, valve, very
w *as in* quiet, west
y *as in* yard, you
z *as in* hazy, please, zip
zh *as in* leisure, pleasure

A

Aachen	**AH** kən
Aalborg	**AWL** bawrg
Aalsmeer	**AHLS** mer
Aalten	**AHL** tən
aardvark	**AHRD** ᴠᴀʜʀᴋ
Aaron	**AIR** ən
Abaco	**AB** ə ᴋᴏʜ
abacus	**AB** ə kəs
Abada, Abdelouahab	ah **BAH** dah, ᴀʜʙ doo lah **HAHB**
abalone	ᴀʙ ə **LOH** nee
abattoir	**AB** ə twahr
Abaya, Hernando	ah **BĪ** ah, air **NAHN** doh
Abbas	ah **BAHS**
abbé	a **BAY**
Abdalla, Abdel-Rahman	ahb **DAH** lah, **AHB** del **RAH** mən
Abdallah	ahb **DAH** lah
Abdelghani, Mohamed Ben Ahmed	ᴀʜʙ dool **HAH** nee, moh **HAH** med bən **AH** med
Abdnor	**ABD** nər
abdomen	**AB** də mən
abdominal	ab **DOM** ə nəl
Abdulah, Frank Owen	ahb **DOO** lah
Abednego	ə **BED** nə ᴄᴏʜ
Abelard	**AB** ə ʟᴀʜʀᴅ
Abello	ah **BE** yaw
Abercrombie, Abercromby	**AB** ər ᴋʀᴏᴍ bee
Aberdeen (Scotland)	ᴀʙ ər **DEEN**
Aberdeen (US)	ᴀʙ ər **DEEN**
aberrant	ə **BER** ənt
aberration	ab ə **RAY** shən
Aberystwyth	ᴀʙ ə **RIST** with
abeyance	ə **BAY** əns
abhor	ab **HOR**
abhorrent	ab **HOR** ənt
Abidin, Tan Sri Zainal	ah bee **DIN**, tahn sree **ZĪ** nahl
Abidjan	ᴀʙ i **JAHN**
Abigail	**AB** ə ᴄᴀʏʟ
Abilene (Syria)	ᴀʙ ə **LEE** nee
Abilene (US)	ᴀʙ ə **LEEN**

25

Abimelech	ə **BIM** ə LEK
Abinoam	ə **BIN** oh əm
Abitibi	AB ə **TIB** ee
abject	**AB** jekt
ablation	ab **LAY** shən
ablative absolute	**AB** lə tiv **AB** sə loot
ablution	ə **BLOO** shən
aboriginal	AB ə **RIJ** ə nəl
aborigine	AB ə **RIJ** ə nee
aborigines	AB ə **RIJ** ə neez
abort	ə **BORT**
abortive	ə **BOR** tiv
Abou ben Adhem	**AH** boo ben **AH** dem
Aboul-Nasr, Mahmoud	ah **BOOL NAH** zər, mah **MOOD**
Abourezk	**AB** ər ESK
abracadabra	AB rə kə **DAB** rə
Abraham	**AY** brə HAM
Abram	**AY** brəm
abrasion	ə **BRAY** _zh_ən
abrogate	**AB** rə gayt
Abruzzi	ah **BROOT** tsee
abscess	**AB** ses
abscissa	ab **SIS** ə
abscond	ab **SKOND**
absent (a)	**AB** sənt
absent (v)	ab **SENT**
absentee	AB sən **TEE**
absinthe	**AB** sinth
absolute	**AB** sə LOOT
absolutely	AB sə **LOOT** lee
absolve	ab **ZOLV**
absorb	ab **SORB**
abstemious	ab **STEE** mee əs
abstract (a, n)	**AB** strakt
abstract (v)	ab **STRAKT**
abstruse	ab **STROOS**
absurd	ab **SURD**
absurdity	ab **SUR** də tee
Abu Dhabi	AH boo **DAH** bee
Abulhassan, Mohammad A.	ah **BOOL HAH** sahn, moh **HAHM** ahd
abuse (n)	ə **BYOOS**
abuse (v)	ə **BYOOZ**

ə ago, a at, ah calm, ahr dark, air care, aw saw, ay say, ch church
e bet, ee me, eer beer, hw what, i is, ī my, _n_ French final n vin,

abusive	ə **BYOO** siv
Abydos (Egypt)	ə **BĪ** dos
abyss	ə **BIS**
Abyssinia	**AB** ə **SIN** ee ə
acacia	ə **KAY** shə
academe	**AK** ə **DEEM**
academician	ə **KAD** ə **MISH** ən
académie (French)	a ka day **MEE**
academy	ə **KAD** ə mee
Acadia	ə **KAY** dee ə
acanthus	ə **KAN** thəs
a cappella	**AH** kə **PEL** ə
a capriccio	**AH** kah **PREET** choh
Acapulco	**AK** ə **PUUL** koh
accelerando	ak **SEL** ə **RAHN** doh
accelerate	ak **SEL** ə **RAYT**
accelerator	ak **SEL** ə **RAY** tər
accelerometer	ak **SEL** ə **ROM** ə tər
accent	**AK** sent
accept	ak **SEPT**
acceptable	ak **SEP** tə bəl
acceptance	ak **SEP** təns
access	**AK** ses
accessory	ak **SES** ə ree
acclamation	**AK** lə **MAY** shən
acclimate	**AK** lə **MAYT**
acclimation	**AK** lə **MAY** shən
acclimatization	ə **KLĪ** mə tə **ZAY** shən
acclimatize	ə **KLĪ** mə **TĪZ**
accolade	**AK** ə **LAYD**
accompaniment	ə **KUM** pə nee mənt
accompanist	ə **KUM** pə nəst
accomplish	ə **KOM** plish
accouchement	ə **KOOSH** mahnt
accoucheur	a koo **SHUR**
accoutre	ə **KOO** tər
accoutrement	ə **KOO** tər mənt
Accra	ə **KRAH**
accredit	ə **KRED** ət
accrue	ə **KROO**
Aceldama	ə **SEL** də mə
acerb	ə **SURB**
acerbate	**AS** ər **BAYT**

---

o **on**, oh **oat**, oi **boy**, oo **soon**, oor **poor**, or **for**, ow **cow**, sh **shush**,
th **thin**, *th* **this**, u **up**, ur **spur**, uu **book**, *zh* **pleasure**

acerbity	ə SUR bi tee
acetanilide	AS ə TAN ə LĪD
acetate	AS ə TAYT
acetic	ə SEE tik
acetylene	ə SET i lən
Achaea	ə KEE ə
Achaean	ə KEE ən
Achaia	ə KAY ə
Achenbach	AH kən bahk
Acheron	AK ə RON
Achilles	ə KIL eez
Achitophel	ə KIT ə FEL
achromatic	AK rə MAT ik
acidity	ə SID ə tee
acidosis	AS ə DOH səs
acidulous	ə SIJ ə ləs
acinus	AS ə nəs
acme	AK mee
acne	AK nee
acolyte	AK ə LĪT
aconite	AK ə NĪT
acorn	AY korn
Acosta	ah KAW stah
acoustics	ə KOO stiks
acquaintance	ə KWAYN təns
acquiesce	AK wee ES
acquisitive	ə KWIZ ə tiv
acrid	AK rid
acrimonious	AK rə MOH nee əs
acrimony	AK rə MOH nee
acromegaly	AK rə MEG ə lee
acronym	AK rə nim
acropolis	ə KROP ə ləs
across	ə KRAWS
acrostic	ə KRAW stik
acrylic	ə KRIL ik
Actaeon	ak TEE ən
actual	AK choo əl
actually	AK choo ə lee
actuary	AK choo ER ee
acuity	ə KYOO ə tee
acumen	ə KYOO mən
acupuncture	AK yə PUNGK chər

ə ago, a at, ah calm, ahr dark, air care, aw saw, ay say, ch church
e bet, ee me, eer beer, hw what, i is, ī my, *n* French final n vin,

acute	ə KYOOT
Ada	AY də
adage	AD ij
adagio	ə DAH joh
Adah	AY də
adamant	AD ə mənt
adamantine	AD ə MAN tən
Adamic, Louis	AD ə mik, LOO is
Adan, Ahmed	ah DAHN, AH med moh HAHM ed
Mohamed	
adapt	ə DAPT
Addabbo	ə DAH boh
addenda	ə DEN də
addendum	ə DEN dəm
addict (n)	AD ikt
addict (v)	ə DIKT
Addis Ababa	AD əs AB ə bə
Addison	AD ə sən
additive	AD ə tiv
addle	AD əl
address (n)	AD res
address (v)	ə DRES
adduce	ə DOOS
Adelaide	AD ə LAYD
Adelphi	ə DEL fi
Aden	AH dən
Adenauer, Konrad	AD now ər, KON rad
adenoid	AD ə NOID
adenoma	AD ə NOH mə
adenosine	ə DEN ə SEEN
adept (a)	ə DEPT
adept (n)	AD ept
adequate	AD ə kwət
à deux	a DUU
adherence	ad HEER əns
adherent	ad HEER ənt
adhesion	ad HEE zhən
adhesive	ad HEE siv
ad hoc	ad HOK
ad hominem	ad HOM ə nəm
adiabatic	AYD ee ə BAT ik
adieu	ə DYUU
adieux	ə DYUUZ

o on, oh oat, oi boy, oo soon, oor poor, or for, ow cow, sh shush,
th thin, *th* this, u up, ur spur, uu book, *zh* pleasure

Adige	**AH** dee je
ad infinitum	ad **IN** fə **NĪ** təm
ad interim	ad **IN** tə rəm
adios	**AD** ee **OHS**
adipose	**AD** ə **POHS**
adiposity	**AD** ə **POS** ə tee
adjacent	ə **JAY** sənt
adjective	**AJ** ik tiv
adjoin	ə **JOIN**
adjourn	ə **JURN**
adjudicate	ə **JOO** di **KAYT**
adjunct	**AJ** ungkt
adjure	ə **JOOR**
adjutant	**AJ** ə tənt
ad libitum	ad **LIB** ə təm
admirable	**AD** mə rə bəl
admiralty, A-	**AD** mə rəl tee
admittance	ad **MIT** əns
admonish	ad **MON** ish
ad nauseam	ad **NAW** zee əm
adobe	ə **DOH** bee
adolescence	**AD** ə **LES** əns
Adolfo	ə **DOL** foh
Adonais	**AD** ə **NAY** is
Adonijah	**AD** ə **NĪ** jə
Adonis	ə **DON** əs
adorable	ə **DOR** ə bəl
adoration	**AD** ə **RAY** shən
Adoula, Cyrille	ah **DOO** lə, see **RIL**
adrenal	ə **DREEN** əl
adrenalin	ə **DREN** ə lən
adrenocorticotrophic	ə **DREE** noh **KOR** tə koh **TROH** fik
adrenocorticotropic	ə **DREE** noh **KOR** tə koh **TROP** ik
Adriatic	**AY** dree **AT** ik
adroit	ə **DROIT**
adulatory	**AJ** ə lə **TOHR** ee
Adullam	ə **DUL** əm
adult	ə **DULT**
Adum, Mohamet Ali	**AH** doom, moh **HAHM** et **AH** lee
adumbrate	a **DUM** brayt
ad valorem	ad və **LOHR** əm
advantage	ad **VAN** tij
advantageous	**AD** vən **TAY** jəs

ə ago, a at, ah calm, ahr dark, air care, aw saw, ay say, ch church
e bet, ee me, eer beer, hw what, i is, ī my, *n* French final n vin,

advent	**AD** vent
adversary	**AD** vər **SER** ee
adverse	ad **VURS**
advertise	**AD** vər **TĪZ**
advertisement	**AD** vər **TĪZ** mənt
advertiser	**AD** vər **TĪZ** ər
advice (n)	ad **VĪS**
advise (v)	ad **VĪZ**
advocacy	**AD** və kə see
advocate (n)	**AD** və kət
advocate (v)	**AD** və **KAYT**
Adzhubei, Alexei	ahd *zh*ə **BAY**, ah **LEK** see
Aegean	i **JEE** ən
aegis	**EE** jis
Aegisthus	i **JIS** thəs
Aeneas	i **NEE** əs
Aeneid	i **NEE** id
Aeolian	ee **OH** lee ən
Aeolus	**EE** ə ləs
aeon	**EE** ən
aerate	**AIR** ayt
aerial	**AIR** ee əl
aerie	**AIR** ee
aeronautics	**AIR** ə **NAW** tik
Aeschines	**ES** kə **NEEZ**
Aeschylus	**ES** kə ləs
Aesculapius	**ES** kyə **LAY** pee əs
Aesop	**EE** səp
aesthete	**ES** theet
aesthetic	es **THET** ik
aestivate	**ES** tə **VAYT**
Aetna	**ET** nə
affair	ə **FAIR**
affaire	a **FAIR**
afferent	**AF** ər ənt
affirm	ə **FURM**
affirmation	**AF** ər **MAY** shən
affix (n)	**AF** iks
affix (v)	ə **FIKS**
affluence	**AF** loo əns
affluent	**AF** loo ənt
affront	ə **FRUNT**
afghan, A-	**AF** gan

---

o on, oh oat, oi boy, oo soon, oor poor, or for, ow cow, sh shush,
th thin, *th* this, u up, ur spur, uu book, *zh* pleasure

Afghanistan	af **GAN** i **STAN**
aficionado	ə **FISH** yə **NAH** doh
a fortiori	ay **FOHR** shee **OHR** ee
Africa	**AF** ri kə
Afrikaans	**AF** ri **KAHNS**
Afrikaner	**AF** ri **KAH** nər
Agag	**AY** gag
again	ə **GEN**
against	ə **GENST**
Aga Khan	ah gə **KAHN**
Agamemnon	**AG** ə **MEM** non
agape (love)	ah **GAH** pay
agape (wide open)	ə **GAYP**
agar, A-	**AH** gər
Agassiz	**AG** ə see
agate	**AG** ət
agave	ə **GAH** vee
Agca, Mehmet Ali	**AHR** jah, **ME** met ah **LEE** (**AHR** *R* barely pronounced)
Agee	**AY** jee
agenda	ə **JEN** də
ageratum	**AJ** ə **RAY** təm
aggrandize	ə **GRAN** dīz
aggrandizement	ə **GRAN** dəz mənt
aggravate	**AG** rə **VAYT**
aggregate (a, n)	**AG** rə gət
aggregate (v)	**AG** rə **GAYT**
aggressor	ə **GRES** ər
aghast	ə **GAST**
agile	**AJ** əl
agility	ə **JIL** ə tee
Agincourt	**AJ** ən **KORT**
agitato	**AJ** ə **TAH** toh
Agnelli	ahn **YEL** ee
Agnew, Spiro	**AG** nyoo, **SPIR** oh
Agnon, Samuel	**AG** non
agnostic	ag **NOS** tik
Agnus Dei	**AG** nəs **DEE** ī
Ago, Roberto	**AH** goh, roh **BAIR** toh
agoraphobia	**AG** ə rə **FOH** bee ə
Agrado	ah **GRAH** doh
agrarian	ə **GRAIR** ee ən
agronomist	ə **GRON** ə məst

ə ago, a at, ah calm, ahr dark, air care, aw saw, ay say, ch church
e bet, ee me, eer beer, hw what, i is, ī my, *n* French final n vin,

Agronsky	ə GRON skee
Agt, Andreas van	AHKT, ahn DRAY ahs vahn
ague	AY gyoo
Aguecheek	AY gyoo cheek
Aguilar	AH gi LAHR
Aguinaldo	AH gi NAHL doh
Aguirre de Carcer, Nuño	ah GEE ray day KAHR ser, NOO nyoh
Ahab	AY hab
Ahasuerus	ə HAZ yoo EER əs
Ahaz	AY haz
Ahithophel	ə HITH ə FEL
Ahmed	AH med
aide	ayd
aide-de-camp	AYD də KAMP
aide-mémoire	AYD mem WAHR
aiguillette	AY gwi LET
Aiken	AY kən
aileron	AY lə RON
ailurophobia	ī LUUR ə FOH bee ə
Aimée, Anouk	e MAY, ah NUUK
Ainsworth	AYNZ wurth
aisle	īl
Aisne	ayn
Aix-la-Chapelle	AYKS lah shah PEL
Ajaccio	ah YAHT chaw
Ajax	AY jaks
Akaka, Daniel K.	ah KAH kah
Akeley	AYK lee
Akihito	ah kee hee toh
akimbo	ə KIM boh
akin	ə KIN
Akuete, Ebenezer	AH koo AY tay, EB ə NEE zər
akvavit	AHK vah VEET
Akyab	ak YAB
Alabama	AL ə BAM ə
alabaster	AL ə BAS tər
à la carte	AL ə KAHRT
alacrity	ə LAK rə tee
Aladdin	ə LAD ən
Al-Ali, Salah Omar	əl ah LEE, sah LAH oh MAHR
Al-Ameri, Abdelkader Braik	ahl ah MAH ree, AHB dool KAH dər bə RĪ eek

Alamo	**AL** ə **MOH**
à la mode	**AL** ə **MOHD**
Aland	**AH** lənd
Alaric	**AL** ər ik
alas	ə **LAS**
Al-Ashtal, Abdalla Saleh	ahl **AHSH** al, **AHB** də lah **SAH** lay
Alaska	ə **LAS** kə
al-Assad, Hafez	əl **AS** sad, **HAH** fə*th*
Alataz, Alex	ahl ah tahz, ah leks
albacore	**AL** bə **KOHR**
Alban	**AWL** bən
Albania	al **BAY** nee ə
Albany	**AWL** bə nee
albatross	**AL** bə **TRAWS**
albedo	al **BEE** doh
Albee	**AWL** bee
albeit	awl **BEE** it
Albemarle	**AL** bə **MAHRL**
Albéniz, Isaac	ahl **VE** neeth, **EE** sah **AHK**
Alberghetti	al bər **GE** tee
Albergue, Pablo Mauricio	ahl **BAIR** gay, **PAHB** loh mow **REES** ee oh
Alberich	**AHL** bər ik
Alberoni	**AHL** be **RAW** nee
Albert (French)	al **BAIR**
Alberta	al **BUR** tə
Alberti	ahl **BER** tee
Albertina	**AL** bər **TEE** nə
Albertinelli	**AHL** bair ti **NEL** ee
Albigenses	**AL** bə **JEN** seez
Albigensian	**AL** bə **JEN** see ən
albinism	**AL** bə niz əm
albino	al **BĪ** noh
Albion	**AL** bee ən
Albornoz, Miguel	ahl bor **NAWS**, mee **GAYL**
Albrecht	**AHL** brekt
Albricht	**AWL** brikt
album	**AL** bəm
albumen	al **BYOO** mən
Albuquerque	**AL** bə **KUR** kee
alcalde	al **KAL** dee
alcántara, A-	ahl **KAHN** tah rah

ə ago, a at, ah calm, ahr dark, air care, aw saw, ay say, ch church
e bet, ee me, eer beer, hw what, i is, ī my, *n* French final n vin,

Alcatraz	**AL** kə **TRAZ**
alcazar, A-	**AL** kə **ZAHR**
Alceste	al **SEST**
Alcestis	al **SES** təs
alchemist	**AL** kə məst
alchemy	**AL** kə mee
Alcibiades	**AL** sə **BĪ** ə **DEEZ**
Alcinoüs	al **SIN** oh əs
Alcmene	alk **MEE** nee
Alcoa	al **KOH** ə
Alcott	**AWL** kət
alcove	**AL** kohv
Aldebaran	al **DEB** ər ən
aldehyde	**AL** də **HĪD**
al dente	al **DEN** tay
alder	**AWL** dər
Alderney	**AWL** dər nee
Aldershot	**AWL** dər **SHOT**
Aldine	**AWL** dīn
Aldrich	**AWL** drich
aldrin, A-	**AWL** drən
Aleichem, Sholem	ə **LAY** kəm, **SHUU** ləm
Aleixandre, Vicente	ah layk **SAHN** dray, bee **SEN** tay
Alemán, Miguel	**AH** le **MAHN**, mee **GEL**
aleph	**AH** ləf
alert	ə **LURT**
Al-Eryani, Mohamad	ahl ee **YAH** nee, moh **HAHM** ahd
Aleut	ə **LOOT**
Aleutian	ə **LOO** shən
Alexander	**AL** ig **ZAN** dər
Alexandria	**AL** ig **ZAN** dree ə
Alexis	ə **LEK** sis
Alfaro	ahl **FAH** roh
Al Fatah	ahl fah **TAH**
Alfonsin, Raúl	**AHL** fawn **SEEN**, rah **OOL**
Alfonso	al **FON** soh
Alfreda	al **FREE** də
Alfredo	ahl **FRAY** doh
alfresco	al **FRES** koh
Alfvén, Hannes	ahl **VEE** ən, **HAH** nes
alga	**AL** gə
algae	**AL** jee
algebraic	**AL** jə **BRAY** ik

o on, oh oat, oi boy, oo soon, oor poor, or for, ow cow, sh shush,
th thin, *th* this, u up, ur spur, uu book, *zh* pleasure

Alger	**AL** jər
Algeria	al **JEER** ee ə
Algerian	al **JEER** ee ən
Algernon	**AL** jər nən
Algol	**AL** gol
Algonquin	al **GONG** kwən
algorithm	**AL** gə RI*TH* əm
Algren	**AWL** grən
Alhambra	al **HAM** brə
al-Hassani, Ali Nasser Mohammed	ahl **HAH** sah nee, **AH** lee **NAH** zər moh **HAHM** ed
Alhegelan, Faisal	ahl **HAHG** layn, **FĪ** sahl
Ali	**AH** lee
Ali, Muhammad	ah **LEE**, mə **HAHM** əd
alias	**AY** lee əs
aliases	**AY** lee əs əz
Ali Baba	**AH** lee **BAH** bah
alibi	**AL** ə **BĪ**
alidade	**AL** ə **DAYD**
alien	**AYL** yən
alienate	**AYL** yə **NAYT**
alienation	**AYL** yə **NAY** shən
Alighieri	**AH** lee **GYAY** ree
alignment	ə **LĪN** mənt
alimentary	**AL** ə **MEN** tə ree
alimony	**AL** ə **MOH** nee
Alison	**AL** ə sən
Alitalia	ah li **TAHL** yə
alkali	**AL** kə **LĪ**
alkaline	**AL** kə **LĪN**
alkaloid	**AL** kə **LOID**
al-Kasim, Marwan	ahl **KAH** sem, mahr **WAHN**
al-Kassem, Abdel-Raouf	el **KAH** sim, **AHB** duul rah **OOF**
al Khalifa, Emir Isa ibn Salman	ahl kah **LEE** fah, ay **MEER** ee **SAH** ee **BEN SAHL** mən
al Khalifa, Khalifa ibn Salman	ahl kah **LEE** fah, kah **LEE** fah ee **BEN SAHL** mən
alkyd	**AL** kəd
alla breve	**AH** lə **BREV** ay
Allagany, Gaafar	ahl **LAH** jah nee, **ZH**AH fər
Allah	**AL** ə
allargando	**AH** lahr **GAHN** doh

ə ago, a at, ah calm, ahr dark, air care, aw saw, ay say, ch church
e bet, ee me, eer beer, hw what, i is, ī my, *n* French final n vin,

allege	ə LEJ
alleged	ə LEJD
allegedly	ə LEJ əd lee
Alleghany	AL ə GAY nee
Allegheny	AL ə GAY nee
allegiance	ə LEE jəns
allegory	AL ə GOR ee
allegretto	AL ə GRET oh
allegro	ə LEG roh
allele	ə LEEL
alleluia	AL ə LOO yə
allemande	AL ə MAND
Allende Gossens	ah YEN de GAW sens
allergic	ə LUR jik
allergy	AL ər jee
Allers, Franz	AH lərs, FRAHNZ
alleviate	ə LEE vee AYT
alliance	ə LĪ əns
allied (a)	AL īd
allied (v)	ə LĪD
allies (pl of *ally*)	AL īz
alliteration	ə LIT ə RAY shən
alliterative	ə LIT ə rə tiv
allium	AL ee əm
allocate	AL ə KAYT
allomorph	AL ə MORF
allopathic	AL ə PATH ik
allopathy	ə LOP ə thee
allophone	AL ə FOHN
alloy (n)	AL oi
alloy (v)	ə LOI
allspice	AWL spīs
allude	ə LOOD
allure	ə LOOR
allusion	ə LOO zhən
allusive	ə LOO siv
alluvial	ə LOO vee əl
ally (n)	AL ī
ally (v)	ə LĪ
Allyev, Geidar	ah LEE yef, GĪ dahr
Allyson	A li sən
al-Maktum, Rashid ibn Said	ahl mahk TOOM, rah SHEED ee BEN sah EED

alma mater	**AL** mə **MAH** tər
almanac	**AWL** mə NAK
almandine	**AL** mən DEEN
Alma-Tadema	AL mə **TAD** ə mə
Almaviva	ahl mah **VEE** vah
Al-Mokarrab, Ahmed	ahl **MOH** kə rahb, **AH** med
almond	**AH** mənd
almoner	**AL** mə nər
alms	ahmz
al-Nahayan, Zaid ibn Sultan	ahl nah **HĪ** yən, **SAH** eed **IB** ən sool **TAHN**
aloe	**AL** oh
aloes	**AL** ohz
aloha	ə **LOH** hah
Alonzo	ə **LON** zoh
aloof	ə **LOOF**
alopecia	AL ə **PEE** shee ə
Aloysius	**AL** oh **ISH** əs
alpaca	al **PAK** ə
alpenhorn	**AL** pən HORN
alpenstock	**AL** pən STOK
alpha	**AL** fə
alphanumeric	AL fə noo **MER** ik
alpine, A-	**AL** pīn
Alpinist	**AL** pə nist
Alpujarras, Alpuxaras	AL puu **HAHR** əs
Al-Qasimi, Fahim Sultan	ahl **HAH** sheem, **FAH** heem sool **TAHN**
Al-Sabah, Saud Nasir	ahl **SHAH** bah, sah **OOD** nah **SHEER**
Al-Sabbagh, Hussein	ahl **SHAH** bah, hoo **SHAYN**
Alsace	al **SAS**
alsatian	al **SAY** shən
Altaic	al **TAY** ik
Altair	al **TAH** ər
Altamira	AL tə **MEER** ə
altar	**AWL** tər
altazimuth	al **TAZ** ə məth
alter	**AWL** tər
altercation	AWL tər **KAY** shən
alter ego	AWL tər **EE** goh
alternate (a, n)	**AWL** tər nət
alternate (v)	**AWL** tər NAYT
alternately	**AWL** tər nət lee

ə ago, a at, ah calm, ahr dark, air care, aw saw, ay say, ch church
e bet, ee me, eer beer, hw what, i is, ī my, *n* French final n vin,

alternation	AWL tər NAY shən
alternative	awl TUR nə tiv
althaea	al THEE ə
al-Thani, Khalifa ibn Hamad	ahl TAH nee, kah LEE fə IB ən HAH məd
Althing	AHL thing
altimeter	al TIM ə tər
altitude	AL tə TOOD
alto	AL toh
Alto Adige	AHL toh AH dee je
Altrocchi	ahl TRAW ki
altruism	AL troo IZ əm
alum	AL əm
aluminium (British)	AL yə MIN ee əm
aluminum	ə LOO mə nəm
alumna (fem sing)	ə LUM nə
alumnae (fem pl)	ə LUM nee
alumni (masc pl)	ə LUM nī
alumnus (masc sing)	ə LUM nəs
Alvarado	AHL vah RAH doh
alveolar	al VEE ə lər
al-Wazzan, Shafiq	ahl wah ZEN, shah FEEK
alyssum	ə LIS əm
Alzheimer's disease	AHLTS HĪ mərz
amàbile	ah MAH bee le
Amadeus	AH mah DAY uus
Amadis	AM ə dis
Amado	ah MAH doh
Amalek	AM ə LEK
Amalekite	AM ə LEK īt
Amalfi	ə MAHL fee
amalgam	ə MAL gəm
amalgamate (v)	ə MAL gə MAYT
Amalthea	AM əl THEE ə
amandine	AH mən DEEN
amanuensis	ə MAN yoo EN səs
Amany, René	ah MAH nee, rə NAY
amaranth	AM ə RANTH
amaranthine	AM ə RAN thən
Amarillo	AM ə RIL oh
amaryllis, A-	AM ə RIL əs
amass	ə MAS
amateur	AM ə chuur

o on, oh oat, oi boy, oo soon, oor poor, or for, ow cow, sh shush, th thin, *th* this, u up, ur spur, uu book, *zh* pleasure

amateurish	AM ə CHUUR ish
Amati	ah MAH tee
Amato	ə MAH toh
amatory	AM ə TOR ee
Amaya	ə MĪ ə
Amaye, Shiro	ah mah ye, shee roh
amazon, A-	AM ə ZON
ambassador	am BAS ə dər
ambassadorial	am BAS ə DOR ee əl
ambergris	AM bər GRIS
ambidexterity	AM bi dek STER i tee
ambidextrous	AM bi DEK strəs
ambience	AM bee əns
ambient	AM bee ənt
ambiguity	AM bə GYOO ə tee
ambiguous	am BIG yoo əs
ambivalence	am BIV ə ləns
amblyopia	AM blee OH pee ə
Amboina	am BOI nə
Amboise	ahm BWAHZ
Ambon	AHM bawn
Ambrose	AM brohz
ambrosia	am BROH zhə
ambulance	AM byə ləns
ambulatory	AM byə lə TOR ee
ambuscade	AM bə SKAYD
ambush	AM buush
Amega, Atsu-Koffi	ah MAY gə, ah CHOO koh FEE
Amelia	ə MEEL yə
ameliorate	ə MEEL yə RAYT
ameliorative	ə MEEL yə RAY tiv
amen (singing)	AH MEN
amen (speaking)	AY MEN
amenable	ə MEE nə bəl
amend	ə MEND
amendment	ə MEND mənt
Amenhotep	AH mən HOH tep
amenity	ə MEN ə tee
amenorrhea	ay MEN ə REE ə
ament (flower spike)	AM ənt
ament (mentally deficient person)	AY ment
Americana	ə MER ə KAN ə

ə ago, a at, ah calm, ahr dark, air care, aw saw, ay say, ch church
e bet, ee me, eer beer, hw what, i is, ī my, n French final n vin,

Americanism	ə MER ə kə NIZ əm
Americanize	ə MER ə kə NĪZ
Amerind	AM ə rind
Amerindian	AM ə RIN dee ən
amethyst	AM ə thəst
Amharic	am HAR ik
Amherst	AM ərst
amiability	AY mee ə BIL ə tee
amiable	AY mee ə bəl
amicability	AM i kə BIL ə tee
amicable	AM i kə bəl
amicus curiae	ə MEE kəs KYUUR ee ī
Amiens	AM ee ənz
amiga	ə MEE gə
amigo	ə MEE goh
Amin, Idi	ah MEEN, EE dee
amine	ə MEEN
amino	ə MEE noh
amir	ə MEER
Amish	AH mish
amiss	ə MIS
amity, A-	AM ə tee
Amman	AH mahn
Ammon	AM ən
ammonia	ə MOHN yə
ammoniac	ə MOH nee AK
ammonium	ə MOH nee əm
amnesia	am NEE *zh*ə
amnesty	AM nə stee
amniocentesis	AM nee oh sen TEE səs
amnion	AM nee on
amniotic	AM nee OT ik
amoeba	ə MEE bə
amok	ə MUK
amoral	ay MOR əl
Amorite	AM ə RĪT
amoroso	AH mə ROH soh
amorous	AM ə rəs
amorphous	ə MOR fəs
amortization	AM ər tə ZAY shən
amortize	AM ər TĪZ
Amory	AY mə ree
Amos	AY məs

---

o on, oh oat, oi boy, oo soon, oor poor, or for, ow cow, sh shush,
th thin, *th* this, u up, ur spur, uu book, *zh* pleasure

amour	ə MOOR
Amoy	ah MOI
amperage	AM pə rij
ampere	AM peer
ampersand	AM pər SAND
amphetamine	am FET ə MEEN
amphibian	am FIB ee ən
amphibious	am FIB ee əs
Amphion	am FĪ ən
amphitheater	AM fə THEE ə tər
Amphitrite	AM fə TRĪ tee
Amphitryon	am FĪ tree ən
amphora	AM fə rə
amplifier	AM plə FĪ ər
amplify	AM plə FĪ
amplitude	AM plə TOOD
ampoule	AM pool
ampule	AM pyool
Amritsar	əm RIT sər
Amsterdam	AM stər DAM
Amtorg	AM tawrg
amuck	ə MUK
amulet	AM yə lət
Amundsen	AH mənd sən
Amur	ah MUUR
amusement	ə MYOOZ mənt
Amy	AY mee
Amytal	AM ə TAWL
Anabaptism	AN ə BAP tiz əm
Anabaptist	AN ə BAP təst
anabasis	ə NAB ə səs
anachronism	ə NAK rə NIZ əm
anaconda, A-	AN ə KON də
Anacreon	ə NAK ree ən
anaerobic	AN ə ROH bik
anagram	AN ə GRAM
anal	AY nəl
analgesia	AN əl JEE zee ə
analgesic	AN əl JEE zik
analog	AN ə LAWG
analogous	ə NAL ə gəs
analogy	ə NAL ə jee
analyses	ə NAL ə SEEZ

ə ago, a at, ah calm, ahr dark, air care, aw saw, ay say, ch church
e bet, ee me, eer beer, hw what, i is, ī my, n French final n vin,

analysis	ə NAL ə səs
analyst	AN ə ləst
analytic	AN ə LIT ik
analyze	AN ə LĪZ
Ananias	AN ə NĪ əs
anapest	AN ə PEST
anarchism	AN ər KIZ əm
anarchist	AN ər kəst
anarchy	AN ər kee
Anasazi	AH nə SAH zee
Anastasia	AN ə STAY zhə
Anastasius	AN ə STAY shəs
anastigmatic	AN as tig MAT ik
anathema	ə NATH ə mə
Anatole	AN ə TOHL
Anatolia	AN ə TOH lee ə
anatomical	AN ə TOM i kəl
anatomist	ə NAT ə məst
anatomy	ə NAT ə mee
Anaxagoras	AN ak SAG ər əs
ancestor	AN ses tər
ancestral	an SES trəl
ancestry	AN ses tree
anchorite	ANG kə RĪT
anchovy	AN choh vee
ancien régime	ahn SYAN ray ZHEEM (SYAN French final *n*)
ancillary	AN sə LER ee
Ancona	ahn KAW nah
Andalusia	AN də LOO zhə
Andaman	AN də mən
andante	ahn DAHN tay
andantino	AHN dahn TEE noh
Andean	an DEE ən
Andes	AN deez
andiron	AND ī ərn
Andorra	an DOR ə
Andover	AN DOH vər
Andrade	ahn DRAH day
Andrassy	ahn DRAHSH ee
André	AHN dray
Andrea del Sarto	ahn DRAY ah del SAHR toh
Andreev	ahn DRE yəf

o on, oh oat, oi boy, oo soon, oor poor, or for, ow cow, sh shush,
th thin, *th* this, u up, ur spur, uu book, *zh* pleasure

Andreotti, Giulio	AHN dre AW tee, JOOL yoh
Andreyev	ahn DRE yəf
Andrić, Ivo	AHN drich, EE vaw
Androcles	AN drə KLEEZ
Androclus	AN drə kləs
androgen	AN drə jən
androgynous	an DROJ ə nəs
android	AN droid
Andromache	an DROM ə KEE
Andromeda	an DROM ə də
Andronicus	AN drə NĪ kəs
Andronicus	an DRON ik əs
(Shakespeare)	
Andropov, Yuri	ahn DRAW pəf, YOO ri
Andvari, Andwari	AHN dwah ree
anecdotal	AN ik DOH təl
anecdote	AN ik DOHT
anecdotist	AN ik DOH təst
anemia	ə NEE mee ə
anemic	ə NEE mik
anemometer	AN ə MOM ə tər
anemone	ə NEM ə NEE
anent	ə NENT
anesthesia	AN əs THEE zhə
anesthesiologist	AN əs THEE zee OL ə jist
anesthesiology	AN əs THEE zee OL ə jee
anesthetic	AN əs THET ik
anesthetist	ə NES thə təst
aneurysm	AN yə RIZ əm
anew	ə NOO
angel	AYN jəl
Angel (Spanish)	AHN hel
Angela	AN jə lə
Angelica	an JEL i kə
Angelico	ahn JAI li koh
Angell	AYN jəl
Angelus, a-	AN jə ləs
Angevin	AN jə vən
angina pectoris	an JĪ nə PEK tə rəs
angiosperm	AN jee ə SPURM
Angkor Wat	ANG kohr WAHT
angle	ANG gəl
angler	ANG glər

ə ago, a at, ah calm, ahr dark, air care, aw saw, ay say, ch church
e bet, ee me, eer beer, hw what, i is, ī my, n French final n vin,

Anglican	**ANG** gli kən
Anglicanism	**ANG** gli kə **NIZ** əm
Anglophile	**ANG** glə **FĪL**
Anglophobe	**ANG** glə **FOHB**
Anglo-Saxon	**ANG** gloh **SAK** sən
Angola	ang **GOH** lə
Angora	ang **GOR** ə
angostura	**ANG** gə **STOOR** ə
angry	**ANG** gree
angst	ahngst
angstrom, A-	**ANG** strəm
Anguilla	ang **GWIL** ə
anguish	**ANG** gwish
angular	**ANG** gyə lər
Angus	**ANG** gəs
Anhalt	**AHN** hahlt
Anhui	ahn hwee
Anhwei	ahn hway
aniline	**AN** ə lən
animadversion	**AN** ə mad **VUR** *zh*ən
animal	**AN** ə məl
animalcule	**AN** ə **MAL** kyool
animate (a)	**AN** ə mət
animate (v)	**AN** ə **MAYT**
animism	**AN** ə **MIZ** əm
animosity	**AN** ə **MOS** ə tee
animus	**AN** ə məs
anion	**AN** **Ī** ən
anionic	**AN** ī **ON** ik
anise	**AN** əs
aniseikonia	**AN** ī sī **KOH** nee ə
anisette	**AN** ə **SET**
anisotropic	an **Ī** sə **TROP** ik
Anita	ə **NEE** tə
Anjou	**AHN** joo
Ankara	**ANG** kə rə
ankh	angk
ankle	**ANG** kəl
Anna	**AN** ə
annalist	**AN** ə ləst
annals	**AN** əlz
Annapolis	ə **NAP** ə ləs
anneal	ə **NEEL**

---

o **on**, oh **oat**, oi **boy**, oo **soon**, oor **poor**, or **for**, ow **cow**, sh **shush**,
th **thin**, *th* **this**, u **up**, ur **spur**, uu **book**, *zh* **pleasure**

annelid	**AN** ə lid
annex (n)	**AN** eks
annex (v)	ə **NEKS**
annnexation	**AN** ek **SAY** shən
annihilate	ə **NĪ** ə **LAYT**
annihilation	ə **NĪ** ə **LAY** shən
anniversary	**AN** ə **VUR** sə ree
anno Domini	**AN** oh **DOM** ə **NEE**
annotate	**AN** oh **TAYT**
annotation	**AN** oh **TAY** shən
annotator	**AN** oh **TAY** tər
annual	**AN** yoo əl
annuity	ə **NOO** ə tee
annul	ə **NUL**
annular	**AN** yə lər
annunciation	ə **NUN** see **AY** shən
Annunzio, Gabriele d'	dahn **NOON** tsyaw, **GAH** bree **E** le
annus mirabilis	**AH** nəs mi **RAH** bə ləs
anode	**AN** ohd
anodize	**AN** ə **DĪZ**
anodyne	**AN** ə **DĪN**
anoint	ə **NOINT**
anomalous	ə **NOM** ə ləs
anomaly	ə **NOM** ə lee
anonymous	ə **NON** ə məs
anorectic	**AN** ə **REK** tik
anorexia nervosa	**AN** ə **REK** see ə nər **VOH** sə
Anouilh, Jean	ah **NOO** yə, **ZH**AHN
anoxia	an **OK** see ə
Anschluss	**AHN** shluus
Ansermet	ahn ser **MAY**
answerable	**AN** sə rə bəl
antacid	ant **AS** əd
antagonism	an **TAG** ə **NIZ** əm
Antananarivo	**AN** tə **NAN** ə **REE** voh
antarctic, A-	ant **AHRK** tik
Antarctica	ant **AHRK** ti kə
Antares	an **TAIR** eez
ante	**AN** tee
antebellum	**AN** ti **BEL** əm
antecedence	**AN** tə **SEED** əns
antecedent	**AN** tə **SEE** dənt
antechamber	**AN** ti **CHAYM** bər

ə ago, a at, ah calm, ahr dark, air care, aw saw, ay say, ch church
e bet, ee me, eer beer, hw what, i is, ī my, *n* French final n vin,

antedate	AN ti DAYT
antediluvian	AN ti də LOO vee ən
antelope	AN tə LOHP
ante meridiem	AN ti mə RID ee əm
antenna	an TEN ə
antennae	an TEN ee
antepenult	AN ti PEE nult
antepenultimate	AN ti pi NUL tə mət
anterior	an TEER ee ər
anteroom	AN ti ROOM
Antheil	AN tīl
anthelion	ant HEE lee ən
anthem	AN thəm
anthill	ANT hil
anthology	an THOL ə jee
Anthony	AN thə nee
anthracite	AN thrə SĪT
anthrax	AN thraks
anthropoid	AN thrə POID
anthropologist	AN thrə POL ə jəst
anthropology	AN thrə POL ə jee
anthropomorphism	AN thrə pə MOR fiz əm
anthropophagi	AN thrə POF ə JĪ
antiaircraft	AN tee AIR KRAFT
Antibes	ahn TEEB
antibiotic	AN ti bī OT ik
antibody	AN ti BOD ee
antic	AN tik
antichrist, A-	AN ti KRĪST
anticipate	an TIS ə PAYT
anticipation	an TIS ə PAY shən
anticipatory	an TIS ə pə TOR ee
anticlimax	AN ti KLĪ maks
anticline	AN ti KLĪN
Anticosti	ANT ə KAW stee
antidote	AN ti DOHT
Antietam	an TEE təm
antigen	AN ti jən
Antigone	an TIG ə NEE
antigravity	AN ti GRAV ə tee
Antigua	an TEE gə
antihero	AN ti HEER oh
antihistamine	AN ti HIS tə MEEN

o on, oh oat, oi boy, oo soon, oor poor, or for, ow cow, sh shush,
th thin, *th* this, u up, ur spur, uu book, *zh* pleasure

antiknock	AN ti NOK
Antillean	an TIL ee ən
Antilles	an TIL eez
antimacassar	AN ti mə KAS ər
antimatter	AN ti MAT ər
antimony	AN tə MOH nee
antinomy	an TIN ə mee
Antioch	AN tee OK
antiparticle	AN ti PAHR ti kəl
antipasto	AN ti PAH stoh
antipathy	an TIP ə thee
antipersonnel	AN ti PUR sə NEL
antiphon	AN tə FON
antiphony	an TIF ə nee
antipodal	an TIP ə dəl
antipodean	an TIP ə DEE ən
antipodes	an TIP ə DEEZ
antipope	AN ti POHP
antiquarian	AN tə KWAIR ee ən
antiquated	AN tə KWAY təd
antique	an TEEK
antiquity	an TIK wə tee
antirrhinum	AN tə RĪ nəm
anti-Semitic	AN ti sə MIT ik
anti-Semitism	AN ti SEM ə TIZ əm
antiseptic	AN tə SEP tik
antisocial	AN ti SOH shəl
antistrophe	an TIS trə fee
antithesis	an TITH ə səs
antithetic	AN tə THET ik
antitoxin	AN ti TOK sən
antitrust	AN ti TRUST
antivivisectionist	AN ti VIV ə SEK shə nəst
antler	ANT lər
Antoinette (US)	AN twə NET
Antoinette (French)	ahn twah NET
Antonescu	AN tə NES koo
Antonov, Sergei	ahn TAW nawv, seer GAY
Antony	AN tə nee
antonym	AN tə nim
antrum	AN trəm
Antwerp	AN twurp
anxiety	ang ZĪ ə tee

ə ago, a at, ah calm, ahr dark, air care, aw saw, ay say, ch church
e bet, ee me, eer beer, hw what, i is, ī my, *n* French final n vin,

anxious	**ANGK** shəs
anybody	**EN** ee **BOD** ee
Anzac	**AN** zak
aorta	ay **OR** tə
aoudad	**AH** uu **DAD**
apace	ə **PAYS**
Apache	ə **PACH** ee
apache (French)	a **PASH**
Apalachicola	**AP** ə **LACH** ə **KOH** lə
Aparri	ah **PAHR** ee
apartheid	ə **PAHR** tayt
apathetic	**AP** ə **THET** ik
apathy	**AP** ə thee
Apel	**AH** pəl
Apennines	**AP** ə **NĪNZ**
apéritif	ə **PER** ə **TEEF**
aperture	**AP** ər chər
apex	**AY** peks
aphasia	ə **FAY** zhə
aphasic	ə **FAY** zik
aphelion	ə **FEE** lee ən
aphid	**AY** fəd
aphonia	ay **FOH** nee ə
aphorism	**AF** ə **RIZ** əm
aphoristic	**AF** ə **RIS** tik
Aphrodite	**AF** rə **DĪ** tee
Apia	ah **PEE** ah
apian	**AY** pee ən
apiary	**AY** pee **ER** ee
apiculture	**AY** pə **KUL** chər
apiece	ə **PEES**
apish	**AY** pish
aplomb	ə **PLOM**
apnea	**AP** nee ə
apocalypse, A-	ə **POK** ə **LIPS**
apocalyptic	ə **POK** ə **LIP** tik
apocope	ə **POK** ə pee
apocrypha, A-	ə **POK** rə fə
apocryphal, A-	ə **POK** rə fəl
apogee	**AP** ə **JEE**
apolitical	**AY** pə **LIT** i kəl
Apollinaire	ə **POL** ə **NAIR**
Apollinaris	a **POL** i **NAIR** is

o on, oh oat, oi boy, oo soon, oor poor, or for, ow cow, sh shush,
th thin, *th* this, u up, ur spur, uu book, *zh* pleasure

Apollo	ə POL oh
Apollyon	ə POL yən
apologetic	ə POL ə JET ik
apologia	AP ə LOH jee ə
apoplectic	AP ə PLEK tik
apoplexy	AP ə PLEK see
apostasy	ə POS tə SEE
apostate	ə POS tayt
apostatize	ə POS tə TĪZ
a posteriori	AH poh STI ree OH ree
apostle, A-	ə POS əl
apostolic	AP ə STOL ik
apothegm, apothem	AP ə them
apotheosis	ə POTH ee OH səs
Appalachian	AP ə LAY chee ən
appall	ə PAWL
Appaloosa	AP ə LOO sə
apparat	AH pə RAHT
apparatchik	AH pə RAHT chik
apparatus	AP ə RAT əs
apparel	ə PAR əl
apparent	ə PAR ənt
apparition	AP ə RISH ən
appeal	ə PEEL
appease	ə PEEZ
appellant	ə PEL ənt
appellate	ə PEL ət
appendage	ə PEN dij
appendectomy	AP ən DEK tə mee
appendices	ə PEN də SEEZ
appendicitis	ə PEN də SĪ təs
appendix	ə PEN diks
apperception	AP ər SEP shən
appertain	AP ər TAYN
appetite	AP ə TĪT
appetizer	AP ə TĪ zər
Appian	AP ee ən
applause	ə PLAWZ
applicable	AP lə kə bəl
applicant	AP lə kənt
application	AP lə KAY shən
applicator	AP lə KAY tər
appliqué	AP lə KAY

ə ago, a at, ah calm, ahr dark, air care, aw saw, ay say, ch church
e bet, ee me, eer beer, hw what, i is, ī my, *n* French final n vin,

appoggiatura	ə POJ ə TUUR ə
appointee	ə poin TEE
Appomattox	AP ə MAT əks
apportionment	ə POR shən mənt
apposite	AP ə zət
apposition	AP ə ZISH ən
appositive	ə POZ ə tiv
appraisal	ə PRAY zəl
appreciable	ə PREE shə bəl
appreciate	ə PREE shee AYT
appreciation	ə PREE shee AY shən
appreciative	ə PREE shə tiv
apprentice	ə PREN təs
apprise	ə PRĪZ
approbation	AP rə BAY shən
appropriate (a)	ə PROH pree ət
appropriate (v)	ə PROH pree AYT
approval	ə PROO vəl
approximate (a)	ə PROK sə mət
approximate (v)	ə PROK sə MAYT
appurtenance	ə PUR tə nəns
apricot	AP rə KOT
April	AY prəl
a priori	AH pree OH ree
à propos	AP rə POH
apse	aps
aptitude	AP tə ᴛᴏᴏD
Apuleius	AP yə LEE əs
Apulia	ə PYOOL yə
Aqaba	AH kah BAH
aqua	AK wə
aquamarine	AK wə mə REEN
aquanaut	AK wə NAWT
aquarium	ə KWAIR ee əm
Aquarius	ə KWAIR ee əs
aquatic	ə KWAHT ik
aquatint	AK wə TINT
aquavit	AH kwə VEET
aqua vitae	AK wə VĪ tee
aqueduct	AK wə DUKT
aqueous	AY kwee əs
aquifer	AK wə fər
Aquila	AK wə lə

o on, oh oat, oi boy, oo soon, oor poor, or for, ow cow, sh shush,
th thin, *th* this, u up, ur spur, uu book, *zh* pleasure

aquilegia	**AK** wə **LEE** jee ə
aquiline	**AK** wə **LĪN**
Aquinas	ə **KWĪ** nəs
Aquino, Benigno	ah **KEEN** oh, bə **NEEN** yoh
Arab	**AR** əb
arabesque	**AR** ə **BESK**
Arabia	ə **RAY** bee ə
Arabic	**AR** ə bik
arable	**AR** ə bəl
Araby	**AR** ə bee
Arafat, Yasir	**AHR** ə **FAHT**, **YAH** sər
Aramaic	**AR** ə **MAY** ik
Aranha	ah **RAH** nyah
Arapaho	ə **RAP** ə **HOH**
Ararat	**AR** ə **RAT**
Arawak	**AR** ə **WAHK**
Arawakan	**AR** ə **WAH** kən
arbiter	**AHR** bə tər
arbitrage	**AHR** bə **TRAHZH**
arbitrament	ahr **BI** trə mənt
arbitrary	**AHR** bə **TRER** ee
arbitrate	**AHR** bə **TRAYT**
arbitration	**AHR** bə **TRAY** shən
arbitrator	**AHR** bə **TRAY** tər
arbor	**AHR** bər
arboreal	ahr **BOR** ee əl
arboretum	**AHR** bə **REE** təm
arbor vitae	**AHR** bər **VĪ** tee
arbutus	ahr **BYOO** təs
Arc, Jeanne d'	dark, *zh*ahn
arcade	ahr **KAYD**
Arcadia	ahr **KAY** dee ə
Arcady	**AHR** kə dee
arcane	ahr **KAYN**
arcanum	ahr **KAY** nəm
Arc de Triomphe	ark də tree **AWNF**
Arce, José	**AHR** say, hoh **SAY**
arch	ahrch
archaeologist	**AHR** kee **OL** ə jəst
archaeology	**AHR** kee **OL** ə jee
archaic	ahr **KAY** ik
archaism	**AHR** kee **IZ** əm
archangel	**AHRK AYN** jəl

ə ago, a at, ah calm, ahr dark, air care, aw saw, ay say, ch church
e bet, ee me, eer beer, hw what, i is, ī my, *n* French final n vin,

archbishop	**AHRCH BISH** əp
archdiocese	**AHRCH DĪ** ə səs
archenemy	ahrch **EN** ə mee
archeologist	**AHR** kee **OL** ə jəst
archeology	**AHR** kee **OL** ə jee
archer, A-	**AHR** chər
archetype	**AHR** ki **TĪP**
archfiend	**AHRCH FEEND**
archiepiscopal	**AHR** kee ə **PIS** kə pəl
archimandrite	**AHR** kə **MAN** drīt
Archimedean	**AHR** kə **MEE** dee ən
Archimedes	**AHR** kə **MEE** deez
arching	**AHR** ching
archipelago	**AHR** kə **PEL** ə **GOH**
Archipenko	**AHR** kə **PENG** koh
architect	**AHR** kə **TEKT**
architectonic	**AHR** kə tek **TON** ik
architecture	**AHR** kə **TEK** chər
architrave	**AHR** kə **TRAYV**
archive	**AHR** kīv
archivist	**AHR** kə vəst
archly	**AHRCH** lee
archon	**AHR** kon
Arciniegas, Germán	ahr see **NYE** gahs, hair **MAHN**
arctic, A-	**AHRK** tik
Arcturus	ahrk **TUUR** əs
Ardennes	ahr **DEN**
ardent	**AHR** dənt
Arditi	ahr **DEE** tee
ardor	**AHR** dər
arduous	**AHR** joo əs
Arecibo	**AR** ə **SEE** boh
Arens, Moshe	**AHR** ənz, **MOH** she
Arensky	ə **REN** skee
Areopagus	**AR** ee **OP** ə gəs
Arethusa	**AR** ə **THOO** zə
Arévalo	ah **RE** vah law
Arezzo	ə **RET** soh
Argana	ahr **GAH** nah
argent	**AHR** jənt
Argentina	**AHR** jen **TEE** nə
argentine, A-	**AHR** jən teen
Argive	**AHR** jīv

o **on**, oh **oat**, oi **boy**, oo **soon**, oor **poor**, or **for**, ow **cow**, sh **shush**, th **thin**, *th* **this**, u **up**, ur **spur**, uu **book**, *zh* **pleasure**

argon	**AHR** gon
Argonaut	**AHR** gə **NAWT**
Argonne	**AHR** gon
argosy	**AHR** gə see
argot	**AHR** goh
argue	**AHR** gyoo
argument	**AHR** gyə mənt
argumentative	**AHR** gyə **MEN** tə tiv
Argus	**AHR** gəs
argyle	**AHR** gīl
Argyll	ahr **GĪL**
aria	**AHR** ee ə
Ariadne	**AR** ee **AD** nee
Arian	**AIR** ee ən
Arias	**AH** ryahs
arid	**AR** əd
aridity	ə **RID** ə tee
Ariel, a-	**AIR** ee əl
Aries	**AIR** eez
Aristarchus	**AR** ə **STAHR** kəs
Aristides	**AR** ə **STĪ** deez
aristocracy	**AR** ə **STOK** rə see
aristocrat	ə **RIS** tə **KRAT**
Aristophanes	**AR** ə **STOF** ə **NEEZ**
Aristotelian	**AR** ə stə **TEEL** yən
Aristotle	**AR** ə **STOT** əl
arithmetic (a)	**AR** ith **MET** ik
arithmetic (n)	ə **RITH** mə tik
arrivederci	**AHR** ree ve **DER** chee
Arizona	**AR** ə **ZOH** nə
Arkansan	ahr **KAN** zən
Arkansas	**AHR** kən **SAW**
armada	ahr **MAH** də
armadillo	**AHR** mə **DIL** oh
Armageddon	**AHR** mə **GED** ən
armament	**AHR** mə mənt
Armas	**AHR** mahs
armature	**AHR** mə chər
Armenia	ahr **MEE** nee ə
armistice	**AHR** mə stəs
armor, A-	**AHR** mər
armory	**AHR** mə ree
Arnhem	**AHRN** hem

ə ago, a at, ah calm, ahr dark, air care, aw saw, ay say, ch church
e bet, ee me, eer beer, hw what, i is, ī my, *n* French final n vin,

arnica	**AHR** ni kə
Arnold	**AHR** nəld
aroma	ə **ROH** mə
aromatic	**AR** ə **MAT** ik
arouse	ə **ROWZ**
Arp	ahrp
arpeggio	ahr **PEJ** ee **OH**
arraign	ə **RAYN**
arrangement	ə **RAYNJ** mənt
arrant	**AR** ənt
arras, A-	**AR** əs
Arrau, Claudio	ahr **RAH** oo, **KLOW** dyaw
array	ə **RAY**
arrears	ə **REERZ**
arrière pensée	**AR** ee **AIR** pahn **SAY**
arrival	ə **RĪ** vəl
arriviste	**AR** ee **VEEST**
arrogance	**AR** ə gəns
arrogant	**AR** ə gənt
arrogate	**AR** ə **GAYT**
arrondissement	a rawn dees **MAHN** (**MAHN** French final *n*)
arroyo	ə **ROI** oh
arroz con pollo	ah **RAWTH** kawn **PAW** lyaw
arsenal	**AHR** sə nəl
arsenic (n)	**AHR** sə nik
arsenic (a)	ahr **SEN** ik
arson	**AHR** sən
Artaxerxes	**AHR** tə **ZURK** seez
Artemis	**AHR** tə məs
arterial	ahr **TEER** ee əl
arteriosclerosis	ahr **TEER** ee oh sklə **ROH** səs
artery	**AHR** tə ree
artesian	ahr **TEE** *zh*ən
arthritis	ahr **THRĪ** təs
arthropod	**AHR** thrə **POD**
Arthurian	ahr **THUUR** ee ən
artichoke	**AHR** tə **CHOHK**
articulate (a)	ahr **TIK** yə lit
articulate (v)	ahr **TIK** yə **LAYT**
artifice	**AHR** tə fəs
artificer	ahr **TIF** ə sər
artificial	**AHR** tə **FISH** əl
artillery	ahr **TIL** ə ree

---

o **on**, oh **oat**, oi **boy**, oo **soon**, oor **poor**, or **for**, ow **cow**, sh **shush**,
th **thin**, *th* **this**, u **up**, ur **spur**, uu **book**, *zh* **pleasure**

artisan	**AHR** tə zən
artist	**AHR** təst
artiste	ahr **TEEST**
artistic	ahr **TIS** tik
artistry	**AHR** tə stree
Art Nouveau	**AHR** noo **VOH**
Artzybasheff	**AHR** tsi **BAH** shef
Artzybashev	**AHR** tsi **BAH** shef
Aruba	ah **ROO** bah
Arundel (England)	**AR** ən dəl
Arundel (Maryland)	ə **RUN** dəl
aryan, A-	**AIR** ee ən
Asa	**AY** sə
Asad	ə **SAHD**
asafetida	**AS** ə **FET** ə də
Asahi	ah sah hee
Asakai, Koichiro	ah sah kī, koh ee chee roh
Asaph	**A** səf
asbestos	as **BES** təs
asbestosis	**AS BES TOH** səs
Ascanius	a **SKAY** nee əs
ascend	ə **SEND**
ascendancy	ə **SEN** dən see
ascension	ə **SEN** shən
ascent	ə **SENT**
ascertain	**AS** ər **TAYN**
ascetic	ə **SET** ik
Asch, Sholem	**ASH, SHOH** ləm
Ascham	**AS** kəm
Asclepius	ə **SKLEE** pee əs
ascorbic	ə **SKOR** bik
ascot, A-	**AS** kət
ascribe	ə **SKRĪB**
aseptic	ay **SEP** tik
Ásgeirsson, Asgeir	**AHS** gair sən, **AHS** gair
ashamed	ə **SHAYMD**
Ashanti	ə **SHAN** tee
Ashdod	**ASH** dod
Ashe	ash
ashen	**ASH** ən
Asher	**ASH** ər
Ashkenazi	**AHSH** kə **NAH** zee
Ashkenazim	**AHSH** kə **NAH** zəm

Ashland	ASH lənd
ashore	ə SHOR
ashram	AHSH rəm
Ashtoreth	ASH tə RETH
Ashur	AH shuur
Asia	AY zhə
Asiatic	AY zhee AT ik
aside	ə SĪD
Asimov	AZ ə mof
asinine	AS ə NĪN
askance	ə SKANS
Askelon	A skə lahn
askew	ə SKYOO
aslant	ə SLANT
Asmara	ahs MAHR ə
asocial	ay SOH shəl
asparagus	ə SPAR ə gəs
Aspasia	a SPAY zhə
aspect	AS pekt
aspen	AS pən
asperity	ə SPER ə tee
aspersion	ə SPUR zhən
asphalt	AS fawlt
asphodel	AS fə DEL
asphyxia	as FIK see ə
asphyxiate	as FIK see AYT
asphyxiation	as FIK see AY shən
aspic	AS pik
aspidistra, A-	AS pə DIS trə
aspirant	ə SPĪR ənt
aspirate (a, n)	AS pə rət
aspirate (v)	AS pə RAYT
aspiration	AS pə RAY shən
aspire	ə SPĪR
aspirin	AS pə rən
Asquith	AS kwith
as-Sabah, Jabir	ahsh SHAH bah, jah BEER ahl AH
al-Ahmad al-Jabir	mahd ahl jah BEER
as-Sabah, Saad	ahsh SHAH bah, sah EED ahl AHB
al-Adbullah al-Salim	doo lah ahl sah LEEM
Assad, Hafez al-	AS sad, HAH fəth
assail	ə SAYL
assailant	ə SAY lənt

o on, oh oat, oi boy, oo soon, oor poor, or for, ow cow, sh shush,
th thin, *th* this, u up, ur spur, uu book, *zh* pleasure

Assam	as **SAM**
Assamese	**AS** ə **MEEZ**
assassin	ə **SAS** ən
assassinate	ə **SAS** ə **NAYT**
assassination	ə **SAS** ə **NAY** shən
assault	ə **SAWLT**
assay (n)	**AS** ay
assay (v)	ə **SAY**
assemblage	ə **SEM** blij
assembly	ə **SEM** blee
assent	ə **SENT**
assert	ə **SURT**
assertion	ə **SUR** shən
asset	**AS** et
asseverate	ə **SEV** ə **RAYT**
assiduous	ə **SIJ** oo əs
assign	ə **SĪN**
assignable	ə **SĪ** nə bəl
assignation	**AS** ig **NAY** shən
assignee	ə sī **NEE**
assimilable	ə **SIM** ə lə bəl
assimilate	ə **SIM** ə **LAYT**
assimilation	ə **SIM** ə **LAY** shən
Assisi	ə **SEE** see
assize	ə **SĪZ**
associate (a, n)	ə **SOH** see ət
associate (v)	ə **SOH** see **AYT**
association	ə **SOH** see **AY** shən
associative	ə **SOH** see **AY** tiv
assonance	**AS** ə nəns
assuage	ə **SWAYJ**
assume	ə **SOOM**
assumption	ə **SUMP** shən
assurance	ə **SHOOR** əns
assure	ə **SHOOR**
Assyrian	ə **SIR** ee ən
Assyriology	ə **SIR** ee **OL** ə jee
astatine	**AS** tə **TEEN**
aster	**AS** tər
asterisk	**AS** tə **RISK**
astern	ə **STURN**
asteroid	**AS** tə **ROID**
asthenia	as **THEE** nee ə

ə ago, a at, ah calm, ahr dark, air care, aw saw, ay say, ch church
e bet, ee me, eer beer, hw what, i is, ī my, n French final n vin,

asthenic	as **THEN** ik
asthma	**AZ** mə
asthmatic	az **MAT** ik
astigmatic	**AS** tig **MAT** ik
astigmatism	ə **STIG** mə **TIZ** əm
astir	ə **STUR**
Astor	**AS** tər
astound	ə **STOWND**
Astraea	a **STREE** ə
astrakhan	**AS** trə **KAN**
Astrakhan (USSR)	**AHS** trah **KAHN**
astral	**AS** trəl
astray	ə **STRAY**
astride	ə **STRĪD**
astringent	ə **STRIN** jənt
astrodome	**AS** trə **DOHM**
astrolabe	**AS** trə **LAYB**
astrologer	as **TROL** ə jər
astrological	**AS** trə **LOJ** i kəl
astrology	ə **STROL** ə jee
astronaut	**AS** trə **NAWT**
astronautics	**AS** trə **NAWT** iks
astrophysics	**AS** trə **FIZ** iks
Asturias	ahs **TOOR** yahs
astute	ə **STOOT**
Asunción	**AH** suun see **AWN**
asunder	ə **SUN** dər
Aswan, Assuan	**AS** wahn
asylum	ə **SĪ** ləm
asymmetric	**AY** sə **ME** trik
asymmetry	ay **SIM** ə tree
asymptote	**AS** əm **TOHT**
Atahualpa	**AH** tah **WAHL** pah
Atalanta	**AT** ə **LAN** tə
Ataturk, Kemal	**AT** ə **TURK**, ke **MAHL**
atavism	**AT** ə **VIZ** əm
ataxia	ə **TAK** see ə
Ate	**AY** tee
atelier	**AT** əl **YAY**
a tempo	ah **TEM** poh
Athanasian	**ATH** ə **NAY** *zh*ən
atheism	**AY** thee **IZ** əm
atheist	**AY** thee əst

---

o on, oh oat, oi boy, oo soon, oor poor, or for, ow cow, sh shush,
th thin, *th* this, u up, ur spur, uu book, *zh* pleasure

Athena	ə **THEE** nə
athenaeum, A-	**ATH** ə **NEE** əm
Athenian	ə **THEE** nee ən
Athens	**ATH** ənz
atherosclerosis	**ATH** ə roh sklə **ROH** səs
athirst	ə **THURST**
athwart	ə **THWORT**
Atiyeh, Victor	ə **TEE** ə
Atlanta	at **LAN** tə
atlantean, A-	**AT** lan **TEE** ən
Atlantic	at **LAN** tik
Atlantis	at **LAN** təs
atlas, A-	**AT** ləs
atmosphere	**AT** məs **FEER**
atmospheric	**AT** məs **FER** ik
atoll	**AT** awl
atomic	ə **TOM** ik
atomizer	**AT** ə **MĪ** zər
atonal	ay **TOH** nəl
atonality	**AY** toh **NAL** ə tee
atone	ə **TOHN**
atonement	ə **TOHN** mənt
atonic	ay **TON** ik
atony	**AT** ən ee
Atreus	**AY** tree əs
atrium	**AY** tree əm
atrocious	ə **TROH** shəs
atrocity	ə **TROS** ə tee
atrophy	**AT** rə fee
atropine, A-	**AT** rə **PEEN**
attach	ə **TACH**
attaché	**AT** ə **SHAY**
attachment	ə **TACH** mənt
attacked	ə **TAKT**
attain	ə **TAYN**
attainable	ə **TAY** nə bəl
attainment	ə **TAYN** mənt
attar	**AT** ər
attempt	ə **TEMPT**
attendance	ə **TEN** dəns
attention	ə **TEN** shən
attentive	ə **TEN** tiv
attenuate (a)	ə **TEN** yoo ət

ə ago, a at, ah calm, ahr dark, air care, aw saw, ay say, ch church
e bet, ee me, eer beer, hw what, i is, ī my, *n* French final n vin,

attenuate (v)	ə TEN yoo AYT
attenuation	ə TEN yoo AY shən
attic, A-	AT ik
Attica	AT ə kə
atticism, A-	AT ə SIZ əm
Attila	ə TIL ə
attire	ə TĪR
attitude	AT ə TOOD
attitudinize	AT ə TOO di NĪZ
attorney	ə TUR nee
attribute (n)	A trə BYOOT
attribute (v)	ə TRIB yoot
attribution	A trə BYOO shən
attributive	ə TRIB yə tiv
attrition	ə TRISH ən
Attu	A too
Attucks, Crispus	AT əks, KRIS pəs
attune	ə TOON
Atuona	AHT ə WOH nə
atypical	ay TIP i kəl
auberge	oh BAIRZH
Aubrey	AW bree
auburn, A-	AW bərn
Aubusson	OH bə SAWN (SAWN French final *n*)
Auchincloss	AW kən KLAWS
Auchinleck	AW kən LEK
Auckland	AWK lənd
au courant	oh koo RAHN (RAHN French final *n*)
audacious	aw DAY shəs
audacity	aw DAS ə tee
Auden	AWD ən
audible	AW də bəl
audience	AW dee əns
audio	AW dee OH
audiology	AW dee OL ə jee
audiophile	AW dee ə FĪL
audit	AW dət
audition	aw DISH ən
auditor	AW də tər
auditorium	AW də TOR ee əm
Audubon	AW də BON
Auer	OW ər
au fait	oh FAY

o **on**, oh **oat**, oi **boy**, oo **soon**, oor **poor**, or **for**, ow **cow**, sh **shush**,
th **thin**, *th* **this**, u **up**, ur **spur**, uu **book**, *zh* **pleasure**

au fond	oh **FAWN** (**FAWN** French final *n*)
auf Wiedersehen	owf **VEE** dər **ZAY** ən
Augean	aw **JEE** ən
auger	**AW** gər
aught	awt
augment	awg **MENT**
au gratin	oh **GRAH** tən
augur	**AW** gər
augury	**AW** gyə ree
August	**AW** gəst
august	aw **GUST**
Augustan	aw **GUS** tən
Auguste, Carlet	oh **GUUST**, kahr **LAY**
Augustine	**AW** gə **STEEN**
Augustus	aw **GUS** təs
au jus	oh *ZHOO*
auk	awk
au lait	oh **LAY**
auld lang syne	**AWLD** lang **ZĪN**
au naturel	oh na tyə **REL**
aunt	ant
auntie	**AN** tee
au pair	oh **PAIR**
aura	**OR** ə
aural	**OR** əl
aureole	**OR** ee **OHL**
aureomycin	**OR** ee oh **MĪ** sən
au revoir	oh rə **VWAHR**
auricular	aw **RIK** yə lər
auriferous	aw **RIF** ə rəs
Auriga	aw **RĪ** gə
Auriol	**OR** ee **OHL**
aurora, A-	aw **ROR** ə
Auschwitz	**OWSH** vits
auscultation	**AW** skəl **TAY** shən
Ausgleich	**OWS** glīk
auspice	**AW** spəs
auspices	**AW** spə səz
auspicious	aw **SPISH** əs
Auster	**AW** stər
austere	aw **STEER**
austerity	aw **STER** ə tee
Austerlitz	**AW** stər lits

ə ago, a at, ah calm, ahr dark, air care, aw saw, ay say, ch church
e bet, ee me, eer beer, hw what, i is, ī my, *n* French final n vin,

Australasia	AW strə LAY *zh*ə
Australasian	AW strə LAY *zh*ən
Australia	aw STRAYL yə
Australian	aw STRAYL yən
Australopithecus	aw STRAY loh PITH ə kəs
Austria	AW stree ə
autarchic	aw TAHR kik
autarchist	AW tahr kəst
autarchy	AW tahr kee
authentic	aw THEN tik
authenticate	aw THEN ti KAYT
authenticity	AW then TIS ə tee
author	AW thər
authoritarian	ə THOR ə TAIR ee ən
authoritative	ə THOR ə TAY tiv
authority	ə THOR ə tee
authorization	AW thə rə ZAY shən
authorize	AW thə RĪZ
autism	AW tiz əm
autistic	aw TIS tik
autobahn	AW toh BAHN
autobiographical	AW toh BĪ ə GRAF i kəl
autobiography	AW toh bī OG rə fee
autochthonous	aw TOK thə nəs
autoclave	AW toh KLAYV
autocracy	aw TOK rə see
autocrat	AW tə KRAT
auto-da-fé	AW toh də FAY
autogiro	AW toh JĪ roh
autoharp	AW toh HAHRP
autoimmune	AW toh i MYOON
Automat	AW tə MAT
automate	AW tə MAYT
automatic	AW tə MAT ik
automation	AW tə MAY shən
automatism	aw TOM ə TIZ əm
automaton	aw TOM ə tən
autonomous	aw TON ə məs
autonomy	aw TON ə mee
autopilot	AW toh PĪ lət
autopsy	AW top see
autosuggestion	AW toh səg JES chən
autumn	AW təm

---

o on, oh oat, oi boy, oo soon, oor poor, or for, ow cow, sh shush,
th thin, *th* this, u up, ur spur, uu book, *zh* pleasure

autumnal	aw **TUM** nəl
auxiliary	awg **ZIL** yə ree
avail	ə **VAYL**
availability	ə **VAY** lə **BIL** ə tee
available	ə **VAY** lə bəl
avalanche	**AV** ə **LANCH**
Avalon	**AV** ə **LON**
avant-garde	**A** vahn **GAHRD**
avarice	**AV** ə rəs
avaricious	**AV** ə **RISH** əs
avast	ə **VAST**
avatar	**AV** ə tahr
ave, A-	**AH** vay
Ave Maria	**AH** vay mə **REE** ə
avenge	ə **VENJ**
avenue	**AV** ən **YOO**
aver	ə **VUR**
average	**AV** ə rij
averse	ə **VURS**
aversion	ə **VUR** *zh*ən
avert	ə **VURT**
avian	**AY** vee ən
aviary	**AY** vee **ER** ee
aviator	**AY** vee **AY** tər
aviatrix	**AY** vee **AY** triks
avid	**AV** əd
avidity	ə **VID** ə tee
Avignon	a vee **NYAWN** (**NYAWN** French final *n*)
Ávila	**AH** vee **LAH**
avionics	**AY** vee **ON** iks
avitaminosis	ay **VĪ** tə mə **NOH** səs
avocado	**AV** ə **KAH** doh
avocation	**AV** ə **KAY** shən
avoidance	ə **VOID** əns
avoirdupois	**AV** ər də **POIZ**
Avon	**AY** vən
avow	ə **VOW**
avowal	ə **VOW** əl
avuncular	ə **VUNG** kyə lər
Awaji	ə **WAHJ** ee
aweigh	ə **WAY**
awesome	**AW** səm
awful	**AW** fəl

ə ago, a at, ah calm, ahr dark, air care, aw saw, ay say, ch church
e bet, ee me, eer beer, hw what, i is, ī my, *n* French final n vin,

awfully	AW fə lee
awhile	ə HWĪL
awkward	AWK wərd
Awolowo, Obafemi	a woh LAW waw, aw BAH fe mee
awry	ə RĪ
ax	aks
axe	aks
axel	AK səl
axes (pl of *ax*)	AK səz
axes (pl of *axis*)	AK seez
axial	AK see əl
axiom	AK see əm
axiomatic	AK see ə MAT ik
axis	AK səs
axle	AK səl
Axminster	AKS MIN stər
axon	AKS on
ayatollah	AH yə TOH lə
Ayling	AY ling
Ayr	air
Ayres	airz
Ayrshire	AIR sheer
Azad	ah ZAHD
azalea, A-	ə ZAYL yə
Azerbaijan	AH zər bī JAHN
Azikwe, Nnamdi	a zee kee WE, nahm DEE
Azim, Ejaz	ah ZEEM, ay JAHZ
azimuth	AZ ə məth
Aziz, Tariq	ah ZEEZ, TAW rik
Azores	AY zorz
Azov	ah ZAWF
Azraai, Zain	AHS rah ee, zayn
Aztec	AZ tek
Aztecan	AZ te kən
Azuma, Tokuho	ahd zoo MAH, toh kuu HOH
azure	A*ZH* ər

---

o on, oh oat, oi boy, oo soon, oor poor, or for, ow cow, sh shush, th thin, *th* this, u up, ur spur, uu book, *zh* pleasure

B

baa	bah
Baal	**BAY** əl
Baalim	**BAY** ə ləm
Baal Shem-Tov	bahl shem tohv
Baba	**BAH** bah
baba au rhum	**BAH** bə oh **RUM**
babbitt, B-	**BAB** ət
babbittry, B-	**BAB** ə tree
babble	**BAB** əl
babel, B-	**BAY** bəl
Babel, Isaac	**BAH** bel, i **SAHK**
Babism	**BAHB** iz əm
Babist	**BAHB** əst
Babite	**BAH** bīt
babka	**BAHB** kə
baboo, B-	**BAH** boo
baboon	ba **BOON**
babu, B-	**BAH** boo
babushka	bə **BUUSH** kə
Babylon	**BAB** ə lən
Babylonia	BAB ə **LOH** nee ə
Bacall	bə **KAWL**
baccalaureate	BAK ə **LOR** ee ət
baccarat	**BAH** kə RAH
Bacchae	**BAK** ee
bacchanal	BAK ə **NAL**
bacchanalia, B-	BAK ə **NAYL** yə
bacchanalian, B-	BAK ə **NAY** lee ən
bacchant	**BAK** ənt
Bacchus	**BAK** əs
Bach	bahk
Bache	baysh
bachelor	**BACH** ə lər
bacilli	bə **SIL** ī
bacillus	bə **SIL** əs
backache	**BAK** ayk
backgammon	**BAK** GAM ən
backstage	**BAK** stayj

ə ago, a at, ah calm, ahr dark, air care, aw saw, ay say, ch church
e bet, ee me, eer beer, hw what, i is, ī my, *n* French final n vin,

Baconian	bay **KOH** nee ən
bacteria	bak **TEER** ee ə
bacteriology	bak **TEER** ee **OL** ə jee
bacteriophage	bak **TEER** ee ə **FAYJ**
bacterium	bak **TEER** ee əm
Bactrian	**BAK** tree ə
bade	bad
Baden (Germany)	**BAHD** ən
Baden (US)	**BAYD** ən
Baden-Powell	**BAYD** ən **POH** əl
badger	**BAJ** ər
badinage	**BAD** ə **NAHZ***H*
badlands, B-	**BAD LANDZ**
badminton	**BAD** min tən
baedeker, B-	**BAY** də kər
Baez	bī **EZ**
Baffin	**BAF** ən
bagasse	bə **GAS**
bagatelle	**BAG** ə **TEL**
Bagaya	bah **GAH** yah
Bagaza	bah **GAH** zah
Bagdad	**BAG** dad
Bagehot	**BAJ** ət
bagel	**BAY** gəl
baggage	**BAG** ij
baggy	**BAG** ee
Baghdad	**BAG** dad
bagnio	**BAHN** yoh
Bagnold, Enid	**BAG** nohld, **EE** nid
bagpipe	**BAG** pīp
baguette	ba **GET**
Baguio	**BAHG** ee **OH**
Bahai	bah **HĪ**
Bahaism	bah **HĪ** iz əm
Bahaist	bah **HĪ** ist
Bahama	bə **HAH** mə
Bahia	bə **HEE** ə
Bahrain	bah **RAYN**
Baikal	bī **KAHL**
bailey, B-	**BAY** lee
bailiff	**BAY** ləf
bailiwick	**BAY** lə wik
Bairam	bī **RAHM**

---

o on, oh oat, oi boy, oo soon, oor poor, or for, ow cow, sh shush,
th thin, *th* this, u up, ur spur, uu book, *zh* pleasure

Bairiki	bī **REE** kee
bairn	bairn
baize	bayz
Bakelite	**BAY** kə **LĪT**
Bakhtiar	**BOK** tee ahr
baksheesh	**BAK** sheesh
Baku	bah **KOO**
Balaam	**BAY** ləm
balaclava	**BAL** ə **KLAH** və
Balaguer, Joaquín	bah lah **GAIR**, hwah **KEEN**
balalaika	**BAL** ə **LĪ** kə
Balanchine	**BAL** ən **SHEEN**
Balaton	**BAH** lah **TAWN**
Balboa	bal **BOH** ə
balbriggan	bal **BRIG** ən
balcony	**BAL** kə nee
baldachin	**BAL** də kən
Balder	**BAWL** dər
balderdash	**BAWL** dər **DASH**
baldpate	**BAWLD** payt
baldric	**BAWL** drik
Baldwin	**BAWLD** wən
bale	bayl
Bâle	bahl
Balearic	**BAL** ee **AR** ik
baleen	bə **LEEN**
baleful	**BAYL** fəl
Balenciaga	ba **LEN** see **AH** gə
Baleta, Abdi	bah **LAY** tah, **AHB** dee
Balewa, Abubakar Tafawa	ba **LAY** wah, a **BOO** ba kahr ta **FAH** wah
Balfour	**BAL** fuur
Bali	**BAH** lee
Balikpapan	**BAH** leek **PAH** pahn
Balinese	**BAH** lə **NEEZ**
balk	bawk
Balkan	**BAWL** kən
ballad	**BAL** əd
ballade	bə **LAHD**
balladeer	**BAL** ə **DEER**
balladry	**BAL** ə dree
Ballantine	**BAL** ən tīn
ballast	**BAL** əst

ə ago, a at, ah calm, ahr dark, air care, aw saw, ay say, ch church
e bet, ee me, eer beer, hw what, i is, ī my, *n* French final n vin,

ballerina	**BAL** ə **REE** nə
ballet	ba **LAY**
Balliol	**BAL** yəl
ballistic	bə **LIS** tik
Ballo in Maschera	**BAH** loh een **MAHS** kay rah
balloon	bə **LOON**
ballyhoo	**BAL** ee **HOO**
balm	bahm
Balmoral, b-	bal **MAWR** əl
baloney	bə **LOH** nee
balsa	**BAWL** sə
balsam	**BAWL** səm
Balthazar	bal **THAY** zər
Baltic	**BAWL** tik
Baltimore	**BAWL** tə **MOR**
Baluchistan	bə **LOO** chə **STAN**
baluster	**BAL** ə stər
balustrade	**BAL** ə **STRAYD**
Balzac	**BAL** zak
Bamako	**BAM** ə **KOH**
bambino	bam **BEE** noh
bamboo	bam **BOO**
bamboozle	bam **BOO** zəl
banal	bə **NAHL**
banality	bə **NAL** ə tee
Banda	**BAHN** dah
bandage	**BAN** dij
bandanna	ban **DAN** ə
bandeau	ban **DOH**
Bandoeng, Bandung	**BAHN** duung
bandolier	**BAN** də **LEER**
bandy-legged	**BAN** dee **LEG** əd
bane	bayn
baneberry	**BAYN BER** ee
baneful	**BAYN** fəl
Banff	bamf
bangalore, B-	**BANG** gə **LOHR**
Bangkok	**BANG** kok
Bangladesh	**BANG** glə **DESH**
bangle	**BANG** gəl
Bangui	bahng **GEE**
Bani-Sadr, Abolhassan	**BAH** nee **SAH** dər, **AH** buul hah **SAHN**
banister	**BAN** ə stər

o on, oh oat, oi boy, oo soon, oor poor, or for, ow cow, sh shush,
th thin, *th* this, u up, ur spur, uu book, *zh* pleasure

Banjermasin	**BAHN** jər **MAH** sən
banjo	**BAN** joh
Banjul	**BAHN** juul
bankruptcy	**BANGK** rupt see
bannock	**BAN** ək
banns	banz
banquet	**BANG** kwət
Banquo	**BANG** kwoh
banshee	**BAN** shee
bantam, B-	**BAN** təm
Bantu	**BAN** too
banyan	**BAN** yən
Banyuwangi	**BAHN** yoo **WAHNG** ee
banzai	bahn **ZĪ**
baobab	**BAY** oh **BAB**
Bao Dai	bow dī (bow as in *cow*)
baptism	**BAP** tiz əm
baptismal	bap **TIZ** məl
baptist, B-	**BAP** təst
baptistery	**BAP** tə stree
baptize	**BAP** tīz
Barabbas	bə **RAB** əs
Baraca	bə **RAH** kə
Baraka, Amiri	bah **RAH** kah, ah **MEER** ee
Baranof	**BA** rə **NAWF**
Barbados	bahr **BAY** dohs
barbarian	bahr **BAIR** ee ən
barbaric	bahr **BAR** ik
barbarism	**BAHR** bə **RIZ** əm
barbarity	bahr **BAR** ə tee
Barbarossa	**BAHR** bə **RAWS** ə
barbarous	**BAHR** bə rəs
Barbary	**BAHR** bə ree
barbecue	**BAHR** bə **KYOO**
barbed	bahrbd
barberry	**BAHR** **BER** ee
Barbiere di Siviglia	bahr **BYE** re dee see **VEE** lyah
barbiturate	bahr **BICH** ə rət
barbituric	**BAHR** bə **TUUR** ik
Barbuda	bahr **BOO** də
barcarole	**BAHR** kə **ROHL**
Barcelona	**BAHR** sə **LOH** nə
Bardot, Brigitte	bahr **DOH**, bri **ZH**EET

ə ago, a at, ah calm, ahr dark, air care, aw saw, ay say, ch church
e bet, ee me, eer beer, hw what, i is, ī my, *n* French final n vin,

barefaced	bair fayst
bareheaded	**BAIR HED** əd
barely	**BAIR** lee
Barents	**BA** rənts
bargain	**BAHR** gən
barge	bahrj
bargeman	**BAHRJ** mən
baritone	**BA** rə **TOHN**
barium	**BA** ree əm
barkentine	**BAHR** kən **TEEN**
barker	**BAHR** kər
Bar-le-Duc	**BAHR** lə **DUUK**
barley	**BAHR** lee
barleycorn, B-	**BAHR** lee **KORN**
barm	bahrm
Barma, Ramadane	**BAHR** mə, **RAH** mə **DAHN**
bar mitzvah	bahr **MITS** və
barmy	**BAHR** mee
Barnabas	**BAHR** nə bəs
barnacle	**BAHR** nə kəl
Barnard	**BAHR** nərd
Barnegat	**BAHR** ni gət
Barnouw	**BAHR** noh
Barnstable	**BAHRN** stə bəl
barnstorm	**BAHRN** storm
barnyard	**BAHRN** yahrd
barometer	bə **ROM** ə tər
barometric	**BA** rə **MET** rik
baroness	**BA** rə nəs
baronet	**BA** rə nət
baronetcy	**BA** rə nət see
baronial	bə **ROH** nee əl
baroque	bə **ROHK**
barouche	bə **ROOSH**
barque	bahrk
barquentine	**BAHR** kən **TEEN**
barracks	**BA** rəks
barracuda	**BA** rə **KOO** də
barrage	bə **RAHZH**
barranca, B-	bə **RANG** kə
Barranquilla	**BA** rən **KEE** ə
Barrault	ba **ROH**
Barré, Mohamed	ba **RAY**, mə **HAH** məd

---

o on, oh oat, oi boy, oo soon, oor poor, or for, ow cow, sh shush,
th thin, *th* this, u up, ur spur, uu book, *zh* pleasure

barred	bahrd
barren	**BA** rən
barricade	**BA** rə **KAYD**
barrier	**BA** ree ər
barrio	**BAHR** ee oh
barrister	**BA** rə stər
barroom	**BAHR ROOM**
Bartholdi	bahr **THOL** dee
Bartholomew	bahr **THOL** ə **MYOO**
Bartlett	**BAHRT** lət
Bartók, Béla	**BAHR** tok, **BAY** lə
Baruch (Bible)	**BAIR** ək
Baruch, Bernard	bə **ROOK**
Baryshnikov, Mikhail	bah **REESH** ni **KOF**, mi kah **EEL**
Barzun, Jacques	**BAHR** zən, *zh*ahk
basal	**BAY** səl
basalt	bə **SAWLT**
base	bays
Basel	**BAH** zəl
baseless	**BAYS** ləs
basement	**BAYS** mənt
baseness	**BAYS** nəs
basenji	bə **SEN** jee
bases (pl of *base*)	**BAY** səz
bases (pl of *basis*)	**BAY** seez
bashful	**BASH** fəl
Bashkir	bahsh **KEER**
Basho	bah shoh
basic	**BAY** sik
basil, B-	**BAZ** əl
basilar	**BAS** ə lər
basilic	bə **SIL** ik
basilica	bə **SIL** i kə
basilisk	**BAZ** ə lisk
basis	**BAY** səs
bas mitzvah	bahs **MITS** və
basque, B-	bask
Basra	**BUS** rə
bas-relief	**BAH** ri **LEEF**
bass (fish)	bas
bass (sound)	bays
basset	**BAS** ət
basso	**BAS** oh

ə ago, a at, ah calm, ahr dark, air care, aw saw, ay say, ch church
e bet, ee me, eer beer, hw what, i is, ī my, *n* French final n vin,

bassoon	bə **SOON**
basso profundo	**BAS** oh proh **FUUN** doh
bastard	**BAS** tərd
bastardize	**BAS** tər **DĪZ**
bastardy	**BAS** tərd ee
baste	bayst
bastille, B-	ba **STEEL**
bastinado	**BAS** tə **NAY** doh
bastion	**BAS** chən
Bastogne	ba **STOHN**
Bataan	bə **TAN**
Batang	bah tahng
Batavia	bə **TAY** vee ə
bateau	ba **TOH**
bated	**BAY** təd
bath	bath
bathe	bay*th*
batholith	**BATH** ə lith
bathos	**BAY** thos
Bathsheba	bath **SHEE** bə
bathyscaphe	**BATH** ə **SKAYF**
bathysphere	**BATH** ə **SFEER**
batik	ba **TEEK**
batiste	ba **TEEST**
bat mitzvah	baht **MITS** və
baton	ba **TON**
Baton Rouge	**BAT** ən **ROOZ***H*
batrachian, B-	bə **TRAY** kee ən
battalion	bə **TAL** yən
batten	**BAT** ən
battery	**BAT** ə ree
battledore	**BAT** əl **DOR**
battue	ba **TOO**
Batum	bah **TUUM**
bauble	**BAW** bəl
baud	bawd
Baudelaire	**BOHD** ə **LAIR**
Baudouin	boh **DWAN** (**DWAN** French final *n*)
Bauhaus	**BOW** hows (**BOW** as in *cow*)
Baumann	**BOW** mən (**BOW** as in *cow*)
bauxite	**BAWK** sīt
Bavaria	bə **VAIR** ee ə
Bavarian	bə **VAIR** ee ən

o on, oh oat, oi boy, oo soon, oor poor, or for, ow cow, sh shush,
th thin, *th* this, u up, ur spur, uu book, *zh* pleasure

Bayard	**BAY** ərd
Bayard (French)	bah **YAHR**
bayberry	**BAY** ber ee
Bayeux	bah **YUU**
bayonet	**BAY** ə nət
Bayonne (France)	bah **YUN**
Bayonne (US)	bay **YOHN**
bayou	**BĪ** oo
Bayreuth	**BĪ** roit
bazaar, bazar	bə **ZAHR**
Bazargan	**BAH** zahr gahn
bazooka	bə **ZOO** kə
bdellium	**DEL** ee əm
beacon	**BEE** kən
Beaconsfield	**BEE** kənz **FEELD**
beadle	**BEED** əl
beagle	**BEE** gəl
beanie	**BEE** nee
bear	bair
bearing	**BAIR** ing
béarnaise	**BAY** ər **NAYZ**
beatific	bee ə **TIF** ik
beatification	bee at ə fə **KAY** shən
beatify	bee **AT** ə **FĪ**
beatitude	bee **AT** ə **TOOD**
beatnik	**BEET** nik
Beatrice	**BEE** ə trəs
beau	boh
Beau Brummel	boh **BRUM** əl
Beauchamp	**BEE** chəm
Beaufort (scale)	**BOH** fərt
Beaufort (North Carolina)	**BOH** fərt
Beaufort (South Carolina)	**BYOO** fərt
beau geste	boh **ZH**EST
Beauharnais	boh ahr **NAY**
beau ideal	**BOH** ī **DEE** əl
Beaujolais	**BOH** zhoh **LAY**
Beaulac	**BOH** lak
Beaulieu (England)	**BYOO** lee
beau monde	boh **MAWND**
Beaumont	**BOH** mont

ə ago, a at, ah calm, ahr dark, air care, aw saw, ay say, ch church
e bet, ee me, eer beer, hw what, i is, ī my, *n* French final n vin,

beauteous	**BYOO** tee əs
beautician	byoo **TISH** ən
beautification	**BYOO** tə fə **KAY** shən
beautiful	**BYOO** ti fəl
beautify	**BYOO** tə **FĪ**
beauty	**BYOO** tee
Beauvoir, Simone de	bohv **WAHR**, see **MUN** də
beaux	bohz
beaux (French)	boh
beaux arts	boh **ZAHR**
bebop	**BEE BOP**
becalm	bi **KAHM**
béchamel	**BAY** shə **MEL**
bêche-de-mer	**BESH** də **MAIR**
Bechuana	**BECH** oo **AH** nə
Bechuanaland	**BECH** oo **AH** nə **LAND**
Becket	**BEK** ət
Beckett	**BEK** ət
beckon	**BEK** ən
becloud	bi **KLOWD**
become	bi **KUM**
Becquerel	be **KREL**
bedaub	bi **DAWB**
Bedaux	bə **DOH**
bedazzle	bi **DAZ** əl
bedclothes	**BED** klohz
bedeck	bi **DEK**
bedevil	bi **DEV** əl
Bedford	**BED** fərd
Bedivere	**BED** ə **VEER**
bedizen	bi **DĪ** zən
bedlam	**BED** ləm
Bedloe	**BED** loh
Bedouin	**BED** oo ən
bedraggled	bi **DRAG** əld
beefeater	**BEEF** ee tər
Beelzebub	bee **EL** zə **BUB**
been	bin
Beerbohm, Max	**BIR** bohm
Beersheba	beer **SHEE** bə
Beethoven	**BAY** toh vən
befall	bi **FAWL**
befitting	bi **FIT** ing

o on, oh oat, oi boy, oo soon, oor poor, or for, ow cow, sh shush,
th thin, *th* this, u up, ur spur, uu book, *zh* pleasure

befog	bi **FOG**
beforehand	bi **FOR** **HAND**
befoul	bi **FOWL**
Begin, Menachem	**BE** geen, me **NAHK** əm (**BE** as in *bet*, me as in *met*)
beginning	bi **GIN** ing
begone	bi **GAWN**
begonia	bi **GOHN** yə
begot	bi **GOT**
begrudge	bi **GRUJ**
beguile	bi **GĪL**
beguine	bi **GEEN**
begum	**BEE** gəm
behalf	bi **HAF**
Behan, Brendan	**BEE** ən, **BREN** dən
behavior	bi **HAYV** yər
behaviorism	bi **HAYV** yə **RIZ** əm
behemoth	bi **HEE** məth
Behistun	**BAY** his **TOON**
Behn	bayn
behoove	bi **HOOV**
beige	bay*zh*
Beijing	bay jeeng
Beirut	bay **ROOT**
Bekaa	bi **KAH**
Békésy, Georg von	**BAY** ke shee, gay **ORG** fawn
belabor	bi **LAY** bər
Belafonte	**BEL** ə **FON** tee
Belasco	bə **LAS** koh
Belaunde Terry, Fernando	bel ow **OON** day **TER** ee, fer **NAHN** doh
bel canto	bel **KAHN** toh
beldam	**BEL** dəm
Belfast	**BEL** fast
belfry	**BEL** free
Belgian	**BEL** jən
Belgic	**BEL** jik
Belgium	**BEL** jəm
Belgrade	bel **GRAYD**
Belgravia	bel **GRAY** vee ə
Belial	**BEE** lee əl
belie	bi **LĪ**
belief	bə **LEEF**

ə ago, a at, ah calm, ahr dark, air care, aw saw, ay say, ch church
e bet, ee me, eer beer, hw what, i is, ī my, *n* French final n vin,

believe	bə **LEEV**
belittle	bi **LIT** əl
Beliveau	be li **VOH**
Belize	bə **LEEZ**
belladonna	**BEL** ə **DON** ə
Bellamy	**BEL** ə mee
belle	bel
Belleau	be **LOH**
Belleek	bə **LEEK**
Bellerophon	bə **LER** ə fən
belles-lettres	bel **LET** rə
bellhop	**BEL** hop
bellicose	**BEL** ə **KOHS**
belligerence	bə **LIJ** ə rəns
belligerent	bə **LIJ** ə rənt
Bellini	bə **LEE** nee
bellman	**BEL** mən
bellow	**BEL** oh
bellows	**BEL** ohz
bellwether	**BEL** **WE**_TH_ ər
Belmondo	bel **MOHN** doh
Belmopan	**BEL** moh **PAN**
beloved (a)	bi **LUVD**
beloved (a, n)	bi **LUV** əd
Bel Paese	**BEL** pah **AY** zə
Belshazzar	bel **SHAZ** ər
beluga	bə **LOO** gə
belvedere, B-	**BEL** və **DEER**
Belvoir (castle)	**BEE** vər
Belvoir (US)	**BEL** vwahr
bemoan	bi **MOHN**
bemuse	bi **MYOOZ**
Benacerraf, Baruj	**BAY** nah se **RAHF**, bah **ROOK**
Benares	bə **NAHR** əs
Ben Bella	ben **BEL** lah
Bendjedid, Chadli	**BEN** **JED** eed, **CHAHD** lee
beneath	bi **NEETH**
benedick, B-	**BEN** ə dik
benedict, B-	**BEN** ə dikt
Benedictine (monk, nun)	**BEN** ə **DIK** tən
Benedictine (liqueur)	**BEN** ə **DIK** **TEEN**
benediction	**BEN** ə **DIK** shən

o **on**, oh **oat**, oi **boy**, oo **soon**, oor **poor**, or **for**, ow **cow**, sh **shush**, th **thin**, _th_ **this**, u **up**, ur **spur**, uu **book**, _zh_ **pleasure**

benedictory	BEN ə DIK tə ree
Benedictus	BEN ə DIK təs
benefaction	BEN ə FAK shən
benefactor	BEN ə FAK tər
benefic	bə NEF ik
benefice	BEN ə fəs
beneficence	bə NEF ə səns
beneficent	bə NEF ə sənt
beneficial	BEN ə FISH əl
beneficiary	BEN ə FISH ee ER ee
benefit	BEN ə fit
Benelux	BEN ə LUKS
Benét	bə NAY
benevolence	bə NEV ə ləns
benevolent	bə NEV ə lənt
Bengal	ben GAWL
Bengalese	BEN gə LEEZ
Bengali	ben GAW lee
bengaline	BENG gə LEEN
Bengasi, Benghazi	ben GAH zee
Bengelloun, Ali	ben GEE loon, AH lee
Ben-Gurion	ben GUUR ee ən
benighted	bi NĪ təd
benign	bi NĪN
benignant	bi NIG nənt
benignity	bi NIG nə tee
Benin	bə NEEN
benison	BEN ə zən
Benites, Leopoldo	be NEE tes, lay oh POHL doh
Benjamin	BEN jə mən
Ben Khedda, Benyoussef	ben KAY də, ben YOO səf
Benoni	bə NOH nee
Bentham	BEN thəm
ben trovato	BEN troh VAHT oh
benumb	bi NUM
Benvenuto, b-	BEN və NOO toh
Ben Yahia, Habib	ben YAH hee ə, hah BEEB
Benzedrine	BEN zə DREEN
benzene	BEN zeen
benzine	BEN zeen
benzoate	BEN zoh AYT
benzoin	BEN zoh in

ə ago, a at, ah calm, ahr dark, air care, aw saw, ay say, ch church
e bet, ee me, eer beer, hw what, i is, ī my, n French final n vin,

benzol	**BEN** zohl
Beowulf	**BAY** ə **WUULF**
bequeath	bi **KWEE***TH*
bequest	bi **KWEST**
berate	bi **RAYT**
Berber	**BUR** bər
berceuse	ber **SUZ**
Berchtesgaden	**BERK** təs **GAHD** ən
Berdyaev	ber **DYAH** yef
Berea	bə **REE** ə
bereave	bi **REEV**
bereft	bi **REFT**
Berenson	**BER** ən sən
beret	bə **RAY**
bergamot	**BUR** gə **MOT**
Berganza	ber **GAHN** zə
Bergen (Norway)	**BER** gən
Bergen (US)	**BUR** gən
Bergerac	ber *zh*ə **RAK**
Bergman	**BURG** mən
Bergonzi, Carlo	bair **GOHN** dzee, **KAHR** loh
Bergson, Henri	berg **SAWN**, ahn **REE** (**SAWN** French final *n*)
Beria (Russian)	**BER** ee ə
beriberi	**BER** ee **BER** ee
Bering	**BEER** ing
Berkeley (California)	**BURK** lee
Berkeley (London)	**BAHRK** lee
Berkshire	**BURK** shir
Berlin (Germany)	bər **LIN**
Berlin (US)	**BUR** lən
Berlioz	**BER** lee **OHZ**
berm	burm
Bermuda	bər **MYOO** də
Bermúdez	ber **MOO** *th*ays
Bern, Berne	burn
Bernadotte	**BUR** nə **DOT**
Bernardin, Joseph Louis	**BER** nar **DAN** (**DAN** French final *n*)
Bernardine	**BUR** nər deen
Bernhardt	**BURN** hahrt
Bernice	bur **NEES**
Bernini	ber **NEE** nee

o **on**, oh **oat**, oi **boy**, oo **soon**, oor **poor**, or **for**, ow **cow**, sh **shush**, th **thin**, *th* **this**, u **up**, ur **spur**, uu **book**, *zh* **pleasure**

Bernoulli	bər **NOO** lee
Bernstein	**BURN** stīn
berserk	bər **SURK**
berth	burth
Bertha	**BUR** thə
Bertillon, Alphonse	**BER** tee **YOHN** (**YOHN** French final *n*)
Bertillon system	**BUR** tə **LON**
beryl	**BER** əl
beryllium	bə **RIL** ee əm
beseech	bi **SEECH**
beset	bi **SET**
beshrew	bi **SHROO**
besides	bi **SĪDZ**
besiege	bi **SEEJ**
besom	**BEE** zəm
Besoyan	bə **SOI** yən
Bessarabia	**BES** ə **RAY** bee ə
Bessemer	**BES** ə mər
besotted	bi **SOT** əd
bestial	**BES** chəl
bestiality	**BES** chee **AL** ə tee
bestiary	**BES** chee **ER** ee
bestir	bi **STUR**
bestow	bi **STOH**
bestride	bi **STRĪD**
beta	**BAY** tə
Betancourt	**BET** ən **KUUR**
Betancur, Belisario	bay tahn **KOOR**, bay lee **SAHR** ee oh
betatron	**BAY** tə **TRON**
betel	**BEE** təl
Betelgeuse	**BET** əl **JOOZ**
bête noire	bet **NWAHR**
Bethany	**BETH** ə nee
Bethe	**BAY** tə
Bethel	**BETH** əl
Bethesda	bə **THEZ** də
bethink	bi **THINGK**
Bethlehem	**BETH** li **HEM**
Bethmann-Hollweg	**BAYT** mahn **HAWL** vayk
Bethsaida	beth **SAY** ə də
betimes	bi **TĪMZ**
bêtise	be **TEEZ**
Betjeman	**BECH** ə mən

ə ago, a at, ah calm, ahr dark, air care, aw saw, ay say, ch church
e bet, ee me, eer beer, hw what, i is, ī my, *n* French final n vin,

betoken	bi **TOH** kən
betray	bi **TRAY**
betroth	bi **TROH***TH*
betrothal	bi **TROH** *th*əl
betrothed (a, n)	bi **TROH***TH*D
betta	**BET** ə
better, bettor	**BET** ər
Beulah	**BYOO** lə
beverage	**BEV** ə rij
Beverwijk	**BAY** vər **VĪK**
bevy	**BEV** ee
bewail	bi **WAYL**
beware	bi **WAIR**
Bewick, Thomas	**BYOO** ik
bewildered	bi **WIL** dərd
bewitched	bi **WICHT**
bey	bay
Beyle	bayl
beyond	bee **OND**
bezant	**BEZ** ənt
bezel	**BEEZ** əl
bezique	bə **ZEEK**
Bhagavad-Gita	**BUG** ə vəd **GEE** tah
bhang	bang
Bhatt, Uddhav Deo	baht, oo **DAHV DAY** oh
Bhopal, Bhopol	boh **PAHL**
Bhumibol, Adulyadej	**POO** mee **POHN**, a **DUUN** lə **DAYT**
Bhutan	boo **TAHN**
Bhutto	**BOO** toh
Biafra	bee **AF** rə
Biaggi	bee **AH** jee
bialy	bee **AH** lee
Bialystok	bee **AH** li **STAWK**
biannual	bī **AN** yoo əl
Biarritz	**BEE** ə **RITS**
bias	**BĪ** əs
biathlon	bī **ATH** lon
bibelot	**BIB** loh
biblical, B-	**BIB** li kəl
bibliographer	**BIB** lee **OG** rə fər
bibliography	**BIB** lee **OG** rə fee
bibliophile	**BIB** lee ə **FĪL**
bibulous	**BIB** yə ləs

o **on**, oh **oat**, oi **boy**, oo **soon**, oor **poor**, or **for**, ow **cow**, sh **shush**,
th **thin**, *th* **this**, u **up**, ur **spur**, uu **book**, *zh* **pleasure**

bicameral	bī **KAM** ər əl
bicarbonate	bī **KAHR** bə nət
bicentenary	bī **SEN** tə **NER** ee
bicentennial	**BĪ** sen **TEN** ee əl
biceps	**BĪ** seps
bichloride	bī **KLOHR** īd
bicker	**BIK** ər
bicuspid	bī **KUS** pəd
bicycle	**BĪ** si kəl
bicycling	**BĪ** si kling
bicyclist	**BĪ** si kləst
bidden	**BID** ən
biddy	**BID** ee
bidet	bee **DAY**
biennial	bī **EN** ee əl
bier	beer
bifilar	bī **FĪ** lər
bifocal	bī **FOH** kəl
bifurcate	**BĪ** fər **KAYT**
bifurcation	**BĪ** fər **KAY** shən
bigamist	**BIG** ə məst
bigamy	**BIG** ə mee
bight	bīt
Bignone, Reynaldo Benito	been **YOHN** ay, ray **NAHL** doh bay **NEE** toh
bignonia	big **NOH** nee ə
bigot	**BIG** ət
bigoted	**BIG** ə təd
bigotry	**BIG** ə tree
Bihać	**BEE** hahch
Bihar	bi **HAHR**
bijou	**BEE** *zh*oo
Bikaner	**BEE** kə **NER**
Bikel	bi **KEL**
bikini, B-	bə **KEE** nee
bilateral	bī **LAT** ə rəl
Bilbao	bil **BAH** oh
Bildad	**BIL** dad
bile	bīl
bilge	bilj
bilingual	bī **LING** gwəl
bilious	**BIL** yəs
billet	**BIL** ət

ə ago, a at, ah calm, ahr dark, air care, aw saw, ay say, ch church
e bet, ee me, eer beer, hw what, i is, ī my, *n* French final n vin,

billet-doux	**BIL** ay **DOO**
billiards	**BIL** yərds
billingsgate, B-	**BIL** ingz **GAYT**
Biloxi	bə **LUK** see
bimetallism	bī **MET** ə **LIZ** əm
bimonthly	bī **MUNTH** lee
binary	**BĪ** nə ree
binaural	bī **NOR** əl
binder	**BĪN** dər
bindery	**BĪN** də ree
Bindzi, Benoit	**BIND** zee, **BEN** wah
Binet	bi **NAY**
binge	binj
Bingen	**BING** ən
bingo	**BING** goh
binnacle	**BIN** ə kəl
binoculars	bə **NOK** yə lərz
binomial	bī **NOH** mee əl
biochemical	**BĪ** oh **KEM** i kəl
biodegradable	**BĪ** oh di **GRAY** də bəl
biogenesis	**BĪ** oh **JEN** ə səs
biogenic	**BĪ** oh **JEN** ik
biographer	bī **OG** rə fər
biography	bī **OG** rə fee
Bioko	bee **OH** koh
biological	**BĪ** ə **LOJ** i kəl
biology	bī **OL** ə jee
biomass	**BĪ** oh **MAS**
biome	**BĪ** ohm
bionics	bī **ON** iks
bionomics	**BĪ** ə **NOM** iks
biophysics	**BĪ** oh **FIZ** iks
biopsy	**BĪ** op see
biorhythm	**BĪ** oh **RITH** əm
biosynthesis	**BĪ** oh **SIN** thə səs
biotin	**BĪ** ə tən
bipartisan	bī **PAHR** tə zən
bipartite	bī **PAHR** tīt
biped	**BĪ** ped
Birabhongse Kasemsri	**PEE** rah pohng kah **SEM** sree
birch	burch
bird's-eye	**BURDZ Ī**
bireme	**BĪ** reem

---

biretta	bə **RET** ə
Birmingham (Alabama)	**BUR** ming **HAM**
Birmingham (England)	**BUR** ming əm
Bisayas	bee **SAH** yahs
Biscay	**BIS** kay
biscuit	**BIS** kət
bisect	bī **SEKT**
bisexual	bī **SEK** shoo əl
Bisho	**BEE** shoh
bishop	**BISH** əp
bishopric	**BISH** əp rik
Bismarck	**BIZ** mahrk
bismuth	**BIZ** məth
bison	**BĪ** sən
bisque	bisk
Bissau	bi **SOW** (**SOW** as in *cow*)
bissextile	bī **SEKS** təl
bistable	bī **STAY** bəl
bister	**BIS** tər
bistro	**BEES** troh
bisulfate	bī **SUL** fayt
Bitsios, Dimitri	**BEET** see ohs, dee **MEE** tree
bittern	**BIT** ərn
bitumen	bə **TOO** mən
bituminous	bə **TOO** mə nəs
bivalence	bī **VAY** ləns
bivalent	bī **VAY** lənt
bivalve	**BĪ** valv
bivouac	**BIV** oo ak
biweekly	bī **WEEK** lee
bizarre	bə **ZAHR**
Bizerte	bə **ZUR** tee
Bizet	bee **ZAY**
blab	blab
blackguard	**BLAG** ərd
blamable	**BLAY** mə bəl
blanch	blanch
blancmange	blə **MAHNJ**
Blanco, Salvador Jorge	**BLAHN** koh, sahl vah **DAWR HOR** hay
bland	bland
blandishment	**BLAN** dish mənt

ə ago, a at, ah calm, ahr dark, air care, aw saw, ay say, ch church
e bet, ee me, eer beer, hw what, i is, ī my, *n* French final n vin,

blanket	**BLANG** kət
blare	blair
Blasco-Ibáñez	**BLAH** skoh ee **BAH** nyeth
blasé	blah **ZAY**
blaspheme	blas **FEEM**
blasphemous	**BLAS** fə məs
blasphemy	**BLAS** fə mee
blastula	**BLAS** chuu lə
blatancy	**BLAY** tən see
blatant	**BLAYT** ənt
blatherskite	**BLA***TH* ər **SKĪT**
Blavatsky	blə **VAHT** skee
blazon	**BLAY** zən
Blenheim	**BLEN** əm
Blériot	**BLAY** ree oh
blessed (a)	**BLES** əd
blessed (v)	blest
blight	blīt
blissful	**BLIS** fəl
blithe	blī*th*
blithering	**BLI***TH* ə ring
blitz	blits
blitzkrieg	**BLITS** kreeg
blizzard	**BLIZ** ərd
bloc	blok
blockade	blo **KAYD**
Bloembergen, Nicolaas	**BLOOM** **BUR** gən, **NIK** ə ləs
Bloemfontein	**BLOOM** fon **TAYN**
Blois	blwah
blond, blonde	blond
blotter	**BLOT** ər
blouse	blows
blowzy	**BLOW** zee (**BLOW** as in *cow*)
blubber	**BLUB** ər
blucher	**BLOO** chər
bludgeon	**BLUJ** ən
Bluebeard	**BLOO** beerd
bluestocking	**BLOO** **STOK** ing
bluish	**BLOO** ish
Blum, Yehuda	**BLOOM**, yə **HOO** də
blunderbuss	**BLUN** dər **BUS**
bluster	**BLUS** tər

o **on**, oh **oat**, oi **boy**, oo **soon**, oor **poor**, or **for**, ow **cow**, sh **shush**,
th **thin**, *th* **this**, u **up**, ur **spur**, uu **book**, *zh* **pleasure**

B'nai B'rith	bə NAY BRITH
boa	BOH ə
Boabdil	BOH ahb *THEEL*
Boadicea	BOH ad ə SEE ə
boar	bor
board	bord
boarish	BOR ish
Boas	BOH az
boatswain	BOH sən
Boaz	BOH az
bobbin	BOB ən
bobolink	BOB ə LINGK
bobsled	BOB sled
Boca Raton	BOH kə rə TOHN
Boccaccio, Giovanni	boh KAH chee OH, JEE ə VAH nee
boche, B-	bosh
bock	bok
bodega	boh DAY gə
Bodensee	BOH dən ZAY
bodice	BOD əs
bodily	BOD ə lee
bodkin	BOD kən
Bodleian	bod LEE ən
Boeing	BOH ing
Boeotia	bee OH shee ə
Boeotian	bee OH shən
Boer	bohr
Boethius	boh EE thee əs
Bogan	BOH gən
bogey	BOH gee
boggle	BOG əl
bogie	BOH gee
Bogota (NJ)	bə GOH tə
Bogotá (Colombia)	BOH gə TAH
bogy	BOH gee
Bohan, Marc	boh AHN, MAHRK
bohème	boh EM
Bohemia	boh HEE mee ə
Bohol	boh HAWL
Bohr, Nils	bohr, neels
Boise	BOI zee
boisterous	BOI stə rəs
Bokhara	boh KAHR ə

ə ago, a at, ah calm, ahr dark, air care, aw saw, ay say, ch church
e bet, ee me, eer beer, hw what, i is, ī my, *n* French final n vin,

bola	**BOH** lə
bolas	**BOH** ləz
Bole, Filipe Nagera	**BOH** lay, fi **LEE** pee nahn **GER** ay
bolero	bə **LAIR** oh
Boleyn	buu **LIN**
bolivar (coin)	**BOL** ə vər
Bolívar, Simón	baw **LEE** vahr, see **MAWN**
Bolivia, b-	bə **LIV** ee ə
Bolivian	bə **LIV** ee ən
boll	bohl
Böll, Heinrich	**BUL, HĪN** rik
bollard	**BOL** ərd
bolo	**BOH** loh
Bologna (Italy)	bə **LOHN** yə
bologna (sausage)	bə **LOH** nee
Bolognese	**BOH** lən **YEEZ**
bolometer	boh **LOM** ə tər
boloney	bə **LOH** nee
bolshevik, B-	**BOHL** shə vik
Bolshoi	**BOHL** shoi
bolster	**BOHL** stər
bolus	**BOH** ləs
Bolzano, Bernhard	bohl **TSAH** noh, **BERN** hahrt
Bomani, Paul	baw **MAHN** ee
bomb	bom
bombard	bom **BAHRD**
bombardier	**BOM** bər **DEER**
bombast	**BOM** bast
bombastic	bom **BAS** tik
Bombay	bom **BAY**
Bombay duck	**BOM** bay **DUK**
bombazine	**BOM** bə **ZEEN**
bombe	bawmb
bomber	**BOM** ər
Bombois	bohm **BWAH**
Bomboko	bəm **BOH** koh
bombproof	**BOM** proof
bombshell	**BOM** shel
bona fide	**BOH** nə **FĪD**
bona fides	**BOH** nə **FĪ** deez
bonanza	bə **NAN** zə
Bonaparte	**BOH** nə **PAHRT**
Bonaventura	**BON** ə ven **CHUUR** ə

---

o on, oh oat, oi boy, oo soon, oor poor, or for, ow cow, sh shush,
th thin, *th* this, u up, ur spur, uu book, *zh* pleasure

Bonaventure, Saint	**BON** ə **VEN** chər
bonbon	**BON** bon
bondage	**BON** dij
bonfire	**BON** fīr
bongo	**BONG** goh
Bongo, El Hadj Omar	**BAWNG** goh, el **HAH** jee oh **MAHR**
Bonheur	bah **NUR**
bonhomie	**BON** ə **MEE**
Bonin	**BOH** nən
bonito	bə **NEE** toh
bonjour	bawn **ZHOOR** (bawn French final *n*)
bon mot	bawn **MOH** (bawn French final *n*)
Bonn	bon
Bonnard	baw **NAHR**
bonnet	**BON** ət
bonsai	**BON** sī
bonsoir	bawn **SWAHR** (bawn French final *n*)
bonus	**BOH** nəs
bon vivant	bawn vee **VAHN** (bawn and **VAHN** French final *n*)
bon voyage	bawn vwah **YAHZH** (bawn French final *n*)
Bonynge	**BON** ing
bonze	bonz
booby	**BOO** bee
boodle	**BOO** dəl
boogie-woogie	**BUUG** ee **WUUG** ee
Boolean	**BOO** lee ən
boomerang	**BOO** mə **RANG**
boondocks	**BOON** doks
boondoggle	**BOON** dah gəl
Boorstin	**BOORS** tən
Boötes	boh **OH** teez
booth, B-	booth
booths	boo*th*z
bootless	**BOOT** ləs
Bophuthatswana	**BOH** poo taht **SWAH** nə
boracic	bə **RAS** ik
borate	**BOR** ayt
borax	**BOR** aks
Borch, Otto	bork
Bordeaux	bor **DOH**
bordelaise	**BAWR** də **LAYZ**

ə ago, a at, ah calm, ahr dark, air care, aw saw, ay say, ch church
e bet, ee me, eer beer, hw what, i is, ī my, *n* French final n vin,

bordello	bor **DEL** oh
boreal	**BOR** ee əl
borealis	**BOR** ee **AL** əs
Boreas	**BOR** ee əs
Borg, Bjorn	borg, jorn
Borges, Jorge Luis	**BOR** hays, **HOR** hay loo **EES**
Borghese	bor **GAY** zay
Borgia	**BOR** jə
Borglum	**BOR** gləm
boric	**BOR** ik
Boris	**BOR** is
Borisoglebsk	**BAW** ree saw **GLEPSK**
Borja, Jacinto Castel	**BOR** hah, hah **SEEN** toh kah **STEL**
Borlaug, Norman	**BOR** lawg
borne	born
Borneo	**BOR** nee **OH**
Bornholm	**BORN** hohm
Borodin	**BOR** ə **DEEN**
boron	**BOR** on
borough	**BUR** oh
borrow	**BAH** roh
borsch	borsh
borscht	borsht
borzoi	**BOR** zoi
boscage	**BOS** kij
Bosch, Hieronymus	**BOSH, HEE** ə **ROH** nə məs
Bose	bohs
bosh	bosh
Bosley	**BOZ** lee
Bosnia	**BOZ** nee ə
bosom	**BUUZ** əm
boson	**BOH** sahn
Bosphorus	**BOS** fər əs
Bosporus	**BOS** pər əs
Bossuet	baw **SWAY**
Boston, b-	**BAW** stən
bosun	**BOH** sən
botanical	bə **TAN** i kəl
botany	**BOT** ə nee
botch	boch
Botha, Pieter	bwə **TAH, PEE** tər
Botha, Roelof	bwə **TAH,** roo **LAWF**
Bothe, Walter	**BOH** tə

o on, oh oat, oi boy, oo soon, oor poor, or for, ow cow, sh shush,
th thin, *th* this, u up, ur spur, uu book, *zh* pleasure

bother	**BAH** *th*ər
Botswana	bot **SWAH** nə
Bottegari	boh tə **GAH** ree
Botticelli	BOT ə **CHEL** ee
Botticini	BOT ə **CHEE** nee
botulism	**BOCH** ə LIZ əm
Botvinnik, Mikhail	**BAWT** vee nik, mi kah **EEL**
Boucher, François	boo **SHAY**, frahn **SWAH** (frahn French final *n*)
bouclé	boo **KLAY**
boudoir	**BOO** dwahr
bougainvillaea	BOO gən **VIL** ee ə
Bougainville (island)	**BOO** gən VIL
bough	bow (as in *cow*)
bought	bawt
bougie	**BOO** jee
Bouguereau	boog ə **ROH**
bouillabaisse	BOO yə **BAYS**
bouillon	**BOOL** yon
Boulanger	boo lahn **ZHAY** (lahn French final *n*)
boulder, B-	**BOHL** dər
boulevard	**BUUL** ə VAHRD
Boulogne	boo **LAWN** yə
Boumédienne	BOO may **DYEN**
bounteous	**BOWN** tee əs
bountiful	**BOWN** tə fəl
bouquet (aroma)	boo **KAY**
bouquet (flowers)	boh **KAY**
Bourbon (European)	**BOOR** bən
Bourbon, b- (US; whiskey)	**BUR** bən
bourgeois	boor **ZH**WAH
bourgeoise	boor **ZH**WAHZ
bourgeoisie	BOOR *zh*wah **ZEE**
Bourget	boor **ZH**AY
Bourguiba, Habib	buur **GEE** bah, hah **BEEB**
Bourke	burk
Bournemouth	**BOORN** məth
bourse	boors
Bouterse, Desire	**BOW** ter sə, **DAY** see ray
boutonniere	BOOT tə **NEER**
Bouvet	**BOO** vay
bouzouki	bə **ZOO** kee

ə ago, a at, ah calm, ahr dark, air care, aw saw, ay say, ch church
e bet, ee me, eer beer, hw what, i is, ī my, *n* French final n vin,

Bovary	**BOH** vah ree
Bovet, Daniel	boh **VAY**, dah **NYEL**
bovine	**BOH** vīn
bow (prow; nod)	bow (as in *cow*)
bow (weapon; curve; knot)	boh
Bowdich, Bowditch	**BOW DICH** (**BOW** as in *cow*)
Bowdler	**BOHD** lər
bowdlerize	**BOHD** lə **RĪZ**
Bowdoin	**BOHD** ən
bowel	**BOW** əl (**BOW** as in *cow*)
bower (arbor; cards; anchor)	**BOW** ər (**BOW** as in *cow*)
bower (violinist)	**BOH** ər
bowery, B-	**BOW** ə ree (**BOW** as in *cow*)
bowie, B-	**BOO** ee
bowl	bohl
bowlegged	**BOH LEG** əd
bowler	**BOH** lər
bowline	**BOH** lən
bowman (archer)	**BOH** mən
bowman (oarsman)	**BOW** mən (**BOW** as in *cow*)
bowsprit	**BOW** sprit (**BOW** as in *cow*)
bowstring	**BOH** string
boxer	**BOK** sər
Boya, Thomas Setondji	**BOH** yə, **TOM** əs sə **TOON** jee
boyar	boh **YAHR**
boycott	**BOI** kot
Boyd, Aquilino	**BOID**, ah kee **LEE** noh
Bo Yibo	baw yee baw
boysenberry	**BOI** zən **BER** ee
bra	brah
Brabant	brə **BANT**
brace	brays
bracelet	**BRAYS** lət
bracero	brah **SAIR** oh
brachial	**BRAY** kee əl
brachiopod	**BRAY** kee ə **POD**
brachium	**BRAY** kee əm
brachycephalic	**BRAK** ee sə **FAL** ik
bracken	**BRAK** ən
brackish	**BRAK** ish
brae	bray

---

o on, oh oat, oi boy, oo soon, oor poor, or for, ow cow, sh shush,
th thin, *th* this, u up, ur spur, uu book, *zh* pleasure

Braganca	brah **GAHN** sə
braggadocio	**BRAG** ə **DOH** shee **OH**
braggart	**BRAG** ərt
Brahe, Tycho	**BRAH**, **TEE** koh
Brahma, b-	**BRAH** mə
Brahman	**BRAH** mən
Brahmaputra	**BRAH** mə **POO** trə
Brahmin	**BRAH** mən
Brahms	brahmz
braid	brayd
braille, B-	brayl
braise	brayz
Bramante	brah **MAHN** tay
Braña	**BRAH** nyah
Brancusi	brahn **KOO** see
Brandeis	**BRAN** dīs
Brandenburg	**BRAN** dən **BURG**
brandied	**BRAN** deed
brandish	**BRAN** dish
Brandt, Willy	**BRAHNT**, **VIL** ee
Braque, Georges	**BRAHK**, *zh*awr*zh*
Brasília	brə **ZIL** yə
brass	bras
brassard	**BRAS** ərd
brasserie	**BRAS** ə **REE**
brassiere	brə **ZEER**
Bratislava	**BRAH** tə **SLAH** və
Brattain, Walter	**BRAT** ən
Braun	brown
Braunschweiger	**BROWN** sʜwī gər
bravado	brə **VAH** doh
bravo	**BRAH** voh
bravura	brə **VYOOR** ə
brawny	**BRAW** nee
braze	brayz
brazier	**BRAY** *zh*ər
Brazil	brə **ZIL**
Brazzaville	**BRAZ** ə **VIL**
breach	breech
breadth	bredth
breadthways	**BREDTH** wayz
breadthwise	**BREDTH** wīz
breakage	**BRAY** kij

ə ago, a at, ah calm, ahr dark, air care, aw saw, ay say, ch church
e bet, ee me, eer beer, hw what, i is, ī my, *n* French final n vin,

breakfast	**BREK** fəst
bream	breem
breast	brest
breath	breth
breathalyzer	**BRETH** ə lī zər
breathe	bree*th*
breathed	bree*th*d
breathing	**BREE*TH*** ing
breathy	**BRETH** ee
breccia	**BRECH** ee ə
Brecht, Bertolt	**BREKT, BER** tohlt
breech	breech
breeches (trousers)	**BRICH** əz
breeches buoy	**BREE** chəz **BOO** ee
breechloader	**BREECH LOH** dər
Bremen (Germany)	**BRAY** mən
Bremen (US)	**BREE** mən
Brenner	**BREN** ər
Brentano	bren **TAH** noh
Brescia	**BRE** shah
Breslau	**BRES** low (low as in *cow*)
Bressoud	bre **SUUD**
Brest	brest
Brest-Litovsk	**BREST** lə **TAWFSK**
brethren	**BRE*TH*** rən
Breton	**BRET** ən
Bretton	**BRET** ən
Breughel	**BROI** gəl
breve	breev
brevet	brə **VET**
breviary	**BREE** vee **ER** ee
brevier	brə **VEER**
brevity	**BREV** ə tee
brewery	**BROO** ə ree
Brezhnev, Leonid	**BREZ*H*** nef, **LAY** oh nid
Briand, Aristide	bree **AHN**, ah ree **STEED** (**AHN** French final *n*)
Briareus	brī **AIR** ee əs
bribery	**BRĪ** bə ree
bric-a-brac	**BRIK** ə **BRAK**
bridal	**BRĪD** əl
bridegroom	**BRĪD** groom
bridesmaid	**BRĪDZ** mayd

bridle	**BRĪD** əl
Brie	bree
brier	**BRĪ** ər
brigade	bri **GAYD**
brigadier	BRIG ə **DEER**
brigand	**BRIG** ənd
brigantine	**BRIG** ən TEEN
brilliance	**BRIL** yəns
brilliant	**BRIL** yənt
brilliantine	**BRIL** yən TEEN
Brindisi	**BREEN** də zee
brindled	**BRIN** dəld
brioche	bree **OHSH**
briquette	bri **KET**
Brisbane (Australia)	**BRIZ** bən
Briseis	brī **SEE** əs
brisket	**BRIS** kət
brisling	**BRIZ** ling
bristle	**BRIS** əl
Bristol	**BRIS** təl
Britannia	bri **TAN** ee ə
Britannic	bri **TAN** ik
Briticism	**BRIT** ə SIZ əm
Britisher	**BRIT** i shər
Briton	**BRIT** ən
Brno	**BUR** noh
broach	brohch
broad gauge	brawd gayj
Brobdingnag	**BROB** ding NAG
Brobdingnagian	BROB ding **NAG** ee ən
brocade	broh **KAYD**
broccoli	**BROK** ə lee
broché	broh **SHAY**
brochette	broh **SHET**
brochure	broh **SHUUR**
brogan	**BROH** gən
Broglio	**BROH** lee oh
brogue	brohg
brokerage	**BROH** kə rij
brome	brohm
bromide	**BROH** mīd
bromine	**BROH** meen
bronchial	**BRONG** kee əl

ə ago, a at, ah calm, ahr dark, air care, aw saw, ay say, ch church
e bet, ee me, eer beer, hw what, i is, ī my, *n* French final n vin,

bronchitis	brong **KĪ** təs
bronchoscope	**BRONG** kə **SKOHP**
bronco	**BRONG** koh
Brontë	**BRON** tee
brontosaurus	**BRON** tə **SOR** əs
Bronx	brongks
bronze	bronz
brooch	brohch
brothel	**BRAHTH** əl
brotherhood	**BRU***TH* ər **HUUD**
brougham	broom
brouhaha	**BROO** hah hah
Broun	broon
browbeat	**BROW BEET** (**BROW** as in *cow*)
browse	browz
Broz	brawz
brucellosis	**BROO** sə **LOH** səs
Bruckner, Anton	**BRUUK** nər, **AN** tohn
Brueghel	**BROI** gəl
Bruges	broo*zh*
bruin	**BROO** ən
bruise	brooz
bruiser	**BROO** zər
bruit	broot
Brumaire	bruu **MAIR**
brumal	**BROO** məl
brume	broom
Brumel, Valery	**BRUU** mil, vah **LAI** ree
Brunei	bruu **NĪ**
Brunelleschi	**BROON** ə **LES** kee
brunet	broo **NET**
Brunetière	**BRUU** nə **TYAIR**
Brunhild	**BRUUN** hilt
Brunnhilde	bruun **HIL** də
brusque	brusk
Brussels	**BRUS** əlz
brut	broot
brute	broot
Bruxelles	broo **SEL**
Bruyère	bruu **YAIR**
Bryansk	bree **AHNSK**
Brynhild	**BRIN** hild
Bryn Mawr	brin **MAHR**

o on, oh oat, oi boy, oo soon, oor poor, or for, ow cow, sh shush,
th thin, *th* this, u up, ur spur, uu book, *zh* pleasure

bryophyte	**BRĪ** ə **FĪT**
Brython	**BRITH** ən
Brythonic	bri **THON** ik
Brzezinski, Zbigniew	brə **ZH**IN skee, zə **BIG** nəf
Buali, Abdulaziz	**BOO** lee, ahb **DOOL** ah **SEEZ**
Buber, Martin	**BOO** bər
Bubiriza, Pascal	boo bee **REE** zah, **PAH** skahl
bubo	**BYOO** boh
buboes	**BYOO** bohz
bubonic	byoo **BON** ik
buccal	**BUK** əl
buccaneer	**BUK** ə **NEER**
buccinator	**BUK** sə **NAY** tər
Bucephalus	byoo **SEF** ə ləs
Buchanan	byoo **KAN** ən
Buchan, John	**BUK** ən
Bucharest	**BOO** kə **REST**
Buchenwald	**BOOK** ən **VAHLT**
Buchholz, Horst	**BUK** hohlts, **HAWRST**
Buchman	**BUUK** mən
Buchmanism	**BUUK** mə **NIZ** əm
Buchmanite	**BUUK** mə **NĪT**
Buchwald	**BOOK** wawld
buckaroo	**BUK** ə **ROO**
Buckeye, b-	**BUK** ī
Buckingham	**BUK** ing əm
bucko	**BUK** oh
buckram	**BUK** rəm
buckwheat	**BUK** hweet
bucolic	byoo **KOL** ik
Bucovina	**BOO** kə **VEE** nə
Bucyk	**BYUU** sik
Budapest	**BOO** də **PEST**
Buddha	**BOO** də
Buddhism	**BOOD** iz əm
buddleia	**BUD** lee ə
Budenny	boo **DEN** ee
budgerigar	**BUJ** ə ree **GAHR**
Budo, Halim	**BUU** doh, **HAL** leem
Budweiser	**BUD** wī zər
Buell	**BYOO** əl
Buenaventura	**BWAY** nə ven **TUUR** ə
Buenos Aires	**BWAY** nəs **ĪR** eez

ə ago, a at, ah calm, ahr dark, air care, aw saw, ay say, ch church
e bet, ee me, eer beer, hw what, i is, ī my, *n* French final n vin,

buffalo, B-	**BUF** ə loh
buffet (blow)	**BUF** ət
buffet (sideboard; meal)	bə **FAY**
buffo	**BOO** foh
buffoon	bə **FOON**
buffoonery	bə **FOO** nə ree
Bug (river)	boog
bugaboo	**BUG** ə **BOO**
Buganda	boo **GAN** də
bugle	**BYOO** gəl
bugloss	**BYOO** glaws
Buitenzorg	**BĪT** ən **ZORG**
Bujumbura	**BOO** jəm **BUUR** ə
Bukharin	boo **KAH** rən
bulbous	**BUL** bəs
bulbul	**BUUL** buul
Bulganin	buul **GAHN** ən
Bulgar	**BUL** gər
Bulgaria	buul **GAIR** ee ə
bulgur	**BUUL** gər
bulimia	byoo **LIM** ee ə
bulkhead	**BULK** hed
bulldoze	**BUUL** dohz
bullion	**BUUL** yən
Bull Moose	buul moos
Bull, Ole	**BOOL, OH** lə
bullock	**BUUL** ək
bulrush	**BUUL** rush
bulwark	**BUUL** wərk
bumblebee	**BUM** bəl **BEE**
bumpkin	**BUM** kən
bumptious	**BUMP** shəs
Buna	**BOO** nə
Bunche	bunch
bunco	**BUNG** koh
buncombe	**BUNG** kəm
Bund	buund
Bundesrat	**BUUN** dəs **RAHT**
Bundestag	**BUUN** dəs **TAHG**
Bundeswehr	**BUUN** dəs **VAIR**
bungalow	**BUNG** gə **LOH**
bunghole	**BUNG HOHL**

o on, oh oat, oi boy, oo soon, oor poor, or for, ow cow, sh shush,
th thin, *th* this, u up, ur spur, uu book, *zh* pleasure

Bunin	**BOON** ən
bunion	**BUN** yən
bunkum	**BUNG** kəm
Bunsen	**BUN** sən
bunting	**BUN** ting
Buñuel, Luis	**BUUN** yoo **EL**, loo **EES**
Bunyan	**BUN** yən
buoy	**BOO** ee
buoyancy	**BOI** ən see
buoyant	**BOI** ənt
Burbage	**BUR** bij
Burbank	**BUR** bank
Burberry	**BUR** bə ree
burdock	**BUR** dok
bureau	**BYOOR** oh
bureaucracy	byuu **ROK** rə see
burette	byuu **RET**
burgeon	**BUR** jən
burgess	**BUR** jəs
burgher	**BUR** gər
Burghley	**BUR** lee
burglar	**BUR** glər
burglarize	**BUR** glə **RĪZ**
burglary	**BUR** glə ree
burgomaster	**BUR** gə **MAS** tər
burgoo	bur **GOO**
Burgoyne	bər **GOIN**
burgrave	**BUR** grayv
Burgundian	bər **GUN** dee ən
Burgundy	**BUR** gən dee
burial	**BER** ee əl
burin	**BYUUR** ən
burka	**BUUR** kə
burl	burl
burlap	**BUR** lap
Burleigh	**BUR** lee
burlesque	bər **LESK**
burley, B-	**BUR** lee
burly	**BUR** lee
Burma	**BUR** mə
Burmese	bər **MEEZ**
burnoose, burnous	bər **NOOS**
burnsides	**BURN** sīdz

ə ago, a at, ah calm, ahr dark, air care, aw saw, ay say, ch church
e bet, ee me, eer beer, hw what, i is, ī my, n French final n vin,

burro	**BUR** oh
burrow	**BUR** oh
bursa	**BUR** sə
bursae	**BUR** see
bursar	**BUR** sər
bursitis	bər **SĪ** təs
Burundi	buu **RUUN** dee
bury	**BER** ee
busby	**BUZ** bee
bushel	**BUUSH** əl
bushido, B-	boo shee doh
bushwhacker	**BUUSH** hwak ər
business	**BIZ** nəs
businessman	**BIZ** nəs **MAN**
buskin	**BUS** kən
Bustamante	**BOO** stah **MAHN** tay
Bustamente	**BOO** stah **MEN** tay
bustard	**BUS** tərd
bustle	**BUS** əl
Busuanga	boo **SWAHNG** gə
busy	**BIZ** ee
busyness	**BIZ** ee nəs
butadiene	**BYOO** tə **DĪ** een
butane	**BYOO** tayn
butchery	**BUUCH** ə ree
Butor, Michel	buu **TAWR**, mee **SHEL**
butt	but
butte, B-	byoot
butterwort	**BUT** ər **WURT**
buttock	**BUT** ək
buttress	**BUT** rəs
butyl	**BYOO** təl
butyrate	**BYOO** tə **RAYT**
butyric	byoo **TIR** ik
buxom	**BUK** səm
buzzard	**BUZ** ərd
Bwakira, Melchior	bgah **TEER** rah, **MEL** kee or (bgah *b* barely pronounced)
bwana	**BWAH** nə
Bydgoszcz	**BID** gawsh
bye	bī
Byelorussia	**BYEL** oh **RUSH** ə
Byelorussian	**BYEL** oh **RUSH** ən

---

o on, oh oat, oi boy, oo soon, oor poor, or for, ow cow, sh shush,
th thin, *th* this, u up, ur spur, uu book, *zh* pleasure

bylaw, byelaw	**BĪ** law
by-line	**BĪ** līn
Byong Hion Lew	byong hyon loo
Byron	**BĪ** rən
Byronic	bī **RON** ik
Bysshe	bish
bystander	**BĪ** stan dər
byte	bīt
Byzantine	**BIZ** ən **TEEN**
Byzantium	bə **ZAN** shee əm

C

cabal	kə **BAL**
cabala	**KAB** ə lə
cabalistic	**KAB** ə **LIS** tik
caballero	**KAB** əl **YAIR** oh
Caballero Tamayo, Jaime	kah bah **YAIR** oh tah **MAH** yoh, **HĪ** may
cabana	kə **BAN** ə
cabaret	**KAB** ə **RAY**
cabbala	**KAB** ə lə
Cabell	**KAB** əl
cabinet	**KAB** ə nət
cabochon	**KAB** ə **SHON**
caboodle	kə **BOO** dəl
caboose	kə **BOOS**
Cabot	**KAB** ət
Cabrera	ka **BRAY** rə
cabriole	**KAB** ree **OHL**
cabriolet	**KAB** ree ə **LAY**
cacao	kə **KAY** oh
Caccia	**KAH** chə
cache	kash
cachet	ka **SHAY**
cachou	kə **SHOO**
cachucha	kə **CHOO** chə
cacique	kə **SEEK**
cacophonous	kə **KOF** ə nəs
cacophony	kə **KOF** ə nee
cacti	**KAK** tī

ə ago, a at, ah calm, ahr dark, air care, aw saw, ay say, ch church
e bet, ee me, eer beer, hw what, i is, ī my, *n* French final n vin,

cactus	**KAK** təs
cadaver	kə **DAV** ər
cadaverous	kə **DAV** ər əs
caddie, caddy	**KAD** ee
cadence	**KAY** dəns
cadenza	kə **DEN** zə
cadet	kə **DET**
cadge	kaj
cadi	**KAH** dee
Cádiz	kə **DIZ**
Cadmean	kad **MEE** ən
cadmium	**KAD** mee əm
Cadmus	**KAD** məs
cadre	**KAD** ree
caduceus	kə **DOO** see əs
Caedmon	**KAD** mən
Caedmonian	kad **MOH** nee ən
Caen	kahn (French final *n*)
Caerleon	kahr **LEE** ən
Caesar	**SEE** zər
Caesarea	SEE zə **REE** ə
Caesarean	si **ZAIR** ee ən
caesura	si **ZHOOR** ə
café	ka **FAY**
café au lait	ka **FAY** oh **LAY**
café noir	ka **FAY NWAHR**
cafeteria	KAF ə **TEER** ee ə
caffeine	ka **FEEN**
caftan	**KAF** tən
cagey, cagy	**KAY** jee
Cagliostro	kah **LYAWS** troh
cahoots	kə **HOOTS**
Caiaphas	**KAY** ə fəs
Caicos	**KAY** kəs
caiman	**KAY** mən
caïque	kah **EEK**
cairn	kairn
Cairo (Egypt)	**KĪ** roh
Cairo (Illinois)	**KAIR** oh
caisson	**KAY** sən
caitiff	**KAY** tif
Caitlin	**KAYT** lin
Caius	**KAY** əs

o **on**, oh **oat**, oi **boy**, oo **soon**, oor **poor**, or **for**, ow **cow**, sh **shush**,
th **thin**, *th* **this**, u **up**, ur **spur**, uu **book**, *zh* **pleasure**

Caius (college)	keez
cajole	kə **JOHL**
cajolery	kə **JOH** lə ree
Cajun	**KAY** jən
calabash	**KAL** ə **BASH**
calaboose	**KAL** ə **BOOS**
Calabria	kə **LAH** bree ə
caladium	kə **LAY** dee əm
Calais (France)	ka **LAY**
Calais (US)	**KA** lis
calamari	**KAHL** ə **MAHR** ee
calamary	**KAL** ə **MER** ee
calamine	**KAL** ə **MĪN**
calamitous	kə **LAM** ə təs
calamity	kə **LAM** ə tee
calamus	**KAL** ə məs
calash	kə **LASH**
calcareous	kal **KAR** ee əs
calceolaria	**KAL** see ə **LAIR** ee ə
calces	**KAL** seez
calcify	**KAL** sə **FĪ**
calcimine	**KAL** sə **MĪN**
calcine	**KAL** sīn
calcite	**KAL** sīt
calcium	**KAL** see əm
calculable	**KAL** kyə lə bəl
calculate	**KAL** kyə **LAYT**
calculation	**KAL** kyə **LAY** shən
calculator	**KAL** kyə **LAY** tər
calculous	**KAL** kyə ləs
calculus	**KAL** kyə ləs
Calcutta	kal **KUT** ə
Calderon (English)	**KAWL** dər ən
Calderón (Spanish)	**KAHL** de **RAWN**
caldron	**KAWL** drən
Caleb	**KAY** ləb
calèche	ka **LESH**
Caledonia	**KAL** i **DOH** nee ə
Caledonian	**KAL** ə **DOH** nee ən
calendar	**KAL** ən dər
calender	**KAL** ən dər
calends	**KAL** əndz
calendula	kə **LEN** jə lə
calf	kaf

Cali	**KAH** lee
Caliban	**KAL** ə **BAN**
caliber	**KAL** ə bər
calibrate	**KAL** ə **BRAYT**
calices	**KAL** i **SEEZ**
calico	**KAL** ə **KOH**
calif	**KAY** lif
California	**KAL** ə **FOR** nyə
californium	**KAL** ə **FOR** nee əm
caliper	**KAL** ə pər
caliph	**KAY** lif
caliphate	**KAL** ə **FAYT**
calisthenic	**KAL** əs **THEN** ik
calix	**KAY** liks
calk	kawk
calla	**KAL** ə
Callaghan	**KAL** ə han
Callao	kah **YAH** oh
Callas	**KAL** əs
Calle y Calle, Juan José	**KAH** yay ee **KAH** yay, **HWAHN** hoh **SAY**
calligraphy	kə **LIG** rə fee
calliope, C-	kə **LĪ** ə **PEE**
Callisto	kə **LIS** toh
callous	**KAL** əs
callow	**KAL** oh
callus	**KAL** əs
calm	kahm
calmative	**KAHM** ə tiv
calomel	**KAL** ə **MEL**
caloric	kə **LAW** rik
calorie	**KAL** ə ree
calumet	**KAL** yə **MET**
calumniate	kə **LUM** nee **AYT**
calumniator	kə **LUM** nee **AY** tər
calumny	**KAL** əm nee
Calvary	**KAL** və ree
Calvin	**KAL** vin
Calvinism	**KAL** və **NIZ** əm
Calvinist	**KAL** və nist
Calvo Sotelo, Leopoldo	**KAHL** boh soh **TEL** oh, lay oh **POHL** doh
calx	kalks

o **on**, oh **oat**, oi **boy**, oo **soon**, oor **poor**, or **for**, ow **cow**, sh **shush**, th **thin**, *th* **this**, u **up**, ur **spur**, uu **book**, *zh* **pleasure**

calyces	KAY lə SEEZ
calycle	KAL i kəl
Calydon	KAL i DON
Calypso, c-	kə LIP soh
calyx	KAY liks
calyxes	KAY liks əz
Camacho	kah MAH choh
Camaguey	KAM ə GWAY
camaraderie	KAH mə RAH də ree
Camargue	kə MAHRG
camarilla	KAM ə RIL ə
camber	KAM bər
cambium	KAM bee əm
Cambodia	kam BOH dee ə
Cambrai	kahm BRAY
Cambrian	KAM bree ən
cambric	KAYM brik
Cambridge	KAYM brij
camellia	kə MEEL yə
Camelot	KAM ə LOT
Camembert	KAM əm BAIR
cameo	KAM ee oh
camera	KAM ə rə
camerlengo	KAM ər LING goh
Cameroon	KAM ə ROON
camisole	KAM i SOHL
camomile	KAM ə MEEL
Camorra	kə MAW rə
camouflage	KAM ə FLAHZH
campagna, C-	kam PAHN yə
campaign	kam PAYN
Campania	kam PAY nee ə
campanile	KAM pə NEE lee
campanula	kam PAN yə lə
Campeche	kam PEE chee
camphor	KAM fər
campion, C-	KAM pee ən
campo	KAM poh
Campora	kahm PAW rah
campus	KAM pəs
Camus	ka MUU
Cana	KAY nə
Canaan	KAY nən

ə ago, a at, ah calm, ahr dark, air care, aw saw, ay say, ch church
e bet, ee me, eer beer, hw what, i is, ī my, n French final n vin,

Canada	**KAN** ə də
Canadian	kə **NAY** dee ən
canaille	kə **NĪ**
canalization	kə **NAL** i **ZAY** shən
canapé	**KAN** ə pee
canard	kə **NAHRD**
Canary, c-	kə **NAIR** ee
Cañas	**KAH** nyahs
canasta	kə **NAS** tə
Canaveral	kə **NAV** ər əl
Canberra	**KAN** bər ə
Canby	**KAN** bee
cancan	**KAN** kan
cancelable	**KAN** sə lə bəl
cancellation	**KAN** sə **LAY** shən
candela	kan **DEE** lə
candelabra	**KAN** də **LAH** brə
candelabrum	**KAN** də **LAH** brəm
candescent	kan **DES** ənt
candid	**KAN** did
Candida	**KAN** di də
candidacy	**KAN** di də **SEE**
candidate	**KAN** di **DAYT**
Candide	kahn **DEED**
Candlemas	**KAN** dəl məs
candor	**KAN** dər
candytuft	**KAN** dee **TUFT**
Canetti	ka **NET** ee
canine	**KAY** nīn
Canis	**KAY** nis
canister	**KAN** ə stər
canker	**KANG** kər
canna	**KAN** ə
cannabis	**KAN** ə bəs
cannel	**KAN** əl
cannelloni	**KAN** ə **LOH** nee
Cannes	kan
canoe	kə **NOO**
canon	**KAN** ən
cañon	**KAN** yən
canonical	kə **NON** i kəl
canonize	**KAN** ə **NĪZ**
Canopic	kə **NOH** pik

o on, oh oat, oi boy, oo soon, oor poor, or for, ow cow, sh shush,
th thin, *th* this, u up, ur spur, uu book, *zh* pleasure

Canopus	kə **NOH** pəs
Canossa	kə **NOS** ə
cant	kant
can't	kant
cantabile	kahn **TAH** bi **LAY**
Cantabrigian	**KAN** tə **BRIJ** ee ən
cantaloupe	**KAN** tə **LOHP**
cantankerous	kan **TANG** kər əs
cantata	kən **TAH** tə
canteen	kan **TEEN**
canter	**KAN** tər
Canterbury	**KAN** tər **BER** ee
canticle	**KAN** ti kəl
cantilever	**KAN** tə **LEE** vər
cantina	kan **TEE** nə
canto	**KAN** toh
Canton (China)	kan **TON**
Canton (US)	**KAN** tən
canton	**KAN** tən
Cantonese	**KAN** tə **NEEZ**
cantonment	kan **TON** mənt
cantor	**KAN** tər
Canuck	kə **NUK**
canvas	**KAN** vəs
canvass	**KAN** vəs
canyon	**KAN** yən
canzone	kahn **TSOH** nay
Caodaism	kow **DĪ** iz əm
capacious	kə **PAY** shəs
capacitance	kə **PAS** ə təns
capacitor	kə **PAS** ə tər
caparison	kə **PAR** ə sən
Capek, Karel	**CHAH** pek, **KAH** rəl
Capella	kə **PEL** ə
caper	**KAY** pər
Capetian	kə **PEE** shən
Cape Verde	**KAYP VURD**
Capezio	kə **PEE** zee oh
capillary	**KAP** ə **LER** ee
capitulate	kə **PICH** ə **LAYT**
capitulation	kə **PICH** ə **LAY** shən
capo	**KAH** poh
capon	**KAY** pon

ə ago, a at, ah calm, ahr dark, air care, aw saw, ay say, ch church
e bet, ee me, eer beer, hw what, i is, ī my, *n* French final n vin,

Caporetto	KAP ə RET oh
Capote	kə POH tee
cappuccino	KAP ə CHEE noh
capriccio	kə PREE chee OH
caprice	kə PREES
capricious	kə PRISH əs
Capricorn	KAP rə KORN
capriole	KAP ree OHL
capsize	KAP sīz
capstan	KAP stən
capsule	KAP səl
captain	KAP tən
caption	KAP shən
captious	KAP shəs
captivate	KAP tə VAYT
captor	KAP tər
capture	KAP chər
Capucci	kah PUU chee
capuchin, C-	KAP yə chin
Capucine	ka pyoo SEEN
Capulet	KAP yə lət
Caputo	kə POOT oh
carabao	KAHR ə BAH oh
carabiniere	KA rə bən YAIR ay
caracal	KA rə KAL
Caracalla	KA rə KAL ə
Caracas	kə RAH kəs
caracul	KA rə kəl
carafe	kə RAF
Caramanlis	KA rə MAN lis
caramel	KA rə məl
caramelize	KA rə mə LĪZ
carapace	KA rə PAYS
carat	KA rət
Caravaggio	KAH rah VAHD joh
caravan	KA rə VAN
caravansary	KA rə VAN sə ree
caravanserai	KA rə VAN sə RĪ
caravel	KA rə VEL
caraway	KA rə WAY
Carazo, Rodrigo	kah RAH soh, rawd REE goh
carbide	KAHR bīd
carbine	KAHR been

o on, oh oat, oi boy, oo soon, oor poor, or for, ow cow, sh shush,
th thin, *th* this, u up, ur spur, uu book, *zh* pleasure

carbohydrate	KAHR boh HĪ drayt
carbolic	kahr BOL ik
carbon	KAHR bən
carbonaceous	KAHR bə NAY shəs
Carbonari	KAHR bə NAHR ee
carboniferous, C-	KAHR bə NIF ər əs
carbonize	KAHR bə NĪZ
carborundum, C-	KAHR bə RUN dəm
carbuncle	KAHR bung kəl
carburetor	KAHR bə RAY tər
carcass	KAHR kəs
Carcassonne	kahr ka SAWN
carcinogen	kahr SIN ə jən
carcinoma	KAHR sə NOH mə
cardamom	KAHR də məm
Cárdenas	KAHR day nahs
cardiac	KAHR dee AK
Cardiff	KAHR dif
cardigan, C-	KAHR də gən
Cardin	kahr DAN (DAN French final *n*)
cardinal	KAHR də nəl
Cardinale, Claudia	kahr dee NAH le, KLOW dee ah
Cardoso, Mario	kahr DOH soh, MAH ree oh
Cardozo	kahr DOH zoh
Carducci	kahr DOO chee
careen	kə REEN
career	kə REER
caress	kə RES
caret	KA rət
Carew	kə ROO
Caria	KAIR ee ə
Carías	kah REE AHS
Caribbean	KA rə BEE ən
caribou	KA rə BOO
caricature	KA rə kə CHUUR
caricaturist	KA rə kə CHUUR əst
caries	KAIR eez
carillon	KA rə LON
carioca	KA ree OH kə
Carlisle	kahr LĪL
Carlos (US)	KAHR ləs
Carlos (Spain)	KAHR lohs
Carlovingian	KAHR lə VINJ ee ən

ə ago, a at, ah calm, ahr dark, air care, aw saw, ay say, ch church
e bet, ee me, eer beer, hw what, i is, ī my, *n* French final n vin,

Carlsbad	**KAHRLZ** bad
Carlstadt	**KAHRL** stat
Carlyle	kahr **LĪL**
Carmel (California)	kahr **MEL**
Carmel (mountain in Israel)	**KAHR** məl
Carmelite	**KAHR** mə **LĪT**
Carmen	**KAHR** mən
Carmichael	**KAHR** mī kəl
carmine	**KAHR** mən
Carmona	kahr **MOH** nə
carnage	**KAHR** nij
carnal	**KAHR** nəl
Carnarvon	kahr **NAHR** vən
carnation	kahr **NAY** shən
carnauba	kahr **NAW** bə
Carnegie, Andrew	kahr **NAY** gee
Carnegie Hall	**KAHR** nə gee
carnelian	kahr **NEEL** yən
carnival	**KAHR** nə vəl
Carnivora	kahr **NIV** ər ə
carnivore	**KAHR** nə **VOR**
carnivorous	kahr **NIV** ər əs
Carolina	**KA** rə **LĪN** ə
Caroline	**KA** rə lin
Carolingian	**KA** rə **LIN** jee ən
Carolinian	**KA** rə **LIN** ee ən
carom	**KA** rəm
carotene	**KA** rə **TEEN**
carotid	kə **ROT** əd
carousal	kə **ROW** zəl (**ROW** as in *cow*)
carouse	kə **ROWZ** (**ROWZ** as in *cows*)
carousel	**KA** rə **SEL**
Carpaccio	kahr **PAHT** choh
Carpathia	kahr **PAY** thee ə
Carpathian	kahr **PAY** thee ən
Carpatho-Ukraine	kahr **PAY** thoh yoo **KRAIN**
carpe diem	**KAHR** pe **DEE** em
Carracci, Annibale	kah **RAHT** chee, ahn **NEE** bah le
Carradine	**KA** rə deen
Carrara	kə **RAHR** ə
carrel	**KA** rəl
Carreon, Camilio	kah rah **OHN**, kah **MEE** lyoh

---

o **on**, oh **oat**, oi **boy**, oo **soon**, oor **poor**, or **for**, ow **cow**, sh **shush**, th **thin**, *th* **this**, u **up**, ur **spur**, uu **book**, *zh* **pleasure**

carriage	**KA** rij
carrier	**KA** ree ər
Carrillo Flores, Antonio	kah **REE** yoh **FLAW** res, ahn **TOH** nyoh
carrion	**KA** ree ən
carrot	**KA** rət
carrousel	**KA** rə **SEL**
Carstens	**KAHR** stəns
Cartagena	**KAHR** tə **HAY** nə
carte	kahrt
carte blanche	kahrt blahnsh
carte du jour	**KAHRT** də **ZH**UUR
cartel	kahr **TEL**
Cartesian	kahr **TEE** zhən
Carthage	**KAHR** thij
Carthaginian	**KAHR** thə **JIN** ee ən
Carthusian	kahr **THOO** zhən
Cartier (French)	kahr **TYAY**
Cartier (US)	**KAHR** tee ay
Cartier-Bresson	kahr tyay bre **SAWN** (**SAWN** French final *n*)
cartilage	**KAHR** tə lij
cartilaginous	**KAHR** tə **LAJ** ə nəs
cartographer	kahr **TOG** rə fər
cartography	kahr **TOG** rə fee
carton	**KAHR** tən
cartoon	kahr **TOON**
cartouche	kahr **TOOSH**
cartridge	**KAHR** trij
Caruso	kə **ROO** soh
Carvalho Silos, Geraldo de	ker **VAH** lyuu **SEE** luush, *zh*ə **RAHL** duu də
carvel	**KAHR** vəl
caryatid	**KA** ree **AT** əd
casaba	kə **SAH** bə
Casablanca	**KAH** sah **BLAHNG** kah
Casals	kah **SAHLZ**
Casanova	**KAZ** ə **NOH** və
Casbah	**KAHZ** bah
cascara	kas **KA** rə
casein	**KAY** seen
casement	**KAYS** mənt
cashew	**KASH** oo
cashmere	**KAZH** meer

ə ago, a at, ah calm, ahr dark, air care, aw saw, ay say, ch church
e bet, ee me, eer beer, hw what, i is, ī my, *n* French final n vin,

Cashmere (India)	kash **MEER**
Casimir	**KAZ** ə mir
Casoria	ka **SOR** ee ə
Caspian	**KAS** pee ən
casque	kask
cassaba	kə **SAH** bə
Cassandra	kə **SAN** drə
Cassatt, Mary	kə **SAT**
cassava	kə **SAH** və
Cassel, Jean-Pierre	kah **SEL**, *zh*ahn pyair (*zh*ahn French final *n*)
casserole	**KAS** ə **ROHL**
cassette	kə **SET**
cassia	**KASH** ə
Cassin, René	ka **SAN**, rə **NAY** (**SAN** French final *n*)
Cassini	kə **SEE** nee
Cassiopeia	**KAS** ee ə **PEE** ə
cassiterite	kə **SIT** ə **RĪT**
cassock	**KAS** ək
cassowary	**KAS** ə **WER** ee
Castaneda, Jorge	kahs tahn **YAY** dah, **HOR** hee
castanet	**KAS** tə **NET**
castaway	**KAS** tə **WAY**
caste	kast
Castelo Branco, Humberto	kahs **TE** luu **BRAHN** kuu, oom **BER** tuu
caster	**KAS** tər
castigate	**KAS** tə **GAYT**
Castiglione	**KAH** stee **LYAW** ne
Castiglioni	**KAH** stee **LYAW** nee
Castile (Spain)	ka **STEEL**
Castile (NY)	ka **STĪL**
Castilian	ka **STIL** yən
Castillo	kahs **TEE** yaw
castle	**KAS** əl
castor, C-	**KAS** tər
castrate	**KAS** trayt
castrato	ka **STRAH** toh
Castries	ka **STREEZ**
Castro	**KAS** troh
casual	**KAZH** oo əl
casualty	**KAZH** oo əl tee
casuist	**KAZH** ə wəst

o **on**, oh **oat**, oi **boy**, oo **soon**, oor **poor**, or **for**, ow **cow**, sh **shush**, th **thin**, *th* **this**, u **up**, ur **spur**, uu **book**, *zh* **pleasure**

casuistry	KAZH ə wəs tree
casus belli	KAY səs BEL ī
catabolism	kə TAB ə LIZ əm
catachresis	KAT ə KREE səs
cataclysm	KAT ə KLIZ əm
catacomb	KAT ə KOHM
catafalque	KAT ə FAWK
Catalan	KAT ə LAN
catalectic	KAT ə LEK tik
catalepsy	KAT ə LEP see
cataleptic	KAT ə LEP tik
catalog	KAT ə LAWG
catalpa	kə TAL pə
catalyses	kə TAL ə SEEZ
catalysis	kə TAL ə səs
catalyst	KAT ə ləst
catamaran	KAT ə mə RAN
catamite	KAT ə MĪT
catapult	KAT ə pəlt
cataract	KAT ə RAKT
catarrh	kə TAHR
catastrophe	kə TAS trə fee
catastrophic	KAT ə STROF ik
catatonic	KAT ə TON ik
Catawba, c-	kə TAW bə
catchup	KACH əp
catechism	KAT ə KIZ əm
categorical	KAT ə GOR i kəl
categorize	KAT ə gə RĪZ
category	KAT ə GOH ree
catenary	KAT ə NER ee
catercorner	KAT ər KOR nər
caterer	KAY tər ər
caterpillar	KAT ə PIL ər
caterwaul	KAT ər WAWL
catharsis	kə THAHR səs
cathartic	kə THAHR tik
Cathay	ka THAY
cathedral	kə THEE drəl
Cather, Willa	KATH ər, WIL ə
catheter	KATH ə tər
cathode	KATH ohd
catholicism, C-	kə THOL ə SIZ əm

ə ago, a at, ah calm, ahr dark, air care, aw saw, ay say, ch church
e bet, ee me, eer beer, hw what, i is, ī my, n French final n vin,

catholicity	KATH ə LIS ə tee
cation	KAT ī ən
Cato	KAY toh
Catroux	ka TROO
catsup	KAT səp
catty-cornered	KAT ee KOR nərd
Catullus	kə TUL əs
Caucasia	kaw KAY zhə
Caucasian	kaw KAY zhən
Caucasus	KAW kə səs
caucus	KAW kəs
caudal	KAWD əl
caudillo, C-	kaw DEEL yoh
caudle	KAWD əl
caul	kawl
cauldron	KAWL drən
cauliflower	KAW lə FLOW ər (FLOW as in *cow*)
caulk	kawk
causal	KAW zəl
causality	kaw ZAL ə tee
causative	KAW zə tiv
cause célèbre	kohz say LEB rə
causerie	KOHZ ə REE
causeway	KAWZ WAY
caustic	KAWS tik
cauterize	KAW tə RĪZ
cautionary	KAW shə NER ee
cavalcade	KAV əl KAYD
cavalier, C-	KAV ə LEER
Cavalleria Rusticana	KAV ə lə REE ə RUUS tə KAHN ə
cavalry	KAV əl ree
cavatina	KAV ə TEE nə
caveat	KAV ee AT
caveat emptor	KAV ee AT EMP tər
caveat venditor	KAV ee AT VEN di tər
Cavell	KAV əl
Cavendish	KAV ən dish
cavern	KAV ərn
cavernous	KAV ər nəs
cavetto	kə VET oh
caviar	KAV ee AHR
cavil	KAV əl
cavitation	KAV ə TAY shən

---

o on, oh oat, oi boy, oo soon, oor poor, or for, ow cow, sh shush,
th thin, *th* this, u up, ur spur, uu book, *zh* pleasure

Cavite	kah **VEE** te
cavort	kə **VORT**
Cavour	kah **VUUR**
Cawdor	**KAW** dər
Caxton	**KAK** stən
cayenne, C-	kī **EN**
cayman, C-	**KAY** mən
Cayuga	kay **YOO** gə
cayuse, C-	kī **YOOS**
Ceausescu, Nicolae	**CHOW** oo **SHES** koo, **NEE** koh **LĪ** ə
Cebu	say **BOO**
Cecil (US)	**SEE** səl
Cecil (British)	**SE** səl
cecum	**SEE** kəm
cedilla	si **DIL** ə
celandine	**SEL** ən **DĪN**
Celebes	**SEL** ə **BEEZ**
celebrant	**SEL** ə brənt
Celebrezze	se lə **BREE** zee
celebrity	sə **LEB** rə tee
celerity	sə **LER** ə tee
celesta	sə **LES** tə
celeste, C-	sə **LEST**
celestial	sə **LES** chəl
celiac	**SEE** lee **AK**
celibacy	**SEL** ə bə see
celibate	**SEL** ə bət
cellar	**SEL** ər
Cellini	chə **LEE** nee
cellist	**CHEL** əst
cello	**CHEL** oh
cellophane	**SEL** ə **FAYN**
cellular	**SEL** yə lər
celluloid, C-	**SEL** yə **LOID**
cellulose	**SEL** yə **LOHS**
Celsius	**SEL** see əs
Celt	kelt
Celtic	**KEL** tik
Celtics (team)	**SEL** tiks
Cenci	**CHEN** chee
Cenis	sə **NEE**
cenobite	**SEN** ə **BĪT**
cenotaph	**SEN** ə **TAF**

ə ago, a at, ah calm, ahr dark, air care, aw saw, ay say, ch church
e bet, ee me, eer beer, hw what, i is, ī my, *n* French final n vin,

Cenozoic	SEE nə ZOH ik
censer	SEN sər
censor	SEN sər
censorable	SEN sər ə bəl
censorious	sen SOR ee əs
censorship	SEN sər SHIP
censure	SEN shər
census	SEN səs
centaur, C-	SEN tor
Centaurus	sen TOR əs
centavo	sen TAH voh
centenary	SEN tə NER ee
centennial	sen TEN ee əl
centigrade	SEN tə GRAYD
centime	sahn TEEM
centimeter	SEN tə MEE tər
centipede	SEN tə PEED
centrifugal	sen TRIF yə gəl
centrifuge	SEN trə FYOOJ
centripetal	sen TRIP ə təl
centrist	SEN trəst
centurion	sen TUUR ee ən
century	SEN chə ree
cephalic	sə FAL ik
cephalopod	SEF ə lə POD
Cephalus	SEF ə ləs
cepheid	SEE fee əd
Cepheus	SEE fee əs
Ceram	say RAHM
ceramic	sə RAM ik
ceramist	SE rə məst
Cerberus	SUR bər əs
cere	seer
cereal	SEER ee əl
cerebellum	SER ə BEL əm
cerebral	SER ə brəl
cerebrate	SER ə BRAYT
cerebrum	SER ə brəm
cerement	SEER mənt
ceremonial	SER ə MOH nee əl
Ceres	SEER eez
cerise	sə REES
cerium	SEER ee əm

cermet	**SUR** met
certification	**SUR** tə fə **KAY** shən
certiorari	**SUR** shee ə **RAIR** ee
certitude	**SUR** tə **TOOD**
cerulean	sə **ROO** lee ən
cerumen	sə **ROO** mən
Cervantes	ser **VAN** teez
cervelat	**SUR** və **LAHT**
cervical	**SUR** vi kəl
cervix	**SUR** viks
cesium	**SEE** zee əm
cessation	se **SAY** shən
cetane	**SEE** tayn
ceteris paribus	**KAY** te **REES PAH** ri **BUUS**
Cetus	**SEE** təs
Ceuta	**SAY OOT** ə
Ceylon	si **LON**
Ceyx	**SEE** iks
Cézanne	say **ZAHN**
chablis, C-	sha **BLEE**
cha-cha	**CHAH** chah
Chaco	**CHAH** koh
chaconne	shah **KAWN**
Chad	chad
chafe	chayf
chaff	chaf
chaffinch	**CHAF** inch
Chagall	shah **GAHL**
Chagres	**CHAH** gres
chagrin	shə **GRIN**
Chahar	chah hahr
chaise	shayz
chaise longue	shayz **LAWNG**
Chai Zemin	chī zu meen
Chakiris	chah **KEE** ris
Chakravarty	chah krah vahr **TEE**
Chalcedon	**KAL** si **DON**
chalcedony	kal **SED** ə nee
chalcopyrite	**KAL** kə **PĪ** rīt
Chaldea	kal **DEE** ə
Chaldean	kal **DEE** ən
Chaldee	kal **DEE**
chalet	sha **LAY**

ə ago, a at, ah calm, ahr dark, air care, aw saw, ay say, ch church
e bet, ee me, eer beer, hw what, i is, ī my, n French final n vin,

Chaliapin	shah **LYAH** pin
chalice	**CHAL** is
chalk	chawk
challis	**SHAL** ee
chamberlain, C-	**CHAYM** bər lən
chambray	**SHAM** bray
chameleon	kə **MEEL** yən
chamfer	**CHAM** fər
chamois	**SHAM** ee
Chamonix	sham ə **NEE**
Chamorro	chə **MAW** roh
champagne, C-	sham **PAYN**
champaign, C-	sham **PAYN**
champion	**CHAM** pee ən
Champlain	sham **PLAYN**
Champs Elysées	shahnz ay lee **ZAY**
chancel	**CHAN** səl
chancellery	**CHAN** sə lə ree
chancellor	**CHAN** sə lər
chancery	**CHAN** sə ree
chancre	**SHANG** kər
chandelier	shan də **LEER**
Chanderli, Abdelkader	chahn dər **LEE**, ahb dəl **KAH** dər
Chandigarh	chun di **GUR**
Chand, Lokendra Bahadur	**CHAHND**, loh **KEN** drə bah hah **DOOR**
Chanel	shə **NEL**
changeable	**CHAYN** jə bəl
changeling	**CHAYNJ** ling
chanson	shahn **SAWN** (both syllables French final *n*)
chanteuse	shahn **TUUZ** (shahn French final *n*)
chantey	**SHAN** tee
chanticleer	**CHAN** tə **KLEER**
Chantilly, c-	shahn tee **YEE** (shahn French final *n*)
chanty	**SHAN** tee
Chanukah	**HAH** nə kə
chaos	**KAY** os
chaotic	kay **OT** ik
chaparajos	shap ə **RAY** ohs
chaparral	shap ə **RAL**
chapbook	**CHAP** buuk
chapeau	sha **POH**

---

o **on**, oh **oat**, oi **boy**, oo **soon**, oor **poor**, or **for**, ow **cow**, sh **shush**,
th **thin**, *th* **this**, u **up**, ur **spur**, uu **book**, *zh* **pleasure**

chaperon	**SHAP** ə **ROHN**
chaplain	**CHAP** lən
Chaplin	**CHAP** lən
Chapultepec	chə **PUUL** tə **PEK**
charabanc	**SHAR** ə **BANG**
characteristic	**KAR** ik tə **RIS** tik
charade	shə **RAYD**
charcoal	**CHAHR KOHL**
chard	chahrd
Chardin, Jean	shar **DAN**, *zh*ahn (**DAN**, *zh*ahn French final *n*)
chargeable	**CHAHR** jə bəl
chargé d'affaires	shahr **ZHAY** da **FAIR**
charioteer	**CHA** ree ə **TEER**
charisma	kə **RIZ** mə
charismatic	**KA** rəz **MAT** ik
charivari	shə **RIV** ə **REE**
charlatan	**SHAHR** lə tən
Charlemagne	**SHAHR** lə **MAYN**
Charles (French)	shahrl
Charleston	**CHAHRL** stən
Charlotte, c-	**SHAHR** lət
Charolais	**SHA** rə **LAY**
Charon	**KAIR** ən
Chartism	**CHAHR** tiz əm
Chartres	**SHAHR** trə
chartreuse, C-	shahr **TRUUZ**
chary	**CHAIR** ee
Charybdis	kə **RIB** dəs
chasm	**KAZ** əm
chassé	sha **SAY**
chassis	**SHAS** ee
chaste	chayst
chasten	**CHAY** sən
chastise	chas **TĪZ**
chastisement	chas **TĪZ** mənt
chastity	**CHAS** tə tee
chasuble	**CHAZ** yə bəl
château	sha **TOH**
chateaubriand	shah **TOH** bree **AHN** (**AHN** French final *n*)
chatelaine	**SHAT** ə **LAYN**
Chatham	**CHAT** əm
Chattahoochee	**CHAT** ə **HOO** chee

ə ago, a at, ah calm, ahr dark, air care, aw saw, ay say, ch church
e bet, ee me, eer beer, hw what, i is, ī my, *n* French final n vin,

Chattanooga	**CHAT** ə **NOO** gə
chattel	**CHAT** əl
Chaucer	**CHAW** sər
Chaucerian	chaw **SEER** ee ən
Chaudet	shoh **DAY**
chauffeur	shoh **FUR**
chaulmoogra	chawl **MOO** grə
Chautauqua	shə **TAW** kwə
chauvinism	**SHOH** və **NIZ** əm
chauvinistic	**SHOH** və **NIS** tik
Chaves	**CHAH** ves
Chavez	**CHAH** vez
Chebrikov, Viktor	**CHEB** ree kawf, **VEEK** tor
Cheddar, c-	**CHED** ər
cheetah	**CHEE** tə
chef	shef
chef-d'oeuvre	she **DURV** rə
Chehab, Fuad	shə **HAB**, **FOO** ahd
Cheka	**CHE** kah
Chekhov	**CHE** kawf
Chekiang	jəj ee ahng
Chelsea	**CHEL** see
chemise	shə **MEEZ**
Chemnitz	**KEM** nits
chemurgy	**KEM** ər jee
Chen-chiang	jun jee ahng
Chengdu	chung doo
Chenier	shay **NYAY**
chenille	shə **NEEL**
Chenoweth	**CHEN** oh weth
Chen Pixian	chun pee shee ahn
Chen Yun	chun yuun
cheongsam	**CHAWNG** sahm
Cheops	**KEE** ops
Cherbourg	**SHAIR** buurg
cherchez la femme	sher **SHAY** la **FAM**
Cherenkov, Pavel	chə **RENG** kof, **PAH** vəl
Chernenko, Konstantin	chər **NYEN** kə, **KON** stan **TEEN**
Cherokee	**CHER** ə **KEE**
cheroot	shə **ROOT**
chert	churt
cherub	**CHER** əb

o on, oh oat, oi boy, oo soon, oor poor, or for, ow cow, sh shush, th thin, *th* this, u up, ur spur, uu book, *zh* pleasure

cherubic	chə ROO bik
chervil	CHUR vəl
Chesapeake	CHES ə PEEK
Cheshire	CHESH ər
chestnut	CHES nut
Chetnik	chet NEEK
chevalier	SHEV ə LEER
Chevalier	shə VAL yay
cheviot (cloth)	SHEV ee ət
cheviot, C- (sheep; Hills)	CHEV ee ət
Chevrolet	SHEV rə LAY
chevron	SHEV rən
Cheyenne	shī EN
Cheysson, Claude	shay SAWN, KLOHD (SAWN French final *n*)
chez	shay
chi	kī
Chiang Ching-kuo	jee ahng jeeng kwoh
Chiang Kai-shek	jee ahng kī shek
Chianti	kee AHN tee
Chiari	kee AH ree
chiaroscuro	kee AHR ə SKYUUR oh
chic	sheek
Chicago	shi KAH goh
chicane	shi KAYN
chicanery	shi KAY nə ree
Chicano	chi KAH noh
Chiceri, Caruncho	chee CHAIR ee, kah RUUN choh
Chichén-Itzá	chə CHEN ət SAH
chichi	SHEE shee
Chichibu	chee chee boo
chickadee	CHIK ə DEE
chicle	CHIK əl
Chico, c-	CHEE koh
chicory	CHIK ə ree
chide	chīd
chieftain	CHEEF tən
chiffon	shi FON
chiffonier	SHIF ə NEER
chigger	CHIG ər
chignon	SHEEN yon
chigoe	CHIG oh

ə ago, a at, ah calm, ahr dark, air care, aw saw, ay say, ch church
e bet, ee me, eer beer, hw what, i is, ī my, *n* French final n vin,

Chihuahua, c-	chi **WAH** wah
chilblain	**CHIL BLAYN**
Chile	**CHIL** ee
chile con carne	**CHIL** ee kon **KAHR** nee
chili	**CHIL** ee
Chillon	shə **LON**
chimera	kə **MIR** ə
chimerical	kə **MER** i kəl
chimpanzee	**CHIM** pan **ZEE**
China	**CHĪ** nə
chinch	chinch
chinchilla	chin **CHIL** ə
Chincoteague	**SHING** kə **TEEG**
Chindit	**CHIN** dit
Chindwin	chin dwin
chine	chīn
Chinese	chī **NEEZ**
Chinghai	jing hī
chino	**CHEE** noh
Chinook	shi **NUUK**
chintz	chints
Chios	**KĪ** os
Chipamaunga, Edmund	**CHEE** pah mah **OONG** gah
Chippendale	**CHIP** ən **DAYL**
Chippewa	**CHIP** ə **WAH**
Chiquita	chə **KEE** tə
Chiriboga	chee ree **BAW** gah
Chirico, Giorgio de	**KEE** ree koh, **JOR** joh də
chiromancy	**KĪ** rə **MAN** see
Chiron	**KĪ** ron
chiropodist	kə **ROP** ə dəst
chiropody	kə **ROP** ə dee
chiropractor	**KĪ** rə **PRAK** tər
chirrup	**CHIR** əp
chisel	**CHIZ** əl
Chisholm	**CHIZ** əm
chiton	**KĪT** ən
Chitradurga	**CHIT** rə **DUR** gə
chitterlings	**CHIT** lənz
chivalric	shə **VAL** rik
chivalrous	**SHIV** əl rəs
chivalry	**SHIV** əl ree

o **on**, oh **oat**, oi **boy**, oo **soon**, oor **poor**, or **for**, ow **cow**, sh **shush**,
th **thin**, *th* **this**, u **up**, ur **spur**, uu **book**, *zh* **pleasure**

chive	chīv
chivy	**CHIV** ee
Chloe, Chloë	**KLOH** ee
chlorate	**KLOR** ayt
chloride	**KLOR** īd
chlorinate	**KLOR** ə **NAYT**
chlorine	**KLOR** een
chloroform	**KLOR** ə **FORM**
chlorophyll	**KLOR** ə fil
Choate	choht
chock-full	chok fuul
chocolate	**CHOK** lət
Choctaw	**CHOK** taw
choir	kwīr
Choiseul	shwah **ZUL**
choler	**KOL** ər
cholera	**KOL** ə rə
choleric	**KOL** ə rik
cholesterol	kə **LES** tə **ROHL**
Cholmondeley	**CHUM** lee
Chongjin	chawng jin
Chongqing	chuung ching
Chookasian, Lili	chuu **KAH** syahn, **LEE** lee
Chopin	**SHOH** pan (pan French final *n*)
chop suey	**CHOP SOO** ee
choral (a)	**KOR** əl
chorale (n)	kə **RAL**
Chorazin	koh **RAY** zin
chordate	**KOR** dayt
chore	chor
chorea	kə **REE** ə
choreographer	**KOR** ee **OG** rə fər
choreography	**KOR** ee **OG** rə fee
choric	**KOR** ik
chorine	**KOR** **EEN**
chorister	**KOR** ə stər
chortle	**CHOR** təl
Choudhury, Humayun Rasheed	**CHOW** də ree, **HOO** mah **YOON** rah **SHEED**
Chou En-lai	joh en lī
chow	chow (as in *cow*)
chowchow	**CHOW** chow
chowder	**CHOW** dər

ə ago, a at, ah calm, ahr dark, air care, aw saw, ay say, ch church
e bet, ee me, eer beer, hw what, i is, ī my, *n* French final n vin,

chow mein	chow **MAYN**
chrestomathy	kre **STOM** ə thee
chrism	**KRIZ** əm
christen	**KRIS** ən
Christendom	**KRIS** ən dəm
Christian	**KRIS** chən
Christiania	**KRIS** chee **AN** ee ə
Christianity	**KRIS** chee **AN** ə tee
Christmas	**KRIS** məs
Christophe	kree **STAWF**
Christopher	**KRIS** tə fər
chromatic	kroh **MAT** ik
chromatin	**KROH** mə tin
chrome	krohm
chromium	**KROH** mee əm
chromosome	**KROH** mə **SOHM**
chromosphere	**KROH** mə **SFEER**
chronic	**KRON** ik
chronicle	**KRON** ə kəl
chronograph	**KRON** ə **GRAF**
chronological	**KRON** ə **LOJ** i kəl
chronology	krə **NOL** ə jee
chronometer	krə **NOM** ə tər
chrysalis	**KRIS** ə lis
chrysanthemum	kri **SAN** thə məm
Chryseis	krī **SEE** is
Chrysler	**KRĪS** lər
Chrysostom	**KRIS** ə stəm
chukker	**CHUK** ər
Chun Doo-Hwan	juun doh hwahn
Churchill	**CHUR** chil
churchman	**CHURCH** mən
Chust	koost
chute	shoot
chutney	**CHUT** nee
chutzpah	**HUUT** spə
ciao	chow
Ciardi	**CHAHR** dee
Cibber, Colley	**SIB** ər, **KOL** ee
Cibola	**SEE** bə lə
ciborium	sə **BOR** ee əm
cicada	sə **KAY** də
cicala	sə **KAH** lə

---

o **on**, oh **oat**, oi **boy**, oo **soon**, oor **poor**, or **for**, ow **cow**, sh **shush**,
th **thin**, *th* **this**, u **up**, ur **spur**, uu **book**, *zh* **pleasure**

cicatrix	**SIK** ə **TRIKS**
Cicero	**SIS** ə **ROH**
cicerone	**SIS** ə **ROH** nee
Ciceronian	**SIS** ə **ROH** nee ən
Cid	sid
ci-devant	seed ə **VAHN** (**VAHN** French final *n*)
Cienfuegos	syen **FWE** gohs
cigarette	**SIG** ə **RET**
Cilicia	sə **LISH** ə
Cimabue	**CHEE** mah **BOO** ay
Cimarron	**SIM** ə **RON**
Cimbri	**SIM** bri
Cimmerian	si **MER** ee ən
cinchona	sin **KOH** nə
Cincinnati	**SIN** sə **NAT** ee
Cincinnatus	**SIN** sə **NAT** əs
cincture	**SINGK** chər
cinema	**SIN** ə mə
Cinerama	**SIN** ə **RAM** ə
cinnabar	**SIN** ə **BAHR**
cinnamon	**SIN** ə mən
cinquefoil	**SINGK FOIL**
Cinque Ports	singk ports
Cinzano	chin **ZAH** noh
cipher	**SĪ** fər
circa	**SUR** kə
circadian	sər **KAY** dee ən
Circassian	sər **KASH** ən
Circe	**SUR** see
circuit	**SUR** kət
circuitous	sər **KYOO** ə təs
circuitry	**SUR** kə tree
circular	**SUR** kyə lər
circulation	**SUR** kyə **LAY** shən
circulatory	**SUR** kyə lə **TOR** ee
circumcise	**SUR** kəm **SĪZ**
circumference	sər **KUM** fə rəns
circumflex	**SUR** kəm **FLEKS**
circumlocution	**SUR** kəm loh **KYOO** shən
circumnavigate	**SUR** kəm **NAV** ə **GAYT**
circumscribe	**SUR** kəm **SKRĪB**
circumspect	**SUR** kəm **SPEKT**
circumstance	**SUR** kəm **STANS**

ə ago, a at, ah calm, ahr dark, air care, aw saw, ay say, ch church
e bet, ee me, eer beer, hw what, i is, ī my, *n* French final n vin,

circumstantial	**SUR** kəm **STAN** shəl
circumvent	**SUR** kəm **VENT**
cirque	surk
cirrhosis	sə **ROH** səs
cirrus	**SIR** əs
cisalpine	sis **AL** pīn
Ciskei	**SIS** kī
Cistercian	sis **TUR** shən
cistern	**SIS** tərn
citadel	**SIT** ə dəl
citation	sī **TAY** shən
citizen	**SIT** ə zən
citizenry	**SIT** ə zən ree
citrate	**SI** trayt
citric	**SI** trik
Citroen	**SI** troh **EN**
citron	**SI** trən
citronella	**SI** trə **NEL** ə
citrus	**SI** trəs
Città Vecchia	cheet **TAH VEK** yah
Ciudad, c-	syoo **DAHD**
civet	**SIV** ət
civvies	**SIV** eez
claimant	**KLAY** mənt
clairvoyance	klair **VOI** əns
clairvoyant	klair **VOI** ənt
clamant	**KLAY** mənt
clamber	**KLAM** bər
clamor	**KLAM** ər
clandestine	klan **DES** tən
clangor	**KLANG** ər
clapboard	**KLAB** ərd
claque	klak
claret	**KLAR** ət
Claretian	klə **REE** shən
clarification	**KLAR** ə fə **KAY** shən
clarinet	**KLAR** ə **NET**
clarion	**KLAR** ee ən
clarity	**KLAR** ə tee
clastic	**KLAS** tik
Claudel	kloh **DEL**
Clausewitz, von	**KLOW** zə vits, fawn
claustrophobia	**KLAWS** trə **FOH** bee ə

o on, oh oat, oi boy, oo soon, oor poor, or for, ow cow, sh shush, th thin, *th* this, u up, ur spur, uu book, *zh* pleasure

clavichord	**KLAV** ə **KORD**
clavicle	**KLAV** ə kəl
clavier	klə **VEER**
cleanliness	**KLEN** lee nəs
cleanly (a)	**KLEN** lee
cleanly (adv)	**KLEEN** lee
cleanse	klenz
cleavage	**KLEE** vij
clef	klef
clematis	**KLEM** ə təs
Clemenceau	**KLEM** ən **SOH**
clemency	**KLEM** ən see
Clemens	**KLEM** ənz
clement, C-	**KLEM** ənt
Cleon	**KLEE** on
Cleone	klee **OH** nee
Cleopatra	**KLEE** ə **PA** trə
clerihew	**KLER** i **HYOO**
Cleveland	**KLEEV** lənd
clew	kloo
Cliburn	**KLĪ** burn
cliché	klee **SHAY**
Clichy	klee **SHEE**
Clicquot	**KLEE** koh
client	**KLĪ** ənt
clientele	**KLĪ** ən **TEL**
climacteric	klī **MAK** tə rik
climactic	klī **MAK** tik
climatology	**KLĪ** mə **TOL** ə jee
climax	**KLĪ** maks
clinician	kli **NISH** ən
Clio	**KLĪ** oh
clique	kleek
clitoris	**KLIT** ə ris
clobber	**KLOB** ər
cloche	klohsh
clod	klod
Cloete	**KLOO** tee
cloisonné	**KLOI** zə **NAY**
cloister	**KLOI** stər
clone	klohn
close (a, adv)	klohs
close (v, n)	klohz

ə ago, a at, ah calm, ahr dark, air care, aw saw, ay say, ch church
e bet, ee me, eer beer, hw what, i is, ī my, n French final n vin,

closure	**KLOH** *zh*ər
cloth	klawth
clothe	kloh*th*
clothes	klohz
clothier	**KLOH***TH* yər
cloture	**KLOH** chər
clout	klowt
Clouzot	kloo **ZOH**
cloven	**KLOH** vən
Clovis	**KLOH** vis
Cluj	kluu*zh*
Cluny	**KLOO** nee
Cluytens	klee **TAHNS**
Clydesdale	**KLĪDZ** dayl
Clytemnestra	ᴋʟī təm **NES** trə
Cnidia	**NĪ** dee ə
coadjutor	koh **AJ** ə tər
coagulate	koh **AG** yə **LAYT**
Coahuila	ᴋᴏʜ ə **WEE** lə
coalesce	ᴋᴏʜ ə **LES**
coalition	ᴋᴏʜ ə **LISH** ən
coarse	kors
coauthor	koh **AW** thər
coax (v)	kohks
coax (electrical)	**KOH** aks
coaxial	koh **AK** see əl
cobalt	**KOH** bawlt
cobbler	**KOB** lər
Cóbh	kohv
Coblenz	**KOH** blents
COBOL	**KOH** bawl
cobra	**KOH** brə
coca	**KOH** kə
cocaine	koh **KAYN**
coccidiosis	kok ꜱɪᴅ ee **OH** səs
coccus	**KOK** əs
coccyx	**KOK** siks
Cochin, c-	**KOH** chən
cochineal	**KOCH** ə neel
cochlea	**KOK** lee ə
Cockaigne	ko **KAYN**
cockatoo	**KOK** ə ᴛᴏᴏ
cockatrice	**KOK** ə trəs

o on, oh oat, oi boy, oo soon, oor poor, or for, ow cow, sh shush,
th thin, *th* this, u up, ur spur, uu book, *zh* pleasure

Cockburn	**KOH** burn
cocker	**KOK** ər
cockerel	**KOK** ər əl
cockeyed	**KOK** īd
cockney, C-	**KOK** nee
coco	**KOH** koh
cocoa	**KOH** koh
coconut	**KOH** kə **NUT**
cocoon	kə **KOON**
cocotte	koh **KAWT**
Cocteau	kawk **TOH**
Cocytus	koh **SĪ** təs
coda	**KOH** də
code	kohd
codeine	**KOH** deen
codex	**KOH** deks
Codex Juris Canonici	**KOH** deks **JOO** ris kə **NON** i **sī**
codger	**KOJ** ər
codicil	**KOD** ə səl
codify	**KOD** ə **FĪ**
coefficient	**KOH** ə **FISH** ənt
coelacanth	**SEE** lə **KANTH**
coelenterate	si **LENT** ə **RAYT**
Coelho	koo **AY** lyoo
coeliac	**SEE** lee **AK**
coerce	koh **URS**
coercion	koh **UR** shən
Coeur d'Alene	**KORD** ə **LAYN**
Coeur de Lion	**KUR** də **LĪ** ən
coeval	koh **EE** vəl
coexist	**KOH** ig **ZIST**
coffee	**KAW** fee
cogency	**KOH** jən see
cogent	**KOH** jənt
cogitate	**KOJ** ə **TAYT**
cogitation	**KOJ** ə **TAY** shən
cogito ergo sum	**KOH** gi **TOH** **ER** goh **SUUM**
cognac	**KOHN** yak
cognate	**KOG** nayt
cognition	kog **NISH** ən
cognitive	**KOG** nə tiv
cognizable	**KOG** nə zə bəl
cognizance	**KOG** nə zəns

ə ago, a at, ah calm, ahr dark, air care, aw saw, ay say, ch church
e bet, ee me, eer beer, hw what, i is, ī my, *n* French final n vin,

cognizant	**KOG** nə zənt
cognomen	kog **NOH** mən
cognoscenti	ᴋᴏɴ yə **SHEN** tee
cohabit	koh **HAB** ət
Cohan, George	**KOH** han
Cohen	**KOH** ən
coherence	koh **HEER** əns
coherent	koh **HEER** ənt
cohesion	koh **HEE** _zh_ən
cohesive	koh **HEE** siv
Cohoes	kə **HOHZ**
cohort	**KOH** hort
coif (head covering)	koif
coif (coiffure)	kwahf
coiffeur	kwah **FUR**
coiffure	kwah **FYUUR**
coincide	ᴋᴏʜ ən **SĪD**
coincidentally	koh ɪɴ sə **DEN** tə lee
coitus	**KOH** ə təs
cola	**KOH** lə
colander	**KUL** ən dər
Colbert	kohl **BAIR**
Colchester	**KOHL** ᴄʜᴇs tər
colchicum	**KOL** chə kəm
Colchis	**KOL** kis
Coleridge	**KOHL** rij
coleus	**KOH** lee əs
colic	**KOL** ik
Coligny	kaw lee **NYEE**
Colima	kə **LEE** mə
coliseum	ᴋᴏʟ ə **SEE** əm
colitis	kə **LĪ** təs
collaborator	kə **LAB** ə ʀᴀʏ tər
collage	kə **LAHZ**_H_
collagen	**KOL** ə jən
collard	**KOL** ərd
collate	koh **LAYT**
collateral	kə **LAT** ə rəl
collation	kə **LAY** shən
colleague	**KOL** eeg
collectivism	kə **LEK** tə ᴠɪᴢ əm
colleen	kol **EEN**
collegian	kə **LEE** jən

---

o on, oh oat, oi boy, oo soon, oor poor, or for, ow cow, sh shush,
th thin, _th_ this, u up, ur spur, uu book, _zh_ pleasure

collegiate	kə **LEE** jət
collier	**KOL** yər
Collier, Gershon	**KOL** yər, **GUR** shən
colliery	**KOL** yə ree
collimate	**KOL** ə **MAYT**
collimator	**KOL** ə **MAY** tər
collinear	kə **LIN** ee ər
collins, C-	**KOL** ənz
collision	kə **LIZ***H* ən
collodion	kə **LOH** dee ən
colloid	**KOL** oid
colloquial	kə **LOH** kwee əl
colloquium	kə **LOH** kwee əm
colloquy	**KOL** ə kwee
Collossians	kə **LOSH** ənz
collude	kə **LOOD**
collusion	kə **LOO** *zh*ən
collusive	kə **LOO** siv
cologne, C-	kə **LOHN**
Colombia	kə **LOHM** bee ə
Colombo	kə **LUM** boh
colon	**KOH** lən
Colón	koh **LOHN**
colonel	**KURN** əl
colonelcy	**KURN** əl see
colonnade	**KOL** ə **NAYD**
colony	**KOL** ə nee
colophon	**KOL** ə fən
Colorado	**KOL** ə **RAD** oh
coloratura	**KUL** ə rə **TUUR** ə
colossal	kə **LOS** əl
Colosseum	**KOL** ə **SEE** əm
colossus	kə **LOS** əs
colostomy	kə **LOS** tə mee
colostrum	kə **LOS** trəm
Colton	**KOHL** tən
Columba	kə **LUM** bə
Columbia	kə **LUM** bee ə
columbine, C-	**KOL** əm **BĪN**
Columbus	kə **LUM** bəs
column	**KOL** əm
columnar	kə **LUM** nər
columnist	**KOL** əm nəst

colure	kə **LUUR**
colza	**KOL** zə
Colzani, Anselmo	kohlt **SAH** nee, ahn **SEL** moh
Coma Berenices	**KOH** mə **BER** ə **NĪ** seez
Comanche	kə **MAN** chee
comatose	**KOH** mə **TOHS**
Comay	koh **MĪ**
comb	kohm
combat (n, a)	**KOM** bat
combat (v)	kəm **BAT**
combatant	kəm **BAT** ənt
combative	kəm **BAT** iv
combine (n)	**KOM** bīn
combine (v)	kəm **BĪN**
combings	**KOH** mingz
combustible	kəm **BUS** tə bəl
combustion	kəm **BUS** chən
comedian	kə **MEE** dee ən
comedienne	kə **MEE** dee **EN**
comedo	**KOM** ə **DOH**
comely	**KUM** lee
Comenius	kə **MEE** nee əs
comestible	kə **MES** tə bəl
comfortable	**KUMF** tə bəl
comforter	**KUM** fə tər
Comines	kaw **MEEN**
Cominform	**KOM** ən **FORM**
Comintern	**KOM** ən **TURN**
comity	**KOM** ə tee
comma	**KOM** ə
commandant	**KOM** ən **DANT**
commandment	kə **MAND** mənt
commando	kə **MAN** doh
comme il faut	**KUM** eel **FOH**
commemorate	kə **MEM** ə **RAYT**
commemorative	kə **MEM** ə rə tiv
commencement	kə **MENS** mənt
commendable	kə **MEN** də bəl
commendation	**KOM** ən **DAY** shən
commendatory	kə **MEN** də **TOR** ee
commensurable	kə **MEN** sə rə bəl
commensurate	kə **MEN** sə rət
commentary	**KOM** ən **TER** ee

o **on**, oh **oat**, oi **boy**, oo **soon**, oor **poor**, or **for**, ow **cow**, sh **shush**,
th **thin**, *th* **this**, u **up**, ur **spur**, uu **book**, *zh* **pleasure**

commentator	KOM ən TAY tər
commerce	KOM ərs
commercial	kə MUR shəl
Commines	kaw MEEN
commingle	kə MING gəl
commiserate	kə MIZ ə RAYT
commiseration	kə MIZ ə RAY shən
commissar	KOM ə SAHR
commissariat	KOM ə SAIR ee ət
commissary	KOM ə SER ee
commissionaire	kə MISH ə NAIR
commissioned	kə MISH ənd
commissioner	kə MISH ə nər
commit	kə MIT
committee	kə MIT ee
commode	kə MOHD
commodious	kə MOH dee əs
commodity	kə MOD ə tee
commodore	KOM ə DOR
common	KOM ən
commons	KOM ənz
commonweal	KOM ən WEEL
commonwealth	KOM ən WELTH
communal	kə MYOO nəl
commune (n)	KOM yoon
commune (v)	kə MYOON
communicable	kə MYOO ni kə bəl
communicant	kə MYOO ni kənt
communicate	kə MYOO nə KAYT
communication	kə MYOO nə KAY shən
communicative	kə MYOO nə kə tiv
communion	kə MYOON yən
communiqué	kə MYOO nə KAY
commutable	kə MYOO tə bəl
commutation	KOM yə TAY shən
commute	kə MYOOT
Como	KOH moh
Comoro	KOM ə ROH
compact (a, v)	kəm PAKT
compact (n)	KOM pakt
comparable	KOM pə rə bəl
comparative	kəm PAR ə tiv
compare	kəm PAIR

ə ago, a at, ah calm, ahr dark, air care, aw saw, ay say, ch church
e bet, ee me, eer beer, hw what, i is, ī my, *n* French final n vin,

comparison	kəm **PAR** ə sən
compass	**KUM** pəs
compatibility	kəm **PAT** ə **BIL** ə tee
compatible	kəm **PAT** ə bəl
compatriot	kəm **PAY** tree ət
compeer	kəm **PEER**
compendium	kəm **PEN** dee əm
compensate	**KOM** pən **SAYT**
compensatory	kəm **PEN** sə **TOR** ee
competence	**KOM** pə təns
competency	**KOM** pə tən see
competitor	kəm **PET** ə tər
Compiègne	kohm **PYAIN**
compilation	**KOM** pə **LAY** shən
complacence	kəm **PLAY** səns
complacency	kəm **PLAY** sən see
complacent	kəm **PLAY** sənt
complaisance	kəm **PLAY** səns
complaisant	kəm **PLAY** sənt
complement (n)	**KOM** plə mənt
complement (v)	**KOM** plə **MENT**
complementary	**KOM** plə **MEN** tə ree
complex (a)	kom **PLEKS**
complex (n)	**KOM** pleks
complexion	kəm **PLEK** shən
compliance	kəm **PLĪ** əns
compliant	kəm **PLĪ** ənt
complicate	**KOM** plə **KAYT**
complicity	kəm **PLIS** ə tee
compliment (n)	**KOM** plə mənt
compliment (v)	**KOM** plə **MENT**
complimentary	**KOM** plə **MEN** tə ree
component	kəm **POH** nənt
comport	kəm **PORT**
compose	kəm **POHZ**
composite	kəm **POZ** ət
composition	**KOM** pə **ZISH** ən
compositor	kəm **POZ** ə tər
compos mentis	**KOM** pəs **MEN** təs
compost	**KOM** pohst
composure	kəm **POH** *zh*ər
compote	**KOM** poht
compound (a, n)	**KOM** pownd

---

o **on**, oh **oat**, oi **boy**, oo **soon**, oor **poor**, or **for**, ow **cow**, sh **shush**,
th **thin**, *th* **this**, u **up**, ur **spur**, uu **book**, *zh* **pleasure**

compound (v)	kəm **POWND**
comprehend	**KOM** pri **HEND**
comprehensible	**KOM** pri **HEN** sə bəl
comprehension	**KOM** pri **HEN** shən
comprehensive	**KOM** pri **HEN** siv
compress (n)	**KOM** pres
compress (v)	kəm **PRES**
compressor	kəm **PRES** ər
comprise	kəm **PRĪZ**
compromise	**KOM** prə **MĪZ**
Compton	**KOMP** tən
comptroller	kən **TROH** lər
compulsion	kəm **PUL** shən
compulsory	kəm **PUL** sə ree
compunction	kəm **PUNGK** shən
computable	kəm **PYOOT** ə bəl
comrade	**KOM** rad
Comus	**KOH** məs
Conakry	**KON** ə kree
con amore	kawn ah **MAW** ray
conative	**KON** ə tiv
concatenation	kon **KAT** ə **NAY** shən
concave	kon **KAYV**
concavity	kon **KAV** ə tee
conceal	kən **SEEL**
concede	kən **SEED**
conceit	kən **SEET**
conceivable	kən **SEE** və bəl
conceive	kən **SEEV**
concentrate	**KON** sən **TRAYT**
concentration	**KON** sən **TRAY** shən
concentric	kən **SEN** trik
Concepción	kən **SEP** see **OHN**
concert (n)	**KON** sərt
concert (v)	kən **SURT**
Concertgebouw	kon **SERT** gə **BOW** (**BOW** as in *cow*)
concertina	**KON** sər **TEE** nə
concertino	**KON** chər **TEE** noh
concertmaster	**KON** sərt **MAS** tər
concerto	kən **CHER** toh
concessionaire	kən **SESH** ə **NAIR**
conch	kongk
concha	**KONG** kə

ə ago, a at, ah calm, ahr dark, air care, aw saw, ay say, ch church
e bet, ee me, eer beer, hw what, i is, ī my, *n* French final n vin,

conchoidal	kong **KOID** əl
concierge	kohn **SYERZ***H*
conciliate	kən **SIL** ee **AYT**
conciliatory	kən **SIL** ee ə **TOR** ee
concise	kən **SĪS**
conclave	**KON** klayv
conclude	kən **KLOOD**
conclusion	kən **KLOO** *zh*ən
conclusive	kən **KLOO** siv
concoct	kən **KOKT**
concomitant	kən **KOM** ə tənt
concord, C- (US other than Massachusetts)	**KON** kord
Concord Massachusetts)	**KONG** kərd
concordance	kən **KOR** dəns
concordat	kən **KOR DAT**
Concorde	kon **KORD**
Concordia	kən **KOR** dee ə
concourse	**KON** kors
concrete	kon **KREET**
concubinage	kon **KYOO** bə nij
concubine	**KONG** kyə **BĪN**
concupiscence	kon **KYOO** pə səns
concur	kən **KUR**
concurrence	kən **KUR** əns
concurrent	kən **KUR** ənt
concussion	kən **KUSH** ən
Conde, Mamadi Lamine	**KOHN** dee, **MAH** mah dee lah **MEEN**
condensation	**KON** den **SAY** shən
condescend	**KON** di **SEND**
condign	kən **DĪN**
condiment	**KON** də mənt
condole	kən **DOHL**
condolence	kən **DOH** ləns
condom	**KUN** dəm
condominium	**KON** də **MIN** ee əm
condone	kən **DOHN**
condor	**KON** dər
condottiere	**KON** də **TYAIR** ee
conduct (n)	**KON** dukt
conduct (v)	kən **DUKT**

o **on**, oh **oat**, oi **boy**, oo **soon**, oor **poor**, or **for**, ow **cow**, sh **shush**, th **thin**, *th* **this**, u **up**, ur **spur**, uu **book**, *zh* **pleasure**

conductive	kən DUK tiv
conductor	kən DUK tər
conduit	KON doo ət
Conestoga	KON ə STOH gə
coney, C-	KOH nee
confabulate	kən FAB yə LAYT
confectionery	kən FEK shə NER ee
confederate, C- (a, n)	kən FED ə rət
confederate (v)	kən FED ə RAYT
confederation	kən FED ə RAY shən
conference	KON fə rəns
confetti	kən FET ee
confidant	KON fə DANT
confidence	KON fə dəns
confident	KON fə dənt
confidential	KON fə DEN shəl
configuration	kən FIG yə RAY shən
confine (n)	KON fin
confine (v)	kən FĪN
confirmation	KON fər MAY shən
confirmatory	kən FUR mə TOR ee
confiscate	KON fə SKAYT
confiscatory	kən FIS kə TOR ee
confiture	KON fə TYUUR
conflagration	KON flə GRAY shən
conflict (n)	KON flikt
conflict (v)	kən FLIKT
confluence	KON floo əns
conformation	KON for MAY shən
confound	kən FOWND
confounded	kən FOWN dəd
confraternity	KON frə TUR nə tee
confrere	KON frair
confront	kən FRUNT
Confucius	kən FYOO shəs
confused	kən FYOOZD
confusion	kən FYOO zhən
confute	kən FYOOT
conga	KONG gə
congé	kohn ZHAY
congeal	kən JEEL
congenial	kən JEEN yəl
congenital	kən JEN ə təl

ə ago, a at, ah calm, ahr dark, air care, aw saw, ay say, ch church
e bet, ee me, eer beer, hw what, i is, ī my, *n* French final n vin,

conger	**KONG** gər
congeries	**KON** jə reez
conglomerate (a, n)	kən **GLOM** ə rət
conglomerate (v)	kən **GLOM** ə **RAYT**
Congo	**KONG** goh
Congolese	**KONG** gə **LEEZ**
congratulate	kən **GRACH** ə **LAYT**
congratulatory	kən **GRACH** ə lə **TOR** ee
congregant	**KON** grə gənt
congregate (a)	**KONG** grə gət
congregate (v)	**KONG** grə **GAYT**
congregation	**KONG** grə **GAY** shən
congress, C-	**KONG** grəs
congressional	kən **GRESH** ə nəl
Congreve	**KON** greev
congruent	**KONG** groo ənt
congruity	kən **GROO** ə tee
congruous	**KONG** groo əs
conic	**KON** ik
conical	**KON** i kəl
conifer	**KON** ə fər
coniferous	kə **NIF** ər əs
conjecture	kən **JEK** chər
conjoin	kən **JOIN**
conjugal	**KON** jə gəl
conjugate (a, n)	**KON** jə gət
conjugate (v)	**KON** jə **GAYT**
conjugation	**KON** jə **GAY** shən
conjunction	kən **JUNGK** shən
conjure (entreat)	kən **JUUR**
conjure (summon)	**KON** jər
Connacht	**KON** ət
connate	**KON** ayt
Connaught	**KON** awt
Connecticut	kə **NET** ə kət
Connemara	**KON** ə **MAHR** ə
connivance	kə **NĪV** əns
connoisseur	**KON** ə **SUR**
connotation	**KON** ə **TAY** shən
connotative	**KON** ə **TAYT** iv
connubial	kə **NOO** bee əl
conqueror	**KONG** kər ər
conquest	**KON** kwest

o **on**, oh **oat**, oi **boy**, oo **soon**, oor **poor**, or **for**, ow **cow**, sh **shush**,
th **thin**, *th* **this**, u **up**, ur **spur**, uu **book**, *zh* **pleasure**

conquistador	kon **KWIS** tə **DOR**
consanguineous	**KON** sang **GWIN** ee əs
consanguinity	**KON** sang **GWIN** ə tee
conscience	**KON** shəns
conscientious	**KON** shee **EN** shəs
conscionable	**KON** shə nə bəl
consciousness	**KON** shəs nəs
conscript (a, n)	**KON** skript
conscript (v)	kən **SKRIPT**
consecrate	**KON** sə **KRAYT**
consensus	kən **SEN** səs
consent	kən **SENT**
consequence	**KON** sə **KWENS**
consequently	**KON** sə **KWENT** lee
conservatoire	kən **SUR** və **TWAHR**
conservatory	kən **SUR** və **TOR** ee
conserve (n)	**KON** surv
conserve (v)	kən **SURV**
considerable	kən **SID** ə rə bəl
consign	kən **SĪN**
consignee	**KON** sī **NEE**
consignor	kən **SĪ** nər
consistency	kən **SIS** tən see
consistory	kən **SIS** tə ree
consolation	**KON** sə **LAY** shən
console (n)	**KON** sohl
console (v)	kən **SOHL**
consommé	**KON** sə **MAY**
consonant	**KON** sə nənt
consort (n)	**KON** sort
consort (v)	kən **SORT**
consortium	kən **SOR** shee əm
conspectus	kən **SPEK** təs
conspicuous	kən **SPIK** yoo əs
conspiracy	kən **SPIR** ə see
conspirator	kən **SPIR** ə tər
conspire	kən **SPĪR**
constable	**KON** stə bəl
Constable, John	**KUN** stə bəl
constabulary	kən **STAB** yə **LER** ee
constancy	**KON** stən see
constantan	**KON** stən **TAN**
Constantinople	**KON** stan tə **NOH** pəl

ə ago, a at, ah calm, ahr dark, air care, aw saw, ay say, ch church
e bet, ee me, eer beer, hw what, i is, ī my, *n* French final n vin,

constellation	**KON** stə **LAY** shən
consternation	**KON** stər **NAY** shən
constituency	kən **STICH** oo ən see
constituent	kən **STICH** oo ənt
constitution	**KON** sti **TOO** shən
constraint	kən **STRAYNT**
constrictor	kən **STRIK** tər
construe	kən **STROO**
consul	**KON** səl
consular	**KON** səl ər
consulate	**KON** səl ət
consultant	kən **SUL** tənt
consume	kən **SOOM**
consummate (a)	kən **SUM** ət
consummate (v)	**KON** sə **MAYT**
consumption	kən **SUMP** shən
consumptive	kən **SUMP** tiv
contagion	kən **TAY** jən
contagious	kən **TAY** jəs
contaminant	kən **TAM** ə nənt
contaminate	kən **TAM** ə **NAYT**
contamination	kən **TAM** ə **NAY** shən
conté (crayon)	**KON** tee
Conte, Silvio	**KON** tee, **SIL** vee oh
contemplate	**KON** təm **PLAYT**
contemplation	**KON** təm **PLAY** shən
contemplative	kən **TEM** plə tiv
contemporaneous	kən **TEM** pə **RAY** nee əs
contempt	kən **TEMPT**
contemptible	kən **TEMP** tə bəl
contemptuous	kən **TEMP** choo əs
contend	kən **TEND**
content (what is contained)	**KON** tent
content (except what is contained)	kən **TENT**
contention	kən **TEN** shən
conterminous	kən **TUR** mə nəs
contest (n)	**KON** test
contest (v)	kən **TEST**
contestant	kən **TES** tənt
context	**KON** tekst
contextual	kən **TEKS** choo əl

---

o **on**, oh **oat**, oi **boy**, oo **soon**, oor **poor**, or **for**, ow **cow**, sh **shush**,
th **thin**, *th* **this**, u **up**, ur **spur**, uu **book**, *zh* **pleasure**

contiguity	KON tə GYOO ə tee
contiguous	kən TIG yoo əs
continent	KON tə nənt
contingency	kən TIN jən see
contingent	kən TIN jənt
continuance	kən TIN yoo əns
continuation	kən TIN yoo AY shən
continue	kən TIN yoo
continuity	KON tə NOO ə tee
continuum	kən TIN yoo əm
contort	kən TORT
contour	KON tuur
contra	KON trə
contraband	KON trə BAND
contrabass	KON trə BAYS
contrabassoon	KON trə bə SOON
contract (n)	KON trakt
contract (v)	kən TRAKT
contradictory	KON trə DIK tə ree
contradistinction	KON trə di STINGK shən
contrail	KON trayl
contraindicate	KON trə IN də KAYT
contralto	kən TRAL toh
contrapuntal	KON trə PUN təl
contrariwise	KON trer ee wĪZ
contrary	KON trer ee
contrast (n)	KON trast
contrast (v)	kən TRAST
contravene	KON trə VEEN
contretemps	KON trə TAHN (TAHN French final *n*)
contributory	kən TRIB yə TOR ee
contrite	kən TRĪT
controller	kən TROH lər
controversial	KON trə VUR shəl
controversy	KON trə VUR see
controvert	KON trə VURT
contumacious	KON tə MAY shəs
contumacy	KON tə mə see
contumely	kon TOO mə lee
contusion	kən TOO *zh*ən
conundrum	kə NUN drəm
convalescence	KON və LES əns
convalescent	KON və LES ənt

ə ago, a at, ah calm, ahr dark, air care, aw saw, ay say, ch church
e bet, ee me, eer beer, hw what, i is, ī my, *n* French final n vin,

convection	kən VEK shən
convene	kən VEEN
converge	kən VURJ
conversant	kən VUR sənt
converse (a, v)	kən VURS
converse (n)	KON vurs
conversely	kən VURS lee
conversion	kən VUR zhən
convert (n)	KON vurt
convert (v)	kən VURT
converter	kən VUR tər
convertible	kən VUR tə bəl
conveyance	kən VAY əns
convict (n)	KON vikt
convict (v)	kən VIKT
conviction	kən VIK shən
convince	kən VINS
convivial	kən VIV ee əl
convocation	KON və KAY shən
convoke	kən VOHK
convolution	KON və LOO shən
convoy	KON voi
convulsion	kən VUL shən
cookie	KUUK ee
coolant	KOO lənt
coolie, cooly	KOO lee
cooper, C-	KOO pər
cooperate	koh OP ə RAYT
cooperative	koh OP ə rə tiv
coopt	koh OPT
coordination	koh OR də NAY shən
cootie	KOO tee
Copacabana	KOH pə kə BA nə
copacetic	KOH pə SET ik
copal	KOH pəl
copeck	KOH pek
Copenhagen	KOH pən HAY gən
Copernican	koh PUR ni kən
Copernicus	koh PUR ni kəs
copier	KOP ee ər
coping	KOH ping
copious	KOH pee əs
Copland	KOHP lənd

---

o on, oh oat, oi boy, oo soon, oor poor, or for, ow cow, sh shush,
th thin, *th* this, u up, ur spur, uu book, *zh* pleasure

Copley	**KOP** lee
copolymer	koh **POL** ə mər
copper	**KOP** ər
coppice	**KOP** əs
copra	**KOH** prə
copse	kops
Copt	kopt
Coptic	**KOP** tik
copula	**KOP** yə lə
copulate	**KOP** yə **LAYT**
copulative	**KOP** yə lə tiv
copyist	**KOP** ee əst
copyright	**KOP** ee **RĪT**
coquet	koh **KET**
coquetry	**KOH** kə tree
coquette	koh **KET**
coquille	koh **KEEL**
coquina	koh **KEE** nə
coquito	koh **KEE** toh
coracle	**KOR** ə kəl
coral	**KOR** əl
coram populo	**KOH** rəm **POP** yə **LOH**
corbel	**KOR** bəl
Corbett	**KOR** bət
Corcoran	**KOR** kər ən
cordage	**KOR** dij
cordate	**KOR** dayt
Corday	kor **DAY**
Cordelia	kor **DEEL** yə
cordial	**KOR** jəl
cordiality	kor **JAL** ə tee
cordillera	**KOR** dəl **YAIR** ə
cordite	**KOR** dīt
cordoba	**KOR** də bə
Córdoba	**KOR** daw vah
cordon	**KOR** dən
cordon bleu	kor dawn **BLUU** (dawn French final *n*)
Cordova	**KOR** də və
cordovan	**KOR** də vən
corduroy	**KOR** də **ROI**
Corelli	koh **REL** ee
coreopsis	**KOR** ee **OP** səs
corespondent	**KOH** ri **SPON** dənt

ə ago, a at, ah calm, ahr dark, air care, aw saw, ay say, ch church
e bet, ee me, eer beer, hw what, i is, ī my, n French final n vin,

Corfu	**KOR** foo
corgi	**KOR** gee
coriander	**KOR** ee **AN** dər
Corinth (Greece)	**KOR** ənth
Corinth (US)	kə **RINTH**
Corinthian	kə **RIN** thee ən
Coriolanus	**KOR** ee ə **LAY** nəs
Coriolis, c-	**KOR** ee **OH** ləs
cork, C-	kork
cormorant	**KOR** mə rənt
cornea	**KOR** nee ə
Corneille	kor **NAY**
cornel	**KOR** nəl
cornelian	kor **NEEL** yən
Cornelius	kor **NEEL** yəs
cornet	kor **NET**
cornice	**KOR** nəs
Cornish	**KOR** nəsh
cornucopia	**KOR** nyə **KOH** pee ə
corolla, C-	kə **ROHL** ə
corollary	**KOR** ə **LER** ee
corona	kə **ROH** nə
coronal (a)	kə **ROH** nəl
coronal (n)	**KOR** ə nəl
coronary	**KOR** ə **NER** ee
coroner	**KOR** ə nər
coronet	**KOR** ə **NET**
Corot	kaw **ROH**
corporal	**KOR** pə rəl
corporate	**KOR** pə rət
corporeal	kor **POR** ee əl
corps (sing)	kor
corps (pl)	korz
corpse	korps
corpulence	**KOR** pyə ləns
corpulent	**KOR** pyə lənt
Corpus Christi	**KOR** pəs **KRIS** tee
corpuscle	**KOR** pə səl
corpus delicti	**KOR** pəs di **LIK** tī
corral	kə **RAL**
Correggio	kor **REJ** oh
Corregidor	kə **REG** ə **DOR**
correlate	**KOR** ə **LAYT**

o **on**, oh **oat**, oi **boy**, oo **soon**, oor **poor**, or **for**, ow **cow**, sh **shush**,
th **thin**, *th* **this**, u **up**, ur **spur**, uu **book**, *zh* **pleasure**

correlation	KOR ə LAY shən
correlative	kə REL ə tiv
correspond	KOR ə SPOND
correspondent	KOR ə SPON dənt
corridor	KOR ə dər
corrigenda	KOR ə JEN də
corrigendum	KOR ə JEN dəm
corrigible	KOR ə jə bəl
corroborate	kə ROB ə RAYT
corroborative	kə ROB ə RAY tiv
corrode	kə ROHD
corrosion	kə ROH zhən
corrosive	kə ROH siv
corrugate	KOR ə GAYT
corrugated	KOR ə GAY təd
corrugation	KOR ə GAY shən
corruptible	kə RUP tə bəl
corsage	kor SAHZH
corsair, C-	KOR sair
Corsica	KOR sə kə
Corsican	KOR sə kən
cortege	kor TEZH
Cortes (parliament)	KOR tes
Cortés (name)	kor TEZ
cortex	KOR teks
cortical	KOR ti kəl
cortices	KOR tə seez
Cortines	kor TEE nes
cortisone	KOR tə ZOHN
corundum	kə RUN dəm
coruscate	KOR ə SKAYT
coruscation	KOR ə SKAY shən
corvée	kor VAY
corvette, C-	kor VET
Corvus	KOR vəs
Corydon	KOR ə dən
coryza	kə RĪ zə
Cos, c-	kos
cosecant	KOH SEE kant
cosignatory	koh SIG nə TOR ee
cosine	KOH sīn
cosmic	KOZ mik
cosmogony	koz MOG ə nee

ə ago, a at, ah calm, ahr dark, air care, aw saw, ay say, ch church
e bet, ee me, eer beer, hw what, i is, ī my, *n* French final n vin,

cosmology	koz **MOL** ə jee
cosmonaut	**KOZ** mə nawt
cosmopolitan	**KOZ** mə **POL** ə tən
cosmopolite	koz **MOP** ə **LĪT**
cosmos	**KOZ** məs
cosmotron	**KOS** mə **TRON**
Cossack	**KOS** ak
costal	**KOS** təl
co-star	**KOH STAHR**
Costa Rica	**KOS** tə **REE** kə
Costello (Ireland)	**KOS** tə **LOH**
Costello (US)	ko **STEL** oh
costermonger	**KOS** tər **MUNG** gər
costume (n)	**KOS** tyoom
costume (v)	kos **TYOOM**
costumer	kos **TYOO** mər
cotangent	**KOH TAN** jənt
coterie	**KOH** tə ree
coterminous	**KOH TUR** mə nəs
cotillion	kə **TIL** yən
Cotswold	**KOTS** wohld
couchant	**KOW** chənt
Coué	koo **AY**
cougar	**KOO** gər
cough	kawf
coulee	**KOO** lee
Coulibaly, Sori	kuu lee **BU** lee, **SAW** ree
coulisse	koo **LEES**
coulomb	**KOO** lom
Coumbassa, Djebel	koom **BAH** sah, **JE** bel
council	**KOWN** səl
councillor	**KOWN** sə lər
counsel	**KOWN** səl
counselor	**KOWN** sə lər
countenance	**KOWN** tə nəns
counterfeit	**KOWN** tər fit
countertenor	**KOWN** tər **TEN** ər
countrified	**KUN** tri **FĪD**
coup	koo
coup de grâce	koo də **GRAHS**
coup d'état	**KOO** day **TAH**
coupe	koop
coupé	koo **PAY**

o on, oh oat, oi boy, oo soon, oor poor, or for, ow cow, sh shush,
th thin, *th* this, u up, ur spur, uu book, *zh* pleasure

couplet	**KUP** lət
coupon	**KOO** pon
coups d'état	**KOO** day **TAH**
courage	**KUR** ij
courant	**KUUR** ənt
Courant (Institute)	kə **RAHNT**
courante	kuu **RAHNT**
Courbet	koor **BAY**
courier	**KUUR** ee ər
Cournand, André	kuur **NAHN**, ahn **DRAY** (ahn and **NAHN** French final *n*)
courteous	**KUR** tee əs
courtesan	**KOR** tə zən
courtesy	**KUR** tə see
courtier	**KOR** tee ər
courtly	**KORT** lee
Cousteau	koo **STOH**
Coutts	koots
couturier	koo **TUU** ree **AY**
couvade	koo **VAHD**
covalent	koh **VAY** lənt
Covarrubias	**KOH** və **ROO** bee əs
covenant	**KUV** ə nənt
Coventry	**KUV** ən tree
covert (n)	**KUV** ərt
covert (a)	**KOH** vərt
covet	**KUV** ət
covetous	**KUV** ə təs
covey	**KUV** ee
coward	**KOW** ərd
cowardice	**KOW** ər dəs
cowl	kowl
Cowley	**KOW** lee
Cowper	**KOO** pər
cowrie	**KOW** ree
coxcomb	**KOKS** kohm
Coxey	**KOK** see
Coxsackie	kok **SAK** ee
coxswain	**KOK** sən
coyote	kī **OH** tee
cozen	**KUZ** ən
Cozumel	**KOH** zə **MEL**
Cozzens	**KUZ** ənz

ə ago, a at, ah calm, ahr dark, air care, aw saw, ay say, ch church
e bet, ee me, eer beer, hw what, i is, ī my, *n* French final n vin,

Cracow	**KRAK** ow
cranium	**KRAY** nee əm
crape	krayp
crapulent	**KRAP** yə lənt
crapulous	**KRAP** yə ləs
Crashaw	**KRA** shaw
crater, C-	**KRAY** tər
cravat	krə **VAT**
craven	**KRAY** vən
crawfish	**KRAW** fish
crayfish	**KRAY** fish
crayon	**KRAY** on
creamery	**KREE** mə ree
crease	krees
creative	kree **AY** tiv
creator, C-	kree **AY** tər
creature	**KREE** chər
crèche	kresh
Crécy	kray **SEE**
credence	**KREED** əns
credential	kri **DEN** shəl
credenza	kri **DEN** zə
credible	**KRED** ə bəl
creditable	**KRED** ət ə bəl
credo	**KREE** doh
credulity	kri **DOO** lə tee
credulous	**KREJ** ə ləs
creek, C-	kreek
creel	kreel
creese	krees
cremate	**KREE MAYT**
crematorium	**KREE** mə **TOR** ee əm
crematory	**KREE** mə **TOR** ee
crème de menthe	**KREM** də **MAHNT**
Cremona	kri **MOH** nə
crenelated	**KREN** ə **LAY** təd
creole, C-	**KREE** ohl
Creon	**KREE** on
creosote	**KREE** ə **SOHT**
crepe de Chine	**KRAYP** də **SHEEN**
crêpe suzette	**KRAYP** soo **ZET**
crepuscular	kri **PUS** kyə lər
crescendo	krə **SHEN** doh

o on, oh oat, oi boy, oo soon, oor poor, or for, ow cow, sh shush,
th thin, *th* this, u up, ur spur, uu book, *zh* pleasure

crescent	**KRES** ənt
Crespin, Régine	kres **PAN**, ray **ZH**EEN (**PAN** French final *n*)
Crespo-Zaldumbide, Ricardo	**KRES** poh **SAL** duum **BEE** day, ree **KAHR** doh
Cressida	**KRES** ə də
Cressy	**KRES** ee
cretaceous	kri **TAY** shəs
Cretan	**KREE** tən
Crete	kreet
cretin	**KREE** tən
cretinism	**KREE** tə **NIZ** əm
cretonne	kri **TON**
Creüsa	kree **OO** sə
crevasse	krə **VAS**
crevice	**KREV** əs
crewel	**KROO** əl
cribbage	**KRIB** ij
Crichton	**KRĪT** ən
Crimea	krī **MEE** ə
crimson	**KRIM** zən
crinoline	**KRIN** ə lən
crises	**KRĪ** seez
Criseyde	kri **SAY** də
crisis	**KRĪ** səs
Cristóbal	kris **TOH** bəl
criteria	krī **TEER** ee ə
criterion	krī **TEER** ee ən
criticism	**KRIT** ə **SIZ** əm
critique	krə **TEEK**
Croat	**KROH** at
Croatia	kroh **AY** shə
Croatian	kroh **AY** shən
Croce, Benedetto	**KROH** chay, **BE** ne **DET** toh
crochet	kroh **SHAY**
Crockett	**KROK** ət
crocodile	**KROK** ə **DĪL**
Croesus	**KREE** səs
croissant	krwah **SAHN** (**SAHN** French final *n*)
croix de guerre	krwah də **GAIR**
Cro-Magnon	kroh **MAG** nən
Cromwell	**KROM** wəl
Cronin	**KROH** nən

ə ago, a at, ah calm, ahr dark, air care, aw saw, ay say, ch church
e bet, ee me, eer beer, hw what, i is, ī my, *n* French final n vin,

Cronyn	**KROH** nən
croquet	kroh **KAY**
croquette	kroh **KET**
crosier	**KROH** *zh*ər
crotchet	**KROCH** ət
croup	kroop
croupier	**KROO** pee **AY**
crouton	**KROO** ton
Crowell	**KROH** əl
crozier	**KROH** *zh*ər
cruces	**KROO** seez
crucial	**KROO** shəl
crucifixion	**KROO** sə **FIK** shən
crucify	**KROO** sə **FĪ**
cruel	**KROO** əl
cruelty	**KROO** əl tee
cruet	**KROO** ət
cruise	krooz
cruiser	**KROO** zər
cruller	**KRUL** ər
crumpet	**KRUM** pət
crusade	kroo **SAYD**
crustacean	krus **TAY** shən
crux	kruks
Cruz	krooz
cruzeiro	kroo **ZAIR** oh
cryogenics	**KRĪ** ə **JEN** iks
cryptic	**KRIP** tik
cryptogram	**KRIP** tə **GRAM**
crystalline	**KRIS** tə lən
crystallization	**KRIS** tə lə **ZAY** shən
Csatorday, Karoly	**CHAH** tohr dī, **KAH** raw lyi
Csongrád	**CHAWNG** grahd
Cuba	**KYOO** bə
Cuban	**KYOO** bən
cubical	**KYOO** bi kəl
cubicle	**KYOO** bi kəl
Cuchulainn, Cuchullin	kuu **KUL** in
cuckold	**KUK** əld
cuckoo	**KOO** koo
cucumber	**KYOO** kum bər
cue	kyoo
Cuernavaca	**KWER** nə **VAHK** ə

cui bono	KWEE BOH noh
cuirass	kwi RAS
cuirassier	KWEER ə SEER
cuisine	kwi ZEEN
cul-de-sac	KUL də SAK
Culiacán	KOOL yə KAHN
culinary	KYOO lə NER ee
culminate	KUL mə NAYT
culottes	koo LOTS
culpability	KUL pə BIL ə tee
culprit	KUL prət
cultivator	KUL tə VAY tər
cultural	KUL chə rəl
culture	KUL chər
culvert	KUL vərt
Cumae	KYOO mee
Cumaean	kyuu MEE ən
cumbersome	KUM bər səm
cumin	KUM ən
cum laude	kuum LOWD ə (LOWD as in *crowd*)
cumulative	KYOO myə lə tiv
cumulus	KYOO myə ləs
Cunard	kyuu NAHRD
cuneiform	kyuu NEE ə FORM
cunnilingus	KUN ə LING gəs
Cuomo, Mario	KWOH moh, MAHR ee oh
cupboard	KUB ərd
Cupid	KYOO pəd
cupidity	kyuu PID ə tee
cupola	KYOO pə lə
Curaçao	KUUR ə SOW (SOW as in *cow*)
curaçao	KYUUR ə SOH
curare	kyuu RAHR ee
curate	KYUUR ət
curative	KYUUR ə tiv
curator	KYUUR ay tər
curé	kyuu RAY
curettage	KYUUR ə TAHZH
curette	kyuu RET
curfew	KUR fyoo
curia, C-	KYUUR ee ə
curie, C-	KYUUR ee
curium	KYUUR ee əm

ə ago, a at, ah calm, ahr dark, air care, aw saw, ay say, ch church
e bet, ee me, eer beer, hw what, i is, ī my, n French final n vin,

curlew	**KUR** loo
curlicue	**KUR** li **KYOO**
curmudgeon	kər **MUJ** ən
currant	**KUR** ənt
current	**KUR** ənt
curricle	**KUR** i kəl
curriculum	kə **RIK** yə ləm
cursive	**KUR** siv
cursor	**KUR** sər
cursorily	**KUR** sə rə lee
cursory	**KUR** sə ree
curtail	kər **TAYL**
curtsy	**KURT** see
curvaceous	kər **VAY** shəs
curvature	**KUR** və chər
curvet	**KUR** vət
cushion	**KUUSH** ən
cuspidor	**KUS** pə dor
cussed (a)	**KUS** əd
cussed (v)	kusd
custodian	kus **TOH** dee ən
custody	**KUS** tə dee
cutaneous	kyuu **TAY** nee əs
cuticle	**KYOO** tə kəl
Cuticura	kyoo tə **KYUU** rə
cutlass	**KUT** ləs
Cuvier	**KYOO** vee **AY**
Cuyp	koip
Cuzco	**KOOS** koh
Cvejic, Biserka	**TSVAY** ich, **BI** sər kah
cyanamide	sī **AN** ə məd
cyanide	**SĪ** ə **NĪD**
cyanosis	sī ə **NOH** sis
Cybele	**SIB** ə **LEE**
cybernetics	sī bər **NET** iks
Cyclades	**SIK** lə **DEEZ**
cyclamate	**SĪ** klə **MAYT**
cyclamen	**SĪ** klə mən
cyclic	**SĪ** klik
cyclical	**SĪ** kli kəl
cyclone	**SĪ** klohn
cyclonic	sī **KLON** ik
Cyclopean	**SĪ** klə **PEE** ən

o **on**, oh **oat**, oi **boy**, oo **soon**, oor **poor**, or **for**, ow **cow**, sh **shush**,
th **thin**, *th* **this**, u **up**, ur **spur**, uu **book**, *zh* **pleasure**

Cyclops	**SĪ** klops
cyclotron	**SĪ** klə **TRON**
cygnet	**SIG** nət
Cygnus	**SIG** nəs
cylinder	**SIL** ən dər
cymbal	**SIM** bəl
Cymbeline	**SIM** bə **LEEN**
Cymric	**KUM** rik
Cynewulf	**KIN** ə **WUULF**
cynic	**SIN** ik
cynical	**SIN** i kəl
cynicism	**SIN** ə **SIZ** əm
cynosure, C-	**SĪ** nə **SHUUR**
Cynthia	**SIN** thee ə
cypress	**SĪ** prəs
Cyprian	**SIP** ree ən
Cyprus	**SĪ** prəs
Cyrankiewicz, Jozef	tsee rahn **KAY** vich, **YOO** zef
Cyrano	**SI** rə **NOH**
Cyrenaica	**SI** rə **NAY** i kə
Cyrillic	sə **RIL** ik
Cyrus	**SĪ** rəs
cyst	sist
cystitis	sis **TĪ** təs
Cytherea	**SITH** ə **REE** ə
cytology	sī **TOL** ə jee
czar	zahr
czardas	**CHAHR** dahs
czarevitch	**ZAHR** ə vich
czarina	zah **REE** nə
czarism	**ZAHR** iz əm
Czech	chek
Czechoslovak	**CHEK** oh **SLOH** vak
Czechoslovakia	**CHEK** ə sloh **VAH** kee ə
Czeladź	**CHE** lahj
Czerny	**CHER** nee
Czestochowa	**CHEN** stə **KOH** və
Czortkow	**CHAWRT** kuuf

ə ago, a at, ah calm, ahr dark, air care, aw saw, ay say, ch church
e bet, ee me, eer beer, hw what, i is, ī my, n French final n vin,

D

da capo	dah **KAH** poh
dacha	**DAH** chə
Dachau	**DAHK** ow
Daché, Lilly	da **SHAY**
dachshund	**DOKS** huund
Dacko, David	**DAK** oh
da Costa, Sérgio Corrêa	da **CAWSH** tə, **SER** *zh*oh kor **HAY** yə
Dacron	**DAY** kron
dactyl	**DAK** təl
Daddah, Abdellah Ould	**DAH** dah, **AHB** də lah **OOL**
Daddah, Moktar	**DAH** dah, **MOHK** tahr
Dadet, Emmanuel	da **DAY**, ə mahn yoo **EL**
Daedalus	**DED** ə ləs
daffodil	**DAF** ə dil
daguerreotype	də **GER** ə **TĪP**
dahlia	**DAL** yə
Dahomey	də **HOH** mee
Dail Eireann	doil **AIR** ən
Daimler	**DĪM** lər
daimyo	**DĪ** myoh
Dai Nippon	**DĪ** ni **PON**
Daiquiri, d-	**DĪ** kə ree
Dairen	dī ren
dais	**DAY** əs
Dakar	da **KAHR**
Daladier	da la **DYAY**
Dalai Lama	**DAH** lī **LAH** mə
Dalhousie	dal **HOO** zee
Dali, Salvador	**DAH** lee, **SAL** və ɾ ʀ
Dallas	**DAL** əs
Dalles, The	dalz
dalliance	**DAL** ee əns
Damascus	də **MAS** kəs
damask	**DAM** əsk
D'Amato, Alphonse	də **MAH** toh, **AL** fons
D'Amboise, Jacques	dahm **BWAHZ**, **ZH**AHK

---

o on, oh oat, oi boy, oo soon, oor poor, or for, ow cow, sh shush,
th thin, *th* this, u up, ur spur, uu book, *zh* pleasure

Dambovita	**DUM** baw veet sah
Damien	**DAYM** yən
Damietta	**DAM** ee **ET** ə
Damocles	**DAM** ə **KLEEZ**
Damon	**DAY** mən
damsel	**DAM** zəl
damson	**DAM** zən
Danilova	dah **NEE** loh vah
Danish	**DAY** nish
d'Annunzio, Gabriele	dah **NOON** tsyoh, **GAH** bree **E** le
danseur	dahn **SUUR** (dahn French final *n*)
danseuse	dahn **SUUZ** (dahn French final *n*)
Dante	**DAHN** tay
Danube	**DAN** yoob
Danzig	**DANT** sig
Daphne	**DAF** nee
Daphnis	**DAF** nəs
d'Arc	dahrk
Dardanelles	**DAHR** də **NELZ**
Dar es Salaam	**DAHR ES** sə **LAHM**
Darian	**DAR** ee ən
Darien	**DAR** ee **EN**
Darius (Persian king)	də **RĪ** əs
Darius (modern name)	**DAR** ee əs
Darmstadt	**DAHRM** stat
Darrieux	dar **YUU**
Darwin	**DAHR** win
Darwinian	dahr **WIN** ee ən
dashiki	də **SHEE** kee
da Silveira, Antonio Azeredo	da sil **VAIR** ə, ahn **TOH** nyoh ah zay **RAY** doh
Dassin, Jules	da **SAN**, **ZHOOL** (**SAN** French final *n*)
data	**DAYT** ə
dative	**DAYT** iv
datum	**DAYT** əm
daub	dawb
d'Aubuisson, Roberto	**DOW** bee sawn, roh **BER** toh
Daudet	doh **DAY**
Daumier	doh **MYAY**
daunt	dawnt
dauphin	doh **FAN** (**FAN** French final *n*)
Dauphin, Claude	doh **FAN**, **KLOHD** (**FAN** French final *n*)

ə ago, a at, ah calm, ahr dark, air care, aw saw, ay say, ch church
e bet, ee me, eer beer, hw what, i is, ī my, *n* French final n vin,

dauphine	doh **FEEN**
David (European)	da **VEED**
Davin, Jean	**DAV** ən, **ZH**AHN (**ZH**AHN French final *n*)
da Vinci	də **VIN** chee
davit	**DAV** it
Davos	dah **VOHS**
Dawalibi, Maarouf	dah wah **LEE** bee, mah **ROOF**
Dayak	**DĪ** ak
Dayan, Moshe	dah **YAHN**, moh **SHE**
dearth	durth
Deauville	**DOH** vil
debacle	di **BAH** kəl
debar	di **BAHR**
de Barentzen	də bah rend **ZEN**
debark	di **BAHRK**
debase	di **BAYS**
debauch	di **BAWCH**
debenture	di **BEN** chər
debilitate	di **BIL** ə **TAYT**
debility	di **BIL** ə tee
debit	**DEB** ət
debonair	**DEB** ə **NAIR**
Deborah	**DEB** ər ə
debouch	di **BOWCH**
Debré	də **BRAY**
debrief	dee **BREEF**
debris	də **BREE**
Debussy	**DAYB** yuu **SEE**
debut	**DAY** byoo
debutante	**DEB** yuu **TAHNT**
Debye	də **BĪ**
decadence	**DEK** ə dəns
decadent	**DEK** ə dənt
decaffeinated	dee **KAF** ə **NAY** təd
decal	**DEE** kal
decant	di **KANT**
decapitate	di **KAP** ə **TAYT**
decathlon	di **KATH** lən
Decatur	di **KAY** tər
Deccan	**DEK** ən
decedent	di **SEE** dənt
December	di **SEM** bər

o on, oh oat, oi boy, oo soon, oor poor, or for, ow cow, sh shush,
th thin, *th* this, u up, ur spur, uu book, *zh* pleasure

decentralization	dee SEN trə lə ZAY shən
decibel	DES ə bəl
deciduous	di SIJ oo əs
decisive	di SĪ siv
declamatory	di KLAM ə TOR ee
declaration	DEK lə RAY shən
déclassé	DAY kla SAY
décolletage	DAY kahl TAHZH
décolleté	DAY kahl TAY
decompose	DEE kəm POHZ
DeConcini	DEE kon SEEN ee
décor	day KOR
decorative	DEK ə rə tiv
decorous	DEK ə rəs
decorum	di KOR əm
découpage	DAY koo PAHZH
decoy (n)	DEE koi
decoy (v)	di KOI
decrease (n)	DEE krees
decrease (v)	di KREES
decrepitude	di KREP ə TOOD
decrescendo	DAY krə SHEN doh
dedicatory	DED i kə TOR ee
deduce	di DOOS
de facto	di FAK toh
defalcate	di FAL kayt
defalcation	DEE fal KAY shən
defamatory	di FAM ə TOR ee
defense	di FENS
deference	DEF ə rəns
Defferre, Gaston	də FAIR, ga STAWN (STAWN French final *n*)
deficit	DEF ə sət
defile	di FĪL
definite	DEF ə nət
Defoe	di FOH
defoliation	dee FOH lee AY shən
defunct	di FUNGKT
dégagé	day ga ZHAY
degas	di GAS
Degas	də GAH
De Gaulle	də GOHL
degauss	dee GOWS (GOWS as in *mouse*)

ə ago, a at, ah calm, ahr dark, air care, aw saw, ay say, ch church
e bet, ee me, eer beer, hw what, i is, ī my, *n* French final n vin,

degenerate (a, n)	di **JEN** ə rət
degenerate (v)	di **JEN** ə **RAYT**
dehydrate	dee **HĪ** drayt
deify	**DEE** ə **FĪ**
deign	dayn
Deimos	**DĪ** mos
Deiphobus	dee **IF** ə bəs
Deirdre	**DEER** drə
déjà vu	day *zh*ah **VOO**
De Jong	də **YAWNG**
de jure	dee **JUUR** ee
de Kooning, Willem	də **KOON** ing, **VIL** əm
Delacroix	də la **KRWAH**
de la Madrid Hurtado, Miguel	day lah mah **DRID** oor **TAH** doh, mee **GEL**
de la Mare	də lə **MAIR**
de Larosière, Jacques	də lah roh **ZYAIR**, **ZH**AHK
Delaware	**DEL** ə **WAIR**
delectation	**DEE** lek **TAY** shən
delegate (n)	**DEL** ə gət
delegate (v)	**DEL** ə **GAYT**
deleterious	**DEL** ə **TEER** ee əs
Delhi	**DEL** ee
deliberate (a)	di **LIB** ə rət
deliberate (v)	di **LIB** ə **RAYT**
deliberative	di **LIB** ə **RAY** tiv
Delibes	də **LEEB**
Delilah	di **LĪ** lə
deliquesce	**DEL** ə **KWES**
Delius	**DEE** lee əs
Dellums	**DEL** əmz
Delock	də **LOK**
Delorean	də **LOR** ee ən
Delos	**DEE** los
De Los Angeles, Victoria	day lohs **AHN** je lez, vik **TAW** ree ə
delphinium	del **FIN** ee əm
Delphinus	del **FĪ** nəs
Delpree-Crespo, Juan Carlos	del **PRAY KRES** poh, hwahn **KAHR** lohs
delude	di **LOOD**
deluge	**DEL** yooj
delusion	di **LOO** *zh*ən

---

o **on**, oh **oat**, oi **boy**, oo **soon**, oor **poor**, or **for**, ow **cow**, sh **shush**,
th **thin**, *th* **this**, u **up**, ur **spur**, uu **book**, *zh* **pleasure**

delusive	di **LOO** siv
de luxe	di **LUUKS**
Delvecchio	del **VEK** ee oh
demagogue	**DEM** ə ɢoɢ
demarcation	**DEE** mahr **KAY** shən
démarche	day **MAHRSH**
de Medina, Rui Barbosa	duu mə **DEE** nə, **ROO** ee bahr **BOH** zə
dementia praecox	di **MEN** shə **PREE** koks
Demerol	**DEM** ə ʀoʜʟ
demesne	di **MAYN**
Demeter	di **MEE** tər
Demetrius	də **MEE** tree əs
Demichev, Pyotr N.	**DE** mi chəf, **PYOH** tər
demimonde	**DEM** ee ᴍoɴᴅ
demise	di **MĪZ**
demitasse	**DEM** ee ᴛᴀs
demoiselle	**DEM** wah **ZEL**
demoniac	di **MOH** nee ᴀᴋ
demoniacal	**DEE** mə **NĪ** ə kəl
demonology	**DEE** mə **NOL** ə jee
demonstrable	di **MON** strə bəl
demonstrate	**DEM** ən sᴛʀᴀʏᴛ
demonstrative	di **MON** strə tiv
Demosthenes	di **MOS** thə ɴᴇᴇᴢ
demur	di **MUR**
demure	di **MYOOR**
demurrer	di **MUR** ər
Demuth	də **MOOTH**
dendritic	den **DRIT** ik
Deneb	**DEN** eb
Deng Liqun	dəng lee choon
dengue	**DENG** gee
Deng Xiaoping	dəng show ping (show as in *how*)
Deng Yingchao	dəng yeeng chow
denier (coin)	də **NEER**
denier (one who denies)	də **NĪ** ər
denier (unit of fineness)	**DEN** yər
denigrate	**DEN** ə ɢʀᴀʏᴛ
denim	**DEN** əm
denizen	**DEN** ə zən

ə ago, a at, ah calm, ahr dark, air care, aw saw, ay say, ch church
e bet, ee me, eer beer, hw what, i is, ī my, *n* French final n vin,

Denmark	**DEN** mahrk
denotation	**DEE** noh **TAY** shən
denote	di **NOHT**
dénouement	**DAY** noo **MAHN** (**MAHN** French final *n*)
de nouveau	də noo **VOH**
de novo	day **NOH** voh
dentifrice	**DEN** tə frəs
denunciation	di **NUN** see **AY** shən
De Oliveira Campos, Roberto	də oh lee **VAIR** ə **KAHMP** ush, rə **BAIR** toh
deoxyribonucleic	dee **OK** si **RĪ** boh noo **KLEE** ik
de Piniés, Jaime	day pee **NYAYS, HĪ** may
depletion	di **PLEE** shən
deponent	di **POH** nənt
deposition	**DEP** ə **ZISH** ən
depot (military)	**DEP** oh
depot (railroad)	**DEE** poh
deprecate	**DEP** rə **KAYT**
depreciate	di **PREE** shee **AYT**
depreciation	di **PREE** shee **AY** shən
depredate	**DEP** rə **DAYT**
depredation	**DEP** rə **DAY** shən
deprivation	**DEP** rə **VAY** shən
de profundis	day proh **FUUN** dees
depute	də **PYOOT**
deputy	**DEP** yə tee
de Quay, Jan	də **KWĪ, YAHN**
derby, D-	**DUR** bee
derby, D- (British)	**DAHR** bee
derelict	**DER** ə likt
dereliction	**DER** ə **LIK** shən
de rigueur	də ree **GUR**
derisive	di **RĪ** siv
derivation	**DER** ə **VAY** shən
dermatologist	**DUR** mə **TOL** ə jəst
dermatology	**DUR** mə **TOL** ə jee
dernier cri	der nyay **KREE**
derogatory	di **ROG** ə **TOR** ee
Derounian	de **ROO** nee ən
descant	**DES** kant
Descartes	day **KAHRT**
Desdemona	**DEZ** də **MOH** nə

---

o **on**, oh **oat**, oi **boy**, oo **soon**, oor **poor**, or **for**, ow **cow**, sh **shush**,
th **thin**, *th* **this**, u **up**, ur **spur**, uu **book**, *zh* **pleasure**

desert (n)	**DEZ** ərt
desert (v)	di **ZURT**
deshabille	**DES** ə **BEEL**
De Sica, Vittorio	də **SEE** kə, vi **TOR** ee **OH**
desiccate	**DES** i **KAYT**
desideratum	di **SID** ə **RAY** təm
designate (a)	**DEZ** ig nət
designate (v)	**DEZ** ig **NAYT**
Des Moines	də **MOIN**
desolate (a)	**DES** ə lət
desolate (v)	**DES** ə **LAYT**
Désormière	day zawr **MYAIR**
desperado	**DES** pə **RAH** doh
despicable	**DES** pi kə bəl
Des Plaines	des **PLAYNZ**
Dessau	**DES** ow (ow as in *cow*)
dessert	di **ZURT**
Dessès	də **SE**
de Stijl, D-	də **STĪL**
desuetude	**DES** wi **TOOD**
desultory	**DES** əl **TOR** ee
detail	di **TAYL**
detent	**DEE** tent
détente	day **TAHNT**
deter	di **TUR**
detergent	di **TUR** jənt
deteriorate	di **TIR** ee ə **RAYT**
determinism	di **TUR** mə **NIZ** əm
deterrent	di **TUR** ənt
de Tocqueville	də **TOHK** vil
detonate	**DET** ə **NAYT**
detonator	**DET** ə **NAY** tər
detour	di **TOOR**
detoxify	dee **TOK** si **FĪ**
Detroit	di **TROIT**
de trop	də **TROH**
deuce	doos
Deukmejian, George	duuk **MAY** jən
deus ex machina	**DE** uus eks **MAH** ki **NAH**
deuterium	doo **TIR** ee əm
Deuteronomy	**DOO** tə **RON** ə mee
Deutsch	doich
Deutschland	**DOICH** lahnt

ə ago, a at, ah calm, ahr dark, air care, aw saw, ay say, ch church
e bet, ee me, eer beer, hw what, i is, ī my, *n* French final n vin,

De Valera, Eamon	DEV ə LAIR ə, AY mən
Devanagari	DAY və NAH gə REE
devastate	DEV ə STAYT
Dev, Birendra Bir Bikram Shah	DEV, bee REN drə beer bee KRAHM shah
Dever, Edmond	də VAIR, ed MAWN (MAWN French final *n*)
deviant	DEE vee ənt
deviate (a, n)	DEE vee ət
deviate (v)	DEE vee AYT
deviationism	DEE vee AY shə NIZ əm
devise	di VĪZ
Devonshire	DEV ən shər
devotee	DEV ə TEE
De Vries, Hugo	də VREES
De Vries, Peter	də VREEZ
dexterous, dextrous	DEK strəs
dextrose	DEK strohs
Dhaka, Dacca	DAK ə
dharma	DAHR mə
dhow	dow (as in *cow*)
Dia, Abdourahmane	JAH, AHB doo rah MAHN
diabetes	DĪ ə BEET eez
diabolic	DĪ ə BOL ik
diacritical	DĪ ə KRIT ə kəl
diadem	DĪ ə DEM
diaeresis	dī ER ə səs
diagnose	DĪ əg NOHS
diagnosis	DĪ əg NOH səs
dialectics	DĪ ə LEK tiks
Diallo Telli	dee AH loh TE lee
dialogue, dialog	DĪ ə LAWG
dialysis	dī AL ə səs
diameter	dī AM ə tər
Diana	dī AN ə
dianthus	dī AN thəs
diapason	DĪ ə PAY zən
diaphragm	DĪ ə FRAM
diarrhea	DĪ ə REE ə
Diaspora	dī AS pər ə
diastole	dī AS tə LEE
diastolic	DĪ ə STOL ik
diatom	DĪ ə TOM

o on, oh oat, oi boy, oo soon, oor poor, or for, ow cow, sh shush,
th thin, *th* this, u up, ur spur, uu book, zh pleasure

diatomaceous	DĪ ə tə MAY shəs
diatonic	DĪ ə TON ik
diatribe	DĪ ə TRĪB
Diaz	DEE ahs
dichotomy	dī KOT ə mee
didactic	dī DAK tik
Diderot	DEE də ROH
Dido, d-	DĪ doh
Diefenbaker	DEE fən BAY kər
Diego	dee AY goh
Diels	deelz
Dien Bien Phu	dyen byen foo
Dieppe	dee EP
dieresis	dī ER ə səs
diesel, D-	DEE zəl
Dies Irae	DEE ays EER ay
diethylstilbestrol	dī ETH əl stil BES trohl
Dietrich, Marlene	DEE trik, mahr LAY nə
differentiate	DIF ə REN shee AYT
differentiation	DIF ə REN shee AY shən
diffident	DIF ə dənt
diffuse (a)	di FYOOS
diffuse (v)	di FYOOZ
digest (n)	DĪ jest
digest (v)	dī JEST
digestion	di JES chən
digitalis	DIJ ə TAL is
digress	di GRES
Dilantin	di LAN tin
dilapidated	di LAP ə DAYT əd
dilate	dī LAYT
dilatory	DIL ə TOR ee
dilemma	di LEM ə
dilettante	DIL ə TAHNT
dilettanti	DIL ə TAHN tee
dilute	də LOOT
dimension	də MEN shən
diminish	də MIN ish
diminuendo	də MIN yoo EN doh
diminution	DIM ə NOO shən
Dimitrov	di MEE trof
dimity	DIM ə tee
Dinesen, Isak	DEE nə sən, EE sahk

ə ago, a at, ah calm, ahr dark, air care, aw saw, ay say, ch church
e bet, ee me, eer beer, hw what, i is, ī my, *n* French final n vin,

dinghy	**DING** gee
diocesan	dī **OS** ə sən
diocese	**DĪ** ə sis
diode	**DĪ** ohd
dioecious	dī **EE** shəs
Diogenes	dī **OJ** ə **NEEZ**
Diomede	**DĪ** ə **MEED**
Diomedes	**DĪ** ə **MEE** deez
Dione	dī **OH** nee
Dionysius	**DĪ** ə **NISH** ee əs
Dionysus	**DĪ** ə **NĪ** səs
Diop, Ousmane Soce	**DYAHP**, oos **MAHN** soh **SAY**
diopter	dī **OP** tər
Dior	dee **OR**
diorama	**DĪ** ə **RAM** ə
Diori, Hamani	dee **AW** ree, **HAH** mah nee
diorite	**DĪ** ə **RĪT**
Dioscuri	**DĪ** ə **SKYUUR** ī
Diouf, Abdou	**JOOF, AHB** doo
dioxin	**DĪ OK** sən
diphtheria	dif **THEER** ee ə
diphthong	**DIF** thawng
diplomacy	də **PLOH** mə see
diplomat	**DIP** lə **MAT**
diplomate	**DIP** lə **MAYT**
diplomatist	də **PLOH** mə təst
dipsomania	**DIP** sə **MAY** nee ə
diptych	**DIP** tik
direct	də **REKT**
direction	də **REK** shən
directly	də **REKT** lee
directorate	də **REK** tə rət
dirge	durj
dirigible	**DIR** ə jə bəl
dirndl	**DURN** dəl
Diroc	di **ROK**
disable	dis **AY** bəl
disaccharide	dī **SAK** ə **RĪD**
disarm	dis **AHRM**
disaster	di **ZAS** tər
disburse	dis **BURS**
discern	di **SURN**
discernible	di **SUR** nə bəl

o **on**, oh **oat**, oi **boy**, oo **soon**, oor **poor**, or **for**, ow **cow**, sh **shush**,
th **thin**, *th* **this**, u **up**, ur **spur**, uu **book**, *zh* **pleasure**

discernment	di SURN mənt
discharge (n)	DIS chahrj
discharge (v)	dis CHAHRJ
Dischinger	DI shing gər
disciplinary	DIS ə plə NER ee
disclosure	dis KLOH zhər
disconsolate	dis KON sə lət
discordant	dis KOR dənt
discothèque	DIS koh TEK
discount (n)	DIS kownt
discount (v)	dis KOWNT
discourse (n)	DIS kors
discourse (v)	dis KORS
discourteous	dis KUR tee əs
discreet	di SKREET
discrepancy	di SKREP ən see
discrepant	di SKREP ənt
discrete	di SKREET
discretion	di SKRESH ən
discursive	dis KUR siv
disdain	dis DAYN
disease	di ZEEZ
diseased	di ZEEZD
disenfranchise	DIS ən FRAN chīz
disfranchise	dis FRAN chīz
disfranchisement	dis FRAN chīz mənt
disgorge	dis GORJ
dishabille	DIS ə BEEL
disheveled	di SHEV əld
disillusion	DIS ə LOO zhən
disintegrate	dis IN tə GRAYT
disinterested	dis IN trəs təd
dismal	DIZ məl
dismantle	dis MAN təl
dismay	dis MAY
dismember	dis MEM bər
disown	dis OHN
disparage	dis PA rij
disparate	DIS pə rət
dispersion	dis PUR zhən
dispossess	dis pə ZES
disputable	dis PYOOT ə bəl
disputant	DIS pyət ənt

ə ago, a at, ah calm, ahr dark, air care, aw saw, ay say, ch church
e bet, ee me, eer beer, hw what, i is, ī my, *n* French final n vin,

disputatious	DIS pyə TAY shəs
Disraeli	diz RAY lee
disreputable	dis REP yə tə bəl
dissect	di SEKT
dissemble	di SEM bəl
disseminate	di SEM ə NAYT
dissident	DIS ə dənt
dissociate	di SOH shee AYT
dissociation	di SOH shee AY shən
dissoluble	di SOL yə bəl
dissolute	DIS ə LOOT
dissolution	DIS ə LOO shən
dissolve	di ZOLV
dissolvent	di ZOL vənt
dissuade	di SWAYD
dissyllabic	DIS ə LAB ik
distich	DIS tik
distillate	DIS tə lət
distingué	dees tang GAY
distrait	di STRAY
distraught	di STRAWT
dither	DITH ər
dithyramb	DITH i RAM
dithyrambic	DITH i RAM bik
diuresis	DĪ yə REE səs
diuretic	DĪ yə RET ik
diurnal	dī UR nəl
diva	DEE və
divagation	DĪ və GAY shən
divan	di VAN
diverge	də VURJ
divergence	də VUR jəns
divers	DĪ vərz
diverse	də VURS
diversion	də VUR zhən
divert	də VURT
divest	də VEST
divination	DIV ə NAY shən
divot	DIV ət
divulge	də VULJ
Djakarta	jə KAHR tə
Djibouti	jə BOO tee
Djilas, Milovan	JEE lahs, MEE loh vahn

---

o on, oh oat, oi boy, oo soon, oor poor, or for, ow cow, sh shush,
th thin, *th* this, u up, ur spur, uu book, *zh* pleasure

Dlamini, Bhekimpi	lah **MEE** nee, bay **GEEM** pee
Dlamini, Mabandla	lah **MEE** nee, mah **BAHND** lah
Dnepr	**NEE** pər
Dnepropetrovsk	**NYE** praw pye **TRAWFSK**
Dnestr	**NEE** stər
Dnieper	**NEE** pər
Dniester	**NEE** stər
Dobi, Istvan	**DOH** bee, **ISHT** vahn
Dobrynin, Anatoly	doh **BREE** nyin, ah nah **TOH** lee
docent	**DOH** sənt
docile	**DOS** əl
doctrinaire	**DOK** trə **NAIR**
Dodecanese	doh **DEK** ə **NEEZ**
Dodgson	**DOJ** sən
doff	dof
doge	dohj
dogged (a)	**DAW** gəd
dogged (v)	dawgd
doggerel	**DAWG** ə rəl
dogma	**DAWG** mə
Doha	**DOH** hah
Dolby	**DAWL** bee
dolce far niente	**DOHL** chay **FAHR NYEN** tay
dolce vita	**DOHL** chay **VEE** tah
doldrums	**DOHL** drəmz
Dolgikh, Vladimir	dohl **GEEK**, vlah **DEE** meer
dollop	**DOL** əp
dolman	**DOHL** mən
dolmen	**DOHL** mən
dolomite	**DOH** lə **MĪT**
doloroso	**DOH** lə **ROH** soh
dolorous	**DOH** lə rəs
Dolukhanova, Zara	doh loo **KAH** noh vah, **ZAH** rah
Domenici, Pete	də **MEN** ə **CHEE**
Domesday Book	**DOOMZ** day
domicile	**DOM** ə **SĪL**
Dominica	**DOM** ə **NEE** kə
Dominican	də **MIN** i kən
Domrémy	dohn ray **MEE** (dohn French final *n*)
Donatello	**DON** ə **TEL** oh
Donau	**DOH** now
Donegal	**DON** i **GAWL**
Donets	dah **NETS**

ə ago, a at, ah calm, ahr dark, air care, aw saw, ay say, ch church
e bet, ee me, eer beer, hw what, i is, ī my, *n* French final n vin,

Don Giovanni	DON joh VAH nee
Donizetti	DON ə ZET ee
Don Juan (Byron)	don JOO ən
Don Juan (Spanish)	dawn HWAHN
donkey	DONG kee
Donna, d-	DON ə
Donne	dun
Donnybrook	DON ee BRUUK
Don Pasquale	don pah SKWAH lay
Don Quixote (English)	don KWIK sət
Don Quixote (Spanish)	DAWN kee HOH tay
dopa	DOH pə
Doppelgänger, d-	DOP əl GANG ər
doppler, D-	DOP lər
Dorcas	DOR kəs
Doré	daw RAY
Doremus	də REE məs
Dorothea	DOR ə THEE ə
Dórticos	DOR ti kaws
dory	DOR ee
dosimeter	doh SIM ə tər
Dos Passos	dohs PAS ohs
dos Santos, José Eduardo	dohs SAN tohs, ZHUU zay ED wahr doh
dossier	DOS ee AY
Dostoevski	DAWS tə YEF skee
dotage	DOHT ij
dotard	DOHT ərd
doth	duth
Douai, Douay	doo AY
douane	dwahn
double entendre	doo blahn TAHN drə
doublet	DUB lət
doubloon	du BLOON
douceur	doo SUR
douche	doosh
doughty	DOW tee
Doukhobors	DOO kə BORZ
Dountas, Mihalis	THOON təs, mee HAH lis
dour	door (as in *poor*)
Dover	DOH vər
dowager	DOW i jər
dowry	DOW ree

---

o **on**, oh **oat**, oi **boy**, oo **soon**, oor **poor**, or **for**, ow **cow**, sh **shush**,
th **thin**, *th* **this**, u **up**, ur **spur**, uu **book**, *zh* **pleasure**

Dowson	**DOW** sən
doxology	dok **SOL** ə jee
doxy	**DOK** see
doyen	**DOI** ən
D'Oyly Carte	**DOI** lee **KAHRT**
drachm	dram
drachma	**DRAK** mə
Draco	**DRAY** koh
Draconian, d-	dray **KOH** nee ən
draconic, D-	dray **KON** ik
dragoon	drə **GOON**
Dragosavac, Dušan	**DRAH** goh **SAH** vahts, **DOO** shahn
drama	**DRAH** mə
Dramamine	**DRAM** ə **MEEN**
dramatic	drə **MAT** ik
dramatis personae	**DRAM** ə təs pər **SOH** nee
dramatist	**DRAM** ə təst
dramaturgy	**DRAM** ə **TURJ** ee
Drambuie	dram **BOO** ee
Drammen	**DRAH** mən
draught	draft
Drava	**DRA** və
Dravidian	drə **VID** ee ən
Dravidic	drə **VID** ik
Drees	drays
Dreier	**DRĪ** ər
Dreiser	**DRĪ** sər
Dresden	**DREZ** dən
dressage	drə **SAHZ**_H_
Dreyfus	**DRAY** fəs
drivel	**DRIV** əl
drogue	drohg
droll	drohl
drollery	**DROH** lə ree
dromedary	**DROM** ə **DER** ee
Drori, Amir	**DRAW** ree, ah **MEER**
droshky	**DROSH** kee
drought	drowt
drouth	drowth
Drozniak	**DRUZ**_H_ nyak
druid, D-	**DROO** əd
Druse	drooz
Drusilla	droo **SIL** ə

Druze	drooz
dryad, D-	DRĪ əd
dual	DOO əl
dualism	DOO ə LIZ əm
Duarte	DWAHR tay
Dubcek	DUUB chek
dubiety	duu BĪ ə tee
dubious	DOO bee əs
Dublin	DUB lən
Dubois, W.E.B.	doo BOIZ
dubonnet, D-	DOO bə NAY
Dubuque	də BYOOK
ducat	DUK ət
duce, D-	DOO chay
Duchamp, Marcel	doo SHAHN, mahr SEL (SHAHN French final *n*)
duchy	DUCH ee
Duclos	doo KLOH
ductile	DUK təl
dude	dood
dudgeon	DUJ ən
Dudintsev, Vladimir	doo DEENT sef, VLAH də meer
duenna	doo EN ə
duet	doo ET
Dufy, Raoul	doo FEE, rah OOL
Dukakis	də KOK əs
Dukhobors	DOO kə BORZ
dulcet	DUL sət
dulcimer	DUL sə mər
Dulcinea	DUL sə NEE ə
Dulles	DUL əs
Duluth	də LOOTH
duma	DOO mə
Dumas	doo MAH
Du Maurier	də MAW ree ay
Dungeness	dunj nes
Dunkirk	DUN kurk
Dunsany	dun SAY nee
Duns Scotus	DUNZ SKOH təs
duodenal	DOO ə DEEN əl
duodenum	DOO ə DEEN əm
duomo	DWAW moh
Dupas	doo PAH

o on, oh oat, oi boy, oo soon, oor poor, or for, ow cow, sh shush,
th thin, *th* this, u up, ur spur, uu book, *zh* pleasure

Duplessis	duu ple **SEE**
duplicate (a, n)	**DOO** pli kət
duplicate (v)	**DOO** pli **KAYT**
Duquesne	doo **KAYN**
durance	**DUUR** əns
durbar	**DUR** bahr
Durenberger	**DUUR** ən **BURG** ər
Dürer, Albrecht	**DUUR** ər, **AHL** brekt
duress	duu **RES**
Durham	**DUR** əm
during	**DUUR** ing
Durocher	də **ROH** shər
Durrell	**DUUR** əl
Dürrenmatt, Friedrich	**DUUR** ən **MAHT**, **FREE** drish
durum	**DUUR** əm
Dussault, Nancy	**DOO** sawlt, **NAN** see
Düsseldorf	**DUUS** əl **DAWRF**
duteous	**DOO** tee əs
Dutra	**DOO** trə
Duvalier, Jean-Claude	duu **VAHL YAY**, **ZHAWN KLOHD** (**ZHAWN** French final *n*)
duvet	duu **VAY**
Dvina	vi **NAH**
Dvinsk	veensk
Dvořák	**DVAWR** *zh*ahk
Dyak	**DĪ** ak
dybbuk	**DIB** ək
Dylan	**DIL** ən
dynamic	dī **NAM** ik
dynamite	**DĪ** nə **MĪT**
dynamo	**DĪ** nə **MOH**
dynamometer	**DĪ** nə **MOM** ə tər
dynast	**DĪ** nast
dynastic	dī **NAS** tik
dynasty	**DĪ** nəs tee
dynatron	**DĪ** nə **TRON**
dyne	dīn
dysentery	**DIS** ən **TER** ee
dyslexia	dis **LEK** see ə
dyslexic	dis **LEK** sik
dysmenorrhea	**DIS MEN** ə **REE** ə
dyspepsia	dis **PEP** see ə
dysprosium	dis **PROH** zee əm

ə ago, a at, ah calm, ahr dark, air care, aw saw, ay say, ch church
e bet, ee me, eer beer, hw what, i is, ī my, *n* French final n vin,

dystrophy	**DIS** trə fee
Dzhugashvili	**JOO** gəsh **VEE** lee

E

Eakins	**AY** kənz
Eanes, Antonio Ramalho	ee **AHN** es, ahn **TOH** nyoh rah **MAHL** luu
Earhart	**AIR** hahrt
eau	oh
Eban, Abba	**EE** bən, **AH** bə
ebon	**EB** ən
ebony	**EB** ə nee
Ebro	**EE** broh
ebullient	i **BUUL** yənt
ebullition	**EB** ə **LISH** ən
ecce homo	**EK** e **HOH** moh
eccentric	ik **SEN** trik
eccentricity	**EK** sen **TRIS** ə tee
Ecclesiastes	i **KLEE** zee **AS** teez
ecclesiastical	i **KLEE** zee **AS** ti kəl
Ecclesiasticus	i **KLEE** zee **AS** ti kəs
ecdysiast	ek **DIZ** ee **AST**
Ecevit, Bulent	ay jay **VEET**, byoo **LENT**
echelon	**ESH** ə **LON**
Echeverria Alvarez, Luis	**AY** chə və **REE** ə **AHL** vah **REZ**, **LWEES**
echidna	i **KID** nə
echinoderm	i **KĪ** nə **DURM**
echoic	e **KOH** ik
éclair	ay **KLAIR**
éclat	ay **KLAH**
eclectic	i **KLEK** tik
eclecticism	i **KLEK** tə **SIZ** əm
eclipse	i **KLIPS**
ecliptic	i **KLIP** tik
eclogue	**EK** lawg
École des Beaux Arts	ay **KUL** day boh **ZAHR**
ecological	**EK** ə **LOJ** ə kəl
ecology	i **KOL** ə jee
economic	**EE** kə **NOM** ik

o on, oh oat, oi boy, oo soon, oor poor, or for, ow cow, sh shush,
th thin, *th* this, u up, ur spur, uu book, *zh* pleasure

economical	**EE** kə **NOM** i kəl
economics	**EE** kə **NOM** iks
economist	i **KON** ə mist
economy	i **KON** ə mee
ecotype	**EK** ə **TĪP**
ecru	**EK** roo
ecstasy	**EK** stə see
ecstatic	ek **STAT** ik
ectoplasm	**EK** tə **PLAZ** əm
Ecuador	**EK** wə **DOR**
ecumenical	**EK** yə **MEN** i kəl
eczema	**EG** zə mə
Edam	**EED** əm
Edda	**ED** ə
eddy, E-	**ED** ee
edelweiss	**AYD** əl **VĪS**
edema	i **DEE** mə
Eden	**EED** ən
edict	**EE** dikt
edifice	**ED** ə fəs
Edinburg (US)	**ED** ən **BURG**
Edinburgh (Scotland)	**ED** ən **BUR** oh
Edo	**E** doh
Edom	**EE** dəm
educate	**EJ** ə **KAYT**
education	**EJ** ə **KAY** shən
eerie	**EER** ee
effect	i **FEKT**
effectual	i **FEK** choo əl
effeminacy	i **FEM** ə nə see
effeminate	i **FEM** ə nət
effendi	e **FEN** dee
efferent	**EF** ə rənt
effervescent	**EF** ər **VES** ənt
effete	i **FEET**
efficacious	**EF** ə **KAY** shəs
efficacy	**EF** ə kə see
effigy	**EF** ə jee
efflorescence	**EF** lə **RES** əns
effluent	**EF** loo ənt
effrontery	i **FRUN** tə ree
effulgence	i **FUL** jəns
effulgent	i **FUL** jənt

ə ago, a at, ah calm, ahr dark, air care, aw saw, ay say, ch church
e bet, ee me, eer beer, hw what, i is, ī my, *n* French final n vin,

effusion	i **FYOO** *zh*ən
effusive	i **FYOO** siv
Efremov	**E** frə mawf
egad	i **GAD**
Eger	**AY** gər
Egeria	i **JEE** ree ə
eglantine	**EG** lən **TĪN**
ego	**EE** goh
egoism	**EE** goh **IZ** əm
egoist	**EE** goh əst
egotism	**EE** goh **TIZ** əm
egotist	**EE** goh təst
egregious	i **GREE** jəs
egregiously	i **GREE** jəs lee
egress	**EE** gres
egret	**EE** grət
Egypt	**EE** jipt
Egyptian	i **JIP** shən
Egyptology	**EE** jip **TOL** ə jee
Ehrenburg	**AIR** ən **BUURG**
Ehrlich (Germany)	**AIR** lik
Ehrlich (US)	**UR** lik
Eichmann	**ĪK** mahn
eider	**Ī** dər
eidetic	ī **DET** ik
eidolon	ī **DOH** lən
Eiffel	**Ī** fəl
eighth	ayth
Eilat	ay **LAHT**
Einstein	**ĪN** stīn
Eire	**AIR** ə
Eisenstein	**Ī** zen **STĪN**
Eissa, Omer Salih	**EE** sah, oo **MAHR SAH** lee
eisteddfod	ī **STE***TH* vod
either	**EE** thər
ejaculate (v)	i **JAK** yə **LAYT**
ejaculate (n)	i **JAK** yə lət
ejaculation	i **JAK** yə **LAY** shən
eject	i **JEKT**
eke	eek
Eke, Abudu Yesufu	**EE** kay, ah **BOO** doo ye **SOO** foo
ekistics	i **KIS** tiks
elaborate (a)	i **LAB** ə rət

elaborate (v)	i **LAB** ə **RAYT**
Elaine	i **LAYN**
El Al	el al
El Alamein	el **AL** ə **MAYN**
Elamite	**EE** lə **MĪT**
élan	ay **LAHN** (**LAHN** French final *n*)
eland	**EE** lənd
Elath	**EE** lath
Elberfeld	**EL** bər **FELT**
El Dorado, Eldorado	**EL** də **RAH** doh
Eleatic	**EL** ee **AT** ik
Eleazar, Eleazer	**EL** ee **AY** zər
elector	i **LEK** tər
electoral	i **LEK** tə rəl
electorate	i **LEK** tə rət
Electra	i **LEK** trə
electrocardiogram	i **LEK** troh **KAHR** dee ə **GRAM**
electrocute	i **LEK** trə **KYOOT**
electrode	i **LEK** trohd
electrolysis	i lek **TROL** ə səs
electrolyte	i **LEK** trə **LĪT**
electromagnet	i **LEK** troh **MAG** nət
electromagnetic	i **LEK** troh mag **NET** ik
electromotive	i **LEK** trə **MOH** təv
electrostatics	i **LEK** trə **STAT** iks
electrovalent	i **LEK** troh **VAY** lənt
eleemosynary	**EL** ə **MOS** ə **NER** ee
elegance	**EL** ə gəns
elegant	**EL** ə gənt
elegiac	**EL** ə **JĪ** ək
elegize	**EL** ə **JĪZ**
elegy	**EL** ə jee
Elekdag, Sukru	el **EK** dah, **SHUUK** ruu
elephantiasis	**EL** ə fən **TĪ** ə səs
elephantine	**EL** ə **FAN** teen
Eleusinian	**EL** yuu **SIN** ee ən
Eleusis	i **LOO** sis
Eleuthera	ə **LOO** thə rə
El-Fattal, Dia-Allah	el fah **TEL**, dyu **OOL** lah
Elgin	**EL** jən
Elgin (British)	**EL** gən
El Greco	el **GREK** oh
Eli	**EE** lī

ə ago, a at, ah calm, ahr dark, air care, aw saw, ay say, ch church
e bet, ee me, eer beer, hw what, i is, ī my, *n* French final n vin,

Elia	**EE** lee ə
Elias	i **LĪ** əs
elicit	i **LIS** ət
elide	i **LĪD**
eligibility	**EL** ə jə **BIL** ə tee
eligible	**EL** ə jə bəl
Elihu	**EL** ə **HYOO**
Elihu (Bible)	i **LĪ** hyoo
Elijah	i **LĪ** jə
Elisha	i **LĪ** shə
elision	i **LI** *zh*ən
Elisir d'Amore	**AY** lee **ZEER** da **MOH** ray
elite	i **LEET**
elixir	i **LIK** sər
Eliza	i **LĪ** zə
Elizabethan	i **LIZ** ə **BEE** thən
Elizalde	e lee **SAHL** de
Elkanah	el **KAH** nə
el-Kodsi, Nazem	ahl **KOH** tsee, **NAH** zem
Ellice	**EL** is
ellipse	i **LIPS**
ellipses	i **LIP** seez
ellipsis	i **LIP** səs
elliptical	i **LIP** ti kəl
Elmi, Hassan Nur	**EL** mee, **HAH** sən **NOOR**
Elmira	el **MĪ** rə
elocution	**EL** ə **KYOO** shən
Elohim	**E** loh **HEEM**
Elohistic	**E** loh **HIS** tik
elongate	i **LAWNG** gayt
eloquence	**EL** ə kwəns
El Paso	el **PAS** oh
Elsa	**EL** sə
El Salvador	el **SAL** və **DOR**
elsewhere	**ELS** hwair
Elsie	**EL** see
Éluard, Paul	**AY** loo **AHR**, **POHL**
elucidate	i **LOO** sə **DAYT**
elude	i **LOOD**
elusion	i **LOO** *zh*ən
elusive	i **LOO** siv
elusory	i **LOO** sə ree
elves	elvz

---

o **on**, oh **oat**, oi **boy**, oo **soon**, oor **poor**, or **for**, ow **cow**, sh **shush**,
th **thin**, *th* **this**, u **up**, ur **spur**, uu **book**, *zh* **pleasure**

Elvira	el VĪR ə
Ely (given name)	EE lī
Ely (place name)	EE lee
Elysian	i LIZH ən
Elysium	i LIZH ee əm
Elytis, Odysseus	ay LEE tees, oh *th*ee SAY əs
emaciate	i MAY shee AYT
emaciation	i MAY shee AY shən
emanate	EM ə NAYT
emanation	EM ə NAY shən
emasculate (a)	i MAS kyə lət
emasculate (v)	i MAS kyə LAYT
embalm	im BAHM
embarrass	im BA rəs
embezzle	im BEZ əl
emblazon	im BLAY zən
emblematic	EM blə MAT ik
embodiment	im BOD i mənt
embolism	EM bə LIZ əm
embolus	EM bə ləs
emboss	im BAWS
embouchure	AHM buu SHUUR
embrasure	im BRAY *zh*ər
embrocate	EM broh KAYT
embroidery	im BROI də ree
embryo	EM bree OH
embryology	EM bree OL ə jee
embryonic	EM bree ON ik
emendation	EE men DAY shən
emerald	EM ə rəld
emerita	i MER ə tə
emeritus	i MER ə təs
emesis	EM ə səs
emetic	i MET ik
émeute	ay MYOOT
emigrant	EM ə grənt
emigrate	EM ə GRAYT
émigré	EM ə GRAY
Emilio	ay MEE lyoh
emir	ə MEER
emirate	EM ə rət
emissary	EM ə SER ee
emission	ə MISH ən

ə ago, a at, ah calm, ahr dark, air care, aw saw, ay say, ch church
e bet, ee me, eer beer, hw what, i is, ī my, *n* French final n vin,

emissivity	**EM** ə **SIV** ə tee
Emmaus	e **MAY** əs
emollient	i **MOL** yənt
emolument	i **MOL** yə mənt
empathy	**EM** pə thee
emphasis	**EM** fə səs
emphatic	em **FAT** ik
emphysema	**EM** fə **SEE** mə
empiric	em **PIR** ik
empirical	em **PIR** i kəl
empiricism	em **PIR** ə **SIZ** əm
employee	em **PLOI** ee
Emporia	em **POR** ee ə
emporium	em **POR** ee əm
empyrean	**EM** pə **REE** ən
emu	**EE** myoo
emulate	**EM** yə **LAYT**
emulation	**EM** yə **LAY** shən
emulsify	i **MUL** sə **FĪ**
emulsion	i **MUL** shən
enamor	i **NAM** ər
enceinte	ahn **SANT** (ahn French final *n*)
Enceladus	en **SEL** ə dəs
encephalitis	en **SEF** ə **LĪ** tis
encephalograph	en **SEF** ə lə **GRAF**
encephalography	en **SEF** ə **LOG** rə fee
encephalon	en **SEF** ə **LON**
encina	en **SEE** nə
Enckell	**ENG** kel
enclave	**EN** klayv
enclitic	en **KLIT** ik
enclosure	en **KLOH** *zh*ər
encomium	en **KOH** mee əm
encompass	in **KUM** pəs
encore	**AHN** kor
encroach	in **KROHCH**
encumbrance	in **KUM** brəns
encyclical	in **SIK** li kəl
encyclopedia	in **SĪ** klə **PEE** dee ə
encyclopedist	in **SĪ** klə **PEE** dəst
endeavor	in **DEV** ər
endemic	in **DEM** ik
endive	**EN** dīv

---

o **on**, oh **oat**, oi **boy**, oo **soon**, oor **poor**, or **for**, ow **cow**, sh **shush**,
th **thin**, *th* **this**, u **up**, ur **spur**, uu **book**, *zh* **pleasure**

endocrine	**EN** də krən
endocrinology	**EN** də krə **NOL** ə jee
endodontia	**EN** də **DON** shə
endogenous	en **DOJ** ə nəs
Endor	**EN** dor
endorse	in **DORS**
endowment	in **DOW** mənt
endure	in **DOOR** (**DOOR** as in *poor*)
Endymion	en **DIM** ee ən
enervate	**EN** ər **VAYT**
Enesco	e **NES** koh
enfant terrible	ahn **FAHN** te **REE** blə (ahn and **FAHN** French final *n*)
enfilade	**EN** fə **LAYD**
enfranchise	en **FRAN** chīz
enfranchisement	en **FRAN** chīz mənt
engagé	ahn gah **ZHAY** (ahn French final *n*)
Engels	**EN** gəlz
England	**ING** glənd
English	**ING** glish
engram	**EN** gram
engross	in **GROHS**
enhance	in **HANS**
Enid	**EE** nid
enigma	i **NIG** mə
enigmatic	**EN** ig **MAT** ik
Eniwetok	**EN** ə **WEE** tok
enjambment	in **JAM** mənt
enlightenment	in **LĪT** ən mənt
enliven	in **LĪ** vən
en masse	ahn **MAS**
enmity	**EN** mə tee
ennui	ahn wee
Enoch	**EE** nək
enormity	i **NOR** mə tee
Enos	**EE** nəs
enow	i **NOW**
en route	ahn **ROOT**
ensconce	in **SKONS**
ensemble	ahn **SAHM** bəl
ensign	**EN** sən
ensilage	**EN** sə lij
ensue	in **SOO**

ə ago, a at, ah calm, ahr dark, air care, aw saw, ay say, ch church
e bet, ee me, eer beer, hw what, i is, ī my, *n* French final n vin,

entablature	in **TAB** lə chər
Entebbe	en **TEB** ee
entente	ahn **TAHNT**
entente cordiale	ahn **TAHNT** kawr **DYAHL** (ahn and **TAHNT** French final *n*)
enteric	en **TER** ik
Entezam, Nasrollah	en tə **ZAHM**, nahs **ROH** lah
enthalpy	**EN** thal pee
enthrall	in **THRAWL**
enthusiasm	in **THOO** zee **AZ** əm
enthusiast	in **THOO** zee **AST**
enthusiastic	in **THOO** zee **AS** tik
enthymeme	**EN** thə **MEEM**
entirety	in **TĪR** tee
entomb	in **TOOM**
entomology	**EN** tə **MOL** ə jee
entourage	**AHN** tuu **RAHZH**
entr'acte	**AHN** trakt
entrails	**EN** traylz
entrance (n)	**EN** trəns
entrance (v)	in **TRANS**
entrechat	**AHN** trə **SHAH**
entree	**AHN** tray
entremets	**AHN** trə **MAY**
entre nous	**AHN** trə **NOO**
entrepreneur	**AHN** trə prə **NUR**
entresol	**EN** trə **SOL**
entropy	**EN** trə pee
enunciate	i **NUN** see **AYT**
enuresis	**EN** yə **REE** səs
envelop (v)	in **VEL** əp
envelope (n)	**EN** və lohp
enviable	**EN** vee ə bəl
environ	in **VĪ** rən
environment	in **VĪ** rən mənt
environs	in **VĪ** rənz
envisage	in **VIZ** ij
envoy	**EN** voi
enzyme	**EN** zīm
Eocene	**EE** ə **SEEN**
Eolian	ee **OH** lee ən
eon	**EE** ən
eparch	**EP** ahrk

o on, oh oat, oi boy, oo soon, oor poor, or for, ow cow, sh shush, th thin, *th* this, u up, ur spur, uu book, *zh* pleasure

epaulet	**EP** ə **LET**
épée	ay **PAY**
ephedrine	i **FED** rən
ephemeral	i **FEM** ə rəl
Ephesian	i **FEE** *zh*ən
Ephesus	**EF** ə səs
ephor	**EF** ər
Ephraim	**EE** free əm
epicene	**EP** ə **SEEN**
Epictetus	**EP** ik **TEE** təs
epicure	**EP** ə kyuur
epicurean, E-	**EP** i kyuu **REE** ən
Epicurus	**EP** ə **KYUUR** əs
epidemiology	**EP** ə **DEE** mee **OL** ə jee
epidermis	**EP** ə **DUR** məs
epiglottis	**EP** ə **GLOT** əs
epigram	**EP** ə **GRAM**
epilepsy	**EP** ə **LEP** see
epilogue	**EP** ə **LAWG**
epinephrine	**EP** ə **NEF** rən
Epiphany, e-	i **PIF** ə nee
Epirus	i **PĪ** rəs
episcopacy	i **PIS** kə pə see
episcopal, E-	i **PIS** kə pəl
episcopate	i **PIS** kə pət
episodic	**EP** ə **SOD** ik
epistemology	i **PIS** tə **MOL** ə jee
epistle, E-	i **PIS** əl
epistolary	i **PIS** tə **LER** ee
epitaph	**EP** ə **TAF**
epithelium	**EP** ə **THEE** lee əm
epithet	**EP** ə **THET**
epitome	i **PIT** ə mee
epizootic	**EP** ə zoh **OT** ik
e pluribus unum	e **PLOO** rə bəs **OO** nəm
epoch	**EP** ək
epochal	**EP** ə kəl
epode	**EP** ohd
eponym	**EP** ə nim
eponymous	ə **PON** ə məs
epopee	**EP** ə **PEE**
epos	**EP** os
epoxy	e **POK** see

ə ago, a at, ah calm, ahr dark, air care, aw saw, ay say, ch church
e bet, ee me, eer beer, hw what, i is, ī my, *n* French final n vin,

epsilon	**EP** sə **LON**
Epsom	**EP** səm
equability	**EK** wə **BIL** ə tee
equable	**EK** wə bəl
equality	i **KWOL** ə tee
equalization	**EE** kwə lə **ZAY** shən
equanimity	**EE** kwə **NIM** ə tee
equate	i **KWAYT**
equator	i **KWAY** tər
equatorial	**EE** kwə **TOR** ee əl
equerry	**EK** wə ree
equestrian	i **KWES** tree ən
equestrienne	i **KWES** tree **EN**
equidistant	**EE** kwə **DIS** tənt
equilateral	**EE** kwə **LAT** ər əl
equilibrium	**EE** kwə **LIB** ree əm
equine	**EE** kwīn
equinoctial	**EE** kwə **NOK** shəl
equinox	**EE** kwə **NOKS**
equipage	**EK** wə pij
equipoise	**EK** wə **POIZ**
equipotential	**EE** kwə pə **TEN** shəl
equitable	**EK** wə tə bəl
equity	**EK** wə tee
equivalent	i **KWIV** ə lənt
equivocal	i **KWIV** ə kəl
equivocate	i **KWIV** ə **KAYT**
equivocation	i **KWIV** ə **KAY** shən
Equuleus	i **KWOO** lee əs
era	**EER** ə
Erasmus	i **RAZ** məs
erasure	i **RAY** shər
Erato	**ER** ə **TOH**
Eratosthenes	**ER** ə **TOS** thə **NEEZ**
erbium	**UR** bee əm
Erdreich	**AIRD** rīsh
ere	air
Erebus	**E** rə bəs
Erechtheum	i **REK** thee əm
Erechtheus	i **REK** thee əs
erectile	i **REK** təl
Erede, Alberto	e **RAY** day, ahl **BER** toh
eremite	**ER** ə **MĪT**

o **on**, oh **oat**, oi **boy**, oo **soon**, oor **poor**, or **for**, ow **cow**, sh **shush**,
th **thin**, *th* **this**, u **up**, ur **spur**, uu **book**, *zh* **pleasure**

Erewhon	**ER** ə hwən
Erfurt	**AIR** fuurt
erg	urg
ergo	**ER** goh
ergosterol	ur **GOS** tə **ROHL**
ergot	**UR** gət
Erhard, Ludwig	**AIR** hahrt, **LUUT** vig
Eric	**ER** ik
Eridanus	i **RID** ən əs
Erie	**IR** ee
Erin	**ER** in
eristic	i **RIS** tik
Eritrea	**ER** i **TREE** ə
Erlander, Tage	er **LAHN** dair, **TAH** gi
erlking	**URL** king
ermine	**UR** mən
Ernani	air **NAH** nee
erogenous	i **ROJ** ə nəs
Eros, e-	**ER** ahs
e-erosion	i **ROH** *zh*ən
erosive	i **ROH** siv
erotic	i **ROT** ik
err	er
errand	**ER** ənd
errant	**ER** ənt
errata	e **RAH** tə
erratic	i **RAT** ik
erratum	e **RAH** təm
erroneous	i **ROH** nee əs
ersatz	**AIR** zahts
Erse	urs
Érsekújvár	**AYR** she **KOO** i **VAHR**
Erskine	**UR** skin
erudite	**ER** yə **DĪT**
Ervin	**UR** vin
Ervine	**UR** vīn
erysipelas	**ER** ə **SIP** ə ləs
erythematosus	**ER** ə **THEE** mə **TOH** səs
erythrocyte	i **RITH** rə **SĪT**
Esau	**EE** saw
escadrille	**ES** kə **DRIL**
escalator	**ES** kə **LAY** tər
escallop	i **SKOL** əp

ə ago, a at, ah calm, ahr dark, air care, aw saw, ay say, ch **church**
e bet, ee me, eer beer, hw what, i is, ī my, *n* French final n vin,

escapade	ES kə **PAYD**
escargot	es kahr **GOH**
escargots	es kahr **GOH**
escarole	ES kə **ROHL**
escarpment	e **SKAHRP** mənt
eschatology	ES kə **TOL** ə jee
escheat	es **CHEET**
eschew	es **CHOO**
Escorial	e **SKOR** ee əl
escort (n)	ES kort
escort (v)	es **KORT**
escritoire	ES krə **TWAHR**
escrow	ES kroh
escudo	e **SKOO** doh
Escurial	e **SKYUUR** ee əl
escutcheon	e **SKUCH** ən
Esdraelon	ES drə **EE** lən
Esdras	EZ drəs
Eshkol, Levi	ESH kawl, **LAY** vee
Eshowe	ESH ə **WAY**
Esmeralda	EZ mə **RAL** də
esophagus	i **SOF** ə gəs
esoteric	ES ə **TER** ik
espalier	i **SPAL** yay
especial	i **SPESH** əl
Esperanto	ES pə **RAHN** toh
espionage	ES pee ə **NAHZH**
Espíritu Santo (Brazil)	ə **SPIR** ə **TOO SAN** too
Espíritu Santo (New Hebrides)	ə **SPIR** ə **TOO SAN** toh
esplanade	ES plə **NAHD**
espousal	i **SPOW** zəl
espouse	i **SPOWZ**
espresso	e **SPRES** oh
Espriella, Ricardo de la	ES pree **AY** yə, ree **KAHR** doh day lah
esprit	es **PREE**
esprit de corps	es **PREE** də **KOR**
esquire, E-	ES kwīr
essay (n)	ES ay
essay (v)	e **SAY**
essayist	ES ay əst
Essegian	ə **SEE** jən

---

o **on**, oh **oat**, oi **boy**, oo **soon**, oor **poor**, or **for**, ow **cow**, sh **shush**,
th **thin**, *th* **this**, u **up**, ur **spur**, uu **book**, *zh* **pleasure**

Essen	ES ən
Essene	i SEEN
Essequibo	ES ə KWEE boh
Essex	ES iks
Essy, Amara	AY see, ah MAHR ə
Este	ES te
Esther	ES tər
esthete	ES theet
estimate (n)	ES tə mət
estimate (v)	ES tə MAYT
Estonia	e STOH nee ə
estovers	e STOH vərz
estrange	e STRAYNJ
Estremadura	ES tre mah THOO rah
estrogen	ES trə jən
estrogenic	ES trə JEN ik
estrone	ES trohn
estrus	ES trəs
estuary	ES choo ER ee
eta	AY tə
étagère	ay tah ZHAIR
Étaples	ay TAH plə
et cetera	et SET ə rə
Eteocles	i TEE ə KLEEZ
Ethan	EE thən
ethanol	ETH ə NAWL
ether	EE thər
ethereal	i THEER ee əl
Ethiopia	EE thee OH pee ə
Ethiopian	EE thee OH pee ən
ethnic	ETH nik
ethnicity	eth NIS ə tee
ethnocentric	ETH noh SEN trik
ethnology	eth NOL ə jee
ethos	EE thos
ethylene	ETH ə LEEN
etiolate	EE tee ə LAYT
etiology	EE tee OL ə jee
etiquette	ET i kət
Etna	ET nə
Eton	EET ən
Etruria	i TRUUR ee ə
Etrurian	i TRUUR ee ən

ə ago, a at, ah calm, ahr dark, air care, aw saw, ay say, ch church
e bet, ee me, eer beer, hw what, i is, ī my, n French final n vin,

Etruscan	i **TRUS** kən
et tu, Brute	et **TOO BROO** te
étude	**AY** tood
etui	ay **TWEE**
etymology	**ET** ə **MOL** ə jee
Euboea	yoo **BEE** ə
eucalyptus	**YOO** kə **LIP** təs
Eucharist	**YOO** kə rəst
euchre	**YOO** kər
Euclid	**YOO** kləd
Euclidean	yuu **KLID** ee ən
Eugene Onegin	yoo **JEEN** oh **NAY** gin
eugenic	yuu **JEN** ik
Euler, Ulf von	**OY** lər, **UULF** fawn
eulogia	yuu **LOH** jee ə
eulogium	yuu **LOH** jee əm
eulogy	**YOO** lə jee
Eumenides	yoo **MEN** ə **DEEZ**
Eunice	**YOO** nis
Eunomia	yoo **NOH** mee ə
eunuch	**YOO** nək
euphemism	**YOO** fə **MIZ** əm
euphonious	yuu **FOH** nee əs
euphony	**YOO** fə nee
euphorbia	yuu **FOR** bee ə
euphoria	yuu **FOR** ee ə
Euphrates	yoo **FRAY** teez
Euphrosyne	yoo **FROS** ə **NEE**
euphuism	**YOO** fyoo **IZ** əm
Eurasia	yuu **RAY** *zh*ə
Euratom	yuu **RAT** əm
eureka	yuu **REE** kə
eurhythmic	yuu **RI***TH* mik
Euripides	yuu **RIP** ə **DEEZ**
Euroclydon	yuu **ROK** li **DON**
Eurodollar	**YUUR** oh **DOL** ər
Europa	yuu **ROH** pə
Europe	**YUUR** əp
European	**YUUR** ə **PEE** ən
Eurydice	yuu **RID** ə **SEE**
Eurystheus	yuu **RIS** thee əs
eurythmic	yuu **RI***TH* mik
Eustace	**YOOS** təs

o on, oh oat, oi boy, oo soon, oor poor, or for, ow cow, sh shush,
th thin, *th* this, u up, ur spur, uu book, *zh* pleasure

Eustachian	yuu **STAY** shən
eutectic	yuu **TEK** tik
Euterpe	yoo **TUR** pee
euthanasia	**YOO** thə **NAY** _zh_ə
eutrophic	yuu **TROH** fik
eutrophy	**YOO** trə fee
evanescent	**EV** ə **NES** ənt
evangelical	**EE** van **JEL** i kəl
Evangeline (name)	i **VAN** jə **LEEN**
Evangeline (poem)	i **VAN** jə lin
evangelism	i **VAN** jə **LIZ** əm
evasion	i **VAY** _zh_ən
evasive	i **VAY** siv
Eve	eev
evening (n)	**EEV** ning
evening (v)	**EE** vən ing
eventual	i **VEN** choo əl
evidential	**EV** ə **DEN** shəl
evidently	**EV** ə dənt lee
evince	i **VINS**
eviscerate	i **VIS** ə **RAYT**
evocative	i **VOK** ə tiv
evolution	**EV** ə **LOO** shən
evolve	i **VOLV**
Evren, Kenan	**EV** ren, ke **NAHN**
ewe	yoo
Ewell	**YOO** əl
ewer	**YOO** ər
Ewing	**YOO** ing
exacerbate	ig **ZAS** ər **BAYT**
exactitude	ig **ZAK** tə **TOOD**
exaggerate	ig **ZAJ** ə **RAYT**
exalt	ig **ZAWLT**
exarch	**EK** sahrk
exasperate	ig **ZAS** pə **RAYT**
Excalibur	ek **SKAL** ə bər
ex cathedra	**EKS** kə **THEE** drə
excellency, E-	**EK** sə lən see
excelsior	ik **SEL** see ər
excerpt (n)	**EK** surpt
excerpt (v)	ek **SURPT**
excess (a)	**EK** ses
excess (n)	ik **SES**

ə ago, a at, ah calm, ahr dark, air care, aw saw, ay say, ch church
e bet, ee me, eer beer, hw what, i is, ī my, _n_ French final n vin,

exchequer, E-	**EKS CHEK** ər
excise (n)	**EK** sīz
excise (v)	ik **SĪZ**
excitant	ik **SĪT** ənt
excitatory	ik **SĪ** tə **TOR** ee
exclamation	**EKS** klə **MAY** shən
exclamatory	iks **KLAM** ə **TOR** ee
exclusive	iks **KLOO** siv
excommunicate	**EKS** kə **MYOO** nə **KAYT**
excoriate	ek **SKOR** ee **AYT**
excrement	**EK** skrə mənt
excrescence	ik **SKRES** əns
excretive	ik **SKREE** tiv
excretory	**EK** skrə **TOR** ee
excruciate	ik **SKROO** shee **AYT**
exculpate	**EK** skul **PAYT**
excursion	ik **SKUR** zhən
excusatory	ik **SKYOO** zə **TOR** ee
execrable	**EK** si crə bəl
executant	ig **ZEK** yə tənt
executive	ig **ZEK** yə tiv
executor (performer)	**EK** sə **KYOO** tər
executor (of a will)	ig **ZEK** yə tər
executrix	ig **ZEK** yə triks
exegesis	**EK** sə **JEE** səs
exegete	**EK** sə **JEET**
exemplar	ig **ZEM** plər
exemplary	ig **ZEM** plə ree
exemplify	ig **ZEM** plə **FĪ**
exempli gratia	ig **ZEM** plee **GRAH** tee **AH**
exempt	ig **ZEMPT**
exequies	**EK** sə kweez
exertion	ig **ZUR** shən
exeunt	**EK** see ənt
exeunt omnes	**EK** see ənt **OM** neez
exfoliate	eks **FOH** lee **AYT**
exhalation	**EKS** hə **LAY** shən
exhilarate	ig **ZIL** ə **RAYT**
exhort	ig **ZORT**
exhortation	**EG** zor **TAY** shən
exhortative	ig **ZOR** tə tiv
exhume	ig **ZOOM**
exigence	**EK** sə jəns

o **on**, oh **oat**, oi **boy**, oo **soon**, oor **poor**, or **for**, ow **cow**, sh **shush**,
th **thin**, *th* **this**, u **up**, ur **spur**, uu **book**, *zh* **pleasure**

exigency	**EK** sə jən see
exigent	**EK** sə jənt
exiguous	ig **ZI** gyoo əs
exile	**EG** zīl
existential	ᴇɢ zis **TEN** shəl
existentialism, E-	ᴇɢ zis **TEN** shə ʟɪᴢ əm
existentialist, E-	ᴇɢ zis **TEN** shə ləst
ex libris	eks **LEE** brəs
exodus, E-	**EK** sə dəs
ex officio	eks ə **FISH** ee **ᴏʜ**
exonerate	ig **ZON** ə **ʀᴀʏᴛ**
exophthalmic	**EK** sof **THAL** mik
exorable	**EK** sər ə bəl
exorbitance	ig **ZOR** bə təns
exorbitant	ig **ZOR** bə tənt
exorcise	**EK** sor **sīz**
exorcism	**EK** sor **sɪᴢ** əm
exorcist	**EK** sor **sɪsᴛ**
exorcize	**EK** sor **sīz**
exordium	ig **ZOR** dee əm
exosphere	**EK** sə **sғᴇᴇʀ**
exoteric	**EK** sə **TER** ik
exotic	ig **ZOT** ik
ex parte	eks **PAHR** tee
expatiate	ek **SPAY** shee **ᴀʏᴛ**
expatriate (a, n)	ek **SPAY** tree ət
expatriate (v)	eks **PAY** tree **ᴀʏᴛ**
expectorant	ik **SPEK** tə rənt
expectorate	ik **SPEK** tə **ʀᴀʏᴛ**
expedient	ik **SPEE** dee ənt
expedite	**EK** spə **ᴅīᴛ**
expenditure	ik **SPEN** di chər
experiential	ik **sᴘᴇᴇʀ** ee **EN** chəl
experiment	ik **SPER** ə mənt
expert	**EK** spurt
expiable	**EK** spee ə bəl
expiate	**EK** spee **ᴀʏᴛ**
expiation	**EK** spee **AY** shən
expiatory	**EK** spee ə **ᴛᴏʀ** ee
expiration	**EK** spə **RAY** shən
expiratory	ik **SPĪR** ə **ᴛᴏʀ** ee
expire	ik **SPĪR**
explanatory	ik **SPLAN** ə **ᴛᴏʀ** ee

ə ago, a at, ah calm, ahr dark, air care, aw saw, ay say, ch church
e bet, ee me, eer beer, hw what, i is, ī my, *n* French final n vin,

expletive	**EK** splə tiv
explicable	**EK** splə kə bəl
explicative	**EK** splə **KAY** tiv
explicit	ik **SPLIS** ət
exploit (n)	**EK** sploit
exploit (v)	ik **SPLOIT**
exploratory	ik **SPLOR** ə **TOR** ee
exponent	ik **SPOH** nənt
exponential	**EK** spə **NEN** shəl
export (n)	**EK** sport
export (v)	ik **SPORT**
expose	ik **SPOHZ**
exposé	**EK** spoh **ZAY**
exposition	**EK** spə **ZISH** ən
expository	ik **SPOZ** ə **TOR** ee
ex post facto	**EKS POHST FAK** toh
expostulate	ik **SPOS** chə **LAYT**
expropriate	eks **PROH** pree **AYT**
expulsion	ik **SPUL** shən
expunge	ik **SPUNJ**
expurgate	**EK** spər **GAYT**
exquisite	**EKS** kwiz it
extant	**EK** stənt
extemporaneous	ek **STEM** pə **RAY** nee əs
extempore	ik **STEM** pə **REE**
extensor	ik **STEN** sər
extenuate	ik **STEN** yoo **AYT**
extinct	ik **STINGKT**
extirpate	**EK** stər **PAYT**
extol	ik **STOHL**
extortion	ik **STOR** shən
extract (n)	**EK** strakt
extract (v)	ik **STRAKT**
extradite	**EK** strə **DĪT**
extradition	**EK** strə **DISH** ən
extrados	**EK** strə **DOS**
extramural	**EK** strə **MYUUR** əl
extraneous	ek **STRAY** nee əs
extraordinary	ik **STROR** də **NER** ee
extrapolate	ik **STRAP** ə **LAYT**
extrasensory	**EK** strə **SEN** sə ree
extravagance	ik **STRAV** ə gəns
extravagancy	ik **STRAV** ə gən see

extravaganza	ik STRAV ə GAN zə
extraversion	EK strə VUR zhən
extravert	EK strə VURT
extremity	ik STREM ə tee
extricate	EK strə KAYT
extrinsic	ek STRIN zik
extroversion	EK strə VUR zhən
extrovert	EK strə VURT
extrude	ik STROOD
exuberance	ig ZOO bər əns
exuberant	ig ZOO bə rənt
exude	ig ZOOD
exult	ig ZULT
exultation	EG zəl TAY shən
exurb	EK surb
Eyadéma, Gnassingbé	ay YAH day mah, gah SING bee
Eyck, van	ĪK, van
eyre, E-	air
eyrie	AIR ee
Eyskens, Gaston	AY skinz, gah STOHN
Eytan, Rafael	ay TAHN, RE fah el
Ezekiel	ə ZEE kyəl
Ezra	EZ rə

F

Faber	FAY bər
Fabian	FAY bee ən
Fabiani	fah bee AH nee
Fabianism	FAY bee ə NI zəm
Fabiola	fah bee OH lah
Fabius	FAY bee əs
fabliau	FAB lee OH
Fabre	FA brə
fabricate	FAB ri KAYT
fabulist	FAB yə ləst
fabulous	FAB yə ləs
facade	fə SAHD
facet	FAS ət
facetious	fə SEE shəs
facia	FAYSH ə

ə ago, a at, ah calm, ahr dark, air care, aw saw, ay say, ch church
e bet, ee me, eer beer, hw what, i is, ī my, n French final n vin,

facial	**FAY** shəl
facile	**FAS** əl
facilitate	fə **SIL** ə **TAYT**
facility	fə **SIL** ə tee
Facio, Gonzalo	fah **SEE** oh, gohn **ZAH** loh
facsimile	fak **SIM** ə lee
factious	**FAK** shəs
factitious	fak **TISH** əs
factor	**FAK** tər
factotum	fak **TOHT** əm
factual	**FAK** choo əl
faculty	**FAK** əl tee
Fadh ibn Abdul Aziz	**FED** ə **IB** ən **AHB** duul ah **ZEEZ** el
al Saud	**SOWD**
Faeroe	**FAIR** oh
Fafnir	**FAHV** nir
Fagin	**FAY** gən
fagot	**FAG** ət
Fahrenheit	**FA** rən **HĪT**
faience	fay **AHNS**
Faisal	**FĪ** səl
fait accompli	**FAYT** ə **KOM PLEE**
Faiyum	fi **YOOM**
faker	**FAY** kər
fakir	fə **KIR**
Falangist	fə **LAN** jəst
Falasha	fə **LAHSH** ə
falcate	**FAL** kayt
falcon	**FAL** kən
falconer	**FAL** kə nər
falconry	**FAL** kən ree
falderal	**FAL** də **RAL**
falderol	**FAL** də **ROL**
Falkland	**FAWK** lənd
fallacious	fə **LAY** shəs
fallacy	**FAL** ə see
Fälldin	**FEL** din
fallible	**FAL** ə bəl
Fallopian	fə **LOH** pee ən
fallow	**FAL** oh
falsetto	fawl **SET** oh
falsify	**FAWL** sə **FĪ**
Falstaff	**FAWL** staf

o **on**, oh **oat**, oi **boy**, oo **soon**, oor **poor**, or **for**, ow **cow**, sh **shush**,
th **thin**, *th* **this**, u **up**, ur **spur**, uu **book**, *zh* **pleasure**

familiarity	fə MIL YA rə tee
familiarize	fə MIL yə RĪZ
famine	FAM ən
fanatic	fə NAT ik
fanaticism	fə NAT ə SIZ əm
fancier	FAN see ər
fancy	FAN see
fandango	fan DANG goh
Faneuil	FAN yəl
Fanfani, Amintore	fahn FAH nee, ah MIN taw re
fanfare	FAN fair
fanfaronade	FAN fə rə NAYD
Fang Yi	fahng yee
fantasy	FAN tə see
farad	FA rəd
faraday, F-	FA rə day
Farah	fə RAH
farandole	FA rən DOHL
farce	fahrs
farina	fə REE nə
faro	FAIR oh
Faroe	FAIR oh
farrago	fə RAH goh
Farragut	FA rə gət
Farrah	FA rə
Farrar	fə RAHR
farrier	FA ree ər
farrow	FA roh
Farsi	FAHR see
farthing	FAHR *th*ing
farthingale	FAHR *th*ən GAYL
Fascell	fay SEL
fasces	FAS eez
fascicle	FAS i kəl
fascinate	FAS ə NAYT
fascism, F-	FASH IZ əm
fascist	FASH əst
Fascisti	fah SHEE stee
Fassi, Allal El	FAH see, ah LAHL el
fasten	FAS ən
fastidious	fa STID ee əs
fatal	FAY təl
fata morgana	FAH tə mor GAH nə

ə ago, a at, ah calm, ahr dark, air care, aw saw, ay say, ch church
e bet, ee me, eer beer, hw what, i is, ī my, *n* French final n vin,

fathom	**FA***TH* əm
fatigue	fə **TEEG**
Fatima	**FA** tə mə
fatuity	fə **TOO** ə tee
fatuous	**FACH** oo əs
faucet	**FAW** sit
Faulkner	**FAWK** nər
fault	fawlt
faun	fawn
fauna	**FAW** nə
Faure	fohr
Fauré	foh **RAY**
Faust	fowst
Faustus	**FOW** stəs
faute de mieux	foht də **MYUU**
fauve, F-	fohv
Fauvist	**FOH** vəst
faux pas	foh **PAH**
favor	**FAY** vər
favorite	**FAY** və rət
Fawkes	fawks
Faya-Largeau	**FĪ** yah lahr **ZHOO**
fealty	**FEE** əl tee
feasible	**FEE** zə bəl
feature	**FEE** chər
febrile	**FEB** rīl
February	**FEB** roo **ER** ee
fecal	**FEE** kəl
feces	**FEE** seez
fecund	**FEE** kənd
fecundity	fi **KUN** də tee
fedayeen	fe dah **YEEN**
federal, F-	**FED** ə rəl
federalist, F-	**FED** ə rə ləst
federation	**FED** ə **RAY** shən
fedora	fi **DOR** ə
Fedorchuk, Vitaly	fee dohr **CHOOK**, vee **TAH** lee
Fedorenko, Nikolai	fe daw **RENG** koh, nee koh **LĪ**
feign	fayn
Feikema, Feike	**FĪ** kə mə, **FĪ** ki
Fekini, Mohieddine	fe **KEE** nee, moh hye **DEEN**
Felice	fə **LEES**
felicitous	fi **LIS** ə təs

---

o on, oh oat, oi boy, oo soon, oor poor, or for, ow cow, sh shush,
th thin, *th* this, u up, ur spur, uu book, *zh* pleasure

felicity	fi **LIS** ə tee
feline	**FEE** līn
Felix	**FEE** liks
fellah	**FEL** ə
fellatio	fə **LAY** shee OH
felon	**FEL** ən
felonious	fə **LOH** nee əs
felony	**FEL** ə nee
felucca	fə **LOO** kə
feminine	**FEM** ə nən
femininity	FEM ə **NIN** ə tee
feminism	**FEM** ə NIZ əm
femme fatale	FEM fə **TAL**
femoral	**FEM** ə rəl
femur	**FEE** mər
Fénelon	fay nə **LAWN** (**LAWN** French final *n*)
fenestration	FEN ə **STRAY** shən
Fenian	**FEE** nee ən
fennel	**FEN** əl
Fenoaltea, Sergio	fe noh **AHL** tay ah, **SAIR** jee oh
feoff	fef
feral	**FEER** əl
fer de lance	FER də **LANS**
ferment (n)	**FUR** ment
ferment (v)	fər **MENT**
Fermi	**FER** mee
fermium	**FER** mee əm
Fernandes	fair **NAHN** des
Fernandez	fer **NAN** diz
Fernós-Isern	fayr **NOHS EE** sern
ferocious	fə **ROH** shəs
ferocity	fə **ROS** ə tee
Ferrara	fə **RAHR** ə
Ferrer	fə **RAIR**
ferret	**FER** ət
ferrous	**FER** əs
ferrule	**FER** əl
ferry	**FER** ee
fertile	**FUR** təl
ferule	**FER** əl
fervent	**FUR** vənt
fervid	**FUR** vəd
fervor	**FUR** vər

ə ago, a at, ah calm, ahr dark, air care, aw saw, ay say, ch church
e bet, ee me, eer beer, hw what, i is, ī my, *n* French final n vin,

Fescennine	FES ə NĪN
fescue	FES kyoo
festoon	fe STOON
festschrift	FEST shrift
Festung	FES tuung
Festus	FES təs
fetal	FEE təl
fete	fayt
fête champêtre	fet shahn PE trə (shahn French final *n*)
fetid	FET əd
fetish	FET ish
fetor	FEE tər
fettuccine Alfredo	FET ə CHEE nee al FRAYD oh
fetus	FEE təs
feud	fyood
feudal	FYOO dəl
fever	FEE vər
fey	fay
fez, F-	fez
Ffrangcon-Davies	FRANG kən DAY veez
fiacre	fee AH krə
fiancé, fiancée	FEE ahn SAY
Fianna Fail	FEE ə nə FOIL
fiasco	fee AS koh
fiat	FEE at
fibrillate	FIB rəl AYT
fibrin	FĪ brən
fibrosis	fi BROH səs
fibula	FIB yə lə
fiche	feesh
Fichte	FIK tə
fichu	FISH oo
fictitious	fik TISH əs
Fidel	fə DEL
Fidelio	fi DAYL yoh
fidelity	fi DEL ə tee
fiducial	fi DOO shəl
fiduciary	fi DOO shee ER ee
fief	feef
fiery	FĪ ə ree
Fiesole	FYE zaw le
fiesta	fee ES tə
fife	fif

o on, oh oat, oi boy, oo soon, oor poor, or for, ow cow, sh shush,
th thin, *th* this, u up, ur spur, uu book, *zh* pleasure

figment	**FIG** mənt
Figueiredo, João Baptista	**FEE** ger **AY** doo **ZH**WOWN ba **TEESH** tə
figurative	**FIG** yə rə tiv
figurine	**FIG** yə **REEN**
Fiji	**FEE** jee
Fijian	**FEE** jee ən
filament	**FIL** ə mənt
filariasis	**FIL** ə **RĪ** ə səs
filbert	**FIL** bərt
filch	filch
filet	fi **LAY**
filial	**FIL** ee əl
filibuster	**FIL** ə **BUS** tər
filigree	**FIL** ə **GREE**
Filipino	**FIL** ə **PEE** noh
fille de joie	**FEE** də **ZH**WAH
fillet (band)	**FIL** it
fillet (slice)	fi **LAY**
fillip	**FIL** əp
fils	fees
finagle	fə **NAY** gəl
finale	fə **NAL** ee
finalist	**FĪ** nə ləst
finality	fi **NAL** ə tee
finance	fə **NANS**
financier	**FIN** ən **SEER**
fin de siècle	fan də **SYE** klə (fan French final *n*)
fines herbes	**FEEN ERB**
finis	**FIN** əs
Finisterre	**FIN** i **STAIR**
finite	**FĪ** nīt
Finland	**FIN** lənd
Finlandia	fin **LAN** dee ə
finnan haddie	**FIN** ən **HAD** ee
Finnbogadottir	**FIN BOH** gə **DAWT** ər
Finno-	**FIN** oh
Finsteraarhorn	**FIN** stər **AHR** horn
Fiona	fee **OH** nə
fiord	fyord
Fiorello	**FEE** ə **REL** oh
Firenze	fee **REND** ze
firing	**FĪR** ing

ə ago, a at, ah calm, ahr dark, air care, aw saw, ay say, ch church
e bet, ee me, eer beer, hw what, i is, ī my, *n* French final n vin,

firkin	**FUR** kən
firth	furth
fiscal	**FIS** kəl
Fischer-Dieskau	**FISH** ər **DEE** skow
fission	**FISH** ən
fissionable	**FISH** ə nə bəl
fissure	**FISH** ər
fistula	**FIS** chə lə
Fiume	**FYOO** me
fjord	fyord
flabellum	flə **BEL** əm
flaccid	**FLAK** sid
flagellant	**FLAJ** ə lənt
flagellate (v)	**FLAJ** ə **LAYT**
flagellate (n, a)	**FLAJ** ə lət
flagellum	flə **JEL** əm
flageolet	**FLAJ** ə **LET**
flagitious	flə **JISH** əs
flagon	**FLAG** ən
flagrant	**FLAY** grənt
Flagstad	**FLAG** stad
flambé	flahm **BAY**
flambeau	**FLAM** boh
flamboyant	flam **BOI** ənt
flamenco	flə **MENG** koh
flamingo	flə **MING** goh
Flanagan	**FLAN** ə gən
flaneur	flah **NUR**
flange	flanj
flatulence	**FLACH** ə ləns
flatus	**FLAY** təs
Flaubert	floh **BAIR**
flaunt	flawnt
flautist	**FLOWT** əst
flavor	**FLAY** vər
fleur-de-lis (sing)	**FLUR** də **LEE**
fleurs-de-lis (pl)	**FLUR** də **LEE**
flexion	**FLEK** shən
Flexner	**FLEKS** nər
flexure	**FLEK** shər
flibbertigibbet	**FLIB** ər tee **JIB** ət
Fliegende Holländer, der	**FLEE** gen də **HOH** layn dair, dair

---

o **on**, oh **oat**, oi **boy**, oo **soon**, oor **poor**, or **for**, ow **cow**, sh **shush**,
th **thin**, *th* **this**, u **up**, ur **spur**, uu **book**, *zh* **pleasure**

flier	FLĪ ər
flimsy	FLIM zee
flippancy	FLIP ən see
flippant	FLIP ənt
flirtatious	flər TAY shəs
flitch	flich
floe	floh
floozy	FLOO zee
Flora, f-	FLOR ə
floral	FLOR əl
Florence	FLOR əns
Florentine	FLOR ən TEEN
Flores	FLAW res
Flores Avendaño, Guillermo	FLAW res ah ben *TH*AH nyoh, gee LYAIR moh
florescence	flor RES əns
florid	FLOR id
Florida	FLOR ə də
Floridian	flə RID ee ən
florin	FLOR ən
Florio	FLOR ee oh
florist	FLOR əst
flotation	floh TAY shən
flotilla	floh TIL ə
Flotow	FLOH toh
flotsam	FLOT səm
flounce	flowns
flourish	FLUR ish
flout	flowt
fluctuate	FLUK choo AYT
fluctuation	FLUK choo AY shən
flue	floo
fluent	FLOO ənt
fluke	flook
flume	floom
flummery	FLUM ə ree
fluorescent	FLOO ə RES ənt
fluoridate	FLUUR ə DAYT
fluoride	FLUUR ĪD
fluoridize	FLUUR ə DĪZ
fluorine	FLUUR EEN
fluoroscope	FLUUR ə SKOHP
fluoroscopy	fluu ROS kə pee

ə ago, a at, ah calm, ahr dark, air care, aw saw, ay say, ch church
e bet, ee me, eer beer, hw what, i is, ī my, *n* French final n vin,

flurry	**FLUR** ee
flute	floot
flutist	**FLOO** təst
fluvial	**FLOO** vee əl
flux	fluks
fluxion	**FLUK** shən
focal	**FOH** kəl
Foch	fawsh
focus	**FOH** kəs
Fogg	fog
fogy	**FOH** gee
foible	**FOI** bəl
foie gras	fwah **GRAH**
foist	foist
Fokine	foh **KEEN**
Fokker	**FOK** ər
folderol	**FOL** də **ROL**
foliage	**FOH** lee ij
foliation	**FOH** lee **AY** shən
Folies Bergères	foh **LEE** bair **ZH**AIR
folk	fohk
folklore	**FOHK** lor
follicle	**FOL** i kəl
foment	foh **MENT**
fomentation	**FOH** men **TAY** shən
fondant	**FON** dənt
fondue	fon **DOO**
Fonseka, Ignatius	fon **SAY** kə
Fontainebleau	**FONT** ən **BLOH**
fontanel	**FON** tə **NEL**
Fonteyn	fon **TAYN**
foolscap	**FOOLZ** kap
forage	**FOR** ij
forbad, forbade	fər **BAD**
forbear (n)	**FOR** bair
forbear (v)	for **BAIR**
force majeure	fawrs ma **ZH**UR
forcemeat	**FORS** meet
forceps	**FOR** səps
forebear	**FOR** bair
forecastle	**FOHK** səl
forehead	**FOR** əd
foreign	**FOR** ən

---

o **on**, oh **oat**, oi **boy**, oo **soon**, oor **poor**, or **for**, ow **cow**, sh **shush**,
th **thin**, *th* **this**, u **up**, ur **spur**, uu **book**, *zh* **pleasure**

forensic	fə REN sik
foreshorten	for SHOR tən
forestation	FOR ə STAY shən
forfeit	FOR fət
forfeiture	FOR fə chər
forgery	FOR jə ree
formaldehyde	for MAL də HĪD
formalin	FOR mə lən
format	FOR mat
formative	FOR mə tiv
formidable	FOR mə də bəl
Formosa	for MOH sə
formula	FOR myə lə
formulae	FOR myə lee
Forquet	fawr KAY
forsooth	for SOOTH
forsythia	for SITH ee ə
Fortaleza	FAWR tə LAY zə
forte (a, adv)	FOR tay
forte (n)	fort
forthwith	forth WI*TH*
fortissimo	for TIS ə MOH
fortitude	FOR tə TOOD
fortuitous	for TOO ə təs
Fortuna	for TOO nə
fortune	FOR chən
forum	FOR əm
forward	FOR wərd
Forza del Destino	FORT sah del de STEE noh
fossa	FOS ə
Foucault	foo KOH
Fouché	foo SHAY
foulard	fuu LAHRD
foulmouthed	fowl mow*th*d (mow as in *cow*)
Fourie, Bernardus	FOO ree, ber NAHR daws
Fourier	FUUR ee AY
Fournier	fuur NYAY
foyer	FOI ər
Fra Angelico	frah ahn JAI li koh
fracas	FRAY kəs
fractious	FRAK shəs
fracture	FRAK chər
Fra Diavolo	frah DYAH voh loh

ə ago, a at, ah calm, ahr dark, air care, aw saw, ay say, ch church
e bet, ee me, eer beer, hw what, i is, ī my, *n* French final n vin,

fragile	**FRAJ** əl
fragmentary	**FRAG** mən **TER** ee
Fragonard	fra gaw **NAHR**
fragrant	**FRAY** grənt
frailty	**FRAYL** tee
Fra Lippo Lippi	frah **LIP** oh **LIP** ee
franc	frangk
Françaix	frahn **SAY** (frahn French final *n*)
France	frans
Francesca	frahn **CHES** kə
Francescatti	**FRAHN** che **SKAH** tee
Franceschi	frahn **CHE** skee
franchise	**FRAN** chīz
Franciscan	fran **SIS** kən
francium	**FRAN** see əm
Franck, César	**FRAHNK**, say **ZAHR**
Franco-	**FRANG** koh
Franconia	frang **KOH** nee ə
Francophile	**FRANG** kə **FĪL**
Francophobe	**FRANG** kə **FOHB**
frangible	**FRAN** jə bəl
frangipane	**FRAN** jə **PAYN**
frangipani	**FRAN** jə **PAN** ee
Franglais	frahn **GLAY**
Franjieh, Suleiman	fran **JEE** ə, **SOO** lay man
Frankenstein	**FRANG** kən **STĪN**
Frankfort	**FRANGK** fərt
Frankfurt am Main	**FRAHNGK** fuurt ahm **MĪN**
frankfurter, F-	**FRANGK** fər tər
frankincense	**FRANGK** ən **SENS**
franklin, F-	**FRANGK** lən
Franz (American)	franz
Franz (European)	frahnts
frappé	fra **PAY**
Fraser	**FRAY** zər
fraternize	**FRAT** ər **NĪZ**
fratricide	**FRAT** rə **SĪD**
Frau	frow
fraud	frawd
fraudulent	**FRAW** jə lənt
Frauen	**FROW** ən
fraught	frawt
Fräulein	**FROI** līn

---

o on, oh oat, oi boy, oo soon, oor poor, or for, ow cow, sh shush,
th thin, *th* this, u up, ur spur, uu book, *zh* pleasure

Frazer	**FRAY** zər
freak	freek
Fredericton	**FRED** ər ik tən
Fredonia	frə **DOHN** yə
freesia	**FREE** *zh*ə
Freiburg (Germany)	**FRĪ** buurk
Frelinghuysen	**FREE** ling **HĪ** zən
Freneau	fri **NOH**
frenetic	frə **NET** ik
frenum	**FREE** nəm
Freon	**FREE** on
frequency	**FREE** kwən see
frequent (a)	**FREE** kwənt
frequent (v)	fri **KWENT**
frequentative	fri **KWEN** tə tiv
frère	frair
fresco	**FRES** koh
freshet	**FRESH** ət
Fresnel	fray **NEL**
Fresno	**FREZ** noh
Freud	froid
Freudian	**FROI** dee ən
Freundlich	**FROIND** lik
Frey	fray
Freya	**FRAY** ə
friable	**FRĪ** ə bəl
friar	**FRĪ** ər
fricassee	**FRIK** ə **SEE**
Frick	frik
Friedan	free **DAN**
Fries	freez
Friesian	**FREE** *zh*ən
frieze	freez
frigate	**FRIG** ət
Frigg	frig
Frigga	**FRIG** ə
frigid	**FRIJ** əd
frijole	free **HOH** lee
Friml	**FRIM** əl
Frisch, Max	frish, mahks
Frisian	**FRI***ZH* ən
frivolity	fri **VOL** ə tee
frivolous	**FRIV** ə ləs

ə **ago**, a **at**, ah **calm**, ahr **dark**, air **care**, aw **saw**, ay **say**, ch **church**
e **bet**, ee **me**, eer **beer**, hw **what**, i **is**, ī **my**, *n* French final n **vin**,

Frobisher	**FROH** bi shər
Froebel	**FROI** bəl
Froissart	frwah **SAHR**
Fromm	frohm
Fronde	frawnd
Frondizi	fron **DEE** zee
frontage	**FRUN** tij
Frontenac	**FRON** tə **NAK**
frontier	frun **TEER**
frontispiece	**FRUN** təs **PEES**
fronton	**FRON** ton
frottage	fraw **TAHZ***H*
Froude	frood
froufrou	**FROO** froo
frow	froh
Fruchtman	**FRUUKT** mən
fructify	**FRUK** tə **FĪ**
frugal	**FROO** gəl
fruition	froo **ISH** ən
Frunze	**FROON** ze
frustrate	**FRUS** trayt
frustum	**FRUS** təm
Fuad	foo **AHD**
Fuchs	fyooks
fuchsia	**FYOO** shə
fuchsine	**FUUK** sən
Fuegian	fyoo **EE** ji ən
fuehrer	**FYUUR** ər
fuel	**FYOO** əl
Fuentes	**FWEN** tays
fugacious	fyoo **GAY** shəs
fugitive	**FYOO** jə tiv
fugue	fyoog
führer, F-	**FYUUR** ər
Fuji	**FOO** jee
Fujiyama	**FOO** jee **YAH** mah
Fukien	foo kyen
Fukuda, Takeo	foo koo dah, tah kay oh
Fukui	foo koo ee
Fukuoka	foo koo oh kah
Fula	**FOO** lə
Fulani	**FOO** lah nee
fulcrum	**FUUL** krəm

---

fulgent	**FUL** jənt
fulminant	**FUUL** mə nənt
fulminate	**FUUL** mə **NAYT**
fulsome	**FUUL** səm
fumarole	**FYOO** mə **ROHL**
fumigate	**FYOO** mə **GAYT**
Funafuti	**FOO** nə **FOO** tee
funambulist	fyuu **NAM** byə ləst
Funchal	fuun **SHAHL**
function	**FUNGK** shən
functionary	**FUNGK** shə **NER** ee
Fundy	**FUN** dee
funeral	**FYOO** nə rəl
funereal	fyuu **NIR** ee əl
fungi	**FUN** jī
fungicide	**FUN** ji **SĪD**
fungus	**FUNG** gəs
funicular	fyuu **NIK** yə lər
furbelow	**FUR** bə **LOH**
furcation	**FUR KAY** shən
furlough	**FUR** loh
furor	**FYUUR** ər
furrier	**FUR** ee ər
furrow	**FUR** oh
Furtwängler	**FUURT** veng lər
furze	furz
fusel	**FYOO** zəl
fuselage	**FYOO** sə **LAHZH**
Fushun	foo shuun
fusil	**FYOO** zəl
fusilier, fusileer	**FYOO** zə **LEER**
fusillade	**FYOO** sə **LAYD**
fusion	**FYOO** zhən
fustian	**FUS** chən
futile	**FYOO** təl
Futuna	fə **TOO** nə
future	**FYOO** chər
futurist	**FYOO** chər əst
futurity	fyuu **TUUR** ə tee
Fuzhou	foo joh

ə ago, a at, ah calm, ahr dark, air care, aw saw, ay say, ch church
e bet, ee me, eer beer, hw what, i is, ī my, *n* French final n vin,

G

gabardine	**GAB** ər **DEEN**
gabbro	**GAB** roh
Gabès	**GAHB** əs
gabion	**GAY** bee ən
gable	**GAY** bəl
Gabon	ga **BOHN**
Gabor	gə **BOR**
Gaboriau	ga baw **RYOH**
Gabriel	**GAY** bree əl
Gabrilowitsch	**GAH** bri **LUV** ich
Gaea	**JEE** ə
Gaekwar	**GĪK** wahr
Gaelic	**GAY** lik
Gaetano	**GAH** e **TAH** noh
Gagarin	gah **GAH** rən
gage	gayj
Gagliano	gah **LYAH** noh
Gaillard (France)	gī **YAHR**
gaillardia	gə **LAHR** dee ə
gainsay	gayn **SAY**
Gainsborough	**GAYNZ** bur ə
Gaius	**GAY** əs
Gajdusek, Daniel	**GĪ** də **SHEK**
gala	**GAY** lə
galactic	gə **LAK** tik
Galahad	**GAL** ə **HAD**
Galápagos	gə **LAH** pə gəs
Galatea	**GAL** ə **TEE** ə
Galatia	gə **LAY** shə
Galatians	gə **LAY** shənz
galaxy, G-	**GAL** ək see
Galbraith	**GAL** brayth
Galen	**GAY** lən
galena	gə **LEE** nə
Galicia	gə **LISH** ə
Galilee	**GAL** ə **LEE**
Galileo	**GAL** ə **LEE** oh
Galitzine	gah leed **ZIN**

o on, oh oat, oi boy, oo soon, oor poor, or for, ow cow, sh shush,
th thin, *th* this, u up, ur spur, uu book, *zh* pleasure

Gallanos	gə **LAH** nohs
gallant (a)	**GAL** ənt
gallant (n, v)	gə **LANT**
gallantly	**GAL** ənt lee
gallantry	**GAL** ən tree
Gallaudet	**GAL** ə **DET**
Gallegos	gah **YAY** gohs
galleon	**GAL** ee ən
galleria	**GAL** ə **REE** ə
gallery	**GAL** ə ree
Gallic	**GAL** ik
Gallicism	**GAL** ə **SIZ** əm
gallimaufry	**GAL** ə **MAW** free
Gallin-Douathe, Michel	gah **LAN** doh **WAHT**, mee **SHEL**
galliot	**GAL** ee ət
Gallipoli	gə **LIP** ə lee
Gallipolis (Ohio)	**GAL** ə pə **LEES**
gallium	**GAL** ee əm
gallivant	**GAL** ə **VANT**
Gallo	**GAL** oh
gallop	**GAL** əp
Galloway	**GAL** ə **WAY**
gallows	**GAL** ohz
galop	**GAL** əp
galore	gə **LOR**
galosh	gə **LOSH**
Galsworthy	**GAWLZ** wur *th*ee
Galtieri	gahl **TYAIR** ee
Galton	**GAWL** tən
Galuppi	gah **LOOP** ee
Galvani	gahl **VAH** nee
galvanic	gal **VAN** ik
Galveston	**GAL** və stən
Galvez	gahl **VES**
Galway	**GAWL** way
Gama	**GAM** ə
Gamaliel	gə **MAY** lee əl
Gamarra	gah **MAH** rah
gamba	**GAHM** bə
gambado	gam **BAY** doh
Gambetta	gam **BET** ə
Gambia	**GAM** bee ə

ə ago, a at, ah calm, ahr dark, air care, aw saw, ay say, ch church
e bet, ee me, eer beer, hw what, i is, ī my, *n* French final n vin,

gambier, G-	**GAM** bir
gambit	**GAM** bət
gamble	**GAM** bəl
gamboge	gam **BOHJ**
gambol	**GAM** bəl
gambrel	**GAM** brəl
Gambrell	gam **BREL**
Gambrinus	gam **BRĪ** nəs
gamete	**GAM** eet
gamin	**GAM** ən
gamma	**GAM** ə
gamut	**GAM** ət
gamy	**GAY** mee
Gandhi, Indira	**GAHN** dee, **IN** də rə
Ganev, Dimiter	**GAH** nef, **DI** mi tər
Ganges	**GAN** jeez
ganglion	**GANG** glee ən
gangrene	**GANG** green
gangrenous	**GANG** grə nəs
Gannett, g-	**GAN** ət
Gansu	gahn soo
gantlet	**GAWNT** lət
gantry, G-	**GAN** tree
Ganymede	**GAN** i **MEED**
gaol	jayl
gaoler	**JAYL** ər
garage	gə **RAHZ**H
Garamond	**GAR** ə **MOND**
Garand	**GAR** ənd
Garango, Tiemoko	gah **RAHN** goh, **TEE** ay **MOH** koh
Garcia	gahr **SEE** ə
Garcia del Solar, Lucio	gahr **SEE** ə **DEL** soh **LAHR, LOO** syoh
Garcia Márquez, Gabriel	gahr **SEE** ə **MAHR** kez, gah bree **EL**
Garcia Robles, Alfonso	gahr **SEE** ə **ROH** bles, al **FON** soh
garçon	gahr **SAWN** (**SAWN** French final *n*)
gardener	**GAHRD** nər
gardenia	gahr **DEEN** yə
Gardiner	**GAHRD** nər
Gareth	**GAR** əth
Garfield	**GAHR** feeld
Gargantua	gahr **GAN** choo ə

gargoyle	**GAHR** goil
Garibaldi, g-	GA rə **BAWL** dee
Garin, Vasco Vieira	gah **RAN, VAHSH** koh vee **AY** rə
garish	**GA** rish
garner	**GAHR** nər
garnet	**GAHR** nət
garnishee	GAHR nə **SHEE**
garniture	**GAHR** nə chər
Garonne	ga **RUN**
garotte	gə **ROT**
garret	**GA** rət
Garrick	**GA** rik
Garrigues	gah **REE** ges
garrison, G-	**GA** rə sən
garrote	gə **ROT**
garrulity	gə **ROO** lə tee
garrulous	**GA** rə ləs
Garźon	gahr **SOHN**
Gascon	**GAS** kən
gasconade	GAS kə **NAYD**
Gascony	**GAS** kə nee
gaseous	**GAS** ee əs
gasohol	**GAS** ə HAWL
gasoline	**GAS** ə LEEN
gasometer	gas **OM** ə tər
Gaspé	ga **SPAY**
Gasperi, Alcide De	**GAHS** pe ree, ahl **CHEE** de de
Gastonia	ga **STOH** nee ə
gastric	**GAS** trik
gastritis	gas **TRĪ** təs
gastronomy	ga **STRON** ə mee
gastropod	**GAS** trə POD
Gath	gath
gather	**GA***TH* ər
Gatling	**GAT** ling
Gatun	gah **TOON**
gauche	gohsh
gaucho, G-	**GOW** choh
gaudeamus igitur	GOW day **AH** muus **IG** ə TUUR
gauge	gayj
Gauguin	goh **GAN** (GAN French final *n*)
Gaul	gawl
gauleiter, G-	**GOW** LĪ tər

ə ago, a at, ah calm, ahr dark, air care, aw saw, ay say, ch church
e bet, ee me, eer beer, hw what, i is, ī my, *n* French final n vin,

gaunt	gawnt
gauntlet	**GAWNT** lət
gauss	gows
Gaussian	**GOW** see ən
Gautama	**GOW** tə mə
Gautier	goh **TYAY**
gauze	gawz
Gaviria, Fernando	gah **VEE** ree ə, fer **NAN** doh
gavotte	gə **VOT**
Gawain	**GAH** win
Gaza	**GAH** zə
gazebo	gə **ZEE** boh
gazelle	gə **ZEL**
gazette	gə **ZET**
gazetteer	**GAZ** ə **TEER**
gazpacho	gəz **PAH** choh
Gazzara	gə **ZA** rə
Gbeho, James Victor	**GBE** hoh (**GBE** *G* barely pronounced)
Gbenye, Christophe	gə **BENG** yay, **KREE** stawf
Gdansk	gə **DAHNSK**
Gdynia	gə **DIN** yə
Gebre-Egzy, Tesfaye	**GAB** rə **EG** zee, tahs **FĪ** ay
Gedda	**GED** ə
Geddes	**GED** eez
gefilte	gə **FIL** tə
Gehenna	gi **HEN** ə
Geiger	**GĪ** gər
geisha	**GAY** shə
Geissler	**GĪS** lər
gel	jel
gelatin	**JEL** ət ən
gelatinous	jə **LAT** ən əs
gelding	**GEL** ding
gelid	**JEL** əd
gelignite	**JEL** ig **NĪT**
Gemara	gə **MAHR** ə
Gemayel, Amin	jə **MĪ** əl, a **MEEN**
Gemini	**JEM** ə **NĪ**
gemutlich	gə **MUUT** lik
gendarme	**ZH**AHN dahrm
genealogy	**JEE** nee **AL** ə jee
genera	**JEN** ə rə
generic	jə **NER** ik

---

o on, oh oat, oi boy, oo soon, oor poor, or for, ow cow, sh shush,
th thin, *th* this, u up, ur spur, uu book, *zh* pleasure

Genesee	**JEN** ə **SEE**
Geneseo	**JEN** ə **SEE** oh
genesis, G-	**JEN** ə səs
genet	**JEN** ət
Genêt	*zh*ə **NAY**
geneticist	jə **NET** ə səst
Geneva	jə **NEE** və
Genghis Khan	**JENG** gəs **KAHN**
genial	**JEEN** yəl
genie	**JEE** nee
genii	**JEE** nee ī
genius	**JEEN** yəs
genius loci	**JEE** nee əs **LOH** sī
Genoa	**JEN** oh ə
genocide	**JEN** ə **SĪD**
genre	***ZH*AHN** rə
gens	jenz
Genscher, Hans Dietrich	**GEN** shər, **HAHNS DEE** trish
gentian	**JEN** shən
gentile, G-	**JEN** tīl
Gentoo	**JEN** too
gentrification	**JEN** trə fə **KAY** shən
gentrify	**JEN** trə **FĪ**
gentry	**JEN** tree
genuflection	**JEN** yə **FLEK** shən
genuine	**JEN** yoo ən
genus	**JEE** nəs
geocentric	**JEE** oh **SEN** trik
geodesy	jee **OD** ə see
geodetic	**JEE** ə **DET** ik
Geoffrey	**JEF** ree
Geoffrion	**JEF** ree ən
geography	jee **OG** rə fee
geology	jee **OL** ə jee
geometer	jee **OM** ə tər
geometric	**JEE** ə **MET** rik
geometry	jee **OM** ə tree
geophysical	**JEE** ə **FIZ** i kəl
geophysics	**JEE** ə **FIZ** iks
geopolitics	**JEE** oh **POL** ə tiks
geoponic	**JEE** ə **PON** ik
Georgetown	**JORJ** town

ə ago, a at, ah calm, ahr dark, air care, aw saw, ay say, ch church
e bet, ee me, eer beer, hw what, i is, ī my, *n* French final n vin,

georgette	jor **JET**
Georgia	**JOR** jə
Georgian	**JOR** jən
geotropism	jee **OT** rə **PIZ** əm
Geraint	jə **RAYNT**
Geraldine	**JER** əl **DEEN**
geranium	jə **RAY** nee əm
Gerard	jə **RAHRD**
gerbil	**JUR** bəl
Gerhardsen, Einar	ge **RAHRD** sen, Ī nahr
geriatrics	**JER** ee **A** triks
Géricault	*zh*ay ree **KOH**
germane	jər **MAYN**
germanium	jər **MAY** nee əm
Germany	**JUR** mə nee
germicide	**JUR** mə **SĪD**
germinate	**JUR** mə **NAYT**
Geronimo	jə **RON** ə **MOH**
gerontocracy	**JER** ən **TOK** rə see
gerontology	**JER** ən **TOL** ə jee
Gerry	**GER** ee
gerrymander	**JER** i **MAN** dər
Gershwin	**GURSH** wən
Gerulaitis	**JER** yuu **LĪT** əs
gerund	**JER** ənd
Geryon	**JER** ee ən
gesso	**JES** oh
gest	jest
Gestalt	gə **SHTAHLT**
Gestapo	gə **STAH** poh
Gesta Romanorum	**JES** tə **ROH** mə **NOR** əm
gestation	je **STAY** shən
gesture	**JES** chər
gesundheit	gə **ZUUNT** hīt
Gethsemane, g-	geth **SEM** ə nee
Gettysburg	**GET** iz **BURG**
gewgaw	**GYOO** gaw
gewürztraminer	gə **VUURTS** **TRAHM** ə nər
geyser	**GĪ** zər
geyser (heater, British)	**GEE** zər
Gezira	jə **ZEER** ə
Ghana	**GAH** nə
ghastly	**GAST** lee

o **on**, oh **oat**, oi **boy**, oo **soon**, oor **poor**, or **for**, ow **cow**, sh **shush**,
th **thin**, *th* **this**, u **up**, ur **spur**, uu **book**, *zh* **pleasure**

ghat, G-	gawt
Ghazala, Abdel Halim Abu	gah **ZAH** lə, ahb **DEL** hah **LEEM** ah **BOO**
Gheber, Ghebre	**GAY** bər
ghee	gee
Ghent	gent
Gheorghiu-Dej, Georghe	dyawr **DYOO** de*zh*, **DYAWR** dyay
gherkin	**GUR** kən
ghetto	**GET** oh
Ghibelline	**GIB** ə lən
Ghiberti	gee **BAIR** tee
Ghirlandajo	**GEER** lahn **DAH** yoh
Ghorbal, Ashraf	**GOR** bahl, **AHSH** rahf
Ghotbzadeh, Sadegh	**KOHT** bə **ZA** də, **SAH** dək ə
ghoul	gool
Giaever, Ivar	**YAY** vər, **EE** vahr
Giaimo	**JĪ** moh
Giaiotti, Bonaldo	jī **OH** tee, boh **NAHL** doh
Giannini	jah **NEE** nee
giantism	**JĪ** ən **TIZ** əm
giaour	jowr
Giauque, William	jee **OHK**
gibber	**JIB** ər
gibberish	**JIB** ə rish
gibbet	**JIB** ət
gibbon, G-	**GIB** ən
gibbous	**GIB** əs
gibe	jīb
Gibeon	**GIB** ee ən
giblet	**JIB** lət
Gibraltar	jə **BRAWL** tər
Gibran, Kahlil	jə **BRAHN**, kah **LEEL**
Gide	*zh*eed
Gideon	**GID** ee ən
Gideonse	**GID** ee ənz
Gielgud	**GEEL** guud
gigantic	jī **GAN** tik
gigolo	*ZH*IG ə **LOH**
gigot	*zh*ee **GOH**
gigue	*zh*eeg
Gila	**HEE** lə
Gilboa	gil **BOH** ə

ə ago, a at, ah calm, ahr dark, air care, aw saw, ay say, ch church
e bet, ee me, eer beer, hw what, i is, ī my, *n* French final n vin,

Gilchrist	**GIL** krist
Gilead	**GIL** ee əd
Giles	jīlz
gilgai	**GIL** gī
Gilgamesh	**GIL** gə **MESH**
gill (anatomy; ravine)	gil
gill (measure)	jil
Gillespie	gə **LES** pee
Gillette	jə **LET**
gillie	**GIL** ee
gillyflower	**JIL** ee **FLOW** ər (**FLOW** as in *cow*)
gimbals	**GIM** bəls
gimcrack	**JIM** krak
gimlet	**GIM** lət
gimmick	**GIM** ik
gimp	gimp
gin	jin
ginger	**JIN** jər
gingham	**GING** əm
gingivitis	**JIN** jə **VĪ** təs
Gingold, Hermione	**GING** gohld, hər **MĪ** ə nee
ginkgo	**GING** koh
Ginn	gin
ginseng	**JIN** seng
Ginza	**GEEN** zah
Gioconda, la	joh **KON** də, lah
Giorgione	jor **JOH** ne
Giotto	**JAWT** toh
Giovanni	joh **VAH** ni
giraffe, G-	ji **RAF**
girandole	**JIR** ən **DOHL**
Girard	jə **RAHRD**
Giraudoux	*zh*ee roh **DOO**
Gironde	*zh*ee **RAWND**
Girondist	jə **RON** dəst
Girosi	ji **RAW** see
Giscard d'Estaing, Valéry	*zh*ees **KAHR** des **TAN**, va lay **REE** (**TAN** French final *n*)
gittern	**GIT** ərn
Giuseppe	joo **ZEP** pay
Givenchy	*ZH*EE vahn shee
Gizenga, Antoine	gi **ZENG** gə, ahn **TWAHN**
Gjellerup	**GEL** ə ruup

glabrous	**GLAY** brəs
glacé	gla **SAY**
glacial	**GLAY** shəl
glacier	**GLAY** shər
gladiator	**GLAD** ee **AY** tər
gladiolus	**GLAD** ee **OH** ləs
Gladstone	**GLAD** stohn
Glamis (Scotland)	glahmz
Glamis (Shakespeare)	**GLAH** mis
glamour	**GLAM** ər
glance	glans
Glarus (Switzerland)	**GLAHR** əs
Glarus (Wisconsin)	**GLA** rəs
Glasgow	**GLAS** goh
Glaspell	**GLAS** pel
glassine	gla **SEEN**
glaucoma	glow **KOH** mə (glow as in *cow*)
glaze	glayz
glazier	**GLAY** *zh*ər
Glazunov	**GLAZ** ə **NAWF**
glebe	gleeb
Glemp, Jozef	**GLEMP, YOO** zef
Glengarry, g-	glen **GAR** ee
Glinka	**GLING** kə
glissade	gli **SAHD**
glissando	gli **SAHN** doh
glitch	glich
gloaming	**GLOH** ming
global	**GLOH** bəl
globin	**GLOH** bən
globular	**GLOB** yə lər
globule	**GLOB** yool
glockenspiel	**GLOK** ən **SHPEEL**
Gloucester (England, Massachusetts)	**GLOS** tər
glow	gloh
glower	**GLOW** ər (**GLOW** as in *cow*)
gloxinia	glok **SIN** ee ə
Gluck	gluuk
glucose	**GLOO** kohs
gluten	**GLOOT** ən
gluteus	**GLOOT** ee əs
glutinous	**GLOOT** ə nəs

ə ago, a at, ah calm, ahr dark, air care, aw saw, ay say, ch church
e bet, ee me, eer beer, hw what, i is, ī my, *n* French final n vin,

glycerin	**GLIS** ə rən
glycine	**GLĪ** seen
glycol	**GLĪ** kohl
glyph	glif
gnarled	nahrld
gnash	nash
gnat	nat
gnathic	**NATH** ik
gnaw	naw
Gneisenau	gə **NĪ** zə now
gneiss	nīs
gnome	nohm
gnomic	**NOH** mik
gnosis	**NOH** səs
gnostic, G-	**NOS** tik
gnu	noo
Goa	**GOH** ə
gobbledygook	**GOB** əl dee **GUUK**
Gobelin	**GOH** bə lən
Gobi	**GOH** bee
Godiva	gə **DĪ** və
Godunov	**GUUD** ə **NAWF**
Goebbels	**GAIR** bəlz
Goering	**GAIR** ing
Goethals	**GOH** thəlz
Goethe	**GAIR** tə
Goetz	gets
Gog	gog
Gogh, van	van **GOH**
Gogol	**GOH** gəl
Goidelic	goi **DEL** ik
goiter	**GOIT** ər
Golan	**GOH** lahn
Golconda	gol **KON** də
Goldhaber, Maurice	**GOHLD** hay bər, maw **REES**
Goldmark	**GOHLD** mahrk
Goldoni	gawl **DOH** nee
golem, G-	**GOH** ləm
Golembiewski	gah ləm **BYOO** skee
Golgi	**GAWL** jee
Golgotha	**GOL** gə thə
goliard	**GOHL** yərd
goliardic	gohl **YAHR** dik

o on, oh oat, oi boy, oo soon, oor poor, or for, ow cow, sh shush,
th thin, _th_ this, u up, ur spur, uu book, _zh_ pleasure

Goliath	gə **LĪ** əth
Gollancz	gə **LANS**
Golovanov	gə lah **VAH** nəf
Goma	**GOH** mə
Gómez	**GOH** mez
Gomorrah	gə **MOR** ə
Gompers	**GOM** pərz
Gomulka	gə **MUUL** kə
gonad	**GOH** nad
Goncourt	gawn **KOOR**
Gond	gond
Gondi	**GON** dee
gondola	**GON** də lə
gondolier	GON də **LEER**
Goneril	**GON** ər il
gonfalon	**GON** fə lən
gonorrhea	GON ə **REE** ə
Gonzalez	gawn **SAH** les
googol	**GOO** gawl
googolplex	**GOO** gawl PLEKS
gook	guuk
goon	goon
goop	goop
gooseberry	**GOOS** BER ee
Gopallawa	goh pah **LAH** wah
gopher	**GOH** fər
Gorbach, Alfons	**GOR** bahk, **AHL** fəns
Gorbachev, Mikhail	gor bah **CHAWF**, mee hī **EEL**
Gorgas	**GOR** gəs
gorget	**GOR** jət
gorgon	**GOR** gən
Gorgonzola	GOR gən **ZOH** lə
Gorky	**GOR** kee
Gorno-Badakhshan	**GOR** noh bah dahk **SHAHN**
goshawk	**GOS** hawk
Goshen	**GOH** shən
gosling	**GOZ** ling
Gosplan	**GAWS** plahn
gospodin	GOS pə **DEEN**
gossamer	**GOS** ə mər
Gosse	gaws
Gotay	goh **TĪ**
Göteborg	YU tə **BOR** yə

ə ago, a at, ah calm, ahr dark, air care, aw saw, ay say, ch church
e bet, ee me, eer beer, hw what, i is, ī my, *n* French final n vin,

Goth	goth
Gotham	**GOTH** əm
Gothenburg	**GOTH** ən **BURG**
Gothic	**GOTH** ik
Gotland	**GAHT** land
Götterdämmerung	**GAIRT** ər **DEM** ə **RUUNG**
Göttingen	**GAIR** ting ən
Gottwald	**GAWT** vahld
gouache	gwahsh
Goucher	**GOW** chər
Gouda	**GOO** də
Goudge	guuj
Goudy	**GOW** dee
gouge	gowj
Goukouni Oueddei	goo **KOO** nee **WAH** dee
Goulart, João	**GOO** lahr, **ZHWOWN**
goulash	**GOO** lahsh
Gould	goold
Gounod	**GOO** noh
gourami	**GUUR** ə mee
gourd	goord
gourmand	**GUUR** mahnd
gourmet	**GUUR** may
Gouverneur	**GOO** vər **NUUR**
government	**GUV** ərn mənt
governor	**GUV** ər nər
Gower	**GOW** ər
Gowon, Yakubu	goh **WAHN**, yah **KOO** boo
Goya	**GOI** ə
graben	**GRAHB** ən
Gracchus	**GRAK** əs
gracious	**GRAY** shəs
gradient	**GRAY** dee ənt
gradual	**GRAJ** oo əl
graduate (a, n)	**GRAJ** oo ət
graduate (v)	**GRAJ** oo **AYT**
gradus	**GRAY** dəs
Graf	grahf
graffiti	grə **FEET** ee
graffito	grə **FEET** oh
graft	graft
graham, G-	**GRAY** əm
Grail	grayl

---

o on, oh oat, oi boy, oo soon, oor poor, or for, ow cow, sh shush,
th thin, *th* this, u up, ur spur, uu book, *zh* pleasure

Grainger	**GRAYN** jər
gramercy	grə **MUR** see
Gramercy Park	**GRAM** ər see
Granada	grə **NAH** də
Granados, Enrique	grah **NAH** dohs, en **REE** ke
granary	**GRAN** ə ree
Gran Chaco	grahn **CHAH** koh
Grand Coulee	grand **KOO** lee
grandee	gran **DEE**
grandeur	**GRAN** jər
grandiloquent	gran **DIL** ə kwənt
grandiose	**GRAN** dee **OHS**
Grand Pré	gran pray
Grand Prix	grahn **PREE** (grahn French final *n*)
Grand Teton	grand **TEE** tahn
granule	**GRAN** yool
grapnel	**GRAP** nəl
grappa	**GRAHP** pah
Gratian	**GRAY** shən
Gratiano	grahsh **YAH** noh
gratis	**GRAT** əs
gratitude	**GRAT** ə **TOOD**
Grattan	**GRAT** ən
gratuitous	grə **TOO** ə təs
gratuity	grə **TOO** ə tee
Grau San Martin	**GROW** san mahr **TEEN** (**GROW** as in *cow*)
Graustark	**GROW** stahrk (**GROW** as in *cow*)
gravamen	grə **VAY** mən
graven	**GRAY** vən
gravity	**GRAV** ə tee
gravure	grə **VYUUR**
Graziano	**GRAHT** see **AH** noh
grazier	**GRAY** *zh*ər
grease	grees
greasy	**GREE** see
grebe	greeb
Grecian	**GREE** shən
Greco-	**GREK** oh
Greece	grees
Greeley	**GREE** lee
Greenland	**GREEN** lənd
Greenock	**GREE** nək
Greenough	**GREE** noh

ə ago, a at, ah calm, ahr dark, air care, aw saw, ay say, ch church
e bet, ee me, eer beer, hw what, i is, ī my, *n* French final n vin,

Greensboro	**GREENZ** **BUR** oh
Greenwich (England)	**GRIN** ij
Greenwich Village	**GREN** ich
gregarious	gri **GA** ree əs
Gregorian	gri **GOR** ee ən
Gregory	**GREG** ə **REE**
Grenada	grə **NAY** də
grenade	grə **NAYD**
grenadier	**GREN** ə **DIR**
grenadine, G-	**GREN** ə **DEEN**
Grendel	**GREN** dəl
Grenoble	grə **NOH** bəl
Grenville	**GREN** vil
Gresham	**GRESH** əm
Gretna	**GRET** nə
gridiron	**GRID** ī ərn
Grieg	greeg
grievance	**GREE** vəns
grievous	**GREE** vəs
griffin, G-	**GRIF** ən
griffon	**GRIF** ən
grimace	**GRIM** əs
Grimes	grīmz
grimly	**GRIM** lee
Grimm	grim
Grimsby	**GRIMZ** bee
grimy	**GRĪ** mee
gringo	**GRING** goh
Grinnell	gri **NEL**
griot	**GREE** ət
gripe	grīp
grippe	grip
Gris, Juan	grees, hwahn
grisaille	gri **ZĪ**
Griselda	gri **ZEL** də
grisette	gri **ZET**
gris-gris	**GREE** gree
Grishin, Viktor	**GREESH** in, **VEEK** tər
grisly	**GRIZ** lee
gristle	**GRIS** əl
Griva	**GREE** və
Griz Nez	gree **NAY**
grizzly	**GRIZ** lee

groat	groht
Grofé, Ferde	**GROH** fay, **FURD** ee
grogram	**GROG** rəm
groin	groin
Grolier	**GROH** lee ər
Gromyko	grə **MEE** koh
Gronchi	**GRONG** kee
Groningen	**GROH** ning ən
Gropius	**GROH** pee əs
grosbeak	**GROHS** beek
groschen	**GROH** shən
grosgrain	**GROH** grayn
gross	grohs
Grosvenor	**GROHV** nər
Grosz	grohs
grotesque	groh **TESK**
Grotius	**GROH** shee əs
Groton	**GROT** ən
grotto	**GROT** oh
groundsel	**GROWN** səl (**GROWN** as in *town*)
grovel	**GRUV** əl
Grozny	**GRAWZ** ni
Grudziadz	**GRUU** jawnts
Gruen	**GROO** ən
Grundy	**GRUN** dee
Grünert, Horst	**GRUUN** ərt, **HORST**
Grunitzky, Yao	groo **NEES** kee, **YOW**
Grus	grus
Gruyère	groo **YAIR**
guacharo	**GWAHCH** ə ʀoh
Guadalajara	ɢwᴀʜᴅ ə lə **HAHR** ə
Guadalcanal	ɢwᴀʜ dəl kə **NAL**
Guadalquivir	ɢwᴀʜ dəl kee **VEER**
Guadalupe	ɢwᴀʜ də **LOOP**
Guadeloupe	ɢwᴀʜ də **LOOP**
Guadiana	ɢwᴀʜ dee **AH** nah
Guadix	gwah **DEESH**
Guam	gwahm
Guanajuato	ɢwᴀʜ nah **HWAH** taw
Guangdong	gwahng dawng
Guangxi	gwahng shee
Guangzhou	gwahng joh
guano	**GWAH** noh

ə ago, a at, ah calm, ahr dark, air care, aw saw, ay say, ch church
e bet, ee me, eer beer, hw what, i is, ī my, *n* French final n vin,

Guantánamo	gwahn **TAHN** ə **MOH**
Guaporé	**GWAH** paw **RAY**
Guarani, g-	**GWAHR** ə **NEE**
guarantee	**GA** rən **TEE**
guarantor	**GA** rən **TOR**
guaranty	**GA** rən **TEE**
Guardi, Francesco	**GWAHR** dee, frahn **CHES** koh
guardian	**GAHR** dee ən
Guarneri	gwahr **NAIR** ee
Guarnerius	gwahr **NAIR** ee əs
Guatemala	**GWAH** tə **MAH** lə
guava	**GWAH** və
Guayaquil	**GWĪ** ah **KEEL**
guayule	gwah **YOO** lee
gubernatorial	**GOO** bə nə **TOR** ee əl
Gubner	**GOOB** nər
Gubser	**GOOB** sər
Gudrun	**GUUD** roon
Gueden, Hilde	**GOO** dən, **HIL** də
Guelich	**GYOO** lik
Guelph, Guelf	gwelf
Guerard	gay **RAHRD**
guerdon	**GUR** dən
Guerin	**GAIR** in
Guernsey, g-	**GURN** zee
guerre	gair
guerrilla	gə **RIL** ə
Guevara	ge **VAH** rah
Guggenheim	**GUUG** ən **HĪM**
Guglielmo	goo **YEL** moh
Guiana	gee **AN** ə
Guido	**GWEE** doh
Guido, José Maria	**GEE** doh, hoh **SAY** mah **REE** ah
guidon	**GĪ** dən
guild	gild
guilder	**GIL** dər
guile	gīl
Guilford	**GIL** fərd
Guillaume	gee **YOHM**
Guillemin	gee yə **MAN** (**MAN** French final *n*)
guillemot	**GIL** ə **MOT**
Guillermo Garcia, José	gə **LYAIR** moh gahr **SEE** ah, hoh **SAY**
guillotine	**GIL** ə **TEEN**

o **on**, oh **oat**, oi **boy**, oo **soon**, oor **poor**, or **for**, ow **cow**, sh **shush**,
th **thin**, *th* **this**, u **up**, ur **spur**, uu **book**, *zh* **pleasure**

Guinea, g-	**GIN** ee
Guinea-Bissau	**GIN** ee bi **SOW** (**SOW** as in *cow*)
Guinevere	**GWIN** ə **VEER**
Guipuzcoa	gee **POOTH** kə wə
guise	gīz
Guise	geez
guitar	gə **TAHR**
Guiyang	gwee yahng
Guizhou	gwee joh
Guizot	gee **ZOH**
Gujarat	**GUUJ** ə **RAHT**
Gujarati	**GUUJ** ə **RAH** tee
gulden	**GUUL** dən
gules	gyoolz
Gullah	**GUL** ə
gullet	**GUL** ət
gullible	**GUL** ə bəl
Gulliver	**GUL** ə vər
gumbo	**GUM** boh
gumption	**GUMP** shən
Gu Mu	goo moo
Gunnar	**GUUN** nahr
Gunther	**GUN** thər
gunwale	**GUN** əl
guppy	**GUP** ee
Gurev, Guriev	**GUUR** yef
Gurkha	**GUR** kə
Gurko	**GUR** koh
Gursel, Cemal	gər **SEL**, ke **MAHL**
guru	**GOO** roo
Gusev, Gussev	**GOO** sef
gusset	**GUS** ət
Gustaf	**GOO** stahf
gustatory	**GUS** tə **TOR** ee
Gustave	**GUS** tahv
Gustavus	gə **STAY** vəs
Gutenberg	**GOOT** ən **BURG**
Gutierrez	guu **TYER** res
gutta-percha	**GUT** ə **PUR** chə
Guyana	gī **AN** ə
Guzmán Blanco	goos **MAHN BLAHN** koh
Gwinnett	gwi **NET**
Gwyn	gwin

ə ago, a at, ah calm, ahr dark, air care, aw saw, ay say, ch church
e bet, ee me, eer beer, hw what, i is, ī my, *n* French final n vin,

gymkhana	jim **KAH** nə
gymnasium (European school)	gim **NAH** zee **UUM**
gymnasium (sports)	jim **NAY** zee əm
gymnast	**JIM** nast
gymnastics	jim **NAS** tiks
gymnosophist	jim **NOS** ə fəst
gymnosperm	**JIM** nə **SPURM**
gynandrous	ji **NAN** drəs
gynecology	**GĪ** nə **KOL** ə jee
Gyöngyös	**DYUN** dyush
Győr	dyur
gypsophila	jip **SOF** ə lə
gypsum	**JIP** səm
gypsy	**JIP** see
gyrate	**JĪ** rayt
gyre	**JĪ** ər
gyrfalcon	**JUR FAL** kən
gyroscope	**JĪ** rə **SKOHP**
gyve	jīv

H

Haakon	**HAW** kuun
Haarlem	**HAHR** ləm
Habakkuk	hə **BAK** ək
habanera	**HAH** bə **NYAIR** ə
habeas corpus	**HAY** bee əs **KOR** pəs
Haber, Fritz	**HAH** bər
habergeon	**HAB** ər jən
Habib	ha **BEEB**
habiliment	hə **BIL** ə mənt
habitat	**HAB** ə **TAT**
habituation	hə **BICH** oo **AY** shən
habitué	hə **BICH** oo **AY**
Habre, Hissen	**HAH** bray, **HEE** sahn
Habsburg	**HAPS** burg
Habyarimana, Juvénal	**HAHB** yah ree **MAHN** ah, *zh*oo ve **NAHL**
hacienda	**HAH** see **EN** də
hackney	**HAK** nee

---

o **on**, oh **oat**, oi **boy**, oo **soon**, oor **poor**, or **for**, ow **cow**, sh **shush**,
th **thin**, *th* **this**, u **up**, ur **spur**, uu **book**, *zh* **pleasure**

Hadassah	hah **DAH** sə
Haddad, Saad	hah **DED**, **SAHD**
hadj	haj
hadji	**HAJ** ee
Hadrian	**HAY** dree ən
Haeckel	**HEK** əl
Ha-erh-pin	hah er bin
hafiz, H-	hah **FIZ**
hafnium	**HAF** nee əm
Haganah	**HAH** gah **NAH**
Hagar	**HAY** gər
Haggadah	hah **GAH** dah
Haggai	**HAG** ee ī
haggard, H-	**HAG** ərd
haggis	**HAG** əs
hagiocracy	**HAG** ee **OK** rə see
Hagiographa	**HAG** ee **OG** rə fə
hagiography	**HAG** ee **OG** rə fee
Hague	hayg
Hahnemann	**HAH** nə mən
hahnium	**HAHN** ee əm
Haidalla, Mohamed	**HĪ** də lah, moh **HAHM** ed **HOO** nə
Khouna Ould	**OOL**
Haifa	**HĪ** fə
Haig	hayg
haik	hīk
haiku	**HĪ** koo
Haile-Mariam,	**HAY** lee **MAIR** ee əm, men **GIT** soo
Mengistu	
Haile Selassie	**HĪ** lee sə **LAS** ee
Hailey, Haley	**HAY** lee
Hainan	hī nahn
Hainaut	ay **NOH**
Haiphong	hī fawng
Haiti	**HAY** tee
Haitian	**HAY** shən
Hajek, Jiri	**HAH** yek, **YEE** ree
Hakim, Georges	hah **KEEM**, **ZHAWRZH**
Hakluyt	**HAK** loot
Halakah, Halacha	hah **LAHK** ə
halakist	**HAH** lə kəst
Halasz	**HAH** lahsh
halberd	**HAL** bərd

ə ago, a at, ah calm, ahr dark, air care, aw saw, ay say, ch church
e bet, ee me, eer beer, hw what, i is, ī my, *n* French final n vin,

halcyon	**HAL** see ən
Haldane	**HAWL** dayn
Haleakala	**HAH** lay ah kah **LAH**
halfpenny	**HAYP** ə nee
halibut	**HAL** ə bət
halide	**HAL** īd
Halifax	**HAL** ə **FAKS**
halite	**HAL** īt
halitosis	**HAL** ə **TOH** səs
Hallam	**HAL** əm
Halle	**HAHL** ə
Halleck	**HAL** ək
hallelujah	**HAL** ə **LOO** yə
Halley	**HAL** ee
hallo	hə **LOH**
halloo	hə **LOO**
hallucination	hə **LOO** sə **NAY** shən
hallucinogen	hə **LOO** sə nə jən
Halmahera	**HAHL** mə **HAIR** ə
halogen	**HAL** ə jən
Hals, Frans	hahlz, frahns
halvah	hahl **VAH**
halve	hav
halyard	**HAL** yərd
Hamadan	**HAM** ə **DAN**
Hamadou, Barkat Gourad	**HAH** mah doo, **BAHR** kaht **GOO** rahd
hamadryad	**HAM** ə **DRĪ** əd
hamal	hə **MAHL**
Haman	**HAY** mən
Hambletonian	**HAM** bəl **TOH** nee ən
Hambro, Edvard Isak	**HAHM** broh, **ED** vahrt **EE** sak
Hamburg	**HAM** burg
Hämeenlinna	**HA** mayn li nə
Hamelin	**HAM** ə lin
Hamilcar	hə **MIL** kahr
Hamitic	ha **MIT** ik
hamlet, H-	**HAM** lət
Hammarskjöld, Dag	**HAH** mər **SHOHLD**, **DAHG**
Hammerfest	**HAHM** ər **FEST**
Hammerschmidt	**HAM** ər **SHMIT**
Hammerstein	**HAM** ər **STĪN**
Hammurabi	**HAH** muu **RAH** bee

Hamody, Mohamed Said Ould	hah **MOH** dee, moh **HAHM** ed sah **EED OOL**
Hampden	**HAM** dən
Hampshire	**HAMP** shər
hamster	**HAM** stər
Hamsun, Knut	**HAHM** sən, **KNUUT**
Hamtramck	ham **TRAM** ik
Han	hahn
Handel	**HAN** dəl
handful	**HAND** fuul
handkerchief	**HANG** kər chəf
handsome	**HAN** səm
hangar	**HANG** ər
Hangchow	hang chow
hanger	**HANG** ər
Hangzhou	hahng joh
Hankow	hang kow
Hannibal	**HAN** ə bəl
Hanoi	hah **NOI**
Hanover	**HAN** oh vər
Hansard	**HAN** sərd
Hanseatic	**HAN** see **AT** ik
Hänsel and Gretel	**HAN** səl and **GRET** əl
Hansen	**HAHN** sən
hansom	**HAN** səm
Hanukkah	**HAH** nə kə
Hapsburg	**HAPS** burg
Harad	**HAHR** əd
Harada, Masahiko	hah rah dah, mah sah hee koh
hara-kiri	**HAHR** ə **KEER** ee
harangue	hə **RANG**
harass	hə **RAS**
harassed	hə **RAST**
harassment	hə **RAS** mənt
Harbin	**HAHR** bən
harbinger	**HAHR** bən jər
harebell	**HAIR** bel
harem	**HA** rəm
haricot	**HA** ri **KOH**
Harleian	**HAHR** lee ən
Harlem	**HAHR** ləm
harlequin, H-	**HAHR** li kwən
harlequinade	**HAHR** li kwə **NAYD**

ə ago, a at, ah calm, ahr dark, air care, aw saw, ay say, ch church
e bet, ee me, eer beer, hw what, i is, ī my, n French final n vin,

Harley Street	**HAHR** lee
harlot	**HAHR** lət
harmonic	hahr **MON** ik
harmonica	hahr **MON** i kə
harmonious	hahr **MOH** nee əs
harpsichord	**HAHRP** si **KORD**
harquebus	**HAHR** kwi bəs
harridan	**HA** rə dən
Harrovian	ha **ROH** vee ən
Harrow, h-	**HA** roh
Harte	hahrt
hartebeest	**HAHRT** ə **BEEST**
Harz	hahrtz
Hasdrubal	**HAZ DROO** bəl
Haseganu, Mihail	hah say **GAH** noo, mi hah **EEL**
hasenpfeffer	**HAH** sən **FEF** ər
Hašhek, Jaroslav	**HAH** shek, **YAH** raw **SLAHF**
Hashemite	**HASH** ə **MĪT**
hashish	**HASH** eesh
Hassam	**HAS** əm
Hassan	**HAH** sahn
hasta la vista	**AH** stah lah **VEE** stah
hasta mañana	**AH** stah mah **NYAH** nah
hasten	**HAY** sən
Hastings	**HAY** stingz
Hathor	**HATH** awr
Hatoyama	hah toh yah mah
Hatteras	**HAT** ər əs
Hatvan	**HAHT** vahn
hauberk	**HAW** burk
Haugesund	**HOW** gə suun
Haughey, Charles	**HAWK** ee
haughty	**HAW** tee
haul	hawl
haunch	hawnch
haunt	hawnt
Hauptmann	**HOWPT** mahn
Hausa	**HOW** sə
hausfrau	**HOWS** frow
hautboy	**HOH** boi
haute couture	oht koo **TUUR**
haute cuisine	oht kwee **ZEEN**
hauteur	hoh **TUR**

---

o on, oh oat, oi boy, oo soon, oor poor, or for, ow cow, sh shush,
th thin, *th* this, u up, ur spur, uu book, *zh* pleasure

haut monde	oh **MAWND**
Havana	hə **VAN** ə
havelock, H-	**HAV** lok
Haverford	**HAV** ər fərd
Haverhill	**HAY** vrəl
haversack	**HAV** ər **SAK**
havoc	**HAV** ək
Havre (France)	**AH** vrə
Havre (US)	**HAV** ər
Havre de Grace	**HAV** ər də **GRAS**
Hawaii	hə **WAH** ee
Hawaiian	hə **WAH** yən
hawser	**HAW** zər
hawthorn	**HAW** thorn
Hawthorne	**HAW** thorn
Haya de la Torre	**Ī** yah day lah **TAW** ray
Hayakawa	hah yah **KAH** wah
Hayashi, Teru	hah yah **SHEE**, **TE** roo
Hayden	**HAYD** ən
Haydn	**HĪD** ən
Hayek	**HĪ** yək
Hayes	hayz
hazardous	**HAZ** ər dəs
Házi, Vencel	**HAH** zee, **VEN** sel
Hazlitt	**HAZ** lət
headcheese	**HED** cheez
hearken	**HAHR** kən
Hearn, Lafcadio	**HURN**, laf **KAD** ee oh
hearse	hurs
Hearst	hurst
hearth	hahrth
heath, H-	heeth
heathen	**HEE** *th*ən
heather	**HE***TH* ər
Hebbel	**HEB** əl
hebdomadal	heb **DOM** ə dəl
Hebe	**HEE** bee
Hebei	hə bay
Hébert	ay **BAIR**
Hebraic	hi **BRAY** ik
Hebrew	**HEE** broo
Hebrides	**HEB** rə **DEEZ**
Hebron	**HEE** brən

ə ago, a at, ah calm, ahr dark, air care, aw saw, ay say, ch church
e bet, ee me, eer beer, hw what, i is, ī my, *n* French final n vin,

Hecate	**HEK** ə tee
Hecate (Shakespeare)	**HEK** ət
hecatomb	**HEK** ə **TOHM**
Hechler	**HEK** lər
Hecht	hekt
hectare	**HEK** tair
hector, H-	**HEK** tər
Hecuba	**HEK** yuu bə
Hedemann, Knut	**HED** ə **MAHN, KNOOT**
Hedmark	**HED** mahrk
hedonism	**HEE** də **NIZ** əm
Hedwig	**HED** vig
Hegel	**HAY** gəl
Hegelian	hay **GAY** lee ən
hegemony	hi **JEM** ə nee
hegira, H-	hi **JĪ** rə
Heidegger	**HĪD** i gər
Heidelberg	**HĪD** əl **BURG**
heifer	**HEF** ər
Heifetz, Jascha	**HĪ** fits, **YAH** shə
height	hīt
Heijo	hay joh
heil	hīl
Heilbroner	**HĪL BROHN** ər
Heilbronn	**HĪL** brawn
Heilongjiang	hay luung jee ahng
Heilungkiang	hay luung jee ahng
Heimdall	**HAYM** dahl
Heine	**HĪ** nə
Heinlein	**HĪN** līn
heinous	**HAY** nəs
Heinsohn	**HĪN** sohn
Heinz	hīnz
heir	air
heirloom	**AIR** loom
Hejaz	hej **AZ**
heldentenor	**HEL** dən **TEN** ər
Helena	**HEL** ə nə
Helgason, Hördur	**HEL** gə **SOON, HAHR** *th*ər
Helgoland	**HEL** goh **LAND**
helianthus	**HEE** lee **AN** *th*əs
Helicon, h-	**HEL** ə **KON**
helicopter	**HEL** ə **KOP** tər

---

o on, oh oat, oi boy, oo soon, oor poor, or for, ow cow, sh shush,
th thin, *th* this, u up, ur spur, uu book, *zh* pleasure

Heligoland	HEL ə goh **LAND**
heliocentric	HEE lee oh **SEN** trik
Heliogabalus	HEE lee ə **GAB** ə ləs
heliometer	HEE lee **OM** ə tər
heliotherapy	HEE lee oh **THER** ə pee
heliotrope	HEE lee ə **TROHP**
heliport	HEL ə **PORT**
helium	HEE lee əm
helix	HEE liks
hellebore	HEL ə **BOR**
Hellenic	he **LEN** ik
Hellespont	HEL ə **SPONT**
hellion	HEL yən
Helmholtz	HELM hohlts
helot, H-	HEL ət
helotry	HEL ə tree
helpmate	HELP mayt
Helsingfors	HEL sing **FORZ**
Helsinki	HEL sing kee
Helvetia	hel **VEE** shə
Helvetii	hel **VEE** shee ī
Hemans	HEM ənz
hematin	HEM ə tən
hematite	HEE mə **TĪT**
hematology	HEE mə **TOL** ə jee
hematoma	HEE mə **TOH** mə
Hemingway	HEM ing **WAY**
hemiplegia	HEM i **PLEE** jee ə
hemistich	HEM i **STIK**
hemoglobin	HEE mə **GLOH** bən
hemophilia	HEE mə **FIL** ee ə
Henan	hu nahn
Henar, Lucien	hay **NAHR**, loo **SYEN**
hendiadys	hen **DĪ** ə dəs
Hengist	**HENG** gist
Henley	**HEN** lee
henna	**HEN** ə
Henslowe	**HENZ** loh
heparin	**HEP** ə rən
hepatic	hi **PAT** ik
hepatica	hi **PAT** i kə
hepatitis	HEP ə **TĪ** təs
Hephaestus	hi **FES** təs

ə ago, a at, ah calm, ahr dark, air care, aw saw, ay say, ch **church**
e bet, ee me, eer beer, hw what, i is, ī my, *n* French final n vin,

Hephzibah	**HEF** zə bə
Hepplewhite	**HEP** əl **HWĪT**
Heptateuch	**HEP** tə **TYOOK**
Hepzibah	**HEP** zə bə
Hera	**HIR** ə
Heracles	**HE** rə **KLEEZ**
Heraclitus	**HE** rə **KLĪ** təs
heraldic	hə **RAL** dik
heraldry	**HE** rəl dree
herb	urb
herbaceous	hur **BAY** shəs
herbage	**UR** bij
herbarium	hur **BAIR** ee əm
herbivore	**HUR** bə **VOR**
herbivorous	hur **BIV** ə rəs
Herculaneum	**HUR** kyə **LAY** nee əm
Herculean, h-	**HUR** kyə **LEE** ən
Hercules, h-	**HUR** kyə **LEEZ**
hereditary	hə **RED** ə **TER** ee
herein	hir **IN**
heresy	**HE** rə see
heretic	**HE** rə tik
heretical	hə **RET** i kəl
heritage	**HE** rə tij
hermaphrodite	hur **MAF** rə **DĪT**
hermeneutics	**HUR** mə **NOO** tiks
Hermes	**HUR** meez
Hermes, Peter	**HER** məs, **PAY** tər
Hermione	hur **MĪ** ə **NEE**
hermitage	**HUR** mə tij
Hermon	**HUR** mən
Hermosa	hər **MOH** sə
Hernandez	er **NAHN** des
hernia	**HUR** nee ə
hero, H-	**HEE** roh
Herod	**HE** rəd
Herodiade	ay roh dee **AD**
Herodias	hi **ROH** dee əs
Herodotus	hi **ROD** ə təs
heroic	hi **ROH** ik
heroin	**HE** roh ən
heroine	**HE** roh ən
heroism	**HE** roh **IZ** əm

heron	**HE** rən
herpes	**HUR** peez
herpetology	**HUR** pə **TOL** ə jee
Herr	hair
Herrenvolk	**HAIR** ən **FAWLK**
Herrera Campins, Luis	ay **RER** ə kam **PEENZ**, loo **EES**
Herrick	**HE** rik
herring	**HE** ring
Herriot, Édouard	e **RYOH**, ay **DWAHR**
Herriot, James	**HE** ree ət
Herschel	**HUR** shəl
Hersey	**HUR** see
Herter	**HUR** tər
Hertford (England)	**HAHR** fərd
Hertford (US)	**HURT** fərd
Hertz, h-	hurts
Hertzog	**HAIRT** zawg
Herzegovina	**HAIR** tsə goh **VEE** nə
Herzl	**HAIRT** səl
Herzog	**HAIRT** zawg
Heshvan	**HESH** vən
Hesiod	**HEE** see əd
hesitant	**HEZ** ə tənt
hesitate	**HEZ** ə **TAYT**
Hesperia	he **SPI** ree ə
Hesperides	he **SPE** rə **DEEZ**
Hesperus	**HES** pər əs
Hess	hes
Hesse	**HES** ə
Hessellund-Jensen, Aage	**HE** se lun **YEN** sen, **AW** gə
Hessian	**HESH** ən
hetaera	hi **TIR** ə
heterodox	**HET** ər ə **DOKS**
heterodoxy	**HET** ər ə **DOK** see
heterodyne	**HET** ər ə **DĪN**
heterogamy	**HET** ə **ROG** ə mee
heterogeneity	**HET** ə roh jə **NEE** ə tee
heterogeneous	**HET** ər ə **JEE** nee əs
Heteroousian	**HET** ər oh **OO** see ən
heterosexual	**HET** ə rə **SEK** shoo əl
heuristic	hyuu **RIS** tik

Hevesy, Georg	HE ve shee, **GAY** org
hexagonal	hek **SAG** ə nəl
hexameter	hek **SAM** ə tər
hey	hay
heyday	**HAY** day
Heyerdahl, Thor	**HĪ** ər **DAHL, THOR**
Heyrovsky, Jaroslav	**HAY RAWF** skee, **YAH** raw **SLAHF**
Heyse	**HĪ** zə
Heywood	**HAY** wuud
Hezekiah	**HEZ** ə **KĪ** ə
Hialeah	**HĪ** ə **LEE** ə
hiatus	hī **AY** təs
Hiawatha	**HĪ** ə **WAH** thə
hibernate	**HĪ** bər **NAYT**
Hibernian	hī **BUR** nee ən
hibiscus	hī **BIS** kəs
hiccup	**HIK** əp
hidalgo, H-	hi **DAL** goh
hideous	**HID** ee əs
hierarchical	**HĪ** ə **RAHR** ki kəl
hierarchy	**HĪ** ə **RAHR** kee
hieratic	**HĪ** ə **RAT** ik
hieroglyph	**HĪ** ə rə **GLIF**
hieroglyphic	**HĪ** ə rə **GLIF** ik
Hieronymus	**HĪ** ə **RON** ə məs
highboy	**HĪ** boi
highfalutin	**HĪ** fə **LOOT** ən
highland, H-	**HĪ** lənd
highwayman	**HĪ** way mən
Hiiumaa	**HEE** uu **MAH**
hilarious	hi **LA** ree əs
hilarity	hi **LA** rə tee
Hilary	**HIL** ə ree
Hildebrand	**HIL** də **BRAND**
Hillyer	**HIL** yər
Hilo	**HEE** loh
Himachal Pradesh	hi **MAH** chəl prə **DAYSH**
Himalaya	**HIM** ə **LAY** ə
Himalayan	**HIM** ə **LAY** ən
Hinckley	**HINGK** lee
Hindemith	**HIN** də məth
Hindenburg	**HIN** dən **BURG**
Hindi	**HIN** dee

o **on**, oh **oat**, oi **boy**, oo **soon**, oor **poor**, or **for**, ow **cow**, sh **shush**,
th **thin**, *th* **this**, u **up**, ur **spur**, uu **book**, *zh* **pleasure**

hindrance	**HIN** drəns
Hindu	**HIN** doo
Hindustan	**HIN** doo **STAN**
Hindustani	**HIN** duu **STAN** ee
hinterland	**HIN** tər **LAND**
Hipparchus	hi **PAHR** kəs
Hippocrates	hi **POK** rə **TEEZ**
Hippocratic	**HIP** ə **KRAT** ik
Hippocrene	**HIP** ə **KREEN**
hippodrome	**HIP** ə **DROHM**
hippogriff	**HIP** ə **GRIF**
Hippolytus	hi **POL** ə təs
Hippomenes	hi **POM** ə **NEEZ**
hippopotamus	**HIP** ə **POT** ə məs
Hiram	**HĪ** rəm
Hirohito	**HI** roh **HEE** toh
Hiroshige	**HI** roh **SHEE** gə
Hiroshima	**HI** roh **SHEE** mə
Hirshhorn	**HURSH** horn
hirsute	**HUR** soot
Hispaniola	**HIS** pən **YOH** lə
histamine	**HIS** tə **MEEN**
histology	hi **STOL** ə jee
historian	hi **STOR** ee ən
historical	hi **STOR** i kəl
historiographer	hi **STOR** ee **OG** rə fər
history	**HIS** tə ree
histrionic	**HIS** tree **ON** ik
hither	**HI***TH* ər
Hitler	**HIT** lər
Hitlerism	**HIT** lə **RIZ** əm
Hittite	**HI** tīt
hives	hīvz
Hjalmar	**YAHL** mahr
hoagie	**HOH** gee
hoary	**HOR** ee
Hobart (Tasmania)	**HOH** bərt
Hobart (US)	**HOH** bahrt
Hobbes	hobz
Hoboken	**HOH** boh kən
Ho Chi Minh	hoh chee min
Hochoy, Solomon	hoh **CHOI, SOL** ə mən
Hoeven	**HOH** vən

ə **ago**, a **at**, ah **calm**, ahr **dark**, air **care**, aw **saw**, ay **say**, ch **church**
e **bet**, ee **me**, eer **beer**, hw **what**, i **is**, ī **my**, *n* French final n **vin**,

Hoffmann	**HOF** mən
Hofstadter	**HOF STAT** ər
Hofstra	**HOF** strə
hogan	**HOH** gahn
Hogan	**HOH** gən
Hogarth	**HOH** gahrth
Hohenzollern	**HOH** ən **ZOL** ərn
hoi polloi	**HOI** pə **LOI**
hoity-toity	**HOI** tee **TOI** tee
Hokkaido	hoh **KĪ** doh
hokku	**HOK** oo
Holbein	**HOHL** bīn
Holinshed	**HOL** inz **HED**
holism	**HOH LIZ** əm
holistic	hoh **LIS** tik
Holland	**HOL** ənd
hollandaise	**HOL** ən **DAYZ**
hollyhock	**HOL** ee **HOK**
holm	hohm
Holmes	hohmz
holocaust	**HOL** ə **KAWST**
Holocene	**HOH** lə **SEEN**
Holofernes	**HOL** ə **FUR** neez
hologram	**HOH** lə **GRAM**
holograph	**HOH** lə **GRAF**
Holstein, h-	**HOHL** stīn
Holyhead	**HAH** lee **HED**
Holyoake	**HOH** lee **OHK**
Holyoke	**HOHL** yohk
Massachusetts)	
homage	**HOM** ij
hombre	**OM** bray
Homburg, h-	**HOM** burg
Home (earls of)	hyoom
homely	**HOHM** lee
homeopath	**HOH** mee ə **PATH**
homeopathic	**HOH** mee ə **PATH** ik
homeopathy	**HOH** mee **OP** ə thee
homer, H-	**HOH** mər
Homeric	hoh **MER** ik
homicide	**HOM** ə **SĪD**
homiletic	**HOM** ə **LET** ik
homily	**HOM** ə lee

o **on**, oh **oat**, oi **boy**, oo **soon**, oor **poor**, or **for**, ow **cow**, sh **shush**,
th **thin**, *th* **this**, u **up**, ur **spur**, uu **book**, *zh* **pleasure**

hominid	**HOM** ə nid
hominy	**HOM** ə nee
homo, H-	**HOH** moh
homogeneity	**HOH** mə jə **NEE** ə tee
homogeneous	**HOH** mə **JEE** nee əs
homologous	hoh **MOL** ə gəs
homonym	**HOM** ə nim
Homoousian	**HOH** moh **OO** see ən
homophone	**HOM** ə **FOHN**
Homo sapiens	**HOH** moh **SAY** pee ənz
Honan	hoh nan
Honda	**HON** də
Honduras	hon **DUUR** əs
Honecker, Erich	**HOH** nə kər, **AY** rik
Honegger	**HOH** ne gər
Hong Kong	**HONG** kong
Honiara	**HOH** nee **AHR** ə
Honolulu	**HON** ə **LOO** loo
honorable	**ON** ə rə bəl
honorarium	**ON** ə **RAIR** ee əm
honorific	**ON** ə **RIF** ik
Honshu	hon shoo
hooch	hooch
Hooch, Pieter de	**HOHK, PEE** tər də
hoodlum	**HUUD** ləm
hoodoo	**HOO** doo
hoodwink	**HUUD** wingk
hoof	huuf
hook	huuk
hookah	**HUUK** ə
hooker	**HUUK** ər
hooligan	**HOO** li gən
hoop	huup
hoopla	**HOO** plah
hoosegow, hoosgow	**HOOS** gow
Hoosier	**HOO** *zh*ər
hootch	hooch
hootenanny	**HOOT** ə **NAN** ee
hooves	hoovz
Hopeh	hoh pay
Hopi	**HOH** pee
Horace	**HAW** rəs
Horatio	hə **RAY** shoh

ə ago, a at, ah calm, ahr dark, air care, aw saw, ay say, ch church
e bet, ee me, eer beer, hw what, i is, ī my, *n* French final n vin,

Horatius	hə **RAY** shəs
Horeb	**HOH** reb
horizon	hə **RĪ** zən
horizontal	**HOR** ə **ZON** təl
hormone	**HOR** mohn
Hormuz	**HOR** məz
hornblende	**HORN** blend
Horney	**HOR** nī
horologist	hə **ROL** ə jəst
horoscope	**HOR** ə **SKOHP**
Horowitz	**HOR** ə wits
horrendous	haw **REN** dəs
horrible	**HOR** ə bəl
horrid	**HOR** əd
horror	**HOR** ər
Horsa	**HOR** sə
hors de combat	or də kohn **BAH** (kohn French final *n*)
hors d'oeuvre	or **DURV**
hors d'oeuvres	or **DURV**
Horst Wessel	**HORST VES** əl
Horszowski, Mieczyslaw	hawr **SHUF** skee, mye **CHI** swahf
hosanna	hoh **ZAN** ə
Hosea	hoh **ZEE** ə
hosiery	**HOH** *zh*ə ree
Hosmer	**HAWZ** mər
hospice	**HOS** pəs
hospitable	**HOS** pi tə bəl
hostage	**HOS** tij
hostel	**HOS** təl
hostelry	**HOS** təl ree
hostile	**HOS** təl
hostler	**HOS** lər
hotel	hoh **TEL**
hôtel de ville	oh **TEL** də **VEEL**
Houdini	hoo **DEE** nee
Houdon	oo **DAWN** (**DAWN** French final *n*)
Hough	huf
Houghton	**HOHT** ən
Hounsfield, Godfrey	**HOWNZ** feeld, **GAHD** free
houri	**HUUR** ee
Housatonic	**HOO** sə **TAHN** ik
Housman	**HOWS** mən

o **on**, oh **oat**, oi **boy**, oo **soon**, oor **poor**, or **for**, ow **cow**, sh **shush**, th **thin**, *th* **this**, u **up**, ur **spur**, uu **book**, *zh* **pleasure**

Houston (English botanist and Scotland)	**HOO** stən
Houston (New York street and Georgia county)	**HOW** stən
Houston (Texas soldier and city)	**HYOO** stən
Houyhnhnm	**HWIN** əm
hovel	**HUV** əl
hover	**HUV** ər
Hovey	**HUV** ee
howdah	**HOW** də
howdy	**HOW** dee
Howe	how
Howells	**HOW** əlz
howitzer	**HOW** ət sər
hoyden	**HOI** dən
Hoyle	hoil
Hrdlička	**HURD** lich ᴋᴀʜ
Hua Guofeng	hwah gwoh feng
Huang Ho	hwahng hoh
huarache	wə **RAH** chee
Huascarán	ᴡᴀʜ skah **RAHN**
Hubbard	**HUB** ərd
hubbub	**HUB** ub
Hubei	hoo bay
hubris	**HYOO** brəs
huckster	**HUK** stər
Hudibras	**HYOO** də ʙʀᴀs
Huelva	**WEL** vah
Huerta, Victoriano	**WER** tah, ʙᴇᴇᴋ taw **RYAH** naw
Huesca	**WES** kah
Hughes	hyooz
Huguenot	**HYOO** gə ɴᴏᴛ
Huila	**WEE** lah
Hui-tsung	hwee dzuung
hula-hula	**HOO** lə **HOO** lə
hullabaloo	**HUL** ə bə ʟᴏᴏ
hullo	hə **LOH**
Hulme (British)	hyoom
Hulme (US)	hulm
humane	hyoo **MAYN**

ə ago, a at, ah calm, ahr dark, air care, aw saw, ay say, ch church
e bet, ee me, eer beer, hw what, i is, ī my, *n* French final n vin,

humanism, H-	**HYOO** mə **NIZ** əm
humanitarian	hyoo **MAN** ə **TAIR** ee ən
humanization	**HYOO** mə nə **ZAY** shən
Humber	**HUM** bər
humble	**HUM** bəl
Humboldt	**HUM** bohlt
humdrum	**HUM** drum
Hume	hyoom
humerus	**HYOOM** ə rəs
humid	**HYOO** məd
humidity	hyoo **MID** ə tee
humidor	**HYOO** mə **DOR**
humiliate	hyoo **MIL** ee **AYT**
humiliation	hyoo **MIL** ee **AY** shən
humility	hyoo **MIL** ə tee
hummock	**HUM** ək
hummus	**HUM** əs
humor	**HYOO** mər
humorist	**HYOO** mər əst
humorous	**HYOO** mə rəs
Humperdinck	**HUUM** pər **DINGK**
humus	**HYOO** məs
Hunan	hoo nahn
hundred	**HUN** drəd
hundredth	**HUN** drədth
Huneker	**HUN** ə kər
Hungarian	hung **GAIR** ee ən
Hungary	**HUNG** gə ree
hunger	**HUNG** gər
Hungnam	huung nahm
hungry	**HUNG** gree
Hupeh	hoo be
Hu Qili	hoo chee lee
Huron	**HYUUR** ən
hurrah	hə **RAH**
hurray	hə **RAY**
hurricane	**HUR** ə **KAYN**
Hurtado Larrea, Osvaldo	oor **TAH** doh lah **RAY** ah, aws **VAHL** doh
Husák, Gustav	**HOO** sahk, **GUUS** tahf
husky	**HUS** kee
Huss	hus
hussar	hə **ZAHR**

o **on**, oh **oat**, oi **boy**, oo **soon**, oor **poor**, or **for**, ow **cow**, sh **shush**, th **thin**, *th* **this**, u **up**, ur **spur**, uu **book**, *zh* **pleasure**

Hussein	hoo **SAYN**
hussy	**HUS** ee
hustings	**HUS** tingz
hustle	**HUS** əl
Huston	**HYOO** stən
Huszt	hoost
Huxley	**HUKS** lee
Hu Yaobang	hoo yah oh bahng
Huygens	**HĪ** gənz
Huysmans (Dutch)	**HOIS** mahns
Huysmans (French)	wees **MAHNS**
huzzah	hə **ZAH**
Hwang Hai	hwahng hī
Hwang Ho	hwahng hoh
hyacinth	**HĪ** ə sinth
Hyacinthus	**HĪ** ə **SIN** thəs
Hyades	**HĪ** ə **DEEZ**
Hyannis	hī **AN** is
hybrid	**HĪ** brəd
hybridization	**HĪ** brə də **ZAY** shən
Hyderabad	**HĪ** dər ə **BAD**
Hydra, h-	**HĪ** drə
hydrangea	hī **DRAYN** jə
hydraulic	hī **DRAW** lik
hydrocephalic	**HĪ** droh sə **FAL** ik
hydrocephalus	**HĪ** droh **SEF** ə ləs
hydrogen	**HĪ** drə jən
hydrogenate	hī **DROJ** ə **NAYT**
hydrographic	**HĪ** drə **GRAF** ik
hydrography	hī **DROG** rə fee
hydrology	hī **DROL** ə jee
hydrometer	hī **DROM** ə tər
hydropathy	hī **DROP** ə thee
hydrophobia	**HĪ** drə **FOH** bee ə
hydroplane	**HĪ** drə **PLAYN**
hydroponic	**HĪ** drə **PON** ik
hydroxyl	hī **DROK** səl
Hydrozoa	**HĪ** drə **ZOH** ə
Hydrus	**HĪ** drəs
hyena	hī **EE** nə
Hygeia	hī **JEE** ə
hygiene	**HĪ** jeen
hygienic	**HĪ** jee **EN** ik

ə ago, a at, ah calm, ahr dark, air care, aw saw, ay say, ch church
e bet, ee me, eer beer, hw what, i is, ī my, *n* French final n vin,

hygienist	hī **JEE** nəst
Hyksos	**HIK** sohs
Hymen, h-	**HĪ** mən
hymeneal	**HĪ** mə **NEE** əl
Hymettus	**HĪ MET** əs
hymn	him
hymnal	**HIM** nəl
hyperbaric	**HĪ** pər **BA** rik
hyperbola	hī **PUR** bə lə
hyperbole	hī **PUR** bə lee
hyperbolic	**HĪ** pər **BOL** ik
hyperborean, H-	**HĪ** pər **BOR** ee ən
hypercritical	**HĪ** pər **KRIT** i kəl
hyperesthesia	**HĪ** pər es **THEE** *zh*ə
hypergolic	**HĪ** pər **GOL** ik
Hyperion	hī **PIR** ee ən
hyperopia	**HĪ** pər **OH** pee ə
hypertension	**HĪ** pər **TEN** shən
hyperthyroid	**HĪ** pər **THĪ** roid
hypertrophy	hī **PUR** trə fee
Hypnos	**HIP** nos
hypnosis	hip **NOH** səs
hypnotic	hip **NOT** ik
hypnotism	**HIP** nə ᴛɪᴢ əm
hypnotist	**HIP** nə təst
hypochondria	**HĪ** pə **KON** dree ə
hypochondriac	**HĪ** pə **KON** dree ᴀᴋ
hypochondriacal	**HĪ** pə kən **DRĪ** ə kəl
hypocrisy	hi **POK** rə see
hypocrite	**HIP** ə krit
hypodermic	**HĪ** pə **DUR** mik
hypoglycemia	**HĪ** poh glī **SEE** mee ə
hypostasis	hī **POS** tə səs
hypotenuse	hī **POT** ə ɴᴏᴏs
hypothecate	hī ᴘᴏᴛʜ ə ᴋᴀʏᴛ
hypothecation	hī ᴘᴏᴛʜ ə **KAY** shən
hypothermia	**HĪ** poh **THUR** mee ə
hypotheses	hī **POTH** ə ꜱᴇᴇᴢ
hypothesis	hī **POTH** ə səs
hypothetical	**HĪ** pə **THET** i kəl
hypothyroid	**HĪ** poh **THĪ** roid
hypoxia	hī **POK** see ə
Hypseus	**HIP** see əs

Hypsipyle	hip **SIP** ə **LEE**
hyrax	**HĪ** raks
Hyrcania	hər **KAY** nee ə
hyson	**HĪ** sən
hyssop	**HIS** əp
hysterectomy	**HIS** tə **REK** tə mee
hysteresis	**HIS** tə **REE** səs
hysteria	hi **STI** ree ə
hysterics	hi **STER** iks
hysterotomy	**HIS** tə **ROT** ə mee

I

Iago	ee **AH** goh
iamb	**Ī** amb
Iambe	**Ī** əm **BEE**
iambic	ī **AM** bik
Iapetus	ī **AP** ə təs
iatrogenic	ī **A** trə **JEN** ik
Ibadan	ee **BAH** dahn
Ibañez	ee **BAH** nyeth
Iberia	ī **BIR** ee ə
Iberian	ī **BIR** ee ən
ibidem	**IB** ə **DEM**
ibis	**Ī** bis
Ibiza	ee **VEE** zə
Ibn Saud, i-	**IB** ən sah **OOD**
Ibo	**EE** boh
Ibrahim, Mohamed Hamid	**IB** rə **HIM**, moh **HAHM** ed hahm **ID**
Ibsen	**IB** sən
Icarian	i **KAIR** ee ən
Icarus	**IK** ər əs
Iceland	**ĪS** lənd
Iceni	ī **SEE** nī
Ichabod	**IK** ə **BOD**
ich dien	ik **DEEN**
I Ching	ee jeeng
ichneumon	ik **NOO** mən
ichor	**Ī** kor
ichthyology	**IK** thee **OL** ə jee

ə ago, a at, ah calm, ahr dark, air care, aw saw, ay say, ch church
e bet, ee me, eer beer, hw what, i is, ī my, *n* French final n vin,

ichthyosaurus	**IK** thee ə **SAW** rəs
ichthyosis	**IK** thee **OH** sis
icicle	**Ī** si kəl
icon	**Ī** kon
iconoclasm	ī **KON** ə **KLAZ** əm
iconoclast	ī **KON** ə **KLAST**
iconolatry	ī kə **NOL** ə tree
icosahedron	ī **KOH** sə **HEE** drən
icterus	**IK** tər əs
ictus	**IK** təs
Ida	**Ī** də
Idaho	**Ī** də **HOH**
idea	ī **DEE** ə
ideal	ī **DEE** əl
idealism	ī **DEE** ə **LIZ** əm
ideality	**Ī** dee **AL** ə tee
idée fixe	ee day **FEEKS**
idem	**Ī** dem
identically	ī **DEN** ti kə lee
ideogram	**ID** ee ə **GRAM**
ideograph	**ID** ee ə **GRAF**
ideologue	**Ī** dee ə **LOG**
ideology	ī dee **OL** ə jee
ides	īdz
id est	id est
idiocy	**ID** ee ə see
idiom	**ID** ee əm
idiomatic	**ID** ee ə **MAT** ik
idiosyncrasy	**ID** ee ə **SING** krə see
idiosyncratic	**ID** ee oh sin **KRAT** ik
idiot	**ID** ee ət
idiot savant	**EE** **DYOH** sa **VAHN** (**VAHN** French final *n*)
Ido	**EE** doh
idolater	ī **DOL** ə tər
idolum	ī **DOH** ləm
Idomeneo	**EE** doh mə **NAY** oh
Idomeneus	ī **DOM** ə **NOOS**
Idris Senussi	i **DREES** se **NOO** see
idyll	**Ī** dəl
idyllic	ī **DIL** ik
Idzumbuir, Theodore	id zuum **BWEER**, tay oh **DAWR**
Ifni	**IF** nee

o **on**, oh **oat**, oi **boy**, oo **soon**, oor **poor**, or **for**, ow **cow**, sh **shush**, th **thin**, *th* **this**, u **up**, ur **spur**, uu **book**, *zh* **pleasure**

Igdrasil	**IG** drə sil
igitur	**IG** ə **TUUR**
Ignacio-Pinto, Louis	ig **NAH** see oh **PEEN** toh, **LWEES**
Ignatia	ig **NAY** shə
Ignatius	ig **NAY** shəs
igneous	**IG** nee əs
ignis fatuus	**IG** nəs **FACH** oo əs
ignition	ig **NISH** ən
ignoble	ig **NOH** bəl
ignominious	**IG** nə **MIN** ee əs
ignominy	**IG** nə **MIN** ee
ignoramus	**IG** nə **RAY** məs
Igorot	**IG** ə **ROHT**
Igraine	i **GRAYN**
iguana	i **GWAH** nə
Iguassú	**EE** gwah **SOO**
ihram	ee **RAHM**
Ijssel	**Ī** səl
Ijsselmeer	**Ī** səl **MAIR**
ikebana	**EE** ke **BAH** nah
Ikeda	ee ke dah
Ileana	eel **YAH** nə
île de France	eel də **FRAHNS**
ileitis	**IL** ee **Ī** təs
Ileo	i **LAY** oh
ileum	**IL** ee əm
ilex	**Ī** leks
Iliad	**IL** ee əd
Ilium, i-	**IL** ee əm
Illampu	ee **YAHM** poo
illative	**IL** ə tiv
illegal	i **LEE** gəl
illegible	i **LEJ** ə bəl
illegitimate	**IL** ə **JIT** ə mit
illicit	i **LIS** ət
Illimani	**EE** yee **MAH** nee
Illinois	**IL** ə **NOI**
illiterate	i **LIT** ə rət
Illueca, Jorge	eel **WEK** ah, **HOR** hay
illuminate	i **LOO** mə **NAYT**
illumination	i **LOO** mə **NAY** shən
illusion	i **LOO** *zh*ən
illusive	i **LOO** siv

ə ago, a at, ah calm, ahr dark, air care, aw saw, ay say, ch church
e bet, ee me, eer beer, hw what, i is, ī my, *n* French final n vin,

illusory	i **LOO** sə ree
illustrate	**IL** ə **STRAYT**
illustrative	i **LUS** trə tiv
illustrator	**IL** ə **STRAY** tər
illustrious	i **LUS** tree əs
Illyria	i **LEER** ee ə
Iloniemi, Jaakko	**EE** loh **NEE** mee, **YAH** koh
image	**IM** ij
imagery	**IM** ij ree
imago	i **MAY** goh
imam	i **MAHM**
imamate	i **MAH** mayt
imbecile	**IM** bə səl
imbecility	**IM** bə **SIL** ə tee
imbroglio	im **BROHL** yoh
imbue	im **BYOO**
immaculate	i **MAK** yə lət
immanent	**IM** ə nənt
Immanuel	i **MAN** yoo əl
immature	**IM** ə **CHUUR**
immeasurable	i **MEZ**H ə rə bəl
immerse	i **MURS**
immersion	i **MUR** zhən
immigrant	**IM** ə grənt
immigrate	**IM** ə **GRAYT**
imminent	**IM** ə nənt
immiscible	i **MIS** ə bəl
immobile	i **MOH** bəl
immolate	**IM** ə **LAYT**
immoral	i **MOR** əl
immortality	**IM** or **TAL** ə tee
immune	i **MYOON**
immunization	**IM** yə nə **ZAY** shən
immunize	**IM** yə **NĪZ**
immunology	**IM** yə **NOL** ə jee
immure	i **MYUUR**
immutable	i **MYOO** tə bəl
Imogen	**IM** ə **JEN**
Imogene	**IM** ə **JEEN**
impala	im **PAL** ə
impartial	im **PAHR** shəl
impartiality	im **PAHR** shee **AL** ə tee
impasse	**IM** pas

o on, oh oat, oi boy, oo soon, oor poor, or for, ow cow, sh shush,
th thin, *th* this, u up, ur spur, uu book, *zh* pleasure

impasto	im **PAS** toh
impatience	im **PAY** shəns
impatiens	im **PAY** shənz
impeccable	im **PEK** ə bəl
impecunious	**IM** pə **KYOO** nee əs
impedance	im **PEE** dəns
impediment	im **PED** ə mənt
impedimenta	im **PED** ə **MEN** tə
impenetrable	im **PEN** ə trə bəl
impenitent	im **PEN** ə tənt
imperial	im **PIR** ee əl
imperialism	im **PIR** ee ə **LIZ** əm
imperialistic	im **PIR** ee ə **LIS** tik
impertinent	im **PUR** tə nənt
imperturbable	**IM** pər **TUR** bə bəl
impervious	im **PUR** vee əs
impetigo	**IM** pə **TĪ** goh
impetuosity	im **PECH** oo **OS** ə tee
impetuous	im **PECH** oo əs
impetus	**IM** pə təs
Imphal	**IMP** həl
impiety	im **PĪ** ə tee
impious	**IM** pee əs
impiousness	**IM** pee əs nəs
implacable	im **PLAK** ə bəl
implement (n)	**IM** plə mənt
implement (v)	**IM** plə **MENT**
implicate	**IM** plə **KAYT**
implicit	im **PLIS** ət
import (n)	**IM** port
import (v)	im **PORT**
important	im **POR** tənt
importunate	im **POR** chə nət
importune	**IM** pər **TOON**
impostor	im **POS** tər
impotence	**IM** pə təns
impotency	**IM** pə tən see
impotent	**IM** pə tənt
imprecatory	**IM** prə kə **TOR** ee
impregnate	im **PREG** nayt
impresario	**IM** prə **SAHR** ee **OH**
impress (n)	**IM** pres
impress (v)	im **PRES**

ə ago, a at, ah calm, ahr dark, air care, aw saw, ay say, ch church
e bet, ee me, eer beer, hw what, i is, ī my, *n* French final n vin,

imprimatur	IM prə MAH tuur
impromptu	im PROMP too
improvisation	im PROV ə ZAY shən
improvvisatore	EEM prawv VEE zah TAW re
imprudent	im PROO dənt
impudence	IM pyə dəns
impudent	IM pyə dənt
impugn	im PYOON
impuissance	im PYOO ə səns
impunity	im PYOO nə tee
impute	im PYOOT
in absentia	IN ab SEN shə
inadvertent	IN əd VUR tənt
inalienable	in AYL yə nə bəl
inane	i NAYN
inanition	IN ə NISH ən
inanity	i NAN ə tee
Inanna	ee NAH nah
inapplicable	in AP li kə bəl
inarticulate	IN ahr TIK yə lət
inaugural	in AW gyə rəl
inaugurate	in AW gyə RAYT
inauspicious	IN aw SPISH əs
Inca	ING kə
incandescence	IN kən DES əns
incandescent	IN kən DES ənt
incarnate (a)	in KAHR nət
incarnate (v)	in KAHR nayt
incendiary	in SEN dee ER ee
incense (n)	IN sens
incense (anger)	in SENS
incestuous	in SES choo əs
inchoate	in KOH ət
incinerate	in SIN ə RAYT
incipient	in SIP ee ənt
incision	in SIZH ən
incisive	in SĪ siv
incisor	in SĪ zər
inclement	in KLEM ənt
incline (n)	IN klīn
incline (v)	in KLĪN
inclusion	in KLOO zhən
inclusive	in KLOO siv

incognito	IN KOG NEE toh
incoherent	IN koh HIR ənt
incommensurate	IN kə MEN shər ət
incommodious	IN kə MOH dee əs
incommunicado	IN kə MYOO nə KAH doh
incomparable	in KOM pə rə bəl
incompatibility	IN kəm PAT ə BIL ə tee
incompatible	IN kəm PAT ə bəl
incompetence	in KOM pə təns
incompetent	in KOM pə tənt
incongruity	IN kong GROO ə tee
incongruous	in KONG groo əs
inconsequential	in KON sə KWEN shəl
inconsolable	IN kən SOH lə bəl
incontinent	in KON tə nənt
incontrovertible	in KON trə VUR tə bəl
incorporate (a)	in KOR pə rət
incorporate (v)	in KOR pə RAYT
incorporeal	IN kor POR ee əl
incorrigible	in KOR ə jə bəl
increase (n)	IN krees
increase (v)	in KREES
incredible	in KRED ə bəl
incredulity	IN krə DOO lə tee
incredulous	in KREJ ə ləs
increment	IN krə mənt
incremental	IN krə MENT əl
incubate	IN kyə BAYT
incubator	IN kyə BAY tər
incubus	IN kyə bəs
inculcate	in KUL kayt
inculpable	in KUL pə bəl
inculpate	in KUL payt
incumbent	in KUM bənt
incunabula	IN kyə NAB yə lə
incursion	in KUR zhən
incus	ING kəs
indecorous	in DEK ə rəs
indefatigable	IN di FAT ə gə bəl
indelible	in DEL ə bəl
indenture	in DEN chər
independence	IN də PEN dəns
indescribable	IN di SKRĪ bə bəl

ə ago, a at, ah calm, ahr dark, air care, aw saw, ay say, ch church
e bet, ee me, eer beer, hw what, i is, ī my, n French final n vin,

India	IN dee ə
Indian	IN dee ən
Indiana	IN dee AN ə
Indianapolis	IN dee ə NAP ə ləs
Indic	IN dik
indicative	in DIK ə tiv
indices	IN də SEEZ
indicia	in DISH ee ə
indict	in DĬT
indictable	in DĬ tə bəl
indictment	in DĬT mənt
indigenous	in DIJ ə nəs
indigent	IN di jənt
indignant	in DIG nənt
indigo	IN də GOH
indiscreet	IN di SKREET
indiscrete	IN di SKREET
indiscretion	IN di SKRESH ən
indiscriminate	IN di SKRIM ə nət
indisputable	IN di SPYOO tə bəl
indissoluble	IN di SOL yə bəl
indite	in DĬT
indium	IN dee əm
indivisible	IN də VIZ ə bəl
Indo-	IN doh
Indochina	IN doh CHĪ nə
indolence	IN də ləns
indomitable	in DOM ə tə bəl
Indonesia	IN də NEE zhə
Indore	in DOR
Indra	IN drə
indubitable	in DOO bə tə bəl
induce	in DOOS
Indus	IN dəs
Indy, d'	dan DEE (dan French final *n*)
inebriate (a, n)	in EE bree ət
inebriate (v)	in EE bree AYT
inebriation	in EE bree AY shən
inedible	in ED ə bəl
ineffable	in EF ə bəl
ineffectual	IN ə FEK choo əl
inefficacy	in EF i kə see
inefficient	IN ə FISH ənt

---

o on, oh oat, oi boy, oo soon, oor poor, or for, ow cow, sh shush,
th thin, *th* this, u up, ur spur, uu book, *zh* pleasure

ineluctable	IN ə **LUK** tə bəl
inequity	in **EK** wə tee
ineradicable	IN ə **RAD** i kə bəl
inert	i **NURT**
inertia	i **NUR** shə
inestimable	in **ES** tə mə bəl
inevitable	in **EV** ə tə bəl
inexorable	in **EK** sə rə bəl
inexplicable	in **EK** splik ə bəl
in extremis	IN ik **STREE** məs
inextricable	in **EK** strik ə bəl
Inez	Ī nez
infallible	in **FAL** ə bəl
infamous	IN fə məs
infamy	IN fə mee
infancy	IN fən see
infanta	in **FANT** ə
infante	in **FANT** ee
infanticide	in **FAN** tə **SĪD**
infantile	IN fən **TĪL**
infarction	in **FAHRK** shən
inference	IN fə rəns
inferiority	in **FIR** ee **OR** ə tee
infernal	in **FUR** nəl
inferno	in **FUR** noh
infest	in **FEST**
infidel	IN fə dəl
infiltrate	in **FIL** trayt
infiltration	IN fil **TRAY** shən
infinite	IN fə nət
infinitesimal	IN fin ə **TES** ə məl
infinity	in **FIN** ə tee
in flagrante delicto	in flah **GRAHN** te di **LIK** toh
inflammable	in **FLAM** ə bəl
inflammation	IN flə **MAY** shən
inflexible	in **FLEK** sə bəl
inflorescence	IN flə **RES** əns
influential	IN floo **EN** shəl
influenza	IN floo **EN** zə
informative	in **FOR** mə tiv
infra dignitatem	IN frah **DIG** ni **TAH** tem
infrangible	in **FRAN** jə bəl
infrared	IN frə **RED**

ə ago, a at, ah calm, ahr dark, air care, aw saw, ay say, ch church
e bet, ee me, eer beer, hw what, i is, ī my, *n* French final n vin,

Infusoria	**IN** fyuu **SOR** ee ə
Inge	inj
Ingelow	**IN** jə **LOH**
Ingeman, -n	**ING** gə mən
Ingemar	**ING** gə **MAHR**
ingenious	in **JEEN** yəs
ingenue	**AN** jə **NOO**
ingenuity	**IN** jə **NOO** ə tee
ingenuous	in **JEN** yoo əs
inglenook	**ING** gəl **NUUK**
Ingold	**IN** gohld
Ingoldsby	**ING** gəlz bee
ingot	**ING** gət
Ingram	**ING** grəm
ingrate	**IN** grayt
ingratiate	in **GRAY** shee **AYT**
ingredient	in **GREE** dee ənt
Ingres	**AN** grə (**AN** French final *n*)
ingress	**IN** gres
inguinal	**ING** gwə nəl
inhere	in **HIR**
inherent	in **HIR** ənt
inheritance	in **HE** rə təns
inhibition	**IN** ə **BISH** ən
inhospitable	in **HOS** pi tə bəl
inimical	i **NIM** i kəl
inimitable	i **NIM** ə tə bəl
iniquitous	i **NIK** wə təs
iniquity	i **NIK** wə tee
initiate (a, n)	i **NISH** ee ət
initiate (v)	i **NISH** ee **AYT**
initiation	i **NISH** ee **AY** shən
initiative	i **NISH** ə tiv
injudicious	**IN** juu **DISH** əs
injunction	in **JUNGK** shən
inlay	**IN** lay
in loco parentis	in **LOH** koh pə **REN** təs
in medias res	in **MAY** dee **AHS** **RAYS**
in memoriam	**IN** mə **MOR** ee əm
Inness	**IN** əs
innocent, I-	**IN** ə sənt
innocuous	i **NOK** yoo əs
innovate	**IN** ə **VAYT**

---

o on, oh oat, oi boy, oo soon, oor poor, or for, ow cow, sh shush,
th thin, *th* this, u up, ur spur, uu book, *zh* pleasure

Innsbruck	**INZ** bruuk
innuendo	**IN** yoo **EN** doh
Innuit	**IN** yoo ət
innumerable	i **NOO** mə rə bəl
Inönü	**EE** noh noo
inordinate	in **OR** də nət
Inouye	i **NOO** ay
in perpetuum	**IN** pər **PET** yoo əm
inquest	**IN** kwest
inquire	in **KWĪR**
inquiry	in **KWĪR** ee
inquisition, I-	**IN** kwə **ZISH** ən
inquisitive	in **KWIZ** ə tiv
inquisitor	in **KWIZ** ə tər
in re	in **RAY**
insalubrious	**IN** sə **LOO** bree əs
insatiable	in **SAY** shə bəl
insatiate	in **SAY** shee ət
inscrutable	in **SKROO** tə bəl
insecticide	in **SEK** tə **SĪD**
Insectivora	**IN** sek **TIV** ər ə
insectivore	in **SEK** tə **VOR**
insentient	in **SEN** shənt
insert (n)	**IN** surt
insert (v)	in **SURT**
insidious	in **SID** ee əs
insigne	in **SIG** nee
insignia	in **SIG** nee ə
insinuation	in **SIN** yoo **AY** shən
insipid	in **SIP** əd
in situ	in **SĪ** too
insolent	**IN** sə lənt
insomnia	in **SOM** nee ə
insomniac	in **SOM** nee **AK**
insouciance	in **SOO** see əns
insouciant	in **SOO** see ənt
in statu quo	in **STAH** too **KWOH**
instinct (a)	in **STINGKT**
instinct (n)	**IN** stingkt
institut	an stee **TOO** (an French final *n*)
institute	**IN** stə **TOOT**
insubordinate	**IN** sə **BOR** də nət
insufferable	in **SUF** ə rə bəl

ə ago, a at, ah calm, ahr dark, air care, aw saw, ay say, ch church
e bet, ee me, eer beer, hw what, i is, ī my, *n* French final n vin,

insular	**IN** sə lər
insularity	**IN** sə **LAR** ə tee
insulate	**IN** sə **LAYT**
insulation	**IN** sə **LAY** shən
insulator	**IN** sə **LAY** tər
insulin	**IN** sə lən
insult (n)	**IN** sult
insult (v)	in **SULT**
insuperable	in **SOO** pə rə bəl
insurable	in **SHUUR** ə bəl
insurgent	in **SUR** jənt
insurrectionary	**IN** sə **REK** shə **NER** ee
intact	in **TAKT**
intaglio	in **TAL** yoh
integer	**IN** tə jər
integral	**IN** tə grəl
integrate	**IN** tə **GRAYT**
integration	**IN** tə **GRAY** shən
integrity	in **TEG** rə tee
integument	in **TEG** yə mənt
intellectual	**IN** tə **LEK** choo əl
intelligentsia	in **TEL** ə **JENT** see ə
intelligible	in **TEL** ə jə bəl
intemperate	in **TEM** pə rət
inter	in **TUR**
inter alia	**IN** tər **AH** lee ə
inter alios	**IN** tər **AH** lee **OHS**
intercede	**IN** tər **SEED**
intercept (n)	**IN** tər **SEPT**
intercept (v)	**IN** tər **SEPT**
interdict (n)	**IN** tər **DIKT**
interdict (v)	**IN** tər **DIKT**
interest	**IN** trəst
interested	**IN** tə ri stid
interesting	**IN** tə ri sting
interface	**IN** tər **FAYS**
interfere	**IN** tər **FIR**
interference	**IN** tər **FIR** əns
interferon	**IN** tər **FIR ON**
interim	**IN** tə rəm
Interlaken	**IN** tər **LAH** kən
interlocutor	**IN** tər **LOK** yə tər
interlocutory	**IN** tər **LOK** yə **TOR** ee

o on, oh oat, oi boy, oo soon, oor poor, or for, ow cow, sh shush,
th thin, *th* this, u up, ur spur, uu book, *zh* pleasure

interloper	IN tər LOH pər
interlude	IN tər LOOD
intermediary	IN tər MEE dee ER ee
intermediate	IN tər MEE dee ət
interment	in TUR mənt
intermezzo	IN tər MET soh
interminable	in TUR mə nə bəl
intern (medical n, v)	IN turn
intern (confine, as in wartime)	in TURN
internecine	IN tər NEE sən
internist	in TUR nəst
internment	in TURN mənt
inter nos	IN tər NOHS
internship	in TURN SHIP
interpolate	in TUR pə LAYT
interpolation	in TUR pə LAY shən
interpretative	in TUR prə TAY tiv
interregnum	IN tər REG nəm
interrogatory	IN tə ROG ə TOR ee
inter se	IN tər SAY
interstice	in TUR stəs
interstices	in TUR stə SEEZ
interstitial	IN tər STISH əl
intestate	in TES TAYT
intimacy	IN tə mə see
intimate (a)	IN tə mət
intimate (v)	IN tə MAYT
intimation	IN tə MAY shən
intimidate	in TIM ə DAYT
intolerable	in TOL ə rə bəl
intonation	IN tə NAY shən
in toto	in TOH toh
intoxicant	in TOK si kənt
intrados	IN trə DOS
intransigence	in TRAN sə jəns
intrauterine	IN trə YOO tə rən
intravenous	IN trə VEE nəs
intrepid	in TREP əd
intrepidity	IN tre PID ə tee
intricacy	IN tri kə see
intricate	IN tri kət
intrigue	in TREEG

ə ago, a at, ah calm, ahr dark, air care, aw saw, ay say, ch church
e bet, ee me, eer beer, hw what, i is, ī my, *n* French final n vin,

intrinsic	in **TRIN** zik
introit	in **TROH** ət
introversion	**IN** trə **VUR** *zh*ən
introvert	**IN** trə **VURT**
intuition	**IN** too **ISH** ən
intuitive	in **TOO** ə tiv
intumescence	**IN** tuu **MES** əns
Inuit	**IN** yoo ət
inundate	**IN** ən **DAYT**
inure	in **YUUR**
in utero	in **YOO** tər **OH**
in vacuo	in **VAK** yoo **OH**
invalid (ill; a, n, v)	**IN** və ləd
invalid (void)	in **VAL** əd
Invalides	an vah **LEED** (an French final *n*)
inveigh	in **VAY**
inveigle	in **VAY** gəl
inventory	**IN** vən **TOR** ee
Inverness, i-	**IN** vər **NES**
inversion	in **VUR** *zh*ən
invert (a, n)	**IN** vurt
invert (v)	in **VURT**
invertebrate	in **VUR** tə brət
investiture	in **VES** tə chər
inveterate	in **VET** ə rət
invidious	in **VID** ee əs
invigorate	in **VIG** ə **RAYT**
inviolable	in **VĪ** ə lə bəl
inviolate	in **VĪ** ə lət
in vitro	in **VEE** troh
in vivo	in **VEE** voh
invoice	**IN** vois
involute	**IN** və **LOOT**
Io	**Ī** oh
iodine	**Ī** ə **DĪN**
Iola	ī **OH** lə
Iolanthe	**Ī** ə **LAN** thee
ion	**Ī** ən
Ionesco	ee ə **NES** koh
Ionia	ī **OH** nee ə
Ionic, i-	ī **ON** ik
ionium	ī **OH** nee əm
ionize	**Ī** ə **NĪZ**

---

o **on**, oh **oat**, oi **boy**, oo **soon**, oor **poor**, or **for**, ow **cow**, sh **shush**,
th **thin**, *th* **this**, u **up**, ur **spur**, uu **book**, *zh* **pleasure**

ionosphere	ī ON ə sᴇᴇʀ
iota	ī OH tə
Iowa	Ī ə wə
Iowan	Ī ə wən
ipecac	IP i ᴋᴀᴋ
Iphigenia	ɪꜰ ə jə NĪ ə
Ippolitov-Ivanov	i paw LEE tawf i VAH nawf
ipse dixit	ɪᴘ see DIK sət
ipso facto	ɪᴘ soh FAK toh
Ipswich	IP swich
Iran	i RAHN
Irani	i RAHN ee
Iranian	i RAY nee ən
Iraq	i RAHK
Iraqi	i RAHK ee
irascible	i RAS ə bəl
irate	ī RAYT
Irazú	ᴇᴇ rah ZOO
ire	īr
Ireland	ĪR lənd
Irene (not myth)	ī REEN
Irene (myth)	ī REE nee
Irgun	ir GUUN
iridescence	ɪʀ ə DES əns
iridium	ir ID ee əm
iris, I-	Ī rəs
Irish	Ī rish
iritis	ī RĪ təs
Irkutsk	ir KUUTSK
Irminger	UR ming gər
iron	Ī ərn
ironic	ī RON ik
irony	Ī rə nee
Iroquois	IR ə ᴋᴡoɪ
irradiate	i RAY dee ᴀʏᴛ
Irrawaddi	ɪʀ ə WOD ee
irreconcilable	i REK ən sĪ lə bəl
Irredentist	ɪʀ i DEN təst
irrefragable	i REF rə gə bəl
irrefutable	i REF yə tə bəl
irrelevant	i REL ə vənt
irremediable	ɪʀ i MEE dee ə bəl
irreparable	i REP ə rə bəl

ə ago, a at, ah calm, ahr dark, air care, aw saw, ay say, ch church
e bet, ee me, eer beer, hw what, i is, ī my, *n* French final n vin,

irresolute	i **REZ** ə **LOOT**
irreverent	i **REV** ə rənt
irrevocable	i **REV** ə kə bəl
irritant	**IR** ə tənt
irruption	ir **RUP** shən
Irtish	ir **TISH**
Irvine	**UR** vin
Irving	**UR** ving
Iryani, Abdel Karim	**EER** ee ah **NEE**, **AHB** del kah **REEM**
Isador, -e	**IZ** ə **DOR**
Isaiah	ī **ZAY** ə
Isaias	ī **ZAY** əs
Isar	**EE** zahr
Iscariot	i **SKAR** ee ət
ischemia	is **KEE** mee ə
Isère	ee **ZAIR**
Iseult	i **SOOLT**
Isfahan	**IS** fə **HAHN**
Ishbosheth	ish **BOH** shith
Isherwood	**ISH** ər **WUUD**
Ishihara	**ISH** ee **HAHR** ə
Ishikawa	**EE** shee **KAH** wah
Ishmael	**ISH** mee əl
Ishtar	**ISH** tahr
Isidor, -e	**IZ** ə **DOR**
isinglass	**Ī** zən **GLAS**
Isis	**Ī** səs
Islam	is **LAHM**
Islamabad	is **LAHM** ə **BAHD**
Islamic	is **LAH** mik
isle	īl
islet	**Ī** lət
Islington	**IZ** ling tən
Islip	**Ī** slip
Ismaili	**IZ** may **IL** ee
isobar	**Ī** sə **BAHR**
Isocrates	ī **SOK** rə **TEEZ**
isolate (v)	**Ī** sə **LAYT**
isolate (n)	**Ī** sə lət
isolation	**Ī** sə **LAY** shən
Isolde	i **SOHLD**
isomer	**Ī** sə mər
isometric	**Ī** sə **MET** rik

---

o on, oh oat, oi boy, oo soon, oor poor, or for, ow cow, sh shush,
th thin, *th* this, u up, ur spur, uu book, *zh* pleasure

isosceles	ī SOS ə LEEZ
isotherm	Ī sə THURM
isotonic	Ī sə TON ik
isotope	Ī sə TOHP
Israel	IZ ree əl
Israeli	iz RAY lee
Israelite	IZ ree ə LĪT
issei	ees say
Issembe, Aristide	EE sem bay, A ris teed
issue	ISH oo
Istanbul	IS tan BOOL
isthmus	IS məs
Istria	IS tree ə
Italian	i TAL yən
italic, I-	ə TAL ik
italicize	ə TAL ə sīz
Italy	IT ə lee
Itasca	ī TAS kə
item	Ī təm
iterate	IT ə RAYT
iteration	IT ə RAY shən
iterative	IT ə rə tiv
Ithaca	ITH ə kə
Ithome	i THOH mee
Ithuriel	i THYUU ree əl
itinerant	ī TIN ə rənt
itinerary	ī TIN ə RER ee
Ivan	Ī vən
Ivan (Russian)	i VAHN
Ivanhoe	Ī vən HOH
Ivanovo	i VAH naw vaw
Ives	īvz
Iwo Jima	EE woh JEE mə
ixia, I-	IK see ə
Ixion	ik SĪ ən
Izmir	iz MIR
Izvestia	iz VES tee ah

ə ago, a at, ah calm, ahr dark, air care, aw saw, ay say, ch church
e bet, ee me, eer beer, hw what, i is, ī my, *n* French final n vin,

J

Jabesh	**JAY** besh
jabot	*zh*a **BOH**
jacaranda	**JAK** ə **RAN** də
jacinth	**JAY** sənth
jackal	**JAK** əl
jackanapes	**JAK** ə **NAYPS**
Jacobean	**JAK** ə **BEE** ən
Jacobin	**JAK** ə bən
Jacoby (British)	**JAK** ə bee
Jacoby (US)	jə **KOH** bee
Jacovides, Andrea	**JA** koh **VEE** deez, an **DRAY** ə
Jacquard	**JAK** ahrd
Jacqueline (French)	*zh*ahk **LEEN**
Jacqueline (US)	**JAK** ə lin
Jacqueminot	**JAK** mi noh
Jacquerie, j-	*zh*ah **KREE**
Jacques	*zh*ahk
Jacquinot	*zh*ah kee **NOH**
Jacuzzi	jə **KOO** zee
jaeger	**YAY** gər
Jael	**JAY** əl
Jaffa	**JAF** ə
Jagan, Cheddi	**HAH** gahn, **CHE** dee
jagged	**JAG** əd
jaguar	**JAG** wahr
Jahve	**YAH** ve
jai alai	**HĪ** lī
Jain	jīn
Jainism	**JĪ** niz əm
Jaipur	**JĪ** puur
Jakarta	jə **KAHR** tə
Jalapa	hah **LAH** pah
Jalisco	hah **LEES** koh
jalopy	jə **LOP** ee
jalousie	**JAL** ə **SEE**
Jamaica	jə **MAY** kə
Jamal, Jasim Yousif	jah **MAHL**, **JAH** seem **YOO** sef
Jamali	jah **MAH** lee

---

o **on**, oh **oat**, oi **boy**, oo **soon**, oor **poor**, or **for**, ow **cow**, sh **shush**,
th **thin**, *th* **this**, u **up**, ur **spur**, uu **book**, *zh* **pleasure**

jamb	jam
jambalaya	JAM bə LĪ ə
jamboree	JAM bə REE
Jamesian	JAYM zee ən
Jamestown	JAYMZ town
Jamie	JAY mee
Jammu	JUM oo
Jan (European)	yahn
Jan (US)	jan
Janáček	YA nah CHEK
jangle	JANG gəl
Janis	JA nis
janissary, J-	JAN ə SER ee
janitor	JAN ə tər
janizary, J-	JAN ə ZER ee
Jansen	JAN sən
January	JA nyoo ER ee
Janus	JAY nəs
Japan	jə PAN
Japanese	JAP ə NEEZ
jape	jayp
Japheth	JAY fəth
japonica	jə PON i kə
Japurá	ZHAHP ə RAH
Jaques (Shakespeare)	JAY kweez
jardiniere	JAHR də NEER
Jared	JA rəd
Jargalsaikhan, Bayaryn	jahr GAHL sī hahn, BĪ ah rin
jargon	JAHR gən
Jaroslav	YAH rə SLAHF
Jaroslaw	YAH rə SLAHF
Jarrell, Randall	jə REL, RAN dəl
Jarrow	JA roh
Jaruzelski, Wojciech	YAHR oo ZEL skee, VOI chek
jasmine	JAZ mən
Jason	JAY sən
jasper, J-	JAS pər
Jataka	JAH tə kə
jato	JAY toh
jaundice	JAWN dəs
jaunt	jawnt
Java	JAH və
Javanese	JAV ə NEEZ

ə ago, a at, ah calm, ahr dark, air care, aw saw, ay say, ch church
e bet, ee me, eer beer, hw what, i is, ī my, n French final n vin,

Javel, -le	*zh*ə **VEL**
javelin	**JAV** ə lən
Javier	hah **VYER**
Javits	**JA** vəts
Jawara, Alhaji Sir Dawda Kairaba	jah **WAHR** ə, ahl **HAH** jee shahr dah **OO** dah kī **EER** ah bah
ja wohl	yah **VOHL**
Jayewardene	jī yə wor di nə
Jean (French)	*zh*ahn (*zh*ahn French final *n*)
Jeanmaire	*zh*ahn **MAIR** (*zh*ahn French final *n*)
Jeanne (French)	*zh*ahn
jehad	ji **HAHD**
Jehoiakim	ji **HOI** ə kim
Jehol	jə **HOHL**
Jehoram	ji **HOH** rəm
Jehoshaphat	ji **HOSH** ə **FAT**
Jehovah	ji **HOH** və
Jehu	**JEE** hyoo
jejune	ji **JOON**
jejunum	ji **JOON** əm
Jekyll	**JEE** kəl
Jellicoe	**JEL** i **KOH**
Jemima	jə **MĪ** mə
Jena	**YAY** nah
Jenner	**JEN** ər
jennet	**JEN** ət
Jennifer	**JEN** ə fər
jenny, J-	**JEN** ee
Jensen (Danish)	**YEN** sən
Jensen (German)	**YEN** zən
Jensen (US)	**JEN** sən
Jens, Salome	**JENZ, SAL** oh may
jeopardize	**JEP** ər **DĪZ**
jeopardy	**JEP** ər dee
Jephthah	**JEF** thə
jerboa	jər **BOH** ə
jeremiad	**JER** ə **MĪ** əd
Jeremiah	**JER** ə **MĪ** ə
Jerez	he **RETH**
Jericho	**JER** ə **KOH**
Jericó (Colombia)	he ri **KOH**
jerkin	**JUR** kin
Jeroboam, j-	**JER** ə **BOH** əm

o **on**, oh **oat**, oi **boy**, oo **soon**, oor **poor**, or **for**, ow **cow**, sh **shush**,
th **thin**, *th* **this**, u **up**, ur **spur**, uu **book**, *zh* **pleasure**

Jerome	jə **ROHM**
Jersey, j-	**JUR** zee
Jerusalem	jə **ROO** sə ləm
Jervis (British)	**JAHR** vəs
Jervis (US)	**JUR** vəs
jessamine, J-	**JES** ə mən
Jesse, Jessie	**JES** ee
Jessica	**JES** i kə
Jesu	**JEE** zoo
Jesuit	**JEZH** oo it
jeté	*zh*ə **TAY**
Jethro	**JETH** roh
jetsam	**JET** səm
jettison	**JET** ə sən
jeu de mots	*zh*uu də **MOH**
jeu d'esprit	*zh*uu des **PREE**
jewel	**JOO** əl
jewelry	**JOO** əl ree
Jewett	**JOO** ət
Jewry	**JOO** ree
Jezebel	**JEZ** ə **BEL**
Jezreel	**JEZ** ree əl
Jhelum	**JAY** ləm
Jiangsu	jee ahng soo
Jiangxi	jee ahng shee
jibe	jīb
Jibuti	ji **BOO** tee
Jicamarca	hee kah **MAHR** kə
Jidda	**JID** ə
Jigme Dorji Wanchuk	**DYIG** me **DOR** jee **VANG** chook
jihad	ji **HAHD**
Jilin	jee leen
Jiménez	hee **MAY** nəs
jimson, J-	**JIM** sən
jingle	**JING** gəl
jingly	**JING** glee
jingo	**JING** goh
jingoism	**JING** goh ɪz əm
jinn	jin
Jinnah	**JIN** ə
jinni	**JEE** nee
jinrikisha	jin **RIK** shaw
jipijapa	**HEE** pee **HOP** ə

ə ago, a at, ah calm, ahr dark, air care, aw saw, ay say, ch **church**
e bet, ee me, eer beer, hw what, i is, ī my, *n* French final n vin,

jitney	**JIT** nee
Joab	**JOH** ab
Joachim (Bible)	**JOH** ə kim
Joachim	**YOH** ə kim
Joanna	joh **AN** ə
Joanne	joh **AN**
Joaquin	wah **KEEN**
job	job
Job	johb
Jocasta	joh **KAS** tə
jocose	joh **KOHS**
jocosity	joh **KOS** ə tee
jocular	**JOK** yə lər
jocund	**JOK** ənd
Jodhpur, j-	**JOD** pər
jodhpurs	**JOD** pərz
Joel	**JOH** əl
Joffre	**ZH**AW frə
Joffrey	**JOF** ree
Jogjakarta	**JOHG** jə **KAHRT** ə
Johann (German)	**YOH** hahn
Johannes (German)	yoh **HAH** nes
Johannesburg	joh **HAN** əs **BURG**
Johore	jə **HOR**
joie de vivre	*zh*wah də **VEE** vrə
joinder	**JOIN** dər
Joinvile (Brazil)	*zh*oin **VEE** lee
Joinville (France)	*zh*wan **VEEL** (*zh*wan French final *n*)
Jókai	**YOH** koi
Joliet	**JOH** lee **ET**
Joliot-Curie	*zh*aw **LYOH** kuu **REE**
Jolo	haw law
Jonah	**JOH** nə
Jonathan	**JON** ə thən
Jones, Abeodu Bowen	**JOHNZ**, ah **BEE** doo **BOH** een
jongleur	**ZH**AWN glər
jonquil	**JONG** kwəl
Joplin	**JOP** lən
Jordaens	**YOR** dahns
Jordan	**JOR** dən
Jordanian	jor **DAY** nee ən
jorum	**JOR** əm
Josephus	joh **SEE** fəs

o on, oh oat, oi boy, oo soon, oor poor, or for, ow cow, sh shush,
th thin, *th* this, u up, ur spur, uu book, *zh* pleasure

Joshua	**JOSH** oo ə
Josiah	joh **SĪ** ə
joss	jos
jostle	**JOS** əl
Jouhaux, Léon	*zh*oo **OH**, lay **AWN** (**AWN** French final *n*)
Joule, j-	jool
Jourdain, Louis	*zh*uur **DAN**, loo **EE** (**DAN** French final *n*)
joust	just
Jove	johv
Jowett	**JOW** ət
Joyce	jois
Juan (French)	*zh*oo **AHN** (**AHN** French final *n*)
Juan (Spanish)	hwahn
Juanita	wah **NEE** tə
Juárez	**HWAH** res
Juba	**JOO** bah
Jubal	**JOO** bəl
Jubilate	**JOO** bə **LAY** tee
jubilate	**JOO** bə **LAYT**
jubilee	**JOO** bə **LEE**
Judaea	joo **DEE** ə
Judah	**JOO** də
Judaic	joo **DAY** ik
Judaica	joo **DAY** ə kə
Judaism	**JOO** dee **IZ** əm
Judas	**JOO** dəs
Judea	joo **DEE** ə
judgment	**JUJ** mənt
judicable	**JOO** di kə bəl
judicial	joo **DISH** əl
judiciary	joo **DISH** ee **ER** ee
judicious	joo **DISH** əs
judo	**JOO** doh
Juggernaut, j-	**JUG** ər **NAWT**
Jugnauth, Aneerood	joo **NOHT**, ah **NEE** rood
jugular	**JUG** yə lər
Juilliard	**JOO** lee ahrd
jujitsu	joo **JIT** soo
juju	**JOO** joo
jujube	**JOO** joob
jukebox	**JOOK** boks

ə ago, a at, ah calm, ahr dark, air care, aw saw, ay say, ch church
e bet, ee me, eer beer, hw what, i is, ī my, *n* French final n vin,

Jukes	jooks
julep	**JOO** ləp
julienne	**JOO** lee **EN**
junco	**JUNG** koh
juncture	**JUNGK** chər
Juneau	**JOO** noh
Jung	yuung
Jungfrau	**YUUNG** frow
Juniata	**JOO** nee **AT** ə
juniper	**JOO** nə pər
Junius	**JOON** yəs
Junker, j-	**YUUNG** kər
junket	**JUNG** kət
Juno	**JOO** noh
Junoesque	**JOO** noh **ESK**
junta	**HUUN** tə
junto	**JUN** toh
Jupiter	**JOO** pə tər
Jura	**JUUR** ə
Jurassic	juu **RAS** ik
jurat	**JUUR** at
Jurgens	**JUR** gənz
juridical	juu **RID** i kəl
jurisdiction	**JOOR** əs **DIK** shən
jurisprudence	**JOOR** əs **PROO** dəns
Juruá	*zh*00 roo **AH**
Jusserand	*zh*oos **RAHN** (**RAHN** French final *n*)
jussive	**JUS** iv
justificatory	jə **STIF** ə kə **TOR** ee
Justin	**JUS** tin
Justinian	jə **STIN** ee ən
Jute, j-	joot
Jutish	**JOO** tish
Jutland	**JUT** lənd
Juvenal	**JOO** və nəl
juvenescence	**JOO** və **NES** əns
juvenile	**JOO** və nəl
juvenilia	**JOO** və **NIL** ee ə
juxtapose	**JUK** stə **POHZ**
juxtaposition	**JUK** stə pə **ZISH** ən

o on, oh oat, oi boy, oo soon, oor poor, or for, ow cow, sh shush,
th thin, *th* this, u up, ur spur, uu book, *zh* pleasure

K

Kaaba	**KAH** bə
Kabaiwanska	kah **BĪ** ee **VAHN** skə
Kabalevsky	**KAH** bah **LYEF** skee
kabob	kə **BOB**
Kabore, John Boureima	kah bə **REE**, **JON** boo **RAY** mə
kabuki	kə **BOO** kee
Kabul	**KAH** buul
Kabyle	kə **BĪL**
kachina	kə **CHEE** nə
Kádár, Janos	**KAH** dahr, **YAH** nohsh
Kaddish	**KOD** ish
Kadesh	**KAY** desh ˙
Kaduna	kə **DOO** nə
Kaesong	**KAY** sawng
Kaffir, k-	**KAF** ər
Kaffraria	kə **FRAIR** ee ə
Kafir, k-	**KAF** ər
Kafka	**KAHF** kah
kaftan	**KAF** tən
Kagawa	kah gah wah
Kagoshima	kah goh shee mah
Kaifeng	kī fung
kaiser, K-	**KĪ** zər
Kakatiya	kah **KAH** tee yah
Kalahari	**KAH** lah **HAH** ree
Kalamazoo	**KAL** ə mə **ZOO**
kalanchoe	kə **LANG** koo ee
Kalat	kə **LAHT**
kaleidoscope	kə **LĪ** də **SKOHP**
kaleidoscopic	kə **LĪ** də **SKOP** ik
Kalevala	**KAH** li **VAH** lah
Kalgan	kahl gahn
Kalinin	kah **LEE** nin
Kalisz	**KAH** lish
Kalmuck	**KAL** muk
Kalonji	kah **LOHN** jee
Kamakura	kah mah koo rah

ə ago, a at, ah calm, ahr dark, air care, aw saw, ay say, ch church
e bet, ee me, eer beer, hw what, i is, ī my, *n* French final n vin,

Kamara, Dauda	kah **MAHR** ə, **DOW** də
Kamchatka	kam **CHAT** kə
Kamehameha	kə **MAY** ə **MAY** hah
Kamerad	**KAH** mə **RAHT**
kamikaze	**KAH** mi **KAH** zee
Kampala	**KAHM PAHL** ə
kampong	**KAHM** pawng
Kanaka	kə **NAK** ə
Kanara	kə **NAHR** ə
Kanarese	**KAN** ə **REEZ**
Kanazawa	kah nah zah wah
Kanchenjunga	**KAHN** chən **JUUNG** gə
Kandahar	**KAN** də **HAHR**
Kandinsky	kan **DIN** skee
kangaroo	**KANG** gə **ROO**
Kanin	**KAY** nin
Kansas	**KAN** zəs
Kansu	kahn soo
Kant	kahnt
Kantian	**KAHN** tee ən
Kantorovich, Leonid	**KAHN** tə **RAWV** ich, lye aw **NYEET**
kaolin	**KAY** ə lən
kaon	**KAY** on
Kapellmeister	kah **PEL MĪ** stər
Kapitonov, Ivan	kap ee **TAWN** awf, ee **VAHN**
Kapitsa, Pyotr	**KOP** yit sə, **PYAW** tər
Kaplan	**KAP** lən
kapok	**KAY** pok
kappa	**KAP** ə
kaput	kə **PUUT**
Kara	**KAHR** ə
Karachi	kə **RAH** chee
Karajan	**KAH** rah **YAHN**
Kara-Kalpak	kah **RAH** kahl **PAHK**
Karakoram	**KAHR** ə **KOH** rəm
karakul	**KA** rə kəl
Kara Kum	**KA** rə **KUUM**
Karamanlis, Constantin	**KAH** rə **MAHN** lees, **KON** stən teen
Karame, Rashid	**KAH** rə may, rah **SHEED**
Karandreas, Nicolas	**KAHR** ahn *TH*RAY əs, nee **KOH** lah **OHSH**
karate	kə **RAH** tee

o **on**, oh **oat**, oi **boy**, oo **soon**, oor **poor**, or **for**, ow **cow**, sh **shush**, th **thin**, *th* **this**, u **up**, ur **spur**, uu **book**, *zh* **pleasure**

Karelian	kə **REE** lee ən
Karenina, Anna	kah **RE** nyi nə, **AH** nah
Karjalainen, Ahti	**KAHR** yə **LĪ** nən, **AH** tee
Karlovac	**KAHR** lə **VAHTS**
Karlsbad	**KAHRLZ** bad
Karlsruhe	**KAHRLZ ROO** ə
karma	**KAHR** mə
Karmal, Babrak	**KAHR** mel, bah **BRAHK**
Karnak	**KAHR** nak
Károlyi	**KAH** roh lyi
Kartawidjaja, Djuanda	**KAHR** tah wee **JĪ** ə, **JOO** ahn də
Kasai	kə **SĪ**
Kasavubu	kah sah **VOO** boo
kasha	**KAH** shə
Kashmir	kash **MIR**
kashruth	**KOSH** ruut
Kassebaum, Nancy	**KAS** ə bowm
Kassem, Abdel-Raouf al-	**KAH** sim, **AHB** duul rah **OOF** el
Kassim	kah **SEEM**
Kastenmeier	**KAH** sten mī ər
Katahdin	kə **TAH** din
Katanga	kə **TAHNG** gə
Katangese	kə tahng **GEEZ**
Katmai	**KAT** mī
Katmandu	**KAHT** mahn **DOO**
Katowice	**KAH** toh **VEET** se
Katrine	**KA** trin
Kattegat	**KAT** ə **GAT**
katydid	**KAY** tee did
Kauai	**KOW** ī
Kauffmann	**KOWF** mahn
Kaufman, George S.	**KAWF** mən
Kaunas	**KOW** nahs
Kaunda, Kenneth	kah **OON** dah
Kavir	kə **VEER**
Kawabata, Yasunari	kah wah bah tah, yah soo nah ree
Kawasaki	**KAH** wah **SAH** kee
kayak	**KĪ** ak
Kaye	kay
Kaysone Phomvihane	kī ee **SAWN** puum vee **HAHN**
Kazak, Kazakh	kə **ZAHK**
Kazan	kə **ZAN**

ə ago, a at, ah calm, ahr dark, air care, aw saw, ay say, ch church
e bet, ee me, eer beer, hw what, i is, ī my, *n* French final n vin,

Kazan (USSR)	kə ZAHN
Kazbek	kaz BEK
Kazin	KAY zin
kazoo	kə ZOO
kea	KAY ə
Kean, Edmund	keen
Kean, Thomas	kayn
Kearny	KAHR nee
Keats	keets
kebab	kə BOB
kebob	kə BOB
Kedah	KAY dah
Kedar	KEE dər
kedge	kej
kedgeree	KEJ ə REE
Kedron	KEE drən
keeshond	KAYS hawnt
Keewatin	kee WAH tin
kefir	kə FIR
Keijo	kay joh
Keita, Modibo	KAY tah, maw DEE baw
Keith	keeth
Kekkonen, Urho	KEK oh NEN, OOR hoh
kelpie	KEL pee
Kelvin, k-	KEL vən
Kemal Ataturk	ke MAHL AH tah TURK
Kemi	KEM ee
Kenilworth	KEN əl WURTH
Kennebec	KEN ə BEK
Kennebunk	KEN ə BUNGK
Kennelly	KEN ə lee
kenning	KEN ing
keno	KEE noh
Kenosha	kə NOH shə
kenosis	ki NOH səs
Kensington	KEN zing tən
Kentucky	kən TUK ee
Kenya	KEN yə
Kenyatta, Jomo	ken YAH tə, JOH moh
Kenyon	KEN yən
Keokuk	KEE ə kək
Keos	KEE os
Keough	KEE oh

---

o on, oh oat, oi boy, oo soon, oor poor, or for, ow cow, sh shush,
th thin, *th* this, u up, ur spur, uu book, *zh* pleasure

kepi	**KAY** pee
Kepler	**KEP** lər
Kerch	kairch
kerchief	**KUR** chəf
Kérékou, Ahmed Mathieu	**KER** ə **KOO**, **AH** med mah tee **YOO**
Kerensky, Kerenski	kə **REN** skee
kerf	kurf
Kerguelen	**KUR** gə lən
Kermanshah	**KUR** mahn **SHAH**
kermis	**KUR** mis
Kermit	**KUR** mit
Kern	kurn
Kerouac	**KER** oo **AK**
Kerr (British)	kahr
Kerr (US)	kur
kestrel	**KES** trəl
Keszthely	**KEST** hay
ketchup	**KECH** əp
ketone	**KEE** tohn
ketosis	kee **TOH** səs
Keturah	kə **TUUR** ə
Keuka	**KYOO** kə
Kevin	**KEV** in
Kew	kyoo
kewpie, K-	**KYOO** pee
Keynes	kaynz
Keynesian	**KAYN** zee ən
Khabarovsk	kah **BAH** rofsk
Khachaturian	**KAH** chə **TUUR** ee ən
Khaibar	**KĪ** bər
khaki	**KAK** ee
Khalkha	**KAL** kə
Khamenei, Hojatolislam Ali	hah **MEE** nee, **HOH** jə **TOOL** is lam **AH** lee
khan, K-	kahn
Khanaqin	**KAN** ə kin
Kharg	karg
Kharkov	**KAHR** kawf
Khartoum, Khartum	kahr **TOOM**
Khayyám	kī **YAHM**
khedive	kə **DEEV**
Khmer	kə **MER**

ə ago, a at, ah calm, ahr dark, air care, aw saw, ay say, ch church
e bet, ee me, eer beer, hw what, i is, ī my, *n* French final n vin,

Khomeini, Ruhollah	hoh **MAY** nee, roo chol **LAH**
Khrushchev	kruush **CHAWF**
Khufu	**KOO** foo
Khurramshahr	KOR əm **SHAHR**
Khust	koost
Khuzistan	**KOO** zis TAHN
Khyber	KĪ bər
Kiangsi	jee ahng see
Kiangsu	jee ahng soo
Kibanda, Simon Pierre	kee **BAHN** də, see **MOHN** pyair
	(**MOHN** French final *n*)
kibbutz	ki **BUUTS**
kibei	kee bay
kibitz	**KIB** əts
kibitzer	**KIB** əts ər
kibosh	KĪ bosh
Kickapoo	**KIK** ə POO
kickshaw	**KIK** shaw
Kiddush	**KID** əsh
Kiel	keel
kielbasa	keel **BAH** sə
Kierkegaard	**KEER** kə GAHRD
Kiesinger, Kurt	**KEE** zing ər, **KUURT**
Kieta	kee **E** tah
Kiev	kee **EV**
Kigali	ki **GAHL** ee
Kigeri	kee **GAIR** ee
Kilauea	KEE low AY ə (low as in *cow*)
Kilimanjaro	KIL ə mən JAHR oh
Kilkenny	kil **KEN** ee
Killarney	ki **LAHR** nee
Killiecrankie	KIL ee **KRANG** kee
Kilmarnock	kil **MAHR** nək
kiln	kil
kilo	**KEE** loh
kilogram	**KIL** ə GRAM
kilometer	kə **LOM** ə tər
kilowatt	**KIL** ə WOT
Kimberley	**KIM** bər lee
Kim Du-bong	kim doo bohng
Kim Il-sung	kim eel sung
Kimny, Nong	**KIM** nee, **NONG**
kimono	kə **MOH** nə

---

o **on**, oh **oat**, oi **boy**, oo **soon**, oor **poor**, or **for**, ow **cow**, sh **shush**,
th **thin**, *th* **this**, u **up**, ur **spur**, uu **book**, *zh* **pleasure**

Kinabalu	KIN ə bə LOO
kindergarten	KIN dər GAHR tən
kinescope, K-	KIN ə SKOHP
kinesics	kə NEE siks
kinesiology	kə NEE see OL ə jee
kinesthesia	KIN əs THEE zhə
kinesthetic	KIN əs THET ik
kinetic	kə NET ik
Kingsley	KINGZ lee
Kingston	KINGZ tən
kinkajou	KING kə JOO
Kinsey	KIN zee
Kinshasa	kin SHAHS ə
Kioga	kee OH gə
kiosk	KEE osk
Kiowa	KĪ ə waw
Kiplinger	KIP ling ər
Kirca, A. Coşkun	kur JAH, jawsh KUUN
Kirchschlaeger, Rudolf	KIRK SHLEG ər, ROO dohlf
Kirghiz	kir GEEZ
Kiribati	KIR ə BAS
Kirilenko	ki ri LENG koh
Kirin	kee reen
kirk	kurk
Kirkcudbright	kər KOO bree
Kirkpatrick	kurk PAT rik
Kirkuk	kir KOOK
Kirman	kər MAHN
Kironde, Apollo	kee RAHN day, ah POH loh
Kirov	KEE rof
kirschwasser	KEERSH VAH sər
Kirsten	KEER stən
Kirsten (US)	KUR stən
kirtle	KUR təl
Kirwan	KUR wən
Kiselev, Tikhon	kee seel YAWF, TEE hən
Kishi, Nobusuke	KEE shee, noh BUU ske
Kishinev	KISH i nef
kishke	KISH kə
Kiska	KIS kə
kismet	KIZ mət
Kissinger	KIS ən jər
kitsch	kich

ə ago, a at, ah calm, ahr dark, air care, aw saw, ay say, ch church
e bet, ee me, eer beer, hw what, i is, ī my, n French final n vin,

Kittikachorn, Thanom	**KEE** tee kah **CHORN**, thah **NOM**
Kiwanis	kə **WAH** nəs
kiwi	**KEE** wee
Kizya, Luka	**KEE** *zh*ah, loo **KAH**
Klagenfurt	**KLAH** gən **FUURT**
Klamath	**KLAM** əth
klaxon, K-	**KLAK** sən
Kléber	klay **BAIR**
Kleberg	**KLAY** bərg
Klee	klay
kleig	kleeg
Klemperer	**KLEM** pər ər
kleptomania	**KLEP** tə **MAY** nee ə
kleptomaniac	**KLEP** tə **MAY** nee **AK**
Klestil, Thomas	**KLES** teel, **TOH** mahs
klieg	kleeg
Klingsor	**KLING** zor
Klondike	**KLON** dīk
klystron	**KLĪS** tron
knapsack	**NAP** sak
knavish	**NAY** vish
knell	nel
Kneller	**NEL** ər
Knesset	kə **NES** et
Knickerbocker	**NIK** ər **BOK** ər
knickknack	**NIK** nak
knish	kə **NISH**
knob	nob
knoll	nohl
Knopf	knahpf
Knossos	**NOS** əs
knout	nowt
knowledge	**NOL** ij
Knowles	nohlz
Knox	noks
knurl	nurl
Knut	kə **NOOT**
koala	koh **AH** lə
koan	**KOH** on
Kobe	**KOH** bee
Koblenz	**KOH** blents
Koch, Edward	koch
Kodak	**KOH** dak

o on, oh oat, oi boy, oo soon, oor poor, or for, ow cow, sh shush,
th thin, *th* this, u up, ur spur, uu book, *zh* pleasure

Kodály, Zoltán	koh DĪ, ZOHL tahn
Kodiak, k-	KOH dee AK
Koestler	KEST lər
Kohinoor	KOH ə NUUR
Kohl, Helmut	KOHL, HEL moot
kohlrabi	kohl RAH bee
Koht	koot
koine, K-	koi NAY
Koirala, Matrika Prasad	kaw RAH lah, MAH tri kah prah SAHD
Koivisto, Mauno	KOY vees toh, MOW noh
Kokoschka	kə KAWSH kə
Kolingba, André-Dieudonne	koh LING bah, ahn DRAY DYUU daw NAY
kolinsky	kə LIN skee
kolkhoz	kawl KAWZ
Kollwitz, Käthe	KOHL vits, KAY tə
Kol Nidre	kohl NID rə
Kolyma	kə LEE mə
Komarno	kaw MAHR naw
Komatina, Miljan	koh MAH tee nah, MEEL yahn
kona	KOH nə
Kondrashin	kahn DRAH shin
Konev	KAW nef
Königsberg	KAYN igz BURG
Konitsa	KAW neet SAH
Kónya, Sándor	KAWN yah, SHAHN dor
kookaburra	KUUK ə BUR ə
Koopmans	KOOP mənz
Kootenay	KOOT ə NAY
kopeck	KOH pek
Kopit	KOH pit
kopje	KOP ee
Koran	kə RAHN
Korea	kə REE ə ·
Kornegay, Horace	KORN gay
Koroma, Abdul	koh ROH mə, ahb DOOL
Korzybski	kor ZIP skee
Kościuszko, Tadeusz	kawsh CHUUSH koh, tah DE uush
kosher	KOH shər
Košice	KAW shit se
Kossuth	KAH sooth
Kostandov, Leonid	kah STAHN dawf, lee ahn YEED

ə ago, a at, ah calm, ahr dark, air care, aw saw, ay say, ch church
e bet, ee me, eer beer, hw what, i is, ī my, *n* French final n vin,

Koster	**KOS** tər
Kosygin	kə **SEE** gən
Kotka	**KAWT** kə
koto	**KOH** toh
koumis	**KOO** məs
Kountché, Seyni	**KOON** chee, **SAY** nee
Koussevitzky	**KOO** sə **VIT** skee
Kovalev, Anatoly	kah vahl **YAWF**, ah nah **TOH** lee
Kovno	**KAWV** naw
Kowalczyk, Edward	koh **VAL** chik, **ED** vahrd
kowtow	**KOW** tow (tow as in *cow*)
kraal	krahl
Krafft-Ebing	**KRAHFT AY** bing
Krag, Jens Otto	**KROW**, **YENS AH** toh
Kragerö	**KRAH** yai **RER**
Krakatoa	**KRAH** kə **TOH** ə
kraken	**KRAH** kən
Kraków (Polish)	**KRAH** kuuf
Krasnodar	**KRAHS** naw **DAHR**
Kravets, Vladimir	**KRAH** vits, vlah **DEE** mir
Krefeld	**KRAY** felt
Kreisky, Bruno	**KRĪS** kee
kremlin, K-	**KREM** lən
Kreutzer, k-	**KROIT** sər
Kreymborg, Alfred	**KRAYM** borg
krieg, K-	kreeg
Kriemhild	**KREEM** hild
kris	krees
Krishna	**KRISH** nə
Krishnan, Natarajan	**KRISH** nən, nat **RAH** jən
Kristiansand	**KRIS** tyahn **SAHN**
Kristiansund	**KRIS** tyahn **SOON**
Krk	kurk
Krnov	**KUR** nawf
Krokodil	kroh koh **DEEL**
krona	**KROH** nə
krone	**KROH** nə
Kronstadt	**KRAWN** staht
Kropotkin	krə **POT** kən
Kruger	**KROO** gər
krugerrand	**KROO** gər rand
Krupp	kruup
Kruševac	**KROO** she **VAHTS**

o **on**, oh **oat**, oi **boy**, oo **soon**, oor **poor**, or **for**, ow **cow**, sh **shush**, th **thin**, *th* **this**, u **up**, ur **spur**, uu **book**, *zh* **pleasure**

Krylov	kri **LAWF**
krypton	**KRIP** tahn
Kuala Lumpur	**KWAH** lə luum **PUUR**
Kubango	kuu **BAHNG** goh
Kubelik	**KUUB** ə lik
Kublai Khan	**KOO** blī **KAHN**
Kubla Khan	**KOO** blə **KAHN**
Kuchel	**KEE** kəl
Kuchta	**KOOSH** tah
kudos	**KYOO** dahs
kudu	**KOO** doo
kudzu	**KUUD** zoo
Kufic	**KOO** fik
kugel	**KUUG** əl
Kuibyshev	**KWEE** bə **SHEF**
Ku Klux Klan	koo kluks klan
kulak	koo **LAHK**
Kuldiga	**KUUL** di gah
Kultur	kuul **TOOR**
kümmel	**KIM** əl
kumquat	**KUM** kwot
Kun, Béla	**KUUN, BAY** lah
Kunayev, Dinmukhamed	koo **NĪ** yef, **DEEN** moo hah **MED**
Kundera, Milan	**KUUN** də rə, **MI** lan
Kundry	**KUUN** dri
Kuner	**KYOO** nər
Kung Fu-tse	kuung foo dzu
Kunming	kuun ming
Kuomintang	kwoh min tahng
Kura	kuu **RAH**
Kural, Adnan	koo **RAHL**, ahd **NAHN**
Kurdish	**KUR** dish
Kurdistan	**KUR** də **STAN**
Kure	**KOO** re
Kuril, -e	**KYUUR** il
Kurosawa	**KUUR** ə **SAH** wah
Kursk	kuursk
Kusch, Polycarp	**KUUSH, POL** i **KAHRP**
Kush (India)	kuush
Kuwait	kə **WAYT**
Kuwatly, Shukri Al	koo **WAHT** lee, **SHOO** kree ahl
Kuznetsk	kuuz **NETSK**

ə ago, a at, ah calm, ahr dark, air care, aw saw, ay say, ch church
e bet, ee me, eer beer, hw what, i is, ī my, *n* French final n vin,

Kuznetsov, Vasily	kooz nyits **AWF**, vah **SEEL** ee
Kuznets, Simon	**KUZ** nets
Kwajalein	**KWAHJ** ə **LAYN**
Kwakiutl	**KWAH** kee **OOT** əl
Kwangchowan	gwahng joh wahn
Kwangsi Chuang	gwahng see jwahng
Kwangtung	gwahng duung
Kwantung	gwahn duung
kwashiorkor	**KWASH** ee **OR** kər
Kweichow	gway joh
Kweilin	kway lin
Kweiyang	gway yahng
Kyd	kid
Kymry	**KIM** ree
Ky, Nguyen Cao	**KEE**, **NOO** yen kow
Kyoto	kee **OH** toh
kyphosis	kī **FOH** səs
Kyprianou, Spyros	**KEE** pree **AH** noo, **SPEE** rohs
Kyrie eleison	**KIR** ee **AY** ə **LAY** ə **SAHN**
Kyushu	**KYOO** shoo

L

laager	**LAH** gər
Laban	**LAY** bən
labia	**LAY** bee ə
labial	**LAY** bee əl
labium	**LAY** bee əm
laboratory	**LAB** rə **TOR** ee
Labrador	**LAB** rə dor
Labuan	**LAH** boo **AHN**
laburnum	lə **BUR** nəm
labyrinth, L-	**LAB** ə rinth
labyrinthine	**LAB** ə **RIN** thən
Laccadive	**LAK** ə **DĪV**
laccolith	**LAK** ə lith
Lacedaemon	**LAS** ə **DEE** mən
Lacedaemonian	**LAS** ə di **MOH** nee ən
Lachaise, La Chaise	la **SHEZ**
Lacharrière, Guy Ladreit de	lah shahr **YAIR**, **GEE** lah **DRAY** də

o **on**, oh **oat**, oi **boy**, oo **soon**, oor **poor**, or **for**, ow **cow**, sh **shush**,
th **thin**, *th* **this**, u **up**, ur **spur**, uu **book**, *zh* **pleasure**

laches	**LACH** əz
Lachesis	**LAK** ə sis
lachrymal	**LAK** rə məl
lachrymose	**LAK** rə **MOHS**
lackadaisical	**LAK** ə **DAY** zi kəl
Lackawanna	**LAK** ə **WAH** nə
lackey	**LAK** ee
Laconia	lə **KOH** nee ə
laconic	lə **KON** ik
lacquer	**LAK** ər
lacrosse	lə **KRAWS**
lactation	lak **TAY** shən
lactose	**LAK** tohs
lacuna	lə **KYOO** nə
lacunae	lə **KYOO** nee
Ladakh	lah **DAHK**
Ladin	lə **DEEN**
Ladino, l-	lə **DEE** noh
Ladoga	**LAD** ə gə
Ladrone, l-	lə **DROHN**
Lae	**LAH** ay
Laertes	lay **ER** teez
Laetare	lay **TAH** ree
laetrile	**LAY** ə tril
La Farge	lə **FAHRZ**H
Lafayette (French general)	lah fah **YET**
Lafayette (US)	**LAF** ee **ET**
Lafcadio	laf **KAD** ee oh
Lafitte, Laffite	lə **FEET**
La Fontaine	la fon **TEN**
lager	**LAH** gər
lagniappe	lan **YAP**
lagoon	lə **GOON**
Lagos (Nigeria)	**LAH** gohs
Lagting, Lagthing	**LAHG** ting
La Guardia, Fiorello	lə **GWAHR** dee ə, **FEE** ə **REL** oh
Lahore	lə **HOR**
laic	**LAY** ək
laird	laird
laissez-faire	**LES** ay **FAIR**
laity	**LAY** ə tee
Laius	**LAY** əs

ə ago, a at, ah calm, ahr dark, air care, aw saw, ay say, ch **church**
e bet, ee me, eer beer, hw what, i is, ī my, *n* French final n vin,

La Jolla	lə **HOI** ə
Lakmé	lak **MAY**
Lalo	la **LOH**
lama, L-	**LAH** mə
Lamarck	lə **MAHRK**
Lamartine	la mahr **TEEN**
lamasery	**LAH** mə **SER** ee
Lamaze	lə **MAHZ**
lambaste	lam **BAYST**
lambda	**LAM** də
lambent	**LAM** bənt
Lambeth	**LAM** bəth
lamé	la **MAY**
Lamech	**LAY** mək
lament	lə **MENT**
lamentable	**LAM** ən tə bəl
laminate (a, n)	**LAM** ə nət
laminate (v)	**LAM** ə **NAYT**
Lamont	lə **MONT**
lampoon	lam **POON**
lamprey	**LAM** pree
Lamy	la **MEE**
lanai, L-	lə **NĪ**
Lanark	**LAN** ərk
Lancashire	**LANG** kə **SHIR**
Lancaster	**LANG** kə stər
Lancastrian	lang **KAS** tree ən
Lancelot	**LAN** sə lət
lancet	**LAN** sət
Lanchow	lahn joh
landau	**LAN** dow
Ländler	**LENT** lər
Lange (North European)	**LAHNG** ə
Langer	**LANG** ər
Langland	**LANG** lənd
Langley	**LANG** lee
Langmuir	**LANG** myuur
langue d'oc	lahng **DAWK**
langue d'oïl	lahng daw **EEL**
languid	**LANG** gwəd
languish	**LANG** gwish
languor	**LANG** gər

---

o **on**, oh **oat**, oi **boy**, oo **soon**, oor **poor**, or **for**, ow **cow**, sh **shush**, th **thin**, *th* **this**, u **up**, ur **spur**, uu **book**, *zh* **pleasure**

Lanier	lə NEER
lanthanide	LAN thə NĪD
lanthanum	LAN thə nəm
Lantos	LAN tohs
lanugo	lə NOO goh
lanyard	LAN yərd
Lanzhou	lahn joh
Lao	low (as in *cow*)
Laoag	lah WAHG
Laocoön	lay AHK ə WAHN
Laodamia	lay OD ə MĪ ə
Laodicea	lay OD ə SEE ə
Laodicean	lay OD ə SEE ən
Laomedon	lay OM ə DON
Laos	LAH ohs
Lao-tzu	lowd zu (ow as in *cow*)
La Paz	lə PAHZ
lapel	lə PEL
lapidary	LAP ə DER ee
lapis lazuli	LAP əs LAZ ə lee
Lapland	LAP land
La Plata	lah PLAH tah
Lapp	lap
lapsus linguae	LAP səs LING gwee
Laputa	lə PYOO tə
Laramie	LA rə mee
larboard	LAHR bərd
larcenous	LAHR sə nəs
larceny	LAHR sə nee
lardoon	lahr DOON
Laredo	lə RAY doh
lares	LAIR eez
largess	lahr ZHES
larghetto	lahr GET oh
largo	LAHR goh
lariat	LA ree ət
La Rocca, Umberto	lah RAWK ah, oom BAIR toh
Laroche	lah ROHSH
La Rochefoucauld	lah RUSH foo KOH
Larousse	lah ROOS
Larvik	LAHR veek
laryngeal	lə RIN jee əl
laryngectomy	LA rən JEK tə mee

laryngitis	**LA** rən **JĪ** təs
laryngology	**LA** rən **GOL** ə jee
larynx	**LA** ringks
lasagna	lə **ZAHN** yə
La Salle	lə **SAL**
La Scala	lah **SKAH** lah
lascivious	lə **SIV** ee əs
Las Cruces	lahs **KROO** səs
laser	**LAY** zər
Lashio	**LAHSH** yoh
La Spezia	lah **SPET** syah
Lassen	**LAS** ən
lassie	**LAS** ee
lasso	**LAS** oh
Las Vegas	lahs **VAY** gəs
Latakia	**LAH** tah **KEE** ah
lateen	la **TEEN**
latent	**LAY** tənt
Lateran	**LAT** ər ən
latex	**LAY** teks
lath	lath
lathe	lay*th*
lather (soap)	**LA***TH* ər
lather (worker)	**LATH** ər
Latimer	**LAT** ə mər
Latium	**LAY** shee əm
Latona	lə **TOH** nə
Latourette	la too **RET**
Latvia	**LAT** vee ə
laud, L-	lawd
laudanum	**LAW** də nəm
Lauder	**LAW** dər
launch	lawnch
laureate	**LOR** ee ət
laurel	**LOR** əl
Laurencin	law rahn **SAN** (rahn and **SAN** French final *n*)
Laurentian	law **REN** shən
Laurents	**LAW** rents
Laurie	**LAWR** ee
Lausanne	loh **ZAN**
Lautenberg	**LOWT** ən **BURG**

o on, oh oat, oi boy, oo soon, oor poor, or for, ow cow, sh shush,
th thin, *th* this, u up, ur spur, uu book, *zh* pleasure

Lautrec	loh **TREK**
lava	**LAH** və
lavaliere	**LAV** ə **LIR**
lavatory	**LAV** ə **TOR** ee
lave	layv
Laver	**LAY** vər
Lavoisier	la vwah **ZYAY**
Laxalt	**LAKS** awlt
Laxness, Halldór	**LAHKS** nes, **HAHL** dohr
Layamon	**LAY** ə mən
lazar	**LAY** zər
lazaret	**LAZ** ə **RET**
lazaretto	**LAZ** ə **RET** oh
Lazarus	**LAZ** ər əs
Lazear	lə **ZEER**
lazulite	**LAZ** ə **LĪT**
lazzarone	**LAZ** ə **ROH** nay
leaden	**LED** ən
league	leeg
Leah	**LEE** ə
Leahy	**LAY** hee
Leander	lee **AN** dər
Lear	leer
learned (a)	**LUR** nəd
leash	leesh
leaven	**LEV** ən
Leavenworth	**LEV** ən **WURTH**
Leavis	**LEEV** əs
Lebanese	**LEB** ə **NEEZ**
Lebanon	**LEB** ə nən
Lebensraum	**LAY** bəns **ROWM** (**ROWM** as in *cow*)
Lebrija	le **BREE** hah
Lech (river)	lek
lecher	**LECH** ər
Lechuga, Carlos	lay **CHOO** gah, **KAHR** lohs
lecithin	**LES** ə thən
Leconte	lə **KAWNT**
Le Corbusier	lə kor buu **ZYAY**
lectern	**LEK** tərn
lecture	**LEK** chər
Leczyca	lan **CHIT** sah
Leda	**LEE** də
Lederberg, Joshua	**LAY** dər **BURG**, **JOSH** ə wə

ə ago, a at, ah calm, ahr dark, air care, aw saw, ay say, ch church
e bet, ee me, eer beer, hw what, i is, ī my, *n* French final n vin,

lederhosen	**LAY** dər **HOH** zən
Lederle	**LED** ər lee
Lee Kuan Yew	lee kwahn yoo
Leeuwenhoek	**LAY** vən **HOOK**
leeward, L-	**LEE** wərd
leeward (nautical)	**LOO** ərd
Lefevre (French)	lə **FEV**
Lefevre, Le Fevre (US)	lə **FEEV** ər
legacy	**LEG** ə see
Le Gallienne	lə **GAL** yən
legate (n)	**LEG** ət
legate (v)	li **GAYT**
legatee	**LEG** ə **TEE**
legato	li **GAH** toh
legend	**LEJ** ənd
legendary	**LEJ** ən **DER** ee
Léger	lay **ZHAY**
legerdemain	**LEJ** ər də **MAYN**
Leghorn (Italy)	**LEG** horn
leghorn, L- (poultry)	**LEG** ərn
legible	**LEJ** ə bəl
legionnaire	**LEE** jə **NAIR**
legislature	**LEJ** əs **LAY** chər
Legree	li **GREE**
legume	**LEG** yoom
Legwaila, Legwaila Joseph	lee kwī **EEL** ah, lee kwī **EEL** ah **JOH** səf
Lehár	**LAY** hahr
Le Havre	lə **HAH** vrə
Lehigh	**LEE** hī
lei	lay
Leibnitz	**LĪB** nits
Leica	**LĪ** kə
Leicester	**LES** tər
Leiden	**LĪ** dən
Leif	leef
Leigh	lee
Leinsdorf	**LĪNZ** dorf
Leinster	**LEN** stər
Leipzig	**LĪP** sig
leisure	**LEE** zhər
Leith	leeth

---

o on, oh oat, oi boy, oo soon, oor poor, or for, ow cow, sh shush,
th thin, *th* this, u up, ur spur, uu book, *zh* pleasure

leitmotiv	**LĪT** moh **TEEF**
Leland	**LEE** lənd
Lely	**LEE** lee
leman	**LEM** ən
Leman	**LEE** mən
Le Mans	lə **MAHN** (**MAHN** French final *n*)
Lemass, Sean	lə **MAHS, SHAWN**
lemming	**LEM** ing
Lemnitzer	**LEM** nit sər
Lemnos	**LEM** nos
Lemoyne	lə **MOIN**
Lemuel	**LEM** yoo əl
lemur	**LEE** mər
Lemuria	li **MYOO** ree ə
Lena (river)	**LYE** nah
Lendl, Ivan	**LEN** dəl, **EE** vahn
L'Enfant	lahn **FAHN** (lahn and **FAHN** French final *n*)
length	lengkth
leniency	**LEE** nee ən see
lenient	**LEE** nee ənt
Lenin	**LEN** in
Leningrad	**LEN** in **GRAD**
lenity	**LEN** ə tee
Lenox, Lennox	**LEN** əks
lens	lenz
lentil	**LEN** təl
lento	**LEN** toh
Lenya, Lotte	**LAY** nyə, **LAH** tə
Leo	**LEE** oh
Leonard	**LEN** ərd
Leonardo	**LEE** ə **NAHR** doh
Leoncavallo	lay **AWN** kah **VAH** loh
Leonid	**LEE** ə nid
Leonidas	lee **ON** ə dəs
Leontief	lee **AWN** tyef
Leopardi, Giacomo	**LAY** aw **PAHR** dee, **JAH** kaw maw
Léopoldville	**LEE** ə pohld **VIL**
leotard	**LEE** ə **TAHRD**
Lepanto	li **PAN** toh
Lepidus	**LEP** i dəs
Lepontine	li **PON** tin
leprechaun	**LEP** rə **KAWN**

ə ago, a at, ah calm, ahr dark, air care, aw saw, ay say, ch church
e bet, ee me, eer beer, hw what, i is, ī my, *n* French final n vin,

leprosy	**LEP** rə see
Lepus	**LEE** pəs
Lermontov	**LER** mən **TAWF**
lesbian, L-	**LEZ** bee ən
Lesbos	**LEZ** bos
Leschetizky	**LE** she **TIT** skee
lese majesty	**LEEZ MAJ** ə stee
lesion	**LEE** zhən
Leslie (American)	**LES** lee
Leslie (British)	**LEZ** lee
Lesotho	lay **SOO** too
Lesseps	**LES** əps
Le Sueur	lə **SUUR**
lethal	**LEE** thəl
lethargic	lə **THAHR** jik
lethargy	**LETH** ər jee
Lethe, l-	**LEE** thee
Letitia	li **TISH** ə
leucocyte	**LOO** kə **SĪT**
leukemia	loo **KEE** mee ə
Levant	lə **VANT**
Levantine	lə **VAN** tin
levee	**LEV** ee
lever	**LEV** ər
leverage	**LEV** ə rij
Levi	**LEE** vī
leviathan, L-	lə **VĪ** ə thən
Levice	**LE** vit **SE**
Levine	lə **VEEN**
Levit, -t	**LE** vit
Leviticus	lə **VIT** ə kəs
levity	**LEV** ə tee
levy	**LEV** ee
Levy	**LEE** vee
lexicography	**LEK** sə **KOG** rə fee
lexicon	**LEK** sə **KON**
lex talionis	**LEKS TAL** ee **OH** nəs
Leyden	**LĪ** dən
Leydig	**LĪ** dig
Leyte	**LAY** tee
Lhasa	**LAH** sə
Lhasa apso	**LAH** sə **AP** soh
liability	**LĪ** ə **BIL** ə tee

---

o on, oh oat, oi boy, oo soon, oor poor, or for, ow cow, sh shush,
th thin, *th* this, u up, ur spur, uu book, *zh* pleasure

liable	LĪ ə bəl
liaison	LEE ə ZON
liana	lee AH nə
Liao	lyow
Liaoning	lyow ning
libation	lī BAY shən
Libby	LIB ee
libelous	LĪ bə ləs
Liberia	lī BEER ee ə
libertine	LIB ər TEEN
libidinous	lə BID ə nəs
libido	lə BEE doh
libra, L-	LEE brə
librarian	lī BRAIR ee ən
library	LĪ BRER ee
librettist	lə BRET əst
libretto	lə BRET oh
Libya	LIB ee ə
Libyan	LIB ee ən
licentiate	lī SEN shee ət
licentious	lī SEN shəs
lichee	lee chee
lichen	LĪ kən
licorice	LIK ə rəs
Li Desheng	lee du shung
Lidice	LEE də CHAY
Lido	LEE doh
liebfraumilch	LEEB frow MILK
Liechtenstein	LIK tən STĪN
lied (song)	leed
lieder (pl of *lied*, song)	LEE dər
Liederkranz	LEE dər KRAHNTS
lief, L-	leef
liege	leej
Liège	lee EZH
lien	leen
lieu	loo
lieutenant	loo TEN ənt
lieutenant (British army)	lef TEN ənt
ligament	LIG ə mənt
ligature	LIG ə chər

ə ago, a at, ah calm, ahr dark, air care, aw saw, ay say, ch church
e bet, ee me, eer beer, hw what, i is, ī my, *n* French final n vin,

lightning	**LĪT** ning
ligneous	**LIG** nee əs
lignite	**LIG** nīt
Ligonier	LIG ə **NEER**
Ligurian	li **GYUUR** ee ən
lilac	**LĪ** lək
Lilith	**LIL** əth
Liliuokalani	lee **LEE** oo oh kah **LAH** nee
Lille	leel
Lilliput	**LIL** ə pət
Lilliputian	LIL ə **PYOO** shən
Lilongwe	li **LAWNG** way
lima (bean)	**LĪ** mə
Lima (Ohio)	**LĪ** mə
Lima (Peru)	**LEE** mə
limbo	**LIM** boh
Limburger (cheese)	**LIM BURG** ər
limerick, L-	**LIM** ə rik
Limoges	li **MOHZ***H*
limousine	**LIM** ə **ZEEN**
limpet	**LIM** pət
limpid	**LIM** pəd
Limpopo	lim **POH** poh
linage	**LĪ** nij
lineage (family)	**LIN** ee ij
lineament	**LIN** ee ə mənt
linear	**LIN** ee ər
Lingayen	LING gah **YEN**
lingerie	**LAN** *zh*ə **REE**
Ling Qing	leeng chung
lingua franca	**LING** gwə **FRANG** kə
Linguaphone	**LING** gwə **FOHN**
linguistic	ling **GWIS** tik
Linley	**LIN** lee
Linlithgow	lin **LITH** goh
Linnaean	lə **NEE** ən
Linnaeus	lə **NEE** əs
linnet, L-	**LIN** ət
Linotype	**LĪ** nə **TĪP**
Lin Piao	leen pyow
lintel	**LIN** təl
Linton	**LIN** tən
Linus	**LĪ** nəs

---

o **on**, oh **oat**, oi **boy**, oo **soon**, oor **poor**, or **for**, ow **cow**, sh **shush**,
th **thin**, *th* **this**, u **up**, ur **spur**, uu **book**, *zh* **pleasure**

Lin Yutang	lin yoo tahng
Linz	lints
Linzer torte	**LIN** zər **TORT**
Lipari	**LIP** ə ree
Lipchitz	**LIP** shits
Lippe	**LIP** ə
Lippi	**LIP** ee
Lippizaner	**LIP** it **SAH** nər
liqueur	li **KUR**
liquidity	li **KWID** ə tee
liquor	**LIK** ər
lira	**LIR** ə
lire	**LIR** ay
Lisa	**LEE** sə
Lisbon	**LIZ** bən
lisle	līl
Lisle (France)	leel
Lisle (US)	līl
Lissajous	**LEE** sə **ZHOO**
lissome	**LIS** əm
Liszt	list
litany, L-	**LIT** ə nee
litchi	**LEE** chee
liter	**LEE** tər
literary	**LIT** ə **RER** ee
literate	**LIT** ə rət
literati	**LIT** ə **RAH** tee
literature	**LIT** ər ə chər
lithe	lī*th*
lithium	**LITH** ee əm
lithograph	**LITH** ə **GRAF**
lithography	li **THOG** rə fee
lithotomy	li **THOT** ə mee
Lithuania	**LITH** oo **AY** nee ə
litigant	**LIT** ə gənt
litigious	lə **TIJ** əs
litmus	**LIT** məs
litotes	**LĪ** tə **TEEZ**
litterateur	**LIT** ə rə **TUR**
littoral	**LIT** ə rəl
liturgical	lə **TUR** ji kəl
liturgy	**LIT** ər jee
Liu Shao-chi	lee oo show chee (show as in *cow*)

ə ago, a at, ah calm, ahr dark, air care, aw saw, ay say, ch church
e bet, ee me, eer beer, hw what, i is, ī my, *n* French final n vin,

livable	**LIV** ə bəl
livelihood	**LĪV** lee **HUUD**
livelong	liv lawng
liven	**LĪ** vən
liver	**LIV** ər
Liverpudlian	**LIV** ər **PUD** lee ən
liverwort	**LIV** ər **WURT**
liverwurst	**LIV** ər **WUURST**
livery	**LIV** ə ree
Livia	**LIV** ee ə
livid	**LIV** əd
Livonia	li **VOH** nee ə
Livorno	lee **VOR** noh
Livy	**LIV** ee
Li Weihan	lee way hahn
Li Xiannian	lee shee ahn nyahn
Ljubljana	lyoo **BLYAH** nah
llama	**LAH** mə
Llanelly	la **NEL** ee
Llanera	lyah **NAY** rah
Lleshi, Haxhi	**LAY** shee, hah **JEE**
Llewellyn	loo **EL** in
Llullaillaco	**YOO YĪ YAHK** oh
loach	lohch
Loanda	loh **AHN** də
loath	lohth
loathe	loh*th*
lobar	**LOH** bər
lobe	lohb
lobectomy	loh **BEK** tə mee
lobelia	loh **BEEL** yə
Lobito	loo **BEE** too
loblolly	**LOB LOL** ee
Lobo, l-	**LOH** boh
lobotomy	loh **BOT** ə mee
locale	loh **KAL**
Locarno	loh **KAHR** noh
locative	**LOK** ə tiv
loch, L-	lok
lochia	**LOH** kee ə
Lochinvar	**LOK** in **VAHR**
Locke	lok
loco	**LOH** koh

o on, oh oat, oi boy, oo soon, oor poor, or for, ow cow, sh shush,
th thin, *th* this, u up, ur spur, uu book, *zh* pleasure

locum tenens	**LOH** kəm **TEN** ənz
locus	**LOH** kəs
locution	loh **KYOO** shən
locutory	**LOK** yə **TOR** ee
Lodge, l-	loj
Lodi (Italy)	**LAW** dee
Lodi (US)	**LOH** dī
Lodz	luuj
Loeb	lohb
Loeffler	**LEF** lər
loess	**LOH** es
Loesser	**LES** ər
Loew	loh
Loewe	loh
Loewy	**LOH** ee
Lofoten	**LOH** **FUUT** ən
Logan	**LOH** gən
logarithm	**LAW** gə **RITH** əm
loge	loh*zh*
loggia	**LOHJ** ə
logic	**LOJ** ik
logistic	loh **JIS** tik
logo	**LOH** goh
logomachy	loh **GOM** ə kee
logos, L-	**LOH** gos
logy	**LOH** gee
Lohengrin	**LOH** ən grin
Loire	lwahr
Loki	**LOH** kee
Lokoloko, Tore	**LOH** koh **LOH** koh, **TOR** ay
Lola	**LOH** lə
Lolita	loh **LEET** ə
loll	lol
Lollard	**LOL** ərd
Lollobrigida, Gina	law law **BREE** *zh*ee dah, **ZH**EE nah
Lombard	**LOM** bərd
Lombardy	**LOM** bər dee
Lombrosian	lom **BROH** zee ən
Lomé	loh **MAY**
Lomond	**LOH** mənd
Loncar, Budimir	**LAWN** chər, **BUU** dee meer
London	**LUN** dən
longevity	lon **JEV** ə tee

ə ago, a at, ah calm, ahr dark, air care, aw saw, ay say, ch church
e bet, ee me, eer beer, hw what, i is, ī my, *n* French final n vin,

Longinus	lon JĪ nəs
longitude	**LON** jə **TOOD**
long-lived	lawng līvd
Longobardi	**LON** goh **BAHR** dee
López	**LOH** pez
López Mateos, Adolfo	**LOH** pez mah **TAY** ohs, ah **DAWL** foh
López Portillo, José	**LOH** pez por **TEE** yoh, hoh **SAY**
loquacious	loh **KWAY** shəs
loquacity	loh **KWAS** ə tee
Lorain	lə **RAYN**
loran, L-	loh **RAN**
Lorca	**LOR** kə
lordosis	lor **DOH** səs
Lorelei	**LOR** ə **LĪ**
Loren, Sophia	**LAW** ren, soh **FEE** ah
lorgnette	lorn **YET**
Lorica	law **REE** kə
Loridan	law ree **DAHN**
lorry	**LOR** ee
Los Alamos	law **SAL** ə **MOHS**
Los Angeles	law **SAN** jə ləs
Los Gatos	law **SGAT** əs
L'Osservatore Romano	loh **SER** vah **TAW** re roh **MAH** noh
Lothario	loh **THA** ree oh
Lothian	**LOH** *th*ee ən
Loti	loh **TEE**
Loudon	**LOW** dən (**LOW** as in *cow*)
lough	lok
Louis (English)	**LOO** is
Louis (French)	lwee
Louisiana	loo **EE** zee **AN** ə
Louisville	**LOO** ee **VIL**
lour	lowr (as in *sour*)
Lourdes	luurd
Louvain	loo **VAN** (**VAN** French final *n*)
louver	**LOO** vər
Louvre	**LOO** vrə
Loveland	**LUV** lənd
Lowell	**LOH** əl
lower (scowl)	**LOW** ər (**LOW** as in *cow*)
lox	loks
Loyola	loi **OH** lə

o **on**, oh **oat**, oi **boy**, oo **soon**, oor **poor**, or **for**, ow **cow**, sh **shush**,
th **thin**, *th* **this**, u **up**, ur **spur**, uu **book**, *zh* **pleasure**

lozenge	**LOZ** ənj
Luanda	loo **AHN** də
Luang Prabang	loo **AHNG** prah **BAHNG**
luau	**LOO** ow
Lubang	loo **BAHNG**
Lubavitcher	luu **BAHV** əch ər
Lubbers, Jan Hendrik	**LUUB** ərs, yahn **HEN** drik
Lubbock	**LUB** ək
Lübeck	**LOO** bek
Lübke, Heinrich	**LOOP** kə, **HĪN** rish
Lublin	**LOO** blin
lubricity	loo **BRIS** ə tee
Lucan	**LOO** kən
Lucania	loo **KAY** nee ə
Lucas	**LOO** kəs
luce, L-	loos
Lucenec	**LOO** che **NETS**
Lucerne, l-	loo **SURN**
Lucia (Italian)	loo **CHEE** ah
Lucian	**LOO** shən
lucid	**LOO** səd
Lucifer, l-	**LOO** sə fər
Lucite	**LOO** sīt
Lucius	**LOO** shəs
Lucknow	**LUK** now
lucrative	**LOO** krə tiv
lucre	**LOO** kər
Lucrece	loo **KREES**
Lucretius	loo **KREE** shəs
Lucrezia	loo **KRAYT** see ə
lucubrate	**LOO** kyə **BRAYT**
lucubration	**LOO** kyə **BRAY** shən
Lucullan	loo **KUL** ən
Lucullus	loo **KUL** əs
Lüda	loo dah
Luddite	**LUD** īt
ludicrous	**LOO** də krəs
Ludwiczak, Zdzislaw	**LOOD** vee chak, **ZDEE** slahv
Ludwig	**LUD** wig
lues	**LOO** eez
Luftwaffe	**LUUFT** vah fə
Luger	**LOO** gər
lugubrious	luu **GOO** bree əs

ə ago, a at, ah calm, ahr dark, air care, aw saw, ay say, ch church
e bet, ee me, eer beer, hw what, i is, ī my, *n* French final n vin,

Lukow	**LUU** kuuf
Lully	luu **LEE**
lumbago	lum **BAY** goh
lumbar	**LUM** bər
Luminal	**LOO** mə nəl
luminescence	**LOO** mə **NES** əns
luminous	**LOO** mə nəs
lummox	**LUM** əks
Lumumba, Patrice	luu **MUUM** bə, pa **TREES**
lunar	**LOO** nər
lunette	loo **NET**
Lupercalia	**LOO** pər **KAY** lee ə
lupine (plant)	**LOO** pən
lupine (wolfish)	**LOO** pīn
lupus	**LOO** pəs
lure	luur
lurid	**LUUR** əd
Lusaka	loo **SAHK** ə
Lusitania	**LOO** sə **TAY** nee ə
lustrous	**LUS** trəs
Lü-ta	loo dah
lutanist, lutenist	**LOOT** ə nəst
lute	loot
Lutece	lyoo **TES**
lutetium	loo **TEE** shee əm
Luthuli	loo **THOO** lee
Lutsk	lootsk
lux, L-	luks
luxe	luuks
Luxembourg	**LUK** səm **BURG**
Luxor	**LUK** sor
luxuriance	lug **ZH**UUR ee əns
luxurious	lug **ZH**UUR ee əs
luxury	**LUG** zhə ree
Luzon	loo **ZON**
Lvov, Lwów	lə **VAWF**
Lwoff, André	**LWAWF, AHN** dray
lycanthropy	lī **KAN** thrə pee
Lycaon	lī **KAY** ən
Lycaonia	**LĪ** kay **OH** nee ə
lycée	lee **SAY**
lyceum	lī **SEE** əm
Lycian	**LISH** ee ən

o **on**, oh **oat**, oi **boy**, oo **soon**, oor **poor**, or **for**, ow **cow**, sh **shush**,
th **thin**, *th* **this**, u **up**, ur **spur**, uu **book**, *zh* **pleasure**

Lycidas	**LIS** ə dəs
Lycurgus	lī **KUR** gəs
Lydgate	**LID GAYT**
Lyle	līl
Lyly	**LIL** ee
lymph	limf
lymphocyte	**LIM** fə **SĪT**
lymphogranulomatosis	**LIM** foh **GRAN** yə **LOH** mə **TOH** səs
Lyndon	**LIN** dən
lynx	lingks
Lyon (France)	lee **AWN** (**AWN** French final *n*)
lyonnaise	**LĪ** ə **NAYZ**
Lyonnesse	**LĪ** ə **NES**
Lyons (France)	lee **AWN** (**AWN** French final *n*)
Lyons (US)	**LĪ** ənz
Lyra	**LĪ** rə
lyre	līr
lyric	**LIR** ik
Lysander	lī **SAN** dər
Lysenko	lə **SENG** koh
lysergic	lə **SUR** jik
Lysistrata	**LIS** i **STRAH** tə
lyssophobia	**LIS** ə **FOH** bee ə
Lystra	**LIS** trə
Lytton	**LIT** ən

M

ma'am	mam
Maas	mahs
Maastricht	**MAHS** trikt
Mabinogion	**MAB** ə **NOH** gee ən
macabre	mə **KAH** brə
macadam	mə **KAD** əm
macadamia	**MAK** ə **DAY** mee ə
Macao	mə **KOW**
Macapagal, Diosdado	**MAH** kah pah **GAHL**, **DEE** ohs **DAH** doh
macaque	mə **KAHK**
macaroni	**MAK** ə **ROH** nee
macaronic	**MAK** ə **RON** ik

ə ago, a at, ah calm, ahr dark, air care, aw saw, ay say, ch church
e bet, ee me, eer beer, hw what, i is, ī my, *n* French final n vin,

macaroon	MAK ə ROON
Macassar	mə KAS ər
Macaulay	mə KAW lee
macaw	mə KAW
Maccabaeus	MAK ə BEE əs
Maccabean	MAK ə BEE ən
Maccabees	MAK ə BEEZ
Macchiarola, Frank	MAK ee ə ROH lə
McCulloch	mə KUL ək
MacDiarmid	mək DUR məd
McDougal, -l	mək DOO gəl
MacDowell	mək DOW əl
macédoine	ma say DWAHN
Macedonia	MAS ə DOH nee ə
maceration	MAS ə RAY shən
McGuffey	mə GUF ee
Mach	mahk
Machel, Samora Moisés	mah SHEL, sah MOR ah MOH zəz
machete	mə SHET ee
Machiavelli	MAK ee ə VEL ee
machination	MAK ə NAY shən
machismo	mah CHEEZ moh
macho	MAH choh
machree	mə KREE
Machu Picchu	MAH choo PEEK choo
Maciejowice	MAH che yaw VEET se
Mackehenie, Carlos	mah KE nee, KAHR lohs
Mackinac	MAK ə NAW
Mackinaw	MAK ə NAW
MacLean, McLean	mə KLAYN
MacLeish	mək LEESH
Macleod, McLeod	mə KLOWD
MacMahon, McMahon	mik MAN
MacMillan, Macmillan	mək MIL ən
MacMonnies	mək MON eez
McNamara	MAK nə MA rə
McNaughton	mək NAWT ən
Macon	MAY kən
MacPherson	mək FUR sən
macramé	MAK rə MAY
Macris	MA kris
macrobiotic	MAK roh bī OT ik

o **on**, oh **oat**, oi **boy**, oo **soon**, oor **poor**, or **for**, ow **cow**, sh **shush**,
th **thin**, *th* **this**, u **up**, ur **spur**, uu **book**, *zh* **pleasure**

Macrobius	mə **KROH** bee əs
macrocosm	**MAK** rə ᴋᴏᴢ əm
macron	**MAY** kron
macula	**MAK** yə lə
macushla	mə **KUUSH** lə
Madagascar	ᴍᴀᴅ ə **GAS** kər
madam	**MAD** əm
madame (French)	ma **DAHM**
Madang	mah **DAHNG**
Madariaga	ᴍᴀʜ *th*ah **RYAH** gah
Madeira	mə **DEER** ə
Madeleine, m-	**MAD** ə lən
mademoiselle	ᴍᴀᴅ ə mə **ZEL**
Madhya Bharat	**MUD** yə **BU** rət
Madhya Pradesh	**MUD** yə prə **DAYSH**
madonna, M-	mə **DON** ə
madras	**MAD** rəs
Madras	mə **DRAS**
Madrid (Spain)	mə **DRID**
madrigal	**MAD** ri gəl
madrilène	ᴍᴀ drə **LEN**
Madura (India)	**MAJ** uu rə
Madura (Indonesia)	mah **DUUR** ah
Maecenas	mi **SEE** nəs
maelstrom, M-	**MAYL** strəm
maenad	**MEE** nad
maestoso	ᴍᴀʜ es **TOH** soh
maestro	**MĪ** stroh
Maeterlinck	**MAY** tər ʟɪɴɢᴋ
Mafeking	**MAH** fə ᴋɪɴɢ
mafia, M-	**MAH** fee ə
Maga, Hubert	**MAH** gah, yoo **BAIRT**
Magallanes	ᴍᴀʜ gah **YAH** nes
Magaña, Alvaro	mah **GAH** nyah, **AHL** vah roh
Magdalen (Oxford)	**MAWD** lin
Magdalena	ᴍᴀʜɢ *th*ah **LE** nah
Magdalene, m-	**MAG** də ʟᴇᴇɴ
Magdalene Cambridge)	**MAWD** lin
Magdeburg	**MAG** də ʙᴜʀɢ
Magellan	mə **JEL** ən
Magellanic	ᴍᴀᴊ ə **LAN** ik
Magen David	ᴍᴀᴡ gən **DAW** vəd

ə ago, a at, ah calm, ahr dark, air care, aw saw, ay say, ch church
e bet, ee me, eer beer, hw what, i is, ī my, *n* French final n vin,

magenta	mə JEN tə
Maggiore	mə JOH ree
Magi	MAY jī
Magindanao	mah GEEN dah NAH oh
Maginot	MA zhə NOH
magisterial	MAJ ə STIR ee əl
Magister Ludi	MAH gis tər LOO dee
magistracy	MAJ i strə see
Magloire	mah GLWAHR
magma	MAG mə
Magna Charta	MAG nə KAHR tə
magna cum laude	MAHG nə kuum LOWD ə (LOWD as in *crowd*)
Magnani	mahn YAH nee
magnanimity	MAG nə NIM ə tee
magnanimous	mag NAN ə məs
magnate	MAG nət
Magnavox	MAG nə voks
magnesium	mag NEE zee əm
magnet	MAG nət
magneto	mag NEE toh
magnetometer	MAG nə TOM ə tər
magnetron	MAG nə TRON
Magnificat, m-	mag NIF i KAT
magnifico	mag NIF ə KOH
magniloquent	mag NIL ə kwənt
Magnin	MAG nən
magnitude	MAG nə TOOD
magnolia	mag NOHL yə
magnum	MAG nəm
magnum opus	MAG nəm OH pəs
Magnus	MAG nəs
Magog	MAY gog
Magsaysay, Ramón	mahg SĪ sī, rah MOHN
Magus, m-	MAY gəs
Magyar	MAG yahr
Magyarorszag	MAWD yahr AWR sahg
Mahabharata	mə HAH BAHR ə tə
Mahan	mə HAN
maharaja	MAH hə RAHJ ə
maharani	MAH hə RAH nee
mahatma, M-	mə HAHT mə
Mahayana	MAH hə YAH nə

o on, oh oat, oi boy, oo soon, oor poor, or for, ow cow, sh shush,
th thin, *th* this, u up, ur spur, uu book, *zh* pleasure

Mahdi	**MAH** dee
Mahendra Bir Bikram Shah Deva	mə **HEN** drah **BEER** bee **KRUM** **SHAH** dee **VAH**
mahjong	**MAH** *zh*ahng
Mahler	**MAH** lər
mahout	mə **HOWT**
Mahovlich	mah **HAHV** lich
Mahratti, Mahrati	mə **RAT** ee
Maia	**MAY** yə
Maidanek	**MĪ** də **NEK**
maigre	**MAY** gər
Mailliard	**MĪ** yahrd
Maillol	mah **YAWL**
maillot	mī **YOH**
maim	maym
Maimonides	mī **MON** ə **DEEZ**
Mainbocher	man boh **SHAY**
mainsail (nautical)	**MAYN** səl
maintain	mayn **TAYN**
maintenance	**MAYN** tə nəns
Mainz	mīntz
Maitama-Sule, Alhaji	mī **TAH** mə **SOO** lay, ahl **HAH** jee
maître d'hôtel	**ME** trə doh **TEL**
Majali, Abdul Hadi	mah **JEL** lee, **AHB** duul **HEH** dee
Majlis	**MUHJ** lis
majolica	mə **JOL** i kə
Majorca	mə **YOR** kah
major-domo	**MAY** jər **DOH** moh
majuscule	**MAJ** ə **SKYOOL**
Makarios	mah **KAH** ree aws
Makarova, Natalia	mah **KAH** rə və, nə **TAL** yə
Makeka, Thabo	mah **KAY** kah, **TAH** boh
Makhachkala	mə **KAHCH** kə **LAH**
Malabar	**MAL** ə **BAHR**
Malabo	mə **LAH** boh
Malacca	mə **LAK** ə
Malachi	**MAL** ə **KĪ**
malachite	**MAL** ə **KĪT**
maladroit	**MAL** ə **DROIT**
Málaga	**MAH** lah **GAH**
Malagasy	**MAL** ə **GAS** ee
malagueña	**MAH** lah **GAY** nyah
malaise	mə **LAYZ**

ə ago, a at, ah calm, ahr dark, air care, aw saw, ay say, ch church
e bet, ee me, eer beer, hw what, i is, ī my, *n* French final n vin,

Malalasekera,	MAH lah lah SAY kə rə, GOO nə
Gunapala	PAH lə PEE yə SAY nə
Piyasena	
Malamud	MAL ə MUUD
malamute	MAL ə MYOOT
Malaprop	MAL ə PROP
malapropism	MAL ə PROP IZ əm
malaria	mə LAIR ee ə
malarkey	mə LAHR kee
malathion	MAL ə THĪ ən
Malawi	mah LAH wee
Malay	MAY lay
Malaya	mə LAY ə
Malayalam	MAL ə YAH ləm
Malaysia	mə LAY zhə
mal de mer	MAL də MAIR
Malden	MAWL dən
Maldive	MAWL deev
Male	MAHL ee
malediction	MAL ə DIK shən
malefactor	MAL ə FAK tər
Malenkov	MAL ən KAWF
malevolent	mə LEV ə lənt
malfeasance	mal FEE zəns
Malherbe	mal ERB
Mali	MAH lee
malign	mə LĪN
malignant	mə LIG nənt
Malinga, Norman	mah LING gə
malinger	mə LING gər
Malinovsky	MAL ə NAWF skee
Malinowski	MAL ə NAWF skee
Malita, Mircea	mah LEET sah, MEERT chah
mall	mawl
mallard	MAL ərd
Mallarmé	ma lahr MAY
malleable	MAL ee ə bəl
Mallorca	mah YOR kah
Mallory	MAL ə ree
Malmédy	mal may DEE
Malmesbury	MAHMZ bə ree
Malmö	MAL moh
malmsey	MAHM zee

o on, oh oat, oi boy, oo soon, oor poor, or for, ow cow, sh shush,
th thin, *th* this, u up, ur spur, uu book, *zh* pleasure

Malory	**MAL** ə ree
Malraux	mal **ROH**
Malta	**MAWL** tə
Malthus	**MAL** thəs
Malthusian	mal **THOO** *zh*ən
maltreat	mal **TREET**
Mamaroneck	mə **MA** rə **NEK**
mamba	**MOM** bə
mambo	**MOM** boh
Mameluke, m-	**MAM** ə **LOOK**
mammary	**MAM** ə ree
Mammon, m-	**MAM** ən
Managua	mah **NAH** gwah
Manama	mə **NAM** ə
mañana	mah **NYAH** nah
Manassas	mə **NAS** əs
Manasseh	mə **NAS** ə
manatee	**MAN** ə **TEE**
Manchu	man choo
Manchukuo	man choo kwoh
Manchuria	man **CHUUR** ee ə
Mancunian	man **KYOO** nee ən
mandala	**MUN** də lə
Mandalay	**MAN** də **LAY**
mandamus	man **DAY** məs
mandarin, M-	**MAN** də rən
mandate	**MAN** dayt
mandatory	**MAN** də **TOR** ee
Mandeville	**MAN** də vil
Mandingo	man **DING** goh
mandolin	**MAN** də lin
manège	ma **NEZH**
manes, M-	**MAY** neez
Manet	ma **NAY**
maneuver	mə **NOO** vər
manganese	**MANG** gə **NEEZ**
Mangano, Silvana	mahn **GAH** noh, seel **VAH** nah
manger	**MAYN** jər
mango	**MANG** goh
Mangope, Chief Lucas	mahn **GOHP** ee, cheef **LOO** kahs
mangrove	**MANG** grohv
mania	**MAY** nee ə
maniacal	mə **NĪ** ə kəl

ə ago, a at, ah calm, ahr dark, air care, aw saw, ay say, ch church
e bet, ee me, eer beer, hw what, i is, ī my, *n* French final n vin,

Manichean	MAN ə KEE ən
manifesto	MAN ə FES toh
manifold	MAN ə FOHLD
Manila	mə NIL ə
manioc	MAN ee OK
Manipur	MUN i PUUR
Manitoba	MAN ə TOH bə
manitou	MAN ə TOO
Manitoulin	MAN ə TOO lən
Mankiewicz	MANG kə wits
mankind	man kīnd
Mann (Thomas)	mahn
Mann (Horace)	man
manna	MAN ə
mannequin	MAN i kən
Mannheim	MAN hīm
Manoah	mə NOH ə
Manolete	MAHN oh LAY tay
manometer	mə NOM ə tər
Manon Lescaut	ma NAWN le SKOH (NAWN French final *n*)
manqué	mahn KAY (mahn French final *n*)
mansard	MAN sahrd
Manson	MAN sən
mansuetude	MAN swi TOOD
manta	MAN tə
manteau	man TOH
Mantegna	mahn TE nyah
mantel	MAN təl
mantilla	man TEE ə
mantle	MAN təl
Mantoux (test)	MAN too
mantra	MAN trə
Mantua, m-	MAN choo ə
manumission	MAN yə MISH ən
Manutius	mə NYOO shee əs
Manx, m-	mangks
Manzanillo	MAHN sah NEE yaw
manzanita	MAN zə NEE tə
Manzoni	mahn DZOH nee
Manzù	mahn ZOO
Maori	MOW ree (MOW as in *cow*)
Mao Zedong	mow dzə duung (mow as in *cow*)
Mapai	mah PĪ

o on, oh oat, oi boy, oo soon, oor poor, or for, ow cow, sh shush,
th thin, *th* this, u up, ur spur, uu book, *zh* pleasure

Maputo	mə **POOT** oh
maquillage	ma kee **YAHZ***H*
Maquis, m-	mah **KEE**
Mara	**MAHR** ə
marabou	**MA** rə **BOO**
maraca	mə **RAH** kə
Maracaibo	**MA** rə **KĪ** boh
Marajó	**MAHR** ə **ZH**AW
maraschino	**MA** rə **SKEE** noh
Marasesti	mə rə **SHESHT**
Marat	mah **RAH**
Maratha	mə **RAH** tə
Marathi	mə **RAH** tee
Marathon, m-	**MAR** ə **THON**
maraud	mə **RAWD**
Marawi	mə **RAH** wee
Marceau, Marcel	mahr **SOH**, mahr **SEL**
Marceline	**MAHR** sə **LEEN**
marchesa	mahr **KAY** zə
marchese	mahr **KAY** zay
marchioness	**MAHR** shə nəs
Marcia	**MAHR** shə
Marckwardt, Marckwart	**MAHR** kwahrt
Marconi	mahr **KOH** nee
Marcos, Ferdinand	**MAHR** kohs
Mardi Gras	**MAHR** dee **GRAH**
mare (sea; moon area)	**MAHR** ay
Marengo	mə **RENG** goh
margarine	**MAHR** jə rən
Margesson	**MAHR** jə sən
marginalia	**MAHR** jə **NAY** lee ə
Margolin	**MAHR** gə lin
maria (seas)	**MAHR** ee ə
Maria	mə **REE** ə
Maria (Black Maria)	mə **RĪ** ə
Mariana Islands	**MA** ree **AN** ə
Marietta	**MA** ree **ET** ə
marigold	**MA** rə **GOHLD**
marijuana	**MA** rə **WAH** nə
marimba	mə **RIM** bə
marina	mə **REE** nə
marinade	**MA** rə **NAYD**

ə ago, a at, ah calm, ahr dark, air care, aw saw, ay say, ch church
e bet, ee me, eer beer, hw what, i is, ī my, *n* French final n vin,

marinara	**MAHR** ə **NAHR** ə
marinate	**MA** rə **NAYT**
marine, M-	mə **REEN**
mariner	**MA** rə nər
Marinescu, Teodor	**MAH** ree **NES** koo, **TAY** oh **DOR**
Marisol	**MA** rə **SOHL**
Maritain	ma ree **TAN** (**TAN** French final *n*)
marital	**MA** rə təl
maritime, M-	**MA** rə **TĪM**
Mariveles	mah ree **VE** les
Marjai, Jozsef	**MAHR** yah ee, **YOH** *zh*ef
marjoram	**MAHR** jə rəm
Markevitch	mahr **KAY** vich
Markham	**MAHR** kəm
Marlborough (British)	**MAWL** brə
Marlborough (US)	**MAHRL** bə rə
Marmara, Marmora	**MAHR** mə rə
marmoset	**MAHR** mə **SET**
marmot	**MAHR** mət
maroon	mə **ROON**
Marquand	mahr **KWAHND**
Marquardt, Marquart	**MAHR** kwahrt
marquee	mahr **KEE**
Marquesas Islands	mahr **KAY** zəs
marquess	**MAHR** kwəs
marquetry	**MAHR** kə tree
Marquette	mahr **KET**
marquis, M-	**MAHR** kwəs
marquis (French)	mahr **KEE**
marquise	mahr **KEEZ**
marquisette	**MAHR** kə **ZET**
Marrakech, Marrakesh	**MA** rə **KESH**
Marriott (hotels)	**MA** ree ət
marron	**MA** rən
Marryat	**MA** ree ət
Marsala	mahr **SAH** lə
Marschner	**MAHRSH** nər
Marseillaise	**MAHR** say **EZ**
Marseille (French)	mahr **SAY**
Marseilles	mahr **SAY**
marshal, M-	**MAHR** shəl
marshmallow	**MAHRSH MEL** oh
marsupial	mahr **SOO** pee əl

o **on**, oh **oat**, oi **boy**, oo **soon**, oor **poor**, or **for**, ow **cow**, sh **shush**,
th **thin**, *th* **this**, u **up**, ur **spur**, uu **book**, *zh* **pleasure**

Martaban	MAHR tə BAHN
Martel	mahr TEL
Martello, m-	mahr TEL oh
marten	MAHR tən
martial, M-	MAHR shəl
Martian	MAHR shən
Martineau	MAHR ti NOH
Martinelli	MAHR ti NEL ee
martinet	MAHR tə NET
Martínez	mahr TEE nes
martingale	MAHR tən GAYL
martini, M-	mahr TEE nee
Martinique	MAHR tə NEEK
Martini Urdaneta,	mahr TEE nee oor dah NAY tah,
Alberto	al BER toh
martyr	MAHR tər
Marvell	MAHR vəl
marzipan	MAHR zə PAN
Masaccio	mah SAHT chaw
Masahiro	mah sah hee roh
Masai	mah SĪ
Masaryk	MAS ə rik
Masbate	mahz BAH tee
Mascagni	mahs KAH nyee
mascara	ma SKA rə
maser	MAY zər
Maseru	MAZ ə ROO
Masharbrum,	MUSH ər BRUUM
Masherbrum	
Mashingaidze, Elleck	mah SHEE ən gah YEE dzee, AY lek
Masire, Quett	ma SEE ray, KWET
masochism	MAS ə KIZ əm
masochist	MAS ə kəst
Masonic, m-	mə SON ik
Masonite	MAY sə NĪT
Masora	mə SOR ə
Masorete	MAS ə REET
masque	mask
Massachusetts	MAS ə CHOO səts
massacre	MAS ə kər
massage	mə SAHZH
Massenet	MAS ə NAY
masseur	ma SUUR

ə ago, a at, ah calm, ahr dark, air care, aw saw, ay say, ch church
e bet, ee me, eer beer, hw what, i is, ī my, n French final n vin,

masseuse	ma SUUZ
massif	ma SEEF
Massine	ma SEEN
mastaba	MAS tə bə
mastectomy	ma STEK tə mee
mastodon	MAS tə DON
mastoid	MAS toid
Mastroianni, Marcello	MAH stroh YAH nee, mahr CHE loh
Matabele	MAT ə BEE lee
matador	MAT ə DOR
Matagalpa	MAT ə GAL pə
Mata Hari	MAH tə HAHR ee
Matamoros	MAT ə MOR əs
Matanuska	MAT ə NOOS kə
Matanzima, Kaiser Daliwonga	mah TAHN zee mah, KĪ zər DAH lee WAHNG gah
Matawan	MAT ə WAHN
matelote	MAT ə LOHT
Mateos	mah TE aws
mater	MAY tər
material	mə TIR ee əl
materia medica	mə TIR ee ə MED i kə
materiel	mə TIR ee EL
Mather	MA*TH* ər
Mathias	mə THĪ əs
matin, M-	MAT ən
matinee	MAT ə NAY
Matisse	ma TEES
Mato Grosso	MAT ə GROH soh
matriarch	MAY tree AHRK
matricide	MAT rə SĪD
matrix	MAY triks
matronly	MAY trən lee
Matsas	MAHT sahs
Matsch, Franz	mahtch, frahns
Matsu	maht soo
Matsui, Robert	mat SOO ee
Matsunaga	mah tsoo nah gah
Matsuoka	mah tsoo oh kah
Matsushita	mah tsoo shee tah
Matterhorn	MAT ər HORN
mature	mə CHUUR
matzo	MAHT sə

---

o on, oh oat, oi boy, oo soon, oor poor, or for, ow cow, sh shush,
th thin, *th* this, u up, ur spur, uu book, *zh* pleasure

matzos	**MAHT** zəs
matzoth	**MAHT** soht
maudlin	**MAWD** lən
Maugham, Somerset	**MAWM, SUM** ər **SET**
Maui	**MOW** ee (**MOW** as in *cow*)
Mau Mau	mow mow (as in *cow*)
Maumee	maw **MEE**
Mauna Kea	**MOW** nah **KAY** ah (**MOW** as in *cow*)
Mauna Loa	**MOW** nah **LOH** ah (**MOW** as in *cow*)
maunder	**MAWN** dər
Maundy	**MAWN** dee
Maupassant	**MOH** pə **SAHN** (**SAHN** French final *n*)
Mauriac	mawr **YAHK**
Maurice	**MOR** əs
Maurice (French)	moh **REES**
Mauritania, Mauretania	**MOR** ə **TAY** nee ə
Mauritius	maw **RISH** əs
Maurois	mohr **WAH**
Mauroy, Pierre	mohr **WAH, PYAIR**
Mauser, m-	**MOW** zər (**MOW** as in *cow*)
mausoleum, M-	**MAW** sə **LEE** əm
mauve	mohv
maven	**MAY** vən
maverick	**MAV** ə rik
mavis, M-	**MAY** vəs
mavourneen	mə **VUUR** neen
maxim, M-	**MAK** səm
Maxim (French)	mak **SEEM**
Maxime	mak **SEEM**
Maximilian	**MAK** sə **MIL** yən
Maya	**MAH** yə
Mayaguez	**MAH** yah **GWES**
Mayakovsky, Vladimir	**MĪ** ah **KUV** skee, **VLAH** də meer
Mayan	**MAH** yən
Mayer, Maria Goeppert	**MĪ** ər, mah **REE** ə **GEP** ərt
Mayo	**MAY** oh
Mayon	mah **YAWN**
mayonnaise	**MAY** ə **NAYZ**
mayoralty	**MAY** ər əl tee
Mayotte	mah **YAHT**
Mazarin	**MAZ** ə rin

ə ago, a at, ah calm, ahr dark, air care, aw saw, ay say, ch church
e bet, ee me, eer beer, hw what, i is, ī my, *n* French final n vin,

Mazatlán	MAH saht LAHN
Mazda, m-	MAZ də
mazel tov	MAH zəl TAWF
mazer	MAY zər
mazurka	mə ZUUR kə
Mazzini	maht TSEE nee
M'Ba, Leon	əm BAH, lee AHN
Mbabane	EM bə BAHN
Mbaye, Kéba	əm BAH ee, KEE bah
Mbogua, John	əm BOH gwah (gwah g barely pronounced)
Mboya	əm BOI ə
mea culpa	MAY ə KUUL pə
mead, M-	meed
meadow	MED oh
meager	MEE gər
meander, M-	mee AN dər
meatus	mee AY təs
Mébiame, Léon	mə bee AHM, lay AWN (AWN French final n)
Mecca, m-	MEK ə
mechanize	MEK ə NĪZ
Mechlin	MEK lin
Mecklenburg, Mecklenberg	MEK lən BURG
Medaglia d'Oro	mə DAL yə DOR oh
medallion	mə DAL yən
Mede	meed
Medea	mə DEE ə
Medellín	me de YEEN
media, M-	MEE dee ə
median, M-	MEE dee ən
mediant	MEE dee ənt
mediate (a)	MEE dee ət
mediate (v)	MEE dee AYT
medicament	mi DIK ə mənt
Medici	MED ə chee
medicinal	mə DIS ə nəl
medicine	MED ə sən
medico	MED i KOH
medieval	MEE dee EE vəl
Medina (Saudi Arabia)	mə DEE nə
Medina (US)	mə DĪ nə

o on, oh oat, oi boy, oo soon, oor poor, or for, ow cow, sh shush,
th thin, _th_ this, u up, ur spur, uu book, _zh_ pleasure

mediocre	MEE dee OH kər
mediocrity	MEE dee OK rə tee
Mediterranean	MED ə tə RAY nee ən
medley	MED lee
Médoc	may DAHK
medulla	mə DUL ə
medullary	MED ə LER ee
Medusa, m-	mə DOO sə
Meehan	MEE ən
meerschaum	MEER shəm
Mefitus	mə FĪ tis
megabyte	MEG ə BĪT
megacycle	MEG ə sĪ kəl
Megaera	mə JEER ə
megahertz	MEG ə HURTS
megalomania	MEG ə loh MAY nee ə
megalopolis	MEG ə LOP ə ləs
Meganthropus	mə GAN thrə pəs
megaton	MEG ə TUN
Megiddo	mə GID oh
megillah	mə GIL ə
megohm	MEG ohm
megrim	MEE grəm
Meguid, Ahmed Esmat Abdel	MAY good, AH med ES maht AHB del (good as in *food*)
Mehta, Ved	MEH tə, VED
Meiji	may jee
Mein Kampf	mīn KAHMPF
meiosis	mī OH səs
Meir, Golda	ME eer, GOHL də
Meissen	MĪ sən
Meistersinger	MĪ stər ZING ər
Meitner, Lise	MĪT nər, LEE zə
Mejias, Roman	mə HEE əs, roh MAHN
Mejia Victores, Oscar	may HEE ə VIK tor es, AWS kər
Méjico	ME hee koh
Meklong	may klawng (klawng *g* barely pronounced)
Meknès	mek NES
Mekong	may kawng (kawng *g* barely pronounced)
melancholia	MEL ən KOH lee ə
melancholy	MEL ən KOL ee

Melanchthon,	mə LANGK thən
Melancthon	
Melanesia	MEL ə NEE *zh*ə
mélange	may LAHNZ*H*
Melba	MEL bə
Melbourne	MEL bərn
Melchers	MEL chərz
Melchizedek,	mel KIZ ə DEK
Melchisedec	
Meleager	MEL ee AY jər
melee	MAY lay
Melilla	mə LEE yə
meliorate	MEEL yə RAYT
mellifluous	mə LIF loo əs
Mellon	MEL ən
Melnik	MYEL neek
(Czechoslovakia)	
melodeon	mə LOH dee ən
melodrama	MEL ə DRAH mə
Melos	MEE los
Melpomene	mel POM ə nee
Melville	MEL vil
membrane	MEM brayn
membranous	MEM brə nəs
Memel	MAY məl
memento	mə MEN toh
memento mori	mə MEN toh MOR ī
Memnon	MEM non
memoir	MEM wahr
memorabilia	MEM ə rə BIL ee ə
memorable	MEM ər ə bəl
Memphis	MEM fəs
memsahib	MEM SAH ib
ménage	may NAHZ*H*
ménage à trois	may NAHZ*H* a TRWAH
menagerie	mə NAJ ə ree
Menam	me NAHM
Menander	mə NAN dər
menarche	mə NAHR kee
Mencius	MEN shee əs
Mencken	MENG kən
mendacious	men DAY shəs
mendacity	men DAS ə tee

---

o on, oh oat, oi boy, oo soon, oor poor, or for, ow cow, sh shush,
th thin, *th* this, u up, ur spur, uu book, *zh* pleasure

Mendeleev	MEN də LAY əf
mendelevium	MEN də LEE vee əm
Mendelian	men DEE lee ən
Mendelssohn	MEN dəl sən
Menderes	MEN de RES
mendicant	MEN də kənt
Mendocino	MEN də SEE noh
Menelaus	MEN ə LAY əs
Menelik	MEN ə lik
menhaden	men HAY dən
menhir	MEN hir
menial	MEE nee əl
meninges	mə NIN jeez
meningitis	MEN in JĪ təs
meninx	MEN ingks
meniscus	mə NIS kəs
Menninger	MEN ing ər
Mennonite	MEN ə NĪT
Menomonee	mə NOM ə nee
Menomonie	mə NOM ə nee
Menotti, Gian-Carlo	mə NOT ee, jahn KAHR loh
menses	MEN seez
menshevik, M-	MEN shə vik
Menshikov, Mikhail	MEN shi kuf, mi KĪL
menstrual	MEN stroo əl
menstruation	MEN stroo AY shən
mensuration	MEN sə RAY shən
menthol	MEN thawl
mentor	MEN tər
menu	MEN yoo
Menuhin, Yehudi	MEN yoo ən, yə HOO dee
Menzies	MEN zeez
Mephisto	mə FIS toh
Mephistopheles	MEF ə STOF ə LEEZ
mephitic	mə FIT ik
mephitis	mə FĪ təs
mercantile	MUR kən TEEL
mercaptan	mər KAP tan
Mercator	mər KAY tər
mercenary	MUR sə NER ee
mercer, M-	MUR sər
merci	mair SEE
Mercian	MUR shee ən

ə ago, a at, ah calm, ahr dark, air care, aw saw, ay say, ch church
e bet, ee me, eer beer, hw what, i is, ī my, n French final n vin,

Mercier (French)	mair **SYAY**
Mercouri, Melina	mer **KOO** ree, mə **LEE** nə
mercurial	mər **KYUUR** ee əl
mercury, M-	**MUR** kyə ree
Mercutio	mər **KYOO** shee oh
merengue	mə **RENG** gay
meretricious	MER ə **TRISH** əs
Mérida	**ME** ree dah
meridian	mə **RID** ee ən
Mérimée	may ree **MAY**
meringue	mə **RANG**
merino	mə **REE** noh
mermaid	**MUR** mayd
Merovingian	MER ə **VIN** jee ən
Merrimac, -k	MER ə MAK
merry	**MER** ee
Mersey	**MUR** zee
mesa, M-	**MAY** sə
Mesabi	mə **SAHB** ee
mescal	mes **KAL**
mescaline	**MES** kə LEEN
mesdames	may **DAHM**
mesenteric	MEZ ən **TER** ik
Meshach	**MEE** shak
Meshed	mə **SHED**
meshuga	mə **SHUUG** ə
mesial	**MEE** zee əl
Mesmer	**MEZ** mər
mesmerize	**MEZ** mə RĪZ
mesne	meen
mesomorph	MEZ ə MORF
meson (elementary particle)	**MEE** zon
Mesopotamia	MES ə pə **TAY** mee ə
mesothelium	MEZ ə **THEE** lee əm
mesotron	**MEZ** ə TRON
Mesozoic	MES ə **ZOH** ik
mesquite	me **SKEET**
Messalina	MES ə **LĪ** nə
messaline	MES ə **LEEN**
Messiah, m-	mə **SĪ** ə
messieurs	may **SYUU**
Messina	mə **SEE** nə

---

o **on**, oh **oat**, oi **boy**, oo **soon**, oor **poor**, or **for**, ow **cow**, sh **shush**,
th **thin**, *th* **this**, u **up**, ur **spur**, uu **book**, *zh* **pleasure**

Messrs.	**MES** ərz
mestiza	me **STEE** zə
mestizo	me **STEE** zoh
Meštrović	**MESH** traw **VICH**
metabolism	mə **TAB** ə **LIZ** əm
metallic	mə **TAL** ik
metallurgy	**MET** ə **LUR** jee
metamorphoses	**MET** ə **MOR** fə **SEEZ**
metamorphosis	**MET** ə **MOR** fə səs
metaphor	**MET** ə **FOR**
metaphorical	**MET** ə **FOR** i kəl
metaphysical	**MET** ə **FIZ** i kəl
metaphysics	**MET** ə **FIZ** iks
metastases	mə **TAS** tə seez
metastasis	mə **TAS** tə səs
metatarsal	**MET** ə **TAHR** səl
metathesis	mə **TATH** ə səs
Metaxas	mə **TAK** səs
metempsychosis	**MET** əm sī **KOH** səs
meteor	**MEE** tee ər
meteorite	**MEE** tee ə **RĪT**
meteorology	**MEE** tee ə **ROL** ə jee
methane	**METH** ayn
Methodist	**METH** ə dəst
Methuen	mə **THYOO** ən
Methuselah	mə **THOO** zə lə
methyl	**METH** əl
meticulous	mə **TIK** yə ləs
métier	may **TYAY**
métis	may **TEE**
métisse	may **TEES**
metonymy	mə **TON** ə mee
metronome	**MET** rə **NOHM**
metropolis	mə **TROP** ə ləs
metropolitan	**MET** rə **POL** ə tən
Metternich	**MET** ər nik
Metuchen	mə **TUCH** ən
Metz	mets
Metzenbaum, Howard	**METS** ən **BOWM** (**BOWM** as in *cow*)
meunière	mun **YAIR**
Meursault	mur **SOH**
Meuse	muuz
Mexico	**MEK** sə **KOH**

ə ago, a at, ah calm, ahr dark, air care, aw saw, ay say, ch church
e bet, ee me, eer beer, hw what, i is, ī my, *n* French final n vin,

Meyerbeer	**MĪ** ər **BEER**
mezuza	mə **ZUUZ** ə
mezzanine	**MEZ** ə **NEEN**
mezzo	**MET** soh
mezzotint	**MET** soh **TINT**
mho	moh
Miami	mī **AM** ee
miasma	mī **AZ** mə
mica	**MĪ** kə
Micah	**MĪ** kə
Micajah	mī **KAY** yə
Micawber	mi **KAW** bər
Michaux	mee **SHOH**
Michel, Robert	**MĪK** əl
Michelangelo	**MĪ** kəl **AN** jə **LOH**
Michener, James	**MICH** nər
Michigan	**MISH** ə gən
Michiko	**MI** chi koh
microbe	**MĪ** krohb
microcephalic	**MĪ** kroh sə **FAL** ik
microcosm	**MĪ** krə **KOZ** əm
microfiche	**MĪ** krə **FEESH**
micrography	mī **KROG** rə fee
micrometer	mī **KROM** ə tər
Micronesia	**MĪ** krə **NEE** zhə
microscope	**MĪ** krə **SKOHP**
microscopy	mī **KROS** kə pee
microwave	**MĪ** kroh **WAYV**
micturate	**MIK** chə **RAYT**
Midas	**MĪ** dəs
Middlebury	**MID** əl **BER** ee
Midi	mee **DEE**
Midianite	**MID** ee ə **NĪT**
Midlothian	mid **LOH** *th*ee ən
midwifery	**MID** **WĪF** ree
mien	meen
Mies van der Rohe	**MEES** **VAHN** də **ROH**
Mifune, Toshiro	mee fuu ne, toh shee roh
mignon	meen **YAWN** (**YAWN** French final *n*)
mignonette	**MIN** yə **NET**
migraine	**MĪ** grayn
migrant	**MĪ** grənt
migratory	**MĪ** grə **TOR** ee

o on, oh oat, oi boy, oo soon, oor poor, or for, ow cow, sh shush,
th thin, *th* this, u up, ur spur, uu book, *zh* pleasure

Miguel	mee **GEL**
mikado, M-	mi **KAH** doh
Miki, Takeo	mee kee, tah kay oh
mikvah	**MIK** və
Milan	mi **LAN**
milanaise	mee lah **NEZ**
Milanese	ᴍɪ lə **NEEZ**
Milano	mee **LAH** naw
Milanov, Zinka	**MEE** lah **NAWF**, **ZING** kah
milch	milch
Miletus	mī **LEET** əs
Milhaud, Darius	mee **YOH**, da **RYUUS**
milieu	meel **YUU**
militant	**MIL** i tənt
militia	mə **LISH** ə
Milla Bermudez	**MEE** lyah bair **MOO** dez
Millais	mi **LAY**
Millard	**MIL** ərd
Millay	mi **LAY**
millennium	mə **LEN** ee əm
millet	**MIL** ət
Millet, Jean François	mee **YAY**, **ZH**AHN frahn **SWAH**
	(**ZH**AHN and frahn French final *n*)
milliampere	ᴍɪʟ ee **AM** pir
Millikan	**MIL** ə kən
millimeter	**MIL** ə ᴍᴇᴇ tər
millimicron	ᴍɪʟ ə **MĪ** kron
millinery	**MIL** ə ᴎᴇʀ ee
Milne	miln
milo, M-	**MĪ** loh
Milo	**MEE** loh
Milosz	**MEE** lawsh
milquetoast, M-	**MILK** tohst
Miltiades	mil **TĪ** ə ᴅᴇᴇᴢ
Miltonic	mil **TON** ik
Milwaukee	mil **WAW** kee
Mimas	**MĪ** məs
mime	mīm
mimeograph, M-	**MIM** ee ə **GRAF**
mimesis	mə **MEE** səs
mimetic	mə **MET** ik
mimic	**MIM** ik
mimicry	**MIM** ik ree

Mimieux, Yvette	mee **MYUU**, ee **VET**
Mimir	**MEE** mir
mimosa	mə **MOH** sə
minaret	**MIN** ə **RET**
minatory	**MIN** ə **TOR** ee
Mindanao	**MIN** də **NAH** oh
Mindoro	min **DOR** oh
Mineola	**MIN** ee **OH** lə
mineralogy	**MIN** ə **RAL** ə jee
Minerva	mə **NUR** və
minestrone	**MIN** ə **STROH** nee
Mineta	mi **NET** ə
Ming	ming
miniature	**MIN** ee ə chər
minion	**MIN** yən
Minneapolis	**MIN** ee **AP** ə lis
minnesinger	**MIN** i **SING** ər
Minnesota	**MIN** ə **SOH** tə
Minoan	mə **NOH** ən
Minorca, m-	mə **NOR** kə
Minos	**MĪ** nəs
Minotaur	**MIN** ə **TOR**
Minow	**MIN** oh
Minsk	minsk
minuend	**MIN** yoo **END**
minuet	**MIN** yoo **ET**
Minuit	**MIN** yoo ət
minuscule	**MIN** ə **SKYOOL**
minute (a)	mī **NOOT**
minute (n, v)	**MIN** ət
minutia	mə **NOO** shee ə
minutiae	mə **NOO** shee **EE**
Miocene	**MĪ** ə **SEEN**
miotic	mī **OT** ik
Miquelon	meek ə **LAWN** (**LAWN** French final *n*)
Mirabeau	**MIR** ə **BOH**
mirabile dictu	mee **RAH** bi **LE DIK** too
Miraflores	**MEE** rah **FLAW** res
mirage	mə **RAH***ZH*
Miranda	mə **RAN** də
Miriam	**MIR** ee əm
Miró Cardona	mee **ROH** kahr **DOH** nə
Miró, Joan	mee **ROH**, *zh*uu **AHN**

o on, oh oat, oi boy, oo soon, oor poor, or for, ow cow, sh shush,
th thin, *th* this, u up, ur spur, uu book, *zh* pleasure

Mirvish	**MUR** vish
misalliance	MIS ə **LĪ** əns
misanthrope	**MIS** ən **THROHP**
miscegenation	mi **SEJ** ə **NAY** shən
miscellaneous	MIS ə **LAY** nee əs
miscellany	**MIS** ə LAY nee
mischief	**MIS** chəf
mischievous	**MIS** chə vəs
miscible	**MIS** ə bəl
miscreant	**MIS** kree ənt
misdemeanor	MIS də **MEE** nər
mise en scène	mee zahn **SEN** (zahn French final *n*)
miser	**MĪ** zər
Misérables, Les	mee zay **RAH** blə, lay
Miserere, m-	MIZ ə **RAIR** ee
misericord	mə **ZER** ə **KORD**
mishap	**MIS** hap
misnomer	mis **NOH** mər
misogamy	mə **SOG** ə mee
misogynist	mə **SOJ** ə nəst
misprision	mis **PRIZ***H* ən
missal	**MIS** əl
missile	**MIS** əl
missilery	**MIS** əl ree
Missouri	mə **ZUUR** i
mistletoe	**MIS** əl **TOH**
mistral	mi **STRAHL**
miter	**MĪ** tər
Mitford	**MIT** fərd
Mithridates	MITH rə **DAY** teez
mitigate	**MIT** ə **GAYT**
mitosis	mī **TOH** səs
Mitsubishi	mit soo **BISH** ee
Mitterrand, François	**MEET** rahn, frahn **SWAH** (rahn and frahn French final *n*)
mittimus	**MIT** ə məs
mitzvah	**MITS** və
Mizere, N. T.	mee **ZER** ee
Mizpah	**MIZ** pə
Mlada Boleslav	mə **LAH** dah **BAW** le slahf
Mmabatho	mah **BAH** toh
mnemonic	ni **MON** ik
Mnemosyne	ni **MOS** ə **NEE**

ə ago, a at, ah calm, ahr dark, air care, aw saw, ay say, ch church
e bet, ee me, eer beer, hw what, i is, ī my, *n* French final n vin,

moa	**MOH** ə
Moab	**MOH** ab
mobile (a)	**MOH** bəl
mobile (sculpture)	moh **BEEL**
Mobile	moh **BEEL**
mobilize	**MOH** bə **LĪZ**
Möbius	**MOH** bee əs
Mobutu Sese Seko	mə **BOO** too **SAY** say **SAY** koh
Mocha, m-	**MOH** kə
modal	**MOHD** əl
mode	mohd
modem	**MOH** dem
Modena	**MAWD** ə nə
moderato	ᴍᴏᴅ ə **RAH** toh
modern	**MOD** ərn
modicum	**MOD** ə kəm
Modigliani	ᴍᴀᴡ dee **LYAH** nee
modiste	moh **DEEST**
Modred	**MOH** drid
modulate	**MOJ** ə **LAYT**
modulation	ᴍᴏᴊ ə **LAY** shən
module	**MOJ** ool
modulus	**MOJ** ə ləs
modus operandi	**MOH** dəs ᴏᴘ ə **RAN** dee
modus vivendi	**MOH** dəs vi **VEN** dee
Mogadishu	ᴍᴏɢ ə **DISH** oo
Mogen David	ᴍᴀᴡ gən **DAW** vəd
Mogul, m-	**MOH** gəl
Mohács	**MOH** hach
Mohamad, Mahathir	moh **HAH** məd, mah **HAH** teer
Mohammed	moh **HAM** əd
Mohammed Da'ud	moh **HAM** əd dah **OOD**
Mohammed Na'im	moh **HAM** əd nah **EEM**
Mohammed Zahir	moh **HAM** əd zah **EER**
Mohave	mə **HAH** vee
mohel	**MOH** əl
Mohican	moh **HEE** kən
Mohieddin, Ahmad Fuad	moh **HEE** din, **AH** mahd fwahd
Moho	**MOH** hoh
Moholy-Nagy	**MOH** hoi **NOD** yə
Mohorovičić	ᴍᴏʜ hə **ROH** və chich
Mohs (scale)	mohz

---

o on, oh oat, oi boy, oo soon, oor poor, or for, ow cow, sh shush,
th thin, *th* this, u up, ur spur, uu book, *zh* pleasure

Mohyeddin, Zia	moi YED in, TSEE ah
Moi, Daniel arap	MAW ee, DAN yəl AR əp
moiety	MOI ə tee
Moira	MOI rə
moire	mwahr
moiré	mwah RAY
Mojave	mə HAH vee
Moji	moh jee
molar	MOH lər
molasses	mə LAS əz
Moldau	MAWL dow
Moldavia	mol DAY vee ə
Molech	MOH lek
molecular	mə LEK yə lər
molecule	MOL ə KYOOL
molest	mə LEST
molestation	MOH le STAY shən
Molière	mohl YAIR
Molina	mə LEE nə
Moline	moh LEEN
mollify	MOL ə FĪ
mollusk	MOL əsk
Molnár, Ferenc	MOHL nahr, FE rənts
Moloch	MOH lok
Molokai	MOH loh KĪ
Molotov	MOL ə TAWF
Molucca	mə LUK ə
moly	MOH lee
molybdenum	mə LIB də nəm
Mombasa	mahm BAH sə
momentous	moh MEN təs
momentum	moh MEN təm
Momus	MOH məs
Monaco	MON ə KOH
monad	MOH nad
monadnock, M-	mə NAD NOK
Monaghan (Ireland)	MON ə gən
Monaghan (family name)	MON ə han
Mona Lisa	MOH nə LEE zə
monarchical	mə NAHR ki kəl
monaural	mon OR əl
Mondjo, Nicolas	MAWN joh, NIK oh LAH

ə ago, a at, ah calm, ahr dark, air care, aw saw, ay say, ch church
e bet, ee me, eer beer, hw what, i is, ī my, n French final n vin,

Mondrian, Piet	**MAWN** dree **AHN, PEET**
Monel	moh **NEL**
Monet, Claude	moh **NAY, KLOHD**
monetarism	**MON** ə tə **RIZ** əm
Monge, Luis Alberto	**MAWNG** hay, loo **EES** ahl **BER** toh
monger	**MUNG** gər
Mongol	**MONG** gəl
Mongolia	mong **GOH** lee ə
mongoloid, M-	**MONG** gə **LOID**
mongoose	**MONG** goos
mongrel	**MUNG** grəl
Monique	moh **NEEK**
monitor	**MON** ə tər
Monmouth	**MON** məth
Monnet	maw **NAY**
monocle	**MON** ə kəl
monocoque	**MON** ə **KOK**
Monod, Jacques	maw **NOH, ZH**AHK
monody	**MON** ə dee
monogamy	mə **NOG** ə mee
monogram	**MON** ə **GRAM**
monograph	**MON** ə **GRAF**
monogyny	mə **NOJ** ə nee
monolatry	mə **NOL** ə tree
monolith	**MON** ə lith
monologue	**MON** ə **LAWG**
monologuist	**MON** ə **LAWG** əst
monomania	**MON** ə **MAY** nee ə
monomial	mə **NOH** mee əl
Monongahela	mə **NONG** gə **HEE** lə
mononucleosis	**MON** oh **NOO** klee **OH** səs
monophonic	**MON** ə **FON** ik
Monophysite	mə **NOF** ə **SĪT**
monoplane	**MON** ə **PLAYN**
monopoly	mə **NOP** ə lee
monosyllabic	**MON** ə sə **LAB** ik
monotheism	**MON** ə thee **IZ** əm
monotony	mə **NOT** ə nee
monotype	**MON** ə **TĪP**
monovalent	**MON** ə **VAY** lənt
Monrovia	mən **ROH** vee ə
Monsarrat	**MAHN** sə **RAHT**

o **on**, oh **oat**, oi **boy**, oo **soon**, oor **poor**, or **for**, ow **cow**, sh **shush**,
th **thin**, *th* **this**, u **up**, ur **spur**, uu **book**, *zh* **pleasure**

Monseigneur, m-	**MOHN** sayn **YUR** (**MOHN** French final *n*)
Monsieur, m-	mə **SYUU**
Monsignor, m-	mon **SEEN** yər
Monson	**MUN** sən
monsoon	mon **SOON**
mons veneris	**MONZ VEN** ə rəs
montage	mohn **TAHZH**
Montagu, -e	**MON** tə **GYOO**
Montaigne	mohn **TEN** yə (mohn French final *n*)
Montale, Eugenio	mohn **TAH** lay, ay oo **JAYN** yoh
Montana	mon **TAN** ə
Montand, Yves	mohn **TAHN, EEV** (mohn and **TAHN** French final *n*)
Montauk	**MON** tawk
Mont Blanc	mohn **BLAHN** (mohn and **BLAHN** French final *n*)
Montcalm	mont **KAHM**
monte	**MON** tee
Monte Cassino	**MAWN** te kah **SEE** noh
Montego Bay	mon **TEE** goh
Montenegro	**MON** tə **NEE** groh
Monterey, Monterrey	**MON** tə **RAY**
Montespan	**MON** tə **SPAN**
Montesquieu	**MOHN** tə **SKYUU** (**MOHN** French final *n*)
Montessori	**MON** tə **SOH** ree
Monteverdi	**MAWN** tə **VAIR** dee
Montevideo	**MON** tə və **DAY** oh
Montezuma	**MON** tə **ZOO** mə
Montfort (English)	**MONT** fərt
Montfort (French)	mohn **FOR** (mohn French final *n*)
Montgomery	munt **GUM** ə ree
Monticello	**MON** tə **SEL** oh
Montmartre	mohn **MAHR** trə (mohn French final *n*)
Montpelier (Vermont)	mont **PEEL** yər
Montpellier (France)	mohn pe **LYAY** (mohn French final *n*)
Montreal	**MON** tree **AWL**
Montserrat	**MONT** sə **RAT**
Mont Tremblant	**MOHN** trahn **BLAHN** (all syllables French final *n*)
moped	**MOH** ped

ə ago, a at, ah calm, ahr dark, air care, aw saw, ay say, ch church
e bet, ee me, eer beer, hw what, i is, ī my, *n* French final n vin,

moraine	mə RAYN
moral	MOR əl
morale	mə RAL
Morales	maw RAH les
Morandi	maw RAHN dee
morass	mə RAS
Morava	MAW rah vah
Moravia	mə RAY vee ə
moray	MOR ay
morbidity	mor BID ə tee
mordant	MOR dənt
Mordecai	MOR də KĪ
mordent	MOR dənt
Mordovian	mor DOH vee ən
Mordred	MOR drid
Morea	moh REE ə
Moreau	maw ROH
morel	mə REL
Morelos	mə RAY ləs
mores	MOR ayz
Moresby	MORZ bee
Morgan	MOR gən
morganatic	MOR gə NAT ik
Morgenthau	MOR gən THAW
Moriah	mə RĪ ə
Moriarty	maw ree AHR tee
moribund	MOR ə bənd
Moriches	mə RICH əz
Morinigo	maw REE nee gaw
Morisot, Berthe	maw ree ZOH, BAIRT
Mormon	MOR mən
Mornay	mor NAY
Morocco, m-	mə ROK oh
moron	MOR on
Moron	mə RAWN
morose	mə ROHS
morpheme	MOR feem
morphemic	mor FEE mik
Morpheus	MOR fee əs
morphine	MOR feen
morphology	mor FOL ə jee
morphosis	mor FOH səs
mortadella	MOR tə DEL ə

o on, oh oat, oi boy, oo soon, oor poor, or for, ow cow, sh shush,
th thin, *th* this, u up, ur spur, uu book, *zh* pleasure

mortgage	**MOR** gij
mortician	mor **TISH** ən
Mortimer	**MOR** tə mər
mortise	**MOR** təs
mortuary	**MOR** choo **ER** ee
mosaic, M-	moh **ZAY** ik
Moscoso	mohs **KOH** zoh
Moscow	**MOS** kow
Moselle	moh **ZEL**
Moshoeshoe	moh **SHOO** shoo
Moslem	**MOZ** ləm
Moson	**MAW** shawn
mosque	mosk
mosquito	mə **SKEET** oh
Moss	maws
Mossadegh	**MOH** sah **DEK**
Mössbauer	**MAWS** bow ər (bow as in *cow*)
Mosul	moh **SOOL**
motet	moh **TET**
Motherwell	**MU***TH* ər **WEL**
motif	moh **TEEF**
motile	**MOH** təl
motive	**MOH** tiv
motley	**MOT** lee
motorcycle	**MOH** tər **SĪ** kəl
moue	moo
moulin, M-	moo **LAN** (**LAN** French final *n*)
moulins, M-	moo **LAN** (**LAN** French final *n*)
Moulmein	muul **MAYN**
moult	mohlt
mountainous	**MOWN** tə nəs
mountebank	**MOWN** tə **BANGK** (**MOWN** as in *town*)
mouser	**MOW** zər (**MOW** as in *cow*)
Moushoutas, Constantine	moo **SHOO** tahs, **KON** stən teen
Moussa	**MOO** sah
mousse	moos
mousseline	moos **LEEN**
Moussorgsky	muu **SORG** skee
mouton	**MOO** ton
mow (cut)	moh
mow (grimace; stack)	mow (as in *cow*)

ə ago, a at, ah calm, ahr dark, air care, aw saw, ay say, ch church
e bet, ee me, eer beer, hw what, i is, ī my, *n* French final n vin,

Mowgli	**MOW** glee (**MOW** as in *cow*)
moxie	**MOK** see
Mozambique	**MOH** zəm **BEEK**
Mozart	**MOHT** sahrt
mozzarella	**MAWT** sə **REL** ə
Mphephu, Patrick	əm **PAY** poo
Mrs.	**MIS** əz
Msuya, Cleopa	əm **SOO** ye, klee **OH** pə
Mubarak, Hosni	muu **BAHR** ək, **HOZ** ni
mucilage	**MYOO** sə lij
mucilaginous	**MYOO** sə **LAJ** ə nəs
mucous, mucus	**MYOO** kəs
Mueller	**MYOO** lər
Muenster	**MUN** stər
muezzin	myoo **EZ** ən
mufti, M-	**MUF** tee
Mugabe, Robert	muu **GAH** bee
mugwump	**MUG** wump
Muir	myuur
Mukacevo	**MOOK** ə **CHEV** aw
Mukden	**MUUK** dən
mukluk	**MUK** luk
mulatto	mə **LAT** oh
mulct	mulkt
Muldoon, Robert	mul **DOON**
muliebrity	**MYOO** lee **EB** rə tee
mullah	**MUL** ə
mullein	**MUL** ən
Muller	**MUL** ər
Müller	**MUUL** ər
mullet	**MUL** ət
mulligan, M-	**MUL** i gən
mulligatawny	**MUL** i gə **TAW** nee
mullion	**MUL** yən
multifarious	**MUL** tə **FA** ree əs
multiparous	**MUL** **TIP** ə rəs
multiplicity	**MUL** tə **PLIS** ə tee
multitudinous	**MUL** tə **TOO** də nəs
multum in parvo	**MUL** təm in **PAHR** voh
Munch, Edvard	**MUUNGK**, **ED** vahrd
Münch	muunsh
Munchausen	**MUN** **CHOW** zən
Muncie	**MUN** see

o **on**, oh **oat**, oi **boy**, oo **soon**, oor **poor**, or **for**, ow **cow**, sh **shush**,
th **thin**, *th* **this**, u **up**, ur **spur**, uu **book**, *zh* **pleasure**

mundane	mun **DAYN**
Mundia, Nalumino	muun **DEE** yə, **NAL** oo **MEE** noh
Munich	**MYOO** nik
municipal	myuu **NIS** ə pəl
municipality	myuu **NIS** ə **PAL** ə tee
munificent	myuu **NIF** ə sənt
munition	myuu **NISH** ən
Muñiz, Carlos Manuel	moo **NEEZ, KAHR** lohs **MAHN** wel
Muñoz Ledo, Porfirio	moo **NYOHZ LAY** doh, por **FEE** ree oh
Muñoz Marín	moon **YAW** smah **REEN**
Munro	mən **ROH**
Münster (Germany)	**MIN** stər
Munster (Ireland)	**MUN** stər
muon	**MYOO** on
mural	**MYUUR** əl
Murasaki	**MOO** rah **SAH** kee
Murat (river)	moo **RAHT**
Murdoch, Rupert	**MUR** dok
Murfreesboro	**MUR** freez **BUR** ə
muriatic	**MYUUR** ee **AT** ik
Murillo	myuu **RIL** oh
Murman	muur **MAHN**
Murmansk	muur **MAHNSK**
murmur	**MUR** mər
murrain	**MUR** ən
Musa	**MOO** sah
Musca	**MUS** kə
muscadine	**MUS** kə **DĪN**
muscat, M-	**MUS** kat
muscatel	**MUS** kə **TEL**
muscle	**MUS** əl
Muscovite, m-	**MUS** kə **VĪT**
Muscovy	**MUS** kə vee
muscular dystrophy	**MUS** kyə lər **DIS** trə fee
muse, M-	myooz
musette	myuu **ZET**
museum	myuu **ZEE** əm
musicale	**MYOO** zi **KAL**
Musici, I	**MOO** zee chee, ee
muskeg	**MUS** keg
Muskegon	mə **SKEE** gən
muskellunge	**MUS** kə **LUNJ**

ə ago, a at, ah calm, ahr dark, air care, aw saw, ay say, ch church
e bet, ee me, eer beer, hw what, i is, ī my, *n* French final n vin,

Muskogee	mus **KOH** gee
muskrat	**MUSK** rat
Muslim	**MUUZ** ləm
muslin	**MUZ** lən
mussel	**MUS** əl
Musset	myoo **SAY**
Mussolini	moo sə **LEE** nee
mustache	**MUS** tash
mustang	**MUS** tang
mutant	**MYOO** tənt
mutation	myoo **TAY** shən
mutineer	**MYOO** tə **NEER**
Mutsuhito	muu tsuu hee toh
mutual	**MYOO** choo əl
muu-muu	**MOO** moo
muzhik	moo **ZH**EEK
Muzorewa	**MUUZ** ə **RAY** wə
Mwambutsa, Mwami	mwahm **BOO** tsah, **MWAH** mee
Mweru	**MWAY** roo
myasthenia	**MĪ** əs **THEE** nee ə
Mycenae	mī **SEE** nee
mycosis	mī **KOH** səs
myelitis	**MĪ** ə **LĪ** təs
myelogram	**MĪ** ə lə **GRAM**
Myint, U Kyee	myint, oo kee
Mykonos	**MEE** kə **NAWS**
mynah	**MĪ** nə
Mynheer, m-	mīn **HAIR**
myopia	mī **OH** pee ə
Myra	**MĪ** rə
Myrdal	**MIR** dahl
myriad	**MIR** ee əd
Myrmidon, m-	**MUR** mə **DON**
Myron	**MĪ** rən
myrrh	mur
Mysore	mī **SOR**
mysticism	**MIS** tə **SIZ** əm
mythical	**MITH** i kəl
Mytilene	**MIT** ə **LEE** nee

o on, oh oat, oi boy, oo soon, oor poor, or for, ow cow, sh shush,
th thin, *th* this, u up, ur spur, uu book, *zh* pleasure

N

Naaman	NAY ə mən
nabob	NAY bob
Nabokov	nə BAW kəf
Naboth	NAY bahth
nacelle	nə SEL
Na Champassak, Sisouk	nah shahm PAH sahk, see SOOK
Nacogdoches	NAK ə DOH chəz
nacre	NAY kər
nacreous	NAY kree əs
Nader	NAY dər
nadir	NAY dir
Naga	NAH gah
Nagasaki	NAH gə SAH kee
Nagoya	nah GAW yah
Nagy (Hungarian)	NOD yə
Nahant	nə HANT
Nahua	NAH wah
Nahuatl	NAH WAH təl
Nahuatlan	nah WAHT lən
Nahum	NAY əm
naiad	NAY əd
naïf	nah EEF
Naipaul	NĪ pawl
Nairobi	nī ROH bee
naive	nah EEV
naiveté	nah EEV TAY
Nakagawa, Ichiro	nah kah gah wah, ee chee roh
Nakasone, Yasuhiro	nah kah soh ne, yah suu hee roh
Nakhichevan	nah KEE chə VAHN
Nama	NAH mah
Namaqua	nah MAH kwə
Namibia	nə MIB ee ə
Nampula	nam POO lə
Nanda Devi	NUN dah DAY vee
Nanga Parbat	NUNG gah PUR bət
Nanjing	nahn jeeng
nankeen	nan KEEN

ə ago, a at, ah calm, ahr dark, air care, aw saw, ay say, ch church
e bet, ee me, eer beer, hw what, i is, ī my, n French final n vin,

Nanking	nan king
Nansen, Fridtjof	NAHN sən, FREET yawf
Nansen Sound	NAN sən
Nantes	nahnt
Nantucket	nan TUK ət
Naomi	nay OH mee
napalm	NAY pahm
nape	nayp
napery	NAY pə ree
Naphtali	NAF tə LĪ
naphtha	NAF thə
Napier	NAY pee ər
Naples	NAY pəlz
napoleon, N-	nə POH lee ən
Nara	nah rah
Narasimhan	nah rah sim HAHN
Narayan	na RĪ an
Narayanan, K. R.	nə RĪ ə nən
Narbonne	nahr BUN
narcissism	NAHR sə SIZ əm
narcissus, N-	nahr SIS əs
narcolepsy	NAHR kə LEP see
narcosis	nahr KOH səs
narcotic	nahr KOT ik
narcotize	NAHR kə TĪZ
Narragansett	NAR ə GAN sət
narrate	na RAYT
Narva	NAHR vah
Narvik	NAHR vik
narwhal	NAHR wəl
narwhale	NAHR hwayl
nascent	NAY sənt
Nashua	NASH oo ə
Nassau	NA saw
Nastase, Ilie	nah STAHZ ee, EE lee
nasturtium	nə STUR shəm
natal	NAY təl
Natal	nə TAL
natatorium	NAY tə TOR ee əm
Natchez	NACH əz
Natchitoches	NAK ə TOSH
nates	NAY teez
Nathan	NAY thən

o on, oh oat, oi boy, oo soon, oor poor, or for, ow cow, sh shush,
th thin, *th* this, u up, ur spur, uu book, *zh* pleasure

Natick	NAY tik
national	NASH ə nəl
nativity, N-	nə TIV ə tee
naturalization	NACH ə rə lə ZAY shən
naturally	NACH ə rə lee
Naugatuck	NAW gə TUK
naught	nawt
Nauru	nah OO roo
nausea	NAW zee ə
nauseate	NAW zee AYT
nauseous	NAW shəs
Nausicaä	naw SIK ee ə
nautch	nawch
nautical	NAW ti kəl
nautilus	NAW tə ləs
Navaho	NAV ə HOH
Navajo	NAV ə HOH
naval	NAY vəl
Navarra	nə VAH rə
Navarre	nə VAHR
navel	NAY vəl
Navon, Yitzhak	nah VAWN, YITS hahk
Navratilova, Martina	NAH vrə tə LOH və, mahr TEEN ə
nawab, N-	nə WAWB
Nawaz, S. Shah	nah WAHZ, shah hə
Naxos	NAH ksaws
Nazarene	NAZ ə REEN
Nazi	NAHT see
N'Djamena	ən JAH may nah
Neanderthal	nee AN dər THAWL
Neapolitan	NEE ə POL ə tən
Nebiim	NEB ee EEM
Nebo	NEE boh
Nebraska	nə BRAS kə
Nebuchadnezzar	NEB ə kəd NEZ ər
nebular	NEB yə lər
nebulous	NEB yə ləs
necessarily	NES ə SER ə lee
necessary	NES ə SER ee
necklace	NEK ləs
necrology	nə KROL ə jee
necromancer	NEK rə MAN sər
necrophilia	NEK rə FIL ee ə

ə ago, a at, ah calm, ahr dark, air care, aw saw, ay say, ch church
e bet, ee me, eer beer, hw what, i is, ī my, n French final n vin,

necropolis	nə **KROP** ə ləs
necrosis	nə **KROH** səs
necrotic	nə **KROT** ik
nectar	**NEK** tər
nectarine	**NEK** tə **REEN**
née	nay
Needham	**NEED** əm
Néel, Louis	nay **EL, LWEE**
ne'er-do-well	**NAIR** doo **WEL**
nefarious	ni **FA** ree əs
Nefertiti	**NEF** ər **TEE** tee
negate	ni **GAYT**
Negev	**NEG** ev
negligee	**NEG** lə **ZH AY**
negligence	**NEG** li jəns
negotiable	ni **GOH** shə bəl
negotiate	ni **GOH** shee **AYT**
negotiation	ni **GOH** shee **AY** shən
Negrillo	ni **GRIL** oh
Negri Sembilan	**NAY** gree **SEM** bee **LAHN**
Negrito	nə **GREE** toh
Negro	**NEE** groh
Negroponte, John	ne groh **PON** tee
Negro, Río	**NAY** groh, **REE** oh
Negros (island)	**NAY** grohs
negus, N-	**NEE** gəs
Nehemiah	**NEE** ə **MĪ** ə
Nehru	**NAY** roo
Neilson	**NEEL** sən
Neiman-Marcus	**NEE** mən **MAHR** kəs
Nei Monggol	**NAY MON** gohl
neither	**NEE** *th*ər
Nejd	nejd
nematode	**NEM** ə **TOHD**
Nembutal	**NEM** byə **TAWL**
Nemea	**NEE** mee ə
nemesis, N-	**NEM** ə səs
Neocene	**NEE** ə **SEEN**
neolithic	**NEE** ə **LITH** ik
neologism	nee **OL** ə **JIZ** əm
neomycin	**NEE** oh **MĪ** sin
neophyte	**NEE** ə **FĪT**
neoprene	**NEE** ə **PREEN**

o on, oh oat, oi boy, oo soon, oor poor, or for, ow cow, sh shush,
th thin, *th* this, u up, ur spur, uu book, *zh* pleasure

Nepal	nə PAWL
Nepalese	NEP ə LEEZ
nepenthe	nə PEN thee
nephew	NEF yoo
nephritis	nə FRĪ təs
nephrosis	nə FROH səs
ne plus ultra	nay pluus UUL trah
nepotism	NEP ə TIZ əm
Neptune	NEP tyoon
Nereid	NIR ee əd
Nereus	NIR ee əs
Nero	NEER oh
Neruda	nay ROO *th*ah
Nesselrode, n-	NES əl ROHD
Nessus	NES əs
n'est-ce pas	nes PAH
nestle	NES əl
Nestor	NES tər
Nestorian	ne STOR ee ən
nether	NE*TH* ər
Netherlands	NE*TH* ər lənds
Neuchâtel	nuu shah TEL
Neufchâtel	nuu shah TEL
Neuilly	nuu YEE
neuralgia	nuu RAL jə
neurasthenia	NUUR əs THEE nee ə
neuritis	nuu RĪ təs
neuroses (pl)	nuu ROH seez
neurosis	nuu ROH səs
neurotic	nuu ROT ik
neutrino	noo TREE noh
neutron	NOO tron
Neva	NEE və
Nevada (state)	nə VAD ə
nevus	NEE vəs
Newark (Delaware)	NOO ahrk
Newark (New Jersey)	NOO ərk
Newcastle	NOO KAS əl
New Delhi	NOO DEL ee
Newfoundland	noo FOWND lənd
Ne Win	nay win
New Orleans	NOO OR lee ənz
New Rochelle	NOO roh SHEL

ə ago, a at, ah calm, ahr dark, air care, aw saw, ay say, ch church
e bet, ee me, eer beer, hw what, i is, ī my, *n* French final n vin,

Nez Percé	nez purs
Ngaio	NĪ oh
Ngarukiyintwali, François	GAHR oo KEE in WAHL ee, frahn SWAH (frahn French final *n*)
Ngonda, Putteho	ən GOHN dah, puu TAY hoh
niacin	NĪ ə sən
Niagara	nī AG rə
Niamey	nee AHM ay
Nibelung	NEE bə LUUNG
Nibelungenlied	NEE bə LUUNG ən LEED
Nicaea	nī SEE ə
Nicaragua	NIK ə RAH gwə
Nice (France)	nees
Nicene	nī SEEN
nicety	NĪ sə tee
niche	nich
Nicobar	NIK ə BAHR
Nicodemus	NIK ə DEEM əs
Nicole	nī KOHL
Nicosia	NIK ə SEE ə
nicotine	NIK ə TEEN
nictitation	NIK tə TAY shən
nidus	NĪ dəs
Niebuhr	NEE buur
Nielsen, Sivert	NEEL sen, SEE vərt
Nietzsche	NEE chə
Nigel	NĪ jəl
Niger	NĪ jər
Nigeria	nī JIR ee ə
niggard	NIG ərd
nightingale, N-	NĪT ən GAYL
nightshade	NĪT shayd
nihilism	NĪ ə LIZ əm
nihilist	NĪ ə ləst
Nihon	nee hawn
Niihau	NEE ee HAH oo
Nijinsky	nə JIN skee
Nijmegen	NĪ MAY gən
Nike	NĪ kee
Niksic	NEE shich
Nikula, Pentti	NI koo lah, PEN tee
Nile	nīl
Nilotic	nī LOT ik

o on, oh oat, oi boy, oo soon, oor poor, or for, ow cow, sh shush, th thin, *th* this, u up, ur spur, uu book, *zh* pleasure

Nilsson, Birgit	NEEL sohn, BEER git
nimbus	NIM bəs
Nimeiry, Gaafar	nee MER ee, GAF ahr moh HAHM
Mohammed al-	ed ahl
Nîmes	neem
Nineveh	NIN ə və
Ningxia Huizu	neeng shee ah hwee zuu
Niobe	NĪ ə BEE
niobium	nī OH bee əm
Nippon	NIP ahn
Nipponese	NIP ə NEEZ
nirvana	nir VAH nə
nisei, N-	nee say
Nishapur	NEE shah PUUR
nisi	NĪ sī
Nissen	NIS ən
niter	NĪ tər
nitric	NĪ trik
nitrogen	NĪ trə jən
nitrogenous	nī TROJ ə nəs
nitroglycerin	NĪ trə GLIS ə rən
nitrous	NĪ trəs
Niue	nee OO ay
Ni Zhifu	nee jee fuu
Nkrumah, Kwame	ən KROO mah, KWAH mee
Noah	NOH ə
Nobel	noh BEL
nobelium	noh BEL ee əm
noblesse oblige	noh BLES oh BLEEZH
nocturnal	nok TUR nəl
nocturne	NOK turn
nocuous	NOK yoo əs
nodal	NOHD əl
nodule	NOJ ool
Noel (personal name)	NOH əl
Noel, n- (Christmas)	noh EL
noesis	noh EE sis
noetic	noh ET ik
Nogales	noh GAL əs
Noguchi	noh GOO chee
noisome	NOI səm
nolens volens	NOH lenz VOH lenz
noli me tangere	NOH lee me TAHNG ge re

ə ago, a at, ah calm, ahr dark, air care, aw saw, ay say, ch church
e bet, ee me, eer beer, hw what, i is, ī my, *n* French final n vin,

nolle prosequi	**NOL** ee **PROS** ə **KWĪ**
nolo contendere	**NOH** loh kən **TEN** də ree
nol-pros	nol **PROS**
nomad	**NOH** mad
nomadic	noh **MAD** ik
nom de guerre	ɴᴏᴍ də **GAIR**
nom de plume	ɴᴏᴍ də **PLOOM**
Nome	nohm
nomenclature	**NOH** mən ᴋʟᴀʏ chər
nominal	**NOM** ə nəl
nomogram	**NOH** mə ɢʀᴀᴍ
nonchalance	ɴᴏɴ shə **LAHNS**
nonchalant	ɴᴏɴ shə **LAHNT**
noncombatant	non **KOM** bə tənt
non compos mentis	non **KOM** pəs **MEN** təs
nonconformist	ɴᴏɴ kən **FOR** məst
nondescript	ɴᴏɴ di **SKRIPT**
nonentity	non **EN** tə tee
nones	nohnz
nonpareil	ɴᴏɴ pə **REL**
nonplus	non **PLUS**
non sequitur	non **SEK** wə tər
nook	nuuk
Norbert	**NOR** bərt
Nordaustlandet	noord **OWST** lahn det
Norfolk	**NOR** fək
normalcy	**NOR** məl see
Norman	**NOR** mən
Norodom Sihanouk	noh roh **DUM SEE** ə ɴᴜᴜᴋ
Norse	nors
Northumberland	nor **THUM** bər lənd
Norton	**NOR** tən
Norwalk	**NOR** wawk
Norway	**NOR** way
Norwegian	nor **WEE** jən
Norwich (Connecticut)	**NOR** wich
Norwich (England)	**NAHR** ij
Nosavan, Phoumi	noh sah **VAHN, POO** mee
nosology	noh **SOL** ə jee
nostalgia	nah **STAL** jə
Nostradamus	ɴᴏs trə **DAY** məs
Nostrand	**NOH** strənd
nostril	**NAHS** trəl

o **on**, oh **oat**, oi **boy**, oo **soon**, oor **poor**, or **for**, ow **cow**, sh **shush**,
th **thin**, *th* **this**, u **up**, ur **spur**, uu **book**, *zh* **pleasure**

nostrum	**NAHS** trəm
nota bene	**NOH** tah **BAY** nay
noteworthy	**NOHT wur** *th*ee
notion	**NOH** shən
notoriety	**NOH** tə **RĪ** ə tee
Notre Dame (Paris)	**NAW** trə **DAHM**
Notre Dame (US)	**NOH** tər **DAYM**
Nottingham	**NOT** ing əm
Nouakchott	nuu **AHK shaht**
nougat	**NOO** gət
nought	nawt
Nouméa	noo **MAY** ə
noumenon	**NOO** mə **NON**
nourish	**NUR** ish
nouveau riche	**NOO** voh **REESH**
nouveaux riches	**NOO** voh **REESH**
nova, N-	**NOH** və
Nova Scotia	**NOH** və **SKOH** shə
Novaya Zemlya	**NAW** vah yah **ZEM** lyah
novel	**NOV** əl
novella	noh **VEL** ə
November	noh **VEM** bər
novena	noh **VEE** nə
Novgorod	**NOV** gə **ROD**
Novi	**NOH** vī
novice	**NOV** is
Novi Sad	**NAW** vee **SAHD**
novitiate	noh **VISH** ət
Novocain	**NOH** və **KAYN**
novocaine	**NOH** və **KAYN**
Novorossiisk	**NAW** vaw raw **SEESK**
Novosibirsk	**NAW** vaw si **BIRSK**
Novotna	nə **VOT** nə
Novotny, Antonin	nah **VUT** nee, ahn **TOH** neen
Nowak, Jerzy	**NOH** vahk, **YER** *zh*e
Nox	noks
noxious	**NOK** shəs
Noyes	noiz
nuance	**NOO** ahns
Nuba	**NOO** bə
Nubian	**NOO** bee ən
nubile	**NOO** bəl
nuclear	**NOO** klee ər

ə ago, a at, ah calm, ahr dark, air care, aw saw, ay say, ch church
e bet, ee me, eer beer, hw what, i is, ī my, *n* French final n vin,

nuclei (pl)	NOO klee ī
nucleic	noo KLEE ik
nucleon	NOO klee ON
nucleonics	NOO klee ON iks
nucleotide	NOO klee ə TĪD
nucleus	NOO klee əs
nude	nood
nudnik	NUUD nik
Nuevo León	NWAY voh lay OHN
nugatory	NOO gə TOR ee
nugget	NUG ət
nuisance	NOO səns
Nukualofa	NOO koo ə LAW fə
Nuku Hiva	NOO koo HEE və
null	nul
nullity	NUL ə tee
numeral	NOO mə rəl
Numidia	noo MID ee ə
numismatic	NOO məz MAT ik
numismatist	noo MIZ mə təst
nunc dimittis	NUNGK di MIT is
nuncio	NUUN see oh
Nuñez	NOO nyes
nuptial	NUP shəl
Nuremberg	NUUR əm BURG
Nureyev, Rudolph	nuu RAY yəf
Nurmi	NUUR mee
Nur, Mohamud Haji	NOOR, moo HAH mood HAH jee
nurture	NUR chər
Nuseibeh, Hazem	noo SAY i bə, HAZ im
nutation	noo TAY shən
nutrient	NOO tree ənt
nutriment	NOO trə mənt
nutrition	nuu TRISH ən
nux vomica	nuks VOM i kə
Nuyen, France	noo YEN, FRANS
Nyack	NĪ ak
Nyasa, Nyassa	nī AS ə
Nyerere	nyə RAIR ay
Nygaard, Hjalmar	NĪ gord, YAHL mahr
Nygaarsdvold	NĪ gawrs vawl
Nyiregyhaza	NYI rej HAH zaw
nymph	nimf

---

o on, oh oat, oi boy, oo soon, oor poor, or for, ow cow, sh shush,
th thin, *th* this, u up, ur spur, uu book, *zh* pleasure

nymphet	nim **FET**
nymphomania	**NIM** fə **MAY** nee ə
nystagmus	ni **STAG** məs
Nyx	niks

O

Oahu	ə **WAH** hoo
oases	oh **AY** seez
oasis	oh **AY** səs
Oates	ohts
oath	ohth
Oaxaca	wah **HAH** kah
Ob	ohb
Obadiah	**OH** bə **DĪ** ə
obbligato	**OB** lə **GAH** toh
obdurate	**OB** duu rət
obeah	**OH** bee ə
obeisance	oh **BEE** səns
obelisk	**OB** ə lisk
Oberammergau	**OH** bər **AH** mər **GOW**
Oberon	**OH** bə **RON**
obese	oh **BEES**
obesity	oh **BEE** sə tee
obfuscate	**OB** fə **SKAYT**
obi	**OH** bee
Obie	**OH** bee
obiit	**OH** bee **IT**
obit	**OH** bit
obiter dictum	**OHB** ə tər **DIK** təm
obituary	ə **BICH** oo **ER** ee
object (n)	**OB** jikt
object (v)	əb **JEKT**
objet d'art	aw *zh*ay **DAHR**
objet trouvé	aw *zh*ay troo **VAY**
objurgate	**OB** jər **GAYT**
oblation	ə **BLAY** shən
obligato	**OB** lə **GAH** toh
obligatory	ə **BLIG** ə **TOR** ee
oblige	ə **BLĪJ**
oblique	ə **BLEEK**

ə ago, a at, ah calm, ahr dark, air care, aw saw, ay say, ch church
e bet, ee me, eer beer, hw what, i is, ī my, *n* French final n vin,

oblique (military)	ə **BLĪK**
obliquity	ə **BLIK** wə tee
obliterate	ə **BLIT** ə **RAYT**
oblivion	ə **BLIV** ee ən
oblivious	ə **BLIV** ee əs
oblong	**OB** lawng
obloquy	**OB** lə kwee
oboe	**OH** boh
Obote, Milton	aw **BAW** te
Obregón	oh bray **GAWN**
obscenity	əb **SEN** ə tee
obscurantism	əb **SKYOOR** ən **TIZ** əm
obsequies	**OB** sə kweez
obsequious	əb **SEE** kwee əs
obsequy	**OB** sə kwee
obsidian	əb **SID** ee ən
obsolescent	**OB** sə **LES** ənt
obsolete	**OB** sə **LEET**
obstacle	**OB** stə kəl
obstetric	əb **STET** rik
obstetrician	**OB** stə **TRISH** ən
obstinate	**OB** stə nət
obstreperous	əb **STREP** ə rəs
obtrusive	əb **TROO** siv
obtuse	əb **TOOS**
obverse	**OB** vurs
obviate	**OB** vee **AYT**
ocarina	**OK** ə **REE** nə
O'Casey, Sean	oh **KAY** see, **SHAWN**
Occam	**OK** əm
occasion	ə **KAY** zhən
occident, O-	**OK** sə dənt
occipital	ok **SIP** ə təl
occult	ə **KULT**
occultation	**OK** əl **TAY** shən
Oceania	**OH** shee **AN** ee ə
oceanographer	**OH** shə **NOG** rə fər
Oceanus	oh **SEE** ə nəs
ocher	**OH** kər
Ochoa, Severo	oh **CHOH** ə, sə **VAIR** oh
Ockham	**OK** əm
octagon	**OK** tə **GON**
octagonal	ok **TAG** ə nəl

o on, oh oat, oi boy, oo soon, oor poor, or for, ow cow, sh shush,
th thin, *th* this, u up, ur spur, uu book, *zh* pleasure

octahedron	OK tə HEE drən
octameter	ok TAM ə tər
octane	OK tayn
Octans	OK tanz
octant	OK tənt
octave	OK tiv
Octavia	ok TAY vee ə
Octavius	ok TAY vee əs
octavo	ok TAY voh
octet	ok TET
octogenarian	OK tə jə NAIR ee ən
octopus	OK tə pəs
ocular	OK yə lər
oculist	OK yə ləst
odalisque	OHD ə lisk
Oda, Shigeru	oh dah, shee ge roo
Odegard	OH də gahrd
Oder	OH dər
Odessa	oh DES ə
odeum	oh DEE əm
Odin	OH din
odious	OH dee əs
odium	OH dee əm
Odoacer	OH doh AY sər
odoriferous	OH də RIF ər əs
odorous	OH dər əs
Odysseus	oh DIS ee əs
Odyssey	OD ə see
Oedipal, o-	ED ə pəl
Oedipus	ED ə pəs
oenology	ee NOL ə jee
Oenone	ee NOH nee
oenophile	EE nə fil
oersted	UR stəd
oeuvre	UUV rə
O'Faoláin, Seán	oh FAL ən, SHAWN
Offenbach	AW fən BAHK
official	ə FISH əl
officious	ə FISH əs
O'Flaherty, Liam	oh FLA ər tee, LEE əm
often	AW fən
Ogbomosho	OG bə MOH shoh
ogee	OH jee

ə ago, a at, ah calm, ahr dark, air care, aw saw, ay say, ch church
e bet, ee me, eer beer, hw what, i is, ī my, n French final n vin,

ogham	OG əm
Ogilvie	OH gəl vee
ogive	OH jīv
Oglala	oh GLAH lə
ogle	OH gəl
Oglethorpe	OH gəl THORP
ogre	OH gər
Ohira, Masayoshi	oh hee rah, mah sah yoh shee
ohm, O-	ohm
Oireachtas	AIR ək thəs
Oise	wahz
Oistrakh	OI strahk
Ojibwa	oh JIB way
okapi	oh KAH pee
Okawara, Yoshio	oh kah wah rah, yoh shee oh
Okazaki, Katsuo	oh kah zah kee, kaht soo oh
Okeechobee	OH kə CHOH bee
Okhotsk	oh KOTSK
Okinawa	OH kə NAH wə
Oklahoma	OH klə HOH mə
okra	OH krə
Olav	OH lahf
Oldham	OHL dəm
Olduvai	AWL duu VĪ
oleaginous	OH lee AJ ə nəs
oleander	OH lee AN dər
olefin	OH lə fən
oleo	OH lee oh
oleomargarine	OH lee oh MAHR jə rən
olfactory	ahl FAK tə ree
oligarchy	AHL ə GAHR kee
Oligocene	AHL ə goh SEEN
oligopoly	ahl ə GOP ə lee
olio	OH lee oh
Olivier	oh LIV ee AY
Ollenauer, Erich	AW lən ow ər, AIR ish
Olmedo	ohl MAY doh
Olympia	oh LIM pee ə
Omaha	OH mə HAH
O'Mahoney	oh MA ə nee
Oman	oh MAHN
Omar Khayyám	OH mahr kī YAHM
ombudsman	OM BUUDZ mən

---

o on, oh oat, oi boy, oo soon, oor poor, or for, ow cow, sh shush,
th thin, *th* this, u up, ur spur, uu book, *zh* pleasure

Omdurman	**AHM** dər **MAN**
omen	**OH** mən
omicron	**OM** ə **KRON**
ominous	**OM** ə nəs
omnibus	**OM** nə bəs
omnifarious	**OM** nə **FA** ree əs
omnipotent	om **NIP** ə tənt
omnipresent	**OM** nə **PREZ** ənt
omniscience	om **NISH** əns
omniscient	om **NISH** ənt
omnivorous	om **NIV** ə rəs
Omphale	**OM** fə **LEE**
Omsk	awmsk
Onan	**OH** nən
onanism	**OH** nə **NIZ** əm
Onassis	oh **NAS** əs
Ondias-Souna, Hubert	awn **DEE** ahs **SOO** nə, oo **BAIR**
Ondine	awn **DEEN**
Onega	oh **NEE** gə
Onegin	oh **NAY** gin
Oneida	oh **NĪ** də
Oneonta	**OH** nee **ON** tə
onerous	**ON** ə rəs
Ong Yoke Lin, Dató	ohng yoh **KAY** leen, dah **TOH**
onomatopoeia	**ON** ə **MAT** ə **PEE** ə
Onondaga	**ON** ən **DAH** gə
Onsager, Lars	**OON** sah gər, lahrs
Ontario	on **TAIR** ee **OH**
ontogenesis	**ON** tə **JEN** ə sis
ontogeny	on **TOJ** ə nee
ontological	**ON** tə **LOJ** ə kəl
ontology	on **TOL** ə jee
onus	**OH** nəs
onyx	**ON** iks
oolite	**OH** ə **LĪT**
oolitic	**OH** ə **LIT** ik
oolong	**OO** lawng
opacity	oh **PAS** ə tee
opal	**OH** pəl
opaque	oh **PAYK**
opera	**OP** ər ə
Opéra	oh pay **RAH**
opéra bouffe	**OP** ər ə **BOOF**

ə ago, a at, ah calm, ahr dark, air care, aw saw, ay say, ch church
e bet, ee me, eer beer, hw what, i is, ī my, *n* French final n vin,

opera buffa	OP ər ə BOO fə
operative (a)	OP ə rə tiv
operative (n)	OP ə RAY tiv
operculum	oh PUR kyə ləm
operetta	OP ə RET ə
Ophelia	oh FEEL yə
Ophir	OH fər
Ophiuchus	AH fi YOO kəs
ophthalmologist	AHF thal MOL ə jəst
opiate (a, n)	OH pee ət
opine	oh PĪN
opium	OH pee əm
Oporto	oh POR toh
opossum	ə POS əm
opportune	OP ər TOON
opportunism	OP ər TOO niz əm
opportunity	OP ər TOO nə tee
oppressor	ə PRES ər
opprobrious	ə PROH bree əs
opprobrium	ə PROH bree əm
optician	op TISH ən
optimism	OP tə MIZ əm
optimum	OP tə məm
option	OP shən
optometrist	op TOM ə trəst
optometry	op TOM ə tree
opulent	OP yə lənt
opuntia	oh PUN shə
opus	OH pəs
oracular	aw RAK yə lər
Oradea	aw RAH dyah
oral, O-	OH rəl
orangutan	ə RANG ə TAN
orator	OR ə tər
oratorio	OR ə TOR ee OH
oratory	OR ə TOR ee
orbital	OR bə təl
orchestra	OR kə strə
orchestral	or KES trəl
orchid	OR kəd
orchidaceous	OR kə DAY shəs
ordeal	or DEEL
ordinal	OR də nəl

o **on**, oh **oat**, oi **boy**, oo **soon**, oor **poor**, or **for**, ow **cow**, sh **shush**,
th **thin**, *th* **this**, u **up**, ur **spur**, uu **book**, *zh* **pleasure**

ordinance	**OR** də nəns
ordinarily	**OR** də **NER** ə lee
ordinary	**OR** də **NER** ee
ordinate	**OR** də nət
ordnance	**ORD** nəns
Ordoñez, Antonio	awr **DOHN** yez, ahn **TOH** nee oh
Ordovician	**OR** də **VISH** ən
ordure	**OR** jər
Ordzhonikidze	or jaw ni **KEED** ze
oread	**OR** ee **AD**
orectic	oh **REK** tik
oregano	ə **REG** ə **NOH**
Oregon	**OR** ə gən
Oregonian	**OR** ə **GOH** nee ən
Orel	oh **REL**
Oreopithicus	**OR** ee oh **PITH** ə kəs
Orestes	ə **RES** teez
organdy, organdie	**OR** gən dee
orgiastic	**OR** jee **AS** tik
orgy	**OR** jee
oriel	**OR** ee əl
orient, O- (a, n)	**OR** ee ənt
orient (v)	**OR** ee **ENT**
oriental, O-	**OR** ee **EN** təl
orientation	**OR** ee ən **TAY** shən
Oriente	**OR** ee **EN** te
orifice	**OR** ə fəs
oriflamme	**OR** ə **FLAM**
origami	**OR** ə **GAH** mee
origan	**OR** ə gən
Origen	**OR** ə jən
origin	**OR** ə jən
Orinoco	**OR** ə **NOH** koh
oriole	**OR** ee **OHL**
Orion	ə **RĪ** ən
Oriskany	oh **RIS** kə nee
orison	**OR** ə zən
Orissa	oh **RIS** ə
Orizaba	**OR** ee **ZAH** bah
Orkney	**ORK** nee
Orlando	or **LAN** doh
Orleans	**OR** lee ənz
Orléans	or lay **AHN** (**AHN** French final *n*)

ə ago, a at, ah calm, ahr dark, air care, aw saw, ay say, ch church
e bet, ee me, eer beer, hw what, i is, ī my, *n* French final n vin,

Orlich	or LEECH
Orlon	OR lon
Orly	or LEE
Ormazd	OR məzd
ormolu	OR mə LOO
Ormuz	OR məz
Ormsby-Gore	ORMZ bee gawr
ornithology	OR nə THOL ə jee
ornithorhynchus	OR nə thə RING kəs
orography	aw ROG rə fee
orology	aw ROL ə jee
Orosius	aw ROH zhee əs
orotund	OR ə TUND
Orozco	aw RAW skaw
Orpen	OR pən
orphan	OR fən
Orpheus	OR fee əs
orris, orrice	OR əs
Ortega Saavedra, Daniel	or TAY gah sah VAYD rah
Ortega y Gasset, José	or TAY gə EE gah SET, haw SE
orthicon	OR thi KON
orthoclase	OR thə KLAYS
orthodontia	OR thə DON shə
orthodox	OR thə DOKS
orthodoxy	OR thə DOK see
orthoepist	or THOH ə pəst
orthoepy	or THOH ə pee
orthographic	OR thə GRAF ik
orthography	or THOG rə fee
orthopedic	OR thə PEE dik
Ortiz, Carlos	awr TEES, KAHR lohs
Orvieto	or VYAY toh
Osage	oh SAYJ
Osaka	oh SAH kə
Osborn, -e	OZ bərn
Oscan	OS kən
Osceola	os ee OH lə
oscillate	OS ə LAYT
oscilloscope	ə SIL ə SKOHP
Osco-Umbrian	OS koh UM bree ən
osculate	OS kyə LAYT
Oshkosh	OSH kosh

o on, oh oat, oi boy, oo soon, oor poor, or for, ow cow, sh shush,
th thin, *th* this, u up, ur spur, uu book, *zh* pleasure

osier	**OH** _zh_ ər
Osijek	**AW** see **YEK**
Osiris	oh **SĪ** rəs
Oslo	**OZ** loh
Osman, Aden Abdulla	**OHS** mən, **AH** dən ahb **DOO** lə
osmosis	oz **MOH** səs
Osnaburg	**OZ** nə **BURG**
Ospina	aw **SPEE** nah
osprey	**OS** pree
Ossa	**OS** ə
Ossetia	ah **SEE** shə
Ossian	**OSH** ən
Ossietzky	os ee **ET** skee
ossify	**OS** ə **FĪ**
Ossining	**OS** ə ning
Ostend	ah **STEND**
ostensible	ə **STEN** sə bəl
ostentatious	os ten **TAY** shəs
osteopath	**OS** tee ə **PATH**
osteopathy	os tee **OP** ə thee
Ostia	**OS** tee ə
ostler	**OS** lər
Ostmark	**AWST** mahrk
ostracize	**OS** trə **SĪZ**
Ostrava	**AW** strah vah
Ostrogoth	**OS** trə **GOTH**
Ostrowiec	aw **STRAW** vyets
Ostwald	**OHST** vahlt
Ostyak, Ostiak	**OS** tee **AK**
Oswego	ah **SWEE** goh
Oswiecim	awsh **VYANT** sim
otalgia	oh **TAL** jee ə
Othello	ə **THEL** oh
otiose	**OH** shee **OHS**
otitis	oh **TĪ** təs
otology	oh **TOL** ə jee
Otranto	oh **TRAHN** toh
Otsego	aht **SEE** goh
ottava rima	oh **TAH** və **REE** mə
Ottawa	**OT** ə wə
Ottoman	**OT** ə mən
Otunnu, Olara	aw **TOO** noo, aw **LAR** rah
Ouachita	**WOSH** i **TAW**
Ouagadougou	**WAH** gə **DOO** goo

ə ago, a at, ah calm, ahr dark, air care, aw saw, ay say, ch church
e bet, ee me, eer beer, hw what, i is, ī my, _n_ French final n vin,

oubliette	oo blee **ET**
Oueddei, Goukouni	**WAH** dee, goo **KOO** nee

Ouedraogo,
    Jean-Baptiste
	WED drah oh **GOH**, *zh*ahn bah
	    TEEST (*zh*ahn French
	    final *n*)

ought	awt
Ouida	**WEE** də
Ouija	**WEE** jə
Oulu	**OH** loo
Oumarou, Idé	oo mah **ROO**, **EE** day
outré	oo **TRAY**
ouzel, ousel	**OO** zəl
ouzo	**OO** zoh
ovarian	oh **VA** ree ən
ovary	**OH** və ree
overt	oh **VURT**
overthrow (v)	**OH** vər **THROH**
overthrow (n)	**OH** vər **THROH**
overture	**OH** vər chər
overwrought	**OH** vər **RAWT**
Ovid	**OV** əd
Oviedo	aw **VYE** *th*aw
oviparous	oh **VIP** ə rəs
ovoid	**OH** void
ovulate	**OV** yə **LAYT**
ovule	**OH** vyool
ovum	**OH** vəm
oxalic	ok **SAL** ik
Oxford	**OKS** fərd
oxidant	**OK** sə dənt
oxidation	**OK** sə **DAY** shən
oxidize	**OK** sə **DĪZ**
Oxnard	**OKS** nahrd
Oxonian	ok **SOH** nee ən
oxyacetylene	**OK** see ə **SET** ə **LEEN**
oxymoron	**OK** si **MOH** ron

Oyono, Ferdinand
    Léopold
	oh **YOH** noh, **FUR** di **NAND** **LEE** oh
	    pohld

Ozark	**OH** zahrk
Ozawa, Seiji	oh **ZAH** wə, **SAY** jee
ozone	**OH** zohn

Ozores Typaldos,
    Carlos
	OH soh res tee **PAHL** dohs, **KAHR**
	    lohs

o on, oh oat, oi boy, oo soon, oor poor, or for, ow cow, sh shush,
th thin, *th* this, u up, ur spur, uu book, *zh* pleasure

P

pabulum	**PAB** yə ləm
Pacelli	pah **CHE** lee
Pachachi, Adnan	pə **SHAH** shee, ahd **NAHN**
pachisi	pə **CHEE** zee
pachyderm	**PAK** i ᴅᴜʀᴍ
pacification	ᴘᴀs ə fə **KAY** shən
pacifism	**PAS** ə ꜰɪᴢ əm
pacify	**PAS** ə ꜰɪ̄
Packard	**PAK** ərd
Padang	pah **DAHNG**
paddock	**PAD** ək
paddy, P-	**PAD** ee
Paderewski, Ignace Jan	ᴘᴀᴅ ə **REF** skee, ee **NYAS YAHN**
Padilla	pah **DEE** yah
padishah	**PAH** di ꜱʜᴀʜ
padre	**PAH** dray
padrone	pah **DROH** nay
Padua	**PAJ** oo ə
Paducah	pə **DOO** kə
paean	**PEE** ən
Paestum	**PES** təm
pagan	**PAY** gən
Paganini	ᴘᴀɢ ə **NEE** nee
pageant	**PAJ** ənt
Paget	**PAJ** ət
paginate	**PAJ** ə ɴᴀʏᴛ
Pagliacci	pah **LYAHT** chee
Pagliaroni	pa glee ə **ROH** nee
pagoda	pə **GOH** də
Pago Pago	**PAHNG** oh **PAHNG** oh
Pahang	pah **HAHNG**
Pahlavi, p-	**PAH** lə ᴠᴇᴇ
paillette	pī **YET**
paisley, P-	**PAYZ** lee
Paiute	**PĪ** yoot
Pakistan	**PAK** i ꜱᴛᴀɴ
Pakistani	ᴘᴀᴋ i **STAN** ee

ə ago, a at, ah calm, ahr dark, air care, aw saw, ay say, ch church
e bet, ee me, eer beer, hw what, i is, ī my, *n* French final n vin,

palabra	pah **LAH** brah
paladin	**PAL** ə dən
palaestra	pə **LES** trə
Palafox, Antonio	**PA** lə fahks, an **TOH** nee oh
Palais-Royal	**PA** lay roi **YAL**
Palamon	**PA** lə mən
palanquin	**PAL** ən **KEEN**
Palar, Lambertus	pah **LAHR**, lahm **BER** təs
palatable	**PAL** ə tə bəl
palatal	**PAL** ə təl
palate	**PAL** ət
palatial	pə **LAY** shəl
palatinate, P-	pə **LAT** ə nət
palatine, P-	**PAL** ə **TĪN**
Palau	pah **LOW** (**LOW** as in *cow*)
palaver	pə **LAV** ər
Palawan	pah **LAH** wahn
palazzo	pah **LAHT** soh
Palembang	**PAH** lem **BAHNG**
Palenque	pah **LENG** kay
Paleocene	**PAY** lee ə **SEEN**
paleography	**PAY** lee **OG** rə fee
paleolithic	**PAY** lee ə **LITH** ik
paleontology	**PAY** lee ən **TOL** ə jee
Paleozoic	**PAY** lee ə **ZOH** ik
Palermo	pah **LER** moh
Palestine	**PAL** ə **STĪN**
palestra	pə **LES** trə
Palestrina	**PAL** ə **STREE** nə
palette	**PAL** ət
palfrey	**PAWL** free
Palgrave	**PAWL** grayv
Pali	**PAH** lee
palimony	**PAL** ə **MOH** nee
palimpsest	**PAL** əm **SEST**
palindrome	**PAL** ən **DROHM**
palisade, P-	**PAL** ə **SAYD**
Palladian	pə **LAY** dee ən
Palladino, Nunzio	**PAH** lah **DEEN** oh, **NUUN** tsee oh
Palladio	pah **LAHD** yoh
palladium, P-	pə **LAY** dee əm
Pallas	**PAL** əs

o on, oh oat, oi boy, oo soon, oor poor, or for, ow cow, sh shush,
th thin, *th* this, u up, ur spur, uu book, *zh* pleasure

pallet	**PAL** ət
palliasse	pal **YAS**
palliative	**PAL** yə tiv
pallid	**PAL** əd
pall-mall, Pall Mall	pel mel
palm	pahm
Palma	**PAHL** mah
Palmas	**PAHL** mahs
Palme, Olof	**PAHL** mə, **OH** lawf
palmer, P-	**PAH** mər
palmetto	pal **MET** oh
palmistry	**PAH** mə stree
Palmyra, p-	pal **MĪ** rə
Palo Alto	**PAL** oh **AL** toh
Palomar	**PAL** ə **MAHR**
palomino	**PAL** ə **MEE** noh
palooka	pə **LOO** kə
Palos	**PAH** laws
palpable	**PAL** pə bəl
palpitation	**PAL** pə **TAY** shən
palsy	**PAWL** zee
palter	**PAWL** tər
paltry	**PAWL** tree
Pamela	**PAM** ə lə
Pamir	pah **MIR**
Pamlico	**PAM** lə кон
pampa, P-	**PAHM** pə
pampas	**PAHM** pəz
pampero	pahm **PE** roh
pamphlet	**PAM** flət
panacea	**PAN** ə **SEE** ə
panache	pə **NASH**
Panama, p-	**PAN** ə **MAH**
Panamanian	**PAN** ə **MAY** nee ən
panatella	**PAN** ə **TEL** ə
Panay	pah **NĪ**
panchromatic	**PAN** kroh **MAT** ik
pancreas	**PAN** kree əs
pancreatic	**PAN** kree **AT** ik
panda	**PAN** də
Pandarus	**PAN** dər əs
pandect, P-	**PAN** dekt
pandemic	pan **DEM** ik

ə ago, a at, ah calm, ahr dark, air care, aw saw, ay say, ch church
e bet, ee me, eer beer, hw what, i is, ī my, *n* French final n vin,

pandemonium, P-	PAN də MOH nee əm
pandit, P-	PUN dət
Pandora	pan DOR ə
pandowdy	pan DOW dee
panegyric	PAN ə JIR ik
panegyrist	PAN ə JIR əst
panegyrize	PAN ə jə RĪZ
panelist	PAN ə ləst
Pango Pango	PAHNG oh PAHNG oh
Panhellenic	PAN hə LEN ik
Panjabi	pun JAH bee
panjandrum	pan JAN drəm
Panmunjom	pahn muun JUM
pannier	PAN yər
pannikin	PAN i kən
panocha	pə NOH chə
panoply	PAN ə plee
panorama	PAN ə RAM ə
Pantagruel	pan TA groo EL
Pantelleria	pahn TE le REE ə
pantheism	PAN thee IZ əm
pantheon, P-	PAN thee ON
Panthéon	pahn tay OHN (pahn and OHN French final *n*)
pantomime	PAN tə MĪM
pantomimic	PAN tə MIM ik
pantothenic	PAN tə THEN ik
Panurge	pan URJ
panzer, P-	PAN zər
papacy	PAY pə see
Papadopoulos, George	PAH pə DOP ə ləs
Papajorgji, Justin	PAH pah YOHR gee, JUUS tin
papal	PAY pəl
Papandreou, Andreas	PAH pahn *TH*RAY oo, ahn DRAY əs
Papanicalaou	PAH pə NEE kə LOW (LOW as in *cow*)
paparazzi	PAH pə RAHT tsee
Papas	PA pəs
papaw	PAW paw
papaya	pə PAH yə
Papeete	PAH pee AY tay
papeterie	PAP ə tree
papier-mâché	PAY pər mə SHAY
papilla	pə PIL ə

---

o on, oh oat, oi boy, oo soon, oor poor, or for, ow cow, sh shush,
th thin, *th* this, u up, ur spur, uu book, *zh* pleasure

papillary	PAP ə LER ee
papilloma	PAP ə LOH mə
papillon	PAP ə LON
papist	PAY pəst
papoose	pa POOS
Papoulias, George	pah POOL yahs
paprika	pə PREE kə
Papua	PAP yoo ə
papule	PAP yool
papyrus	pə PĪ rəs
Pará	pah RAH
parable	PA rə bəl
parabola	pə RAB ə lə
parabolic	PA rə BOL ik
Paracelsus	PA rə SEL səs
paraclete	PA rə KLEET
paradichlorobenzene	PA rə dī KLOR ə BEN zeen
paradigm	PA rə DĪM
paradigmatic	PA rə dig MAT ik
paradise, P-	PA rə DĪS
paradisiac	PA rə DIZ ee AK
paradisiacal	PA rə də SĪ ə kəl
paradox	PA rə DOKS
paradoxical	PA rə DOK si kəl
paraffin	PA rə fən
paragon	PA rə GON
Paraguay	PA rə GWAY
parakeet	PA rə KEET
parallax	PA rə LAKS
parallel	PA rə LEL
parallelogram	PA rə LEL ə GRAM
paralysis	pə RAL ə səs
paralytic	PA rə LIT ik
Paramaribo	PA rə MA rə BOH
paramecium	PA rə MEE see əm
parameter	pə RAM ə tər
paramount	PA rə MOWNT
paramour	PA rə MUUR
Paramus	pə RAM əs
Paraná	PA rə NAH
paranoia	PA rə NOI ə
paranoiac	PA rə NOI AK
Paranthropus	PA rən THROH pəs

ə ago, a at, ah calm, ahr dark, air care, aw saw, ay say, ch church
e bet, ee me, eer beer, hw what, i is, ī my, *n* French final n vin,

parapet	**PA** rə pət
paraphernalia	**PA** rə fə **NAYL** yə
paraphrase	**PA** rə **FRAYZ**
paraphrastic	**PA** rə **FRAS** tik
paraplegia	**PA** rə **PLEE** jə
paraplegic	**PA** rə **PLEE** jik
parapsychology	**PA** rə sī **KOL** ə jee
parasite	**PA** rə **SĪT**
parasitic	**PA** rə **SIT** ik
parasitism	**PA** rə sə **TIZ** əm
parasol	**PA** rə **SAWL**
parataxis	**PA** rə **TAK** səs
parathyroid	**PA** rə **THĪ** roid
Paray	pah **RAY**
parboil	**PAHR** boil
Parcae	**PAHR** see
Parcheesi, p-	pahr **CHEE** zee
paregoric	**PA** rə **GOR** ik
paresis	pə **REE** səs
par excellence	**PAHR EK** sə **LAHNS**
parfait	pahr **FAY**
parhelion	pahr **HEE** lee ən
pariah	pə **RĪ** ə
Paricutín	pah ree koo **TEEN**
parietal	pə **RĪ** ə təl
pari-mutuel	**PA** ri **MYOO** choo əl
pari passu	**PAH** ree **PAHS** soo
Paris	**PA** rəs
parish	**PA** rish
parishioner	pə **RISH** ə nər
Parisian	pə **REE** *zh* ən
parka	**PAHR** kə
Park Chung Hee	pahrk chung hee
parlance	**PAHR** ləns
parlay	**PAHR** lay
parley	**PAHR** lee
parliament	**PAHR** lə mənt
parliamentarian	**PAHR** lə mən **TAIR** ee ən
parliamentary	**PAHR** lə **MEN** tə ree
Parma	**PAHR** mə
Parmesan	**PAHR** mə **ZAHN**
parmigiana	**PAHR** mi **JAH** nə
Parnassian	pahr **NAS** ee ən

---

o **on**, oh **oat**, oi **boy**, oo **soon**, oor **poor**, or **for**, ow **cow**, sh **shush**,
th **thin**, *th* **this**, u **up**, ur **spur**, uu **book**, *zh* **pleasure**

Parnassus	pahr NAS əs
Parnu	PAR noo
parochial	pə ROH kee əl
parody	PA rə dee
parole	pə ROHL
paroxysm	PA rək SIZ əm
parquet	pahr KAY
parquetry	PAHR kə tree
Parran	PA rən
parricide	PA rə SĪD
parrot	PA rət
parry, P-	PA ree
parse	pahrs
parsec	PAHR sek
Parsi	PAHR see
Parsifal	PAHR si FAHL
parsimonious	PAHR sə MOH nee əs
parsimony	PAHR sə MOH nee
parsley	PAHRS lee
parsnip	PAHR snəp
parterre	pahr TAIR
parthenogenesis	PAHR thə noh JEN ə səs
Parthenon	PAHR thə NON
Parthenope	pahr THEN ə PEE
Parthenos	PAHR thə NOS
Parthian	PAHR thee ən
participial	PAHR tə SIP ee əl
participle	PAHR tə SIP əl
particular	pər TIK yə lər
partisan	PAHR tə zən
partite	PAHR tīt
partitive	PAHR tə tiv
partridge	PAHR trij
parturient	pahr TYUUR ee ənt
parturition	PAHR chə RISH ən
parvenu	PAHR və NOO
pas (French)	pah
Pasadena	PAS ə DEE nə
Pascal, Blaise	pas KAL, BLEZ
paschal	PAS kəl
pasha	PAH shə
Pashayan	pə SHAY ən
Pashto	PUSH toh (PUSH as in *slush*)

ə ago, a at, ah calm, ahr dark, air care, aw saw, ay say, ch church
e bet, ee me, eer beer, hw what, i is, ī my, *n* French final n vin,

Pasiphaë	pə SIF ə EE
paso doble	PAH soh DOH blay
Pasquale	pah SKWAH lay
passacaglia	PAH sə KAHL yə
passade	pə SAYD
passado	pə SAH doh
Passaic	pə SAY ik
Passamaquoddy	PAS ə mə KWOD ee
passé	pa SAY
passel	PA səl
passementerie	pas MEN tree
passe-partout	PAS pahr TOO
passerine	PAS ə RĪN
passim	PAS əm
passivity	pa SIV ə tee
Passover	PAS OH vər
passus	PAS əs
Passy	pa SEE
pasta	PAH stə
pastel	pa STEL
Pasternak	PAS tər NAK
Pasteur	pa STUR
pasteurize	PAS chə RĪZ
pasticcio	pa STEE choh
pastiche	pa STEESH
pastille	pa STEEL
pastime	PAS tīm
Pastinen, Ilkka Olavi	PAHS tee nən, EEL kə OH lah vee
Pasto	PAHS taw
pastoral	PAS tə rəl
pastorale	PAS tə RAL
pastorate	PAS tə rət
pastrami	pə STRAH mee
Patachou	pah tah SHOO
Patagonia	PAT ə GOH nee ə
Patchogue	PA chog
patchouli	PA chuu lee
pate	payt
pâté	pah TAY
pâté de foie gras	pah TAY də FWAH GRAH
patella	pə TEL ə
paten	PAT ən
patent (obvious)	PAY tənt

---

o on, oh oat, oi boy, oo soon, oor poor, or for, ow cow, sh shush,
th thin, *th* this, u up, ur spur, uu book, *zh* pleasure

patent (except obvious)	**PAT** ənt
patently	**PAY** tənt lee
Pater, p-	**PAY** tər
paterfamilias	**PAT** ər fə **MIL** ee əs
paternoster, Pater Noster	**PAH** tər **NOS** tər
Paterson	**PAT** ər sən
pathetic	pə **THET** ik
Pathet Lao	**PAH** tət **LAH** oh
pathogen	**PATH** ə jən
pathogenesis	**PATH** ə **JEN** ə səs
pathological	**PATH** ə **LOJ** ə kəl
pathology	pə **THOL** ə jee
pathos	**PAY** thos
Patiala	**PUT** ee **AH** lə
patina	pə **TEE** nə
Patiño	pah **TEE** nyaw
patio	**PAT** ee **OH**
patisserie	pah tees **REE**
Patmos	**PAT** məs
Patna	**PUT** nə (**PUT** as in *but*)
patois	**PA** twah
Paton, Alan	**PAYT** ən
Patras	pə **TRAS**
patriarch	**PAY** tree **AHRK**
patriarchal	**PAY** tree **AHR** kəl
patrician	pə **TRISH** ən
patricidal	**PA** trə **SĪ** dəl
patricide	**PA** tri **SĪD**
patrimony	**PA** trə **MOH** nee
patriot	**PAY** tree ət
patriotic	**PAY** tree **OT** ik
patriotism	**PAY** tree ə **TIZ** əm
patristic	pə **TRIS** tik
Patroclus	pə **TROH** kləs
patronage	**PAY** trə nij
patroness	**PAY** trə nəs
patronize	**PAY** trə **NĪZ**
patronymic	**PA** trə **NIM** ik
patroon	pə **TROON**
paucity	**PAW** sə tee
Pauli, Wolfgang	**POW** lee, **VUULF** gahng

ə ago, a at, ah calm, ahr dark, air care, aw saw, ay say, ch church
e bet, ee me, eer beer, hw what, i is, ī my, *n* French final n vin,

Pauling, Linus	**PAW** ling, **LĪ** nəs
Paumotu	pah uu **MOH** too
paunch	pawnch
pauper	**PAW** pər
Pausanias	paw **SAY** nee əs
pavane	pa **VAHN**
Pavarotti, Luciano	**PAH** vah **RAW** tee, loo **CHAH** noh
pavé	pa **VAY**
Pavia	pah **VEE** ah
Pavicevic, Miso	pah **VI** chay vich, **MEE** shoh
pavilion	pə **VIL** yən
Pavlov	**PAHV** lawf
Pavlova	pahv **LOH** və
Pawnee	paw **NEE**
Pawtucket	pə **TUK** ət
Pax Romana	**PAHKS** roh **MAH** nah
pax vobiscum	**PAHKS** woh **BIS** kuum
payola	pay **OH** lə
Paz Estenssoro	**PAHS** es ten **SAW** roh
Pazhwak, Abdul Rahman	pa*zh* **WAWK**, ahb **DUUL** rah **MAHN**
Pearson	**PIR** sən
Peary	**PIR** ee
peasant	**PEZ** ənt
pease	peez
pecan	pi **KAHN**
peccadillo	**PEK** ə **DIL** oh
peccary	**PEK** ə ree
peccavi	pe **KAY** vee
Pecksniffian	pek **SNIF** ee ən
Pecos	**PAY** kəs
Pecs	paych
pectin	**PEK** tən
pectoral	**PEK** tə rəl
peculation	**PEK** yə **LAY** shən
peculiar	pi **KYOOL** yər
peculiarity	pi **KYOOL YA** rə tee
pecuniary	pi **KYOO** nee **ER** ee
pedagogue	**PED** ə **GOG**
pedagogy	**PED** ə **GOH** jee
pedant	**PED** ənt
pedantic	pi **DAN** tik
pedantry	**PED** ən tree

---

o on, oh oat, oi boy, oo soon, oor poor, or for, ow cow, sh shush,
th thin, *th* this, u up, ur spur, uu book, *zh* pleasure

pederast	**PED** ə **RAST**
pediatric	**PEE** dee **AT** rik
pediatrician	**PEE** dee ə **TRISH** ən
pediatrist	**PEE** dee **AT** rəst
pedicure	**PED** ə **KYUUR**
pedology	pi **DOL** ə jee
pedometer	pi **DOM** ə tər
peduncle	pi **DUNG** kəl
peerage	**PEER** ij
Pegasus	**PEG** ə səs
pegmatite	**PEG** mə **TĪT**
peignoir	payn **WAHR**
Pei, I. M.	pay
Peiping	pay ping
pejorative	pi **JOR** ə tiv
Pekin, p-	**PEE** kin
Peking	pee king
Pekingese	**PEE** kə **NEEZ**
pekoe	**PEE** koh
pelage	**PEL** ij
pelagic	pə **LAJ** ik
pelargonium	**PEL** ahr **GOH** nee əm
Pele	**PE** lay
Pelée	pə **LAY**
Peleliu	**PEL** ə lyoo
Peleus	**PEE** lee əs
Pelew	pee **LOO**
Pelham	**PEL** əm
Pelias	**PEE** lee əs
pelican	**PEL** i kən
Pelion	**PEE** lee ən
pelisse	pə **LEES**
pellagra	pə **LAY** grə
Pelletier, Gérard	pel **TYAY**, *zh*ay **RAHR**
pellmell	pel mel
pellucid	pə **LOO** səd
Peloponnesian	**PEL** ə pə **NEE** *zh*ən
Peloponnesus	**PEL** ə pə **NEE** səs
Pelops	**PEE** lops
pelota	pə **LOH** tə
Pelshe, Arvid	**PEL** shə, **AHR** vid
Pemba	**PEM** bə
pemmican	**PEM** i kən

Peña	**PE** nyah
penal	**PEE** nəl
penalize	**PEE** nə **LĪZ**
penalty	**PEN** əl tee
penance	**PEN** əns
Penang	pi **NANG**
penates	pə **NAY** teez
penchant	**PEN** chənt
pendant	**PEN** dənt
pendragon, P-	pen **DRAG** ən
pendulous	**PEN** jə ləs
pendulum	**PEN** jə ləm
Penelope	pə **NEL** ə pee
Peneus	pə **NEE** əs
penguin	**PEN** gwən
Peng Zhen	pung jun
penicillin	**PEN** ə **SIL** ən
peninsula	pə **NIN** sə lə
penitence	**PEN** ə təns
penitentiary	**PEN** ə **TEN** shə ree
Pennario	pe **NAH** ree oh
Pennine	**PEN** īn
pennon	**PEN** ən
Pennsylvania	**PEN** səl **VAY** nyə
Penobscot	pə **NOB** skot
penology	pi **NOL** ə jee
Pensacola	**PEN** sə **KOH** lə
pensée	pahn **SAY**
Penseroso	**PEN** sə **ROH** soh
pension (boarding house)	pahn **SYAWN** (pahn and **SYAWN** French final *n*)
penstemon	pen **STEE** mən
pentagon, P-	**PEN** tə **GON**
pentameter	pen **TAM** ə tər
Pentateuch	**PEN** tə **TYOOK**
Pentecost	**PEN** ti **KAWST**
pentimento	**PEN** tə **MEN** toh
Pentothal	**PEN** tə **THAWL**
pentstemon	pent **STEE** mən
penuche	pə **NOO** chee
penult	**PEE** nult
penultimate	pi **NUL** tə mət
penumbra	pə **NUM** brə

o **on**, oh **oat**, oi **boy**, oo **soon**, oor **poor**, or **for**, ow **cow**, sh **shush**, th **thin**, *th* **this**, u **up**, ur **spur**, uu **book**, *zh* **pleasure**

penurious	pə **NUUR** ee əs
penury	**PEN** yə ree
Penzance	pen **ZANS**
Penzias, Arno	**PENT** see əs, **AHR** noh
peon	**PEE** ən
peonage	**PEE** ə nij
peony	**PEE** ə nee
Pepin	**PEP** ən
peplum	**PEP** ləm
peppercorn	**PEP** ər **KORN**
pepperidge	**PEP** ər ij
peptic	**PEP** tik
peptide	**PEP** tīd
Pepys	peeps
Pequot	**PEE** kwot
Perak	**PE** rak
per annum	pər **AN** əm
percale	pər **KAYL**
per capita	pər **KAP** ə tə
percentile	pər **SEN** tīl
Perceval	**PUR** sə vəl
Percheron	**PUR** chə **RON**
percipient	pər **SIP** ee ənt
Percival, -e	**PUR** sə vəl
percolate	**PUR** kə **LAYT**
percolator	**PUR** kə **LAY** tər
percussion	pər **KUSH** ən
per diem	pər **DEE** əm
perdition	pər **DISH** ən
père, P-	pair
peregrinate	**PER** ə grə **NAYT**
peregrination	**PER** ə grə **NAY** shən
peregrine	**PER** ə grən
pereira	pə **RAIR** ə
Pereira	pe **RAY** rah
Perelman	**PURL** mən
peremptory	pə **REMP** tə ree
perennial	pə **REN** ee əl
Peres, Shimon	**PE** res, **SHI** mawn
Perez	pə **REZ**
Pérez de Cuellar, Javier	**PAY** rez day **KWAY** yahr, hah **VYAIR**
Pérez Esquivel, Aldolpho	**PAY** rez **ES** kee **VEL**, a **DAWL** foh

ə ago, a at, ah calm, ahr dark, air care, aw saw, ay say, ch church
e bet, ee me, eer beer, hw what, i is, ī my, *n* French final n vin,

Pérez Jiménez, Marcos	**PAY** rez hee **MAY** nez, **MAHR** kohs
perfect (a)	**PUR** fikt
perfect (v)	pər **FEKT**
perfecto	pər **FEK** toh
perfervid	pər **FUR** vəd
perfidious	pər **FID** ee əs
perfidy	**PUR** fə dee
perforate (a)	**PUR** fə rət
perforate (v)	**PUR** fə **RAYT**
perforce	pər **FORS**
perfume (n)	**PUR** fyoom
perfume (v)	pər **FYOOM**
perfunctory	pər **FUNGK** tə ree
pergola	**PUR** gə lə
Pergolesi	**PAIR** gə **LAY** see
perhaps	pər **HAPS**
pericardium	**PE** rə **KAHR** dee əm
Periclean	**PE** rə **KLEE** ən
Pericles	**PE** rə **KLEEZ**
pericranium	**PE** rə **KRAY** nee əm
perigee	**PE** rə jee
perihelion	**PE** rə **HEE** lee ən
peril	**PE** ril
perimeter	pə **RIM** ə tər
perineum	**PE** rə **NEE** əm
periodic	**PEER** ee **OD** ik
periodical	**PEER** ee **OD** i kəl
periosteum	**PE** ree **OS** tee əm
peripatetic	**PE** rə pə **TET** ik
periphery	pə **RIF** ə ree
periphrasis	pə **RIF** rə səs
periphrastic	**PE** rə **FRAS** tik
periscope	**PE** rə **SKOHP**
perish	**PE** rish
peristalsis	**PE** rə **STAWL** səs
peristyle	**PE** rə **STĪL**
peritoneum	**PE** rə tə **NEE** əm
peritonitis	**PE** rə tə **NĪ** təs
perjure	**PUR** jər
perjury	**PUR** jə ree
Perlis	pər **LIS**
perlite	**PUR** līt
perm	purm

o on, oh oat, oi boy, oo soon, oor poor, or for, ow cow, sh shush,
th thin, *th* this, u up, ur spur, uu book, *zh* pleasure

Perm (USSR)	perm
permalloy	PUR mə LOI
permanganate	pər MANG gə NAYT
permeability	PUR mee ə BIL ə tee
permeable	PUR mee ə bəl
permeate	PUR mee AYT
Permian	PUR mee ən
permit (n)	PUR mit
permit (v)	pər MIT
permutation	PUR myə TAY shən
Pernambuco	PUR nəm BYOO koh
pernicious	pər NISH əs
Pernod	pair NOH
Perón	pe ROHN
peroration	PE rə RAY shən
perpetual	pər PECH oo əl
perpetuity	PUR pə TOO ə tee
perquisite	PUR kwə zət
Perrault	pe ROH
Perrier	PE ree ay
per se	pər SAY
Perseid	PUR see əd
Persephone	pər SEF ə nee
Persepolis	pər SEP ə ləs
Perse, St.-John	PURS, SIN jən
Perseus	PUR see əs
perseverance	PUR sə VIR əns
persevere	PUR sə VIR
Pershing	PUR shing
Persia	PUR zhə
Persian	PUR zhən
persiflage	PUR sə FLAHZH
persimmon	pər SIM ən
persist	pər SIST
persona	pər SOH nə
personae	pər SOH nee
personal	PUR sə nəl
persona non grata	pər SOH nə nohn GRAH tə
personification	pər SON ə fə KAY shən
personify	pər SON ə FĪ
personnel	PUR sə NEL
perspective	pər SPEK tiv
perspicacious	PUR spə KAY shəs

ə ago, a at, ah calm, ahr dark, air care, aw saw, ay say, ch church
e bet, ee me, eer beer, hw what, i is, ī my, n French final n vin,

perspicacity	PUR spə **KAS** ə tee
perspicuity	PUR spə **KYOO** ə tee
perspicuous	pər **SPIK** yoo əs
perspiration	PUR spə RAY shən
perspire	pər **SPIR**
persuade	pər **SWAYD**
persuasion	pər **SWAY** *zh*ən
persuasive	pər **SWAY** siv
Perth	purth
pertinacious	PUR tə **NAY** shəs
pertinacity	PUR tə **NAS** ə tee
pertinent	PUR tə nənt
Pertini, Alessandro	pair **TEE** nee, AH lay **SAHN** droh
perturbation	PUR tər **BAY** shən
pertussis	pər **TUS** əs
Peru	pə **ROO**
Perugia	pe **ROO** jah
Perugino	PE roo **JEE** noh
peruke	pə **ROOK**
perusal	pə **ROO** zəl
peruse	pə **ROOZ**
Perutz	PE rəts
Peruvian	pə **ROO** vee ən
pervasive	pər **VAY** siv
perverse	pər **VURS**
perversion	pər **VUR** *zh*ən
pervert (n)	PUR vurt
pervert (v)	pər **VURT**
pervious	PUR vee əs
Pesach	PAY sahk
Pescadores	PES kah **DOR** es
peseta	pə **SAY** tə
Peshawar	pe **SHAH** wər
peso	PAY soh
Pestalozzi	PES tə **LOT** see
pestiferous	pe **STIF** ə rəs
pestilence	PES tə ləns
pestilential	PES tə **LEN** shəl
pestle	PES əl
pesto	PES toh
petard	pə **TAHRD**
petiole	PET ee OHL
petit	PET ee

---

o on, oh oat, oi boy, oo soon, oor poor, or for, ow cow, sh shush,
th thin, *th* this, u up, ur spur, uu book, *zh* pleasure

petite	pə **TEET**
petit four	**PET** ee **FOR**
petition	pə **TISH** ən
petit point	**PET** ee **POINT**
petits pois	pə tee **PWAH**
Petöfi, Sándor	**PE** tuu fee, **SHAHN** dor
Petran, Janos	**PET** ran, **YAH** nohsh
Petrarch	**PEE** trahrk
Petrarchan	pi **TRAHR** kən
petrel	**PE** trəl
petri	**PEE** tree
Petrides, Avra	pe **TREE** *th*is, **AH** vrah
Petrie	**PEE** tree
petrify	**PET** rə **FĪ**
Petrignani, Rinaldo	pe treen **YAH** nee, ree **NAHL** doh
petroglyph	**PET** rə **GLIF**
Petrograd	**PE** trə **GRAD**
petrography	pə **TROG** rə fee
petrol	**PET** rəl
petrolatum	**PET** rə **LAY** təm
petroleum	pə **TROH** lee əm
petrology	pə **TROL** ə jee
Petronius	pi **TROH** nee əs
Petropavlovsk	**PE** traw **PAHV** lawfsk
Petrosani	**PE** traw **SHAHN**
Petrouchka	pə **TROOSH** kə
Petrozavodsk	**PE** trə zə **VAHTSK**
Petruchio	pə **TROO** kee oh
Petsamo	**PET** sah maw
pettifoggery	**PET** ee **FOG** ə ree
petulance	**PECH** ə ləns
petulant	**PECH** ə lənt
petunia	pə **TOO** nyə
pewter	**PYOO** tər
peyote	pay **OH** tee
Pfeiffer	**FĪ** fər
pfennig	**FEN** ig
Pfizer	**FĪ** zər
Phaedra	**FEE** drə
Phaëthon	**FAY** ə thən
phaeton	**FAY** ə tən
phagocyte	**FAG** ə **SĪT**
phalanx	**FAY** langks

ə ago, a at, ah calm, ahr dark, air care, aw saw, ay say, ch church
e bet, ee me, eer beer, hw what, i is, ī my, *n* French final n vin,

phalarope	**FAL** ə **ROHP**
phallic	**FAL** ik
phallus	**FAL** əs
Pham Van Dong	fahm vahn dahng
phantasm	**FAN TAZ** əm
phantasmagoria	fan **TAZ** mə **GOR** ee ə
phantasmal	fan **TAZ** məl
phantom	**FAN** təm
Pharaoh	**FAIR** oh
Pharaonic	**FAIR** ay **ON** ik
pharisaic, P-	**FA** rə **SAY** ik
Pharisee, p-	**FA** rə **SEE**
pharmaceutical	**FAHR** mə **SOO** ti kəl
pharmacopoeia	**FAHR** mə kə **PEE** ə
Pharos, p-	**FAI** rahs
Pharpar	**FAHR** pahr
Pharsalus	fahr **SAY** ləs
pharyngeal	fə **RIN** jee əl
pharyngitis	**FA** rən **JĪ** təs
pharynx	**FA** ringks
Phebe	**FEE** bee
Phèdre	**FE** drə
phenacetin	fə **NAS** ə tən
phenobarbital	**FEE** noh **BAHR** bə tawl
phenol	**FEE** nohl
phenology	fi **NOL** ə jee
phenomena	fi **NOM** ə nə
phenomenal	fi **NOM** ə nəl
phenomenon	fi **NOM** ə **NON**
phial	**FĪ** əl
Phidias	**FID** ee əs
philanderer	fə **LAN** də rər
philanthropic	**FIL** ən **THROP** ik
philanthropist	fə **LAN** thrə pəst
philanthropy	fə **LAN** thrə pee
philatelic	**FIL** ə **TEL** ik
philatelist	fə **LAT** ə ləst
philately	fə **LAT** ə lee
Philemon	fə **LEE** mən
philharmonic	**FIL** hahr **MON** ik
Philippi	fə **LIP** ī
Philippian	fə **LIP** ee ən
Philippic, p-	fə **LIP** ik

o on, oh oat, oi boy, oo soon, oor poor, or for, ow cow, sh shush,
th thin, *th* this, u up, ur spur, uu book, *zh* pleasure

Philippine	**FIL** ə **PEEN**
Philistine	**FIL** ə **STEEN**
philodendron	**FIL** ə **DEN** drən
philogyny	fə **LOJ** ə nee
philologian	**FIL** ə **LOH** jən
philologist	fə **LOL** ə jəst
philology	fə **LOL** ə jee
philomel	**FIL** ə **MEL**
Philomela	**FIL** ə **MEE** lə
philosophical	**FIL** ə **SOF** i kəl
philosophy	fə **LOS** ə fee
philter	**FIL** tər
Phineas	**FIN** ee əs
phlebitis	flə **BĪ** təs
phlebotomy	flə **BOT** ə mee
Phlegethon	**FLEG** ə **THON**
phlegm	flem
phlegmatic	fleg **MAT** ik
phlogiston	floh **JIS** tən
phlox	floks
Phnom Penh	nom pen
phobia	**FOH** bee ə
Phobos	**FOH** bos
phocomelia	**FOH** koh **MEE** lee ə
Phoebe, p-	**FEE** bee
Phoebus	**FEE** bəs
Phoenicia	fə **NEE** shə
Phoenix, p-	**FEE** niks
phonation	foh **NAY** shən
phoneme	**FOH** neem
phonemic	fə **NEE** mik
phonetic	fə **NET** ik
phonetician	**FOH** nə **TISH** ən
phonic	**FON** ik
phosgene	**FOZ** jeen
phosphate	**FOS** fayt
phosphorescence	**FOS** fə **RES** əns
phosphoric	fos **FOR** ik
phosphorous (a)	**FOS** fə rəs
phosphorus (n)	**FOS** fə rəs
photogenic	**FOH** tə **JEN** ik
photography	fə **TOG** rə fee
photogravure	**FOH** tə grə **VYUUR**

ə ago, a at, ah calm, ahr dark, air care, aw saw, ay say, ch church
e bet, ee me, eer beer, hw what, i is, ī my, *n* French final n vin,

photolytic	FOH tə LIT ik
photometer	foh TOM ə tər
photometry	foh TOM ə tree
photon	FOH tahn
photostat, P-	FOH tə STAT
phraseology	FRAY zee OL ə jee
phrenetic	fri NET ik
phrenic	FREN ik
phrenology	fri NOL ə jee
Phrygia	FRIJ ee ə
phthalic	THAL ik
phthisic	TIZ ik
phthisis	TIS əs
Phyfe	fīf
phylactery	fə LAK tə ree
phylogeny	fī LOJ ə nee
phylum	FĪ ləm
physiatrist	FIZ ee A trəst
physiognomy	FIZ ee OG nə mee
physiography	FIZ ee OG rə fee
physiological	FIZ ee ə LOJ i kəl
physiology	FIZ ee OL ə jee
physiotherapy	FIZ ee oh THER ə pee
physique	fə ZEEK
pi	pī
Piacenza	pyah CHEN tsah
Piaget	pyah ZHAY
pianissimo	PEE ə NIS ə MOH
pianist	pee AN əst
piano (a, adv)	pee AH noh
piano (n)	pee AN oh
pianoforte	pee AN oh FOR tay
piaster	pee AS tər
piazza	pee AZ ə
Piazza Navone	PYAHT sah nah VOH ne
pibroch	PEE brok
pica	PĪ kə
picador	PIK ə DOR
Picardy	PIK ər dee
picaresque	PIK ə RESK
Picasso	pi KAH soh
picayune	PIK ə YOON
Piccadilly	PIK ə DIL ee

o on, oh oat, oi boy, oo soon, oor poor, or for, ow cow, sh shush,
th thin, *th* this, u up, ur spur, uu book, *zh* pleasure

Piccadilly Circus	**PIK** ə **DIL** ee **SUR** kəs
piccalilli	**PIK** ə **LIL** ee
Piccard, Auguste	pee **KAR,** oh **GUUST**
piccolo	**PIK** ə loh
Pickwickian	pik **WIK** ee ən
picot	**PEE** koh
Pict	pikt
Pictor	**PIK** tər
pictorial	pik **TOR** ee əl
picture	**PIK** chər
picturesque	**PIK** chə **RESK**
picul	**PIK** əl
Pidgin, p-	**PIJ** ən
piebald	**PĪ** bawld
pièce de résistance	**PYES** də ray zees **TAHNS (TAHNS** French final *n*)
Pieck	peek
pied	pīd
pied-à-terre	pye da **TAIR**
Piedmont, p-	**PEED** mont
Piemonte	pye **MAWN** te
Pierian	pī **IR** ee ən
Pierre	pyair
Pierre (South Dakota)	pir
Pierrot	**PEE** ə **ROH**
Piers Plowman	**PEERZ PLOW** mən
Piestany	**PYESH** tyah nee
Pietà, p-	**PEE** ay **TAH**
Pietermaritzburg	**PEE** tər **MA** rits **BURG**
pietism	**PĪ** ə **TIZ** əm
pietistic	**PĪ** ə **TIS** tik
piety	**PĪ** ə tee
piezoelectric	pee **AY** zoh ə **LEK** trik
Pigalle	pee **GAL**
pigeon	**PIJ** ən
Pigmy, p-	**PIG** mee
pignoli	peen **YOH** lee
pignolia	peen **YOH** lee ə
pilaf	**PEE** lahf
pilaster	pə **LAS** tər
Pilate, Pontius	**PĪ** lət, **PON** chəs
pilau	**PEE** lahf
pilchard	**PIL** chərd

ə ago, a at, ah calm, ahr dark, air care, aw saw, ay say, ch church
e bet, ee me, eer beer, hw what, i is, ī my, *n* French final n vin,

Pilcomayo	PEEL kaw MAH yaw
pileus	PĪ lee əs
pilgrimage	PIL grə mij
pili	pee LEE
pillion	PIL yən
pillory	PIL ə ree
pilose	PĪ lohs
pilot	PĪ lət
Pilote, Pierre	pee LAHT, PYAIR
Pilsen	PIL zən
Pilsudski	pil SOOT skee (SOOT as in *boot*)
Piltdown	PILT down
Pima	PEE mə
pimento	pə MEN toh
pimiento	pə MEN toh
pimpernel, P-	PIM pər NEL
piña	PEE nyah
pinaceous	pī NAY shəs
pinafore	PIN ə FOR
piñata	peen YAH tah
pince-nez	PANS nay
pincers	PIN sərz
Pindar	PIN dahr
Pindaric	pin DA rik
pineal	PIN ee əl
Pinero	pə NE roh
Piñero	pee NYE roh
pinion	PIN yən
pinnace	PIN əs
pinnacle	PIN ə kəl
pinnate	PIN ayt
Pinochet Ugarte, Augusto	PEE noh CHET oo GAHR tay, ow GOOS toh
pinochle	PEE NUK əl
pinole	pi NOH lee
Pinot	PEE noh
pinta	PIN tə
Pinta	PEEN tah
pintle	PIN təl
pion	PĪ on
pioneer	PĪ ə NIR
pious	PĪ əs
pipette	pī PET

---

o **on**, oh **oat**, oi **boy**, oo **soon**, oor **poor**, or **for**, ow **cow**, sh **shush**, th **thin**, *th* **this**, u **up**, ur **spur**, uu **book**, *zh* **pleasure**

pipit	**PIP** ət
Pippa	**PIP** ə
Piqua	**PIK** way
piquancy	**PEE** kən see
piquant	**PEE** kənt
pique	peek
piqué	pi **KAY**
piquet	pi **KAY**
piracy	**PĪ** rə see
Piraeus	pī **REE** əs
piragua	pə **RAH** gwə
Pirandello	**PIR** ən **DEL** oh
Piranesi	**PEE** rah **NAY** zee
piranha	pə **RAHN** yə
piratical	pə **RAT** i kəl
Pirithous	pī **RITH** oh əs
pirogen	pə **RUG** ən
pirogue	**PEE** rohg
piroshki	pə **RUSH** kee
pirouette	**PIR** oo **ET**
Pisa	**PEE** zə
pis aller	pee za **LAY**
Pisano	pee **ZAH** noh
piscatorial	**PIS** kə **TOR** ee əl
Pisces	**PĪ** seez
piscine	**PĪ** seen
Pisgah	**PIZ** gə
Pisistratus	pi **SIS** trə təs
pismire	**PIS** mīr
Pissarro	pi **SAHR** oh
pissoir	pee **SWAHR**
pistachio	pə **STASH** ee oh
piston	**PIS** tən
Pitcairn	**PIT** kairn
pitchblende	**PICH** blend
piteous	**PIT** ee əs
Pithecanthropus	**PITH** i **KAN** thrə pəs
pithy	**PITH** ee
pitiable	**PIT** ee ə bəl
piton	**PEE** ton
Pitot	**PEE** toh
Pitri	**PI** tree
pittance	**PIT** əns

ə ago, a at, ah calm, ahr dark, air care, aw saw, ay say, ch church
e bet, ee me, eer beer, hw what, i is, ī my, *n* French final n vin,

pituitary	pə **TOO** ə **TER** ee
Pius	**PĪ** əs
pivot	**PIV** ət
pivotal	**PIV** ə təl
pixie	**PIK** see
Pizarro	pə **ZAHR** oh
pizza	**PEET** sə
pizzeria	**PEET** sə **REE** ə
pizzicato	**PIT** si **KAH** toh
placable	**PLAK** ə bəl
placard	**PLAK** ahrd
placate	**PLAY** kayt
placebo	plə **SEE** boh
placenta	plə **SEN** tə
placet	**PLAY** sit
placid	**PLAS** əd
placket	**PLAK** ət
plagiarism	**PLAY** jə **RIZ** əm
plagiarize	**PLAY** jə **RĪZ**
plague	playg
plaice	plays
plaid	plad
plaint	playnt
plaintiff	**PLAYN** təf
plait	playt
planarian	plə **NA** ree ən
planchette	plan **SHET**
Planck, Max	plahngk, maks
planetarium	**PLAN** ə **TAIR** ee əm
planetary	**PLAN** ə **TER** ee
planetesimal	**PLAN** ə **TES** ə məl
plangent	**PLAN** jənt
planimeter	plə **NIM** ə tər
Planinc, Milka	plah **NEENS, MEEL** kə
planish	**PLAN** ish
plankton	**PLANGK** tən
planometer	plə **NOM** ə tər
Plantagenet	plan **TAJ** ə nət
plantain	**PLAN** tən
plaque	plak
plasma	**PLAZ** mə
plasmodium	plaz **MOH** dee əm
Plassey	**PLAH** see

o on, oh oat, oi boy, oo soon, oor poor, or for, ow cow, sh shush,
th thin, *th* this, u up, ur spur, uu book, *zh* pleasure

plastic	**PLAS** tik
plasticity	plas **TIS** ə tee
Plata	**PLAH** tah
plat du jour	**PLAH** də **ZH**OOR
plateau	pla **TOH**
Plate, Juan	**PLAH** tay, **HWAHN**
platen	**PLAT** ən
platinum	**PLAT** ə nəm
platitude	**PLAT** ə **TOOD**
platitudinous	**PLAT** ə **TOO** də nəs
Plato	**PLAY** toh
Platonic, p-	plə **TON** ik
Platonism	**PLAYT** ən **IZ** əm
platoon	plə **TOON**
Plattdeutsch	**PLAHT** doich
Platte	plat
platy	**PLAT** ee
platypus	**PLAT** i pəs
Platzer, Wilfried	**PLAHT** sər, **VIL** freet
plaudit	**PLAW** dət
plausible	**PLAW** zə bəl
Plautus	**PLAW** təs
playa	**PLĪ** ə
plaza	**PLAZ** ə
Plaza (Latin America)	**PLAH** sah
pleasant	**PLEZ** ənt
pleasure	**PLEZ**_H_ ər
pleat	pleet
pleb	pleb
plebe	pleeb
plebeian	plə **BEE** ən
plebiscite	**PLEB** ə **SĪT**
plebs	plebz
plectrum	**PLEK** trəm
Pleiades	**PLEE** ə **DEEZ**
Pleistocene	**PLĪ** stə **SEEN**
plenary	**PLEE** nə ree
plenipotentiary	**PLEN** ə pə **TEN** shee **ER** ee
plenitude	**PLEN** ə **TOOD**
plenteous	**PLEN** tee əs
plenum	**PLE** nəm
pleonasm	**PLEE** ə **NAZ** əm
pleonastic	**PLEE** ə **NAS** tik

ə ago, a at, ah calm, ahr dark, air care, aw saw, ay say, ch church
e bet, ee me, eer beer, hw what, i is, ī my, *n* French final n vin,

plesiosaur	**PLEE** see ə **SAWR**
plesiosaurus	**PLEE** see ə **SOR** əs
plethora	**PLETH** ə rə
plethoric	plə **THOR** ik
pleurisy	**PLUUR** ə see
Plexiglas	**PLEK** si **GLAS**
plexus	**PLEK** səs
pliable	**PLĪ** ə bəl
pliant	**PLĪ** ənt
plié	plee **AY**
Plimsoll	**PLIM** səl
plinth	plinth
Pliny	**PLIN** ee
Pliocene	**PLĪ** ə **SEEN**
Plisetskaya, Maya	plee **SETS** **KĪ** ə, **MĪ** ə
Ploesti	plaw **YESHT**
Plotinus	ploh **TĪ** nəs
Plovdiv	**PLAWV** dif
plover	**PLUV** ər
plow	plow
plumb	plum
plumbago	plum **BAY** goh
plumber	**PLUM** ər
plummet	**PLUM** ət
plumose	**PLOO** mohs
plumule	**PLOOM** yool
pluperfect	ploo **PUR** fikt
plural	**PLUUR** əl
plurality	pluu **RAL** ə tee
Plutarch	**PLOO** tahrk
Pluto	**PLOO** toh
plutocracy	ploo **TOK** rə **SEE**
plutocrat	**PLOO** tə **KRAT**
Plutonic, p-	ploo **TON** ik
plutonium	ploo **TOH** nee əm
Plutus	**PLOO** təs
pluvial	**PLOO** vee əl
Pluvius	**PLOO** vee əs
ply	plī
Plymouth	**PLIM** əth
pneumatic	nuu **MAT** ik
pneumoconiosis	**NOO** moh **KOH** nee **OH** səs
pneumonectomy	**NOO** mə **NEK** tə mee

pneumonia	nuu **MOHN** yə
Pnom-Penh	nom pen
Pnyx	niks
Po	poh
Pocahontas	**POH** kə **HON** təs
pococurante	**POH** koh kuu **RAN** tee
podagra	pə **DAG** rə
podesta	poh **DES** tə
Podgorny, Nikolai	pod **GAWR** nee, nee koh **LĪ**
podiatrist	pə **DĪ** ə trəst
podium	**POH** dee əm
podsol	**POD** sol
Podunk	**POH** dungk
podzol	**POD** zol
poem	**POH** əm
Poena	**PEE** nə
poesy	**POH** ə zee
poet	**POH** ət
poetaster	**POH** ət **AS** tər
poetess	**POH** ət əs
poetic	poh **ET** ik
poet laureate	**POH** ət **LOR** ee ət
poetry	**POH** ə tree
pogrom	**POH** grəm
Pohai	poh hī
poi	poi
poignancy	**POIN** yən see
poignant	**POIN** yənt
poilu	pwah **LOO**
poinciana	**POIN** see **AN** ə
poinsettia	poin **SET** ee ə
pointillism	**POIN** tə **LIZ** əm
Poisson	pwah **SAWN** (**SAWN** French final *n*)
Poitier	**PWAH** tyay
Poitiers	pwah **TYAY**
Poitou	pwah **TOO**
polacca	poh **LAK** ə
Poland	**POH** lənd
polar	**POH** lər
Polaris	pə **LAR** əs
polarity	pə **LAR** ə tee
Polaroid	**POH** lə **ROID**
polder	**POHL** dər

ə ago, a at, ah calm, ahr dark, air care, aw saw, ay say, ch church
e bet, ee me, eer beer, hw what, i is, ī my, *n* French final n vin,

polemic	pə **LEM** ik
polenta	poh **LEN** tə
polio	**POH** lee oʜ
poliomyelitis	**POH** lee oh **MĪ** ə **LĪ** təs
Politburo	**POL** it **BYUUR** oh
politesse	**POL** i **TES**
Politian	poh **LISH** ən
politic	**POL** ə tik
politico	pə **LIT** i **KOH**
polity	**POL** ə tee
Polk	pohk
polka (dance)	**POHL** kə
polka (dot)	**POH** kə
poll	pohl
pollack	**POL** ək
pollen	**POL** ən
polliwog	**POL** ee **WOG**
Pollock	**POL** ək
pollute	pə **LOOT**
Pollux	**POL** əks
polonaise	**POL** ə **NAYZ**
polonium	pə **LOH** nee əm
Polonius	pə **LOH** nee əs
Pol Pot	pol pot
Poltava	pol **TAH** vah
poltergeist	**POHL** tər **GĪST**
poltroon	pol **TROON**
polyandry	**POL** ee **AN** dree
Polybius	pə **LIB** ee əs
Polycarp	**POL** i **KAHRP**
polychrome	**POL** i **KROHM**
polyclinic	**POL** i **KLIN** ik
Polyclitus, Polycleitus	**POL** i **KLĪ** təs
Polycrates	pə **LIK** rə **TEEZ**
polydactyl	**POL** i **DAK** təl
Polydorus	**POL** i **DOR** əs
polyester	**POL** ee **ES** tər
polyethylene	**POL** ee **ETH** ə **LEEN**
polygamy	pə **LIG** ə mee
polyglot	**POL** i **GLOT**
Polygnotus	**POL** ig **NOH** təs
polygon	**POL** i **GON**
polygraph	**POL** i **GRAF**

o on, oh oat, oi boy, oo soon, oor poor, or for, ow cow, sh shush,
th thin, *th* this, u up, ur spur, uu book, *zh* pleasure

polygyny	pə **LIJ** ə nee
Polyhymnia	**POL** i **HIM** nee ə
polymer	**POL** ə mər
polymerization	pə **LIM** ər ə **ZAY** shən
Polymnia	pə **LIM** nee ə
Polynesia	**POL** ə **NEE** *zh*ə
Polynices	**POL** i **NĪ** seez
polynomial	**POL** ee **NOH** mee əl
polyp	**POL** əp
Polyphemus	**POL** ə **FEE** məs
polyphonic	**POL** i **FON** ik
polyphony	pə **LIF** ə nee
polypropylene	**POL** i **PROH** pə **LEEN**
polyptych	**POL** əp **TIK**
polystyrene	**POL** i **STĪ** reen
polysyllabic	**POL** i sə **LAB** ik
polysyllable	**POL** i **SIL** ə bəl
polytechnic	**POL** i **TEK** nik
polytheism	**POL** i thee **IZ** əm
Polyxena	pə **LIK** sə nə
pomade	pə **MAYD**
pomander	**POH** **MAN** dər
pomegranate	**POM** ə **GRAN** ət
pomelo	**POM** ə **LOH**
Pomerania	**POM** ə **RAY** nee ə
pommel	**PUM** əl
pomology	poh **MOL** ə jee
Pomona	pə **MOH** nə
pompadour, P-	**POM** pə **DOR**
Pompeii	pom **PAY**
Pompeius	pom **PEE** əs
Pompey	**POM** pee
Pompidou, Georges	pohm pee **DOO**, **ZHAWRZH**
pom-pom	**POM** pom
pompon	**POM** pon
pomposity	pom **POS** ə tee
pompous	**POM** pəs
Ponca	**PONG** kə
ponce	pons
Ponce	**PAWN** se
Ponce de León	**PAWN** sə day le **AWN**
Ponchielli	pawng **KYEL** ee
poncho	**PON** choh

ə ago, a at, ah calm, ahr dark, air care, aw saw, ay say, ch church
e bet, ee me, eer beer, hw what, i is, ī my, *n* French final n vin,

ponderous	PON dər əs
Pondicherry	PON di CHER ee
pongee	pon JEE
poniard	PON yərd
Ponomaryov, Boris	PON ə mahr YAWF, bah REES
pons, P-	ponz
Ponta Delgada	PAWN tə del GAH də
Pontchartrain	PON chər TRAYN
Pontiac	PON tee AK
pontifex	PON tə FEKS
pontifical	pon TIF i kəl
pontificate (n)	pon TIF i kət
pontificate (v)	pon TIF ə KAYT
Pontius	PON chəs
pontoon	pon TOON
Pontoppidan	pon TOP i DAHN
Pontus	PON təs
Poona	POO nə
poplar	POP lər
poplin	POP lən
Popocatepetl	POH pə KAT ə PET əl
Popovic	PAW paw vich
populace	POP yə ləs
popular	POP yə lər
popularity	POP yə LAR ə tee
populous	POP yə ləs
porcelain	POR sə lən
porcine	POR sīn
porcupine	POR kyə PĪN
porgy, P-	POR gee
Pori	POR ee
pornographic	POR nə GRAF ik
pornography	por NOG rə fee
porosity	pə ROS ə tee
porous	POR əs
porphyry	POR fə ree
porpoise	POR pəs
porridge	POR ij
porringer	POR ən jər
Porsena, Lars	POR si nə, LAHRZ
Port-au-Prince	PORT oh PRINS
portcullis	port KUL əs
Port du Salut	POR də sal OO

o on, oh oat, oi boy, oo soon, oor poor, or for, ow cow, sh shush,
th thin, *th* this, u up, ur spur, uu book, *zh* pleasure

porte-cochère	PORT koh SHAIR
portend	por TEND
Porteño	por TAY nyoh
portent	POR tent
portentous	por TEN təs
portfolio	port FOH lee OH
Portia	POR shə
portico	POR ti KOH
portiere	por TYAIR
Portland	PORT lənd
portmanteau	port MAN toh
Porto (Portugal)	POR tuu
Porto Alegre	POR tuu ah LE gri
portrait	POR trət
portraiture	POR trə CHUUR
Port Said	PORT sah EED
Portsmouth	PORTS məth
Portugal	POR chə gəl
Portuguese	POR chə GEEZ
portulaca	POR chə LAK ə
Porumbeanu	PAW rəm bee AH noo
Poseidon	pə SĪ dən
Posen	POH zən
poseur	poh ZUR
posit	POZ ət
positive	POZ ə tiv
positively	POZ ə tiv lee
positively (emphatic)	POZ ə TIV lee
positron	POZ ə TRON
posse	POS ee
possess	pə ZES
possession	pə ZESH ən
posset	POS ət
possible	POS ə bəl
possum	POS əm
post bellum	POHST BEL əm
postdiluvian	POHST də LOO vee ən
posterity	pos TER ə tee
postern	POH stərn
post hoc ergo propter hoc	pohst HOHK AIR goh PROHP tər HOHK
posthumous	POS chuu məs
postiche	paw STEESH

ə ago, a at, ah calm, ahr dark, air care, aw saw, ay say, ch church
e bet, ee me, eer beer, hw what, i is, ī my, n French final n vin,

postilion, postillion	poh **STIL** yən
postmeridian	**POHST** mə **RID** ee ən
post meridiem	**POHST** mə **RID** ee əm
postmortem	pohst **MOR** təm
postprandial	pohst **PRAN** dee əl
postulant	**POS** chə lənt
postulate (n)	**POS** chə lət
postulate (v)	**POS** chə **LAYT**
posture	**POS** chər
posy	**POH** zee
potable	**POH** tə bəl
potage	poh **TAHZ***H*
potash	**POT** ash
potassium	pə **TAS** ee əm
potato	pə **TAY** toh
pot-au-feu	poht oh **FUU**
poteen	poh **TEEN**
Potemkin	pə **TEM** kən
potency	**POH** tən see
potent	**POH** tənt
potentate	**POH** tən **TAYT**
potential	pə **TEN** shəl
potentiality	pə **TEN** shee **AL** ə tee
potentially	pə **TEN** shə lee
potentiometer	pə **TEN** shee **OM** ə tər
potheen	poh **THEEN**
pother	**PO***TH* ər
potherb	**POT** urb
potiche	poh **TEESH**
potion	**POH** shən
Potiphar	**POT** ə fər
Potomac	pə **TOH** mək
Potosi	pə **TOH** see
Potosí	**PAW** taw **SEE**
potpie	**POT** pī
potpourri	**POH** puu **REE**
Potsdam	**POTS** dam
potsherd	**POT** shurd
pottage	**POT** ij
pouf	poof
Poughkeepsie	pə **KIP** see
Poulenc	poo **LANGK**
poult	pohlt

o on, oh oat, oi **boy**, oo **soon**, oor **poor**, or **for**, ow **cow**, sh **shush**,
th **thin**, *th* **this**, u **up**, ur **spur**, uu **book**, *zh* **pleasure**

poultice	**POHL** təs
pourboire	puur **BWAHR**
pourparler	puur pahr **LAY**
pousse-café	**POOS** ka **FAY**
Poussin	poo **SAN** (**SAN** French final *n*)
Powhatan	**POW** ə **TAN**
Powys	**POH** əs
Pozarevac	**PAW** *zh*ah re vahts
Pozega	**PAW** *zh*e gah
Poznań	**PAWZ** nahn yə
practitioner	prak **TISH** ə nər
Pradhan, Om	prah **DAHN**, awm
praetor	**PREE** tər
praetorian, P-	pree **TOR** ee ən
pragmatic	prag **MAT** ik
pragmatism	**PRAG** mə **TIZ** əm
Prague	prahg
Praha	**PRAH** hah
Praia	**PRĪ** ə
prairie	**PRAIR** ee
Prajadhipok	prə **CHAH** ti **POK**
Prakrit	**PRAH** krit
praline	**PRAY** leen
prance	prans
prandial	**PRAN** dee əl
praseodymium	**PRAY** zee oh **DIM** ee əm
pratfall	**PRAT** fawl
pratique	pra **TEEK**
Pravda	**PRAHV** dah
praxis	**PRAK** səs
Praxiteles	prak **SIT** ə **LEEZ**
prayer (act of praying)	prair
prayer (one who prays)	**PRAY** ər
prebendary	**PREB** ən **DER** ee
Precambrian	pree **KAM** bree ən
precarious	pri **KA** ree əs
precatory	**PREK** ə **TOR** ee
precedence	pri **SEED** əns
precedent (a)	pri **SEED** ənt
precedent (n)	**PRES** ə dənt
precept	**PREE** sept
preceptor	pri **SEP** tər

ə ago, a at, ah calm, ahr dark, air care, aw saw, ay say, ch church
e bet, ee me, eer beer, hw what, i is, ī my, *n* French final n vin,

precession	pree SESH ən
precinct	PREE singkt
preciosity	PRES ee OS ə tee
precipice	PRES ə pəs
precipitant	pri SIP ə tənt
precipitate (v)	pri SIP ə TAYT
precipitate (a, n)	pri SIP ə tit
precipitous	pri SIP ə təs
précis	pray SEE
precise	pri SĪS
precisely	pri SĪS lee
precision	pri SIZH ən
preclude	pri KLOOD
precocious	pri KOH shəs
precocity	pri KOS ə tee
precognition	PREE kog NISH ən
precursor	pri KUR sər
predator	PRED ə tər
predatory	PRED ə TOR ee
predecessor	PRED ə SES ər
predestination	pree DES tə NAY shən
predicament	pri DIK ə mənt
predicate (a, n)	PRED ə kət
predicate (v)	PRED ə KAYT
predilection	PRED ə LEK shən
preeminence	pree EM ə nəns
preempt	pree EMPT
preface	PREF əs
prefatory	PREF ə TOR ee
prefect	PREE fekt
prefecture	PREE FEK chər
preferable	PREF ər ə bəl
preferably	PREF ər ə blee
preference	PREF ər əns
preferential	PREF ə REN shəl
prefix (n)	PREE fiks
prefix (v)	pree FIKS
pregnancy	PREG nən see
prehensile	pree HEN səl
prehistory	pree HIS tə ree
prejudge	pree JUJ
prejudice	PREJ ə dəs
prejudicial	PREJ ə DISH əl

o on, oh oat, oi boy, oo soon, oor poor, or for, ow cow, sh shush,
th thin, *th* this, u up, ur spur, uu book, *zh* pleasure

prelacy	**PREL** ə see
prelate	**PREL** ət
preliminary	pri **LIM** ə **NER** ee
Prelog, Vladimir	**PRE** lohg, **VLA** də mir
prelude	**PREL** yood
Premadasa, Ranasinghe	pree mə dah sə, rah nah sing ə
premature	**PREE** mə **CHUUR**
premier	pri **MIR**
premiere	pri **MYER**
premise	**PREM** əs
premium	**PREE** mee əm
premonition	**PREE** mə **NISH** ən
Prem Tinsulanonda	praym **TIN** suul ah **NON**
prenatal	pree **NAYT** əl
Prentice	**PREN** təs
Prentiss	**PREN** təs
preparative	pri **PA** rə tiv
preparatory	pri **PA** rə **TOR** ee
preponderance	pri **PON** dər əns
preposition	**PREP** ə **ZISH** ən
prepossession	**PREE** pə **ZESH** ən
preposterous	pri **POS** tər əs
prepuce	**PREE** pyoos
Pre-Raphaelite	pree **RAF** ee ə **LĪT**
prerequisite	pri **REK** wə zət
prerogative	pri **ROG** ə tiv
presage (n)	**PRES** ij
presage (v)	pri **SAYJ**
presbyter	**PREZ** bə tər
Presbyterian	**PREZ** bə **TEER** ee ən
presbytery	**PRES** bə **TER** ee
prescience	**PRESH** əns
prescient	**PRESH** ənt
Prescott	**PRES** kət
present (a, n)	**PREZ** ənt
present (v)	pri **ZENT**
presentation	**PREZ** ən **TAY** shən
presentiment	pri **ZEN** tə mənt
preside	pri **ZĪD**
presidency	**PREZ** ə dən see
presidential	**PREZ** ə **DEN** shəl
presidio	pri **SID** ee **OH**

ə ago, a at, ah calm, ahr dark, air care, aw saw, ay say, ch church
e bet, ee me, eer beer, hw what, i is, ī my, *n* French final n vin,

presidium	pri **SID** ee əm
pressure	**PRESH** ər
prestidigitation	**PRES** tə **DIJ** ə **TAY** shən
prestidigitator	**PRES** tə **DIJ** ə **TAY** tər
prestige	pre **STEEZ***H*
prestissimo	pre **STIS** ə **MOH**
presto	**PRES** toh
Preston	**PRES** tən
presume	pri **ZOOM**
presumptive	pri **ZUM** tiv
presumptuous	pri **ZUM** choo əs
presupposition	**PREE SUP** ə **ZISH** ən
pretense	**PREE** tens
pretentious	pri **TEN** shəs
preterit	**PRET** ər ət
preternatural	**PREE** tər **NACH** ə rəl
pretext	**PREE** tekst
Pretoria	pri **TOR** ee ə
pretzel	**PRET** səl
prevalence	**PREV** ə ləns
prevalent	**PREV** ə lənt
prevaricator	pri **VAR** ə **KAY** tər
preventive	pri **VEN** tiv
Prévost	pray **VOH**
Priam	**PRĪ** əm
priapic	prī **AY** pik
priapism	**PRĪ** ə **PIZ** əm
Priapus, p-	prī **AY** pəs
Pribilof	**PRIB** ə **LOF**
prie-dieu	pree dyuu
Prigogine, Ilya	prə **GOH** *zh*ən, **EEL** yə
prima	**PREE** mə
primacy	**PRĪ** mə see
prima donna	**PRĪ** mə **DON** ə
prima facie	**PRĪ** mə **FAY** shee
primarily	prī **MER** ə lee
primary	**PRĪ MER** ee
primate	**PRĪ** mayt
primer (book)	**PRIM** ər
primer (except book)	**PRĪ** mər
primeval	prī **MEE** vəl
primipara	prī **MIP** ə rə
primogenitor	**PRĪ** mə **JEN** ə tər

o on, oh oat, oi boy, oo soon, oor poor, or for, ow cow, sh shush,
th thin, *th* this, u up, ur spur, uu book, *zh* pleasure

primogeniture	**PRĪ** mə **JEN** ə chər
primordial	prī **MOR** dee əl
primula	**PRIM** yə lə
primus, P-	**PRĪ** məs
primus inter pares	**PREE** məs **IN** tər **PA** reez
prince	prins
princes	**PRINS** əz
princess	**PRINS** əs
princesses	**PRINS** əs əz
Princeton	**PRINS** tən
principal	**PRIN** sə pəl
principality	**PRIN** sə **PAL** ə tee
Principe	**PRIN** sə pee
principle	**PRIN** sə pəl
prior, P-	**PRĪ** ər
priorate	**PRĪ** ər ət
prioress	**PRĪ** ər əs
priority	prī **OR** ə tee
priory	**PRĪ** ə ree
Pripet	**PREE** pet
Priscian	**PRISH** ən
prism	**PRIZ** əm
prismatic	priz **MAT** ik
pristine	**PRIS** teen
prithee	**PRI***TH* ee
privacy	**PRĪ** və see
privateer	**PRĪ** və **TEER**
privation	prī **VAY** shən
privet	**PRIV** ət
privilege	**PRIV** ə lij
privy	**PRIV** ee
prix fixe	pree feeks
probably	**PROB** ə blee
probate	**PROH** bayt
probationary	proh **BAY** shə **NER** ee
probity	**PROH** bə tee
problematical	**PROB** lə **MAT** ə kəl
pro bono publico	proh **BOH** noh **POOB** lə **KOH**
proboscis	proh **BOS** əs
procaine	**PROH** kayn
procedural	prə **SEE** jər əl
procedure	prə **SEE** jər
proceeds (goes forward)	proh **SEEDS**

ə ago, a at, ah calm, ahr dark, air care, aw saw, ay say, ch church
e bet, ee me, eer beer, hw what, i is, ī my, *n* French final n vin,

proceeds (money)	**PROH** seeds
process	**PROS** es
Prochnik	**PRAHCH** nik
proclitic	proh **KLIT** ik
proclivity	proh **KLIV** ə tee
Procne	**PROK** nee
Procopius	proh **KOH** pee əs
procrastinate	proh **KRAS** tə **NAYT**
procreant	**PROH** kree ənt
Procrustean	proh **KRUS** tee ən
Procrustes	proh **KRUS** teez
proctology	prok **TOL** ə jee
proctor	**PROK** tər
procurance	prə **KYUUR** əns
procuration	**PROK** yə **RAY** shən
procurator	**PROK** yə **RAY** tər
procure	prə **KYUUR**
procurer	prə **KYUUR** ər
procuress	prə **KYUUR** əs
Procyon	**PROH** see **ON**
prodigal	**PROD** ə gəl
prodigality	**PROD** ə **GAL** ə tee
prodigious	prə **DIJ** əs
prodigy	**PROD** ə jee
produce (n)	**PROD** oos
produce (v)	prə **DOOS**
proem	**PROH** em
profanation	**PROF** ə **NAY** shən
profane	proh **FAYN**
profanity	proh **FAN** ə tee
profess	prə **FES**
profession	prə **FESH** ən
professorial	**PROH** fə **SOR** ee əl
proffer	**PROF** ər
proficiency	prə **FISH** ən see
proficient	prə **FISH** ənt
profile	**PROH** fil
profiteer	**PROF** ə **TIR**
profligacy	**PROF** lə gə see
profligate	**PROF** lə gət
pro forma	proh **FOR** mə
profound	prə **FOWND**
profundity	prə **FUN** də tee
profuse	prə **FYOOS**

---

o on, oh oat, oi boy, oo soon, oor poor, or for, ow cow, sh shush,
th thin, *th* this, u up, ur spur, uu book, *zh* pleasure

profusion	prə **FYOO** *zh*ən
progenitor	proh **JEN** ə tər
progeny	**PROJ** ə nee
progesterone	proh **JES** tə **ROHN**
prognathous	**PROG** nə thəs
prognosis	prog **NOH** səs
prognostic	prog **NOS** tik
prognosticate	prog **NOS** tə **KAYT**
program	**PROH** gram
programmatic	**PROH** grə **MAT** ik
progress (n)	**PROG** rəs
progress (v)	prə **GRES**
progression	prə **GRESH** ən
progressive	prə **GRES** iv
prohibition	**PROH** ə **BISH** ən
prohibitive	proh **HIB** ə tiv
project (n)	**PROJ** ekt
project (v)	prə **JEKT**
projectile	prə **JEK** təl
Prok Amaranand	prohk **AHM** ah rah **NAHN**
Prokofieff, Prokofiev	praw **KAW** fyef
Prokopievsk	praw kaw **PYEFSK**
prolapse	proh **LAPS**
prolegomenon	**PROH** li **GOM** ə **NON**
prolepsis	proh **LEP** səs
proletarian	**PROH** lə **TAIR** ee ən
proletariat	**PROH** lə **TAIR** ee ət
proliferate	prə **LIF** ə **RAYT**
prolific	prə **LIF** ik
prolix	proh **LIKS**
prolixity	proh **LIK** sə tee
prolocutor	proh **LOK** yə tər
prologue	**PROH** lawg
prolong	prə **LAWNG**
prolongation	**PROH** lawng **GAY** shən
promenade	**PROM** ə **NAYD**
Promethean	prə **MEE** thee ən
Prometheus	prə **MEE** thee əs
prominence	**PROM** ə nəns
prominent	**PROM** ə nənt
promiscuity	**PROM** ə **SKYOO** ə tee
promiscuous	prə **MIS** kyoo əs
promissory	**PROM** ə **SOR** ee

ə ago, a at, ah calm, ahr dark, air care, aw saw, ay say, ch church
e bet, ee me, eer beer, hw what, i is, ī my, *n* French final n vin,

promontory	**PROM** ən **TOR** ee
promulgate	**PROM** əl **GAYT**
promulgation	**PROM** əl **GAY** shən
promulgator	**PROM** əl **GAY** tər
pronto	**PRON** toh
pronunciamento	proh **NUN** see ə **MEN** toh
pronunciation	prə **NUN** see **AY** shən
propaganda	**PROP** ə **GAN** də
propagate	**PROP** ə **GAYT**
propane	**PROH** payn
propel	prə **PEL**
propellant	prə **PEL** ənt
propensity	prə **PEN** sə tee
Propertius	proh **PUR** shəs
prophecy (n)	**PROF** ə see
prophesy (v)	**PROF** ə sī
prophet	**PROF** ət
prophetic	prə **FET** ik
prophylactic	**PROH** fə **LAK** tik
prophylaxis	**PROH** fə **LAK** səs
propinquity	prə **PING** kwə tee
propitiate	prə **PISH** ee **AYT**
propitious	prə **PISH** əs
proponent	prə **POH** nənt
proportionate (a)	prə **POR** shə nət
proportionate (v)	prə **POR** shə **NAYT**
proprietary	prə **PRĪ** ə **TER** ee
proprietor	prə **PRĪ** ə tər
propriety	prə **PRĪ** ə tee
propulsion	prə **PUL** shən
pro rata	proh **RAY** tə
prorogue	prə **ROHG**
prosaic	proh **ZAY** ik
proscenium	proh **SEE** nee əm
prosciutto	proh **SHOO** toh
proselyte	**PROS** ə **LĪT**
proselytize	**PROS** ə lə **TĪZ**
Proserpina	prə **SUR** pə nə
Proserpine	**PROS** ər **PĪN**
prosit	**PROH** zət
prosodic	prə **SOD** ik
prosodist	**PROS** ə dəst
prosody	**PROS** ə dee

o on, oh oat, oi boy, oo soon, oor poor, or for, ow cow, sh shush,
th thin, *th* this, u up, ur spur, uu book, *zh* pleasure

prospectus	prə **SPEK** təs
Prospero	**PROS** pə **ROH**
prostate	**PROS** tayt
prostatitis	**PROS** tə **TĪT** əs
prosthesis	pros **THEE** səs
prosthetic	pros **THET** ik
Prostigmin, p-	proh **STIG** min
prostitute	**PROS** tə **TOOT**
prostrate	**PROS** trayt
prostyle	**PROH** stīl
prosy	**PROH** zee
protactinium	**PROH** tak **TIN** ee əm
protagonist	proh **TAG** ə nəst
Protagoras	proh **TAG** ər əs
protamine	**PROH** tə **MEEN**
protean, P-	**PROH** tee ən
protectorate	prə **TEK** tə rət
protégé	**PROH** tə **ZHAY**
protein	**PROH** teen
pro tempore	proh **TEM** pə **RE**
Proterozoic	**PROT** ər ə **ZOH** ik
protest (n)	**PROH** test
protest (v)	prə **TEST**
Protestant, p-	**PROT** ə stənt
protestation	**PROT** ə **STAY** shən
Proteus	**PROH** tee əs
prothalamion	**PROH** thə **LAY** mee **ON**
prothesis	**PROTH** ə səs
protium	**PROH** tee əm
protocol	**PROH** tə **KAWL**
proton	**PROH** ton
protoplasm	**PROH** tə **PLAZ** əm
prototype	**PROH** tə **TĪP**
Protozoa	**PROH** tə **ZOH** ə
protozoan	**PROH** tə **ZOH** ən
protract	proh **TRAKT**
protrude	proh **TROOD**
protrusion	proh **TROO** *zh*ən
protrusive	proh **TROO** siv
protuberance	proh **TOO** bə rəns
Proudhon	proo **DAWN** (**DAWN** French final *n*)
Proust	proost
provenance	**PROV** ə nəns

ə ago, a at, ah calm, ahr dark, air care, aw saw, ay say, ch church
e bet, ee me, eer beer, hw what, i is, ī my, *n* French final n vin,

Provençal	proh vahn **SAHL**
Provence	proh **VAHNS**
provender	**PROV** ən dər
proverb	**PROV** urb
proverbial	prə **VUR** bee əl
providence, P-	**PROV** ə dəns
provident	**PROV** ə dənt
province	**PROV** əns
provincial	prə **VIN** shəl
provision	prə **VIZH** ən
proviso	prə **VĪ** zoh
Provo	**PROH** voh
provocation	**PROV** ə **KAY** shən
provocative	prə **VOK** ə tiv
provolone	**PROH** və **LOH** nee
provost	**PROH** vohst
provost (military)	**PROH** voh
prowess	**PROW** əs
proximal	**PROK** sə məl
proximate	**PROK** sə mət
proximity	prok **SIM** ə tee
proximo	**PROK** sə **MOH**
proxy	**PROK** see
prudery	**PROO** də ree
Prud'hon	proo **DAWN** (**DAWN** French final *n*)
prudish	**PROOD** ish
prunella	proo **NEL** ə
prurient	**PRUUR** ee ənt
Prussia	**PRUSH** ə
Prussian	**PRUSH** ən
prussic	**PRUS** ik
Pruszkow	**PRUUSH** kuuf
Prut, -h	proot
Prynne	prin
psalm	sahm
psalmodist	**SAH** mə dəst
psalmody	**SAH** mə dee
psalter, P-	**SAWL** tər
psaltery, P-	**SAWL** tə ree
pseudo	**SOO** doh
pseudonym	**SOO** də nim
pseudonymous	soo **DON** ə məs
pseudopod	**SOO** də **POD**

o on, oh oat, oi boy, oo soon, oor poor, or for, ow cow, sh shush,
th thin, *th* this, u up, ur spur, uu book, *zh* pleasure

pseudopodium	soo də POH dee əm
pshaw	shaw
psi	sī
psilocybin	SĪL ə SĪ bən
psittacosis	SIT ə KOH səs
psoriasis	sə RĪ ə səs
psyche, P-	SĪ kee
psychedelic	sī kə DEL ik
psychiatric	sī kee AT rik
psychiatrist	si KĪ ə trəst
psychiatry	si KĪ ə tree
psychic	SĪ kik
psychoanalysis	sī koh ə NAL ə səs
psychoanalyst	sī koh AN ə ləst
psychogenic	sī koh JEN ik
psychological	sī kə LOJ i kəl
psychologist	sī KOL ə jəst
psychology	sī KOL ə jee
psychometry	sī KOM ə tree
psychoneuroses	sī koh nuu ROH seez
psychoneurosis	sī koh nuu ROH səs
psychopath	SĪ kə PATH
psychopathic	sī kə PATH ik
psychopathology	sī koh pə THOL ə jee
psychoses	sī KOH seez
psychosis	sī KOH səs
psychosomatic	sī kə sə MAT ik
psychotherapy	sī koh THER ə pee
psychotic	sī KOT ik
Ptah	pə TAH
ptarmigan	TAHR mi gən
pterodactyl	TER ə DAK təl
pteropod	TER ə POD
Ptolemaic	TOL ə MAY ik
Ptolemy	TOL ə mee
ptomaine	TOH mayn
ptosis	TOH səs
puberty	PYOO bər tee
pubescent	pyoo BES ənt
pubic	PYOO bik
publican	PUB li kən
Pucci, Emilio	POO chee, ay MEE lyoh
Puccini	poo CHEE nee

ə ago, a at, ah calm, ahr dark, air care, aw saw, ay say, ch church
e bet, ee me, eer beer, hw what, i is, ī my, n French final n vin,

puce	pyoos
pudendum	pyuu **DEN** dəm
Puebla	**PWE** blah
pueblo, P-	**PWEB** loh
puerile	**PYUUR** əl
puerperal	pyoo **UR** pə rəl
Puerto Rican	**PWER** toh **REE** kən
Puerto Rico	**PWER** toh **REE** koh
Puerto Vallarta	**PWER** toh vah **YAHR** tah
puffin	**PUF** ən
Puget	**PYOO** jit
puggaree	**PUG** ə ree
pugilist	**PYOO** jə ləst
pugnacious	pug **NAY** shəs
pugree	**PUG** ree
puisne	**PYOO** nee
puissance	**PYOO** ə səns
puissant	**PYOO** ə sənt
pukka	**PUK** ə
Pulaski	pə **LAS** kee
pulchritude	**PUL** krə **TOOD**
pulchritudinous	**PUL** krə **TOO** də nəs
pule	pyool
puli	**POO** lee
Pulitzer	**PUUL** ət sər
pullet	**PUUL** ət
Pullman	**PUUL** mən
pullulate	**PUL** yə **LAYT**
pulmonary	**PUUL** mə **NER** ee
pulpit	**PUUL** pit
pulque	**PUUL** kay
pulsate	**PUL** sayt
Pultusk	**PUUL** tuusk
pulverize	**PUL** və **RĪZ**
puma	**PYOO** mə
pumice	**PUM** əs
pummel	**PUM** əl
pumpernickel	**PUM** pər **NIK** əl
pumpkin	**PUMP** kən
puna	**POO** nah
puncheon	**PUN** chən
punchinello, P-	**PUN** chə **NEL** oh
punctilio	pungk **TIL** ee **OH**

o on, oh oat, oi boy, oo soon, oor poor, or for, ow cow, sh shush, th thin, *th* this, u up, ur spur, uu book, *zh* pleasure

punctilious	pungk **TIL** ee əs
punctual	**PUNGK** choo əl
punctuality	**PUNGK** choo **AL** ə tee
punctuate	**PUNGK** choo **AYT**
punctuation	**PUNGK** choo **AY** chən
puncture	**PUNGK** chər
pundit	**PUN** dət
pungent	**PUN** jənt
Punic	**PYOO** nik
punitive	**PYOO** nə tiv
Punjab	pun **JAHB**
Punjabi	pun **JAH** bee
punkah	**PUNG** kə
Punta Arenas	**POON** tah ah **RE** nahs
Punxsutawney	**PUNGK** sə **TAW** nee
puny	**PYOO** nee
pupa	**PYOO** pə
Pupin	pyuu **PEEN**
puppet	**PUP** ət
Puppis	**PUP** is
purblind	**PUR** blīnd
Purcell (composer)	**PUR** səl
purdah	**PUR** də
purée	pyuu **RAY**
purgative	**PUR** gə tiv
purgatory	**PUR** gə **TOR** ee
Purim	**PUUR** im
puritanical, P-	**PYUUR** ə **TAN** i kəl
Puritanism, p-	**PYUUR** ə tə **NIZ** əm
purl	purl
purlieu	**PURL** yoo
purloin	pər **LOIN**
purport (n)	**PUR** port
purport (v)	pər **PORT**
purposive	**PUR** pə siv
purpura	**PUR** pyə rə
purslane	**PURS** lən
pursuance	pər **SOO** əns
pursuant	pər **SOO** ənt
pursue	pər **SOO**
pursuit	pər **SOOT**
pursuivant	**PUR** swi vənt
purulence	**PYUUR** ə ləns

ə ago, a at, ah calm, ahr dark, air care, aw saw, ay say, ch church
e bet, ee me, eer beer, hw what, i is, ī my, *n* French final n vin,

purulent	**PYUUR** ə lənt
purveyor	pər **VAY** ər
purview	**PUR** vyoo
Pusan	poo sahn
Pusey	**PYOO** zee
Pushkin	**PUUSH** kən
Pushto	**PUSH** toh (**PUSH** as in *hush*)
Pushtu	**PUSH** too (**PUSH** as in *hush*)
pusillanimity	**PYOO** sə lə **NIM** ə tee
pusillanimous	**PYOO** sə **LAN** ə məs
pustule	**PUS** chool
putative	**PYOO** tə tiv
Putnam	**PUT** nəm
putrefaction	**PYOO** trə **FAK** shən
putrescent	pyoo **TRES** ənt
putrid	**PYOO** trəd
Putsch, p-	puuch
putt	put (as in *nut*)
puttee	pu **TEE**
putty	**PUT** ee (**PUT** as in *nut*)
Putumayo	**POO** too **MAH** yaw
Pu-yi	poo yee
Pydna	**PID** nə
pyelitis	**PĪ** ə **LĪ** təs
pyemia	pī **EE** mee ə
Pygmalion	pig **MAYL** yən
Pygmy, p-	**PIG** mee
pyknic	**PIK** nik
pylon	**PĪ** lon
pylorus	pī **LOR** əs
Pylos	**PĪ** lahs
Pynchon	**PINCH** ən
Pyongyang	pyung yahng
pyorrhea	**PĪ** ə **REE** ə
pyramid	**PIR** ə mid
pyramidal	pə **RAM** ə dəl
Pyramus	**PIR** ə məs
pyre	pīr
Pyrenean	**PIR** ə **NEE** ən
Pyrenees	**PIR** ə **NEEZ**
pyretic	pī **RET** ik
Pyrex	**PĪ** reks
pyrexia	pī **REK** see ə

---

o on, oh oat, oi boy, oo soon, oor poor, or for, ow cow, sh shush,
th thin, *th* this, u up, ur spur, uu book, *zh* pleasure

pyridine	**PIR** ə **DEEN**
pyridoxine	**PIR** ə **DOK** seen
pyriform	**PIR** ə **FORM**
pyrite	**PĪ** rīt
pyrites	pə **RĪ** teez
pyrogenic	**PĪ** rə **JEN** ik
pyrography	pī **ROG** rə fee
pyrolysis	pī **ROL** ə sis
pyrolyze	**PĪ** rə **LĪZ**
pyromania	**PĪ** rə **MAY** nee ə
pyrophobia	**PĪ** rə **FOH** bee ə
pyrosis	pī **ROH** səs
pyrotechnic	**PĪ** rə **TEK** nik
Pyrrha	**PIR** ə
pyrrhic, P-	**PIR** ik
Pyrrhonism	**PIR** ə **NIZ** əm
Pyrrhus	**PIR** əs
Pythagoras	pə **THAG** ər əs
Pythagorean	pə **THAG** ə **REE** ən
Pythia	**PITH** ee ə
Pythian	**PITH** ee ən
Pythias	**PITH** ee əs
python, P-	**PĪ** thon
pythoness	**PĪ** thə nəs
pyuria	pī **YUUR** ee ə
pyx	piks
Pyxis, p-	**PIK** səs

Q

Qaddafi, Muammar al-	kə **DAHF** ee, **MOO** ə **MAHR** ahl
Qantas	**KWON** təs
Qara Qum	kah **RAH** **KUUM**
Qatar	**KAH** tahr
Qattara	kah **TAH** rah
Qeshm	**KESH** əm
Qingdao	ching dow
Qinghai	ching hī
Qin Shi Huang	chin shuu hwahng
Qirghiz	kir **GEEZ**
Qishm	**KISH** əm

ə ago, a at, ah calm, ahr dark, air care, aw saw, ay say, ch church
e bet, ee me, eer beer, hw what, i is, ī my, *n* French final n vin,

Qizil Qum	ki ZIL KUUM
qua	kwah
Quaalude	KWAY lood
quad	kwod
quadragenarian	KWOD rə jə NA ree ən
Quadragesima	KWOD rə JES ə mə
quadrangle	KWOD rang əl
quadrangular	kwod RANG gyə lər
quadrant	KWOD rənt
quadraphonic	KWOD rə FON ik
quadrate	KWOD rayt
quadrate (v)	KWOD rayt
quadratic	kwo DRAT ik
quadrature	KWOD rə chər
quadrennial	kwo DREN ee əl
quadricentennial	KWOD rə sen TEN ee əl
quadrille	kwo DRIL
quadriplegia	KWOD rə PLEE jee ə
quadriplegic	KWOD rə PLEE jik
quadrivium	kwo DRIV ee əm
quadroon	kwo DROON
Quadros, Jânio	KWAH drohsh, ZHA nee oh
quadruped	KWOD rə PED
quadruple	kwo DROO pəl
quadruplet	KWOD rə plət
quadruplicate (a, n)	kwo DROO plə kət
quadruplicate (v)	kwo DROO plə KAYT
quaestor	KWES tər
quaff	kwahf
quagmire	KWAG mīr
quahog	KWAW hawg
Quai d'Orsay	KAY dor SAY
quaint	kwaynt
Quaison-Sackey, Alex	KWE sən SA kay, A leks
qualitative	KWOL ə TAY tiv
qualm	kwahm
quandary	KWON də ree
quandong	KWON dong
quant	kwant
quanta	KWON tə
quantic	KWON tik
quantitative	KWON tə TAY tiv
quantity	KWON tə tee

---

o on, oh oat, oi boy, oo soon, oor poor, or for, ow cow, sh shush,
th thin, *th* this, u up, ur spur, uu book, *zh* pleasure

quantum	**KWON** təm
quarantine	**KWOR** ən **TEEN**
quark	kwork (as in *stork*)
Quarnero	kwahr **NE** raw
quarrel	**KWOR** əl
quarry	**KWOR** ee
quart (measure)	kwort (as in *sort*)
quartan	**KWOR** tən
quartile	**KWOR** tīl
quarto	**KWOR** toh
quartz	kworts (as in *sorts*)
quasar	**KWAY** zahr
quash	kwosh
quasi	**KWAY** zī
Quasimodo, Salvatore	**KWAH** zee **MAW** daw, **SAHL** vah **TAW** re
quassia	**KWOSH** ə
quaternary	**KWAH** tər **NER** ee
Quathlamba	kwaht **LAHM** bah
quatrain	**KWAH** trayn
quatrefoil	**KAT** ər **FOIL**
quattrocento	**KWAH** troh **CHEN** toh
quay	kee
queasy	**KWEE** zee
Quebec	kwi **BEK**
Quebecois	**KAY** be **KWAH**
quebracho	kay **BRAH** choh
Quechua	**KECH** wə
Quechuan	**KECH** wən
Queensland	**KWEENZ** lənd
Quelpart	**KWEL** pahrt
Quemoy	kee **MOI**
quenelle	kə **NEL**
Querétaro	ke **RE** tah **ROH**
querulous	**KWER** ə ləs
query	**KWIR** ee
questionnaire	**KWES** chə **NAIR**
questor	**KWES** tər
Quetta	**KWET** ah
quetzal	ket **SAHL**
Quetzalcoatl	ket **SAHL** **KWAHT** əl
queue	kyoo
Quezon	**KAY** zon
quiche	keesh

ə ago, a at, ah calm, ahr dark, air care, aw saw, ay say, ch church
e bet, ee me, eer beer, hw what, i is, ī my, *n* French final n vin,

Quiché	kee **CHAY**
quiddity	**KWID** ə tee
quidnunc	**KWID** nungk
quid pro quo	**KWID** proh **KWOH**
quién sabe	kyen **SAH** be
quiescence	kwī **ES** əns
quiescent	kwī **ES** ənt
quietude	**KWĪ** ə **TOOD**
quietus	kwī **EE** təs
quinacrine	**KWIN** ə **KREEN**
quincunx	**KWIN** kungks
Quincy (Illinois)	**KWIN** see
Quincy (Massachusetts)	**KWIN** zee
quindecagon	kwin **DEK** ə **GON**
quindecennial	**KWIN** di **SEN** ee əl
quinidine	**KWIN** ə **DEEN**
quinine	**KWĪ** nīn
quinquagenarian	**KWING** kwə jə **NA** ree ən
Quinquagesima	**KWING** kwə **JES** ə mə
quinquennial	kwin **KWEN** ee əl
quinquennium	kwin **KWEN** ee əm
quinquereme	**KWING** kwə **REEM**
quinsy	**KWIN** zee
quintal	**KWIN** təl
Quintana Roo	keen **TAHN** ə **ROO**
quintessence	kwin **TES** əns
quintessential	**KWIN** tə **SEN** shəl
Quintilian	kwin **TIL** yən
quintillion	kwin **TIL** yən
quintuple	kwin **TOO** pəl
quintuplet	**KWIN** tə plət
quire	kwīr
Quirinal	**KWIR** ə nəl
Quirinus	kwə **RĪ** nəs
Quirites	kwə **RĪ** teez
quirk	kwurk
quirt	kwurt
quisling	**KWIZ** ling
Quito	**KEE** toh
qui vive	kee **VEEV**
Quixote (see Don Quixote)	
quixotic	kwik **SOT** ik

---

o **on**, oh **oat**, oi **boy**, oo **soon**, oor **poor**, or **for**, ow **cow**, sh **shush**,
th **thin**, *th* **this**, u **up**, ur **spur**, uu **book**, *zh* **pleasure**

Qum	kuum
Qumran	kuum **RAHN**
quo animo	**KWOH AH** ni **MOH**
quodlibet	**KWOD** lə **BET**
quoin	koin
quoit	kwoit
quondam	**KWON** dəm
Quonset	**KWON** sət
quorum	**KWOR** əm
quota	**KWOH** tə
quotation	kwoh **TAY** shən
quoth	kwohth
quotidian	kwoh **TID** ee ən
Quo Vadis	kwoh **WAH** dəs

R

Ra	rah
Rabat	rah **BAHT**
Rabaul	rah **BOWL** (**BOWL** as in *howl*)
Rabbath	**RAB** əth
rabbi	**RAB** ī
Rabbinic, r-	rə **BIN** ik
rabbinical	rə **BIN** i kəl
rabbinist	**RAB** ə nəst
Rabelais	**RAB** ə **LAY**
Rabelaisian	**RAB** ə **LAY** *zh*ən
rabid	**RAB** əd
rabies	**RAY** beez
Rabi, I. I.	**RAH** bee
Rabin, Yitzhak	rah **BEEN**, **YEETS** hahk
raccoon	ra **KOON**
raceme	ray **SEEM**
Rachel	**RAY** chəl
Rachel (French)	ra **SHEL**
rachis	**RAY** kəs
rachitic	rə **KIT** ik
rachitis	rə **KĪ** təs
Rachmaninoff, Rachmaninov	rahk **MAH** nə **NAWF**
Racine (Wisconsin)	rə **SEEN**

ə ago, a at, ah calm, ahr dark, air care, aw saw, ay say, ch church
e bet, ee me, eer beer, hw what, i is, ī my, *n* French final n vin,

Racine, Jean Baptiste	ra **SEEN**, *zh*ahn ba **TEEST** (*zh*ahn French final *n*)
racket	**RAK** ət
Rackham	**RAK** əm
racon	**RAY** kon
raconteur	**RAK** on **TUR**
racquet	**RAK** ət
Rácz, Pál	rahs, pal
radar	**RAY** dahr
Radauti	**RAHD** ə **OOTS**
Radek	**RAH** dek
Radhakrishnan	rah dah **KRISH** nən
radial	**RAY** dee əl
radian	**RAY** dee ən
radiant	**RAY** dee ənt
radiate	**RAY** dee **AYT**
radiation	**RAY** dee **AY** shən
radiator	**RAY** dee **AY** tər
radical	**RAD** i kəl
radii (pl)	**RAY** dee ī
radioactive	**RAY** dee oh **AK** tiv
radiogram	**RAY** dee oh **GRAM**
radiography	**RAY** dee **OG** rə fee
radioisotope	**RAY** dee oh Ī sə **TOHP**
radiology	**RAY** dee **OL** ə jee
radiosonde	**RAY** dee oh **SOND**
radium	**RAY** dee əm
radius	**RAY** dee əs
radix	**RAY** diks
Radnor	**RAD** nər
Radom	**RAH** dawm
radome	**RAY** dohm
radon	**RAY** don
Radrodro, J. F.	rahn draw **DOH**
Radványi, János	**ROHD** vah nyee, **YAH** nohsh
raffia	**RAF** ee ə
raffinate	**RAF** ə **NAYT**
raffish	**RAF** ish
Rafsanjani, Hashemi	ruf sen **JAN** ee, **HASH** ə mee
raga	**RAH** gə
ragamuffin	**RAG** ə **MUF** ən
ragged	**RAG** əd
raglan	**RAG** lən

o on, oh oat, oi boy, oo soon, oor poor, or for, ow cow, sh shush, th thin, *th* this, u up, ur spur, uu book, *zh* pleasure

Ragnarok	**RAHG** nə **ROK**
ragout	ra **GOO**
Ragusa	rah **GOO** zah
raillery	**RAY** lə ree
raiment	**RAY** mənt
Raimondi	rī **MOHN** dee
Rainier (Mount)	rə **NEER**
Rainier (Prince)	re **NYAY**
raison d'être	**RAY** zohn **DET** rə (zohn French final *n*)
raj	rahj
raja	**RAH** jə
Rajaie-Khorassani, Said	rah **JE** ee **HOH** rah **SEN** ee, sah **EED**
Rajasthan	**RAH** jə **STAHN**
Rajput	**RAHJ** poot
Rajputana	**RAHJ** puu **TAH** nə
raki	rah **KEE**
rakish	**RAY** kish
Rakotomalala, Louis	**RAH** koh toh **MAH** lahl, loo **EE**
rale (disease)	rahl
Raleigh	**RAW** lee
rallentando	**RAH** lən **TAHN** doh
Ralston	**RAWL** stən
Rama	**RAH** mə
Ramachandra	**RAH** mə **CHUN** drə
Ramadan	**RAM** ə **DAHN**
Ramapo	**RAM** ə poh
Rama Rau, Santha	**RAH** mah **ROW**, **SAHN** tə (**ROW** as in *cow*)
Ramayana	rah **MAH** yə nə
Rambouillet	rahn boo **YAY** (rahn French final *n*)
rambunctious	ram **BUNGK** shəs
Ramdat-Misier, Lachmipersad	**RAHM** daht mis **EER**, **LAHCH** mee pər **SAHD**
Rameau	ra **MOH**
ramekin	**RAM** ə kən
Rameses	**RAM** ə **SEEZ**
ramification	**RAM** ə fə **KAY** shən
Ramirez Pane, Ruben	rah **MEER** ez **PAH** nay, **ROO** ben
Ramón	rah **MAWN**
ramose	**RAY** mohs
rampage (n)	**RAM** payj

ə ago, a at, ah calm, ahr dark, air care, aw saw, ay say, ch church
e bet, ee me, eer beer, hw what, i is, ī my, *n* French final n vin,

rampage (v)	ram **PAYJ**
rampant	**RAM** pənt
Ramsay	**RAM** zee
Ramses	**RAM** seez
Ramsey	**RAM** zee
ramshackle	**RAM SHAK** əl
ranchero	rahn **CHAIR** oh
rancho	**RAHN** choh
rancid	**RAN** səd
rancor	**RANG** kər
random	**RAN** dəm
ranee	**RAH** nee
Rangel	**RANG** gəl
Rangoon	rang **GOON**
rani	**RAH** nee
Rank, Otto	rahnk
Rankine	**RANG** kən
ransack	**RAN** sak
ranunculus	rə **NUNG** kyə ləs
Raoul, Raúl	ra **OOL**
rapacious	rə **PAY** shəs
rapacity	rə **PAS** ə tee
Rapacki, Adam	rah **PAHT** see, ah **DAHM**
Rapallo	rah **PAH** law
Raphael	**RAY** fee əl
Raphael (painter)	**RAH** fah el
Rapidan	**RAP** ə **DAN**
rapidity	rə **PID** ə tee
rapier	**RAY** pee ər
rapine	**RAP** ən
Rappahannock	**RAP** ə **HAN** ək
rappel	rə **PEL**
rapport	ra **POR**
rapprochement	ra prohsh **MAHN** (**MAHN** French final *n*)
rapscallion	rap **SKAL** yən
rapture	**RAP** chər
rapturous	**RAP** chər əs
rara avis	**RAR** ə **AY** vəs
rarebit	**RAR** bət
rarefaction	**RAR** ə **FAK** shən
rarefy	**RAR** ə **FĪ**
Raritan	**RAR** ət ən
rarity	**RAR** ə tee

o **on**, oh **oat**, oi **boy**, oo **soon**, oor **poor**, or **for**, ow **cow**, sh **shush**,
th **thin**, *th* **this**, u **up**, ur **spur**, uu **book**, *zh* **pleasure**

Rarotonga	RAR ə TONG gə
rascality	ra SKAL ə tee
rasher	RASH ər
Rashi	RAH shee
Rashidov, Sharaf	rah SHEE dof, shah RAHF
Rasmussen, Knud	RAHS muu sən, KNOOTH
raspberry	RAZ BER ee
Rasputin	ra SPYOO tən
Rastafarian	RAS tə FA ree ən
raster	RAS tər
ratafia	RAT ə FEE ə
ratatouille	rah tah TOO yə
ratchet	RACH ət
rather	RATH ər
rathskeller	RAHT SKEL ər
ratiné	RAT ə NAY
ratio	RAY shee oh
ratiocinate	RASH ee OS ə NAYT
ratiocination	RASH ee OS ə NAY shən
ration	RASH ən
rational	RASH ə nəl
rationale	RASH ə NAL
rationalism	RASH ən əl IZ əm
rationality	RASH ə NAL ə tee
rationalization	RASH ən əl ə ZAY shən
ratline	RAT lən
ratsbane	RATS bayn
Ratsiraka, Didier	RAHT see RAH kah, dee dee AY
rattan	ra TAN
raucous	RAW kəs
Rauschenburg	ROW shən BURG (ROW as in *cow*)
rauwolfia	raw WUUL fee ə
ravage	RAV ij
ravel	RAV əl
Ravel	ra VEL
raven (n, a)	RAY vən
raven (v)	RAV ən
Ravenna	rə VEN ə
ravenous	RAV ə nəs
ravigote	ra vee GAWT
ravine	rə VEEN
ravioli	RAV ee OH lee
ravish	RAV ish

ə ago, a at, ah calm, ahr dark, air care, aw saw, ay say, ch church
e bet, ee me, eer beer, hw what, i is, ī my, n French final n vin,

Rawalpindi	RAH wəl PIN dee
rayah	RAH yə
Rayburn	RAY bərn
Rayleigh	RAY lee
rayon	RAY on
Re, r-	ray
reactance	ree AK təns
reaction	ree AK shən
reactionary	ree AK shə NER ee
reactor	re AK tər
Reading (Pennsylvania, England)	RED ing
Reading Gaol	RED ing JAYL
Reagan	RAY gən
reagent	ree AY jənt
real	REE əl
realign	REE ə LĪN
realism	REE ə LIZ əm
reality	ree AL ə tee
realization	REE ə lə ZAY shən
really	REE ə lee
realm	relm
realpolitik	ray AHL POH li TEEK
realtor, R-	REE əl tər
realty	REE əl tee
Réaumur	RAY oh MYUUR
rebec	REE bek
Rebecca, Rebekah	ri BEK ə
rebel (n)	REB əl
rebel (v)	ri BEL
rebellion	ri BEL yən
rebellious	ri BEL yəs
rebozo, R-	ri BOH zoh
rebuke	ri BYOOK
rebus	REE bəs
rebut	ri BUT
rebuttal	ri BUT əl
recalcitrance	ri KAL sə trəns
recalcitrant	ri KAL sə trənt
recall	ri KAWL
recamier	RAY kə MYAY
Récamier	ray ka MYAY

o on, oh oat, oi boy, oo soon, oor poor, or for, ow cow, sh shush,
th thin, *th* this, u up, ur spur, uu book, *zh* pleasure

recant	ri **KANT**
recapitulate	**REE** kə **PICH** ə **LAYT**
receipt	ri **SEET**
recency	**REE** sən see
recension	ri **SEN** shən
receptacle	ri **SEP** ti kəl
recess (n)	**REE** ses
recess (v)	ri **SES**
recessional	ri **SESH** ə nəl
réchauffé	ray shoh **FAY**
recherché	rə **SHAIR SHAY**
recidivism	ri **SID** ə **VIZ** əm
recidivist	ri **SID** ə vəst
Recife	re **SEE** fə
recipe	**RES** ə **PEE**
recipient	ri **SIP** ee ənt
reciprocal	ri **SIP** rə kəl
reciprocate	ri **SIP** rə **KAYT**
reciprocity	**RES** ə **PROS** ə tee
recital	ri **SĪ** təl
recitation	**RES** ə **TAY** shən
recitative (music)	**RES** ə tə **TEEV**
reclamation	**REK** lə **MAY** shən
recluse	**REK** loos
reclusive	ri **KLOO** siv
recognition	**REK** əg **NISH** ən
recognizable	**REK** əg **NĪ** zə bəl
recognizance	ri **KOG** nə zəns
recoil (v)	ri **KOIL**
recoil (n)	**REE** koil
recollect (recall)	**REK** ə **LEKT**
re-collect (collect again)	**REE** kə **LEKT**
recollection	**REK** ə **LEK** shən
recombinant	ree **KOM** bə nənt
recompense	**REK** əm **PENS**
reconcilable	**REK** ən **SĪ** lə bəl
reconciliation	**REK** ən **SIL** ee **AY** shən
recondite	**REK** ən **DĪT**
reconnaissance	ri **KON** ə səns
reconnoiter	**REE** kə **NOI** tər
record (a, n)	**REK** ərd
record (v)	ri **KORD**

ə ago, a at, ah calm, ahr dark, air care, aw saw, ay say, ch church
e bet, ee me, eer beer, hw what, i is, ī my, *n* French final n vin,

recorder	ri **KOR** dər
recoup	ri **KOOP**
recourse	**REE** kors
recreant	**REK** ree ənt
recreate (relax)	**REK** ree **AYT**
re-create (create again)	**REE** kree **AYT**
recreation (relaxation)	**REK** ree **AY** shən
re-creation (creation anew)	**REE** kree **AY** shən
recrimination	ri **KRIM** ə **NAY** shən
recriminatory	ri **KRIM** ə nə **TOR** ee
recrudesce	**REE** kroo **DES**
recrudescence	**REE** kroo **DES** əns
recruit	ri **KROOT**
rectangle	**REK TANG** gəl
rectangular	rek **TANG** gyə lər
rectify	**REK** tə **FĪ**
rectilinear	**REK** tə **LIN** ee ər
rectitude	**REK** tə **TOOD**
recto	**REK** toh
rector	**REK** tər
rectory	**REK** tə ree
rectum	**REK** təm
recumbent	ri **KUM** bənt
recuperate	ri **KOO** pə **RAYT**
recuperative	ri **KOO** pər ə tiv
recur	ri **KUR**
recurrence	ri **KUR** əns
recusant	**REK** yə zənt
redact	ri **DAKT**
redaction	ri **DAK** shən
Reddy, Sanjiva	**RED** ee, sən **JEE** və
redeploy	**REE** di **PLOI**
redingote	**RED** ing **GOHT**
redolent	**RED** ə lənt
Redon, Odilon	rə **DOHN**, oh dee **LOHN** (**DOHN** and **LOHN** French final *n*)
redoubt	ri **DOWT**
redoubtable	ri **DOW** tə bəl
redound	ri **DOWND**
redress	ri **DRES**
reductio ad absurdum	ri **DUUK** tee oh ad ab **SUURD** əm

o on, oh oat, oi boy, oo soon, oor poor, or for, ow cow, sh shush,
th thin, *th* this, u up, ur spur, uu book, *zh* pleasure

redundancy	ri **DUN** dən see
redundant	ri **DUN** dənt
reefer	**REE** fər
refectory	ri **FEK** tə ree
referee	**REF** ə **REE**
reference	**REF** ə rəns
referendum	**REF** ə **REN** dəm
referent	**REF** ə rənt
referential	**REF** ə **REN** shəl
referral	ri **FUR** əl
reflection	ri **FLEK** shən
reflector	ri **FLEK** tər
reflex	**REE** fleks
reflexive	ri **FLEK** siv
reflux (n)	**REE** fluks
reflux (v)	ri **FLUKS**
reforestation	ree **FOR** ə **STAY** shən
reformation	**REF** ər **MAY** shən
reformatory	ri **FOR** mə **TOR** ee
refraction	ri **FRAK** shən
refractory	ri **FRAK** tə ree
refrain	ri **FRAYN**
refrangible	ri **FRAN** jə bəl
refuge	**REF** yooj
refugee	**REF** yuu **JEE**
refulgent	ri **FUL** jənt
refund (n)	**REE** fund
refund (v)	ri **FUND**
refurbish	ri **FUR** bish
refusal	ri **FYOO** zəl
refuse (a, n)	**REF** yoos
refuse (v)	ri **FYOOZ**
refutable	ri **FYOO** tə bəl
refutation	**REF** yuu **TAY** shən
refute	ri **FYOOT**
regal	**REE** gəl
regale	ri **GAYL**
regalia	ri **GAYL** yə
Regan	**REE** gən
regatta	ri **GAT** ə
Régence	ray **ZHAHNS**
regency, R-	**REE** jən see
regenerate (n)	ri **JEN** ər ət

ə ago, a at, ah calm, ahr dark, air care, aw saw, ay say, ch church
e bet, ee me, eer beer, hw what, i is, ī my, *n* French final n vin,

regenerate (v)	ri **JEN** ə **RAYT**
Regensburg	**RAY** gənz burg
regent	**REE** jənt
Reggio di Calabria	**RE** jaw **DEE** kah **LAH** bree ah
regicide	**REJ** ə **SĪD**
regime	rə **ZH**EEM
regimen	**REJ** ə mən
regiment (n)	**REJ** ə mənt
regiment (v)	**REJ** ə **MENT**
Regina	ri **JĪ** nə
region	**REE** jən
régisseur	ray zhee **SUR**
registrant	**REJ** ə strənt
registrar	**REJ** ə **STRAHR**
registry	**REJ** ə stree
regius, R-	**REE** jəs
regnant	**REG** nənt
regress (n)	**REE** gres
regress (v)	ri **GRES**
regression	ri **GRESH** ən
regular	**REG** yə lər
regularity	**REG** yə **LAR** ə tee
regularly	**REG** yə lər lee
regulatory	**REG** yə lə **TOR** ee
Regulus, r-	**REG** yə ləs
regurgitate	ri **GUR** jə **TAYT**
rehabilitate	**REE** hə **BIL** ə **TAYT**
rehabilitation	**REE** hə **BIL** ə **TAY** shən
Rehan	**REE** ən
rehash (n)	**REE** hash
rehash (v)	ree **HASH**
rehearsal	ri **HUR** səl
Rehnquist, William	**REN** kwist
Rehoboam	**REE** ə **BOH** əm
Rehoboth	rə **HOH** bəth
Rehovot	rə **HOH** voht
Reich	rīk
Reichstag	**RĪKS** tahg
Reichstein, Tadeus	**RĪK** stīn, tah **DE** uush
Reichswehr	**RĪKS** vair
Reifel	**RĪ** fəl
reify	**REE** ə fī
Reik	rīk

---

o on, oh oat, oi boy, oo soon, oor poor, or for, ow cow, sh shush,
th thin, *th* this, u up, ur spur, uu book, *zh* pleasure

Reikjavik	**RAY** kyə **VEEK**
Reims	rans (rhymes with *dance*)
reindeer	**RAYN** deer
reiterate	ree **IT** ə **RAYT**
reiteration	ree **IT** ə **RAY** shən
rejoinder	ri **JOIN** dər
rejuvenate	ri **JOO** və **NAYT**
rejuvenescence	ri **JOO** və **NES** əns
relativism	**REL** ə ti **VIZ** əm
relativity	**REL** ə **TIV** ə tee
relaxation	**REE** lak **SAY** shən
relay (a, n)	**REE** lay
relay (pass along)	**REE** lay
relay (lay again)	ree **LAY**
relegate	**REL** ə **GAYT**
relegation	**REL** ə **GAY** shən
relent	ri **LENT**
relevance	**REL** ə vəns
relevant	**REL** ə vənt
reliable	ri **LĪ** ə bəl
relic	**REL** ik
relict	**REL** ikt
relief	ri **LEEF**
relieve	ri **LEEV**
relievo	rel **YAY** voh
religieuse	ray lee **ZHUUZ**
religieux	ray lee **ZHUU**
religiosity	ri **LIJ** ee **OS** ə tee
relinquish	ri **LING** kwish
reliquary	**REL** ə **KWER** ee
reliquiae	ri **LIK** wi **EE**
remanent	**REM** ə nənt
Remarque	ri **MAHRK**
Rembrandt van Rijn	**REM** brahnt vahn **RĪN**
remedial	ri **MEE** dee əl
remedy	**REM** ə dee
remembrance	ri **MEM** brəns
reminisce	**REM** ə **NIS**
reminiscence	**REM** ə **NIS** əns
remiss	ri **MIS**
remission	ri **MISH** ən
remittance	ri **MIT** əns
remnant	**REM** nənt

ə ago, a at, ah calm, ahr dark, air care, aw saw, ay say, ch church
e bet, ee me, eer beer, hw what, i is, ī my, *n* French final n vin,

remonstrance	ri **MON** strəns
remonstrate	ri **MON STRAYT**
remonstrative	ri **MON** strə tiv
remora	**REM** ər ə
remorse	ri **MORS**
rémoulade	**RAY** moo **LAHD**
remuneration	ri **MYOO** nə **RAY** shən
remunerative	ri **MYOO** nər ə tiv
Remus	**REE** məs
Renais, Alain	rə **NAY**, ah **LAN** (LAN French final *n*)
Renaissance	**REN** ə **SAHNS**
renaissance	ri **NAY** səns
renal	**REE** nəl
Renan, Joseph	rə **NAHN**, *zh*oh **SEF** (NAHN French final *n*)
Renard	**REN** ərd
renascence, R-	ri **NAY** səns
Renata	rə **NAH** tə
Renault	rə **NOH**
rendezvous (n, v)	**RAHN** day **voo**
rendezvous (n pl)	**RAHN** day **voo**
René, Renée	rə **NAY**
renegade	**REN** ə **GAYD**
renege	ri **NEG**
Reni, Guido	**RE** nee, **GWEED** oh
Rennes	ren
rennet	**REN** ət
rennin	**REN** ən
Renoir	rə **NWAHR**
renovate	**REN** ə **VAYT**
renown	ri **NOWN**
renowned	ri **NOWND**
Rensselaer	**REN** sə **LEER**
rentier	rahn **TYAY**
renunciation	ri **NUN** see **AY** shən
repairable	ri **PAIR** ə bəl
reparable	**REP** ər ə bəl
reparation	**REP** ə **RAY** shən
repartee	**REP** ahr **TAY**
repast	ri **PAST**
repatriate (v)	ree **PAY** tree **AYT**
repatriate (n)	ree **PAY** tree ət
repay	ree **PAY**

---

o on, oh oat, oi boy, oo soon, oor poor, or for, ow cow, sh shush,
th thin, *th* this, u up, ur spur, uu book, *zh* pleasure

repellent	ri **PEL** ənt
repercussion	**REE** pər **KUSH** ən
repertoire	**REP** ər **TWAHR**
repertory	**REP** ər **TOR** ee
repetitive	ri **PET** ə tiv
repine	ri **PĪN**
replete	ri **PLEET**
repletion	ri **PLEE** shən
replevin	ri **PLEV** ən
replica	**REP** li kə
replicate (a, n)	**REP** li kət
replicate (v)	**REP** lə **KAYT**
replicative	**REP** li **KAY** tiv
reportage	**REP** or **TAHZ***H*
reportorial	**REP** ər **TOR** ee əl
repository	ri **POZ** ə **TOR** ee
repoussé	rə poo **SAY**
Repplier	**REP** lir
reprehend	**REP** ri **HEND**
reprehensible	**REP** ri **HEN** sə bəl
reprehension	**REP** ri **HEN** shən
representation	**REP** ri zen **TAY** shən
representative	**REP** ri **ZEN** tə tiv
reprieve	ri **PREEV**
reprimand	**REP** rə **MAND**
reprint (n)	**REE** print
reprint (v)	ree **PRINT**
reprisal	ri **PRĪ** zəl
reprise (law)	ri **PRĪZ**
reprise (music)	ri **PREEZ**
reprobate	**REP** rə **BAYT**
reprobation	**REP** rə **BAY** shən
reproof	ri **PROOF**
reprove	ri **PROOV**
reptile	**REP** təl
reptilian	rep **TIL** ee ən
republic	ri **PUB** lik
république, R-	ray puu **BLEEK**
repudiate	ri **PYOO** dee **AYT**
repugnance	ri **PUG** nəns
repugnant	ri **PUG** nənt
repulse	ri **PULS**
repulsion	ri **PUL** shən

ə ago, a at, ah calm, ahr dark, air care, aw saw, ay say, ch church
e bet, ee me, eer beer, hw what, i is, ī my, *n* French final n vin,

repulsive	ri **PUL** siv
reputable	**REP** yə tə bəl
reputation	**REP** yə **TAY** shən
repute	ri **PYOOT**
requiem, R-	**REK** wee əm
requiescat in pace	**RE** kwee **ES** kaht in **PAH** kay
requisite	**REK** wə zət
requisition	**REK** wə **ZISH** ən
requital	ri **KWĪT** əl
requite	ri **KWĪT**
reredos	**RIR** dos
rescind	ri **SIND**
rescission	ri **SIZ***H* ən
research	ri **SURCH**
resemblance	ri **ZEM** bləns
resent	ri **ZENT**
reserpine	ri **SUR** peen
reservist	ri **ZUR** vəst
reservoir	**REZ** ər **VWAHR**
residence	**REZ** ə dəns
residential	**REZ** ə **DEN** shəl
residual	ri **ZIJ** oo əl
residue	**REZ** ə **DOO**
residuum	ri **ZIJ** oo əm
resignation	**REZ** ig **NAY** shən
resilient	ri **ZIL** yənt
resin	**REZ** ən
resistor	ri **ZIS** tər
resolute	**REZ** ə **LOOT**
resolution	**REZ** ə **LOO** shən
resolve	ri **ZOLV**
resolvent	ri **ZOL** vənt
resonance	**REZ** ə nəns
resonant	**REZ** ə nənt
resonator	**REZ** ə **NAY** tər
resort	ri **ZORT**
resound	ri **ZOWND**
resource	**REE** sors
resourceful	ri **SORS** fəl
Respighi	re **SPEE** gee
respirable	**RES** pər ə bəl
respiration	**RES** pə **RAY** shən
respirator	**RES** pə **RAY** tər

o on, oh oat, oi boy, oo soon, oor poor, or for, ow cow, sh shush,
th thin, *th* this, u up, ur spur, uu book, *zh* pleasure

respiratory	RES pə rə **TOR** ee
respite	RES pət
resplendent	ri **SPLEN** dənt
respondent	ri **SPON** dənt
responsory	ri **SPON** sə ree
res publica	rays **POO** bli **KAH** (rays ryhmes with *space*)
restaurant	RES tə rənt
restaurateur	RES tə rə **TUR**
restitution	RES tə **TOO** shən
Reston	RES tən
restoration	RES tə **RAY** shən
restorative	ri **STOR** ə tiv
resume	ri **ZOOM**
résumé	REZ ə **MAY**
resumption	ri **ZUMP** shən
resurgam	re **SOOR** gahm
resurgence	ri **SUR** jəns
resurrect	REZ ə **REKT**
resuscitate	ri **SUS** ə **TAYT**
resuscitation	ri SUS ə **TAY** shən
retail	REE tayl
retailer	REE tayl ər
retake (n)	REE tayk
retake (v)	ree **TAYK**
retaliate	ri **TAL** ee **AYT**
retaliatory	ri **TAL** ee ə **TOR** ee
retard	ri **TAHRD**
retardant	ri **TAHR** dənt
retardation	REE tahr **DAY** shən
reticence	RET ə səns
reticent	RET ə sənt
reticle	RET i kəl
reticular	ri **TIK** yə lər
reticule	RET i **KYOOL**
reticulum, R-	ri **TIK** yə ləm
retina	RET ə nə
retinitis pigmentosa	RET ən ĪT əs PIG mən TOH sə
retinue	RET ən yoo
retort	ri **TORT**
retrench	ri **TRENCH**
retribution	RE trə **BYOO** shən
retrieve	ri **TREEV**

retroactive	**RET** roh **AK** tiv
retroflex	**RET** rə **FLEKS**
retrograde	**RET** rə **GRAYD**
retrogress	**RET** rə **GRES**
retrospect	**RET** rə **SPEKT**
retroussé	rə **TROO SAY**
Reuben	**ROO** bin
Réunion	ree **YOON** yən
Reuss	rois
Reuters	**ROI** tərz
reveille	**REV** ə lee
revel	**REV** əl
revenue	**REV** ən **YOO**
reverberatory	ri **VUR** bər ə **TOR** ee
revere, R-	ri **VEER**
reverence	**REV** ər əns
reverend	**REV** ər ənd
reverent	**REV** ər ənt
reverential	**REV** ə **REN** shəl
reverie	**REV** ə ree
reversion	ri **VUR** *zh*ən
revetment	ri **VET** mənt
revision	ri **VI***ZH* ən
revival	ri **VĪ** vəl
revivify	ri **VIV** ə **FĪ**
revocable	**REV** ə kə bəl
revocation	**REV** ə **KAY** shən
revolt	ri **VOHLT**
revue	ri **VYOO**
revulsion	ri **VUL** shən
rex, R-	reks
Rexist	**REKS** əst
Reye's syndrome	**RĪZ SIN** drohm
Reykjavik	**RAY** kyə **VEEK**
Reymont	**RAY** mont
Reynard	**RAY** nahrd
Reynolds	**REN** əldz
Reza Shah Pahlavi	ri **ZAH SHAH** pah lah **VEE**
rhabdomancy	**RAB** də **MAN** see
Rhadamanthine, r-	**RAD** ə **MAN** thən
Rhadamanthus, Rhadamanthys	**RAD** ə **MAN** thəs
Rhaetian	**REE** shən

---

o on, oh oat, oi boy, oo soon, oor poor, or for, ow cow, sh shush,
th thin, *th* this, u up, ur spur, uu book, *zh* pleasure

Rhaetic	**REE** tik
Rhaeto-Romanic	REE toh roh **MAN** ik
rhapsodic	rap **SOD** ik
rhapsody	**RAP** sə dee
rhatany	**RAT** ə nee
Rhea	**REE** ə
Rheims	rans (rhymes with *dance*)
Rhein	rīn
Rheingold	**RĪN** gohld
rhematic	ri **MAT** ik
Rhenish	**REN** ish
rhenium	**REE** nee əm
rheostat	**REE** ə **STAT**
rhesus, R-	**REE** səs
rhetoric	**RET** ər ik
rhetorical	ri **TOR** i kəl
rhetorician	RET ə **RISH** ən
rheumatic	ruu **MAT** ik
rheumatism	**ROO** mə **TIZ** əm
rhinal	**RĪN** əl
Rhine	rīn
rhinestone	**RĪN** stohn
rhinitis	rī **NĪ** təs
rhinoceros	rī **NOS** ə rəs
rhinology	rī **NOL** ə jee
rhizome	**RĪ** zohm
rhizotomy	rī **ZOT** ə mee
rho	roh
Rhoda	**ROH** də
Rhodes	rohdz
Rhodesia	roh **DEE** *zh*ə
rhodium	**ROH** dee əm
rhododendron	ROH də **DEN** drən
rhodolite	**ROH** də **LĪT**
rhodonite	**ROH** də **NĪT**
Rhodope, Rhodopi	**ROD** ə pee
rhombic	**ROM** bik
rhombus	**ROM** bəs
rhonchus	**RONG** kəs
Rhone	rohn
rhubarb	**ROO** bahrb
rhumb	rum
rhumba	**RUUM** bə

ə ago, a at, ah calm, ahr dark, air care, aw saw, ay say, ch church
e bet, ee me, eer beer, hw what, i is, ī my, *n* French final n vin,

rhyme	rīm
rhyolite	**RĪ** ə **LĪT**
Rhys	rees
rhythm	**RI***TH* əm
Riad, Mahmoud	ree **AHD, MAH** mood
Rialto	ree **AL** toh
riant	**RĪ** ənt
riata	ree **AH** tə
ribald	**RIB** əld
ribaldry	**RIB** əl dree
Ribas Reig, Oscar	ree **BAHS RAY, OS** kahr
riboflavin	**RĪ** bə **FLAY** vən
ribonucleic	**RĪ** boh nuu **KLEE** ik
ribose	**RĪ** bohs
ribosome	**RĪ** bə soнм
Ricardo	ri **KAHR** doh
Ricci	**REE** chee
Riccio	**REE** choh
Richard, Henri	ree **SHAHR, AHN** ree (**AHN** French final *n*)
Richelieu	reesh ə **LYUU**
Richter	**RIK** tər
rickets	**RIK** əts
rickettsia	ri **KET** see ə
rickettsial	ri **KET** see əl
rickety	**RIK** ə tee
rickey	**RIK** ee
Rickover, Hyman	**RIK** oh vər, **HĪ** mən
ricksha	**RIK** shaw
ricochet	**RIK** ə **SHAY**
ricotta	ree **KAWT** tah
Riegger	**REEG** ər
Riegle	**REEG** əl
Rienzi	ree **EN** zee
Riesling	**REEZ** ling
Rifa'i, Abdul Monem	ree **FĪ, AHB** dəl moh **NEM**
Riga	**REE** gə
rigamarole	**RIG** ə mə **ROHL**
righteous	**RĪ** chəs
rigmarole	**RIG** mə **ROHL**
Rigoletto	**RIG** ə **LET** oh
rigor	**RIG** ər
rigorous	**RIG** ər əs

o on, oh oat, oi boy, oo soon, oor poor, or for, ow cow, sh shush,
th thin, *th* this, u up, ur spur, uu book, *zh* pleasure

Rigsdag	**RIGZ** dahg
Rig-Veda	rig **VAY** də
Riis	rees
Rikhoff	**RIK** hawf
Riksdag	**RIKS** dahg
rilievo	ril **YE** voh
Rilke, Rainer	**RIL** kə, **RĪ** nər
rill	ril
Rimbaud	ran **BOH** (ran French final *n*)
Rimini	**RIM** ə nee
Rimmon	**RIM** ən
Rimsky-Korsakov	**RIM** skee **KOR** sə ᴋᴀᴡꜰ
Rinaldo	ri **NAL** doh
rind	rīnd
Rio Bravo	**REE** oh **BRAH** voh
Rio de Janeiro	**REE** oh day *zh*ə **NAIR** oh
Rio de Oro	**REE** oh de **AW** raw
Rio Gallegos	**REE** oh gah **YAY** gəs
Rio Grande (Brazil)	ʀᴇᴇ uu **GRAHN** di
Rio Grande (US)	**REE** oh **GRAND**
Rio Muni	**REE** aw **MOO** nee
Ríos Montt, Efraín	**REE** ohs **MONT**, ᴇꜰ rah **EEN**
riotous	**RĪ** ə təs
riparian	ri **PAIR** ee ən
Ripon	**RIP** ən
riposte	ri **POHST**
risibility	ʀɪᴢ ə **BIL** ə tee
risible	ʀɪᴢ ə bəl
Risorgimento	ʀᴇᴇ sor jee **MEN** toh
risotto	ree **SAW** toh
risqué	ri **SKAY**
rissole	**RI** sohl
rissolé	ree saw **LAY**
ritardando	ʀᴇᴇ tahr **DAHN** doh
ritual	**RICH** oo əl
Rivas	**REE** vahs
Rivas-Gallont, Ernesto	**REE** vahs ga **LAWNT**, air **NES** toh
Rivera	ree **VE** rah
rivet	**RIV** ət
Riviera, r-	ʀɪᴠ ee **AIR** ə
rivière	ree **VYAIR**
rivulet	**RIV** yə lət
Riyadh	ree **YAHD**

ə ago, a at, ah calm, ahr dark, air care, aw saw, ay say, ch church
e bet, ee me, eer beer, hw what, i is, ī my, *n* French final n vin,

riyal	ree **YAHL**
Rizal	ree **SAHL**
Rizzio	**REET** see OH
Rizzo	**RIZ** oh
Roanoke	**ROH** ə NOHK
Robbia	**ROH** bee ə
Robeson	**ROHB** sən
Robespierre	**ROHBZ** pyair
robot	**ROH** bot
roburite	**ROH** bə RĪT
robust	roh **BUST**
rocambole	**ROK** əm BOHL
Rocha	**RAW** chah
Rochambeau (French)	raw shahn **BOH** (shahn French final *n*)
Rochambeau (US)	ROH sham **BOH**
Rochdale	**ROCH** dayl
Rochefoucauld, La	rawsh foo **KOH**, la
Rochelle	roh **SHEL**
Rockefeller	**ROK** ə FEL ər
rococo	rə **KOH** koh
rodent	**ROHD** ənt
rodeo	**ROH** dee OH
rodeo (southwestern US)	roh **DAY** oh
Rodin	roh **DAN** (DAN French final *n*)
Rodino, Peter	roh **DEEN** oh
rodomontade	ROD ə mon **TAYD**
Roebling	**ROH** bling
roentgen, R-	**RENT** gən
Roethke, Theodore	**RET** kee
rogation	roh **GAY** shən
Roget	roh **ZHAY**
rogue	rohg
roguery	**ROH** gə ree
roguish	**ROH** gish
roil	roil
roister	**ROI** stər
Rojas	**ROH** hahs
role	rohl
roll	rohl
Rolland, Romain	raw **LAHN**, raw **MAN** (**LAHN** and **MAN** French final *n*)

---

o on, oh oat, oi boy, oo soon, oor poor, or for, ow cow, sh shush,
th thin, *th* this, u up, ur spur, uu book, *zh* pleasure

Rollo	**ROL** oh
Rölvaag, Ole	**ROHL** vahg, **OH** lə
roly-poly	**ROH** lee **POH** lee
Romaic	roh **MAY** ik
romaine	roh **MAYN**
Romains, Jules	raw **MAN, ZH**UUL (**MAN** French final *n*)
Roman	**ROH** mən
roman	roh **MAHN** (**MAHN** French final *n*)
roman à clef	roh **MAHN** ah **KLAY** (**MAHN** French final *n*)
romance, R-	roh **MANS**
Romanesque	ʀᴏʜ mə **NESK**
Romania	roh **MAY** nee ə
Romanic	roh **MAN** ik
Romanism	**ROH** mə ɴɪᴢ əm
Romano	roh **MAHN** oh
Romanov, Romanoff	**ROH** mə ɴᴀᴡꜰ
Romansh	roh **MANSH**
romantic	roh **MAN** tik
Romany	**ROM** ə nee
Rome	rohm
Romeo	**ROH** mee ᴏʜ
romero	roh **MAIR** oh
Rommany	**ROM** ə nee
Rommel	**ROM** əl
Romney	**ROM** nee
Romola	**ROM** ə lə
Romualdez, Benjamin	rom **WAHL** dez
Romulo	**ROM** yuu ʟᴏʜ
Romulus	**ROM** yə ləs
Roncalli, Angelo Giuseppe	rohn **KAH** lee, **AHN** jə loh jə **ZEP** ee
Roncesvalles	**RAHN** sə ᴠᴀʟᴢ
rondeau	**RON** doh
rondel	**RON** dəl
rondo	**RON** doh
Ronsard	rohn **SAHR** (rohn French final *n*)
Röntgen, r-	**RENT** gən
rood, R-	rood
Roodepoort-Maraisburg	**ROO** də ᴘᴜᴜʀᴛ mah **RAY** burk
rook	ruuk

ə ago, a at, ah calm, ahr dark, air care, aw saw, ay say, ch church
e bet, ee me, eer beer, hw what, i is, ī my, *n* French final n vin,

rookery	**RUUK** ə ree
rookie	**RUUK** ee
Roosevelt	**ROH** zə **VELT**
roque	rohk
Roquefort	**ROHK** fərt
roquet	roh **KAY**
rorqual	**ROR** kwəl
Rorschach	**ROR** shok
rosaceous	roh **ZAY** shəs
Rosales-Rivera, Mauricio	roh **SAH** les ree **VER** ə, maw **REE** see oh
Rosario	roh **ZAHR** ee **OH**
rosary	**ROH** zə ree
rosé	roh **ZAY**
Roseau	roh **ZOH**
Rosecrans	**ROHZ** krans
roseola	**ROH** zee **OH** lə
Rosetta	roh **ZET** ə
rosette	roh **ZET**
Rosh Hashana	**ROHSH** hah **SHAH** nah
Rosicrucian	**ROH** zə **KROO** shən
rosin	**ROZ** ən
Rosina	roh **ZEE** nə
Rosinante	**ROZ** ə **NAN** tee
Roslyn	**ROZ** lən
rosolio	roh **ZAW** lyoh
Rossel, Agda	**RU** sel, **AHG** dah
Rossetti	roh **SET** ee
Rossides, Zenon	roh **SEE** *th*ees, **ZEE** nuun
Rossi-Drago	**ROH** see **DRAH** goh
Rossini	roh **SEE** nee
Rostand	raw **STAHN** (**STAHN** French final *n*)
Rostenkowski, Daniel	**ROS** tən **KOW** skee
roster	**ROS** tər
Rostock	**ROS** tok
Rostov	**ROS** tof
Rostropovich, Mstislav	rah strah **PAW** veech, stis **LAHV**
rostrum	**ROS** trəm
rota, R-	**ROH** tə
Rotarian	roh **TAIR** ee ən
rotary, R-	**ROH** tə ree
rotative	**ROH** **TAY** tiv
rotatory	**ROH** tə **TOR** ee

o on, oh oat, oi boy, oo soon, oor poor, or for, ow cow, sh shush,
th thin, *th* this, u up, ur spur, uu book, *zh* pleasure

rote	roht
Rothschild	**RAWTH** chīld
Rothschild (French)	rawt **SHEELD**
rotifer	**ROH** tə fər
rotisserie	roh **TIS** ə ree
rotl	**ROT** əl
rotogravure	ROH tə grə **VYUUR**
rotor	**ROH** tər
Rotterdam	**ROT** ər DAM
rotund	roh **TUND**
rotunda	roh **TUN** də
Rouault	roo **OH**
Roubaix	roo **BE**
rouble	**ROO** bəl
roué	roo **AY**
Rouen	roo **AHN** (**AHN** French final *n*)
rouge	roo*zh*
Rouget de Lisle	roo **ZHAY** də **LEEL**
roulade	roo **LAHD**
rouleau	roo **LOH**
Rouleau, Raymond	roo **LOH**, ray **MOHN** (**MOHN** French final *n*)
roulette	roo **LET**
Roumania	roo **MAY** nee ə
roundel	**ROWN** dəl
roundelay	**ROWN** də LAY
roup	roop
rouse	rowz
Rousseau	roo **SOH**
Roussillon	ROO see **YOHN** (**YOHN** French final *n*)
route	root
routine	roo **TEEN**
roux	roo
Rovno	**RAWV** naw
rowan	**ROH** ən
rowdy	**ROW** dee (**ROW** as in *cow*)
Rowe	roh
rowel	**ROW** əl (**ROW** as in *cow*)
rowen	**ROW** ən (**ROW** as in *cow*)
Rowena	roh **WEE** nə
Rowne	**RUUV** ne
Roxana	rok **SAN** ə
Roxane	rok **SAN**

ə ago, a at, ah calm, ahr dark, air care, aw saw, ay say, ch church
e bet, ee me, eer beer, hw what, i is, ī my, *n* French final n vin,

Roxas	**ROH** hahs
Ruanda-Urundi	roo **AHN** də uu **RUUN** dee
Rubaiyat	**ROO** bī **YAHT**
rubato	roo **BAH** toh
rubble	**RUB** əl
rubefacient	**ROO** bə **FAY** shənt
rubella	roo **BEL** ə
Rubens	**ROO** bənz
rubeola	**ROO** bee **OH** lə
rubescent	ruu **BES** ənt
Rubicon	**ROO** bi **KON**
rubicund	**ROO** bī kənd
rubidium	ruu **BID** ee əm
rubiginous	ruu **BIJ** ə nəs
ruble	**ROO** bəl
rubric	**ROO** brik
ruche	roosh
rucksack	**RUK** sak
ruckus	**RUK** əs
ruction	**RUK** shən
rudbeckia	rud **BEK** ee ə
rudiment	**ROO** də mənt
rudimentary	**ROO** də **MEN** tə ree
Rudyard	**RUD** yərd
rue	roo
rueful	**ROO** fəl
ruffian	**RUF** ee ən
rufous	**ROO** fəs
Rugby	**RUG** bee
rugose	**ROO** gohs
Ruhr	ruur
ruinous	**ROO** ə nəs
Ruis	ruu **EES**
Ruisdael	**ROIS** dahl
Rukeyser	**ROO** kī zər
Rumania	roo **MAY** nee ə
rumba	**RUUM** bə
Rumelia	roo **MEEL** yə
ruminate	**ROO** mə **NAYT**
rummage	**RUM** ij
rummy	**RUM** ee
Rumpelstiltskin	**RUM** pəl **STILT** skin
runcible	**RUN** sə bəl

o on, oh oat, oi boy, oo soon, oor poor, or for, ow cow, sh shush,
th thin, *th* this, u up, ur spur, uu book, *zh* pleasure

runcinate	**RUN** sə **NAYT**
rune	roon
runic	**ROO** nik
runnel	**RUN** əl
Runnymede	**RUN** i **MEED**
Runyon	**RUN** yən
rupee	roo **PEE**
rupiah	roo **PEE** ə
Rupia, Paul Milyango	roo **PEE** ya, pawl mee lee **YAHN** goh
rupture	**RUP** chər
rural	**RUUR** əl
Rurik	**RUUR** ik
Rusakov, Konstantin	roo sah **KAWF**, kon ston **TYEEN**
ruse	rooz
rusk, R-	rusk
Ruskin	**RUS** kən
russet	**RUS** ət
Russia	**RUSH** ə
Russian	**RUSH** ən
Russophile	**RUS** ə **FĪL**
Russophobe	**RUS** ə **FOHB**
rustic	**RUS** tik
rusticate	**RUS** ti **KAYT**
rusticity	rus **TIS** ə tee
rustle	**RUS** əl
rut	rut
rutabaga	**ROO** tə **BAY** gə
ruth, R-	rooth
Ruthenia	roo **THEE** nee ə
ruthenium	roo **THEE** nee əm
Rutherford, Rutherfurd	**RU*TH*** ər fərd
rutherfordium	**RU*TH*** ər **FOR** dee əm
ruthless	**ROOTH** ləs
Rutland	**RUT** lənd
Rutledge	**RUT** lij
Ruwenzori	**ROO** wən **ZOR** ee
Ruysdael	**ROIS** dahl
Ruyter	**ROI** tər
Ruzicka, Leopold	**ROO** *ZH*EECH kah, **LAY** oh pawlt
Rwanda	ruu **WAHN** də
Ryazan	ryah **ZAHN**
Ryder	**RĪ** dər

ə ago, a at, ah calm, ahr dark, air care, aw saw, ay say, ch church
e bet, ee me, eer beer, hw what, i is, ī my, *n* French final n vin,

ryot	**RĪ** ət
Ryswick	**RIZ** wik
Ryukyu	ryoo kyoo
Rzeszow	**ZH**E shuuf

S

Saar	sahr
Saarbrucken	**SAHR** bruuk ən
Saarinen	**SAHR** ə nən
Saba	**SAY** bə
Sabac	**SHAH** bahts
Sabaean	sə **BEE** ən
Sabaoth	**SAB** ee **OTH**
sabbath	**SAB** əth
Sabbatical, s-	sə **BAT** i kəl
Sabean	sə **BEE** ən
Sabena	sə **BEE** nə
saber	**SAY** bər
Sabin	**SAY** bin
Sabina	sə **BEE** nə
Sabine (ancient Italy)	**SAY** bīn
Sabine (Texas)	sə **BEEN**
sabot	**SA** boh
sabotage	**SAB** ə **TAHZH**
saboteur	**SAB** ə **TUR**
sabra, S-	**SAH** brə
sabre	**SAY** bər
sabretache	**SAY** bər **TASH**
Sabrina	sə **BREE** nə
sac, S-	sak
Sacagawea	**SAK** ə jə **WEE** ə
saccharide	**SAK** ə **RĪD**
saccharine	**SAK** ə rən
Sacco	**SAK** oh
sacerdotal	**SAS** ər **DOHT** əl
sachem	**SAY** chəm
sachet	sa **SHAY**
Sacheverell	sə **SHEV** ər əl
Sachs (German)	zahks
Sachs (US)	saks

---

o **on**, oh **oat**, oi **boy**, oo **soon**, oor **poor**, or **for**, ow **cow**, sh **shush**,
th **thin**, *th* **this**, u **up**, ur **spur**, uu **book**, *zh* **pleasure**

sacral (near the sacrum)	SAK rəl
sacral (holy)	SAYK rəl
sacrament	SAK rə mənt
sacramental	SAK rə MEN təl
Sacramento	SAK rə MEN toh
sacrarium	sə KRAIR ee əm
sacrifice	SAK rə FĪS
sacrificial	SAK rə FISH əl
sacrilege	SAK rə lij
sacrilegious	SAK rə LEE jəs
sacristan	SAK rə stən
sacristy	SAK rə stee
sacroiliac	SAK roh IL ee AK
sacrosanct	SAK roh SANGT
sacrum	SAK rəm
Sadat, Anwar	sah DOT, ON wahr
Sadducean	SAJ ə SEE ən
Sadducee	SAJ ə SEE
Sade	sahd
sadism	SAY diz əm
sadist	SAY dəst
sadistic	sə DIS tik
Sadowa	SAH daw VAH
safari	sə FAHR ee
saffron	SAF rən
Safid Rud	sa FEED ROOD
Safire, William	SAF īr
saga	SAH gə
sagacious	sə GAY shəs
sagacity	sə GAS ə tee
sagamore	SAG ə MOR
Sagan, Carl	SAY gən
Sagan, Françoise	sa GAHN, frahn SWAHZ (GAHN and frahn French final n)
Saghalien	SAH gahl YEN
Saginaw	SAG ə NAW
Sagitta	sə JIT ə
sagittal	SAJ ə təl
Sagittarius	SAJ ə TAIR ee əs
sago, S-	SAY goh
saguaro	sə WAH roh
Saguenay	SAG ə NAY

ə ago, a at, ah calm, ahr dark, air care, aw saw, ay say, ch church
e bet, ee me, eer beer, hw what, i is, ī my, n French final n vin,

Sahara	sə HAR ə
sahib, S-	SAH ib
said	sed
Saida	SAH ee DAH
saiga	SĪ gə
Saigon	sī GON
St. Albans	saynt AWL bənz
St. Augustine	saynt AW gə STEEN
Saint Bernard	SAYNT bər NAHRD
St.-Cloud (France)	san KLOO (san French final *n*)
St. Cloud (US)	saynt KLOWD (KLOWD rhymes with *loud*)
St. Croix	saynt KROI
St. Denis	SAN də NEE (SAN French final *n*)
Ste. Anne de Beaupré	saynt AN də boh PRAY
Sainte-Beuve	sant BUUV
St.-Étienne	SAN tay TYEN (SAN French final *n*)
Saint-Exupéry	SAN teg zuu pay REE (SAN French final *n*)
Saint-Gaudens	saynt GAWD ənz
St.-Germain	san *zh*air MAN (san and MAN French final *n*)
St. Gotthard	saynt GOT ərd
St. Helena	SAYNT hə LEE nə
St. Helier	saynt HEL yər
St. Laurent	san loh RAHN (san and RAHN French final *n*)
St.-Lô	san LOH (san French final *n*)
St. Louis (Missouri)	saynt LOO əs
Saint Lucia	saynt LOO shə
St.-Malo	san ma LOH (san French final *n*)
St.-Mihiel	san mee YEL (san French final *n*)
St.-Moritz	SAYNT mə RITS
St.-Nazaire	san na ZAIR (san French final *n*)
St.-Ouen	san TWAHN (san and TWAHN French final *n*)
St.-Pierre	san PYAIR (san French final *n*)
Saint-Saëns	san SAHN (san and SAHN French final *n*)
Saintsbury	SAYNTS bə ree
Saint-Simon	san see MAWN (san and MAWN French final *n*)
St. Tropez	san troh PAY (san French final *n*)

o on, oh oat, oi boy, oo soon, oor poor, or for, ow cow, sh shush,
th thin, *th* this, u up, ur spur, uu book, *zh* pleasure

Saipan	sī **PAN**
saith	seth
sake (drink)	**SAH** ke
Sakhalin	**SAK** ə LEEN
Sakharov, Andrei	**SAH** kə RAWF, ahn **DRAY**
Saki	**SAH** kee
Sakurauchi, Yoshio	sah koo rah oo chee, yoh shee oh
salaam	sə **LAHM**
salacious	sə **LAY** shəs
salacity	sə **LAS** ə tee
Saladin	**SAL** ə din
Salado	sah **LAH** doh
Salam, Abdus	sah **LAHM**, **AHB** duus
Salamanca	SAL ə **MANG** kə
salamander	**SAL** ə MAN dər
Salambria	sə **LAM** bree ə
salami	sə **LAH** mee
Salamis	**SAL** ə mis
salary	**SAL** ə ree
Sala y Gómez	SAHL ə ee **GOH** MAYS
Salazar	SAL ə **ZAHR**
Salcedo, Luis Moreno	sal **SAY** doh, loo **EES** moh **RE** noh
Saleh, Ali Abdullah	**SAH** lay, **AH** lee **AHB** doo lah
Salem	**SAY** ləm
saleratus	SAL ə **RAY** təs
Salerno	sə **LER** noh
Salesian	sə **LEE** zhən
Salic	**SAY** lik
salicylate	sə **LIS** ə LAYT
Salida	sə **LĪ** də
salience	**SAY** lyəns
salient	**SAY** lyənt
Salim, Salim Ahmed	sah **LEEM**, sah **LEEM AH** med
Salina, s-	sə **LĪ** nə
Salinas	sə **LEE** nəs
saline	**SAY** leen
Salinger	**SAL** ən jər
Salisbury	**SAWLZ** ber ee
Salish	**SAY** lish
Salishan	**SAY** lish ən
saliva	sə **LĪ** və
salivary	**SAL** ə VER ee
salivate	**SAL** ə VAYT

ə ago, a at, ah calm, ahr dark, air care, aw saw, ay say, ch church
e bet, ee me, eer beer, hw what, i is, ī my, *n* French final n vin,

Salk	sawk
Sallah, Ousman Ahmadou	SAH lah, OOS mahn AH mah doo
Sallam, Mohamed Abdulaziz	sah LAHM, moh HAHM ed AHB dool ah SEEZ
Sallust	SAL əst
salmagundi	SAL mə GUN dee
salmi	SAL mee
salmon, S-	SAM ən
salmonella	SAL mə NEL ə
Salome	sə LOH mee
Salomé (opera)	SAL ə MAY
salon	sə LON
Salonika	SAL ə NEE kə
salsa	SAWL sə
salsify	SAL sə FĪ
saltarello	SAL tə REL oh
Saltillo	sahl TEE yaw
Salton	SAWL tən
salubrious	sə LOO bree əs
salubrity	sə LOO brə tee
Saluki	sə LOO kee
Salus	SAY ləs
salutary	SAL yə TER ee
salutation	SAL yə TAY shən
salutatorian	sə LOO tə TOR ee ən
salute	sə LOOT
Salvador, El	SAL və DOR, el
salvage	SAL vij
salve (hail)	SAHL way
salve (ointment)	sav
salve (salvage)	salv
salver	SAL vər
salvia	SAL vee ə
salvo	SAL voh
Salween	SAL ween
Salzburg	SAWLZ burg
samadhi	sə MAH dee
Samantha	sə MAN thə
Samar	SAH mahr
Samaria	sə MA ree ə
Samaritan	sə MA rə tən
samarium	sə MA ree əm

o on, oh oat, oi boy, oo soon, oor poor, or for, ow cow, sh shush,
th thin, *th* this, u up, ur spur, uu book, *zh* pleasure

Samarkand	SAM ər KAND
Samarra	sə MAHR ə
samarskite	sə MAHR skīt
samba	SAHM bə
samisen	SAM ə SEN
samite	SAM īt
samizdat	SAH meez DOT
Samoa	sə MOH ə
Samos	SAY mos
Samothrace	SAM ə THRAYS
samovar	SAM ə VAHR
Samoyed	SAM ə YED
sampan	SAM pan
Sampang	SAHM pahng
samphire	SAM fīr
Samson	SAM sən
Samsun	sahm SUUN
samurai	SAM ə RĪ
Sanaa, San'a	sah NAH
San Agustín	sahn AH guu STEEN
San Andreas	san an DRAY əs
San Andrés	sahn ahn DRES
San Angelo	san AN jə loh
San Antonio	SAN an TOH nee oh
sanatorium	SAN ə TOR ee əm
San Benito	SAN bə NEE toh
San Bernardino	SAN BUR nər DEE noh
Sancho Panza	SAHN choh PAHN zə
San Clemente	SAN klə MEN tee
San Cristóbal	SAN kris TOH bəl
sanctify	SANGK tə FĪ
sanctimonious	SANGK tə MOH nee əs
sanctimony	SANGK tə MOH nee
sanctuary	SANGK choo ER ee
sanctum	SANGK təm
sanctum sanctorum	SANGK təm SANGK TOR əm
Sanctus	SANGK təs
sandarac	SAN də RAK
Sandefjord	SAH nə FYOR
sandhi	SAN dee
San Diego	SAN dee AY goh
Sandinist	SAN də nəst
Sandinista	SAN də NEES tə

ə ago, a at, ah calm, ahr dark, air care, aw saw, ay say, ch church
e bet, ee me, eer beer, hw what, i is, ī my, n French final n vin,

Sandino, Augusto César	sahn DEE noh, ow GOOS toh SAY sahr
Sándor, Šandor	SHAHN dor
Sandor (US)	SAN dər
Sandusky	san DUS kee
Sandys, Duncan	SANDZ, DUNG kən
San Fernando	SAN fər NAN doh
San Francisco	SAN frən SIS koh
San Gabriel	san GAY bree əl
sangaree	SANG gə REE
San Gennaro	SAN jen NAIR oh
Sanger	SANG ər
sang-froid	sahn FRWAH (sahn French final *n*)
Sangre de Cristo	SANG gre de KRIS toh
sangria	sang GREE ə
Sangsomsack, Bounkeut	sahng suum sahk, boon kuut
sanguinary	SANG gwə NER ee
sanguine	SANG gwən
sanguineous	sang GWIN ee əs
Sanhedrin	san HED rən
sanitarium	SAN ə TAIR ee əm
sanitary	SAN ə TER ee
sanitation	SAN ə TAY shən
sanity	SAN ə tee
San Jacinto	SAN jə SIN toh
San Joaquín	SAN waw KEEN
San Jorge	sahn HAWR he
San Jose (California)	SAN hoh ZAY
San José (Spanish)	SAHN haw SE
San Juan	san HWAHN
Sankhya	SAHNG kyə
San Luis Obispo	san LOO əs ə BIS poh
San Luis Potosí	sahn loo EES paw taw SEE
San Marino	SAN mə REE noh
San Martín	SAHN mahr TEEN
San Remo	san REE moh
sans	sanz
San Salvador	san SAL və DOR
sans-culotte	sahn kuu LUT (sahn French final *n*)
San Sebastian	SAN si BAS chən
sansei	sahn say
Sanskrit	SAN skrit

o on, oh oat, oi boy, oo soon, oor poor, or for, ow cow, sh shush,
th thin, *th* this, u up, ur spur, uu book, *zh* pleasure

sans serif	SANZ SER əf
sans souci	sahn soo SEE (sahn French final *n*)
Santa (in English names)	SAN tə
Santa (in Spanish and Italian names)	SAHN tah
Santa Barbara	SAN tə BAHR bə rə
Santa Catalina	SAN tə KAT ə LEE nə
Santa Claus	SAN tə KLAWZ
Santa Cruz	SAN tə KROOZ
Santa Fe	SAN tə FAY
Santa María	SAHN tah mah REE ah
Santa Monica	SAN tə MON ə kə
Santander	SAHN tahn DAIR
Santayana	SAN tee AN ə
Santiago	SAN tee AH goh
Santiago de Cuba	SAHN tee AH goh de KOO bah
Santo Domingo	SAN toh də MING goh
Santos	SAHN tuus
São Francisco	SOWN frahn SEES kuu (SOWN as in *town*)
São Luiz	sown LWEES (sown as in *town*)
São Miguel	SOWN mee GEL (SOWN as in *town*)
Saône	sohn
São Paulo	sown POW luu (sown as in *town*)
Saorstat Eireann	SAIR stawt AIR ən
São Salvador	sown SAHL və DAWR (sown as in *town*)
São Tomé	SOWN tə MAY (SOWN as in *town*)
sapajou	SAP ə JOO
sapid	SAP əd
sapience	SAY pee əns
sapient	SAY pee ənt
sapodilla	SAP ə DIL ə
saponaceous	SAP ə NAY shəs
saponify	sə PON ə FĪ
sapor	SAY pər
saporific	SAP ə RIF ik
sapota	sə POH tə
sapper	SAP ər
Sapphic, s-	SAF ik
Sapphira	sə FĪ rə
sapphire	SAF īr

ə ago, a at, ah calm, ahr dark, air care, aw saw, ay say, ch church
e bet, ee me, eer beer, hw what, i is, ī my, *n* French final n vin,

sapphism	**SAF** iz əm
Sappho	**SAF** oh
Sapporo	sah poh roh
saprolite	**SAP** rə **LĪT**
saprophyte	**SAP** rə **FĪT**
sapsago	sap **SAY** goh
Saqqara	sə **KAH** rə
saraband	**SA** rə **BAND**
Saracen	**SA** rə sən
Saracoglu	sah **RAH** jaw gluu
Saragossa	**SAR** ə **GOS** ə
Sarajevo	**SA** rə **YAY** voh
Saran	sə **RAN**
Saranac	**SAR** ə **NAK**
Sarasota	**SAR** ə **SOH** tə
Saratoga	**SAR** ə **TOH** gə
Saratov	sah **RAH** tawf
Sarawak	sə **RAH** wahk
Sarbanes, Paul	**SAHR** baynz
sarcasm	**SAHR** kaz əm
sarcastic	sahr **KAS** tik
sarcenet	**SAHRS** nət
sarcoma	sahr **KOH** mə
sarcomatosis	sahr **KOH** mə **TOH** sis
sarcomatous	sahr **KOH** mə təs
sarcophagi	sahr **KOF** ə **GĪ**
sarcophagus	sahr **KOF** ə gəs
sarcous	**SAHR** kəs
sardine	sahr **DEEN**
Sardinia	sahr **DIN** ee ə
sardonic	sahr **DON** ik
sardonyx	sahr **DON** iks
Sardou	sahr **DOO**
sargasso, S-	sahr **GAS** oh
sargassum	sahr **GAS** əm
Sargent	**SAHR** jənt
sari	**SAH** ree
Sarkis, Elias	**SAHR** kəs
sarong	sə **RONG**
Sarouk	sər **OOK**
Sarpedon	sahr **PEE** dən
Sarrante, Nathalie	sah **RAHNT**, nah tah **LEE**
Sarré, Massamba	**SAHR**, mah **SAHM** bah

o on, oh oat, oi boy, oo soon, oor poor, or for, ow cow, sh shush,
th thin, *th* this, u up, ur spur, uu book, *zh* pleasure

sarsaparilla	SAS pə RIL ə
sarsenet	SAHRS nət
Sarto	SAHR toh
sartorial	sahr TOR ee əl
sartorius	sahr TOR ee əs
Sartre	SAHR trə
sashay	sa SHAY
Saskatchewan	sas KACH ə WAHN
Saskatoon, s-	SAS kə TOON
sasquatch, S-	SAS kwach
sassaby	SAS ə bee
sassafras	SAS ə FRAS
Sassenach	SAS ə nak
Sassoon	sa SOON
Sassou-Nguesso, Denis	SA soo ən GWAY soo, də NEE
satanic, S-	sə TAN ik
Satanism, s-	SAY tə NIZ əm
sateen	sa TEEN
satellite	SAT ə LĪT
satiate (a)	SAY shee ət
satiate (v)	SAY shee AYT
Satie	sa TEE
satiety	sə TĪ ə tee
satire	SA tīr
satirical	sə TIR i kəl
satirize	SAT ə RĪZ
Sato, Eisaku	sah toh, ay sah koo
satori	sah TOR ee
satrap	SAY trap
satrapy	SAY trə pee
Satsuma, s-	sah tsoo mah
saturant	SACH ər ənt
saturate	SACH ə RAYT
Saturday	SAT ər DAY
Saturn	SAT ərn
Saturnalia, s-	SAT ər NAY lee ə
Saturnian, s-	sə TUR nee ən
saturnine	SAT ər NĪN
Satyagraha	SUT yə GRU hə
satyr	SAY tər
satyriasis	SAY tə RĪ ə sis
satyric	sə TIR ik
Saud	sah OOD

ə ago, a at, ah calm, ahr dark, air care, aw saw, ay say, ch church
e bet, ee me, eer beer, hw what, i is, ī my, n French final n vin,

Saudi Arabia	sah **OO** dee ə **RAY** bee ə
sauerbraten	**SOW** ər **BRAH** tən (**SOW** as in *cow*)
sauerkraut	**SOW** ər **KROWT** (**SOW** as in *cow*, **KROWT** as in *out*)
Sauk	sawk
Sault Sainte Marie	**SOO SAYNT** mə **REE**
sauna	**SOW** nə (**SOW** as in *cow*)
saunter	**SAWN** tər
Saurashtra	sow **RUSH** trə (sow as in *cow*)
saurian	**SOR** ee ən
sauropod	**SOR** ə **POD**
sausage	**SAW** sij
sauté	soh **TAY**
sauterne	soh **TURN**
Sauternes	soh **TAIRN**
sauve qui peut	sohv kee **PUU**
sauvignon blanc	**SOH** veen **YAWN BLAHN** (**YAWN** and **BLAHN** French final *n*)
Sava	**SAH** vah
savage	**SAV** ij
Savaii	sah **VI** ee
Savalas, Telly	sə **VAH** ləs, **TEL** ee
Savang Vatthana	sah **VAHNG** vah **TAH** nah
savanna	sə **VAN** ə
savant	sa **VAHN** (**VAHN** French final *n*)
savate	sa **VAHT**
savior, S-	**SAY** vyər
savoir faire	**SAV** wahr **FAIR**
Savonarola	**SAV** ə nə **ROH** lə
savor	**SAY** vər
savory	**SAY** və ree
Savoy, s-	sə **VOI**
Savoyard	**SA** voi **AHRD**
savvy	**SAV** ee
Sawatch	sə **WACH**
Saw Hlaing	saw hling
Saxe-Coburg-Gotha	**SAKS KOH** burg **GOH** thə
saxifrage	**SAK** sə frij
Saxon	**SAK** sən
Saxony	**SAK** sə nee
saxophone	**SAK** sə **FOHN**
Sayan	sah **YAHN**
says	sez

---

o on, oh oat, oi boy, oo soon, oor poor, or for, ow cow, sh shush,
th thin, *th* this, u up, ur spur, uu book, *zh* pleasure

Scaasi	**SKAH** see
scabies	**SKAY** beez
scabious	**SKAY** bee əs
scabrous	**SKAB** rəs
Scafell	**SKAW** fel
scaffold	**SKAF** əld
scagliola	skal **YOH** lə
scaife	skayf
scalar	**SKAY** lər
scalawag	**SKAL** ə **WAG**
scald	skawld
scalene	**SKAY** leen
scallion	**SKAL** yən
scallop	**SKAL** əp
scallywag	**SKAL** ə **WAG**
scalpel	**SKAL** pəl
Scanderbeg	**SKAN** dər **BEG**
Scandia	**SKAN** dee ə
Scandian	**SKAN** dee ən
Scandinavia	**SKAN** də **NAY** vee ə
scandium	**SKAN** dee əm
scansion	**SKAN** shən
Scapa Flow	**SKAP** ə **FLOH**
scapegoat	**SKAYP** goht
scapula	**SKAP** yə lə
scapular	**SKAP** ə lər
scarab	**SKAR** əb
scarce	skairs
scarify	**SKAR** ə **FĪ**
Scarlatti	skahr **LAHT** ee
scathe	skay*th*
scatological	**SKAT** ə **LOJ** i kəl
scatology	skə **TOL** ə jee
scavenge	**SKAV** ənj
scavenger	**SKAV** ən jər
scenario	sə **NA** ree oh
scenic	**SEE** nik
scepter	**SEP** tər
Schaghticoke	**SKAT** ə **KOHK**
Scharnhorst	**SHAHRN** howrst
Schawlow, Arthur	**SHAW** loh
schedule	**SKEJ** ool
Scheherazade	shə **HER** ə **ZAH** də (**HER** as in *herring*)

ə ago, a at, ah calm, ahr dark, air care, aw saw, ay say, ch church
e bet, ee me, eer beer, hw what, i is, ī my, *n* French final n vin,

Scheldt	skelt
Schell	shel
Scheltema, Hugo	**SKEL** tə mə, **HYOO** hoh (**SKEL** *K* almost an *H* sound)
schema	**SKEE** mə
schematic	ski **MAT** ik
schematize	**SKEE** mə **TĪZ**
scheme	skeem
Schenectady	skə **NEK** tə dee
Scherchen	**SHAIR** shin
scherzando	skair **TSAHN** doh
scherzo	**SKAIR** tsoh
Scheyven	**SHI** vən
Schiaffino, Rosanna	shah **FEE** noh, roh **ZAH** nah
Schick	shik
Schiller, s-	**SHIL** ər
schilling	**SHIL** ing
schipperke	**SKIP** ər kee
Schippers	**SHIP** ərz
schism	**SIZ** əm
schismatic	siz **MAT** ik
schist	shist
schistosome	**SHIS** tə **SOHM**
schistosomiasis	**SHIS** tə soh **MĪ** ə səs
schizoid	**SKIT** soid
schizomycete	**SKIZ** oh mī **SEET**
schizomycosis	**SKIZ** oh mī **KOH** səs
schizophrenia	**SKIT** sə **FREE** nee ə
schizophrenic	**SKIT** sə **FREN** ik
schlemiel	shlə **MEEL**
Schleswig	**SHLES** wig
Schliemann	**SHLEE** mahn
Schluter, Poul	**SHLOO** tər, pohl
schmaltz	shmahlts
Schmidt, Helmut	**SHMIT, HEL** moot
schmierkase	**SHMEER KAYZ** ə
schnapps	shnahps
schnauzer	**SHNOW** zər
schnitzel	**SHNIT** səl
Schnitzler	**SHNITS** lər
schnorkel	**SHNOR** kəl
schnorrer	**SHNOR** ər
Schoenberg	**SHURN** burg

o on, oh oat, oi boy, oo soon, oor poor, or for, ow cow, sh shush,
th thin, *th* this, u up, ur spur, uu book, *zh* pleasure

scholastic	skə **LAS** tik
scholasticism	skə **LAS** tə **SIZ** əm
scholia	**SKOH** lee ə
scholiast	**SKOH** lee **AST**
scholium	**SKOH** lee əm
Schönberg	**SHURN** burg
schoolhouse	**SKOOL** hows
schooner	**SKOO** nər
Schoonover	**SKOO** noh vər
Schopenhauer	**SHOH** pən **HOW** ər
schottische	**SHOT** ish
Schottky	**SHOT** kee
Schrödinger	**SHRAY** ding ər
Schroeder, Patricia	**SHROHD** ər
Schubert	**SHOO** bərt
Schueler	**SHOO** lər
Schumann	**SHOO** mahn
Schurmann	**SHUR** mahn
Schurz	shurts
schuss	shuus
Schuster	**SHOO** stər
Schutzstaffel	**SHUUTS SHTAH** fəl
Schuyler	**SKĪ** lər
Schuylkill	**SKOOL** kil
schwa	shwah
Schwab	shwahb
Schwarzkopf	**SHVAHRTS** kupf
Schweitzer	**SHVĪT** zər
Schwengel	**SHWENG** gəl
Schwinger	**SHWING** ər
Schwitters	**SHVIT** ərz
sciamachy	sī **AM** ə kee
sciatica	sī **AT** i kə
sciential	sī **EN** shəl
scientology	**SĪ** ən **TOL** ə jee
scilicet	**SIL** i **SET**
Scilla	**SIL** ə
Scilly	**SIL** ee
scimitar	**SIM** ə tər
scintilla	sin **TIL** ə
scintillate	**SIN** tə **LAYT**
sciolism	**SĪ** ə **LIZ** əm
sciolist	**SĪ** ə ləst

ə ago, a at, ah calm, ahr dark, air care, aw saw, ay say, ch church
e bet, ee me, eer beer, hw what, i is, ī my, *n* French final n vin,

scion	SĪ ən
Scioto	sī OH tə
Scipio	SIP ee OH
Scituate	SICH oo it
scleritis	sklə RĪ təs
scleroma	sklə ROH mə
sclerosis	sklə ROH səs
Scofield	SKOH feeld
scoliosis	SKOH lee OH səs
sconce	skons
scone	skohn
Scone	skoon
scopolamine	skə POL ə MEEN
scorbutic	skor BYOO tik
scoria	SKOR ee ə
Scorpio	SKOR pee OH
scorpion	SKOR pee ən
Scorpius	SKOR pee əs
scotia, S-	SKOH shə
Scotism	SKOH tiz əm
Scotland	SKOT lənd
scotoma	skə TOH mə
Scourby	SKOR bee
scourge	skurj
Scowcroft	SKOW krawft (SKOW as in *cow*)
scrabble	SKRAB əl
scrag	skrag
scrapple	SKRAP əl
Scriabin	skree AH bin
scrimshaw	SKRIM shaw
scriptorium	skrip TOR ee əm
scrivener	SKRIV nər
scrod	skrod
scrofula	SKROF yə lə
scrofulous	SKROF yə ləs
Scrooge	skrooj
scrotum	SKROH təm
scrounge	skrownj
scrumptious	SKRUM shəs
scrunch	skrunch
scruple	SKROO pəl
scrupulous	SKROO pyə ləs
scuba	SKOO bə

o on, oh oat, oi boy, oo soon, oor poor, or for, ow cow, sh shush,
th thin, *th* this, u up, ur spur, uu book, *zh* pleasure

scull	skul
scullery	**SKUL** ə ree
scullion	**SKUL** yən
sculptor	**SKULP** tər
sculpture	**SKULP** chər
sculpturesque	**SKULP** chə **RESK**
scurrility	skə **RIL** ə tee
scurrilous	**SKUR** ə ləs
scurry	**SKUR** ee
scurvy	**SKUR** vee
Scutari	**SKOO** tah **REE**
scutcheon	**SKUCH** ən
scuttlebutt	**SKUT** əl **BUT**
scutum, S-	**SKYOO** təm
Scylla	**SIL** ə
scyphus	**SĪ** fəs
scythe	sī*th*
Scythian	**SITH** ee ən
Sealyham	**SEE** lee əm
seamstress	**SEEM** strəs
Seanad Eireann	**SAN** ahd **AIR** ən
séance	**SAY** ahns
Seattle	see **AT** əl
sebaceous	si **BAY** shəs
Sebastopol	si **BAS** tə **POHL**
Sebe, Chief Lennox	**SAY** bay, cheef **LEN** əks
seborrhea	**SEB** ə **REE** ə
Sebrell	se **BREL**
sebum	**SEE** bəm
secant	**SEE** kant
secco	**SEK** oh
secession	si **SESH** ən
seclude	si **KLOOD**
Seconal	**SEK** ə **NAWL**
second	**SEK** ənd
secondary	**SEK** ən **DER** ee
secondhand	**SEK** ənd **HAND**
secondo	si **KOHN** doh
Secrest	**SEE** krəst
secretaire	**SEK** rə **TAIR**
secretarial	**SEK** rə **TA** ree əl
secretariat	**SEK** rə **TA** ree ət
secretary	**SEK** rə **TER** ee

ə ago, a at, ah calm, ahr dark, air care, aw saw, ay say, ch church
e bet, ee me, eer beer, hw what, i is, ī my, *n* French final n vin,

secrete	si **KREET**
secretion	si **KREE** shən
secretive	**SEE** krə tiv
secretiveness	**SEE** krə tiv nəs
sectarian	sek **TA** ree ən
sector	**SEK** tər
secular	**SEK** yə lər
Secunderabad	sə **KUN** dər ə **BAD**
Sedalia	si **DAY** lee ə
sedan, S-	si **DAN**
sedate	si **DAYT**
sedation	si **DAY** shən
sedative	**SED** ə tiv
sedentary	**SED** ən **TER** ee
Seder	**SAY** dər
sediment	**SED** ə mənt
sedition	si **DISH** ən
seduce	si **DOOS**
seductive	si **DUK** tiv
sedulity	si **DYOO** lə tee
sedulous	**SEJ** ə ləs
sedum	**SEE** dəm
Seferis, Giorgos	se **FE** rees, ye **OR** ee uus
Segni, Antonio	**SAY** nyee, ahn **TOH** nyoh
segno	**SAY** nyoh
sego	**SEE** goh
Segovia	sə **GOH** vee ə
Segré, Emilio	say **GRAY**, ay **MEE** lyoh
segregate (n)	**SEG** ri gət
segregate (v)	**SEG** ri **GAYT**
segregation	**SEG** ri **GAY** shən
segregationist	**SEG** ri **GAY** shə nist
segregative	**SEG** ri **GAY** tiv
segue	**SEG** way
seguidilla	**SEG** ə **DEEL** yah
seicento	say **CHEN** toh
seiche	saysh
seidel, S-	**SID** əl
Seidlitz	**SED** ləts
seigneur	say **NYUR**
seignior	**SAYN** yər
seigniorage	**SAYN** yər ij
seigniory	**SAYN** yə ree

---

o on, oh oat, oi boy, oo soon, oor poor, or for, ow cow, sh shush,
th thin, *th* this, u up, ur spur, uu book, *zh* pleasure

Seine	sen
seine	sayn
seismic	SĪZ mik
seismograph	SĪZ mə GRAF
seismology	sīz MOL ə jee
selah	SEE lə
Selangor	sə LAHNG gawr
Selene	sə LEE nee
selenite	SEL ə NĪT
selenium	sə LEE nee əm
selenology	SEL ə NOL ə jee
Seleucus	sə LOO kəs
Seljuk	sel JOOK
Selma	SEL mə
Seltzer, s-	SELT sər
selvage	SEL vij
semantic	si MAN tik
semaphore	SEM ə FOR
Semarang	sə MAHR ahng
semasiology	si MAY see OL ə jee
semblance	SEM bləns
Sembrich	ZEM brik
semé	sə MAY
Semedo, Inacio	se MEE doo, in NAH see oh
Semele	SEM ə LEE
semen	SEE mən
Semenov, Nikolai	sə MYAW nof, nee koh LĪ
semester	sə MES tər
seminal	SEM ə nəl
seminar	SEM ə NAHR
seminary	SEM ə NER ee
Seminole	SEM ə NOHL
semiology	SEE mee OL ə jee
semiotic	SEE mee OT ik
semiotics	SEE mee OT iks
Semiramis	si MIR ə mis
Semite	SEM īt
Semitic	sə MIT ik
Semitism	SEM ə TIZ əm
semolina	SEM ə LEE nə
semper fidelis	SEM pər fə DAY ləs
semper paratus	SEM pər pə RAH təs
sempiternal	SEM pi TUR nəl

ə ago, a at, ah calm, ahr dark, air care, aw saw, ay say, ch church
e bet, ee me, eer beer, hw what, i is, ī my, n French final n vin,

senate	**SEN** ət
senator	**SEN** ə tər
Sendai	sen dī
Seneca	**SEN** ə kə
Senecan	**SEN** ə kən
Senegal	**SEN** ə **GAWL**
Senegalese	**SEN** ə gə **LEEZ**
Senegambia	**SEN** ə **GAM** bee ə
senescent	si **NES** ənt
seneschal	**SEN** ə shəl
Senghor, Leopold	seng **GAWR**, lee oh **POHLD**
senhor	si **NYOR**
senhora	si **NYOR** ə
senhorita	**SEE** nyə **REE** tə
senile	**SEE** nīl
senility	si **NIL** ə tee
Senlac	**SEN** lak
senna	**SEN** ə
Sennacherib	sə **NAK** ər əb
senor	sayn **YOR**
senora	sayn **YOR** ə
senorita	sayn yə **REET** ə
senseless	**SENS** ləs
sensibility	**SEN** sə **BIL** ə tee
sensorium	sen **SOR** ee əm
sensory	**SEN** sə ree
sensual	**SEN** shoo əl
sensuality	**SEN** shoo **AL** ə tee
sensuous	**SEN** shoo əs
sentential	sen **TEN** shəl
sententious	sen **TEN** shəs
sentience	**SEN** shəns
sentient	**SEN** shənt
sentimental	**SEN** tə **MEN** təl
sentinel	**SEN** tə nəl
sentry	**SEN** tree
Senusi, Senussi	se **NOO** see
Seoul	sohl
sepal	**SEE** pəl
separate (a, n)	**SEP** ə rət
separate (v)	**SEP** ə **RAYT**
separatist	**SEP** ə rə təst
Sephardic	sə **FAHR** dik

---

o on, oh oat, oi boy, oo soon, oor poor, or for, ow cow, sh shush,
th thin, *th* this, u up, ur spur, uu book, *zh* pleasure

Sephardim	sə **FAHR** dəm
sepia	**SEE** pee ə
Sepik	**SAY** pik
sepiolite	**SEE** pee ə **LĪT**
sepoy	**SEE** poi
Seppälä	**SE** pa la
seppuku	se poo koo
sepsis	**SEP** səs
September	sep **TEM** bər
septenary	**SEP** tə **NER** ee
septennial	sep **TEN** ee əl
septet	sep **TET**
septic	**SEP** tik
septicemia	**SEP** tə **SEE** mee ə
septuagenarian	**SEP** choo ə jə **NAIR** ee ən
Septuagesima	**SEP** choo ə **JES** ə mə
Septuagint	**SEP** too ə **JINT**
septum	**SEP** təm
septuple	**SEP** tə pəl
sepulcher	**SEP** əl kər
sepulchral	sə **PUL** krəl
sepulture	**SEP** əl chər
Sepulveda, Bernardo	sep ool **VAY** də, ber **NAHR** doh
sequacious	si **KWAY** shəs
sequel	**SEE** kwəl
sequela	si **KWEL** ə
sequelae	si **KWEL** ee
sequence	**SEE** kwəns
sequential	si **KWEN** shəl
sequester	si **KWES** tər
sequestration	**SEK** wəs **TRAY** shən
sequin	**SEE** kwən
sequoia	si **KWOI** ə
Serafina	**SER** ə **FEE** nə
seraglio	sə **RAL** yoh
serai	sə **RAH** ee
seral	**SI** rəl
Serang	se **RAHNG**
serape	sə **RAH** pee
seraph	**SER** əf
seraphic	sə **RAF** ik
seraphim	**SER** ə fim
Serapis	sə **RAY** pəs

ə ago, a at, ah calm, ahr dark, air care, aw saw, ay say, ch church
e bet, ee me, eer beer, hw what, i is, ī my, *n* French final n vin,

Serb	surb
Serbia	**SUR** bee ə
Serbo-Croatian	**SUR** boh kroh **AY** shən
sere	seer
Serena	sə **REE** nə
serenade	**SER** ə **NAYD**
serendipity	**SER** ən **DIP** ə tee
serene	sə **REEN**
Serengeti	**SER** ən **GET** ee
serenity	sə **REN** ə tee
serf	surf
serge, S-	surj
sergeant	**SAHR** jənt
seriatim	**SI** ree **AY** təm
sericulture	**SER** ə **KUL** chər
serif	**SER** əf
serigraph	**SER** ə **GRAF**
serigraphy	sə **RIG** rə fee
Serkin	**SUR** kin
serology	sə **ROL** ə jee
serous	**SI** rəs
Serov	**SE** rof
Serpens	**SUR** pənz
serpent	**SUR** pənt
serpentine	**SUR** pən **TEEN**
serpiginous	sər **PIJ** ə nəs
serried	**SER** eed
serum	**SI** rəm
serval	**SUR** vəl
serviette	**SUR** vee **ET**
servile	**SUR** vəl
servility	sur **VIL** ə tee
sesame	**SES** ə mee
sesquicentennial	**SES** kwi sen **TEN** ee əl
sesquipedalian	**SES** kwi pi **DAYL** yən
sesterce	**SES** tərs
sestet	ses **TET**
sestina	ses **TEE** nə
setaceous	si **TAY** shəs
settecento	se te **CHEN** taw
settee	se **TEE**
Seurat	suu **RAH**
Sevareid	**SEV** ə **RĪD**

o on, oh oat, oi boy, oo soon, oor poor, or for, ow cow, sh shush,
th thin, *th* this, u up, ur spur, uu book, *zh* pleasure

Sevastopol	sə **VAS** tə **POHL**
sever	**SEV** ər
several	**SEV** ə rəl
severance	**SEV** ə rəns
severe	sə **VIR**
severity	sə **VER** ə tee
Severn	**SEV** ərn
Severnaya Zemlya	**SEV** ər nə **YAH ZEM** lee **AH**
seviche	sə **VEE** chay
Sévigné	say vee **NYAY**
Sevilla	say **VEE** lyah
Sevilla-Sacasa,	say **VEEL** yah sah **KAH** sah, gil
Guillermo	**YAIR** moh
Seville	sə **VIL**
Sèvres	**SE** vrə
sewage	**SOO** ij
Seward	**SOO** ərd
sewerage	**SOO** ər ij
Sewrajsing, Inderdew	**SOO** rahj **SING, IN** dər **DOO**
sexagenarian	**SEK** sə jə **NAIR** ee ən
Sexagesima	**SEK** sə **JES** ə mə
sexennial	sek **SEN** ée əl
sexology	sek **SOL** ə jee
sextain	**SEKS** tayn
Sextans	**SEKS** tənz
sextant	**SEKS** tənt
sextet	seks **TET**
sextuple	seks **TOO** pəl
sextuplet	seks **TUP** lət
sexuality	**SEK** shoo **AL** ə tee
Seychelles	say **SHELZ**
Seydoux, Roger	say **DOO**, roh **ZHAY**
sforzando	sfort **SAHN** doh
sforzato	sfort **SAH** toh
Shaanxi	shahn shee
Shabuoth	shə **VOO** oht
shadchan	**SHAHD** kən
shaddock	**SHAD** ək
Shadrach	**SHAD** rak
Shaerf, Adolph	**SHAIRF, AH** dawlf
Shaftesbury	**SHAFTS** bə ree
Shagari, Alhaji Shehu	shah **GAH** ree, ahl **HAH** jee she **HOO**
shagreen	sha **GREEN**

ə ago, a at, ah calm, ahr dark, air care, aw saw, ay say, ch church
e bet, ee me, eer beer, hw what, i is, ī my, *n* French final n vin,

shah, S-	shah
Shahada	shah **HAH** dah
Shahjahanpur	**SHAH** jə **HAHN PUUR**
shaitan, S-	shī **TAHN**
Shakespeare	**SHAYK** spir
Shakespearean	shayk **SPIR** ee ən
shako	**SHAK** oh
Shakti, s-	**SHUK** tee
shalloon	sha **LOON**
shallop	**SHAL** əp
shallot	shə **LOT**
shalom	shah **LOHM**
shaman	**SHAH** mən
Shamash	**SHAH** mahsh
Shamir, Yitzhak	shah **MEER**, **YITS** hahk
shammes	**SHAH** məs
shamus	**SHAY** məs
Shan	shahn
Shandong	shahn dawng
shandrydan	**SHAN** dree **DAN**
shandygaff	**SHAN** dee **GAF**
Shanghai	shang **HĪ**
Shangri-La	**SHANG** gri **LAH**
Shansi	shahn see
shan't	shant
Shantung, s-	shan **TUNG**
Shanxi	shahn shi
Shara	**SHAHR** ə
Shari	**SHAH** ree
sharif	shə **REEF**
Sharon	**SHA** rən
Sharon, Ariel	shah **ROHN**, **AHR** ee əl
Sharra	**SHAHR** ə
shashlik	shahsh **LIK**
Shasta	**SHAS** tə
Shatt-al-Arab	**SHAT** al **AHR** ahb
Shavian	**SHAY** vee ən
Shavuoth	shə **VOO** oht
Shaw, s-	shaw
Shcharansky, Anatoly	shah **RAHN** skee, ah nah **TOH** lee
Shcherbakov	**CHER** bə **KAWF**
Shcherbitsky, Vladimir	shair **BEET** skee, vlah **DEE** mir
shea (tree)	shee

o on, oh oat, oi boy, oo soon, oor poor, or for, ow cow, sh shush,
th thin, *th* this, u up, ur spur, uu book, *zh* pleasure

Shea (stadium)	shay
sheath	sheeth
sheathe	shee*th*
Sheba	**SHEE** bə
shebang	shə **BANG**
shebeen	shə **BEEN**
Shebeli	shay **BE** li
Sheboygan	shi **BOI** gən
Shechinah	shə **KEE** nə
Shehu, Mehmet	**SHAY** hoo, **MEM** et
sheik (handsome man)	sheek
sheikh (Arab chief)	shayk
Sheila	**SHEE** lə
sheitel	**SHAY** təl
shekel	**SHEK** əl
Shekinah	shə **KEE** nə
Sheldov, Anatoly	**SHEL** dawf, ah nah **TOH** lee
shellac	shə **LAK**
Shenandoah	SHEN ən **DOH** ə
shenanigan	shə **NAN** ə gən
Shensi	shen see
Shenyang	shən yahng
Sheol, s-	**SHEE** ohl
Shepard	**SHEP** ərd
shepherd	**SHEP** ərd
Sheraton	**SHER** ə tən
sherbet	**SHUR** bət
sherif	shə **REEF**
sheriff	**SHER** əf
Sherpa	**SHUR** pə
Shetland	**SHET** lənd
Shevardnadze, Eduard	shev ahrd **NAHD** zeh, ed **WAHRD**
Shevtsova, Ludmila	sheft **SOH** vah, lood **MEE** lah
Shevuoth	shə **VOO** oht
Shiah	**SHEE** ə
shiatsu	shee aht soo
shibboleth	**SHIB** ə ləth
shield	sheeld
shigellosis	SHIG ə **LOH** səs
Shih Tzu	shee **TSOO**
Shiite	**SHEE** īt
Shikoku	shee **KOH** koo
shillelagh	shə **LAY** lee

ə ago, a at, ah calm, ahr dark, air care, aw saw, ay say, ch church
e bet, ee me, eer beer, hw what, i is, ī my, *n* French final n vin,

Shillong	shi **LAWNG**
Shiloh	**SHĪ** loh
Shimizu	shi mee zoo
Shimonoseki	**SHEE** mə noh **SEK** ee
Shinnecock	**SHIN** ə kok
Shinto	**SHIN** toh
Shiraz	shee **RAHZ**
shirr	shur
shish kebab	**SHISH** kə **BOB**
shittah	**SHIT** ə
shittim	**SHIT** əm
Shiva	**SHEE** və
shivaree	**SHIV** ə **REE**
Shizuoka	shee zoo oh kah
shoal	shohl
shoat	shoht
shofar	**SHOH** fahr
shogun	**SHOH** guun
shogunate	**SHOH** gən ət
Sholapur	**SHOH** lə **PUUR**
Sholokhov	**SHAW** lə kawf
Sholom Aleichem	**SHOH** ləm ah **LAY** kəm
shone	shohn
shoran	**SHOR** an
short-lived	short līvd
Shoshone	shoh **SHOH** nee
Shostakovich	**SHOS** tə **KOH** vich
shrapnel	**SHRAP** nəl
Shreveport	**SHREEV** port
Shrewsbury	**SHROOZ** bə ree
shrive	shrīv
shrivel	**SHRIV** əl
shriven	**SHRIV** ən
Shriver	**SHRĪ** vər
Shropshire	**SHROP** shər
shroud	shrowd (rhymes with *crowd*)
Shuf (mountains)	shoof
Shukairy, Ahmed	shoo **KĪ** ree, **AH** med
Shulamite	**SHOO** lə **MĪT**
Shuster	**SHUU** stər
Shvernik	**SHVAIR** nik
Sialkot	see **AHL** koht
Siam	sī **AM**

o on, oh oat, oi boy, oo soon, oor poor, or for, ow cow, sh shush,
th thin, *th* this, u up, ur spur, uu book, *zh* pleasure

siamang	SEE ə MANG
Sian	shee ahn
Sibelius	sə BAYL yəs
Siberia	sī BEER ee ə
sibilant	SIB ə lənt
sibling	SIB ling
Sibomana, Jean-Marie	see boh MAH nah, zhahn mah REE (zhahn French final n)
Sibyl, s-	SIB əl
sibylline, S-	SIB ə LEEN
sic	sik
siccative	SIK ə tiv
Sichuan	sich oo ahn
Sicilian	si SIL yən
Sicily	SIS ə lee
sickle	SIK əl
sic semper tyrannis	sik SEM pər tə RAN əs
sic transit gloria mundi	sik TRAN sət GLOH ree ah MUUN dee
Siddhartha	si DAHR tə
Siddons	SID ənz
siddur	SID uur
sidereal	sī DIR ee əl
siderite	SID ə RĪT
siderosis	SID ə ROH səs
sidewinder	SĪD WĪN dər
Sidi Barrani	SEE dee bah RAH nee
Sidikou, Abdou	see dee KOO, AHB doo
sidle	SĪ dəl
Sidon	SĪ dən
Sidonian	sī DOH nee ən
Sidra	SID rə
siècle	SYE klə
Siegbahn	SEEG bahn
Siegel	SEE gəl
Siegfried	SEEG freed
Sieglinde	see GLIN də
Siemens	SEE mənz
Siena	see EN ə
sienna	see EN ə
sierra, S-	see ER ə
Sierra Leone	see ER ə lee OH nee
Sierra Madre	see ER ə MAH dray

ə ago, a at, ah calm, ahr dark, air care, aw saw, ay say, ch church
e bet, ee me, eer beer, hw what, i is, ī my, n French final n vin,

Sierra Nevada	see **ER** ə nə **VAD** ə
siesta	see **ES** tə
sieve	siv
Sighisoara	**SEE** gee **SHWAH** rah
Sigismund	**SIJ** əs mənd
sigma	**SIG** mə
sigmoid	**SIG** moid
Sigmund	**SIG** mənd
signatory	**SIG** nə **TOR** ee
signet	**SIG** nət
significance	sig **NIF** i kəns
signor	seen **YOR**
signora	seen **YOR** ə
signore	seen **YOR** ay
Signoret, Simone	see nyaw **RAY**, see **MUN**
signorina	**SEEN** yə **REE** nə
signorino	**SEEN** yə **REE** noh
Sigurd	**SIG** ərd
Sihanouk, Norodom	**SEE** ə **NUUK**, **NOR** ə **DOM**
Sikandarabad	see **KUN** də rah **BAHD**
Sikh	seek
Sikkim	**SIK** im
Sikorsky	si ̲**KOR** skee
silage	**SĪ** lij
silenus, S-	sī **LEE** nəs
Siles, Hernan	**SEE** les, air **NAN**
Silesia, s-	sī **LEE** zhə
silhouette	**SIL** oo **ET**
silica	**SIL** i kə
silicate	**SIL** ə kayt
siliceous	sə **LISH** əs
silicic	sə **LIS** ik
silicon	**SIL** i kən
silicone	**SIL** ə **KOHN**
silicosis	**SIL** ə **KOH** səs
sillabub	**SIL** ə **BUB**
Sillanpää	**SIL** ən **PA**
Sillitoe	**SIL** i **TOH**
silo	**SĪ** loh
Siloam	sī **LOH** əm
Silone	si **LOH** nee
Silurian	sī **LUUR** ee ən
silva	**SIL** və

---

o on, oh oat, oi boy, oo soon, oor poor, or for, ow cow, sh shush,
th thin, *th* this, u up, ur spur, uu book, *zh* pleasure

Silvana	sil **VA** nə
Silvanus	sil **VAY** nəs
Silvia	**SIL** vee ə
silviculture	**SIL** və KUL chər
s'il vous plaît	seel voo **PLE**
Simchas Torah	SIMK əs **TOH** rə
Simenon, Georges	seem ə **NAWN, ZHAWRZH** (**NAWN** French final *n*)
Simeon	**SIM** ee ən
Simferopol	sim fe **RAW** pawl
simian	**SIM** ee ən
similar	**SIM** ə lər
similarity	SIM ə **LAR** ə tee
simile	**SIM** ə lee
similitude	si **MIL** ə TOOD
Simonetta	see moh **NE** tah
simoniac	sə **MOH** nee AK
Simonides	sī **MON** ə DEEZ
simonize, Simoniz	**SĪ** mə NĪZ
Simon Legree	**SĪ** mən lə **GREE**
Simonov, Konstantin	**SEE** mə nuf, kahn stahn **TEEN**
simony	**SIM** ə nee
simoom	sə **MOOM**
simoon	sə **MOON**
Simplon	**SIM** plon
simulacrum	SIM yə **LAY** krəm
simulcast	**SĪ** məl KAST
simultaneity	sī məl tə **NEE** ə tee
simultaneous	sī məl **TAY** nee əs
Sinai	**SĪ** nī
Sinaloa	SEEN ə **LOH** ə
Sinarquist	**SIN** ahr kist
Sinarquista	SIN ahr **KEES** tə
Sinbad	**SIN** bad
sincerity	sin **SER** ə tee
sine	sīn
sinecure	**SĪ** nə KYUUR
sine die	**SĪ** nee **DĪ** ee
sine qua non	**SEE** ne kwah **NOHN**
sinew	**SIN** yoo
sinewy	**SIN** yoo ee
sinfonia	SIN fə **NEE** ə
sinfonietta	SIN fən **YET** ə

ə ago, a at, ah calm, ahr dark, air care, aw saw, ay say, ch church
e bet, ee me, eer beer, hw what, i is, ī my, *n* French final n vin,

Singapore	**SING** gə **POR**
Singaraja, Singaradja	**SING** gah **RAH** jah
singe	sinj
Singer, Isaac Bashevis	**SING** ər, $\overline{I}$**Z** ək bah **SHAY** vəs
Singh	sing
Singhalese	**SING** gə **LEEZ**
singularity	**SING** gyə **LAR** ə tee
Sinhalese	**SIN** hə **LEEZ**
Sinicism	**SIN** i **SIZ** əm
sinister	**SIN** ə stər
sinistral	**SIN** ə strəl
sinistrality	**SIN** ə **STRAL** ə tee
Sinitic	si **NIT** ik
Sinkiang Uighur	**SHIN** jee ahng **WEE** gər
Sinn Fein	shin fayn
Sino-	**S**$\overline{I}$ noh
Sinology, s-	s$\overline{i}$ **NOL** ə jee
Sinon	**S**$\overline{I}$ non
sinuosity	**SIN** yoo **OS** ə tee
sinuous	**SIN** yoo əs
sinus	**S**$\overline{I}$ nəs
sinusitis	s$\overline{i}$ nə **S**$\overline{I}$ təs
sinusoidal	s$\overline{i}$ nə **SOID** əl
Siouan	**S**́**OO** ən
Sioux	soo
siphon	**S**$\overline{I}$ fən
Siqueiros	see **KAY** raws
siren	**S**$\overline{I}$ rən
Sirena	sə **REE** nə
sirenian	s$\overline{i}$ **REE** nee ən
Siret	si **RET**
Sirhan	**SEER** hahn
Sirius	**S**$\overline{I}$ ree əs
sirloin	**SUR** loin
sirocco	sə **ROK** oh
Siroky, Viliam	shee **ROH** kee, **VEEL** yahm
sirrah	**S**$\overline{I}$ rə
sisal	**S**$\overline{I}$ səl
Sisley	**SIZ** lee
Sismondi	sis **MON** dee
Sistine	**SIS** teen
sistrum	**SIS** trəm
Sisyphean	**SIS** ə **FEE** ən

o **on**, oh **oat**, oi **boy**, oo **soon**, oor **poor**, or **for**, ow **cow**, sh **shush**,
th **thin**, *th* **this**, u **up**, ur **spur**, uu **book**, *zh* **pleasure**

Sisyphus	**SIS** ə fəs
sitar	si **TAHR**
Sitka	**SIT** kə
sitology	sī **TOL** ə jee
sitomania	**sī** tə **MAY** nee ə
sitophobia	**sī** tə **FOH** bee ə
Sittang	**SI** tong
situate (a)	**SICH** oo ət
situate (v)	**SICH** oo **AYT**
situs	**SĪ** təs
Sitwell	**SIT** wəl
sitz	sits
Siva	**SEE** və
Sivas	see **VAHZ**
Siwa	**SEE** wə
Sixtine	**SIKS** teen
Sixtus	**SIKS** təs
sizar	**SĪ** zər
sjambok	sham **BOK**
Skagen	**SKAH** gən
Skagerrak	**SKAG** ə **RAK**
skald	skawld
skaldic	**SKAWL** dik
Skaneateles	**SKAN** ee **AT** ləs
skein	skayn
skeletal	**SKEL** ə təl
skew	skyoo
skewer	**SKYOO** ər
ski	skee
skirl	skurl
skirmish	**SKUR** mish
skiver	**SKĪ** vər
skivvy	**SKIV** ee
skoal	skohl
Skokie	**SKOH** kee
Skoplje	**SKAWP** lye
skulduggery	skul **DUG** ə ree
skulk	skulk
Skye	skī
slalom	**SLAH** ləm
slather	**SLA***TH* ər
slattern	**SLAT** ərn
Slav	slahv

slavey	**SLAY** vee
Slavic	**SLAH** vik
slavish	**SLAY** vish
Slavonia	slə **VOH** nee ə
Slavonic	slə **VON** ik
Slavophile	**SLAH** və **FĪL**
Slavophobe	**SLAH** və **FOHB**
Slavophobia	**SLAH** və **FOH** bee ə
sleazy	**SLEE** zee
sleigh	slay
sleight	slīt
sleuth	slooth
slew	sloo
Sligo	**SLĪ** goh
Slim, Mongi	sə **LEEM, MOHN** jee
Slim, Taïeb	sə **LEEM, TĪ** yəb
slither	**SLI***TH* ər
slithery	**SLI***TH* ə ree
sliver	**SLIV** ər
slivovitz	**SLIV** ə vits
Sliwa	**SLEE** wə
sloe	sloh
Sloka	**SLAW** kah
sloth	slawth
slough (cast off)	sluf
slough (marsh)	sloo
Slough of Despond	slow (as in *cow*)
Slovak	**SLOH** vak
Slovakia	sloh **VAH** kee ə
sloven	**SLUV** ən
Slovene	**SLOH** veen
Slovenia	sloh **VEE** nee ə
slovenly	**SLUV** ən lee
sluggard	**SLUG** ərd
sluice	sloos
slur	slur
Smetana	**SMET** ə nə
Smethwick	**SME***TH* ik
smidgen	**SMIJ** ən
smilax	**SMĪ** laks
smirch	smurch
smirk	smurk
smithy	**SMITH** ee

o **on**, oh **oat**, oi **boy**, oo **soon**, oor **poor**, or **for**, ow **cow**, sh **shush**,
th **thin**, *th* **this**, u **up**, ur **spur**, uu **book**, *zh* **pleasure**

smolder	**SMOHL** dər
Smolensk	smo **LENSK**
Smollett	**SMOL** ət
smolt	smohlt
smooch	smooch
smooth	smoo*th*
smorgasbord	**SMOR** gəs **BORD**
smorzando	smort **SAHN** doh
smother	**SMU***TH* ər
Smuts	smuts
Smyrna	**SMUR** nə
snafu	sna **FOO**
snivel	**SNIV** əl
snood	snood
snooker	**SNUUK** ər
snorkel	**SNOR** kəl
soave	soh **AH** vay
Sobhuza	soh **BOO** zə
Sobolev	**SAW** bah lef
sobriety	sə **BRĪ** ə tee
sobriquet	**SOH** bri **KAY**
soccer	**SOK** ər
Sochi	**SAW** chi
social	**SOH** shəl
sociality	soh shee **AL** ə tee
socialize	**SOH** shə **LĪZ**
societal	sə **SĪ** ə təl
society	sə **SĪ** ə tee
Socinian	soh **SIN** ee ən
Socinus	soh **SĪ** nəs
sociological	soh see ə **LOJ** i kəl
sociology	soh see **OL** ə jee
sociometry	soh see **OM** ə tree
sockdolager	sok **DOL** i jər
socket	**SOK** ət
sockeye	**SOK** ī
Socorro	sə **KAW** roh
Socotra	soh **KOH** trə
Socrates	**SOK** rə **TEEZ**
Socratic	sə **KRAT** ik
sodality	soh **DAL** ə tee
sodium	**SOH** dee əm
Sodom	**SOD** əm

ə ago, a at, ah calm, ahr dark, air care, aw saw, ay say, ch church
e bet, ee me, eer beer, hw what, i is, ī my, *n* French final n vin,

Sodomite, s-	SOD ə MĪT
sodomy	SOD ə mee
Soemba	SOOM bah
Soembawa	soom BAH wah
Soenda	SOON dah
Soerabaja	soo rah BAH yah
Soerakarta	soo rah KAHR tah
soffit	SOF ət
Sofia	SOH fee ə
soft	sawft
soften	SAW fən
Sogdian	SOG dee ən
Sogdiana	sog dee AY nə
soggy	SOG ee
Soho	SOH hoh
soi-disant	swah dee ZAHN (ZAHN French final *n*)
soigné	swahn YAY
soiree	swah RAY
Soissons	swah SAWN (SAWN French final *n*)
sojourn (n)	SOH jurn
sojourn (v)	soh JURN
solace	SOL əs
solar	SOH lər
solarium	soh LA ree əm
solarize	SOH lə RĪZ
Solarz	SOH lahrz
solder	SOD ər
solecism	SOL ə SIZ əm
Soledad	SOL ə DAD
solemn	SOL əm
solemnify	sə LEM nə FĪ
solemnity	sə LEM nə tee
solemnize	SOL əm NĪZ
solenoid	SOH lə NOID
Solent	SOH lənt
sol-fa	sohl FAH
solfatara	SOHL fə TAHR ə
solfeggio	sol FEJ oh
solicitor	sə LIS ə tər
solicitous	sə LIS ə təs
solidarity, S-	SOL ə DAR ə tee
solidify	sə LID ə FĪ
solidity	sə LID ə tee

o **on,** oh **oat,** oi **boy,** oo **soon,** oor **poor,** or **for,** ow **cow,** sh **shush,**
th **thin,** *th* **this,** u **up,** ur **spur,** uu **book,** *zh* **pleasure**

solidus	**SOL** ə dəs
solifidian	**SOL** ə **FID** ee ən
soliloquist	sə **LIL** ə kwəst
soliloquize	sə **LIL** ə **KWĪZ**
soliloquy	sə **LIL** ə kwee
solipsism	**SOL** əp **SIZ** əm
solipsist	**SOL** əp səst
solitaire	**SOL** ə **TAIR**
solitary	**SOL** ə **TER** ee
solo, S-	**SOH** loh
Solomentsev, Mikhail	səl am **YENT** sef, mee hī **EEL**
Solomon	**SOL** ə mən
Solon, s-	**SOH** lən
solstice	**SOHL** stəs
Solti	**SOHL** tee
soluble	**SOL** yə bəl
solus	**SOH** ləs
solute	**SOL** yoot
solution	sə **LOO** shən
Solvay	**SOL** vay
solve	solv
solvent	**SOL** vənt
Solway Firth	**SOL** way **FURTH**
Solzhenitsyn	**SOHL** zhə **NEET** sən
soma	**SOH** mə
Somali	soh **MAH** lee
Somalia	soh **MAH** lee ə
Somaliland	soh **MAH** lee **LAND**
somatic	soh **MAT** ik
somatology	**SOH** mə **TOL** ə jee
somber	**SOM** bər
sombrero	som **BRAIR** oh
somersault	**SUM** ər **SAWLT**
Somerset	**SUM** ər **SET**
Somerville	**SUM** ər **VIL**
somewhat	**SUM** hwot
Somme	sum
sommelier	**SUM** əl **YAY**
somnambulate	som **NAM** byə **LAYT**
somnambulation	som **NAM** byə **LAY** shən
somniferous	som **NIF** ər əs
somnolence	**SOM** nə ləns
Somnus	**SOM** nəs

ə ago, a at, ah calm, ahr dark, air care, aw saw, ay say, ch church
e bet, ee me, eer beer, hw what, i is, ī my, *n* French final n vin,

Somoza	saw **MAW** sah
sonant	**SOH** nənt
sonar	**SOH** nahr
sonata	sə **NAH** tə
sonatina	**SAHN** ə **TEE** nə
song	sawng
Song Renqiong	sawng run chee awng
sonic	**SAHN** ik
soniferous	sə **NIF** ər əs
Sonnambula, La	soh **NAHM** byoo **LAH**, lah
sonnet	**SAHN** ət
sonobuoy	**SAHN** oh **BOO** ee
Sonora (Mexico)	saw **NAW** rah
Sonora (US)	sə **NOR** ə
sonority	sə **NOR** ə tee
sonorous	**SAHN** ər əs
Soochow	soo joh
Soong	suung
soot	suut
sooth	sooth
soothe	soo*th*
Sophia	soh **FĪ** ə
sophism	**SOF** iz əm
sophist	**SOF** əst
sophisticate (n)	sə **FIS** ti kət
sophisticate (v)	sə **FIS** tə **KAYT**
sophistry	**SOF** ə stree
Sophocles	**SOF** ə **KLEEZ**
sophomore	**SOF** ə **MOR**
sophomoric	**SOF** ə **MOR** ik
soporific	**SOP** ə **RIF** ik
soprano	sə **PRAN** oh
Sopron	**SHAW** prawn
Sorata	saw **RAH** tə
sorbefacient	**SOR** bə **FAY** shənt
Sorbian	**SOR** bee ən
Sorbonne	sor **BUN**
sorcerer	**SOR** sə rər
sordid	**SOR** dəd
sordino	sor **DEE** noh
Sorenson	**SOR** ən sən
sorghum	**SOR** gəm
sorites	soh **RĪ** teez

o on, oh oat, oi boy, oo soon, oor poor, or for, ow cow, sh shush,
th thin, *th* this, u up, ur spur, uu book, *zh* pleasure

soroban	soh roh bahn
Soroptimist	sə **ROP** tə məst
sororicide	sə **ROR** ə **SĪD**
sorority	sə **ROR** ə tee
sorosis	sə **ROH** sis
sorrel	**SOR** əl
Sorrento	sə **REN** toh
sorrow	**SAHR** oh
sorry	**SAHR** ee
Sorsa, Kalevi	**SOR** sə, **KAH** lay vee
sortie	**SOR** tee
sortilege	**SOR** tə lij
Sosa-Rodriguez	**SOH** sah roh **DREE** gez
Sosnowiec	saws **NAW** vyets
sostenuto	**sos** tə **NOO** toh
Sotheby	S**UTH** bee
Sothern	S**UTH** ərn
sotto voce	**SOT** oh **VOH** chee
sou	soo
soubrette	soo **BRET**
soubriquet	**SOH** brə **KAY**
souchong	soo shawng
soufflé	soo **FLAY**
sough	sow (as in *cow*)
sought	sawt
souk	sook
Soulat, Robert	**SOO** lah, roh **BAIR**
Souleymane Ould Cheikh Sidya	soo lay **MAHN OOLT** chayk **SEE** dyah
soupçon	soop **SAWN** (**SAWN** French final *n*)
Souphanouvong	suu **FAH** noo vawng
sourdough	**SOWR** doh
Sousa	**SOO** zə
sousaphone	**SOO** zə **FOHN**
souse	sows (as in *louse*)
soutache	soo **TASH**
soutane	soo **TAHN**
Southampton	sowth **AMP** tən
southerly	S**UTH** ər lee
southern	S**UTH** ərn
Southey	**SOW** *th* ee (**SOW** as in *cow*)
Southwark	S**UTH** ərk

ə ago, a at, ah calm, ahr dark, air care, aw saw, ay say, ch church
e bet, ee me, eer beer, hw what, i is, ī my, *n* French final n vin,

Soutine	soo **TEEN**
Souvanna Phouma	suu **VAH** nə **FOO** mə
Souvannavong	suu vah nə **VAWNG**
souvenir	**SOO** və **NEER**
sou'wester	**SOW** **WES** tər (**SOW** as in *cow*)
sovereign	**SOV** ə rən
sovereignty	**SOV** ər ən tee
soviet, S-	**SOH** vee **ET**
sovietize	**SOH** vee ə **TĪZ**
sow (pig)	sow (as in *cow*)
sow (plant)	soh
Sow, Adam Malick	**SOH**, ə **DAHM MA** leek
Soweto	soh **WET** oh
spa, S-	spah
spado	**SPAY** doh
Spadolini, Giovanni	**SPAHD** əl **EE** nee, joh **VAHN** ni
spaetzle	**SHPET** slə
spaghetti	spə **GET** ee
Spain	spayn
Spalato	**SPAH** lah taw
spaniel	**SPAN** yəl
spanner	**SPAN** ər
Spartacus	**SPAHR** tə kəs
spasm	**SPAZ** əm
spasmodic	spaz **MOD** ik
spasmolytic	**SPAZ** mə **LIT** ik
Spasowski, Romuald	spa **SOF** skee, rom **OO** ahld
spastic	**SPAS** tik
spatial	**SPAY** shəl
spatterdash	**SPAT** ər **DASH**
spatterdock	**SPAT** ər **DOK**
spatula	**SPACH** ə lə
spatulate	**SPACH** ə lət
spavin	**SPAV** ən
spavined	**SPAV** ənd
spécialité	spe syah lee **TAY**
specialty	**SPESH** əl tee
specie	**SPEE** shee
species	**SPEE** sheez
specific	spi **SIF** ik
specify	**SPES** ə **FĪ**
specimen	**SPES** ə mən
speciosity	**SPEE** shee **OS** ə tee

o **on**, oh **oat**, oi **boy**, oo **soon**, oor **poor**, or **for**, ow **cow**, sh **shush**, th **thin**, *th* **this**, u **up**, ur **spur**, uu **book**, *zh* **pleasure**

specious	**SPEE** shəs
spectacle	**SPEK** tə kəl
spectacular	spek **TAK** yə lər
spectator	**SPEK** tay tər
specter	**SPEK** tər
spectral	**SPEK** trəl
spectre	**SPEK** tər
spectroscope	**SPEK** trə **SKOHP**
spectroscopic	**SPEK** trə **SKOP** ik
spectroscopy	spek **TROS** kə pee
spectrum	**SPEK** trəm
speculate	**SPEK** yə **LAYT**
speculum	**SPEK** yə ləm
speedometer	spi **DOM** ə tər
speiss	spīs
speleology	**SPEE** lee **OL** ə jee
spelunker	spi **LUNG** kər
Spencer, s-	**SPEN** sər
Spencerian	spen **SI** ree ən
Spengler	**SPENG** glər
Spenser	**SPEN** sər
Spenserian	spen **SEER** ee ən
sperm	spurm
spermaceti	**SPUR** mə **SET** ee
spermatozoon	**SPUR** mə tə **ZOH** ən
sphagnum	**SFAG** nəm
sphalerite	**SFAL** ə **RĪT**
sphenic	**SFEE** nik
sphere	sfeer
spherical	**SFER** i kəl
sphericity	sfe **RIS** ə tee
spheroid	**SFER** oid
spherule	**SFER** ool
spherulite	**SFER** ə **LĪT**
sphincter	**SFINGK** tər
sphinx, S-	sfingks
sphygmograph	**SFIG** mə **GRAF**
sphygmomanometer	**SFIG** moh mə **NOM** ə tər
sphygmus	**SFIG** məs
spica, S-	**SPĪ** kə
spiccato	spi **KAH** toh
spicule	**SPIK** yool
Spiegel, Der	**SHPEE** gəl, der

ə ago, a at, ah calm, ahr dark, air care, aw saw, ay say, ch church
e bet, ee me, eer beer, hw what, i is, ī my, n French final n vin,

spiegeleisen	**SPEE** gəl **Ī** zən
spiel	speel
Spielberg	**SPEEL** burg
spigot	**SPIG** ət
spikenard	**SPĪK** nahrd
spillage	**SPIL** ij
spillikin	**SPIL** ə kən
spinach	**SPIN** ich
spinal	**SPĪ** nəl
spindly	**SPIND** lee
spinel	spə **NEL** ---
spinet	**SPIN** ət
spinnaker	**SPIN** ə kər
Spinoza	spi **NOH** zə
Spinozism	spi **NOH** ziz əm
spiracle	**SPĪ** rə kəl
spiral	**SPĪ** rəl
spirant	**SPĪ** rənt
spirea	spī **REE** ə
spirit	**SPIR** ət
spiritoso	ꜱᴘɪʀ ə **TOH** soh
spiritual	**SPIR** i choo əl
spirituous	**SPIR** i choo əs
spiritus	**SPIR** i təs
spirochete	**SPĪ** rə ᴋᴇᴇᴛ
Spitsbergen	**SPITS** ʙᴜʀ gən
spittoon	spi **TOON**
spitz	spits
spitzenburg	**SPIT** sən ʙᴜʀɢ
splanchnic	**SPLANGK** nik
splanchnology	splangk **NOL** ə jee
splendor	**SPLEN** dər
splenetic	spli **NET** ik
splenius	**SPLEE** nee əs
Split	spleet
splurge	splurj
Spode	spohd
Spokane	spoh **KAN**
Spoleto	spoh **LE** toh
spoliate	**SPOH** lee ᴀʏᴛ
spoliation	ꜱᴘᴏʜ lee **AY** shən
spondaic	spon **DAY** ik
spondee	**SPON** dee

---

o on, oh oat, oi boy, oo soon, oor poor, or for, ow cow, sh shush,
th thin, *th* this, u up, ur spur, uu book, *zh* pleasure

spondylitis	SPON də LĪ təs
sponsion	SPON shən
sponson	SPON sən
spontaneity	SPON tə NEE ə tee
spontaneous	spon TAY nee əs
spoonerism	SPOO nə RIZ əm
spoor	spuur
Sporades	SPOR ə DEEZ
sporadic	spə RAD ik
spore	spor
Spotsylvania	SPOT sil VAY nee ə
springbok	SPRING bok
springe	sprinj
sprue	sproo
spumante	spoo MAHN te
spume	spyoom
spumoni	spuu MOH nee
spumous	SPYOO məs
spurious	SPYUUR ee əs
sputnik	SPUUT nik
sputum	SPYOO təm
Spuyten Duyvil	SPĪT ən DĪ vəl
squab	skwob
squad	skwod
squadron	SKWOD rən
squalid	SKWOL əd
squall	skwawl
squalor	SKWOL ər
squama	SKWAY mə
squamous	SKWAY məs
squander	SKWAHN dər
squash	skwosh
squeegee	SKWEE jee
squirearchy	SKWĪR AHR kee
squirrel	SKWUR əl
sri	shree
Sri Lanka	sree LAHNG kə
Srinagar	sree NUG ər
Srithirath, Soubanh	sree tee RAHT, soo bahn
Stabat Mater	STAH baht MAH ter
stabile (sculpture)	stay BEEL
stabilize	STAY bə LĪz
staccato	stə KAH toh

ə ago, a at, ah calm, ahr dark, air care, aw saw, ay say, ch church
e bet, ee me, eer beer, hw what, i is, ī my, n French final n vin,

Stader	**STAY** dər
stadia	**STAY** dee ə
stadium	**STAY** dee əm
Staebler	**STAY** blər
Staël, de	**STAHL**, də
stagnant	**STAG** nənt
staid	stayd
Stakhanovism	stə **KAH** nə **VIZ** əm
Stakhanovite	stə **KAH** nə **VĪT**
stalactite	stə **LAK** tĭt
stalag	**STAHL** ahg
stalagmite	stə **LAG** mīt
Stalin	**STAH** lən
Stalingrad	**STAH** lən **GRAD**
stalk	stawk
stallion	**STAL** yən
stalwart	**STAWL** wərt
Stambolić, Petar	**STAHM** boh leech, **PET** ər
Stamboul, Stambul	stahm **BOOL**
stamen	**STAY** mən
stamina	**STAM** ə nə
stampede	stam **PEED**
stanch	stawnch
stanchion	**STAN** chən
Standish	**STAN** dish
Stanford-Binet	**STAN** fərd bi **NAY**
Stanhope, s-	**STAN** əp
Stanislaus	**STAN** əs **LAWS**
Stanislav	stah ni **SLAHF**
Stanislavsky	**STAN** i **SLAHF** skee
Stanley	**STAN** lee
Stanovoi	**STAH** naw **VOI**
stanza	**STAN** zə
stanzaic	stan **ZAY** ik
stapes	**STAY** peez
staphylococci	**STAF** ə lə **KOK** sī
staphylococcus	**STAF** ə lə **KOK** əs
stasis	**STAY** səs
Stasiuk	**STAY** see ək
Staten Island	**STAT** ən
stationary, stationery	**STAY** shə **NER** ee
statism	**STAYT** iz əm
statist	**STAYT** əst

o on, oh oat, oi boy, oo soon, oor poor, or for, ow cow, sh shush,
th thin, *th* this, u up, ur spur, uu book, *zh* pleasure

statistic	stə TIS tik
statistician	STAT ə STISH ən
Statius	STAY shee əs
stator	STAY tər
statoscope	STAT ə SKOHP
statuary	STACH oo ER ee
statue	STACH oo
statuesque	STACH oo ESK
statuette	STACH oo ET
stature	STACH ər
status	STAYT əs
status quo	STAYT əs KWOH
status quo ante	STAH təs KWOH AHN tay
statute	STACH oot
statutory	STACH ə TOR ee
staunch	stawnch
Staunton	STAWN tən
Stavanger	stah VAHNG ər
stave	stayv
stead	sted
steak tartare	STAYK tahr TAHR
stealth	stelth
stealthy	STEL thee
stearic	stee AR ik
Stearns	sturnz
steatite	STEE ə TĪT
steatopygia	stee AT ə PIJ ee ə
steatopygic	stee AT ə PIJ ik
Steen, Jan	stayn, yahn
steenbok	STEEN bok
Stefanie	STEF ə nee
Stefansson	STEF ən sən
Steffens	STEF ənz
stegosaurus	STEG ə SOR əs
Steichen	STĪ kən
stein, S-	stīn
Steinbeck	STĪN bek
steinbok	STĪN bok
Steinem	STĪN əm
Steinmetz	STĪN mets
Steinway	STĪN way
stela	STEE lə
stelae	STEE lee

ə ago, a at, ah calm, ahr dark, air care, aw saw, ay say, ch church
e bet, ee me, eer beer, hw what, i is, ī my, *n* French final n vin,

stele (burial stone)	**STEE** lee
stele (botany)	steel
Stendhal	sten **DAHL**
stenographer	stə **NOG** rə fər
stenographic	**STEN** ə **GRAF** ik
stenosis	stə **NOH** səs
stenotype	**STEN** ə **TĪP**
stenotypy	**STEN** ə **TĪ** pee
Stentor, s-	**STEN** tor
stentorian	sten **TOR** ee ən
Stephanie	**STEF** ə nee
Stephen	**STEE** vən
steppe	step
stercoraceous	**STUR** kə **RAY** shəs
stereo	**STER** ee **OH**
stereophonic	**STER** ee ə **FON** ik
stereopticon	**STER** ee **OP** ti kən
stereoscope	**STER** ee ə **SKOHP**
stereotype	**STER** ee ə **TĪP**
sterile	**STER** əl
sterility	stə **RIL** ə tee
sterilize	**STER** ə **LĪz**
Stern	sturn
Sterne, Laurence	**STURN, LAW** rəns
sternum	**STUR** nəm
steroid	**STI** roid
sterol	**STI** rawl
stertorous	**STUR** tə rəs
stet	stet
stethoscope	**STETH** ə **SKOHP**
Stettin	shte **TEEN**
Steuben	**STOO** bən
Steubenville	**STOO** bən vil
stevedore	**STEE** və **DOR**
steward	**STOO** ərd
stewardess	**STOO** ərd əs
Stewart	**STOO** ərt
sthenic	**STHEN** ik
Stheno	**STHEE** noh
stibium	**STIB** ee əm
stibnite	**STIB** nīt
stich	stik
stichic	**STIK** ik

o on, oh oat, oi boy, oo soon, oor poor, or for, ow cow, sh shush, th thin, *th* this, u up, ur spur, uu book, *zh* pleasure

stichomythia	**STIK** ə **MITH** ee ə
Stieglitz	**STEEG** ləts
stifle	**STĪ** fəl
stigma	**STIG** mə
stigmata	stig **MAH** tə
stigmatic	stig **MAT** ik
stigmatism	**STIG** mə **TIZ** əm
stigmatize	**STIG** mə **TĪZ**
Stikker, Dirk	**STIK** ər, **DURK**
stilbestrol	stil **BES** trawl
stiletto	stə **LET** oh
Stilton	**STIL** tən
Stilwell	**STIL** wel
stimulant	**STIM** yə lənt
stimulus	**STIM** yə ləs
stipend	**STĪ** pend
stipulation	**STIP** yə **LAY** shən
stirpes	**STUR** peez
stirpiculture	**STUR** pə **KUL** chər
stirps	sturps
stirrup	**STI** rəp
stoa	**STOH** ə
stoat	stoht
stochastic	stoh **KAS** tik
stockade	stah **KAYD**
Stockholm	**STOK** hohm
stodgy	**STOJ** ee
stogy	**STOH** gee
Stoic, s-	**STOH** ik
stoichiometric	**STOI** kee ə **MET** rik
stoichiometry	**STOI** kee **OM** ə tree
Stoicism, s-	**STOH** ə **SIZ** əm
stolid	**STOL** əd
stolidity	stə **LID** ə tee
stolon	**STOH** lən
Stoltenberg, Gerhard	**SHTOHL** tən berg, **GAIR** hahrt
stoma	**STOH** mə
stomach	**STUM** ək
stomacher	**STUM** ə kər
stomachic	stə **MAK** ik
stomata	**STOH** mə tə
stomatitis	**STOH** mə **TĪ** təs
Stonehenge	**STOHN** henj

ə ago, a at, ah calm, ahr dark, air care, aw saw, ay say, ch church
e bet, ee me, eer beer, hw what, i is, ī my, n French final n vin,

stony	**STOH** nee
Stoph, Willi	**SHTAWF, VEE** lee
storied	**STOR** eed
Storting, Storthing	**STOR** ting
Stouffer	**STOH** fər
stoup	stoop
Stowe	stoh
strabismus	strə **BIZ** məs
Strabo	**STRAY** boh
strabotomy	strə **BOT** ə mee
Strachey	**STRAY** chee
Stradivari	**STRAH** dee **VAH** ree
Stradivarius	**STRAD** ə **VA** ree əs
strafe	strayf
straight	strayt
strait	strayt
straitjacket	**STRAYT JAK** ət
stramonium	strə **MOH** nee əm
straphanger	**STRAP HANG** ər
strappado	strə **PAY** doh
Strasbourg	strahz **BOOR**
strata	**STRAY** tə
stratagem	**STRAT** ə jəm
strategic	strə **TEE** jik
strategist	**STRAT** ə jəst
strategy	**STRAT** ə jee
Stratford-on-Avon	**STRAT** fərd on **AY** vən
strathspey	strath **SPAY**
stratification	**STRAT** ə fə **KAY** shən
stratocracy	strə **TOK** rə see
stratocumulus	**STRAY** toh **KYOO** myə ləs
stratosphere	**STRAT** ə **SFEER**
stratum	**STRAY** təm
stratus	**STRAY** təs
Straus, -s	strows (rhymes with *louse*)
Straus, -s (German)	shtrows (rhymes with *louse*)
Stravinsky	strə **VIN** skee
Streich	strīk
Streisand	**STRĪ** sənd
strength	strengkth
strenuous	**STREN** yə wəs
streptococcal	**STREP** tə **KOK** əl
streptococci	**STREP** tə **KOK** ī

o on, oh oat, oi boy, oo soon, oor poor, or for, ow cow, sh shush,
th thin, *th* this, u up, ur spur, uu book, *zh* pleasure

streptococcus	**STREP** tə **KOK** əs
streptomycin	**STREP** tə **MĪ** sən
stretta	**STRET** ə
stretto	**STRET** oh
stria	**STRĪ** ə
striated	**STRĪ** ay təd
stricture	**STRIK** chər
stringendo	strin **JEN** doh
stroboscope	**STROH** bə **SKOHP**
Stroessner, Alfredo	**STRES** nər, ahl **FRAY** *th*oh
Stromboli	**STRAWM** baw lee
stronger	**STRAWNG** gər
strongest	**STRAWNG** gəst
strontium	**STRON** chəm
strophe	**STROH** fee
strophic	**STROF** ik
Strozzi	**STRAWT** tsee
structure	**STRUK** chər
strudel	**SHTROO** dəl
strychnine	**STRIK** nīn
Stuart	**STOO** ərt
stubborn	**STUB** ərn
stucco	**STUK** oh
studding	**STUD** ing
studdingsail (nautical)	**STUN** səl
studio	**STOO** dee **OH**
studious	**STOO** dee əs
Stuka	**STOO** kə
stultification	**STUL** tə fə **KAY** shən
stultify	**STUL** tə **FĪ**
stumpage	**STUM** pij
stupa	**STOO** pə
stupe	stoop
stupefacient	**STOO** pə **FAY** shənt
stupefaction	**STOO** pə **FAK** shən
stupefy	**STOO** pə **FĪ**
stupendous	stuu **PEN** dəs
stupid	**STOO** pəd
stupor	**STOO** pər
sturgeon	**STUR** jən
Sturm und Drang	**SHTUURM** uunt **DRAHNG**
Stuttgart	**SHTUUT** gahrt
Stuyvesant	**STĪ** və sənt

ə ago, a at, ah calm, ahr dark, air care, aw saw, ay say, ch church
e bet, ee me, eer beer, hw what, i is, ī my, *n* French final n vin,

Stygian, s-	STIJ ee ən
stylet	STĪ lət
stylite	STĪ lit
stylograph	STĪ lə GRAF
stylus	STĪ ləs
stymie, stymy	STĪ mee
styptic	STIP tik
Styr	steer
styrene	STĪ reen
Styrofoam	STĪ rə FOHM
Styx	stiks
Suakin	SWAH kin
suasion	SWAY zhən
suave	swahv
suavity	SWAH və tee
subaltern	sub AWL tərn
subdue	səb DOO
Subic	SOO bik
subito	SOO bi TOH
subject (a, n)	SUB jikt
subject (v)	səb JEKT
subjective	səb JEK tiv
sub judice	sub JOO di SEE
subjugate	SUB jə GAYT
sublimate	SUB lə MAYT
subliminal	sub LIM ə nəl
subordinate (a, n)	sə BOR də nət
subordinate (v)	sə BOR də NAYT
suborn	sə BORN
Subotica, Subotitsa	SOO BAW tit sah
subpoena	sə PEE nə
sub rosa	sub ROH zə
subroutine	SUB roo TEEN
subsequent	SUB si kwənt
subsidence	səb SĪD əns
subsidiary	səb SID ee ER ee
subsidy	SUB sə dee
substance	SUB stəns
substantiate	səb STAN shee AYT
substantiation	səb STAN shee AY shən
substantive	SUB stən tiv
subterfuge	SUB tər FYOOJ
subterranean	SUB tə RAY nee ən

---

o **on,** oh **oat,** oi **boy,** oo **soon,** oor **poor,** or **for,** ow **cow,** sh **shush,**
th **thin,** *th* **this,** u **up,** ur **spur,** uu **book,** *zh* **pleasure**

subtle	**SUT** əl
subtlety	**SUT** əl tee
suburb	**SUB** urb
suburban	sə **BUR** bən
suburbanite	sə **BUR** bə **NĪT**
subversion	səb **VUR** *zh*ən
succedaneum	**SUK** sə **DAY** nee əm
succeed	sək **SEED**
success	sək **SES**
succinct	suk **SINGKT**
succor	**SUK** ər
succotash	**SUK** ə **TASH**
Succoth	**SUUK** əs
succuba	**SUK** yə bə
succubus	**SUK** yə bəs
succulent	**SUK** yə lənt
succumb	sə **KUM**
Suceava	suu **CHAH** vah
Süchow	soo joh
sucrose	**SOO** krohs
Sudan	soo **DAN**
Sudanese	soo də **NEEZ**
Sudanic	soo **DAN** ik
sudarium	soo **DAIR** ee əm
sudatorium	**SOOD** ə **TOR** ee əm
sudatory	**SOOD** ə **TOR** ee
Sudbury	**SUD** ber ee
Sudermann	**ZOO** dər **MAHN**
Sudeten	soo **DAY** tən
Sudetes	soo **DEE** teez
sudorific	soo də **RIF** ik
sue, S-	soo
suede	swayd
suet	**SOO** ət
Suetonius	**SOO** ə **TOH** nee əs
Suez	soo **EZ**
suffice	sə **FĪS**
sufficient	sə **FISH** ənt
suffix	**SUF** iks
suffocate	**SUF** ə **KAYT**
Suffolk	**SUF** ək
suffragan	**SUF** rə gən
suffrage	**SUF** rij

ə ago, a at, ah calm, ahr dark, air care, aw saw, ay say, ch church
e bet, ee me, eer beer, hw what, i is, ī my, *n* French final n vin,

suffragette	**SUF** rə **JET**
suffuse	sə **FYOOZ**
Sufi	**SOO** fee
Sufism	**SOO** fiz əm
suggest	səg **JEST**
suggestion	səg **JES** chən
Suharto	suu **HAHR** toh
suicidal	**SOO** ə **SĪ** dəl
suicide	**SOO** ə **sĪD**
sui generis	**soo** ee **JEN** ər əs
suitable	**SOO** tə bəl
suite	sweet
suitor	**SOO** tər
Sukarno	soo **KAHR** noh
sukiyaki	**SUUK** ee **YAH** kee
sukkah	**SUUK** ə
Sukkoth	**SUUK** əs
Sulaiman, Sadek	soo **LAY MAHN**, sah **DAY** jah **WAHD**
Jawad	
sulcus	**SUL** kəs
Suleiman	**SOO** lay **MAHN**
sulfa	**SUL** fə
sulfadiazine	**SUL** fə **DĪ** ə **ZEEN**
sulfanilamide	**SUL** fə **NIL** ə **MĪD**
sulfapyrazine	**SUL** fə **PIR** ə **ZEEN**
sulfapyridine	**SUL** fə **PIR** ə **DEEN**
sulfate	**SUL** fayt
sulfathiazole	**SUL** fə **THĪ** ə **ZOHL**
sulfide	**SUL** fīd
sulfonamide	sul **FON** ə **MĪD**
sulfonate	**SUL** fə **NAYT**
sulfone	**SUL** fohn
sulfonic	sul **FON** ik
sulfur	**SUL** fər
sulfureous	sul **FYUUR** ee əs
sulfuric	sul **FYUUR** ik
sulfurous	**SUL** fə rəs
Sulla	**SUL** ə
sullen	**SUL** ən
Sully, s-	**SUL** ee
sulphur	**SUL** fər
sultan, S-	**SUL** tən
sultana	sul **TAN** ə

---

o **on**, oh **oat**, oi **boy**, oo **soon**, oor **poor**, or **for**, ow **cow**, sh **shush**,
th **thin**, *th* **this**, u **up**, ur **spur**, uu **book**, *zh* **pleasure**

sultanate	**SUL** tə **NAYT**
Sulu	**SOO** loo
sumac	**SOO** mak
Sumatra	suu **MAH** trə
Sumba	**SOOM** bah
Sumbawa	soom **BAH** wah
Sumer	**SOO** mər
Sumerian	soo **MER** ee ən
sumi	soo mee
sumi-e	soo mee e
summa cum laude	**SUUM** ə kuum **LOWD** ə (**LOWD** as in *crowd*)
summary	**SUM** ə ree
summation	sə **MAY** shən
summersault	**SUM** ər **SAWLT**
summum bonum	**SUUM** əm **BOH** nəm
sumo	**SOO** moh
sumptuary	**SUMP** choo **ER** ee
sumptuous	**SUMP** choo əs
Sunda	**SUN** də
sundae	**SUN** day
Sunday	**SUN** day
Sunde	**SUUN** də
sundry	**SUN** dree
Sung	suung
Sun Myung Moon	sun myung moon
Sunna, -h	**SUUN** ə
Sunni	**SUUN** ee
Sunnite	**SUUN** īt
Sun Yat-sen	suun yaht sen
Sun Yün-hsüan	suun yuun shuu ahn
Suomenlinna	suu **AW** men **LIN** ə
Suomi	suu **AW** mee
super	**SOO** pər
superb	suu **PURB**
supercilious	soo pər **SIL** ee əs
superficial	soo pər **FISH** əl
superfluity	soo pər **FLOO** ə tee
superfluous	suu **PUR** floo əs
superheterodyne	soo pər **HET** ə rə **DĪN**
superintendent	soo pər in **TEN** dənt
superior, S-	suu **PIR** ee ər
superiority	suu **PIR** ee **OR** ə tee

ə ago, a at, ah calm, ahr dark, air care, aw saw, ay say, ch church
e bet, ee me, eer beer, hw what, i is, ī my, *n* French final n vin,

superlative	suu **PUR** lə tiv
supernal	suu **PUR** nəl
supernova	**soo** pər **NOH** və
supernumerary	**soo** pər **NOO** mə **RER** ee
supersede	**soo** pər **SEED**
supersonic	**soo** pər **SON** ik
superstition	**soo** pər **STISH** ən
superstitious	**soo** pər **STISH** əs
supine (a)	suu **PĪN**
supine (n)	**SOO** pīn
supplant	sə **PLANT**
supple	**SUP** əl
supplement (n)	**SUP** lə mənt
supplement (v)	**SUP** lə **MENT**
supplementary	**SUP** lə **MEN** tə ree
suppliant	**SUP** lee ənt
supplicant	**SUP** lə kənt
supplication	**SUP** lə **KAY** shən
supposition	**SUP** ə **ZISH** ən
suppository	sə **POZ** ə **TOR** ee
suppurate	**SUP** yə **RAYT**
suprarenal	**soo** prə **REEN** əl
supremacy	sə **PREM** ə see
supreme	sə **PREEM**
sura	**SUUR** ə
Surabaya	**SUUR** ə **BAH** yə
surah	**SUUR** ə
Surakarta	**SUUR** ə **KAHR** tə
Surat	sə **RAT**
surcease	sur **SEES**
surcingle	**SUR SING** gəl
surcoat	**SUR** koht
surd	surd
surety	**SHUUR** ə tee
surface	**SUR** fəs
surfactant	sər **FAK** tənt
surfeit	**SUR** fət
surgeon	**SUR** jən
surgery	**SUR** jə ree
Suribachi	**SUUR** ə **BAH** chee
Surinach	**SOO** ri nahk
Surinam	**SUUR** ə **NAHM**
Suriname	**SUUR** ə **NAHM** ə

o on, oh oat, oi boy, oo soon, oor poor, or for, ow cow, sh shush,
th thin, *th* this, u up, ur spur, uu book, *zh* pleasure

surly	SUR lee
surmise	sər MĪZ
surmount	sər MOWNT (MOWNT as in *count*)
surpass	sər PAS
surplice	SUR pləs
surplus	SUR pləs
surprise	sər PRĪZ
surrealism	sə REE ə LIZ əm
surrealist	sə REE ə ləst
surrealistic	sə REE ə LIS tik
surreptitious	SUR əp TISH əs
surrey, S-	SUR ee
surrogate (a, n)	SUR ə gət
surrogate (v)	SUR ə GAYT
sursum corda	SUUR səm KOR də
surtax	SUR taks
surtout	sər TOO
surveillance	sər VAY ləns
survey (n)	SUR vay
survey (v)	sər VAY
surveyor	sər VAY ər
Susa	SOO sah
susceptible	sə SEP tə bəl
sushi	soo shee
Suslov, Mikhail	SOOS lahf, mi kah EEL
suspect (a, n)	SUS pekt
suspect (v)	sə SPEKT
suspire	sə SPĪR
Susquehanna	SUS kwə HAN ə
Sussex	SUS iks
sustain	sə STAYN
sustenance	SUS tə nəns
susurration	SOO sə RAY shən
susurrus	suu SUR əs
Sutherland	SU*TH* ər lənd
sutler	SUT lər
sutra	SOO trə
suttee	su TEE
Sutter	SUT ər
suture	SOO chər
Suva	SOO vah
Suvorov	suu VAW rahf
Suwannee	sə WAH nee

ə ago, a at, ah calm, ahr dark, air care, aw saw, ay say, ch church
e bet, ee me, eer beer, hw what, i is, ī my, n French final n vin,

Suwon	soo wahn
suzerain	**SOO** zə rən
suzerainty	**SOO** zə rən tee
Suzhou	soo joh
Suzuki, Zenko	sə **ZOOK** ee, **ZEN** koh
Svalbard	**SVAHL** bahr
svelte	sfelt
Svengali	sfen **GAHL** ee
Svenska	**SVEN** skah
Sverdlovsk	sverd **LAWFSK**
Svoboda	svah **BAW** dah
Swabia	**SWAY** bee ə
swaddle	**SWOD** əl
Swadeshi, s-	swə **DAY** shee
Swahili	swah **HEE** lee
Swai, Nsilo	**SWĪ**, ən **SEE** loh
swami	**SWAH** mee
Swanee	**SWAH** nee
Swansea	**SWAHN** see
swaraj, S-	swə **RAHJ**
sward	swawrd
swarm	swawrm
swart, S-	swawrt
swarthy	**SWAWR** *th*ee
swastika	**SWAH** sti kə
Swat, s-	swaht
swatch	swahch
swath	swahth
swathe	swah*th*
Swazi	**SWAH** zee
Swaziland	**SWAH** zee **LAND**
Sweden	**SWEE** dən
Swedenborg	**SWEE** dən **BORG**
Swedenborgian	**SWEE** dən **BOR** gee ən
sweetbread	**SWEET** bred
swerve	swurv
Swigert, Jack	**SWĪ** gərt
Swinburne	**SWIN** bərn
Swithin, Swithun	**SWI***TH* ən
Switzerland	**SWIT** sər lənd
sword	sawrd
Sybarite, s-	**SIB** ə **RĪT**
Sybaritic, s-	**SIB** ə **RIT** ik

---

o on, oh oat, oi boy, oo soon, oor poor, or for, ow cow, sh shush,
th thin, *th* this, u up, ur spur, uu book, *zh* pleasure

Sybil	**SIB** əl
sycamore	**SIK** ə **MOR**
sycophancy	**SIK** ə fən see
sycophant	**SIK** ə fənt
sycophantic	**SIK** ə **FAN** tik
sycosis	sī **KOH** səs
Sydney	**SID** nee
syllabary	**SIL** ə **BER** ee
syllabic	si **LAB** ik
syllabify	sə **LAB** ə **FĪ**
syllabub	**SIL** ə **BUB**
syllabus	**SIL** ə bəs
syllepsis	sə **LEP** səs
syllogism	**SIL** ə **JIZ** əm
sylph	silf
sylphid	**SIL** fəd
Sylphides	seel **FEED**
sylvan	**SIL** vən
sylvite	**SIL** vīt
symbiosis	**SIM** bee **OH** sis
symbiotic	**SIM** bee **OT** ik
symbol	**SIM** bəl
symbolism	**SIM** bə **LIZ** əm
symmetrical	sə **MET** ri kəl
symmetry	**SIM** ə tree
symposium	sim **POH** zee əm
symptom	**SIMP** təm
symptomatic	**SIM** tə **MAT** ik
synagogical	**SIN** ə **GOJ** i kəl
synagogue	**SIN** ə **GOG**
Synanon	**SIN** ə **NON**
synapse	**SIN** aps
synapses	sə **NAP** seez
synapsis	sə **NAP** səs
synchronic	sin **KRON** ik
synchronism	**SING** krə **NIZ** əm
synchronize	**SING** krə **NĪZ**
synchronous	**SING** krə nəs
synchrotron	**SING** krə **TRON**
synclinal	sin **KLĪN** əl
syncline	**SIN** klīn
syncopate	**SING** kə **PAYT**
syncope	**SING** kə pee

ə ago, a at, ah calm, ahr dark, air care, aw saw, ay say, ch church
e bet, ee me, eer beer, hw what, i is, ī my, n French final n vin,

syncretism	SIN krə TIZ əm
syndetic	sin DET ik
syndic	SIN dik
syndicalism	SIN di kə LIZ əm
syndicate (a, n)	SIN də kət
syndicate (v)	SIN də KAYT
syndrome	SIN drohm
synecdoche	sə NEK də kee
synergism	SIN ər JIZ əm
synergistic	SIN ər JIS tik
synergy	SIN ər jee
synesis	SIN ə səs
Synge	sing
synizesis	SIN ə ZEE səs
synod	SIN əd
synodical	sə NOD i kəl
synonymity	SIN ə NIM ə tee
synonymous	sə NON ə məs
synonymy	sə NON ə mee
synopses	sə NOP seez
synopsis	sə NOP səs
syntactic	sin TAK tik
syntheses	SIN thə seez
synthesis	SIN thə səs
synthesize	SIN thə sīz
synthetic	sin THET ik
syphilis	SIF ə ləs
syphilitic	SIF ə LIT ik
syphilology	SIF ə LOL ə jee
Syracuse	SI rə KYOOS
Syr Darya	sir DAHR yah
Syria	SI ree ə
Syriac	SI ree AK
Syrian	SI ree ən
syringa	sə RING gə
syringe	sə RINJ
syrinx, S-	SI ringks
syrup	SI rəp
systaltic	si STAWL tik
systematic	SIS tə MAT ik
systematist	SIS tə mə tist
systemic	si STEM ik
systole	SIS tə LEE

---

o **on**, oh **oat**, oi **boy**, oo **soon**, oor **poor**, or **for**, ow **cow**, sh **shush**, th **thin**, *th* **this**, u **up**, ur **spur**, uu **book**, *zh* **pleasure**

systolic	si **STOL** ik
syzygy	**SIZ** ə jee
Szczecin	**SHCHET** seen
Szechwan	sech wahn
Szent-Györgyi	saynt **JOR** jee
Szepes	**SE** pesh
Szilard	**ZIL** ahrd
Szold	zohld
Szolnok	**SAWL** nawk
Szombathely	**SAWM** baht **HAY**
Szulc	shuults
Szydlowiec	shid **LAW** vyets

T

Taal (language)	tahl
Taal (volcano)	tah **AHL**
tabard	**TAB** ərd
tabaret	**TAB** ə rət
Tabasco	tə **BAS** koh
tabes	**TAY** beez
Tabitha	**TAB** ə thə
tablature	**TAB** lə chər
tableau	**TAB** loh
tableau vivant	ta **BLOH** vee **VAHN** (**VAHN** French final *n*)
tableaux	**TAB** lohz
table d'hôte	**TAB** əl **DOHT**
taboo	tə **BOO**
tabor	**TAY** bər
taboret	**TAB** ə **RET**
Tabriz	tah **BREEZ**
tabular	**TAB** yə lər
tabula rasa	**TAB** yə lə **RAH** zə
tacet	**TAH** ket
tachistoscope	tə **KIS** tə **SKOHP**
tachometer	tə **KOM** ə tər
tachycardia	**TAK** i **KAHR** dee ə
tachymeter	ta **KIM** ə tər
tacit	**TAS** ət
taciturn	**TAS** ə **TURN**
taciturnity	**TAS** ə **TUR** nə tee

ə ago, a at, ah calm, ahr dark, air care, aw saw, ay say, ch church
e bet, ee me, eer beer, hw what, i is, ī my, *n* French final n vin,

Tacitus	**TAS** ə təs
tackle	**TAK** əl
Tacna	**TAK** nə
taco	**TAH** koh
Tacoma	tə **KOH** mə
Taconic	tə **KON** ik
taconite	**TAK** ə **NĪT**
tactical	**TAK** ti kəl
tactician	tak **TISH** ən
tactile	**TAK** təl
Tacubaya	**TAH** koo **BAH** yah
Tadzhik, Tadjik	tah **JEEK**
Taegu	tī **GOO**
taenia	**TEE** nee ə
taffeta	**TAF** ə tə
tafia	**TAF** ee ə
Tafti	**TAF** tee
Tag (German)	tahk
Tagal	tah **GAHL**
Tagalog	tə **GAH** ləg
Taganrog	**TAH** gahn **RAWK**
Taggard	**TAG** ərd
Tagliavini	**TAH** lyah **VEE** nee
Tagore, Rabindranath	tə **GOR**, rə **BIN** drə **NAHT**
Tagus	**TAYG** əs
Tahiti	tə **HEE** tee
Tahitian	tə **HEE** shən
Tahoe	**TAH** hoh
t'ai chi	tī jee
Taif	**TAH** if
taiga	**TĪ** gə
taille	tayl
Taimyr, Taimir	tī **MEER**
Tainan	tī nahn
Taine	tayn
taipan	**TĪ** pan
Taipeh, Taipei	tī pay
Taiping	tī ping
Taisho	tī shoh
Taiwan	tī wahn
Taiyuan	**TĪ** yuu **AHN**
Taiz	ta **EEZ**
Tajik	tah **JIK**

o on, oh oat, oi boy, oo soon, oor poor, or for, ow cow, sh shush,
th thin, *th* this, u up, ur spur, uu book, *zh* pleasure

Taj Mahal	*TAHZH* mə **HAHL**
Takamatsu	tah kah maht soo
talapoin	**TAL** ə **POIN**
talaria	tə **LAIR** ee ə
Talcahuano	**TAHL** kah **WAH** noh
talcum	**TAL** kəm
tales (jury)	**TAY** leez
talesman	**TAYLZ** mən
Taliesin	**TAL** ee **ES** ən
talion	**TAL** ee ən
taliped	**TAL** ə **PED**
talipes	**TAL** ə **PEEZ**
talipot	**TAL** ə **POT**
talisman	**TAL** əs mən
talkathon	**TAW** kə **THON**
Talkeetna	tal **KEET** nə
Tallahassee	**TAL** ə **HAS** ee
Talleyrand	**TAL** i **RAND**
Tallinn	**TAHL** lin
tallith	**TAH** ləs
Tall, Maki Koreissi Aguibou	**TAL**, **MAH** kee koh **REE** see ah **GEE** boo
Talmud	**TAHL** muud
Talmudic	tahl **MUUD** ik
talon	**TAL** ən
Talos	**TAY** lahs
talus	**TAY** ləs
tamale	tə **MAH** lee
Tamar	**TAY** mər
Tamara	tə **MAHR** ə
tamarack	**TAM** ə **RAK**
tamarind	**TAM** ə rənd
tamarisk	**TAM** ə risk
tamasha	tə **MAH** shə
Tamatave	**TAH** mah **TAHV**
Tamaulipas	**TAH** mow **LEE** pahs (mow as in *cow*)
Tamayo	tah **MAH** yoh
Tambora	tahm **BOR** ə
tambour	**TAM** buur
tambourin	**TAM** buu rən
tambourine	**TAM** bə **REEN**
Tamerlane	**TAM** ər **LAYN**
Tamil	**TAM** əl

ə ago, a at, ah calm, ahr dark, air care, aw saw, ay say, ch church
e bet, ee me, eer beer, hw what, i is, ī my, *n* French final n vin,

Tammuz	**TAH** muuz
Tampa	**TAM** pə
Tampere	**TAHM** pe re
Tampico	tam **PEE** koh
tampion	**TAM** pee ən
tampon	**TAM** pon
Tana	**TAH** nah
tanager	**TAN** i jər
Tanaka, Kakuei	tah nah kah, kah kway
Tanana	**TAN** ə **NAW**
Tananarive	tə **NAN** ə **REEV**
Tancred	**TANG** krəd
tandem	**TAN** dəm
Tang (dynasty)	tahng
Tanganyika	**TAN** gən **YEE** kə
tangelo	**TAN** jə **LOH**
tangent	**TAN** jənt
tangential	tan **JEN** shəl
tangerine	**TAN** jə **REEN**
tangible	**TAN** jə bəl
Tangier	tan **JIR**
Tangiers	tan **JIRZ**
tangle	**TANG** gəl
tango	**TANG** goh
Tangshan	dahng shahn
Tanguy, Yves	tahn **GEE**, **EEV** (tahn French final *n*)
Tanis	**TAY** nis
Tanner, Väinö	**TAH** nair, **VĪ** nə
Tannhäuser	**TAHN** **HOI** zər
Tannu Tuva	**TAN** oo **TOO** və
Tanqueray	**TANK** ə ray
tansy	**TAN** zee
tantalum	**TAN** tə ləm
Tantalus, t-	**TAN** tə ləs
tantamount	**TAN** tə **MOWNT** (**MOWNT** as in *count*)
tant mieux	tahn **MYUU** (tahn French final *n*)
tanto	**TAHN** toh
tant pis	tahn **PEE** (tahn French final *n*)
tantra, T-	**TUN** trə
tantrum	**TAN** trəm
Tanzania	**TAN** zə **NEE** ə
Tan Zhenlin	tahn jun leen
Tao	dow

o **on**, oh **oat**, oi **boy**, oo **soon**, oor **poor**, or **for**, ow **cow**, sh **shush**,
th **thin**, *th* **this**, u **up**, ur **spur**, uu **book**, *zh* **pleasure**

Taoism	**DOW** iz əm
Taos	tows (rhymes with *louse*)
Tapajoz	**TAH** pə **ZHAWS**
taper	**TAY** pər
tapestry	**TAP** ə stree
tapioca	**TAP** ee **OH** kə
tapir	**TAY** pər
tapis	**TAP** ee
Tapuyan	tah **POO** yən
taramosalata	**TAH** rah moh sah **LAH** tah
tarantas	**TAH** rahn **TAHS**
tarantella	**TA** rən **TEL** ə
Taranto	**TAH** rahn **TOH**
tarantula	tə **RAN** chə lə
Tarawa	tah **RAH** wah
Tarazi, Salah El Dine	**TAH** rah zee, sah **LAHK** əl **DEEN**
tarboosh	tahr **BOOSH**
Tardieu	tahr **DYUU**
tardo	**TAHR** doh
tare	tair
Targoviste	**TUR** goh **VESH** te
Targum	**TAHR** guum
Tarim	tah **REEM**
tarlatan	**TAHR** lə tən
taro	**TAHR** oh
tarot	**TA** roh
tarpaulin	tahr **PAW** lən
Tarpeia	tahr **PEE** ə
tarpon	**TAHR** pən
Tarquin	**TAHR** kwin
tarragon	**TA** rə gən
tarry (like tar)	**TAHR** ee
tarry (delay)	**TA** ree
Tarshish	**TAHR** shish
tarsier	**TAHR** see ər
Tarsus, t-	**TAHR** səs
tartan	**TAHR** tən
Tartar	**TAHR** tər
tartar (sauce)	**TAHR** tər
Tartarus	**TAHR** tər əs
Tartini	tahr **TEE** nee
Tartu	**TAHR** too
Tartuffe	tahr **TUUF**

ə ago, a at, ah calm, ahr dark, air care, aw saw, ay say, ch church
e bet, ee me, eer beer, hw what, i is, ī my, *n* French final n vin,

Tashkent, Tashkend	tahsh **KENT**
Tasman	**TAZ** mən
Tasmania	taz **MAY** nee ə
tass	tas
Tass	tahs
tassel	**TAS** əl
Tasso	**TAS** oh
tatami	tah **TAH** mee
Tatar	**TAH** tər
Tatiana	tah **TYAH** nah
Tatra	**TAH** trah
tatterdemalion	TAT ər di **MAYL** yən
tattersall	TAT ər SAWL
tattoo	ta **TOO**
Tatum	**TAYT** əm
tau	tow (as in *cow*)
taunt	tawnt
taupe	tohp
Taurus	**TOR** əs
Taussig	**TOW** sig (**TOW** as in *cow*)
taut	tawt
tautologous	taw **TOL** ə gəs
tautology	taw **TOL** ə jee
Taxco	**TAHS** koh
taxeme	**TAK** seem
taxidermy	**TAK** sə DUR mee
taxonomy	tak **SON** ə mee
Taygeta	tay **IJ** i tə
Tbilisi	tə **BIL** ə see
Tchaikovsky	chī **KAWF** skee
Tchebycheff	che **BISH** ef
Tchelitchew, Tchelitsheff	**CHU** lee chef
Tcherina, Ludmila	**CHE** ree nah, lood **MEE** lə
Tchobanov, Yordan	choh **BAH** nawf, **YOR** dahn
Tczew	chef (ch as in *chest*)
tear (weep)	teer
tear (rend)	tair
Tebaldi, Renata	tə **BAHL** dee, rə **NAH** tə
technetium	tek **NEE** shee əm
technic	**TEK** nik
technique	tek **NEEK**
technocracy	tek **NOK** rə see

o on, oh oat, oi boy, oo soon, oor poor, or for, ow cow, sh shush,
th thin, *th* this, u up, ur spur, uu book, *zh* pleasure

tectonic	tek **TAHN** ik
Tecumseh	tə **KUM** sə
Te Deum	tay **DAY** əm
tedious	**TEE** dee əs
tedium	**TEE** dee əm
teepee	**TEE** pee
Tees	teez
teeth	teeth
teethe	tee*th*
teetotaler	tee **TOH** tə lər
Tegal	te **GAHL**
Tegucigalpa	te **GOO** see **GAHL** pah
tegument	**TEG** yə mənt
Tehachapi	tə **HACH** ə pee
Teheran, Tehran	**TAY** ə **RAN**
Tehuantepec	te **WAHN** tə **PEK**
Tehuelche	te **WEL** che
Teilhard de Chardin	**TAY YAR** də shar **DAN** (**DAN** French final *n*)
tektite	**TEK** tīt
Telamon, t-	**TEL** ə **MON**
telangiectasis	**TEL AN** jee **EK** tə səs
Tel Aviv	**TEL** ə **VEEV**
telecast	**TEL** ə **KAST**
telega	tə **LEG** ə
telegenic	**TEL** ə **JEN** ik
telegraph	**TEL** ə **GRAF**
telegrapher	tə **LEG** rə fər
telegraphy	tə **LEG** rə fee
Telegu	**TEL** ə **GOO**
telekinesis	**TEL** ə kə **NEE** səs
Telemachus	tə **LEM** ə kəs
Telemann	**TAY** lə **MAHN**
Telemark, t-	**TEL** ə **MAHRK**
telemeter	**TEL** ə **MEET** ər
telemetry	tə **LEM** ə tree
teleological	**TEL** ee ə **LOJ** i kəl
teleology	**TEL** ee **OL** ə jee
telepathic	**TEL** ə **PATH** ik
telepathy	tə **LEP** ə thee
telephonic	**TEL** ə **FON** ik
telephony	tə **LEF** ə nee
telephoto	**TEL** ə **FOH** toh

ə ago, a at, ah calm, ahr dark, air care, aw saw, ay say, ch church
e bet, ee me, eer beer, hw what, i is, ī my, *n* French final n vin,

TelePrompTer	TEL ə PROM tər
telescopic	TEL ə SKOP ik
telescopy	tə LES kə pee
telesthesia	TEL əs THEE zhə
telethon	TEL ə THON
Teletron	TEL ə TRON
televise	TEL ə VĪZ
telic	TEL ik
Téllez	TEL yeth
tellurian	tə LUUR ee ən
tellurium	tə LUUR ee əm
Tellus	TEL əs
telpherage	TEL fər ij
Telugu	TEL uu GOO
temblor	TEM blər
temerarious	TEM ə RAIR ee əs
temerity	tə MER ə tee
Tempe	TEM pee
tempera	TEM pər ə
temperament	TEM pə rə mənt
temperamental	TEM pə rə MEN təl
temperance	TEM pə rəns
temperate	TEM pə rət
temperature	TEM pə rə chuur
tempestuous	tem PES choo əs
tempi	TEM pee
Templar, t-	TEM plər
template	TEM plət
tempo	TEM poh
temporal	TEM pə rəl
temporarily	TEM pə RER ə lee
temporize	TEM pə RĪZ
temptress	TEM trəs
tempura	TEM puu RAH
tempus fugit	TEM pəs FYOO jət
Temuco	tay MOO koh
tenable	TEN ə bəl
tenacious	tə NAY shəs
tenacity	tə NAS ə tee
Tenafly	TEN ə FLĪ
tenant	TEN ənt
tendency	TEN dən see
tendentious	ten DEN shəs

---

o on, oh oat, oi boy, oo soon, oor poor, or for, ow cow, sh shush,
th thin, *th* this, u up, ur spur, uu book, *zh* pleasure

tendon	TEN dən
tendonitis	TEN də NĪT əs
Tenebrae	TEN ə BREE
tenebrous	TEN ə brəs
Tenedos	TEN ə DOS
tenement	TEN ə mənt
Tenerife, Teneriffe	TEN ə REE fay
tenet	TEN ət
Teng Hsiao-p'ing	dəng show ping (show as in *how*)
Teniers	TEN yərz
Tenniel	TEN yəl
Tennyson	TEN ə sən
Tennysonian	TEN ə SOHN ee ən
tenon	TEN ən
tenonitis	TEN ə NĪ təs
tenor	TEN ər
tenorrhaphy	tə NOR ə fee
tensile	TEN səl
tension	TEN shən
tensor	TEN sər
tentacle	TEN ti kəl
tentative	TEN tə tiv
tenuis	TEN yoo əs
tenuity	ten YOO ə tee
tenuous	TEN yoo əs
tenure	TEN yər
tenuto	tə NOO toh
teocalli	TEE ə KAL ee
Teotihuacán	TAY oh TEE wah KAHN
tepee	TEE pee
tepid	TEP əd
tequila	tə KEE lah
Terah	TEER ə
teraphim	TER ə fim
teratism	TER ə TIZ əm
teratogenic	TER ə tə JEN ik
teratology	TER ə TOL ə jee
terbium	TUR bee əm
Ter Borch, Terborch	tər BORK
Terceira	ter SAY rə
tercel	TUR səl
tercentenary	tur SEN tə NER ee
tercentennial	TUR sen TEN ee əl

ə ago, a at, ah calm, ahr dark, air care, aw saw, ay say, ch church
e bet, ee me, eer beer, hw what, i is, ī my, n French final n vin,

tercet	**TUR** sət
teredo	tə **REE** doh
Terence	**TER** əns
Tereshkova, Valentina	TE resh **KAW** vah, **VAH** len **TEE** nah
terga	**TUR** gə
tergiversate	**TUR JIV** ər **SAYT**
tergiversation	**TUR JIV** ər **SAY** shən
tergum	**TUR** gəm
Terhune	tər **HYOON**
Terkel, Studs	**TUR** kəl
termagant	**TUR** mə gənt
terminology	**TUR** mə **NOL** ə jee
terminus	**TUR** mə nəs
ternary	**TUR** nə ree
Ternate	ter **NAH** tay
terneplate	**TURN** playt
Ter-Ovanesyan, Igor	**TER** ah ven ye **SYAHN, EE** gor
Terpsichore	turp **SIK** ə ree
terpsichorean, T-	**TURP** si kə **REE** ən
terra, T-	**TER** ə
terrace	**TER** əs
terra cotta	**TER** ə **KOT** ə
terra firma	**TER** ə **FUR** mə
terrain	tə **RAYN**
terra incognita	**TER** ə in **KOG** nə tə
Terramycin	**TER** ə **MĪ** sən
terrapin	**TER** ə pən
terrarium	tə **RA** ree əm
terrazzo	tə **RAHT** soh
Terre Haute	**TER** ə **HOHT**
terrene	te **REEN**
terreplein	**TER** ə playn
terrestrial	tə **RES** tree əl
terrible	**TER** ə bəl
terrify	**TER** ə **FĪ**
terrigenous	te **RIJ** ə nəs
terrine	tə **REEN**
territorial	**TER** ə **TOR** ee əl
territory	**TER** ə **TOR** ee
terror	**TER** ər
terrorist	**TER** ə rəst
terrorize	**TER** ə **RĪZ**
terry, T-	**TER** ee

o **on**, oh **oat**, oi **boy**, oo **soon**, oor **poor**, or **for**, ow **cow**, sh **shush**,
th **thin**, *th* **this**, u **up**, ur **spur**, uu **book**, *zh* **pleasure**

tertiary, T-	**TUR** shee **ER** ee
Tertullian	tər **TUL** yən
terza rima	**TER** tsə **REE** mə
Terzin	**TAIR** zin
Tesla	**TES** lə
tessellate (v)	**TES** ə **LAYT**
tessera	**TES** ər ə
tessitura	**TES** ə **TUUR** ə
testate	**TES** tayt
testator	**TES TAY** tər
testes	**TES** teez
testicle	**TES** ti kəl
testimonial	**TES** tə **MOH** nee əl
testimony	**TES** tə **MOH** nee
testis	**TES** təs
testosterone	te **STOS** tə **ROHN**
testudo	te **STOO** doh
Tet	tet
tetanic	te **TA** nik
tetanus	**TET** nəs
tetany	**TET** ə nee
tête-à-tête	**TAYT** ə **TAYT**
tête-bêche	tet besh
tether	**TE***TH* ər
Tethys	**TEE** thəs
tetra	**TET** rə
tetrachloride	**TET** rə **KLOR** īd
tetrachord	**TET** rə **KORD**
tetracycline	**TET** rə **SĪ KLEEN**
tetraethyl	**TET** rə **ETH** əl
Tetragrammaton	**TET** rə **GRAM** ə **TAHN**
tetrahedron	**TET** rə **HEE** drən
tetralogy	te **TRAL** ə jee
tetrameter	te **TRAM** ə tər
tetrarch	**TE** trahrk
tetrarchy	**TE TRAHR** kee
tetrastich	**TE** trə stik
Tetrazzini, t-	**TE** trə **ZEE** nee
tetrode	**TE** trohd
tetter	**TET** ər
Tetuán	te **TWAHN**
Teufelsdröckh, Teufelsdroeckh	**TOI** fəlz **DREK**

Teuton	**TOO** tən
Teutonic	too **TON** ik
Tewkesbury	**TYOOKS** ʙᴇʀ ee
Texarkana	ᴛᴇᴋ sahr **KAN** ə
textile	**TEKS** təl
textual	**TEKS** choo əl
texture	**TEKS** chər
Teyde, Teide	**TAY** *th*e
Teyte	tayt
Thackeray	**THAK** ə ree
Thaddeus, Thadeus	**THAD** ee əs
Thai	tī
Thailand	**TĪ** land
Thais (pl of *Thai*)	tīz
Thaïs	**THAY** is
Thaïs (opera)	tah **EES**
thalamus	**THAL** ə məs
thalassic	thə **LAS** ik
Thales	**THAY** leez
Thalia (feminine name)	**THAY** lee ə
Thalia (Muse)	thə **LĪ** ə
thalidomide	thə **LID** ə ᴍ**ĪD**
thallium	**THAL** ee əm
thallus	**THAL** əs
Thamae, Tseliso	tah **MĪ** ee, tsee **LEE** soh
Thames (Connecticut)	thaymz
Thames (England, Canada)	temz
Thanarat, Sarit	tah nah **RAHT**, sah **REET**
thanatology	ᴛʜᴀɴ ə **TOL** ə jee
thanatophobia	ᴛʜᴀɴ ə tə **FOH** bee ə
thanatopsis	ᴛʜᴀɴ ə **TOP** sis
Thanatos	**THAN** ə ᴛᴏѕ
thane	thayn
Thapa, Bekh Bahadur	**TAH** pə, **BEK** bah hah **DOOR**
Thapa, Surya Bahadur	**TAH** pə, **SOOR** yə bah hah **DOOR**
Thapsus	**THAP** səs
Thar	tur
Thasos	**THAH** saws
thaumatology	**THAW** mə **TOL** ə jee
thaumaturge	**THAW** mə ᴛᴜʀᴊ
thaumaturgy	**THAW** mə ᴛᴜʀ jee

---

o on, oh oat, oi boy, oo soon, oor poor, or for, ow cow, sh shush,
th thin, *th* this, u up, ur spur, uu book, zh pleasure

Thea	**THEE** ə
theanthropic	**THEE** an **THROP** ik
theanthropism	thee **AN** thrə **PIZ** əm
thearchy	**THEE** ahr kee
theater	**THEE** ə tər
theatrical	thee **AT** ri kəl
Thebaid	**THEE** bay **ĪD**
Theban	**THEE** bən
Thebes	theebz
thé dansant	tay dahn **SAHN** (dahn and **SAHN** French final *n*)
theine	**THEE** in
theism	**THEE** iz əm
theistic	thee **IS** tik (**IS** as in *hiss*)
thematic	thi **MAT** ik
Themis	**THEE** mis
Themistocles	thə **MIS** tə **KLEEZ**
thence	*th*ens
Theobald	**THEE** ə **BAWLD**
theocracy, theocrasy	thee **OK** rə see
Theocritus	thee **OK** rə təs
theodolite	thee **OD** ə **LĪT**
Theodoric	thee **OD** ə rik
Theodosius	**THEE** ə **DOH** shee əs
theogony	thee **OG** ə nee
theologian	**THEE** ə **LOH** jən
theology	thee **OL** ə jee
theophany	thee **AH** fə **NEE**
Theophilus	thee **AH** fə ləs
Theophrastus	**THEE** ə **FRAS** təs
theorem	**THEE** ə rəm
theoretical	**THEE** ə **RET** i kəl
theoretician	**THEE** ə rə **TISH** ən
theory	**THEE** ə ree
theosophical	**THEE** ə **SOF** i kəl
theosophy	thee **OS** ə fee
therapeutic	**THER** ə **PYOO** tik
therapist	**THER** ə pəst
therapy	**THER** ə pee
Theravada	**THER** ə **VAH** də
theremin, T-	**THER** ə mən
therianthropic	**THIR** ee an **THROP** ik
theriomorphic	**THIR** ee ə **MOR** fik

ə ago, a at, ah calm, ahr dark, air care, aw saw, ay say, ch church
e bet, ee me, eer beer, hw what, i is, ī my, *n* French final n vin,

thermae	THUR mee
thermal	THUR məl
thermion	THURM Ī ən
thermionic	THURM ī ON ik
thermistor	thər MIS tər
thermocline	THUR mə KLĪN
thermocouple	THUR mə KUP əl
thermodynamic	THUR moh dī NAM ik
thermography	thər MOG rə fee
thermolysis	thər MOL ə sis
thermometer	thər MOM ə tər
thermonuclear	THUR moh NOO klee ər
Thermopylae	thər MOP ə LEE
Thermos	THUR məs
thermostat	THUR mə STAT
Thersites	thər SĪ teez
thesauri	thi SOR ī
thesaurus	thi SOR əs
Theseus	THEE see əs
Thespian, t-	THES pee ən
Thespis	THES pəs
Thessalonians	THES ə LOH nee ənz
Thessalonica	THES ə LON ə kə
Thessaly	THES ə lee
theta	THAY tə
Thetis	THEE təs
theurgy	THEE ur jee
thew	thyoo
thews	thyooz
thiamine	THĪ ə mən
thiazine	THĪ ə ZEEN
thiazole	THĪ ə ZOHL
Thibet	tə BET
Thiers	tyair
Thimbu	THIM boo
Thimphu	THIM poo
thine	*th*īn
Thisbe	THIZ bee
thistle	THIS əl
thither	THI*TH* ər
Thohoyandou	TOI yoo yon DOH
Thomism	TOH MIZ əm
Thor	thor

o on, oh oat, oi boy, oo soon, oor poor, or for, ow cow, sh shush,
th thin, *th* this, u up, ur spur, uu book, *zh* pleasure

thoracic	thə **RAS** ik
thorax	**THOR** aks
Thoreau	thə **ROH**
thorium	**THOR** ee əm
Thoroddsen, Gunnar	**TOR** əd sən, **GUUN** ər
thoron	**THOR** on
thorough	**THUR** oh
Thorshavn	tors **HOWN**
Thoth	thohth
Thotmes	**THOHT** mes
thou	*th*ow
though	*th*oh
Thracian	**THRAY** shən
thrall	thrawl
threnody	**THREN** ə dee
threshold	**THRESH** ohld
thrombin	**THROM** bən
thrombosis	throm **BOH** səs
thrombotic	throm **BOT** ik
thrombus	**THROM** bəs
throstle	**THROS** əl
throttle	**THROT** əl
Thucydides	thoo **SID** ə **DEEZ**
Thule (Greenland)	**TOO** lee
Thule (ancient world)	**THOO** lee
thulium	**THOO** lee əm
Thummim	**THUM** im
Thun	toon
Thunborg, Anders	**TYOON** bor ee, **AHN** ders
Thurber	**THUR** bər
thurible	**THUUR** ə bəl
Thuringia	thuu **RIN** jee ə
Thursday	**THURZ** day
Thutmose	thut **MOH** sə
Thyestes	thī **ES** teez
thylacine	**THĪ** lə **SĪN**
thyme	tīm
thymus	**THĪ** məs
thyroid	**THĪ** roid
thyrsus	**THUR** səs
Tia Juana	**TEE** ə **WAH** nə
Tianjin	tee ahn jeen
tiara	tee **AR** ə
Tiber	**TĪ** bər

ə ago, a at, ah calm, ahr dark, air care, aw saw, ay say, ch church
e bet, ee me, eer beer, hw what, i is, ī my, *n* French final n vin,

Tiberius	tī **BIR** ee əs
Tibet	tə **BET**
Tibetan	tə **BET** ən
tibia	**TIB** ee ə
Tibullus	tə **BUL** əs
Ticino	tee **CHEE** noh
Ticonderoga	**TĪ** kon də **ROH** gə
Tien Shan	tee en shahn
Tientsin	tin tsin
Tiepolo	**TYEP** ə loh
tierce	teers
tiercel	**TIR** səl
Tierra del Fuego	tee **ER** ə del **FWAY** goh
Tiffany	**TIF** ə nee
tiffin	**TIF** ən
Tiflis	**TIF** ləs
Tiglath-pileser	**TIG** lath pī **LEE** zər
tiglon	**TĪ** glən
Tigrinya	tə **GREEN** yə
Tigris	**TĪ** grəs
Tijuana	**TEE** ə **WAHN** ə
Tikhonov, Nikolai	**TYEE** hən əv, nee koh **LĪ**
tiki	**TEE** kee
tilde	**TIL** də
Till Eulenspiegel	**TIL OI** lən ꜱʜᴘᴇᴇ gəl
Tilsit	**TIL** zət
timbal	**TIM** bəl
timbale	**TIM** bəl
timber	**TIM** bər
timbre	**TAN** brə (**TAN** French final *n*)
Timbuktu	ᴛɪᴍ buk **TOO**
Timisoara	ᴛᴇᴇ mee **SHWAH** rah
timocracy	tī **MOK** rə see
Timon	**TĪ** mən
Timor	**TEE** mor
timorous	**TIM** ər əs
Timotheus	tə **MOH** thee əs
Timothy	**TIM** ə thee
timpani	**TIM** pə nee
timpanist	**TIM** pə nəst
tinamou	**TIN** ə ᴍᴏᴏ
Tinbergen, Jan	**TIN** ber ken, yahn (ken *k* almost an *h* sound)
tincture	**TINGK** chər

---

o **on**, oh **oat**, oi **boy**, oo **soon**, oor **poor**, or **for**, ow **cow**, sh **shush**, th **thin**, *th* **this**, u **up**, ur **spur**, uu **book**, *zh* **pleasure**

tinea	**TIN** ee ə
tinnitus	tə **NĪ** təs
Tintagel	tin **TAJ** əl
Tintern	**TIN** tərn
tintinnabulation	**TIN** tə **NAB** yə **LAY** shən
Tintoretto	**TIN** tə **RET** oh
tiny	**TĪ** nee
Tippecanoe	**TIP** ə kə **NOO**
Tipperary	**TIP** ə **RAIR** ee
tirade	tĭ **RAYD**
tirailleur	tee rah **YUUR**
Tirana, Tiranë	tee **RAH** nə
Tiresias	tĭ **REE** see əs
Tiros	**TĪ** rohs
Tirzah	**TUR** zə
tisane	tĭ **ZAN**
Tiselius, Arne	tee **SAY** lee **UUS, AHR** nə
Tishah b'Av	**TISH** ə **BAWV**
Tishbite	**TISH** bīt
Tisiphone	tə **SIF** ə nee
tissue	**TISH** oo
Tisza	**TEE** sah
titan, T-	**TĪT** ən
Titania	tə **TAY** nee ə
Titanic, t-	tĭ **TAN** ik
titanium	tĭ **TAY** nee əm
tithe	tī*th*
tithing	**TĪ** *th*ing
Tithonus	tĭ **THOH** nəs
Titian	**TISH** ən
Titicaca	**TI** tĭ **KAH** kə
titillate	**TIT** ə **LAYT**
Tito	**TEE** toh
titubation	**TICH** uu **BAY** shən
titular	**TICH** ə lər
Titus	**TĪ** təs
Tivoli	**TIV** ə lee
tizzy	**TIZ** ee
Tlaxcala	tlahs **KAHL** ə
tmesis	**MEE** səs
tobacco	tə **BAK** oh
Tobago	tə **BAY** goh
Tobiah	tə **BĪ** ə

ə ago, a at, ah calm, ahr dark, air care, aw saw, ay say, ch church
e bet, ee me, eer beer, hw what, i is, ī my, *n* French final n vin,

Tobias	tə BĪ əs
Tobit	TOH bət
toboggan	tə BOG ən
Toby, t-	TOH bee
Tocantins	TAW kahn TEENS
toccata	tə KAH tə
Tocharian	toh KA ree ən
tocology	toh KOL ə jee
tocopherol	toh KOF ə ROHL
Tocqueville, de	TOHK vil, də
tocsin	TOK sən
toffee	TAW fee
tofu	TOH foo
Togo	TOH goh
toile	twahl
Tokay, t-	toh KAY
toke	tohk
Tokelau	TOH kə LOW (LOW as in *cow*)
Tokharian	toh KAIR ee ən
Tokyo	TOH kee OH
tole	tohl
Tolima	tə LEE mə
Tolkien	TAHL keen
toll	tohl
Tolstoy, Tolstoi	tawl STOI
Toltec	TOL tek
Toluca	tə LOO kə
toluene	TOL yoo EEN
Tomalbaye, François	toh mahl BĪ, frahn SWAH (frahn French final *n*)
Toma, Maiva Lulai	TOH mə, mī AH və YOO lī
tomato	tə MAY toh
Tomaz, Americo	TOO mahsh, ə MER i koo
Tombigbee	tom BIG bee
tome	tohm
tomography	tə MOG rə fee
Tomonaga, Shinichiro	toh moh nah gah, shee nee chee roh
tomorrow	tə MOR oh
Tomsk	tawmsk
tonality	toh NAL ə tee
Tonga, t-	TONG gə
tongue	tung
tonight	tə NĪT

---

o on, oh oat, oi boy, oo soon, oor poor, or for, ow cow, sh shush,
th thin, *th* this, u up, ur spur, uu book, *zh* pleasure

Tonkin, t-	tahn kin
Tonle Sap	**TAHN** lay **SAP**
tonneau	tə **NOH**
Tonsberg	**TUNZ** bair
tonsil	**TAHN** səl
tonsillectomy	**TAHN** sə **LEK** tə mee
tonsillitis	**TAHN** sə **LĪ** təs
tonsorial	tahn **SOR** ee əl
tonsure	**TAHN** shər
tontine	tahn **TEEN**
tonus	**TOH** nəs
toothed	too*th*d
topaz	**TOH** paz
topectomy	tə **PEK** tə mee
topee (helmet)	toh **PEE**
Topeka	tə **PEE** kə
Tophet, -h	**TOH** fət
tophus	**TOH** fəs
topi (antelope)	**TOH** pee
topiary	**TOH** pee **ER** ee
topography	tə **POG** rə fee
toponym	**TOP** ə nim
toponymy	tə **PON** ə mee
Toppazzini	tah pə **SEE** nee
topsail	**TOP** səl
toque	tohk
Torah	**TOH** rə
torchier	tor **CHEER**
torchon	**TOR** shon
Tordesillas	**TOR** *th*e **SEE** lyahs
toreador	**TOR** ee ə **DOR**
torero	taw **RAIR** oh
toreutic	tə **ROO** tik
torii	**TOH** ree **EE**
torment (n)	**TOR** ment
torment (v)	tor **MENT**
tornadic	tor **NAY** dik
tornado	tor **NAY** doh
Tornio	**TOR** nee **OH**
toroid	**TOR** oid
toroidal	taw **ROID** əl
Toronto	tə **RON** toh
torpedo	tor **PEE** doh

ə ago, a at, ah calm, ahr dark, air care, aw saw, ay say, ch church
e bet, ee me, eer beer, hw what, i is, ī my, *n* French final n vin,

torpid	**TOR** pəd
torpor	**TOR** pər
torque	tork
Torquemada	**TOR** kə **MAHD** ə
torr	tor
Torrelio, Celso	toh **REL** yoh, **SEL** soh
torrefy	**TOR** ə **FĪ**
Torrens	**TOR** ənz
torrent	**TOR** ənt
Torrente	taw **REN** tay
torrential	taw **REN** shəl
Torricelli	**TOR** ə **CHEL** ee
torrid	**TOR** əd
torsade	tor **SAYD**
torsion	**TOR** shən
torso	**TOR** soh
tort	tort
torte	tort
torticollis	**TOR** tə **KOL** əs
tortilla	tor **TEE** yə
tortoise	**TOR** təs
Tortola	tor **TOH** lə
tortoni	tor **TOH** nee
Tortuga	tor **TOO** gə
tortuous	**TOR** choo əs
torture	**TOR** chər
torturous	**TOR** chə rəs
torus	**TOR** əs
Tory	**TOR** ee
Toscanini	**TOS** kə **NEE** nee
totalitarian	toh **TAL** ə **TAIR** ee ən
totem	**TOH** təm
Tottenham	**TOT** ən əm
toucan	**TOO** kan
touché	too **SHAY**
tough	tuf
Toulon	too **LAWN** (**LAWN** French final *n*)
Toulouse	too **LOOZ**
Toulouse-Lautrec	too **LOOZ** loh **TREK**
Toungoo	towng goo
toupee	too **PAY**
tour	tuur
touraco	**TUUR** ə **KOH**

o **on**, oh **oat**, oi **boy**, oo **soon**, oor **poor**, or **for**, ow **cow**, sh **shush**,
th **thin**, *th* **this**, u **up**, ur **spur**, uu **book**, *zh* **pleasure**

tour de force	TUUR də FORS
Touré, Sekou	too RAY, se KOO
Tourel	too REL
tourmaline	TUUR mə lən
tournament	TUUR nə mənt
tournedos (sing)	TUUR nə DOH
tournedos (pl)	TUUR nə DOHZ
tourney	TUUR nee
tourniquet	TUR nə kət
Tours	toor
Toussaint L'Ouverture	too SAN loo ver TYUUR (SAN French final *n*)
tout	towt
tout à fait	too ta FE
tout de suite	toot SWEET
tout ensemble	too tahn SAHN blə (tahn and SAHN French final *n*)
tout le monde	too lə MAWND
tovarich	toh VAH rish
tow	toh
toward	tord
towards	tordz
towel	TOW əl (TOW as in *cow*)
towhead	TOH hed
towhee	TOH hee
towline	TOH līn
Townes	townz
Townsend	TOWN zənd
Towson	TOW sən (TOW as in *cow*)
toxemia	tok SEE mee ə
toxicology	TOK si KOL ə jee
toxicosis	TOK sə KOH səs
toxin	TOK sən
toxophilite	tok SOF ə LĪT
Toynbee	TOIN bee
trabeation	TRAY bee AY shən
trachea	TRAY kee ə
tracheal	TRAY kee əl
tracheostomy	TRAY kee OS tə mee
tracheotomy	TRAY kee OT ə mee
trachoma	trə KOH mə
tractable	TRAK tə bəl
tractile	TRAK təl

ə ago, a at, ah calm, ahr dark, air care, aw saw, ay say, ch church
e bet, ee me, eer beer, hw what, i is, ī my, *n* French final n vin,

traduce	trə **DOOS**
Trafalgar	trə **FAL** gər
tragacanth	**TRAJ** ə **KANTH**
tragedian	trə **JEE** dee ən
tragedienne	trə **JEE** dee **EN**
tragicomedy	**TRAJ** i **KOM** ə dee
tragus	**TRAY** gəs
traipse	trayps
traitorous	**TRAY** tər əs
Trajan	**TRAY** jən
trajectory	trə **JEK** tə ree
Tralee	trə **LEE**
trammel	**TRAM** əl
tramontane	trə **MON** tayn
trampoline	**TRAM** pə **LEEN**
tramway	**TRAM** way
tranquil	**TRANG** kwəl
tranquility	trang **KWIL** ə tee
tranquilizer	**TRANG** kwə **LĪ** zər
Transcaucasia	**TRANS** kaw **KAY** *zh*ə
transceiver	tran **SEE** vər
transcendent	tran **SEN** dənt
transcendental	**TRAN** sen **DEN** təl
transducer	trans **DOO** sər
transect	tran **SEKT**
transept	**TRAN** sept
transfer (n)	**TRANS** fər
transfer (v)	trans **FUR**
transferable	trans **FUR** ə bəl
transference	trans **FUR** əns
transfiguration	trans **FIG** yə **RAY** shən
transfix	trans **FIKS**
transform (n)	**TRANS** form
transform (v)	trans **FORM**
transformation	**TRANS** fər **MAY** shən
transformer	trans **FOR** mər
transgress	trans **GRES**
transience	**TRAN** shəns
transient	**TRAN** shənt
transistor	tran **ZIS** tər
transit	**TRAN** sət
transition	tran **ZISH** ən
transitive	**TRAN** sə tiv

---

o on, oh oat, oi boy, oo soon, oor poor, or for, ow cow, sh shush,
th thin, *th* this, u up, ur spur, uu book, *zh* pleasure

transitory	TRAN sə TOR ee
Transjordan	trans JOR dən
Transjordania	TRANS jor DAY nee ə
Transkei	trans KĪ
transliterate	trans LIT ə RAYT
translucent	trans LOO sənt
transmigration	TRANS mī GRAY shən
transmission	trans MISH ən
transmitter	trans MIT ər
transmogrification	trans MOG rə fə KAY shən
transmontane	trans MON tayn
transmutation	TRANS myuu TAY shən
transoceanic	TRANS OH shee AN ik
transom	TRAN səm
transonic	trans SAHN ik
transplant (n)	TRANS plant
transplant (v)	trans PLANT
transport (n)	TRANS port
transport (v)	trans PORT
transubstantiation	TRAN səb STAN shee AY shən
Transvaal	trans VAHL
transverse	trans VURS
transvestism	trans VES tiz əm
transvestite	trans VES tīt
Transylvania	TRAN səl VAY nee ə
Traoré, Moussa	TRAH wah lay, moo SAH
Traoré, Seydou	TRAH wah lay, SAY doo
Trapani	TRAH pah nee
trapeze	tra PEEZ
trapezium	trə PEE zee əm
trapezius	trə PEE zee əs
trapezoid	TRAP ə ZOID
Trappist	TRAP əst
trauma	TROW mə (TROW as in *cow*)
traumatic	trow MAT ik (trow as in *cow*)
Träumerei	TROI mə RĪ
travail	trə VAYL
travelog, -ue	TRAV ə LAWG
traverse (n, a)	TRAV ərs
traverse (v)	trə VURS
Traverse (lake)	TRAV ərs
travertine	TRAV ər TEEN
travesty	TRAV ə stee

ə ago, a at, ah calm, ahr dark, air care, aw saw, ay say, ch church
e bet, ee me, eer beer, hw what, i is, ī my, *n* French final n vin,

Traviata, La	trah **VYAH** tah, lah
travois	trə **VOI**
treacherous	**TRECH** ər əs
treachery	**TRECH** ə ree
treacle	**TREE** kəl
treadle	**TRED** əl
treasure	**TREZ***H* ər
Trebizond	**TREB** ə **ZOND**
treble	**TREB** əl
Treblinka	tre **BLEENG** kah
trecento	tre **CHEN** taw
trefoil	**TREE** foil
Treiki, Ali	tray̆ **KEE**, ah **LEE**
Treitschke	**TRĬCH** kə
trek	trek
Tremblant	trahn **BLAHN** (trahn and **BLAHN** French final *n*)
tremendous	tri **MEN** dəs
tremolite	**TREM** ə **LĪT**
tremolo	**TREM** ə **LOH**
tremor	**TREM** ər
tremulous	**TREM** yə ləs
trenchant	**TREN** chənt
Trengganu	treng **GAH** noo
Trentino	tren **TEE** naw
Trenton	**TREN** tən
trepan	tri **PAN**
Trepczynski, Stanislaw	trep **SIN** skee, stah **NEE** slahf
trephination	**TREF** ə **NAY** shən
trephine	**TREE** fin
trepidation	**TREP** ə **DAY** shən
trespass	**TRES** pəs
trestle	**TRES** əl
Trevelyan	tri **VEL** yən
Trevor	**TREV** ər
trey	tray̆
triad	**TRĪ** ad
triage	**TREE** ah*zh*
trial	**TRĪ** əl
triangle	**TRĪ ANG** gəl
triangulation	trī **ANG** gyə **LAY** shən
Triangulum	trī **ANG** gyə ləm
triarchy	**TRĪ AHR** kee

o on, oh oat, oi boy, oo soon, oor poor, or for, ow cow, sh shush, th thin, *th* this, u up, ur spur, uu book, *zh* pleasure

Trias	TRĪ əs
Triassic	trī A sik
tribade	TRIB əd
tribadism	TRIB ə DIZ əm
tribal	TRĪ bəl
tribalism	TRĪ bəl IZ əm
tribrach	TRĪ brak
tribulation	TRIB yə LAY shən
tribunal	trī BYOO nəl
tribune	TRIB yoon
tributary	TRIB yə TER ee
tribute	TRIB yoot
triceps	TRĪ seps
Triceratops	trī SER ə TOPS
trichiasis	trī KĪ ə səs
trichina	trik Ī nə
trichinosis	TRIK ə NOH səs
trichotomy	trī KOT ə mee
triclinic	trī KLIN ik
triclinium	trī KLIN ee əm
tricot	TREE koh
tricycle	TRĪ si kəl
trident, T-	TRĪD ənt
triennial	trī EN ee əl
Trier, t-	treer
Trieste	tree EST
trifle	TRĪ fəl
Trigère	tree ZHAIR
trigon	TRĪ gon
trigonometric	TRIG ə nə MET rik
trigonometry	TRIG ə NOM ə tree
trihedral	trī HEE drəl
trilateral	trī LAT ə rəl
trilingual	trī LING gwəl
trillium	TRIL ee əm
trilobate	trī LOH BAYT
trilobite	TRĪ lə BĪT
trilogy	TRIL ə jee
trimester	trī MES tər
trimeter	TRIM ə tər
trimetric	trī MET rik
Trimurti	trī MUUR tee
Trinacria	trə NAK ree ə

ə ago, a at, ah calm, ahr dark, air care, aw saw, ay say, ch church
e bet, ee me, eer beer, hw what, i is, ī my, n French final n vin,

trinal	TRĪN əl
trinary	TRĪ nə ree
Trincomalee	TRING koh mə LEE
Trinidad	TRIN ə DAD
trinitrotoluene	TRĪ NĪ troh TOL yoo EEN
Trinity	TRIN ə tee
trinomial	trī NOH mee əl
trio	TREE oh
triode	TRĪ ohd
triolet	TRĪ ə lət
tripartite	trī PAHR tīt
tripe	trīp
triphibian	trī FIB ee ən
triphthong	TRIF thawng
triplet	TRIP lət
triplicate (a, n)	TRIP lə kət
triplicate (v)	TRIP lə KAYT
tripod	TRĪ pod
tripodal	TRIP ə dəl
Tripoli, t-	TRIP ə lee
Tripolitania	TRIP ə lə TAYN yə
tripos	TRĪ pos
tripterous	TRIP tər əs
Triptolemus, Triptolemos	trip TOL ə məs
triptych	TRIP tik
Tripura	TRIP ə rə
trireme	TRĪ reem
trisaccharide	trī SAK ə RĪD
triskaidekaphobia	TRIS KĪ DEK ə FOH bee ə
triskelion	trī SKEL ee ən
Trismegistus	TRIS mə JIS təs
trismus	TRIZ məs
Tristan	TRIS tən
triste	treest
tristesse	trees TES
tristich	TRIS tik
Tristram	TRIS trəm
tritheism	TRĪ thee IZ əm
tritium	TRIT ee əm
Triton	TRĪT ən
triturate	TRICH ə RAYT
triumvir	trī UM vər

---

o on, oh oat, oi boy, oo soon, oor poor, or for, ow cow, sh shush,
th thin, *th* this, u up, ur spur, uu book, *zh* pleasure

triumvirate	trī UM vər ət
Trivandrum	tri VAN drəm
trivia	TRIV ee ə
trivial	TRIV ee əl
trivium	TRIV ee əm
Trnava	TUR nah vah
Trnovac	TUR naw vahts
Troad	TROH ad
Troas	TROH as
Trobriand	TROH bree AHND
Trobriander	TROH bree AHND ər
trochaic	troh KAY ik
troche	TROH kee
trochee	TROH kee
troglodyte	TROG lə DĪT
troika	TROI kə
Troilus	TROI ləs
Trois Rivières	TRWAH ree VYAIR
Trojan	TROH jən
troll	trohl
trollop	TROL əp
Trollope	TROL əp
Trombe	trawmb
trombone	trom BOHN
trompe l'oeil	trawmp LU ee
Tromsö	TRUUM soh
Trondheim	TRAWN haym
tropaeolum	trə PEE ə ləm
trope	trohp
trophy	TROH fee
tropism	TROH piz əm
tropology	troh POL ə jee
troposphere	TROHP ə SFIR
troppo	TRAW poh
Trossachs	TROS əks
troth	trawth
Trotsky	TROT skee
troubadour	TROO bə DOR
trou-de-loup (sing)	TROO də LOO
trough	trawf
trounce	trowns
troupe	troop
trous-de-loup (pl)	TROO də LOO

ə ago, a at, ah calm, ahr dark, air care, aw saw, ay say, ch church
e bet, ee me, eer beer, hw what, i is, ī my, n French final n vin,

trousseau	troo **SOH**
trouvère	troo **VAIR**
Trouville	troo **VEEL**
Trovatore	**TROH** vah **TOH** ray
trowel	**TROW** əl (**TROW** as in *cow*)
Troyanovsky, Oleg	**TROI** ə **NOF** skee, **OH** leg
truant	**TROO** ənt
Trucial Oman	**TROO** shəl oh **MAHN**
truculence	**TRUK** yə ləns
Trudeau, Pierre	troo **DOH**, **PYAIR**
trudgen	**TRUJ** ən
Truffaut, François	troo **FOH**, frahn **SWAH** (frahn French final *n*)
truffle	**TRUF** əl
Trujillo	truu **HEE** yoh
Truk	truk
trullisatio	**TROO** li **SAH** shoh
Trumbo	**TRUM** boh
Trumbull	**TRUM** bəl
truncheon	**TRUN** chən
Truro	**TRUUR** oh
trypanosome	trip **AN** ə **SOHM**
trypanosomiasis	trip **AN** ə sə **MĪ** ə səs
trypsin	**TRIP** sən
tryst	trist
tsar	zahr
Tsarapkin, Semyon	tse **RAHP** kin, sem **YOHN**
Tsavo	**SAHV** oh
Tschaikovsky, Tschaikowsky	chī **KAWF** skee
tsetse	**TSET** see
Tshombe, Moise	**CHOM** bay, moh **EES**
Tsiang, Tingfu	jahng, ting foo
Tsinan	jee nahn
Tsinghai	ching hī
Tsingtao	ching dow
Tsinling Shan	sin ling shahn
Tsiranana, Philibert	tsee **RUN** ən, pi lee **BAIR**
Tsongas, Paul	**SAHN** gəs
Tsouderos	soo *th*e **RAWS**
Tsountas, Chrestos	**TSOON** dahs, **KREE** staws
Tsuga	**TSOO** gə
Tsugaru	soo gah roo

o **on**, oh **oat**, oi **boy**, oo **soon**, oor **poor**, or **for**, ow **cow**, sh **shush**,
th **thin**, *th* **this**, u **up**, ur **spur**, uu **book**, *zh* **pleasure**

tsunami	suu **NAH** mee
Tsuruga	tsoo roo gah
Tsushima	tsoo shee mah
tsutsugamushi (disease)	**SOOT** sə gə **MOO** shee
Tsvetkov, Boris	sə vet **KAWF**, baw **REES**
Tuamotu	**TOO** ə **MOH** too
tuan	twahn
Tuapse	too ahp **SE**
Tuareg	**TWAH** reg
tuba	**TOO** bə
tubal, T-	**TOO** bəl
tube	toob
tubercle	**TOO** bər kəl
tubercular	tuu **BUR** kyə lər
tuberculin	tuu **BUR** kyə lən
tuberculosis	tuu **BUR** kyə **LOH** səs
tuberose	**TOOB** rohz
tuberosity	**TOO** bə **RAH** sə tee
tubular	**TOO** byə lər
tubule	**TOO** byool
Tucana	too **KAY** nə
Tuchman	**TUK** mən
Tucson	**TOO** sahn
Tucumcari	**TOO** kəm **KA** ree
Tudor	**TOO** dər
Tuesday	**TOOZ** day
tufa	**TOO** fə
Tuguegarao	**TOO** ge gah **ROW** (**ROW** as in *cow*)
Tuileries	**TWEE** lə reez
Tukums	**TUU** kuums
Tula	**TOO** lah
Tulagi	too **LAHG** ee
tularemia	**TOO** lə **REE** mee ə
tule	**TOO** lee
tulip	**TOO** lip
tulle	tool
Tully	**TUL** ee
Tumacacori	**TOO** mə **KAH** kə ree
tumbril	**TUM** brəl
tumefacient	**TOO** mə **FAY** shənt
tumescent	too **MES** ənt
tumor	**TOO** mər

ə ago, a at, ah calm, ahr dark, air care, aw saw, ay say, ch church
e bet, ee me, eer beer, hw what, i is, ī my, *n* French final n vin,

tumult	**TOO** məlt
tumultuous	tuu **MUL** choo əs
tumulus	**TOO** myə ləs
tuna	**TOO** nə
tundra	**TUN** drə
tune	toon
Tungliao	toong lyow
tungsten	**TUNG** stən
Tungting	duung ting
Tungus	tuun **GUUZ**
Tunguska	tuun **GUUS** kah
tunic	**TOO** nik
tunicate	**TOO** ni kət
Tunis	**TOO** nis
Tunisia	too **NEE** *zh*ə
Tupamaro	**TOO** pah **MAH** roh
tupelo	**TOO** pə **LOH**
Tupi	too **PEE**
Tupi-Guarani	too **PEE GWAHR** ə **NEE**
tu quoque	too **KWOH** kwe
Turandot	**TUUR** ən **DOT**
Turanian	tuu **RAY** nee ən
turban	**TUR** bən
turbid	**TUR** bəd
turbine	**TUR** bən
turbojet	**TUR** boh **JET**
turbot	**TUR** bət
turbulence	**TUR** byə ləns
turbulent	**TUR** byə lənt
Turco	**TUR** koh
tureen	tə **REEN**
Turgenev, Turgeniev	tuur **GE** nyəf
turgid	**TUR** jəd
Turgot	tuur **GOH**
Turin	**TUUR** ən
turista	tuu **REE** stə
Turkestan	**TUR** kə **STAN**
Turkey, t-	**TUR** kee
Turki	**TUR** kee
Turkic	**TUR** kik
Turkmen (USSR)	**TURK** mən
Turkoman	**TUR** kə mən
Turku	**TUUR** koo

o on, oh oat, oi boy, oo soon, oor poor, or for, ow cow, sh shush,
th thin, *th* this, u up, ur spur, uu book, z*h* pleasure

turmeric	**TUR** mər ik
turnip	**TUR** nəp
turnkey	**TURN** kee
Turnverein	**TUURN** fer **ĪN**
turpentine	**TUR** pən **TĪN**
turpitude	**TUR** pə **TOOD**
turquoise	**TUR** kwoiz
turret	**TUR** ət
Tuscaloosa	**TUS** kə **LOO** sə
Tuscan	**TUS** kən
Tuscany	**TUS** kə nee
Tuscarora	**TUS** kə **ROR** ə
Tuscumbia	tus **KUM** bee ə
Tuskegee	tus **KEE** gee
Tussaud	too **SOH**
tussive	**TUS** iv
Tutankhamen	**TOOT** ahngk **AH** mən
tutelage	**TOO** tə lij
tutelary	**TOO** tə **LER** ee
tutor	**TOO** tər
tutorial	too **TOR** ee əl
tutti	**TOO** tee
tutti-frutti	**TOO** ti **FROO** tee
tutu	**TOO** too
Tutuila	**TOO** too **EE** lah
Tuva	**TOO** və
Tuvalu	too **VAHL** oo
tuxedo, T-	tuk **SEE** doh
Tweedsmuir	**TWEEDZ** myuur
Twickenham	**TWIK** ən əm
Tyburn	**TĪ** bərn
Tyche	**TĪ** kee
tycoon	tī **KOON**
Tylenol	**TĪ** lə **NOHL**
tympanic	tim **PAN** ik
tympanites	**TIM** pə **NĪ** teez
tympanum	**TIM** pə nəm
Tynan	**TĪ** nən
Tyndale, Tyndall	**TIN** dəl
Tyndareus	tin **DA** ree əs
Tyne	tīn
Tynemouth	**TĪN** məth
Typee	tī **PEE**

ə ago, a at, ah calm, ahr dark, air care, aw saw, ay say, ch church
e bet, ee me, eer beer, hw what, i is, ī my, *n* French final n vin,

typhoid	TĪ foid
Typhon	TĪ fon
typhoon	tī **FOON**
typhus	TĪ fəs
typical	**TIP** i kəl
typify	**TIP** ə **FĪ**
typographer	tī **POG** rə fər
typographical	**TĪ** pə **GRAF** ik əl
typography	tī **POG** rə fee
typology	tī **POL** ə jee
Tyr	tir
tyrannical	tə **RAN** i kəl
tyrannize	**TIR** ə **NĪZ**
tyrannosaur	tə **RAN** ə **SOR**
tyrannous	**TIR** ə nəs
tyranny	**TIR** ə nee
tyrant	**TĪ** rənt
Tyre	tīr
Tyrian	**TIR** ee ən
tyro, T-	**TĪ** roh
Tyrol	tə **ROHL**
Tyrolean	tə **ROH** lee ən
Tyrolese	**TIR** ə **LEEZ**
Tyrone (place)	tī **ROHN**
Tyrone (boy's name)	**TĪ** rohn
Tyrrhenian	tə **REE** nee ən
tzar	zahr
Tzigane, t-	tsee **GAHN**

U

Ubangi	yoo **BANG** gee
Ubangi-Shari	yoo **BANG** gee **SHAHR** ee
Ubeda	**OO** be *THAH*
ubiety	yoo **BĪ** ə tee
ubiquitous	yoo **BIK** wə təs
Ucayali	oo kah **YAH** lee
Udaipur	uu **DĪ PUUR**
Udall (US)	**YOO** dawl
Udall, Udale (England)	**YOOD** əl
Udmurt	**UUD** muurt

o **on**, oh **oat**, oi **boy**, oo **soon**, oor **poor**, or **for**, ow **cow**, sh **shush**, *th* **thin**, *th* **this**, u **up**, ur **spur**, uu **book**, *zh* **pleasure**

udometer	yoo **DOM** ə tər
Uele	**WAY** lee
Uelses	**YUUL** səs
Ufa	oo **FAH**
Uffizi	oo **FEE** tsee
UFOlogy, ufology	yoo **FOL** ə jee
Uganda	yoo **GAN** də
Ugaritic	oo gə **RIT** ik
ugli	**UG** lee
Ugrian	**OO** gree ən
Ugric	**OO** grik
uhlan	**OO** lahn
Uigur, Uighur	**WEE** guur
Uinta	yoo **IN** tə
uitlander, U-	**OIT** lan dər
Ujiji	oo **JEE** jee
Ujpest	**OO** ee pesht
ukase	yoo **KAYS**
Ukraine	yoo **KRAYN**
Ukrainian	yoo **KRAY** nee ən
ukulele	yoo kə **LAY** lee
Ulan Bator	**OO** lahn **BAH** tor
Ulanhu	oo lahn hoo
Ulan-Ude	oo lahn uu **DAY**
Ulbricht	**UUL** brikt
ulcer	**UL** sər
ulema	oo lə **MAH**
Ulfilas	**UL** fi ləs
ullage	**UL** ij
Ulm	uulm
ulna	**UL** nə
Ulotrichi	yoo **LOT** ri kī
ulotrichous	yoo **LOT** ri kəs
Ulrica	**UL** ri kə
Ulrichsen, Wilhelm	**OOL** rik sən, **WIL** helm
Ulster, u-	**UL** stər
ulterior	ul **TIR** ee ər
ultimate	**UL** tə mət
ultima Thule	**UUL** tə mah **TOO** le
ultimatum	ul tə **MAY** təm
ultimo	**UL** tə moh
ultra	**UL** trə
ultramontane	ul trə **MON** tayn

ə ago, a at, ah calm, ahr dark, air care, aw saw, ay say, ch church
e bet, ee me, eer beer, hw what, i is, ī my, *n* French final n vin,

ultrasonic	UL trə SAHN ik
ultraviolet	UL trə VĪ ə lət
ultra vires	UL trə VĪ reez
ululate	YOOL yə LAYT
Ulusu, Bülend	OOL oo SOO, buu LEND
Ulysses	yuu LIS eez
Umatilla	YOO mə TIL ə
umber	UM bər
umbilical	um BIL i kəl
umbilicus	um BIL i kəs
umbra	UM brə
umbrage	UM brij
umbrageous	um BRAY jəs
umbrella	um BREL ə
Umbria	UM bree ə
Umbriel	UM bree EL
Umeki, Myoshi	oo me kee, mee oh shee
umiak	OO mee AK
umlaut	UUM lowt (lowt as in *out*)
Umtata	uum TAHT ə
Una	OO nə
Unalaska	UN ə LAS kə
Unamuno	oo nah MOO noh
unanimity	YOO nə NIM ə tee
unanimous	yuu NAN ə məs
unbiased	UN BĪ əst
uncial	UN shəl
unconscionable	un KON shə nə bəl
uncouth	un KOOTH
unction	UNGK shən
unctuous	UNGK choo əs
undine, U-	un DEEN
undoubtedly	un DOW təd lee
undulant	UN jə lənt
undulate (a)	UN jə lət
undulate (v)	UN jə LAYT
undulatory	UN jə lə TOR ee
unequivocal	UN i KWIV ə kəl
unerring	UN ER ing
unfrequented	UN fri KWENT əd
ungual	UNG gwəl
unguent	UNG gwənt
ungulate	UNG gyə lət

o on, oh oat, oi boy, oo soon, oor poor, or for, ow cow, sh shush,
th thin, *th* this, u up, ur spur, uu book, *zh* pleasure

Uniat, Uniate	**YOO** nee **AT**
unicameral	**YOO** ni **KAM** ə rəl
unicorn, U-	**YOO** nə **KORN**
unicycle	**YOO** ni **SĪ** kəl
unilateral	**YOO** ni **LAT** ə rəl
unique	yoo **NEEK**
unisex	**YOO** nə **SEKS**
unison	**YOO** nə sən
Unitarian, u-	**YOO** nə **TAIR** ee ən
unity	**YOO** nə tee
universal	**YOO** nə **VUR** səl
universality	**YOO** nə vər **SAL** ə tee
universe	**YOO** nə **VURS**
unmitigated	**UN MIT** ə **GAY** təd
unobtrusive	**UN** əb **TROO** siv
unprecedented	**UN PRES** ə **DEN** təd
unrighteous	**UN RĪ** chəs
Unruh, Jess	**UN** rə
unruly	**UN ROO** lee
unsavory	**UN SAY** və ree
Unter den Linden	**UUN** tər den **LIN** dən
Unterseeboot	**UUN** ter zay boht
untoward	un **TORD**
unwarranted	**UN WOR** ən təd
unwonted	**UN WAWN** təd
Upanishad	oo **PAHN** i **SHAHD**
upas	**YOO** pəs
upholster	up **HOHL** stər
upland, U-	**UP** lənd
uplander	**UP** lənd ər
Upolu	oo **POH** loo
Uppsala, Upsala	**UP** sə **LAH**
uproarious	up **ROR** ee əs
upset (n)	**UP** set
upset (v, a)	up **SET**
upshot	**UP** shot
upsilon	**YOOP** sə **LON**
Ur	ur
uraeus	yuu **REE** əs
Ural	**YUUR** əl
Uralic	yuu **RAL** ik
Urania	yuu **RAY** nee ə
uranic	yuu **RAN** ik

ə ago, a at, ah calm, ahr dark, air care, aw saw, ay say, ch church
e bet, ee me, eer beer, hw what, i is, ī my, *n* French final n vin,

uranium	yuu **RAY** nee əm
Uranus	**YUU** rə nəs
urban, U-	**UR** bən
Urbana	**UR BAN** ə
urbane	ur **BAYN**
urbanity	**UR BAN** ə tee
urbanize	**UR** bən īz
urbi et orbi	**OOR** bee **ET OR** bee
urchin	**UR** chən
Urdu	**UUR** doo
urea	yuu **REE** ə
uremia	yuu **REE** mee ə
ureter	yuu **REE** tər
urethra	yuu **REE** thrə
Urey	**YUUR** ee
Urfa	uur **FAH**
Urga	**UUR** gah
Uriah	yuu **RĪ** ə
Uriel	**YUUR** ee əl
Urim	**YUUR** əm
urinal	**YUUR** ə nəl
urinalysis	**YUUR** ə **NAL** ə səs
Uris	**YUUR** əs
Urmia	**UUR** mee ə
urology	yuu **ROL** ə jee
Urquhart	**UR** kərt
Ursa	**UR** sə
ursine	**UR** sīn
Ursprache	**UUR SHPRAH** kə
Ursula	**UR** sə lə
Ursuline	**UR** sə lən
urticaria	**UR** tə **KA** ree ə
Uruguay	**UUR** ə **GWĪ**
Urundi	uu **RUUN** dee
urus	**YUUR** əs
usage	**YOO** sij
U San Yu	oo sahn yoo
use (n)	yoos
use (v)	yooz
Ushant	**USH** ənt
Ushas	**UUSH** əs
Usk	usk
Uspallata	**oos** pah **YAH** tah

---

o **on**, oh **oat**, oi **boy**, oo **soon**, oor **poor**, or **for**, ow **cow**, sh **shush**,
th **thin**, *th* **this**, u **up**, ur **spur**, uu **book**, *zh* **pleasure**

usquebaugh	US kwi **BAW**
Ussuri	oo **SOO** ree
Ustinov, Peter	**YOO** stə **NAWF**
usual	**YOO** *zh*oo əl
usufruct	**YOO** zə **FRUKT**
usurer	**YOO** *zh*ə rər
usurious	yuu **ZH**UUR ee əs
usurp	yuu **SURP**
usurpation	**YOO** sər **PAY** shən
usurper	yuu **SURP** ər
usury	**YOO** *zh*ə ree
Utah	**YOO** taw
Utamaro, Kitagawa	oo tah mah roh, kee tah gah wah
Ute	yoot
utensil	yuu **TEN** səl
uterine	**YOO** tər ən
uterus	**YOO** tər əs
Uther	**YOO** thər
Utica	**YOO** ti kə
utilitarian	yoo **TIL** ə **TAIR** ee ən
utility	yoo **TIL** ə tee
utilize	**YOO** tə **LĪZ**
uti possidetis	**YOO** tī **POS** i **DEE** tis
Uto-Aztecan	**YOO** toh **AZ** **TEK** ən
Utopia	yuu **TOH** pee ə
Utrecht	**YOO** trekt
Utrillo	yoo **TRIL** oh
Utt	ut
Uttar Pradesh	**UUT** ər prə **DAYSH**
utterance	**UT** ər əns
Uusikaupunki	oo see **KOW** puung kee
uvea	**YOO** vee ə
uvula	**YOO** vyə lə
U Win Maung	oo win mowng (mowng as in *town*)
Uxmal	oosh **MAHL**
uxoricide	UK **SOR** ə **SĪD**
uxorious	UK **SOR** ee əs
Uzbek	**UUZ** bek
Uzbekistan	uuz **BEK** i **STAN**
Uzhorod	**UUZ***H* haw **RAWT**
Uzice	**OO** *zh*it se

ə ago, a at, ah calm, ahr dark, air care, aw saw, ay say, ch church
e bet, ee me, eer beer, hw what, i is, ī my, *n* French final n vin,

V

Vaal	vahl
Vaasa	**VAH** sah
vacant	**VAY** kənt
vacate	**VAY** kayt
vacation	vay **KAY** shən
vaccinate	**VAK** sə **NAYT**
vaccine	vak **SEEN**
Vachel	**VAY** chəl
vacillate	**VAS** ə **LAYT**
vacuity	va **KYOO** ə tee
vacuole	**VAK** yoo **OHL**
vacuous	**VAK** yoo əs
vacuum	**VAK** yoo əm
vade mecum	**VAY** dee **MEE** kəm
Vaduz	**VAH** duuts
vagary	**VAY** gə ree
vagina	və **JĪ** nə
vaginal	**VAJ** ə nəl
vaginitis	**VAJ** ə **NĪT** əs
vagrancy	**VAY** grən see
vagrant	**VAY** grənt
vagus	**VAY** gəs
Vakil, Mehdi	va **KEEL**, med **EE**
valance	**VAL** əns
Valdai	vahl **DĪ**
Valdepeñas	**VAHL** də **PE** nyahs
Valdés, Valdéz	vahl **DES**
Valdez (Alaska)	val **DEEZ**
vale (farewell)	**WAH** lay
valediction	**VAL** ə **DIK** shən
valedictory	**VAL** ə **DIK** tə ree
valence	**VAY** ləns
Valencia	və **LEN** see ə
Valencia, Guillermo	vah **LEN** syah, gee **LYAIR** moh
Valenciennes lace	və **LEN** see **ENZ**
Valenzuela, Enrique	**VAL** ən **ZWAY** lə, en **REE** kay
valerian, V-	və **LIR** ee ən
valeric	və **LER** ik

o on, oh oat, oi boy, oo soon, oor poor, or for, ow cow, sh shush,
th thin, *th* this, u up, ur spur, uu book, *zh* pleasure

Valerie	**VAL** ə ree
Valéry	va lay **REE**
valet	**VAL** ət
valetudinarian	**VAL** ə **TOO** də **NER** ee ən
Valga	**VAHL** gə
valgus	**VAL** gəs
Valhalla	val **HAL** ə
valiant	**VAL** yənt
valise	və **LEES**
Valium	**VAL** ee əm
Valkyrie	val **KIR** ee
Vallauris	**VAL** aw **REES**
Vallejo	va **LAY** hoh
Valletta	vahl **LET** tah
Vallombrosa	**VAL** əm **BROH** sə
Valmiera	**VAHL** myer ah
Valois	val **WAH**
Valparaiso (Chile)	**VAL** pə **RĪ** zoh
Valparaiso (Indiana)	**VAL** pə **RAY** zoh
valpolicella, V-	**VAHL POH** li **CHEL** ah
valse	vahls
valuable	**VAL** yə bəl
valvulitis	**VAL** vyə **LĪ** təs
vanadium	və **NAY** dee əm
Vanbrugh	van **BROO**
Van Buren	van **BYUUR** ən
Vancouver	van **KOO** vər
vandal, V-	**VAN** dəl
Van Deerlin	van **DEER** lin
Vander Jagt	**VAN** dər **JAK**
Van Dyck, Vandyke	van **DĪK**
Van Eyck	van **ĪK**
van Gogh	van **GOH**
vanguard	**VAN** gahrd
Vanier	va **NYAY**
vanilla	və **NIL** ə
vanillin	və **NIL** ən
Vanir, v-	**VAH** nir
vanquish	**VANG** kwish
Vansittart	van **SIT** ərt
vantage	**VANT** ij
Vanua Levu	vah **NOO** ah **LE** voo
Vanuatu	**VAN** ə **WAHT** oo

ə ago, a at, ah calm, ahr dark, air care, aw saw, ay say, ch church
e bet, ee me, eer beer, hw what, i is, ī my, *n* French final n vin,

van Well, Guenter	fahn **VEL**, **GUUN** tər
Vanzetti	van **ZET** ee
vapid	**VAP** əd
vapor	**VAY** pər
vaporetti	**VAP** ə **RET** ee
vaporetto	**VAP** ə **RET** oh
vaporous	**VAY** pər əs
vaquero	vah **KAIR** oh
varactor	va **RAK** tər
Varese	vah **RE** se
Varèse, Edgard	və **REZ**, ed **GAHR**
variable	**VA** ree ə bəl
variance	**VA** ree əns
variation	**VA** ree **AY** shən
varicocele	**VA** rə koh **SEEL**
varicose	**VA** rə **KOHS**
variegate	**VA** ree ə **GAYT**
varietal	və **RĪ** ə təl
variety	və **RĪ** ə tee
Varig	**VA** rig
variorum	**VA** ree **OR** əm
varistor	va **RIS** tər
varlet	**VAHR** lət
Varna	**VAHR** nə
Varro	**VA** roh
Varuna	**VA** ruu nə
varus	**VA** rəs
vary	**VA** ree
vasa murrhina	**VAY** sə mə **RĪ** nə
Vasari	vah **ZAH** ree
Vasco da Gama	**VA** skoh də **GAM** ə
vascular	**VAS** kyə lər
vas deferens	**VAS** **DEF** ə **RENZ**
vasectomy	va **SEK** tə mee
Vaseline	**VAS** ə **LEEN**
Vashti	**VASH** tī
vasomotor	**VAS** oh **MOH** tər
vassal	**VAS** əl
vassalage	**VAS** ə lij
Vassilevsky	**VAH** si **LEF** skee
Vatican	**VAT** i kən
Vaucluse	voh **KLOOZ**
vaudeville	**VAWD** vəl

o on, oh oat, oi boy, oo soon, oor poor, or for, ow cow, sh shush,
th thin, *th* this, u up, ur spur, uu book, *zh* pleasure

Vaughan	vawn
vault	vawlt
vaunt	vawnt
Veblen	**VEB** lən
vector	**VEK** tər
Veda	**VAY** də
Vedanta	və **DON** tə
vedette	vi **DET**
Vedic	**VAY** dik
Vega (star)	**VEE** gə
Vega, Lope de	**VAY** gah, **LOH** pay day
vegetable	**VEJ** tə bəl
vegetarian	**VEJ** ə **TER** ee ən
Vegh-Villegaz, Aleandro	**VAYG** vee **ZHAY** gahs, ahl ay **HAHN** droh
vehemence	**VEE** ə məns
vehement	**VEE** ə mənt
vehicle	**VEE** i kəl
vehicular	vee **HIK** yə lər
vein	vayn
Vela	**VEE** lə
velar	**VEE** lər
Velasco	ve **LAHS** koh
Velázquez, Diego	vay **LAHTH** keth, **DYAY** goh
Velázquez, Guaroa	bay **LAHS** kez, gwah **ROH** ah
veld, veldt	velt
velleity	və **LEE** ə tee
vellum	**VEL** əm
velocipede	və **LOS** ə **PEED**
velocity	və **LOS** ə tee
velour	və **LUUR**
velouté	və loo **TAY**
velum	**VEE** ləm
velure	və **LUUR**
velveteen	**VEL** və **TEEN**
vena cava	**VEE** nə **KAY** və
venal	**VEEN** əl
venality	vi **NAL** ə tee
venation	vee **NAY** shən
Venda	**VEN** də
vendetta	ven **DET** ə
Vendôme	vahn **DOHM**
vendor	**VEN** dər

ə ago, a at, ah calm, ahr dark, air care, aw saw, ay say, ch church
e bet, ee me, eer beer, hw what, i is, ī my, *n* French final n vin,

vendue	ven **DOO**
veneer	və **NIR**
venerate	**VEN** ə **RAYT**
venereal	və **NIR** ee əl
venery	**VEN** ə ree
Venetian	və **NEE** shən
Veneto	**VEN** ə **TOH**
Venezia	ve **NE** tsyah
Venezuela	**VEN** ə **ZWAY** lə
vengeance	**VEN** jəns
venial	**VEE** nee əl
Venice	**VEN** əs
venipuncture	**VEEN** ə **PUNGK** chər
venire	və **NĪ** ree
venireman	və **NĪ** ree mən
venison	**VEN** ə sən
Venite	və **NEE** tay
veni, vidi, vici	**WAY** nee, **WEE** dee, **WEE** kee
venom	**VEN** əm
venous	**VEE** nəs
Venta	**VEN** tah
ventral	**VEN** trəl
ventricle	**VEN** tri kəl
ventricular	ven **TRIK** yə lər
ventriloquism	ven **TRIL** ə **KWIZ** əm
ventriloquist	ven **TRIL** ə kwəst
Ventspils	**VENTS** peels
venture	**VEN** chər
Venturi	ven **TUUR** ee
venturous	**VEN** chər əs
venue	**VEN** yoo
Venus	**VEE** nəs
veracious	və **RAY** shəs
veracity	və **RAS** ə tee
Veracruz	**VER** ə **KROOZ**
veranda	və **RAN** də
verbal	**VURB** əl
verbatim	vər **BAY** təm
verbena	vər **BEE** nə
verbiage	**VUR** bee ij
verbose	vər **BOHS**
verbosity	vər **BOS** ə tee
verboten	fər **BOHT** ən

o on, oh oat, oi boy, oo soon, oor poor, or for, ow cow, sh shush,
th thin, *th* this, u up, ur spur, uu book, *zh* pleasure

Vercingetorix	**VUR** sin **JET** ə riks
verdant	**VUR** dənt
Verde (cape)	vurd
Verdi	**VAIR** dee
verdigris	**VUR** də **GREES**
Verdun	vər **DUN**
verdure	**VUR** jər
Verein	fer **ĪN**
verge	vurj
verger	**VUR** jər
Vergil	**VUR** jəl
verglas	ver **GLAH**
verisimilitude	**VER** ə sə **MIL** ə **TOOD**
veritable	**VER** ə tə bəl
vérité	**VAY** ree **TAY**
Verlaine	ver **LEN**
Vermeer	vər **MEER**
vermeil	**VUR** məl
vermicelli	**VUR** mə **CHEL** ee
vermicular	vər **MIK** yə lər
vermiculite	vər **MIK** yə **LĪT**
vermiform	**VUR** mə **FORM**
vermifuge	**VUR** mə **FYOOJ**
vermilion	vər **MIL** yən
vermin	**VUR** mən
Vermont	vər **MONT**
vermouth	vər **MOOTH**
vernacular	vər **NAK** yə lər
vernal	**VUR** nəl
Verne	vurn
Verner	**VUR** nər
Vernier	**VUR** nee ər
Vernier-Palliez, Bernard	vair **NYAY** pahl **YAY**, bair **NAHR**
Vernon	**VUR** nən
Verona	və **ROH** nə
Veronal	**VER** ə nəl
Veronese	**VER** ə **NEEZ**
Veronese, Paolo	vay roh **NAY** ze, **PAH** oh loh
veronica, V-	və **RON** i kə
Véronique	**VAY** raw **NEEK**
Verrazano Bridge	**VER** ə **ZAH** noh
Verrocchio	və **ROH** kee **OH**

ə ago, a at, ah calm, ahr dark, air care, aw saw, ay say, ch church
e bet, ee me, eer beer, hw what, i is, ī my, *n* French final n vin,

verruca	və **ROO** kə
Versailles (France)	ver **SĪ**
Versailles (US)	vər **SAYLZ**
versatile	**VUR** sət əl
version	**VUR** zhən
vers libre	vair **LEEB** rə
verso	**VUR** soh
versus	**VUR** səs
vertebra	**VUR** tə brə
vertebral	**VUR** tə brəl
vertebrate	**VUR** tə brət
vertiginous	vər **TIJ** ə nəs
vertigo	**VUR** tə **GOH**
Vertumnus	vər **TUM** nəs
vervain	**VUR** vayn
Verwoerd, Hendrik	fair **FUUT, HEN** drik
vesical	**VES** i kəl
vesicle	**VES** i kəl
Vespasian	ves **PAY** zhən
vesper	**VES** pər
Vespucci, Amerigo	ve **SPOO** chee, ə **MER** ə **GOH**
Vesta	**VES** tə
vestibule	**VES** tə **BYOOL**
vestige	**VES** tij
vestigial	ves **TIJ** ee əl
vestment	**VEST** mənt
vesture	**VES** chər
Vesuvius	və **SOO** vee əs
veterinarian	**VET** ər ə **NER** ee ən
veterinary	**VET** ər ə **NER** ee
via	**VĪ** ə
viable	**VĪ** ə bəl
viaduct	**VĪ** ə **DUKT**
vial	**VĪ** əl
viand	**VĪ** ənd
viaticum	vī **AT** i kəm
Via Veneto	**VEE** ə **VEN** ə **TOH**
Viborg	**VEE** bor
vibrant	**VĪ** brənt
vibrato	vi **BRAH** toh
viburnum	vī **BUR** nəm
vicar	**VIK** ər
vicarious	vī **KA** ree əs

o **on**, oh **oat**, oi **boy**, oo **soon**, oor **poor**, or **for**, ow **cow**, sh **shush**,
th **thin**, *th* **this**, u **up**, ur **spur**, uu **book**, *zh* **pleasure**

vicegerent	vīs **JIR** ənt
vicennial	vī **SEN** ee əl
vice-regent	vīs **REE** jənt
vicereine	**VĪS** rayn
viceroy	**VĪS** roi
vice versa	**VĪ** si **VUR** sə
Vichy	**VEESH** ee
vichyssoise	vee shee **SWAHZ**
Vichy water	**VISH** ee
vicinity	və **SIN** ə tee
vicious	**VISH** əs
vicissitude	və **SIS** ə **TOOD**
Victoria, v-	vik **TOR** ee ə
victual	**VIT** əl
victualler	**VIT** ə lər
vicuña	vī **KOO** nə
Vidal, Gore	vee **DAHL, GOR**
vide	**VEE** day
videlicet	vi **DAY** li **KET**
Vidzeme	**VEED** ze me
vie (French)	vee
vie (strive)	vī
Vienna	vee **EN** ə
Vientiane	vyen **TYAHN**
Vietcong	vyet **KONG**
Vietminh	vyet **MIN**
Viet-Nam, Vietnam	vyet **NAHM**
Vigan	**VEE** gahn
vigesimal	vī **JES** ə məl
vigil	**VIJ** əl
vigilant	**VIJ** ə lənt
vigilante	**VIJ** ə **LAN** tee
vignette	vin **YET**
Vigny	vee **NYEE**
vigor	**VIG** ər
vigoroso	**VIG** ə **ROH** soh
Viipuri	**VEE** puu **REE**
Viking, v-	**VĪ** king
Vila	**VEE** lah
vilify	**VIL** ə **FĪ**
Viljandi	**VIL** yahn dee
Viljoen, Marais	fuul **YOON**, mah **RAY**
villa	**VIL** ə

ə ago, a at, ah calm, ahr dark, air care, aw saw, ay say, ch church
e bet, ee me, eer beer, hw what, i is, ī my, *n* French final n vin,

village	**VIL** ij
villain	**VIL** ən
Villa-Lobos, Heitor	**VEE** lah **LOH** bohs, **AY** tuur
villanelle	**VIL** ə **NEL**
Villa, Pancho	**VEE** yah, **PAHN** choh
Villard	və **LAHRD**
Villeda Morales, Ramón	vee **LYAY** *th*ah moh **RAH** les, rah **MOHN**
Villiers	**VIL** ərz
Villon	vee **YAWN** (**YAWN** French final *n*)
Vilna	**VIL** nə
vimpa	**VIM** pə
vinaigrette	**VIN** ə **GRET**
vin blanc	van **BLAHN** (van and **BLAHN** French final *n*)
Vincennes (France)	van **SEN** (van French final *n*)
Vincennes (Indiana)	vin **SENZ**
Vinci, da	**VIN** chee, də
Vindhya	**VIND** yah
vindicatory	**VIN** di kə **TOR** ee
vindictive	vin **DIK** tiv
vineyard	**VIN** yərd
viniculture	**VIN** ə **KUL** chər
vinifera	vī **NIF** ə rə
vin ordinaire	van or dee **NAIR** (van French final *n*)
vinous	**VĪ** nəs
vin rouge	van **ROOZ***H* (van French final *n*)
vintage	**VIN** tij
vinyl	**VĪ** nəl
viol	**VĪ** əl
viola (instrument)	vee **OH** lə
viola (plant)	vī **OH** lə
violable	**VĪ** ə lə bəl
viola da gamba	vee **OH** lə də **GOM** bə
viola d'amore	vee **OH** lə dah **MOR** ay
violate (v)	**VĪ** ə **LAYT**
violate (a)	**VĪ** ə lət
violet, V-	**VĪ** ə lət
violin	vī ə **LIN**
violoncello	vī ə lən **CHEL** oh
virago	və **RAH** goh
vireo	**VIR** ee oh
Virgil	**VUR** jəl

---

o **on,** oh **oat,** oi **boy,** oo **soon,** oor **poor,** or **for,** ow **cow,** sh **shush,**
th **thin,** *th* **this,** u **up,** ur **spur,** uu **book,** *zh* **pleasure**

Virgilian	vər **JIL** yən
virginal	**VUR** jə nəl
Virgo	**VUR** goh
virgule	**VUR** gyool
viridescent	**VIR** ə **DES** ənt
virile	**VIR** əl
virility	və **RIL** ə tee
Virtanen, Artturi	**VIR** tah **NEN**, **AHRT** tuu ree
virtu	vur **TOO**
virtual	**VUR** choo əl
virtue	**VUR** choo
virtuosa	**VUR** choo **OH** sə
virtuosi	**VUR** choo **OH** see
virtuosic	**VUR** choo **OH** sik
virtuosity	**VUR** choo **OS** ə tee
virtuoso	**VUR** choo **OH** soh
virtuous	**VUR** choo əs
virulent	**VIR** yə lənt
virus	**VĪ** rəs
visa	**VEE** zə
visage	**VIZ** ij
vis-à-vis	**VEE** zə **VEE**
Visayan	və **SĪ** ən
viscera	**VIS** ə rə
viscid	**VIS** əd
viscosity	vis **KOS** ə tee
viscount	**VĪ** kownt
viscous	**VIS** kəs
viscus	**VIS** kəs
Vishnevskaya, Galina	veesh **NYEV** **SKĪ** ə, gah **LEE** nə
Visigoth	**VIZ** ə **GOTH**
vision	**VIZH** ən
visionary	**VIZH** ə **NER** ee
visor	**VĪ** zər
Vistula	**VIS** chuu lə
visual	**VIZH** oo əl
vitamin	**VĪ** tə min
Vitebsk	**VEE** tepsk
vitiate	**VISH** ee **AYT**
viticulture	**VIT** ə **KUL** chər
Viti Levu	**VEE** tee **LE** voo
vitreous	**VI** tree əs
vitrify	**VI** trə **FĪ**
vitriol	**VIT** ree əl

ə ago, a at, ah calm, ahr dark, air care, aw saw, ay say, ch church
e bet, ee me, eer beer, hw what, i is, ī my, *n* French final n vin,

vitriolic	**VIT** ree **OL** ik
Vitti	**VEE** tee
Vittorio	vi **TAW** ree oh
vituperation	vī **TOO** pə **RAY** shən
vituperative	vī **TOO** pə rə tiv
viva	**VEE** və
vivace	vee **VAH** chay
vivacious	və **VAY** shəs
vivacity	və **VAS** ə tee
Vivaldi	vi **VAHL** dee
vivarium	vī **VA** ree əm
viva voce	**VĪ** və **VOH** see
vivax	**VĪ** vaks
vivify	**VIV** ə **FĪ**
viviparous	və **VIP** ə rəs
vivisection	**VIV** ə **SEK** shən
vixen	**VIK** sən
vizier	və **ZEER**
vizsla	**VIZH** lə
Vladimir	**VLAD** ə **MIR**
Vladivostok	**VLAD** ə **VOS** tok
vocalic	voh **KAL** ik
vocalize	**VOH** kə **LĪZ**
vocative	**VOK** ə tiv
vociferous	voh **SIF** ər əs
vodka	**VOD** kə
voilà	vwah **LAH**
voile	voil
voir dire	vwahr **DEER**
Volans	**VOH** lanz
volant	**VOH** lənt
Volapuk	**VOH** lə **PUUK**
volatile	**VOL** ə təl
vol-au-vent	vaw loh **VAHN** (**VAHN** French final *n*)
volcanic	vol **KAN** ik
volcanism	**VOL** kə **NIZ** əm
volcano, V-	vol **KAY** noh
Volcker, Paul	**VOHL** kər
Volga	**VOL** gə
Volgograd	**VOL** gə **GRAD**
Volio Jiménez, Fernando	voh **LEE** oh hee **MAY** nez, fair **NAHN** doh
volition	və **LISH** ən

---

o **on**, oh **oat**, oi **boy**, oo **soon**, oor **poor**, or **for**, ow **cow**, sh **shush**, th **thin**, *th* **this**, u **up**, ur **spur**, uu **book**, *zh* **pleasure**

volitive	**VOL** ə tiv
Volk (German)	fawlk
Volkswagen	**VOHKS WAG** ən
Vologda	**VAW** ləg dah
Volpe	**VOHL** pee
volplane	**VOL** playn
Volpone	vol **POH** nee
Volsunga	**VOL** suung gə
Volta, Alessandro	**VOHL** tə, **AH** les **SAHN** draw
voltaic	vol **TAY** ik
Voltaire	vohl **TAIR**
volte-face	vawlt **FAHS**
Volturno	vawl **TUUR** noh
voluble	**VOL** yə bəl
volume	**VOL** yəm
voluminous	və **LOO** mə nəs
voluntarism	**VOL** ən tə **RIZ** əm
voluptuary	və **LUP** choo **ER** ee
voluptuous	və **LUP** choo əs
volute	və **LOOT**
vomitus	**VOM** ə təs
von, V- (German)	fawn
von Hassel, Kai-Uwe	fawn **HAH** səl, kī **OO** və
Vonnegut, Kurt	**VAHN** i gət, **KUURT**
voodoo	**VOO** doo
voracious	vaw **RAY** shəs
voracity	vaw **RAS** ə tee
vorlage	**FOR LAHG** ə
Voronezh	vaw **RAW** nesh
Vorster	**FAWR** stər
vortex	**VOR** teks
Vosges	voh*zh*
votary	**VOH** tə ree
Votyak	vaw **TYAHK**
vouchsafe	vowch **SAYF**
vox populi	**VOKS POP** yə **LĪ**
voyage	**VOI** ij
voyager	**VOI** i jər
voyageur	**VWAH** yah *ZH*UR
voyeur	vwah **YUR**
voyeurism	vwah **YUR IZ** əm
Voznesensky, Andrei	**VAWZ** nyə **SEN** skee, **AHN** dray
Vraalsen, Tom Eric	**VROL** sən

ə ago, a at, ah calm, ahr dark, air care, aw saw, ay say, ch church
e bet, ee me, eer beer, hw what, i is, ī my, *n* French final n vin,

Vries	vrees
Vrsac	**VUR** shahts
Vuelta Abajo	**VWEL** tə ə **BAH** hoh
Vuillard	vwee **YAHR**
Vulcan	**VUL** kən
vulgar	**VUL** gər
vulgarian	**VUL GA** ree ən
vulgarism	**VUL** gə **RIZ** əm
vulgarity	**VUL GA** rə tee
Vulgate, v-	**VUL** gayt
vulnerable	**VUL** nər ə bəl
Vulpecula	vul **PEK** yə lə
vulpine	**VUL** pīn
vulva	**VUL** və
Vyatka	**VYAHT** kah
Vyazma	**VYAHZ** mah
Vyborg	**VEE** borg
Vychegda	**VICH** ig də

W

Waal	vahl
Waals, Johannes	**WAWLZ**, yoh **HON** əs
Wabash	**WAW** bash
Wabuge, Wafula	wah **BOO** ge, wah **FOO** lah (ge *g* almost silent)
Waco	**WAY** koh
Wadai	wah **DĪ**
wadi	**WAH** dee
Wafd	wahft
waft	wahft
Wagner (German)	**VAHG** nər
Wagner (US)	**WAG** nər
Wagnerian	vahg **NIR** ee ən
wagoner, W-	**WAG** ə nər
wagon-lit	va gawn **LEE** (gawn French final *n*)
Wahhabi	wah **HAH** bee
wahine	wah **HEE** nee
waif	wayf
Waikiki	**wī** kee **KEE**
wainscot	**WAYN** skət

o on, oh oat, oi boy, oo soon, oor poor, or for, ow cow, sh shush,
th thin, *th* this, u up, ur spur, uu book, *zh* pleasure

wainwright, W-	**WAYN** rīt
waistcoat	**WES** kət
Wakashan	waw **KASH** ən
Wakayama	wah kah yah mah
Waksman, Selman	**WAKS** mən, **SEL** mən
Walachia, Wallachia	wah **LAY** kee ə
Walden	**WAWL** dən
Waldenses	wawl **DEN** seez
Waldheim, Kurt	**VAHLT** hīm, **KUURT**
Waldorf	**WAWL** dorf
Walesa, Lech	vah **WEN** sah, lek
Walker, w-	**WAW** kər
Walküre, Die	vahl **KIR** ee, dee
Wallace	**WOL** əs
Wallachia	wah **LAY** kee ə
wallah	**WOL** ə
walleye	**WAWL** ī
Wallhauser	**WAWL** how zər
Wallis	**WOL** əs
Walloon	wol **OON**
Wallops (island)	**WOL** əps
wallow	**WOL** oh
Walpurgis	vahl **PUUR** gəs
Walpurgisnacht	vahl **PUURG** əs **NAHKT**
Walsingham	**WAWL** sing əm
waltz	wawlts
Walvis	**WAWL** vəs
Wampanoag	**WOM** pə **NOH** ag
wampum	**WOM** pəm
wan	wahn
Wanamaker	**WAH** nə **MAY** kər
wander	**WAHN** dər
Wanderjahr	**VAHN** dər **YAHR**
wanderlust	**WAHN** dər **LUST**
wangan	**WAHN** gən
Wang Zhen	wahng jun
wanigan	**WAHN** i gən
Wankel	**VAHN** kəl
Wan Li	wahn lee
Wanne-Eickel	**VAH** nə **ĪK** əl
Wantagh	**WAHN** taw
wanton	**WAHN** tən
wantonness	**WAHNT** ən nəs

ə ago, a at, ah calm, ahr dark, air care, aw saw, ay say, ch church
e bet, ee me, eer beer, hw what, i is, ī my, n French final n vin,

wapentake	WOP ən TAYK
wapiti	WOP ə tee
Warburton	WOR BUR tən
warlock	WOR lok
Warnke, Paul	WORN kee
warrant	WOR ənt
warranty	WOR ən tee
warrior	WOR ee ər
Warsaw	WOR saw
Warszawa	vahr SHAH vah
Warwick	WOR ik
wary	WAIR ee
Wasatch	WAW sach
Wasell	wah SEL
Wasiuddin, Khwaja	WAH see yoo DEEN, KWAH jah
wassail	WAH səl
Wassermann	WAH sər mən
wastrel	WAY strəl
Watanabe, Kiichi	wah tah nah be, kee eech ee
Waterbury	WAW tər BER ee
Waterloo	WAW tər LOO
Watling	WOT ling
Watteau	wah TOH
Waugh	waw
Waukegan	waw KEE gən
waxen	WAKS ən
Waziristan	wah ZIR i STAN
weal	weel
weald, W-	weeld
wean	ween
weaponry	WEP ən ree
wear	wair
wearisome	WIR ee səm
weary	WIR ee
Weber (German)	VAY bər
weber (physics)	WEB ər
Wechmar, Rudiger von	VEK mahr, RUUD i gər fawn
Wechsler	WEKS lər
Wedgwood	WEJ wuud
Wednesday	WENZ day
weevil	WEE vəl
Weicker, Lowell	WĪK ər, LOH əl

o on, oh oat, oi boy, oo soon, oor poor, or for, ow cow, sh shush,
th thin, *th* this, u up, ur spur, uu book, *zh* pleasure

Weifang	way fahng
weigela	wī **JEE** lə
Weihai	way hī
Weil, Simone	**VAY**, see **MUN**
Weill, Kurt	vīl, kuurt
Weimar	**VĪ** mahr
Weimaraner	**VĪ** mə **RAH** nər
Weinberger, Caspar	**WĪN BUR** gər, **KAS** pər
Wei Quoqing	way choh ching
weir	wir
weird	wird
Weismann, Weissmann (German)	**VĪS** mahn
Weizmann, Chaim	**VĪTS** mahn, **HĪ** əm
welkin	**WEL** kən
Wellesley	**WELZ** lee
Wellington	**WEL** ing tən
Welsbach	**WELZ** bak
Weltanschauung	**VELT** ahn **SHOW** uung (**SHOW** as in *cow*)
Weltansicht	**VELT AHN** zikt
Weltpolitik	**VELT** pawl i **TEEK**
Weltschmerz	**VELT** shmerts
Welty, Eudora	**WEL** tee, yoo **DOR** ə
Wemys, -s	weemz
Wenceslaus	**WEN** sə **SLAWS**
Wenchow, Wenzhou, Wen-chou	wun joh
Wend, w-	wend
Werther (German)	**VAIR** tər
Weser	**VAY** zər
Wesley	**WES** lee
Wesleyan	**WES** lee ən
Westminster	**WES MIN** stər
Westphalia	wes **FAYL** yə
Wetterhorn	**VET** ər **HORN**
whale	hwayl
wharf	hworf
wharfinger	**HWORF** ən jər
Wharton	**HWORT** ən
what	hwot
whatever	hwot **EV** ər

ə ago, a at, ah calm, ahr dark, air care, aw saw, ay say, ch church
e bet, ee me, eer beer, hw what, i is, ī my, *n* French final n vin,

wheat	hweet
whelp	hwelp
when	hwen
whence	hwens
whenever	hwen EV ər
where	hwair
whereas	hwair AZ
whereof	hwair UV
wherever	hwair EV ər
wherewithal	HWAIR with AWL
whether	HWE*TH* ər
whey	hway
which	hwich
whiffletree	HWIF əl TREE
Whig	hwig
while	hwīl
whilom	HWĪ ləm
whimsical	HWIM zi kəl
whimsy	HWIM zee
whine	hwīn
whinny	HWIN ee
whippet	HWIP ət
whippoorwill	HWIP ər WIL
whir	hwur
whirl	hwurl
whisper	HWIS pər
whist	hwist
whistle	HWIS əl
Whistler, w-	HWIS lər
whit	hwit
white	hwīt
whited	HWĪT əd
whither	HWI*TH* ər
Whitsunday	HWIT sən DAY
Whittier	HWIT ee ər
whoa	hwoh
whole	hohl
wholesome	HOHL səm
wholly	HOHL ee
whom	hoom
whoop	hoop
whoosh	hwoosh
whore	hawr

o on, oh oat, oi boy, oo soon, oor poor, or for, ow cow, sh shush,
th thin, *th* this, u up, ur spur, uu book, *zh* pleasure

whortleberry	**HWUR** təl **BER** ee
whose	hooz
why	hwī
Wichita	**WICH** ə **TAW**
Wickersham	**WI** kər shəm
wickiup	**WIK** ee **UP**
Wicklow	**WIK** loh
widgeon	**WIJ** ən
widget	**WIJ** ət
wie geht's	vee **GAYTS**
Wien (German)	veen
wiener	**WEE** nər
Wiener, Norbert	**WEE** nər, **NOR** bərt
Wiener schnitzel, w-	**VEE** nər **SHNIT** səl
Wiesbaden	**VEES BAHD** ən
Wigglesworth	**WIG** əlz **WURTH**
wight, W-	wīt
wildebeest	**WIL** də **BEEST**
Wilder	**WĪL** dər
wilderness	**WIL** dər nəs
Wilhelmina	**WIL** hel **MEE** nə
Wilhelm Meister	**VIL** helm **MĪ** stər
Wilhelmshaven	**VIL** helms **HAH** fən
Wilhelmstrasse	**VIL** helm **SHTRAH** sə
Wilkes	wilks
Wilkes-Barre	**WILKS BA** rə
Willamette	wə **LAM** ət
Willard	**WIL** ərd
Willemstad	**WIL** əm **STAHT**
Willesden	**WILZ** dən
Willis	**WIL** əs
Willoch, Kåre	**VIL** ək, **KOR** ə
willowy	**WIL** ə wee
Wiltshire	**WILT** shər
wily	**WĪ** lee
Wimbledon	**WIM** bəl dən
wimple	**WIM** pəl
Winchester	**WIN CHES** tər
windage	**WIN** dij
Windermere	**WIN** dər **MIR**
Windhoek	**VINT** huuk
windlass	**WIND** ləs
Windsor	**WIN** zər

ə ago, a at, ah calm, ahr dark, air care, aw saw, ay say, ch church
e bet, ee me, eer beer, hw what, i is, ī my, n French final n vin,

windward, W-	**WIND** wərd
Winnebago	**WIN** ə **BAY** goh
Winnepesaukee	**WIN** ə pə **SAW** kee
Winnipeg	**WIN** ə **PEG**
Winnipegosis	**WIN** ə pə **GOH** səs
Winona	wə **NOH** nə
Winooski	wə **NOOS** kee
Winslow	**WINZ** loh
winsome	**WIN** səm
Winston-Salem	**WIN** stən **SAY** ləm
Winterthur	**VINT** ər **TUUR**
(Switzerland)	
Winthrop	**WIN** thrəp
winy	**WĪ** nee
wiry	**WĪR** ee
wisdom	**WIZ** dəm
Wisla	**VEE** slah
wisteria	wis **TIR** ee ə
with	wi*th*
withal	wi*th* **AWL**
withdraw	wi*th* **DRAW**
wither	**WI*TH*** ər
withstand	with **STAND**
Wittenberg	**WIT** ən **BURG**
Witwatersrand	**WIT** **WAWT** ərz **RAND**
wizard	**WIZ** ərd
wizened	**WIZ** ənd
Wodehouse	**WUUD** hows
Woden, Wodan	**WOHD** ən
Wojtyla, Karol	voi **TEE** wah, **KAHR** əl
wolfram	**WUUL** frəm
Wolfram von	**VAWL** frahm fawn **ESH** ən **BAHK**
Eschenbach	
Wollstonecraft	**WUUL** stən **KRAFT**
Wolseley	**WUULZ** lee
Wolsey	**WUUL** zee
wombat	**WOM** bat
wonder	**WUN** dər
Wonsan	**WUN** sahn
wont	wawnt
won't	wohnt
wonted	**WAWNT** əd
wonton	**WAHN** **TAHN**

---

o **on**, oh **oat**, oi **boy**, oo **soon**, oor **poor**, or **for**, ow **cow**, sh **shush**,
th **thin**, *th* **this**, u **up**, ur **spur**, uu **book**, *zh* **pleasure**

Woodward	**WUUD** wərd
woof	wuuf
woofer	**WUUF** ər
Woolf	wuulf
Woollcott, Alexander	**WUUL** kət
Woolwich	**WUUL** ij
Woolworth	**WUUL** wurth
Woomera	**WUUM** ə rə
Woonsocket	woon **SOK** ət
Woosung	woo suung
Worcester	**WUUS** tər
Worcestershire	**WUUS** tər **SHIR**
Worms	wurmz
worship	**WUR** shəp
worsted (yarn)	**WUUS** təd
Worthington	**WUR** *th*ing tən
worthy	**WUR** *th*ee
Wotan	**VOH** tahn
Wotton	**WUUT** ən
Wouk, Herman	wohk
Wozzeck	**VAW** tsek
wraith	rayth
Wrangel, -l	**RANG** gəl
wrath	rath
wreak	reek
wreath	reeth
wreathe	ree*th*
Wren, w-	ren
wrestle	**RES** əl
wretched	**RECH** əd
writhe	rī*th*
Wroclaw	**VRAWT** slahf
wroth	rawth
wrought	rawt
wry	rī
Wuchang	woo chahng
Wuhan	woo hahn
wunderkind	**VUUN** dər **KINT**
Wuppertal	**VUUP** ər **TAHL**
Württemberg	**WUR** təm **BURG**
Würzburg	**WURTS** burg
Wuzhou	woo joh
Wyandot, -te	**WĪ** ən **DOT**

Wyatt	**WĪ** ət
Wycherley	**WICH** ər lee
Wyclif, -fe	**WIK** lif
Wyeth	**WĪ** əth
Wyndham	**WIN** dəm
Wynyard	**WIN** yərd
Wyoming	wī **OH** ming
Wyszynski, Cardinal Stefan	və **SHIN** skee, **STEF** ahn

X

Xanadu	**ZAN** ə doo
xanthic	**ZAN** thik
Xanthippe, Xantippe	zan **TIP** ee
Xavier	**ZAY** vee ər
Xavier (Spanish)	hah **VYER**
xebec	**ZEE** bek
Xenocrates	zi **NOK** rə **TEEZ**
xenon	**ZEE** non
xenophobia	**ZEN** ə **FOH** bee ə
Xenophon	**ZEN** ə fən
Xeres	**SHER** eez
xeric	**ZI** rik
xerography	zə **ROG** rə fee
xerophilous	zə **ROF** ə ləs
xerophthalmia	**ZI ROF THAL** mee ə
xerophyte	**ZI** rə **FĪT**
Xerox	**ZI** roks
Xerxes	**ZURK** seez
Xhosa	**KOH** sah
xi	zī
Xi (river)	shee
Xi'an	shee ahn
Xiang	shee ahng
Xi Chongxun	shee chawng shoon
Xingú	sheeng **GOO**
Xining	shee ning
Xinjiang Uygur	**SHIN** jee **AHNG WEE** gər
Xinxiang	shin shee ahng
xiphoid	**ZĪ** foid

---

o **on**, oh **oat**, oi **boy**, oo **soon**, oor **poor**, or **for**, ow **cow**, sh **shush**, th **thin**, *th* **this**, u **up**, ur **spur**, uu **book**, *zh* **pleasure**

Xizang	shee zahng
Xi Zhongxun	shee jawng shoon
Xmas	**KRIS** məs
Xochimilco	**SOH** shi **MEEL** koh
Xosa	**KOH** sah
Xuanhua	shoo ahn hwah
Xu Shiyou	shoo shu yoh
Xu Xiangqian	shoo shee ahng chee ahn
Xuzhou	shoo joh
xylem	$\overline{\text{ZI}}$ ləm
xylene	$\overline{\text{ZI}}$ leen
xylography	zī **LOG** rə fee
xylophone	$\overline{\text{ZI}}$ lə **FOHN**
xyster	**ZIS** tər
Xystus	**ZIS** təs

Y

Yablonoi	**YAH** blaw **NOI**
yacht	yot
Yadkin	**YAD** kən
yagi	**YAH** gee
Yahoo	**YAH** hoo
Yahweh	**YAH** we (we as in *wet*)
Yaker, Layachi	**YAH** kah, lī **AH** chee
Yakima	**YAK** ə mə
Yakut	yah **KOOT**
Yakutsk	yah **KOOTSK**
Yalow, Rosalyn	**YAL** oh
Yalta	**YAWL** tə
Yalu	**YAH** loo
Yalung	yah luung
Yamani, Ahmed Zaki	yah **MEN** ee, **AHK** med **ZEK** ee
Yameogo, Maurice	yah may **OH** goh, maw **REES**
Yang Chen Ning	yahng jun ning
Yang Dezhi	yahng du ju
Yang Shangkun	yahng shahng koon
Yangtze	yang tsee
Yang Yong	yahng yawng
Yanqui, y-	**YAHN** kee
Yaoundé	yah uun **DAY**

ə ago, a at, ah calm, ahr dark, air care, aw saw, ay say, ch church
e bet, ee me, eer beer, hw what, i is, ī my, *n* French final n vin,

Yao Yilin	yow yee leen (yow as in *cow*)
yap	yap
Yap	yop
Yaqui	**YAH** kee
Yarborough	**YAHR** bə roh
yare	yair
Yarmouth	**YAHR** məth
yarmulke	**YAHR** məl kə
Yaroslavl	**YAH** rə **SLAHV** əl
yaupon	**YAW** pən
Yazoo	ya **ZOO**
yclept	i **KLEPT**
Ydígoras Fuentes, Miguel	ee **DEE** gaw rahs **FWEN** tes, mee **GEL**
yea	yay
yearling	**YEER** ling
Yeats	yayts
Ye Jiangying	yu jee ahng yeeng
Yemen	**YEM** ən
Yenisei, Yenisey	**YEN** ə **SAY**
yeoman	**YOH** mən
Yerba Buena	**YAIR** bə **BWAY** nə
Yerevan	**YER** ə **VON**
Yesenin-Volpin	ye **SAY** nyin **VOHL** pin
Yeshiva, y-	yə **SHEE** və
yeti	**YET** ee
Yevtushenko, Yevgeni	**YEV** tə **SHENG** koh, yev **GAY** nee
yew	yoo
Yggdrasill	**IG** drə **SIL**
Ymir	**EE** mir
yoga	**YOH** gə
yogi	**YOH** gee
yogurt	**YOH** gərt
Yoknapatawpha	**YOK** nə pə **TAW** fə
Yokohama	**YOH** kə **HAH** mə
Yokosuka	yoh **KOH** sə kə
yolk	yohk
Yom Kippur	**YOHM KIP** ər
Yorkshire	**YORK** shir
Yoruba	**YOR** ə bə
Yosemite	yoh **SEM** ə tee
Yoshihito	yoh shee hee toh
Yost	yohst

---

o on, oh oat, oi boy, oo soon, oor poor, or for, ow cow, sh shush, th thin, *th* this, u up, ur spur, uu book, *zh* pleasure

Youlou, Abbe	**YOO** luu, **AH** be
youth	yooth
youths	yoo*th*z
Ypres	**EE** prə
Ypsilanti	**IP** sə **LAN** tee
Yquem	ee **KEM**
Yser	ee **ZER**
Yseult	i **SOOLT**
ytterbium	i **TUR** bee əm
yttrium	**I** tree əm
Yucatan, Yucatán	**YOO** kə **TAN**
Yucatec	**YOO** kə **TEK**
Yucatecan	**YOO** kə **TEK** ən
yucca	**YUK** ə
Yuen	yoo **EN**
Yuga	**YUUG** ə
Yugoslavia	**YOO** goh **SLAH** vee ə
Yugov, Anton	**YOO** gawf, **AHN** tohn
Yukon	**YOO** kon
Yuma	**YOO** mə
Yunnan	yoo nahn
Yu Qiuli	yoo chee oo lee
yurt	yuurt

Z

zabaglione	**ZAH** bəl **YOH** nee
Zabulon	**ZAB** yə lən
Zacatecas	**SAH** kah **TE** kahs
Zachariah	**ZAK** ə **RĪ** ə
Zacharias	**ZAK** ə **RĪ** əs
Zagazig	**ZAHG** ah **ZEEG**
Zagreb	**ZAHG** reb
zaibatsu	zī **BAHT** soo
Zaire	zah **IR**
Zambezi	zam **BEE** zee
Zambia	**ZAM** bee ə
Zamboanga	**ZAM** boh **AHN** gə
Zangwill, Israel	**ZANG** wil
Zanzibar	**ZAN** zə **BAHR**
Zaporozhe	**ZAH** paw **RAWZH** yə

ə ago, a at, ah calm, ahr dark, air care, aw saw, ay say, ch church
e bet, ee me, eer beer, hw what, i is, ī my, *n* French final n vin,

Zapotec	**ZAHP** ə **TEK**
Zarathustra	**ZA** rə **THOOS** trə
zareba	zə **REE** bə
Zarif, Mohammad Farid	*th*ə **REEF**, moh **HAM** med fe **REED**
Zarubin	zah **ROO** bin
Zatec	**ZH**AH tets
zealot	**ZEL** ət
zealous	**ZEL** əs
zebra	**ZEE** brə
zebu	**ZEE** byoo
Zebulon	**ZEB** yə **LON**
Zebulun	**ZEB** yə lən
Zeebrugge	**ZEE** bruug ə
Zeitgeist	**TSĪT** gīst
Zeitschrift	**TSĪT** shrift
Zeitung	**TSĪ** tuung
Zelaya, Jorge Luis	say **LĪ** ə, **HOR** gay loo **EES**
Zellerbach	**ZEL** ər bak
Zelotes	zi **LOH** teez
Zemgale	**ZEM** gah le
Zen	zen
zenana	zə **NAH** nə
Zend	zend
Zend-Avesta	**ZEN** də **VES** tə
zener	**ZEE** nər
Zenger, John Peter	**ZENG** ər
zenith	**ZEE** nəth
Zeno	**ZEE** noh
zephyr	**ZEF** ər
Zephyrus	**ZEF** ər əs
zeppelin, Z-	**ZEP** ə lən
Zerbo, Sayé	zer **BOH**, sī **YAY**
Zermatt	tser **MAHT**
Zernike, Frits	**ZAIR** nə kə, **FRITS**
zero	**ZEE** roh
Zetterling, Mai	**ZE** tər **LING**, **MĪ**
zeugma	**ZOOG** mə
Zeus	zoos
Zhang Aiping	jahng ī peeng
Zhang Tingfa	jahng teeng fah
Zhang Wenjin	jahng wun jeen
Zhao Ziyang	jow zee yahng (jow as in *cow*)

o on, oh oat, oi boy, oo soon, oor poor, or for, ow cow, sh shush, th thin, *th* this, u up, ur spur, uu book, *zh* pleasure

Zhejiang	ju jee ahng
Zhivkov, Todor	**ZH**EEV kawf, **TOH** tawr
Zhulev, Stoyan	**ZH**OO lev, stoh **YAHN**
Zia ul-Haq, Mohammad	**ZEE** ah ool **HAHK**, moh **HAH** məd
Ziegler, Karl	**TSEEG** lər
ziggurat	**ZIG** ə **RAT**
Zimbabwe	zim **BAH** bway
Zimyanin, Mikhail	zeem **YAH** nyin, mee hī **YEEL**
zinnia	**ZIN** ee ə
Zinzendorf	**TSIN** tsən **DORF**
Zionism	**ZĪ** ə **NIZ** əm
Zipangu	zə pang goo
zircon	**ZUR** kon
zither	**ZI***TH* ər
ziti	**ZEE** tee
zloty	**ZLAW** tee
zlotys	**ZLAW** teez
zoanthropy	zoh **AN** thrə pee
zodiac	**ZOH** dee **AK**
zodiacal	zoh **DĪ** ə kəl
Zoe, Zoë	**ZOH** ee
Zola, Émile	**ZOH** lə, ay **MEEL**
Zollverein	**TSAWL** fer **ĪN**
Zomba	**ZOM** bə
zombie	**ZOM** bee
zone	zohn
Zonta	**ZON** tə
zoolatry	zoh **OL** ə tree
zoological	**ZOH** ə **LOJ** i kəl
zoology	zoh **OL** ə jee
zoomorphic	**ZOH** ə **MOR** fik
zoomorphism	**ZOH** ə **MOR** fiz əm
zoophyte	**ZOH** ə **FĪT**
Zoppi, Vittorio	**DZOH** pee, vee **TAW** ree oh
Zorin, Valerian	**ZOR** in, vah lair ee **AHN**
Zorn	sorn
Zoroaster	**ZOH** roh **A** stər
zoster	**ZOH** stər
Zouave	zoo **AHV**
Zschau	show (as in *cow*)
Zubin	**ZUUB** ən
zucchetto	zuu **KET** oh

ə ago, a at, ah calm, ahr dark, air care, aw saw, ay say, ch church
e bet, ee me, eer beer, hw what, i is, ī my, *n* French final n vin,

zucchini	zuu **KEE** nee
Zug	tsook
Zuider Zee	z**ĪD** ər **ZEE**
Zumbado-Jimenez, Fernando	suum **BAH** doh hee **MEN** ez, fer NAN doh
Zuñi	**ZOO** nee
Zurich	**ZUUR** ik
Zweig	zwīg
zwieback	**ZWĪ** bak
Zwingli	**ZWING** lee
zygote	**ZĪ** goht
zymurgy	**ZĪ** mur jee